500 MANGA VILLAINS AND HEROES

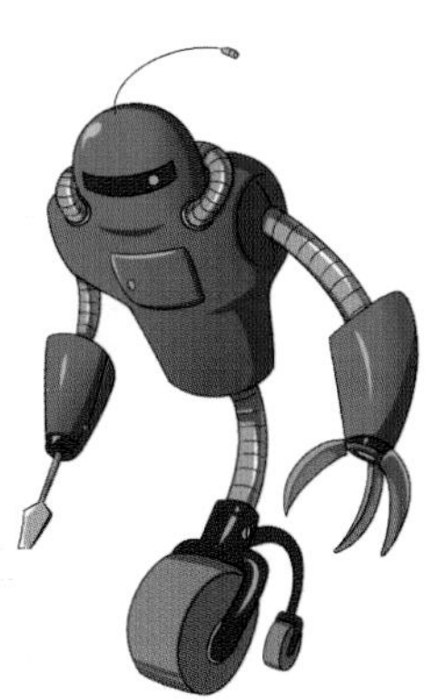

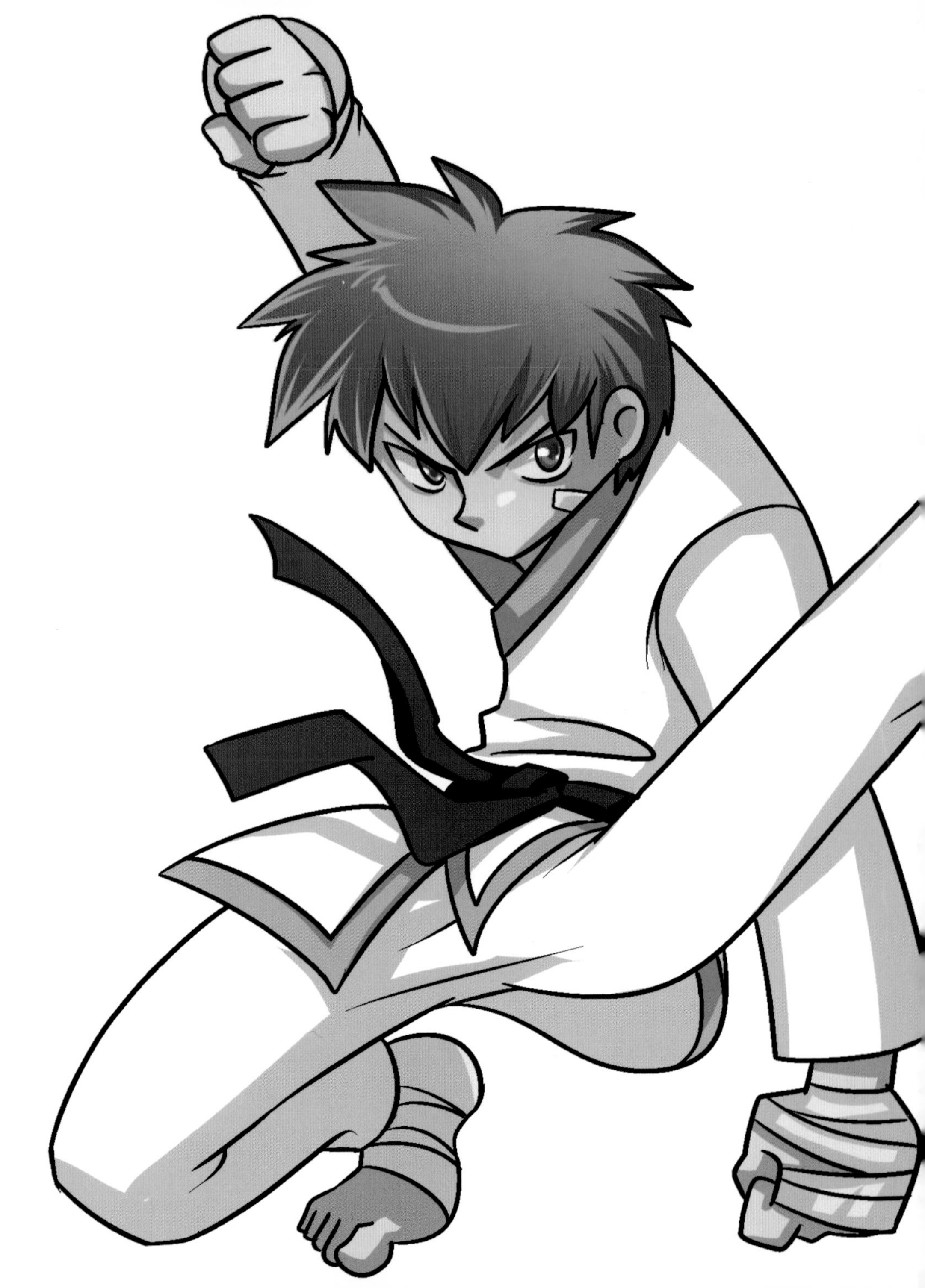

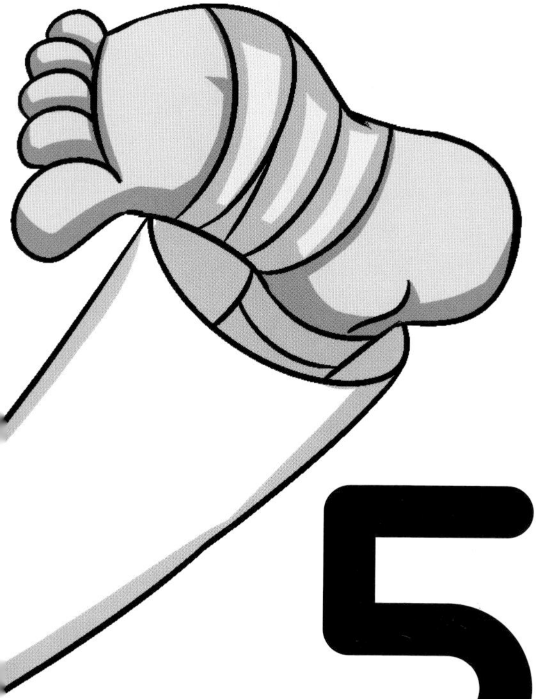

500
MANGA VILLAINS AND HEROES

YISHAN LI
WITH YISHAN STUDIO

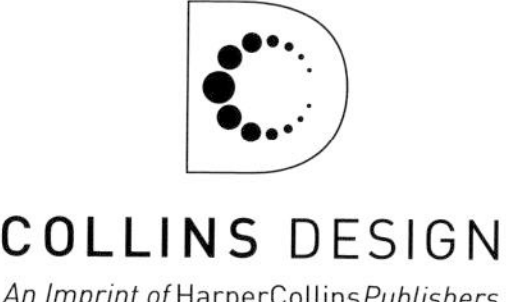

COLLINS DESIGN
An Imprint of HarperCollins*Publishers*

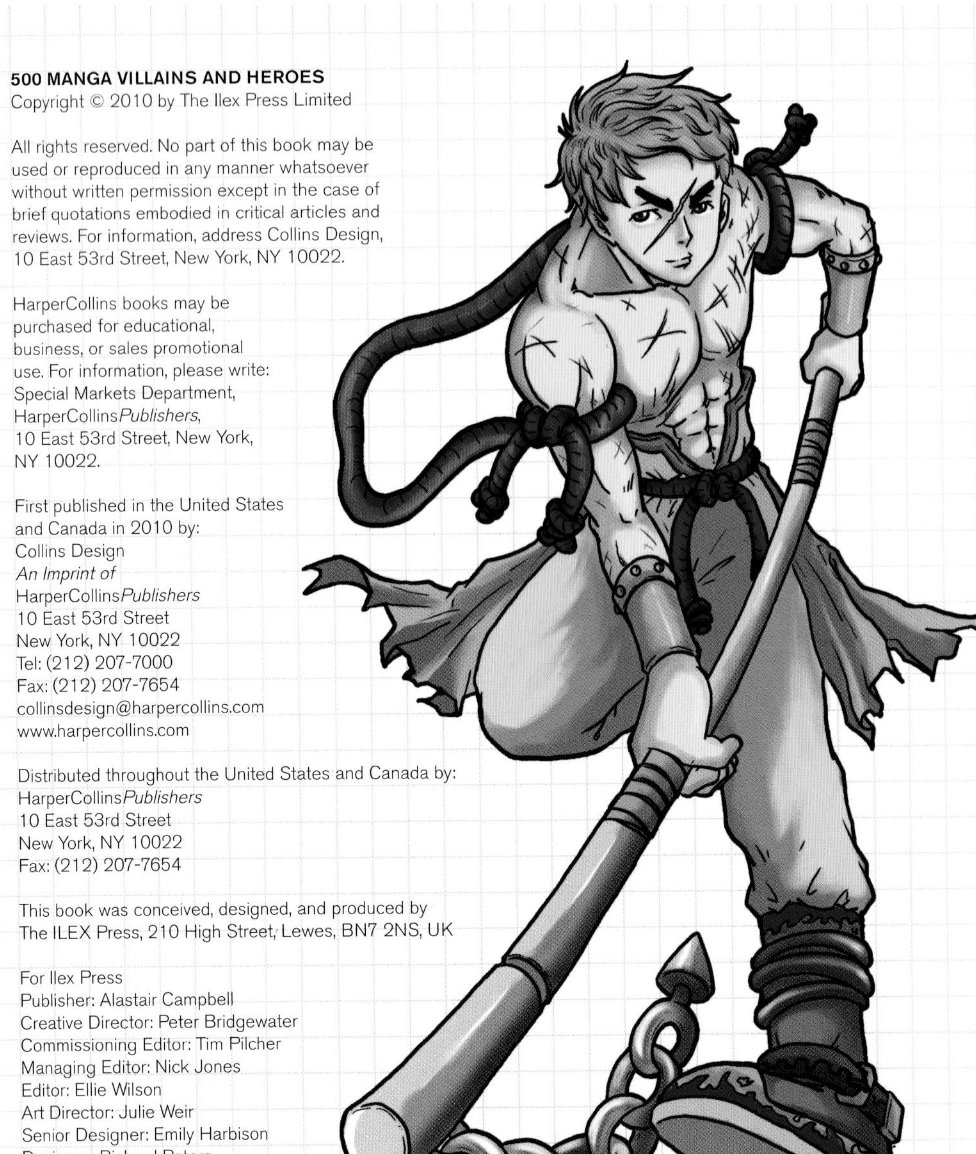

500 MANGA VILLAINS AND HEROES

HarperCollins books may be purchased for educational, business, or sales promotional use. For information, please write: Special Markets Department, HarperCollins*Publishers*, 10 East 53rd Street, New York, NY 10022.

First published in the United States and Canada in 2010 by:
Collins Design
An Imprint of
HarperCollins*Publishers*
10 East 53rd Street
New York, NY 10022
Tel: (212) 207-7000
Fax: (212) 207-7654
collinsdesign@harpercollins.com
www.harpercollins.com

Distributed throughout the United States and Canada by:
HarperCollins*Publishers*
10 East 53rd Street
New York, NY 10022
Fax: (212) 207-7654

This book was conceived, designed, and produced by
The ILEX Press, 210 High Street, Lewes, BN7 2NS, UK

For Ilex Press
Publisher: Alastair Campbell
Creative Director: Peter Bridgewater
Commissioning Editor: Tim Pilcher
Managing Editor: Nick Jones
Editor: Ellie Wilson
Art Director: Julie Weir
Senior Designer: Emily Harbison
Designer: Richard Peters

Library of Congress Control Number:
2010930349

ISBN: 978-0-06-196880-8

Printed in China
Colour Origination by Ivy Press Reprographics.
First Printing, 2010

For more information on this title please visit:
http://www.web-linked.com/mahv

contents

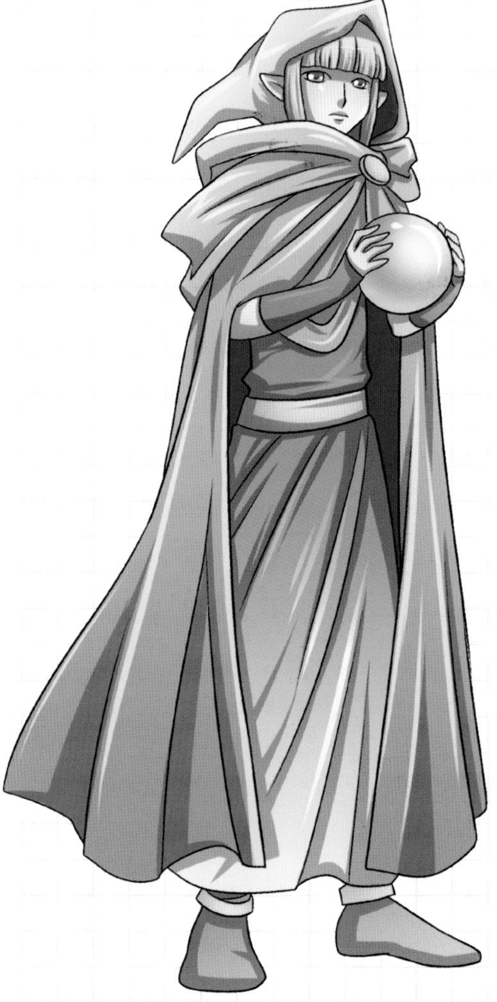

Introduction

Image gallery

Computer coloring basics

introduction

"Manga" is simply the Japanese word for "comics," referring solely to printed comics. The word, however, has become internationally recognized to refer to the art style, subject matter, and method of presentation, and manga-style artists can be found all over the world.

Manga in its present form has existed for over 50 years, but the origins of Japanese sequential art date back to ukiyo-e painting from the 19th century. Hokusai, probably the most famous ukiyo-e artist, is generally credited with coining the term "manga," literally meaning "irresponsible pictures." The development of this style into mass-produced sequential art in the early 20th century, combined with influences from European and American strip-panel comics, evolved the form into what is now commonly accepted as manga. Anime, referring to Japanese animated films and cartoons, is also a big influence on manga artists. Both manga and anime share many visual traits, so it's natural for the two to be associated.

The flexibility within manga is part of its appeal, and there's manga-style artwork to suit all tastes. From the gritty and realistic to the cute and exaggerated, and every step in between, there's always something interesting about every new picture drawn in this uniquely versatile art form. This book offers you a massive selection of 500 manga villains and heroes illustrated in a wide range of styles, themes, and poses.

using the cd

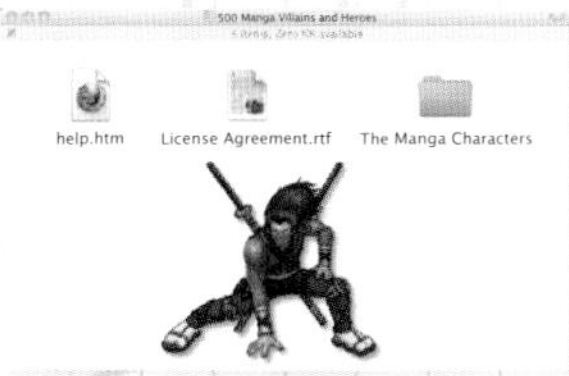

Getting Started

All of the images on the CD are stored as .psd documents that can be opened in leading image-editing programs, Adobe Photoshop and Photoshop Elements. They are named according to their category and position in the book. For example, 104ninja.psd is image number 104 in the book, and is in the *Ninja* characters category. Each of the categories has its own folder on the CD, so you can easily find the files that you are looking for.

Searching Metadata

Another easy way to find the files that you are looking for is to search through the metadata tags. Metadata sounds complicated, but it just means data that describes other data—in this case, keywords that describe the content of the images. This means that you can search through all of the images on the CD to find, say, all of the characters with wings. Most image-editing and cataloging software will allow you to browse through your images and view the metadata. In Adobe Photoshop an external application called Bridge is used to browse images. Bridge is used by Adobe Photoshop Elements on the Macintosh, but Photoshop Elements on Windows uses the Organizer workspace. Corel Paint Shop Pro uses the Organizer window. They all work in broadly the same way, and we will use Photoshop Elements as an example.

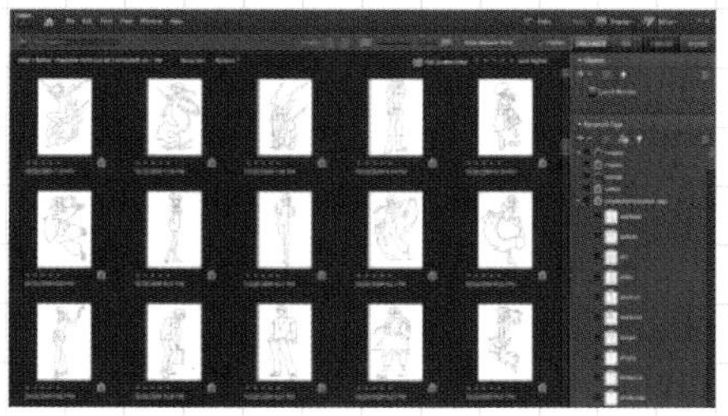

1 Open Photoshop Elements and go to the Organizer workspace. When it has opened, go to *File > Get Photos > From Files and Folders*, and navigate to the CD that contains the images. Select all the subfolders within The Manga Characters folder and click *Get Photos*. Choose to *Import all Tags* when prompted to make sure that all of the metadata keywords are loaded into Elements.

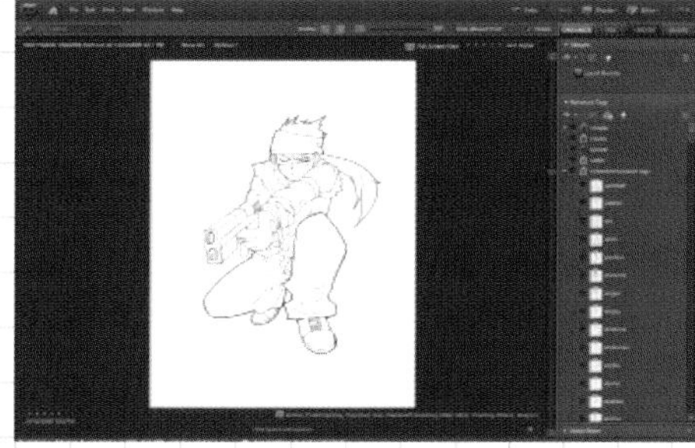

2 Scroll through the thumbnails of the images on the CD. If you double-click on one of these images it will expand to fill the window and give a list of all the attached keywords describing the image below it.

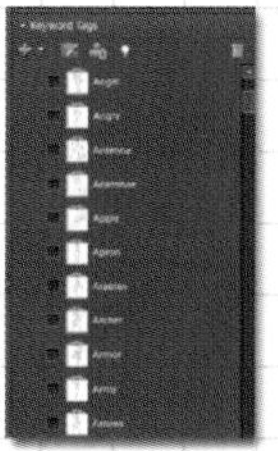

3 To search for all images that are tagged with a certain keyword, simply click the icon next to the keyword tag on the right, and the photo list will be restricted to only those images that include the selected keyword. You can search by chapter name or by specific keywords such as "Assassin."

image gallery

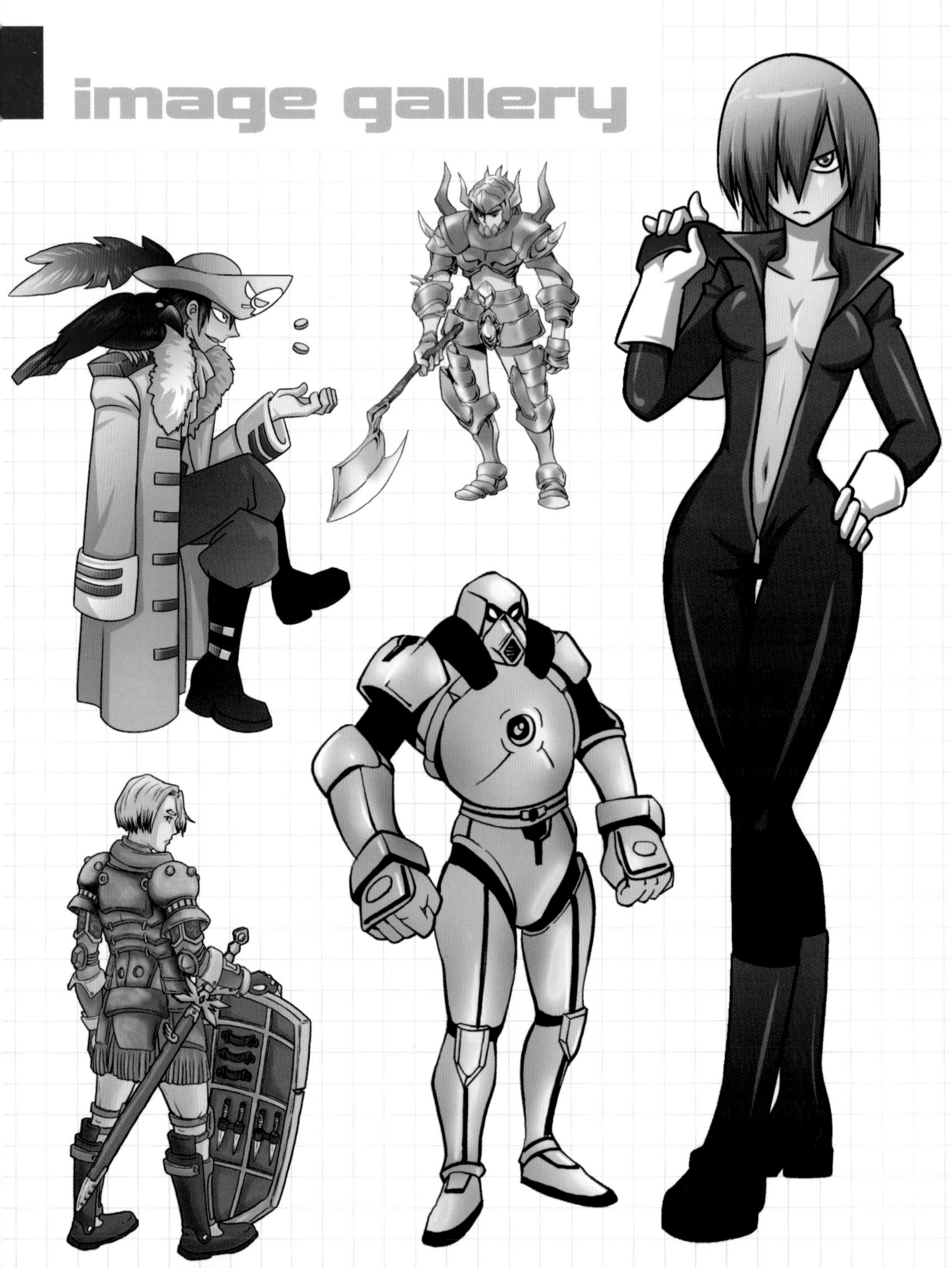

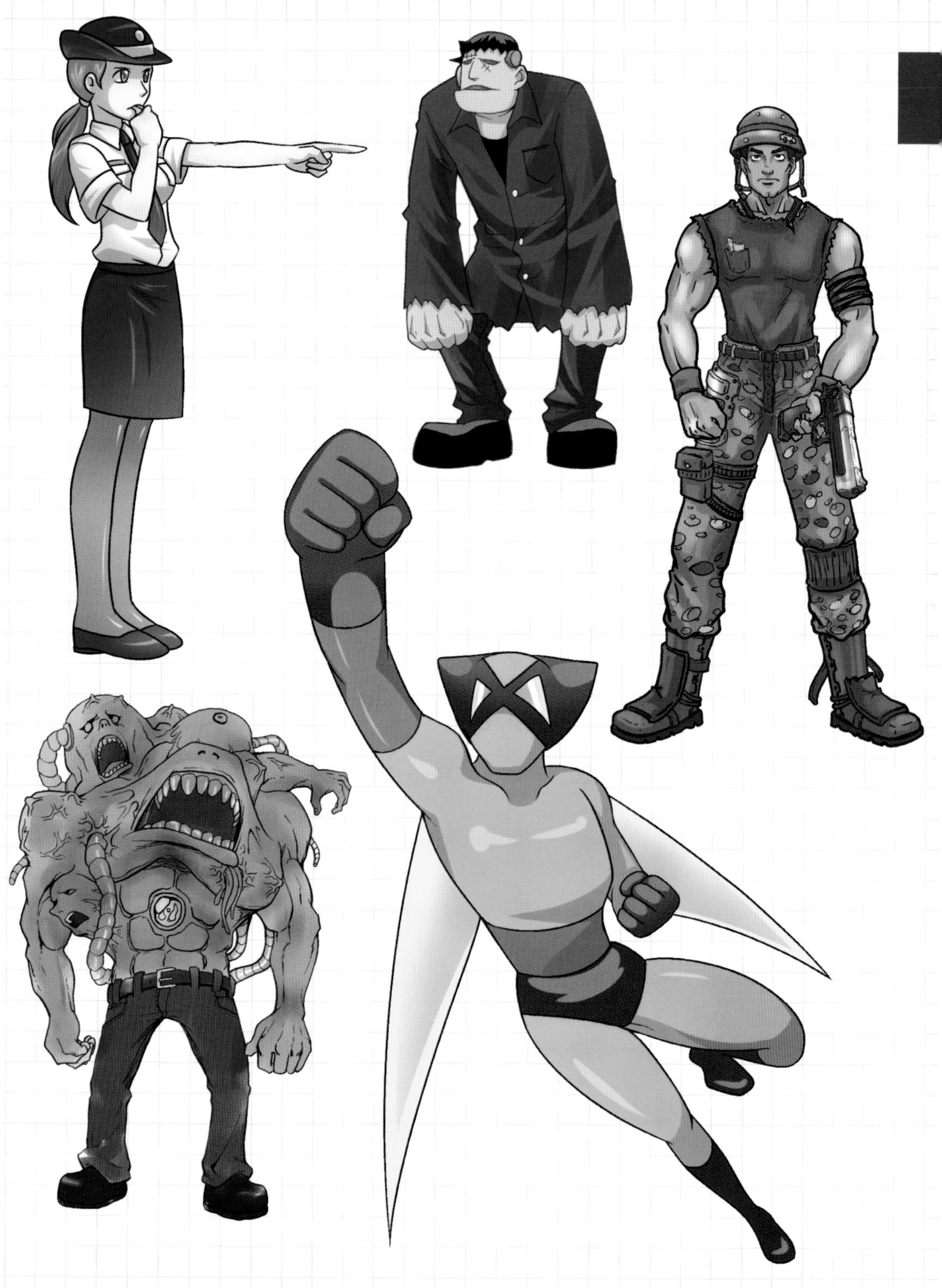

001

sci-fi and cyber punk villains

search criteria

male. kneeling. cyborg. futuristic. sunglasses. evil.

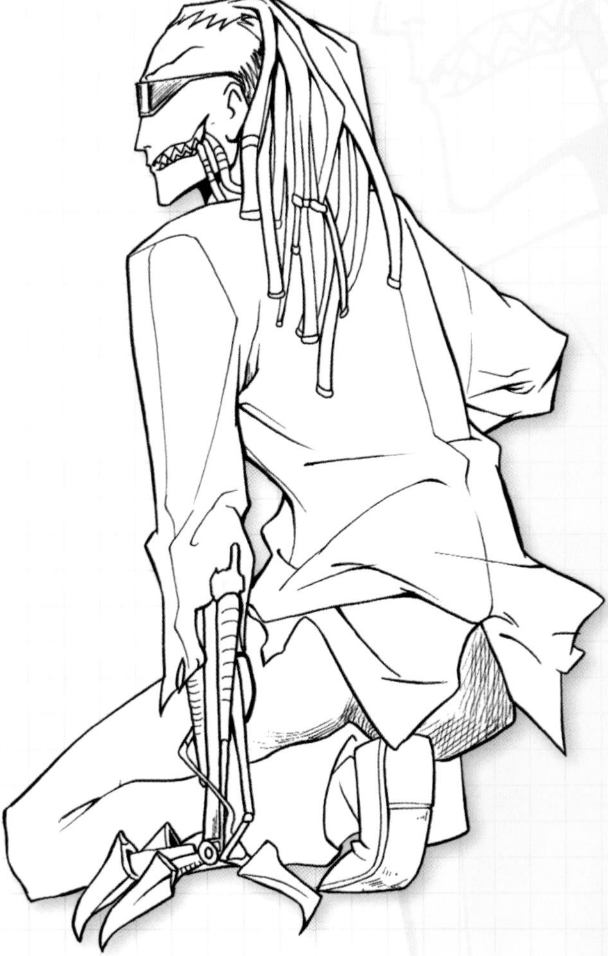

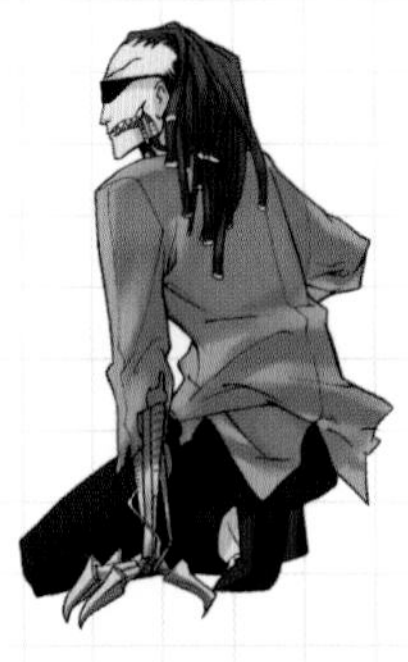

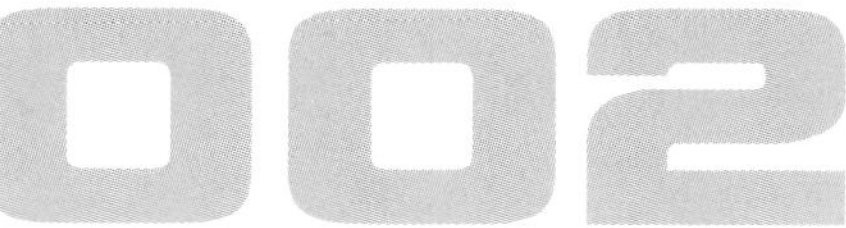

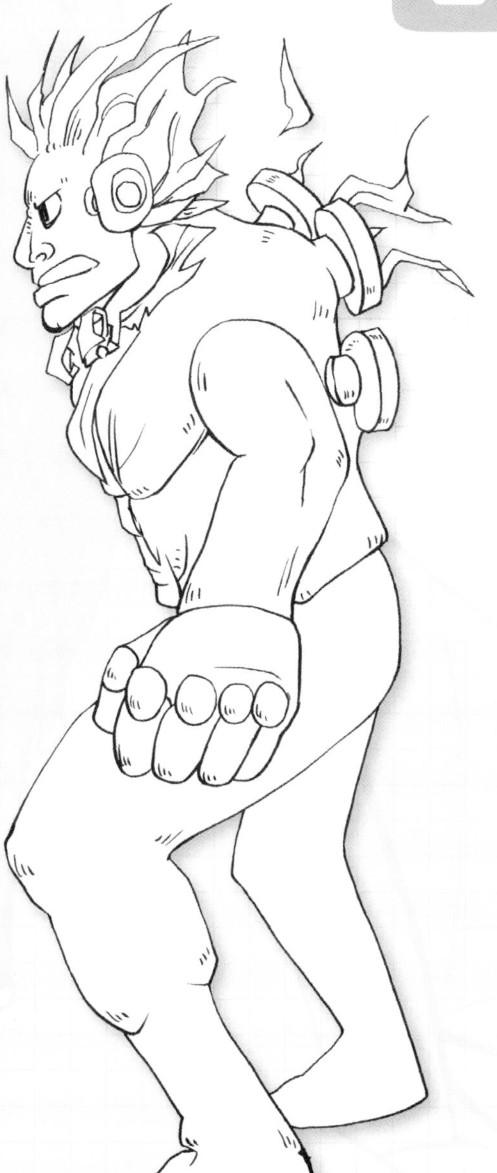

sci-fi and cyber punk villains

search criteria

male. standing. fire. angry. beast. muscle.

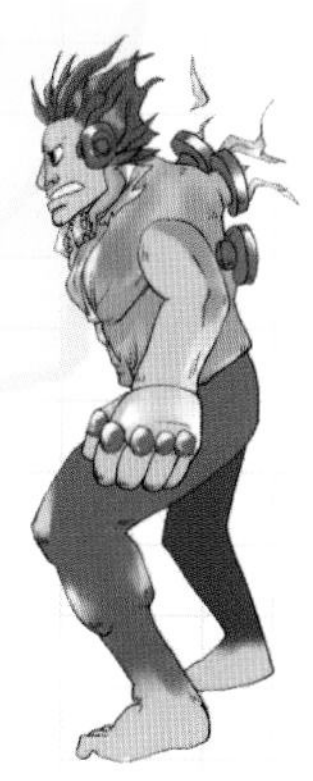

003

sci-fi and cyber punk villains

search criteria

male. standing. beast. monster. muscle. horror.

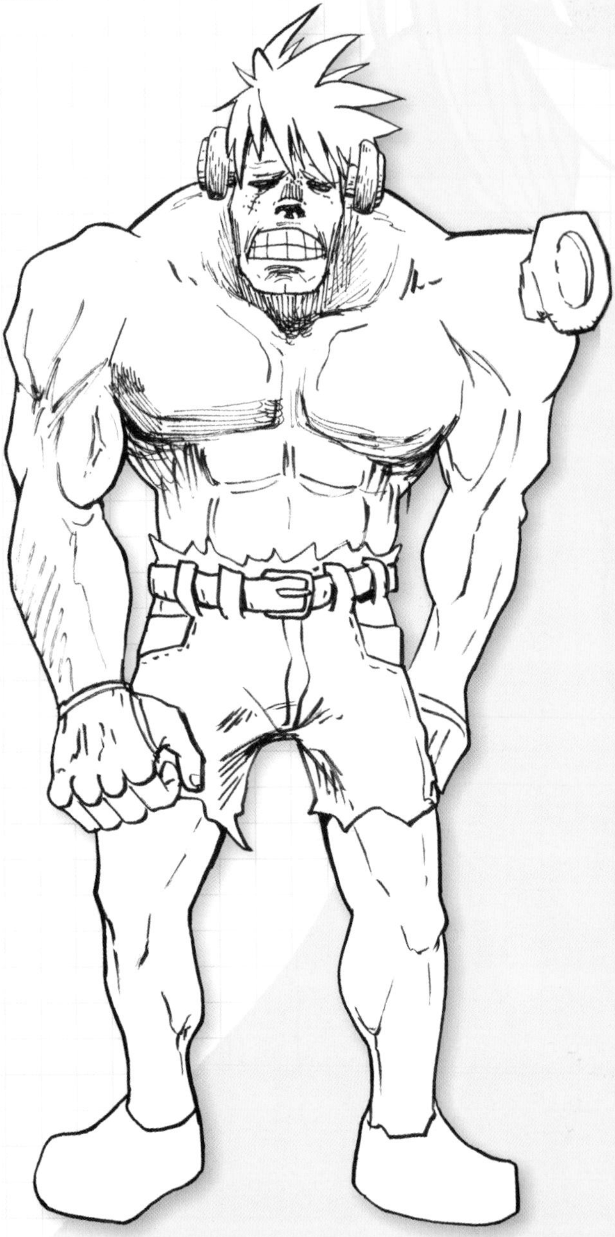

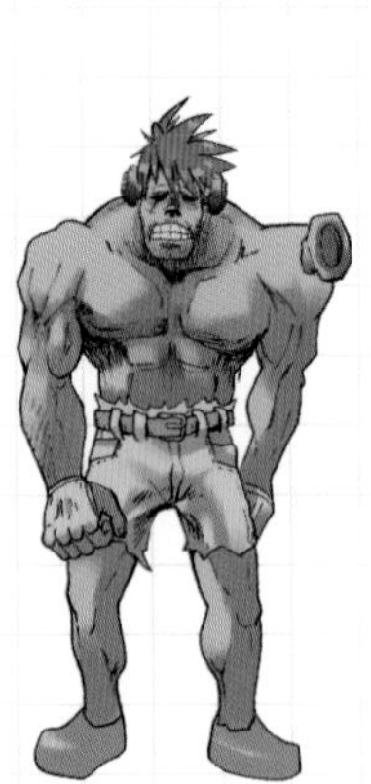

sci-fi and cyber punk villains

search criteria

female. standing. shoujo. pointing. sunglasses. sinister.

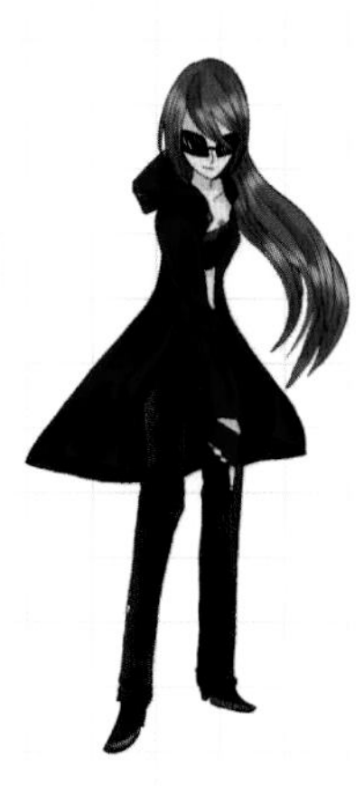

005

sci-fi and cyber punk villains

search criteria

robot. standing. android. weapon. gun. futuristic.

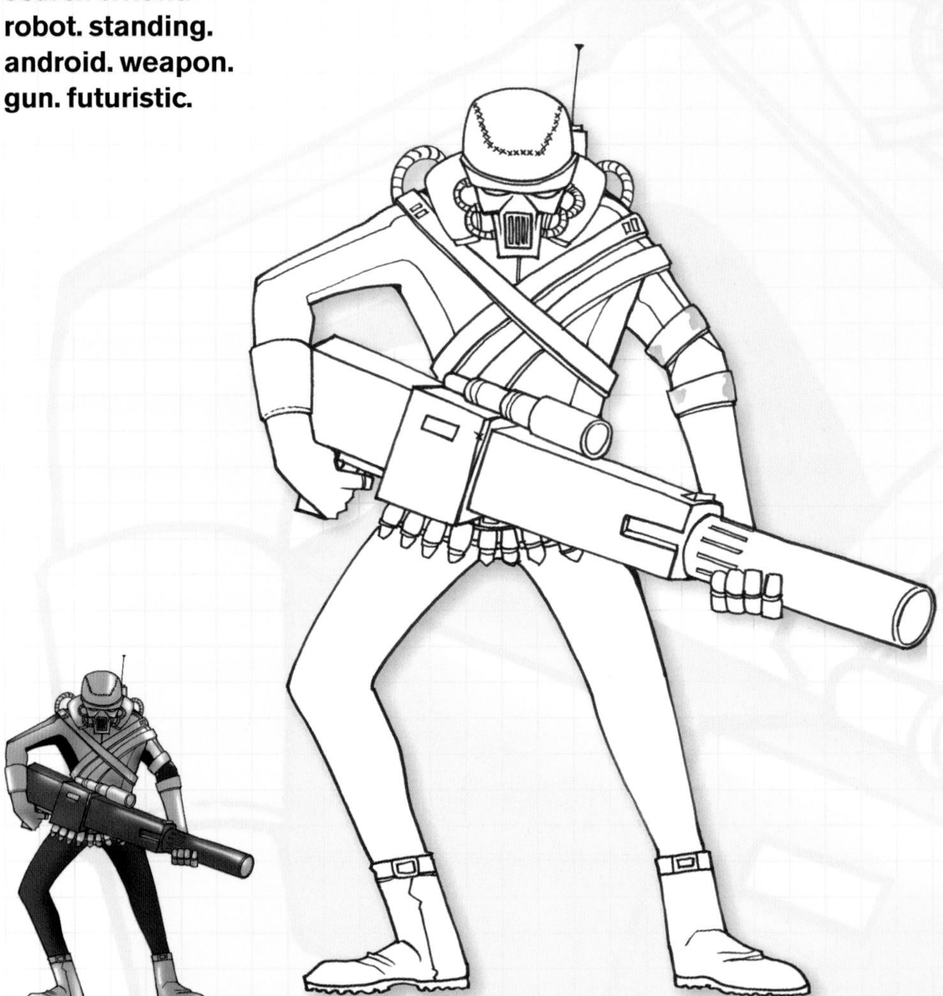

006

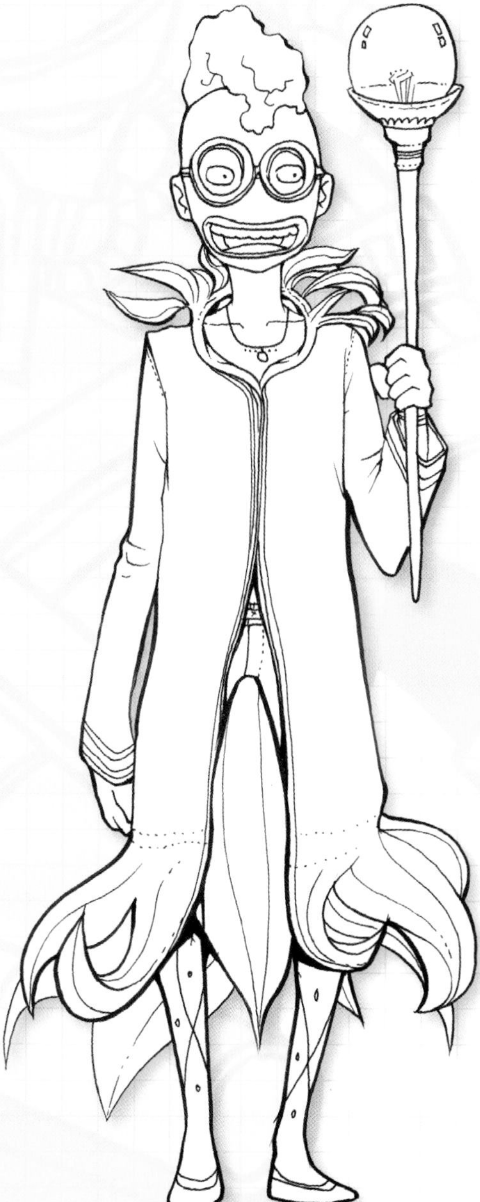

sci-fi and cyber punk villains

search criteria

male. standing. staff. wizard. goofy. glasses.

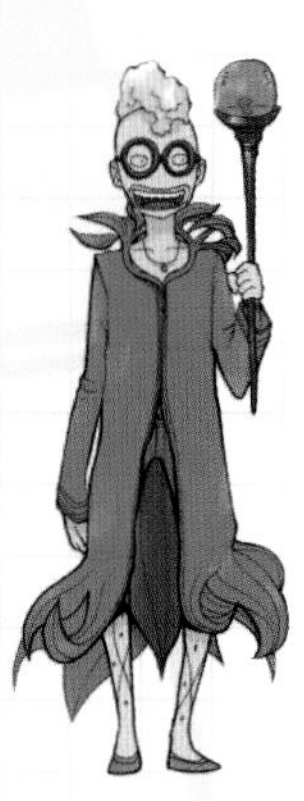

sci-fi and cyber punk villains

search criteria

robot. standing. female. android. futuristic.

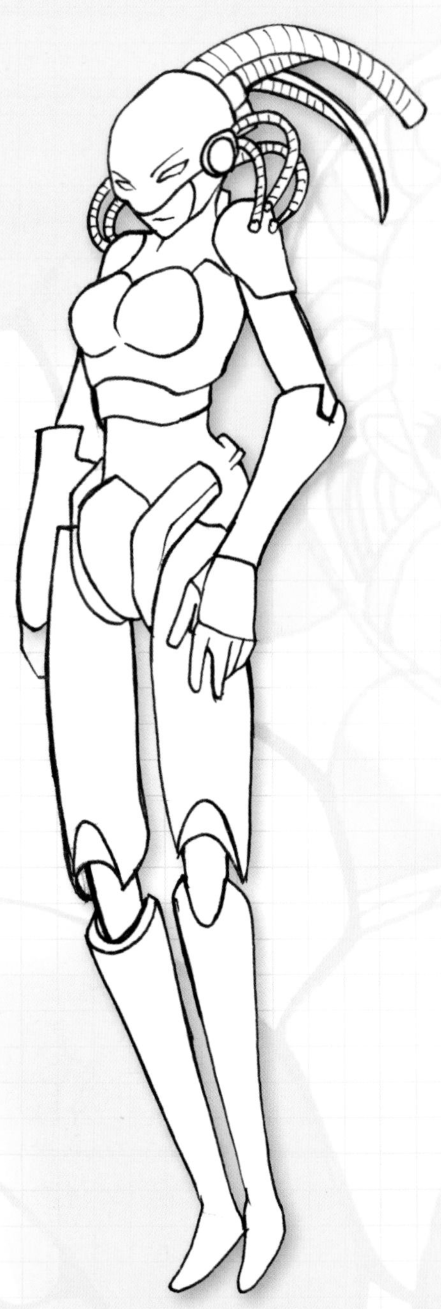

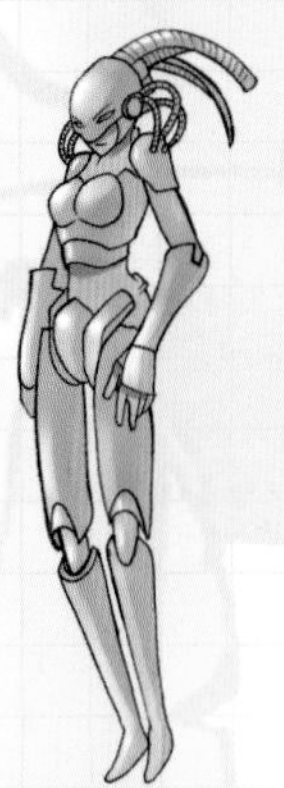

008

sci-fi and cyber punk villains

search criteria

standing. robot. weapon. chainsaw. futuristic. tentacles.

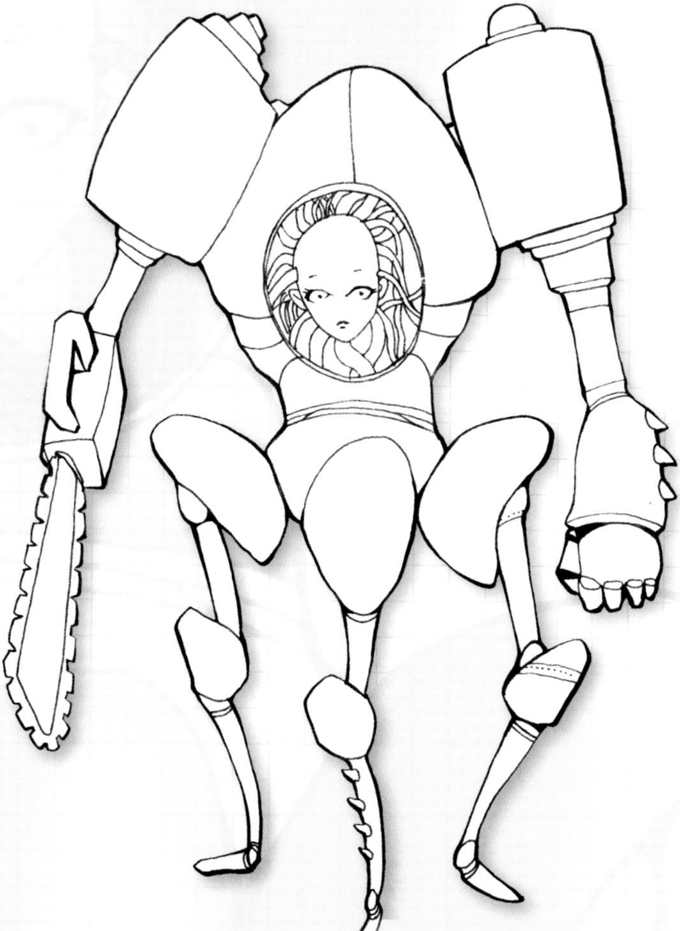

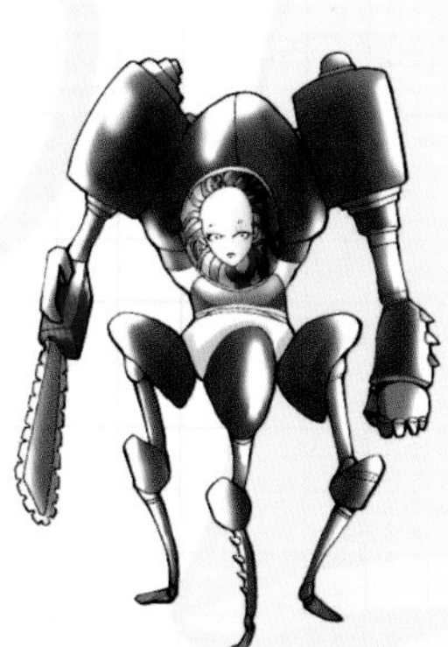

009

sci-fi and cyber punk villains

search criteria

female. standing. robot. futuristic. wheels. angry.

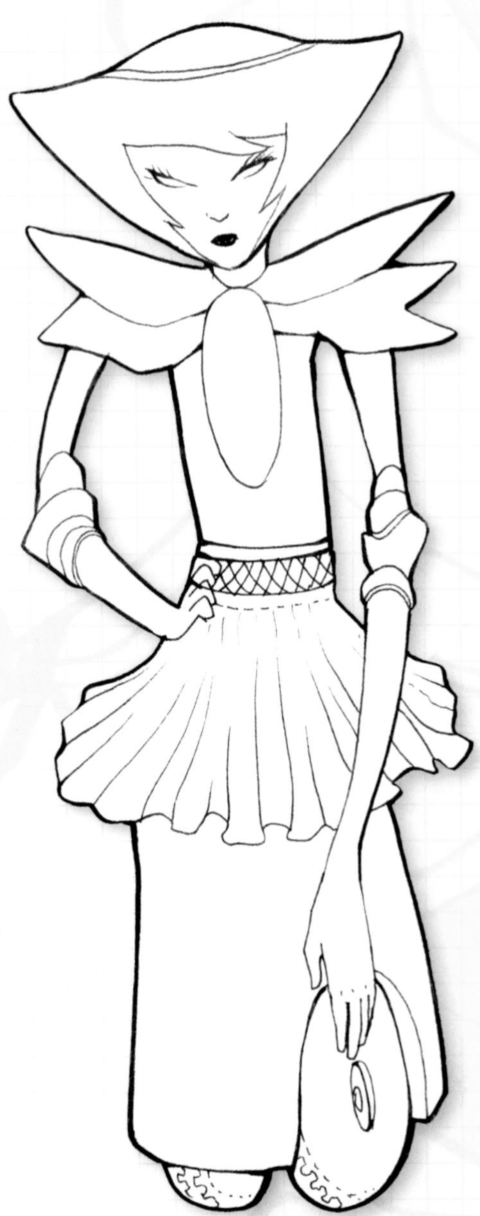

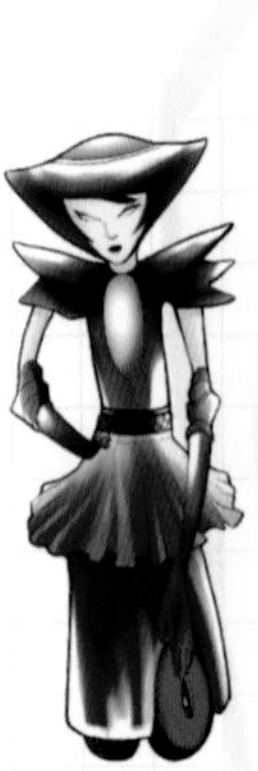

010

sci-fi and cyber punk villains

search criteria

male. standing. robot. weapons. swords. cyborg.

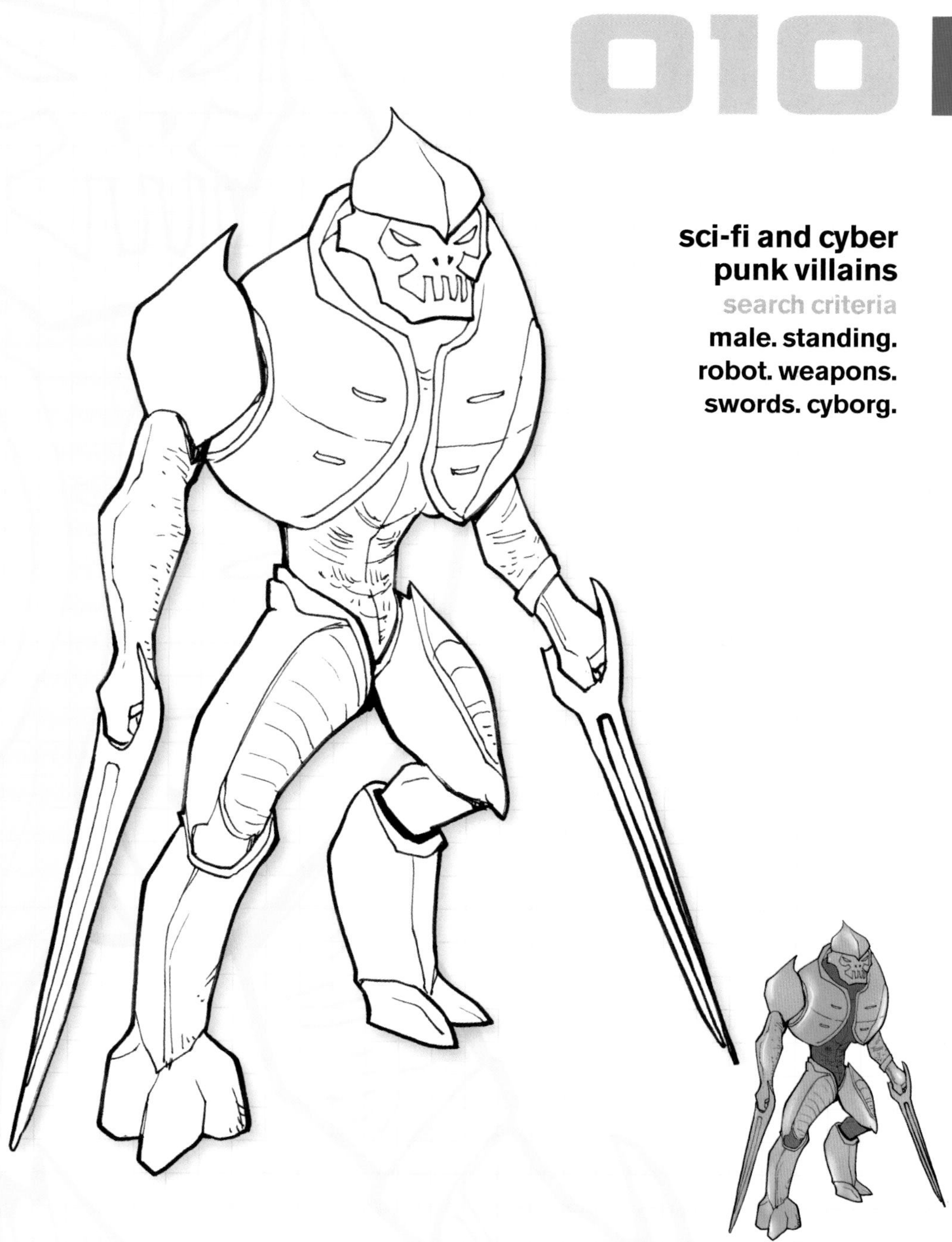

011

sci-fi and cyber punk villains

search criteria

male. floating. futuristic. tentacles. monster. alien.

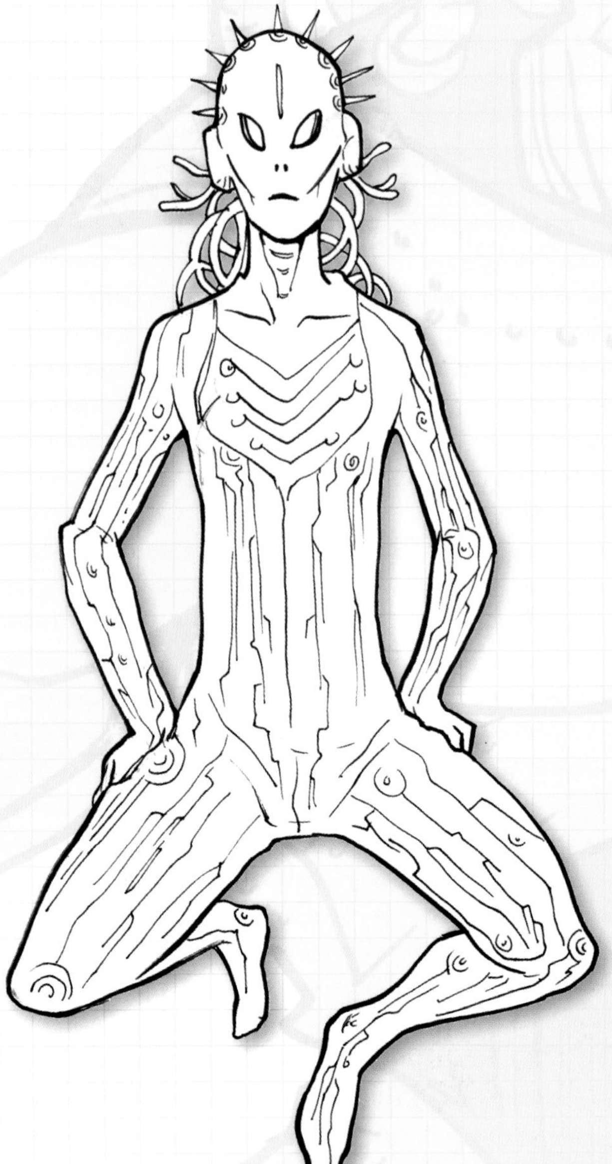

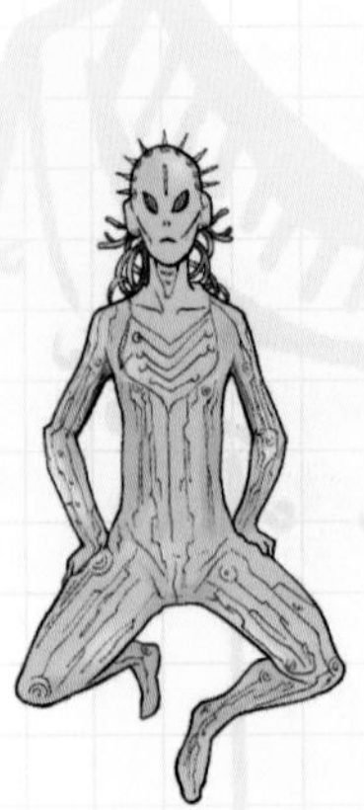

012

sci-fi and cyber punk villains

search criteria

male. standing. robot. muscle. weapon. angry.

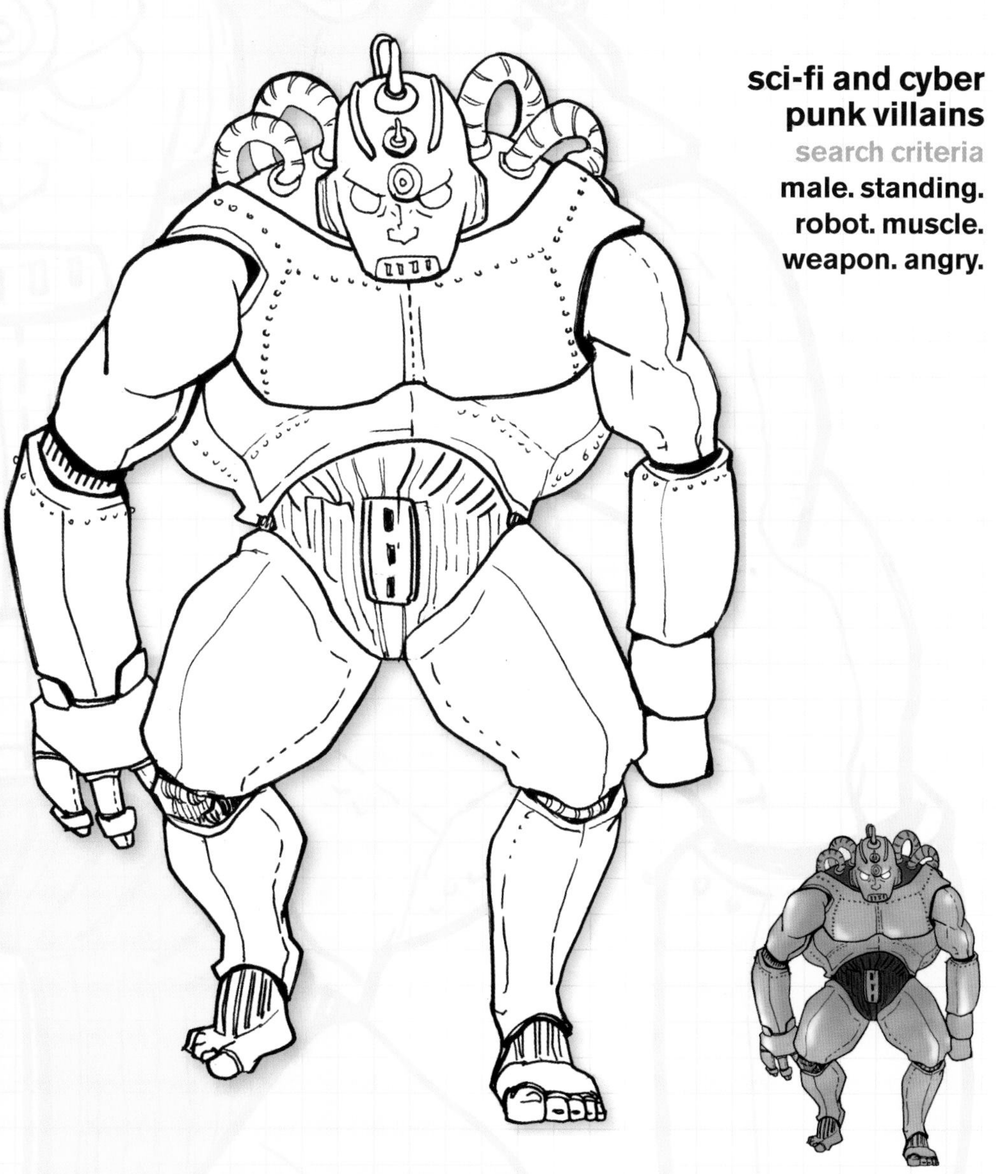

013

sci-fi and cyber punk villains

search criteria

male. standing. side. cyborg. boy. headphones.

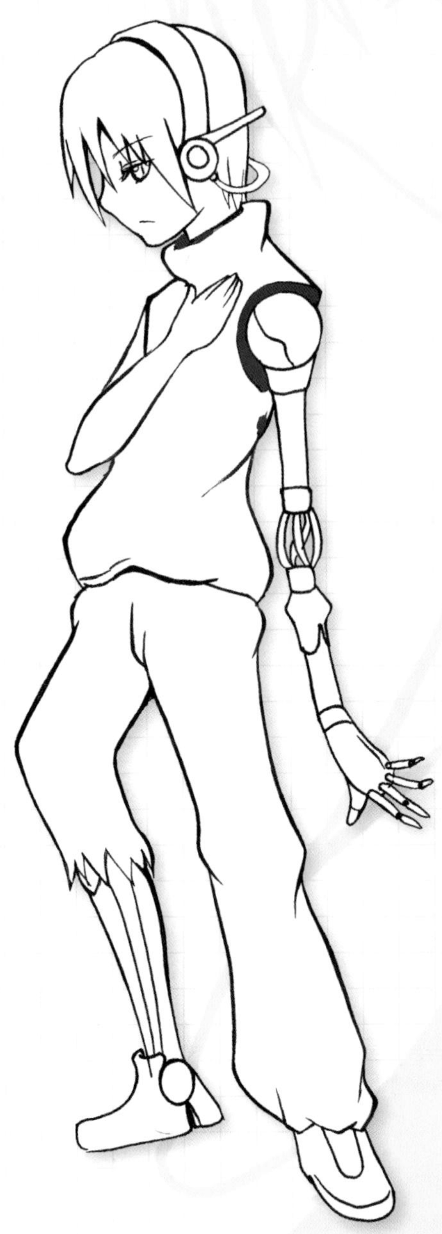

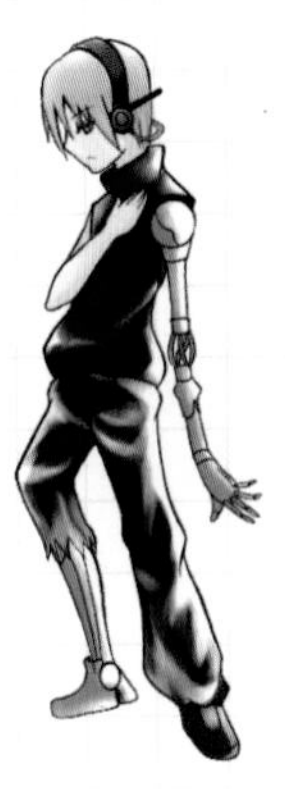

014

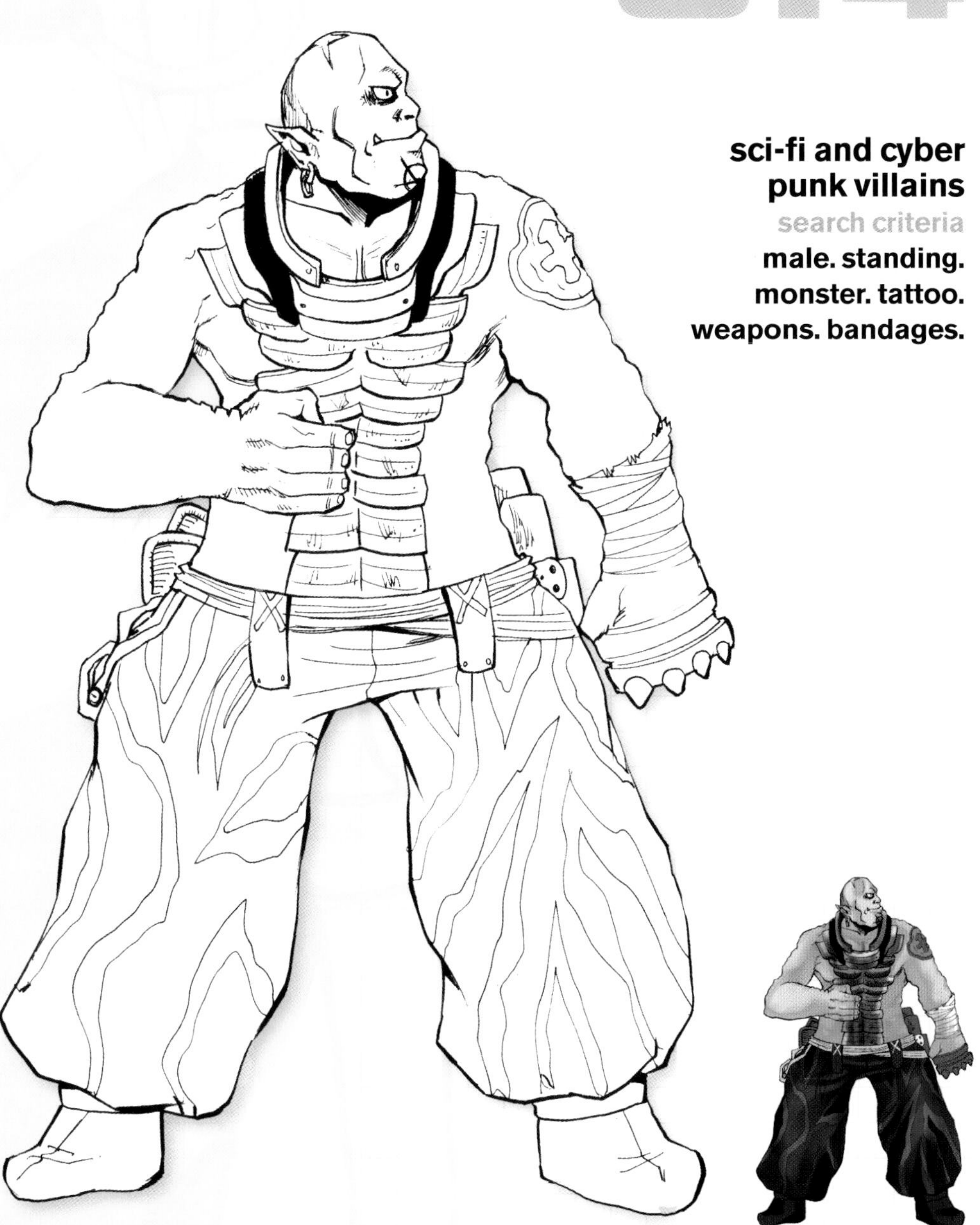

sci-fi and cyber punk villains

search criteria

male. standing. monster. tattoo. weapons. bandages.

015

sci-fi and cyber punk villains

search criteria

male. walking. cyborg. futuristic. razors. blades.

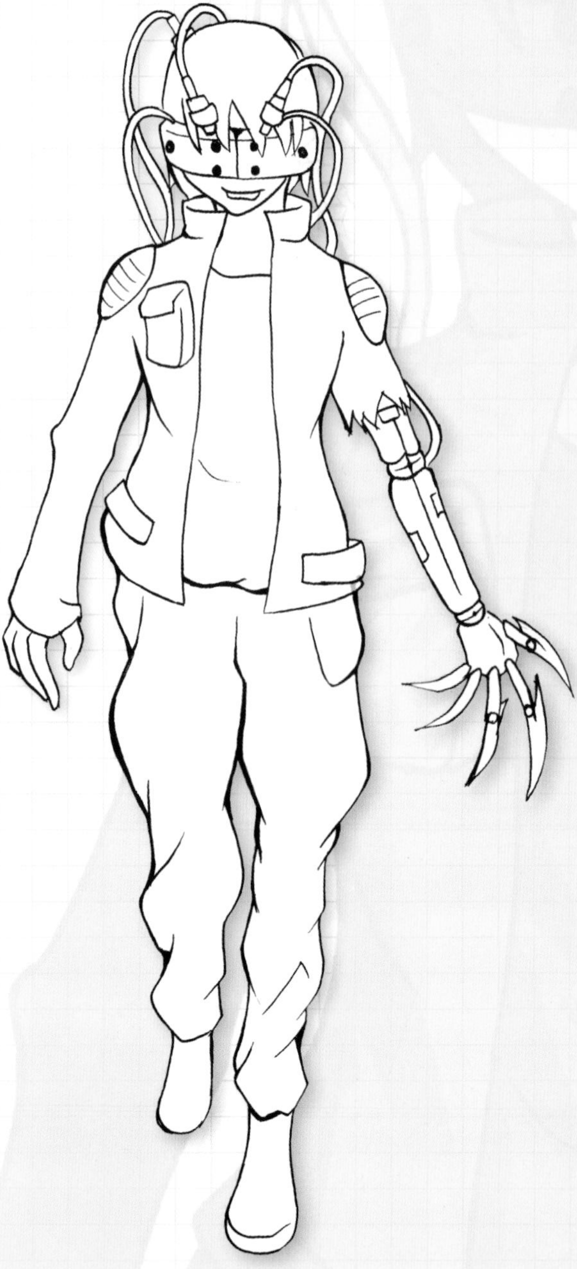

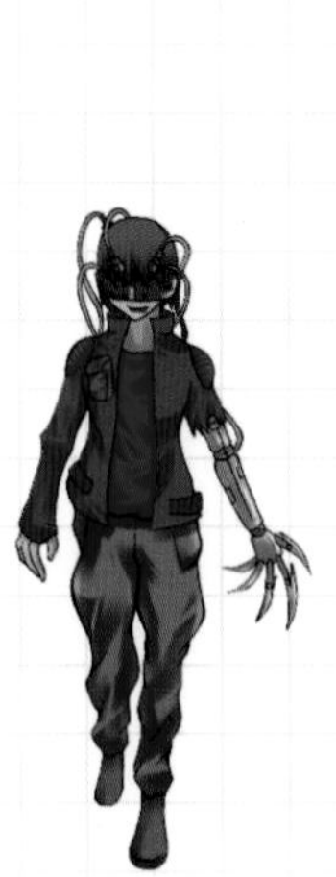

016

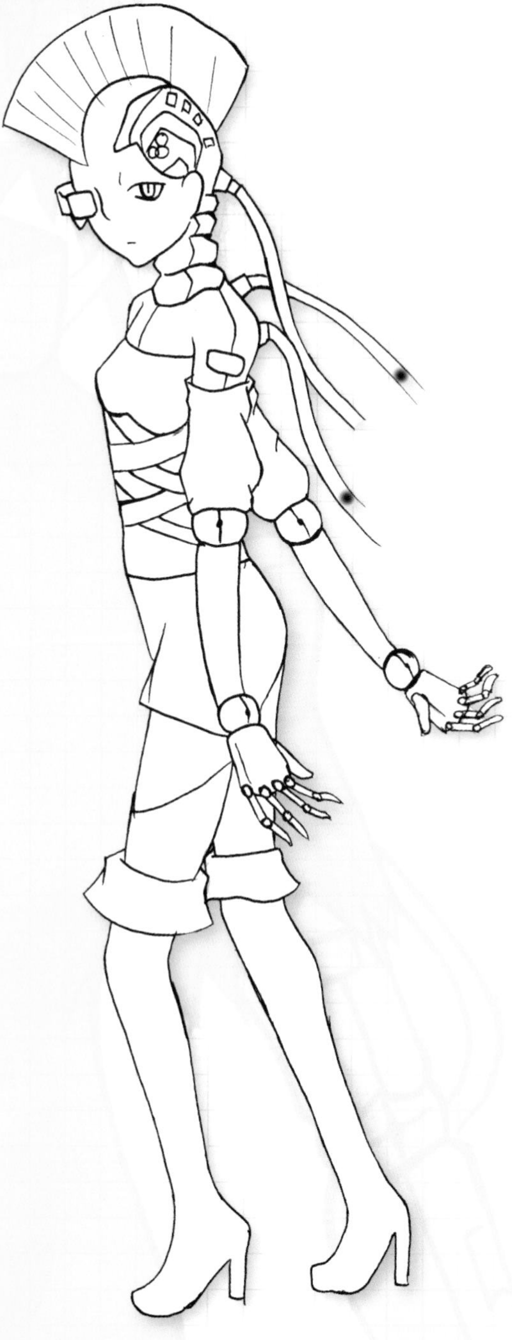

sci-fi and cyber punk villains

search criteria

female. robot. side. android. walking. tentacles. futuristic.

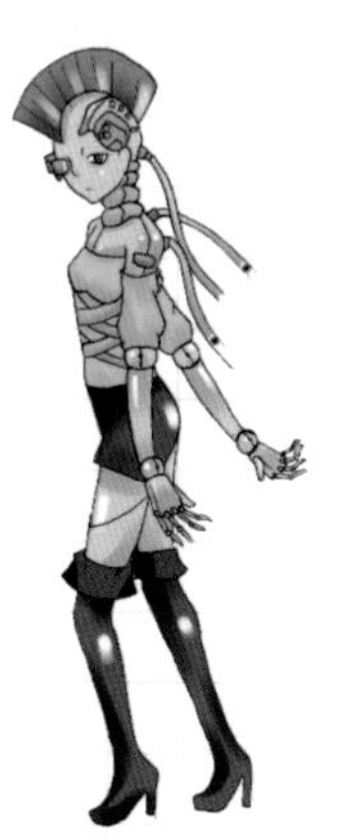

017

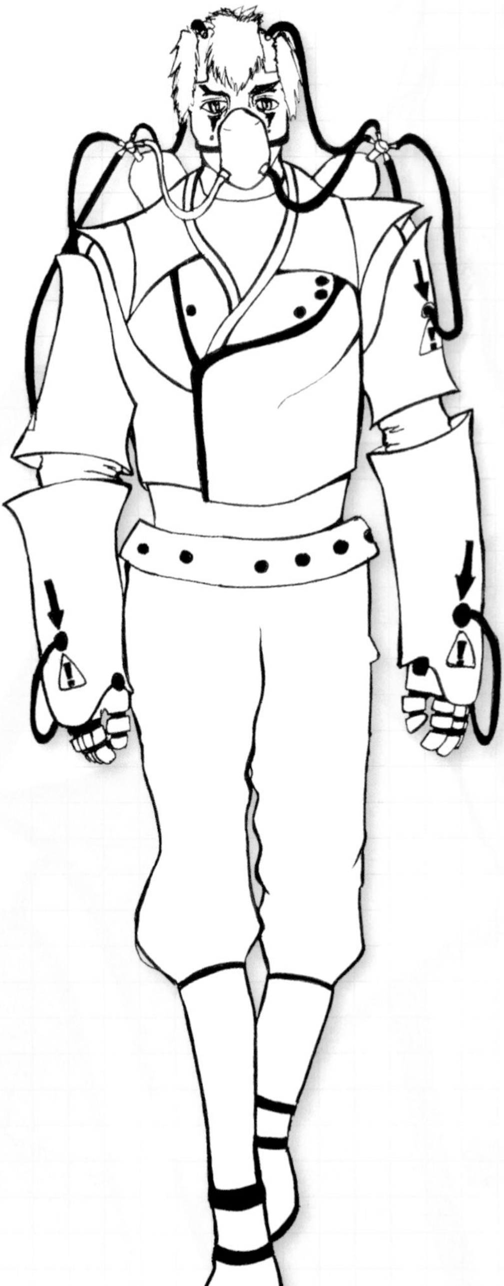

sci-fi and cyber punk villains

search criteria

male. walking. fighter. gas. danger. mask.

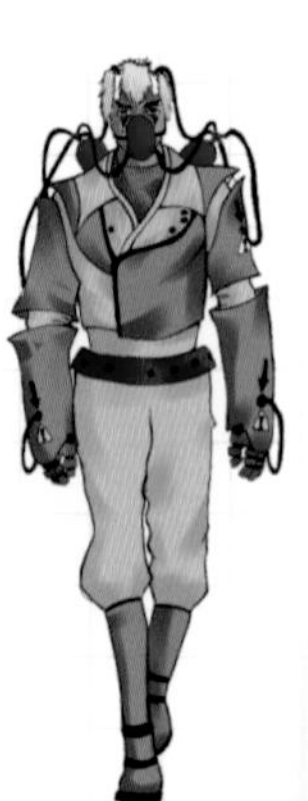

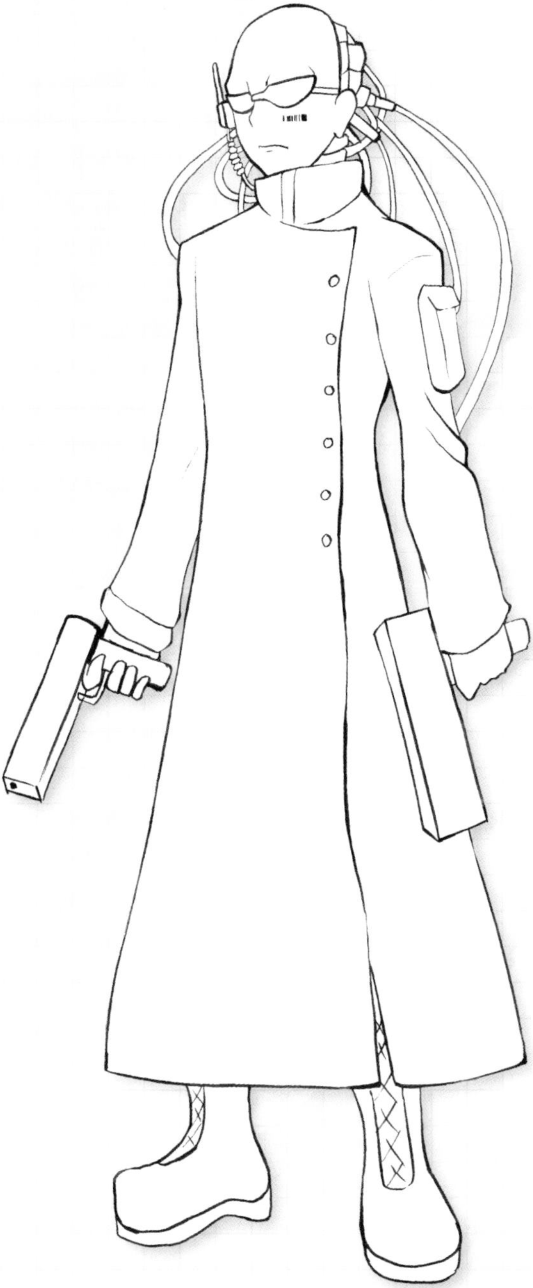

018

sci-fi and cyber punk villains

search criteria

male. standing. weapons. guns. sunglasses. cyborg. futuristic.

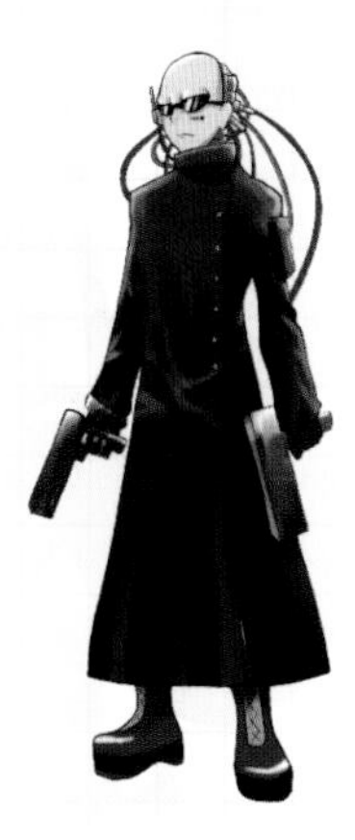

019

sci-fi and cyber punk villains

search criteria

male. sitting. sad. monster. doll. stitches. boy. horror.

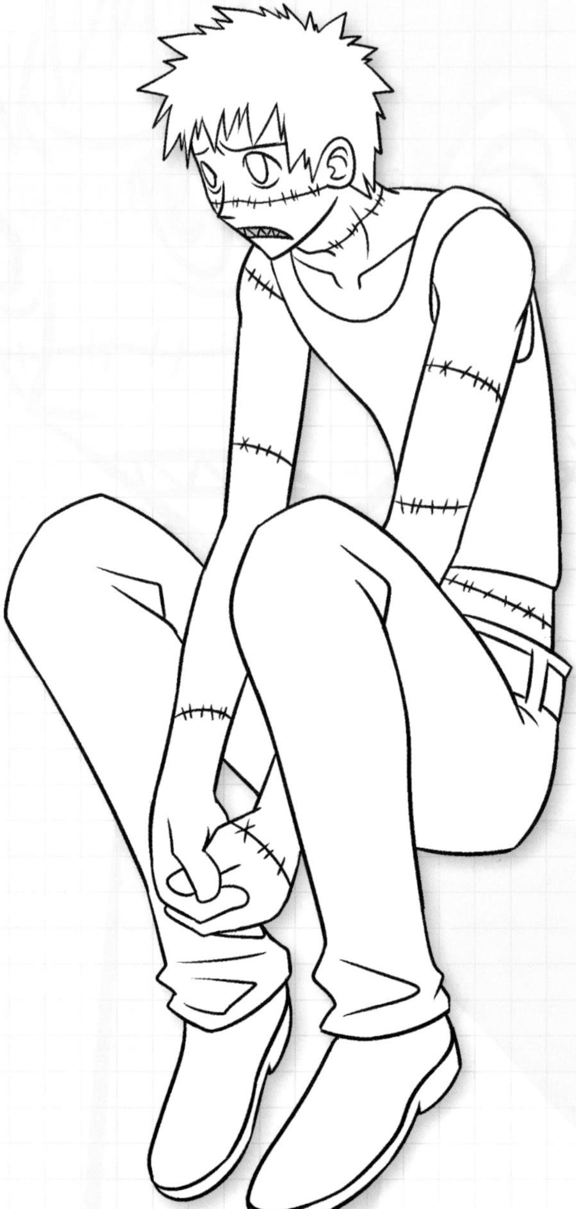

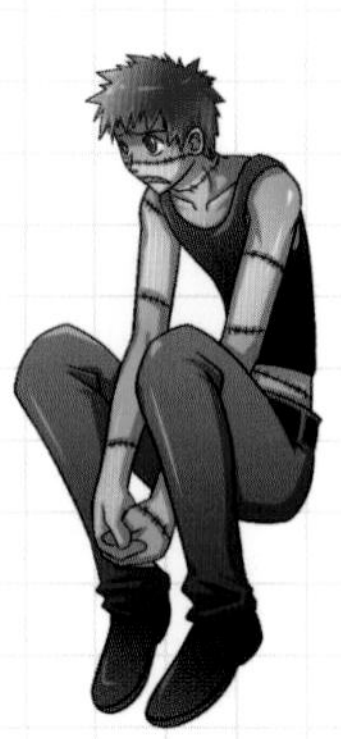

020

sci-fi and cyber punk villains

search criteria

female. sitting. horror. monster. doll. girl.

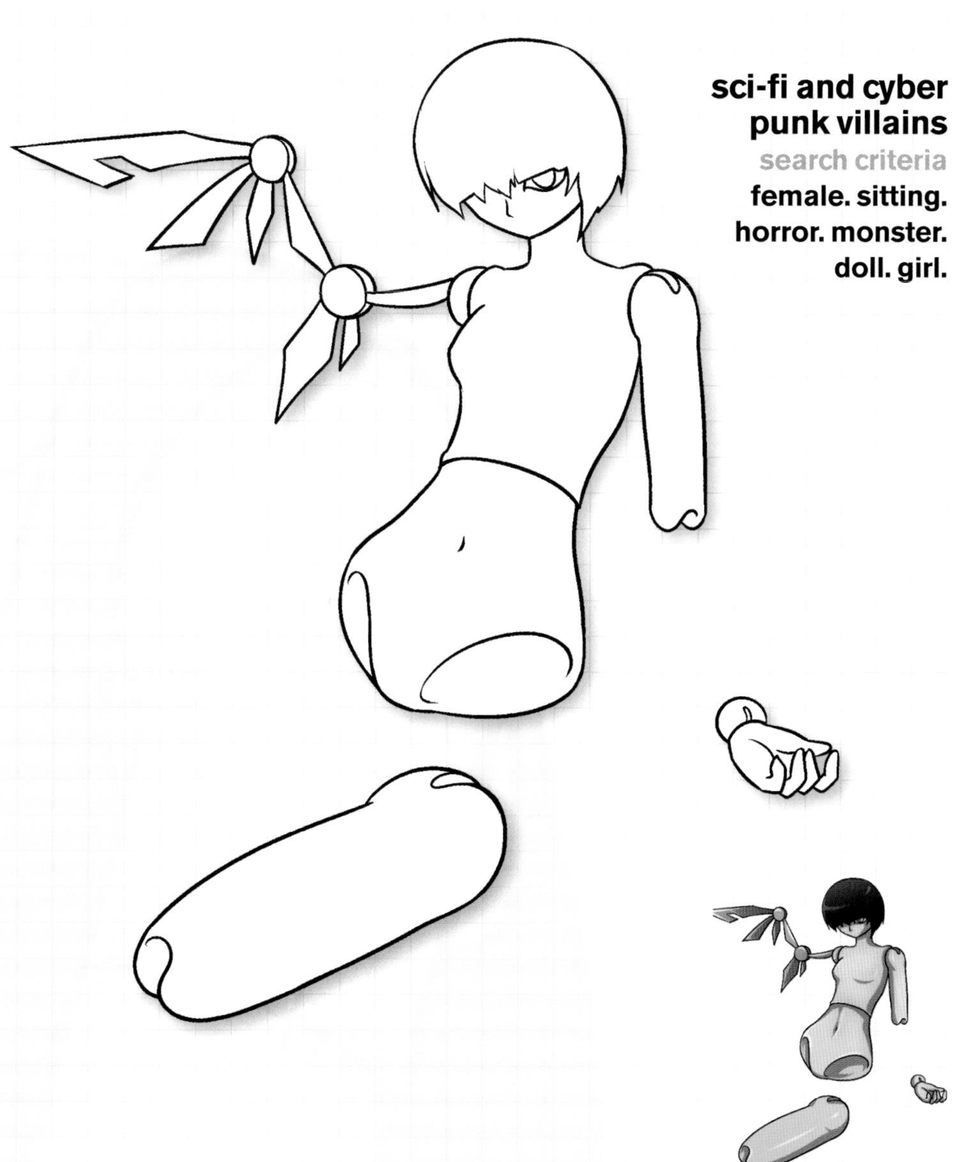

021

sci-fi and cyber punk villains

search criteria

female. standing. monster. doll. stitches. vamp. gothic. horror.

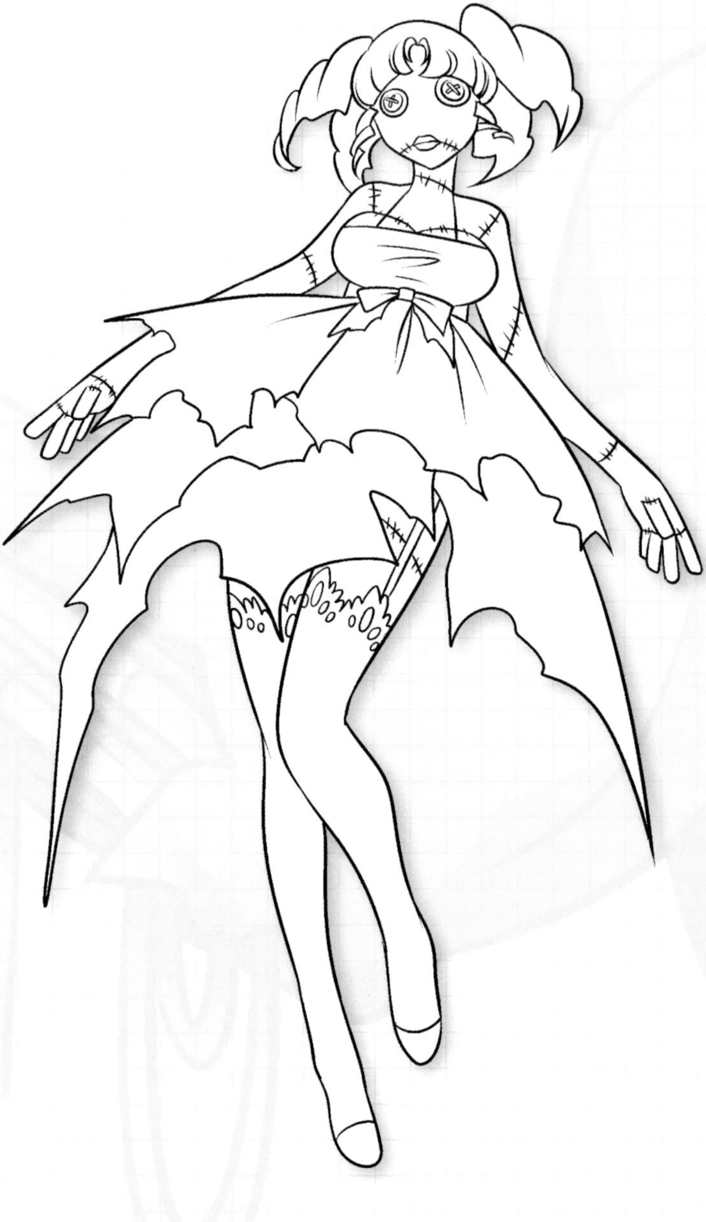

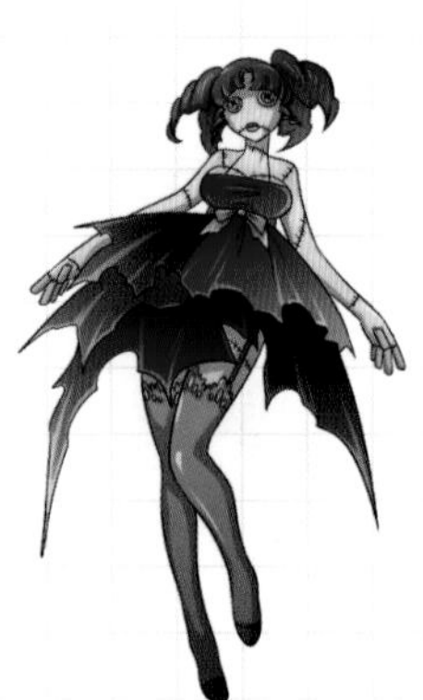

022

sci-fi and cyber punk villains

search criteria

male. standing. side. muscle. cyborg.

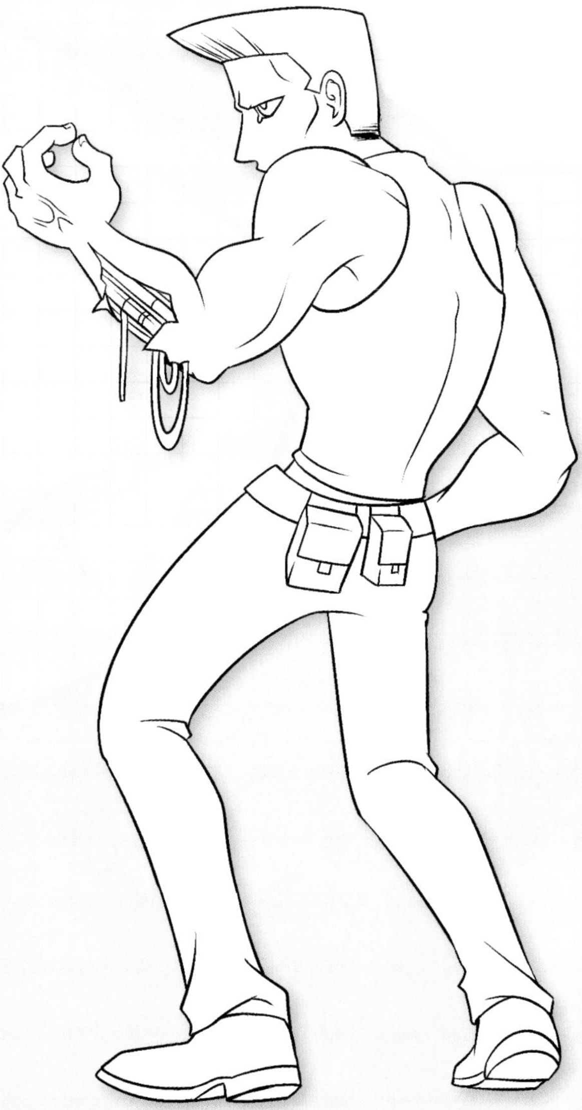

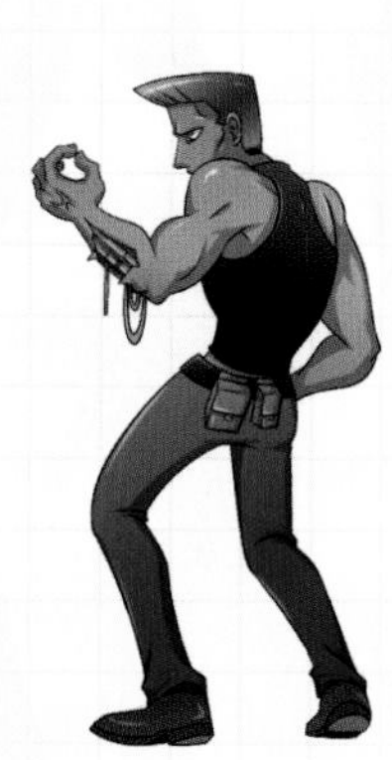

023

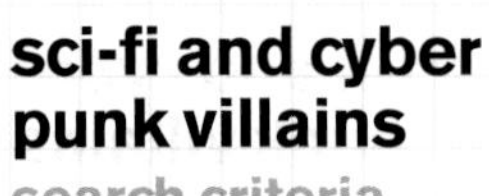

sci-fi and cyber punk villains

search criteria

female. floating. monster. doll. strings. girl. horror.

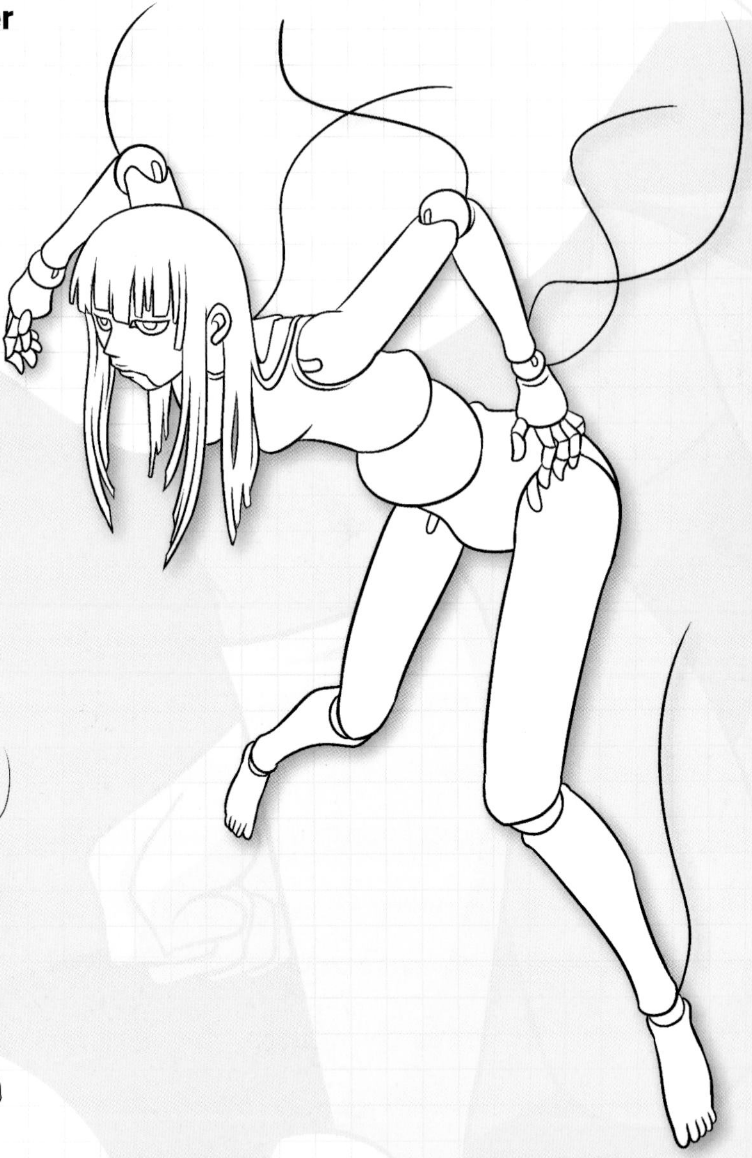

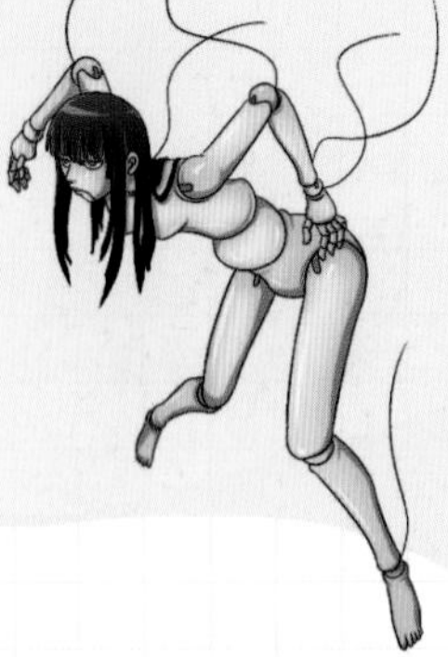

024

sci-fi and cyber punk villains

search criteria

male. flying. cape. shout. jump. mask. superhuman.

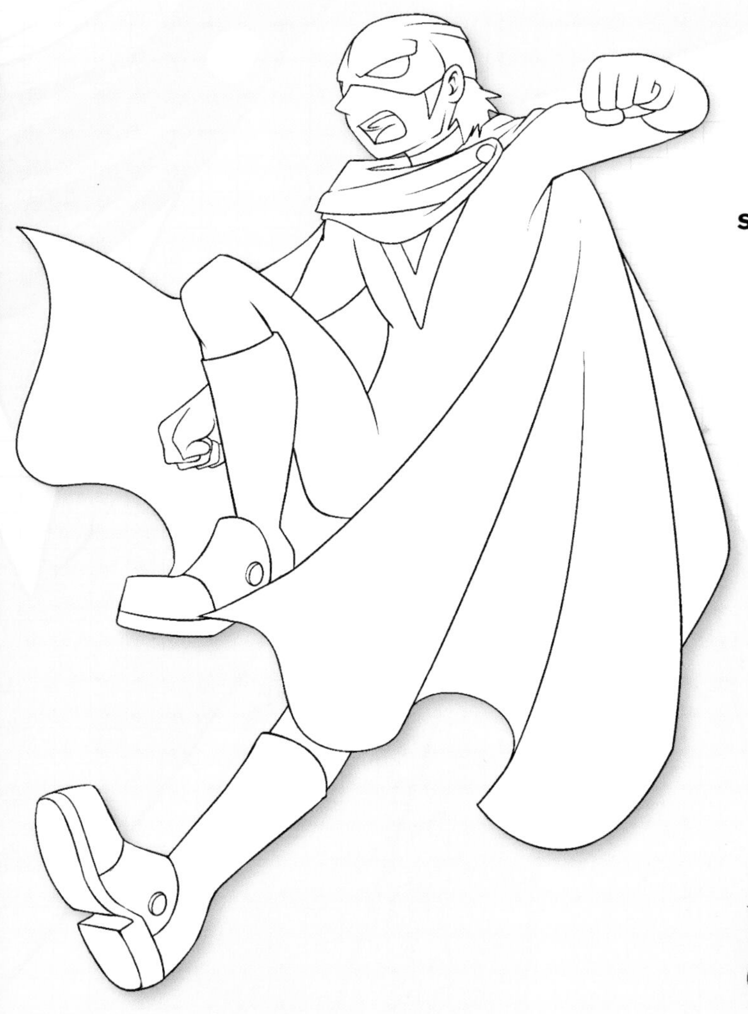

025

sci-fi and cyber punk villains

search criteria

male. standing. tail. monster. alien.

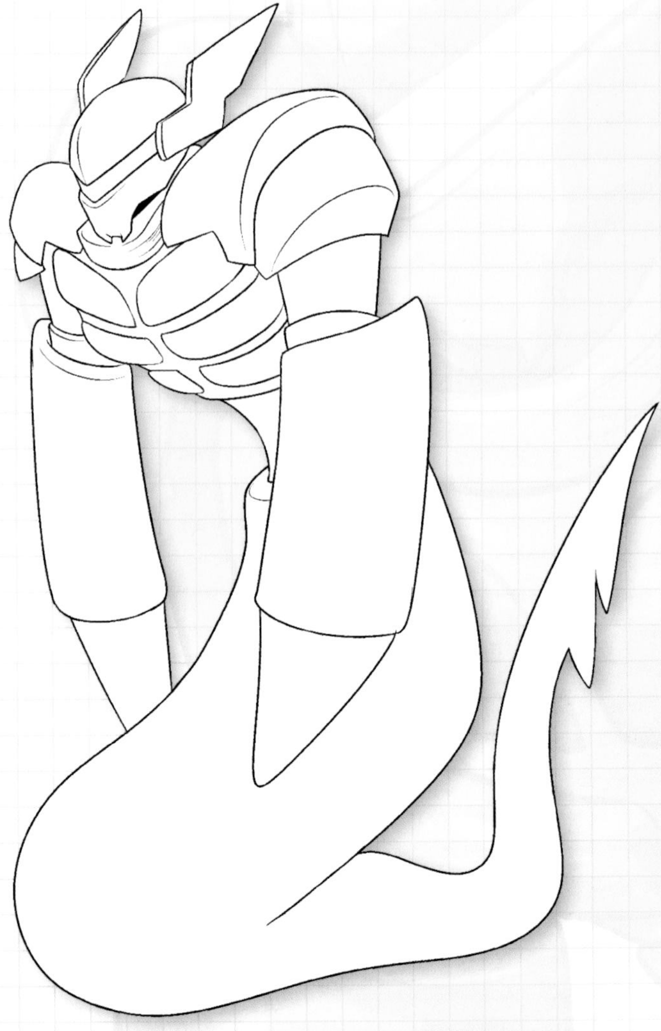

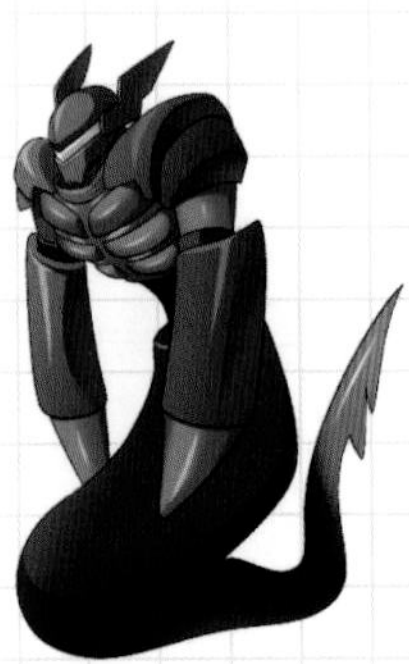

026

sci-fi and cyber punk villains

search criteria

male. standing. staff. monster. alien. wizard. tail.

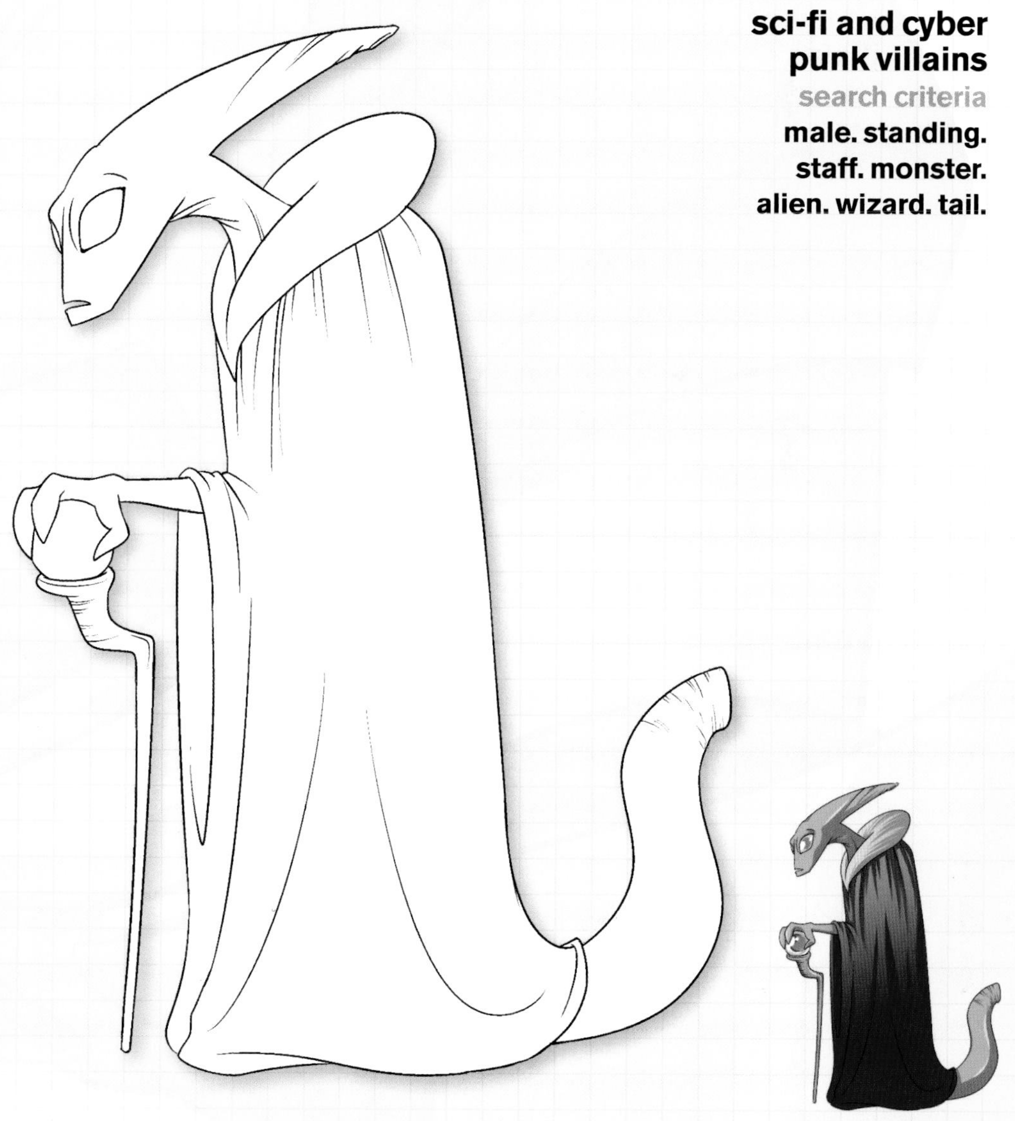

027

sci-fi and cyber punk villains

search criteria

floating. cyborg. monster. evil. futuristic. alien.

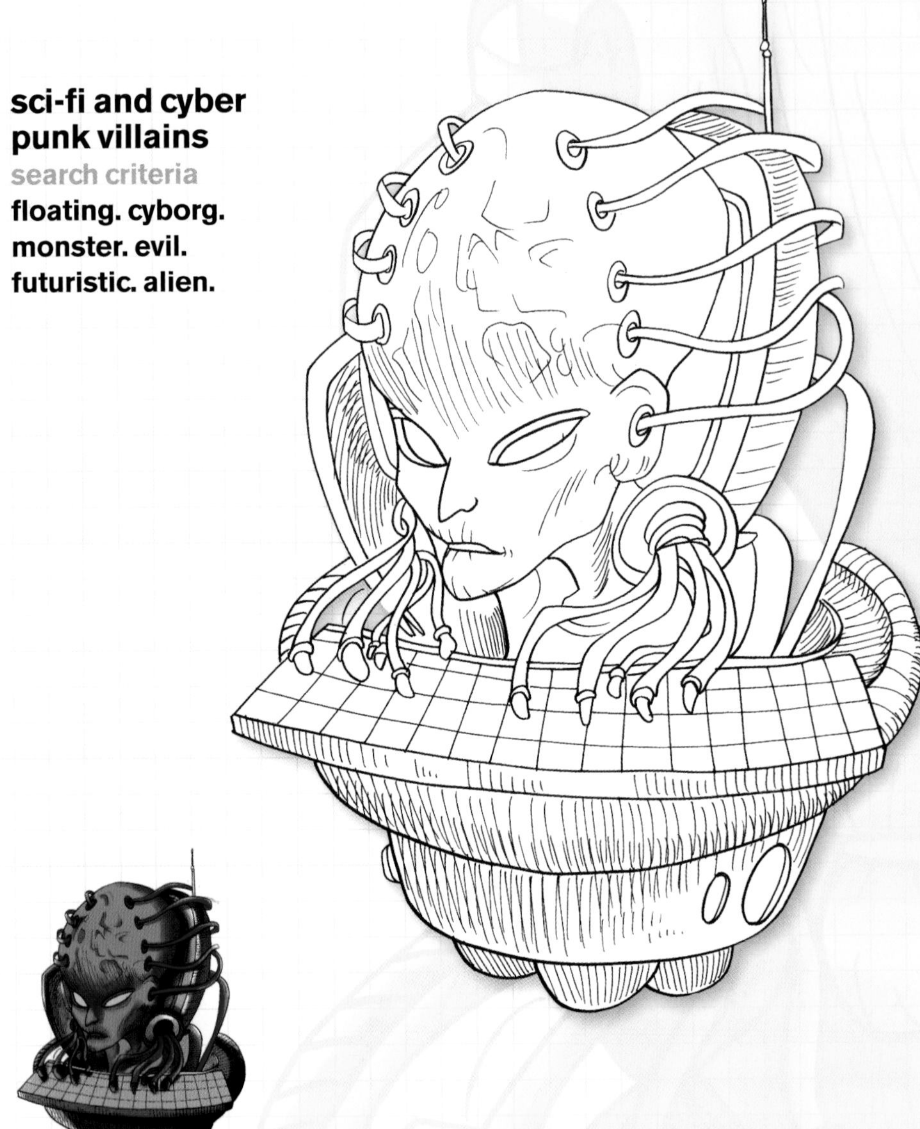

028

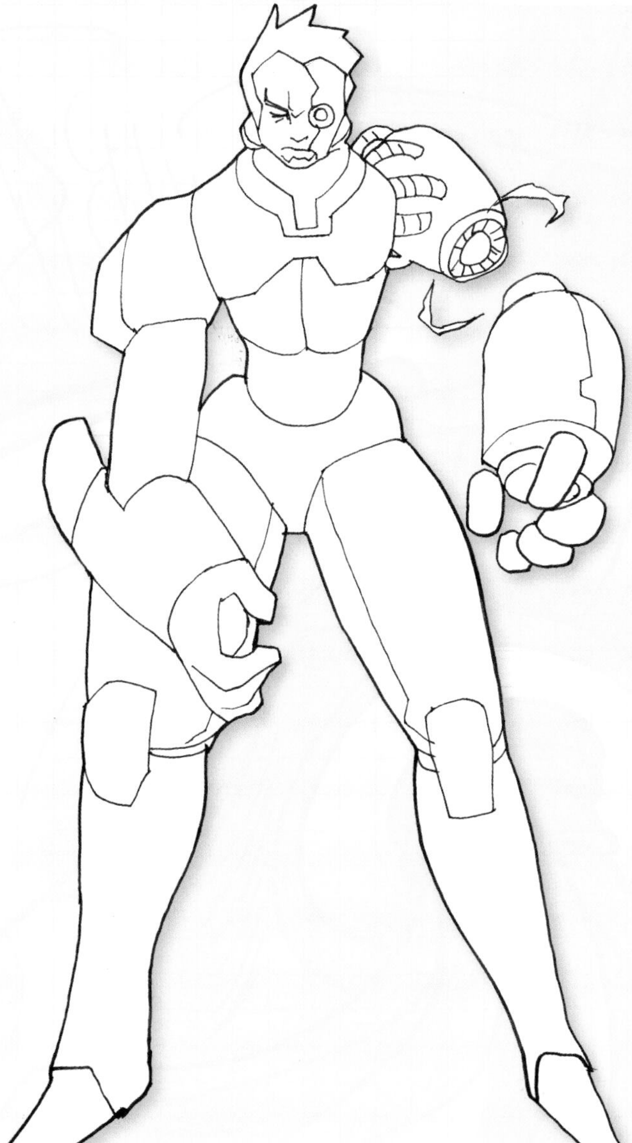

sci-fi and cyber punk villains

search criteria

male. standing. cyborg. muscle.

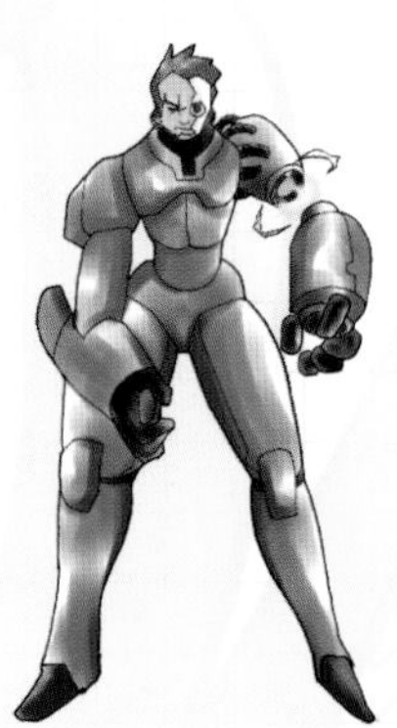

029

sci-fi and cyber punk villains

search criteria

male. standing. staff. wizard. alien. monster. cyber.

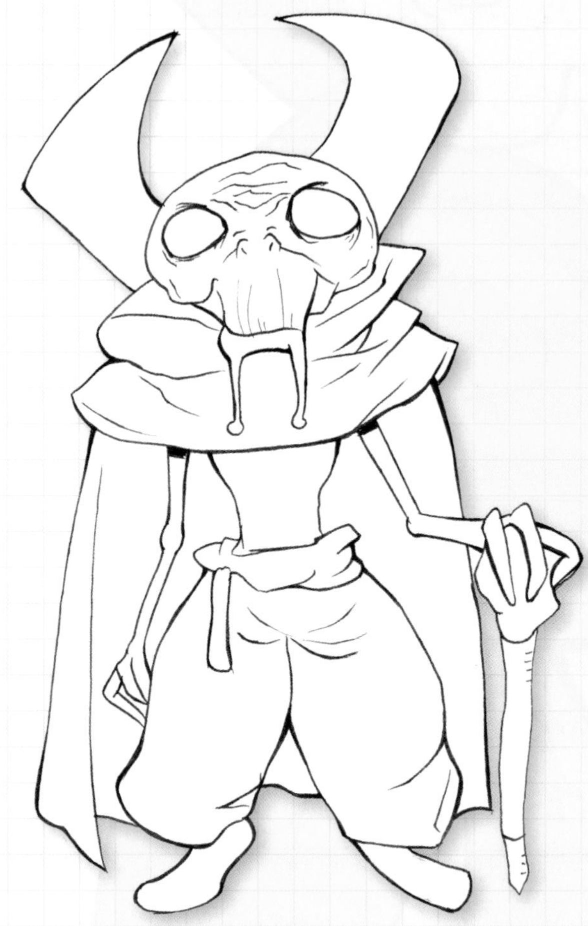

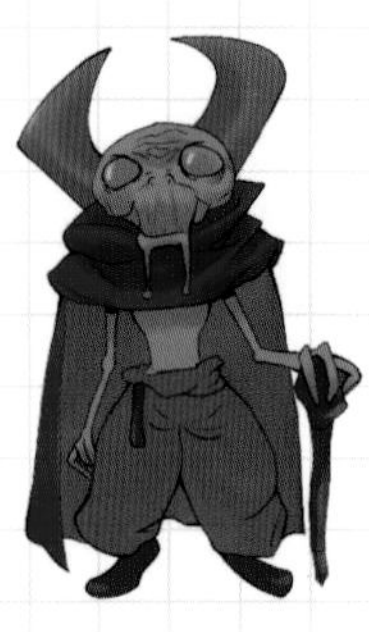

030

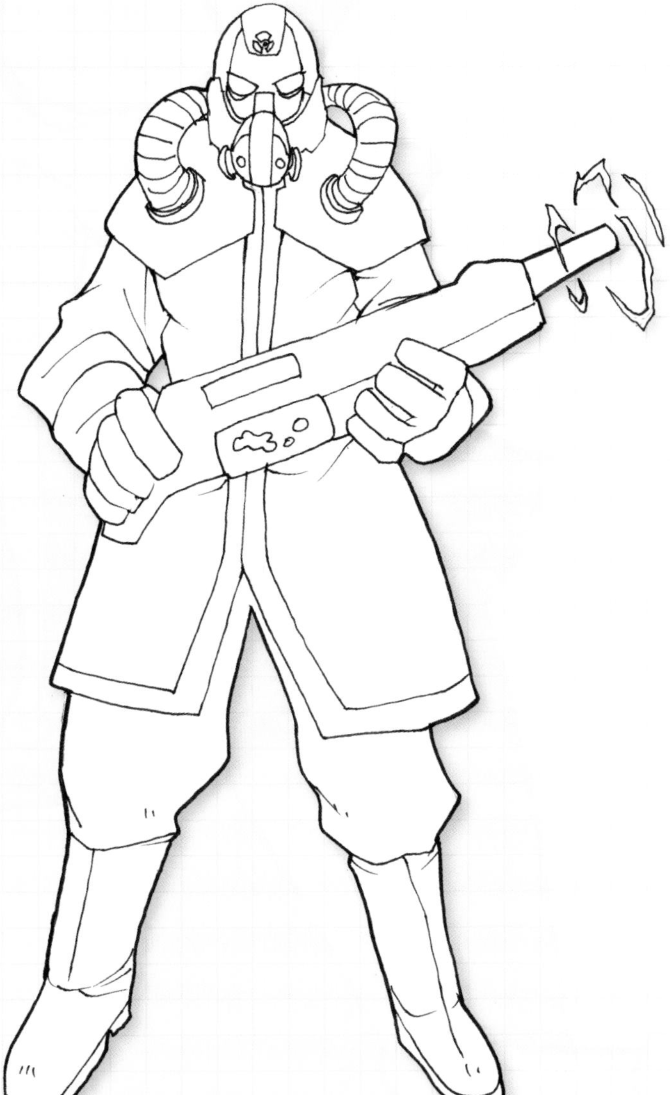

sci-fi and cyber punk villains

search criteria

male. standing. android. fighter. weapon. gun. mask. gas.

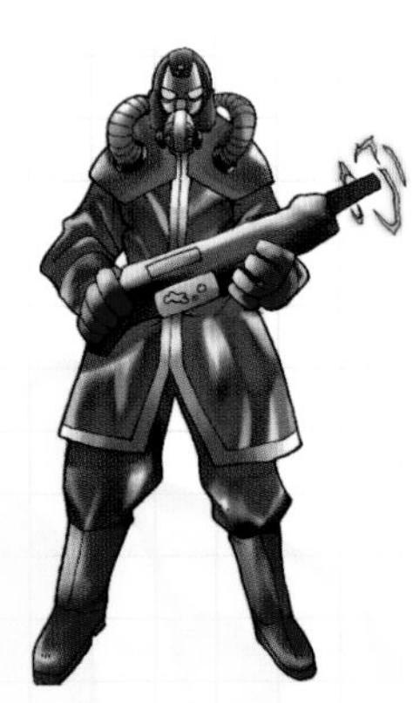

031

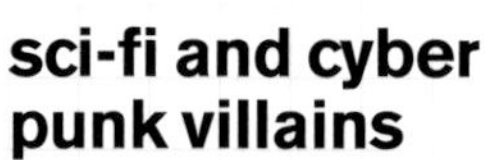

sci-fi and cyber punk villains

search criteria

male. posed. weapon. sword. mask. gas. jump.

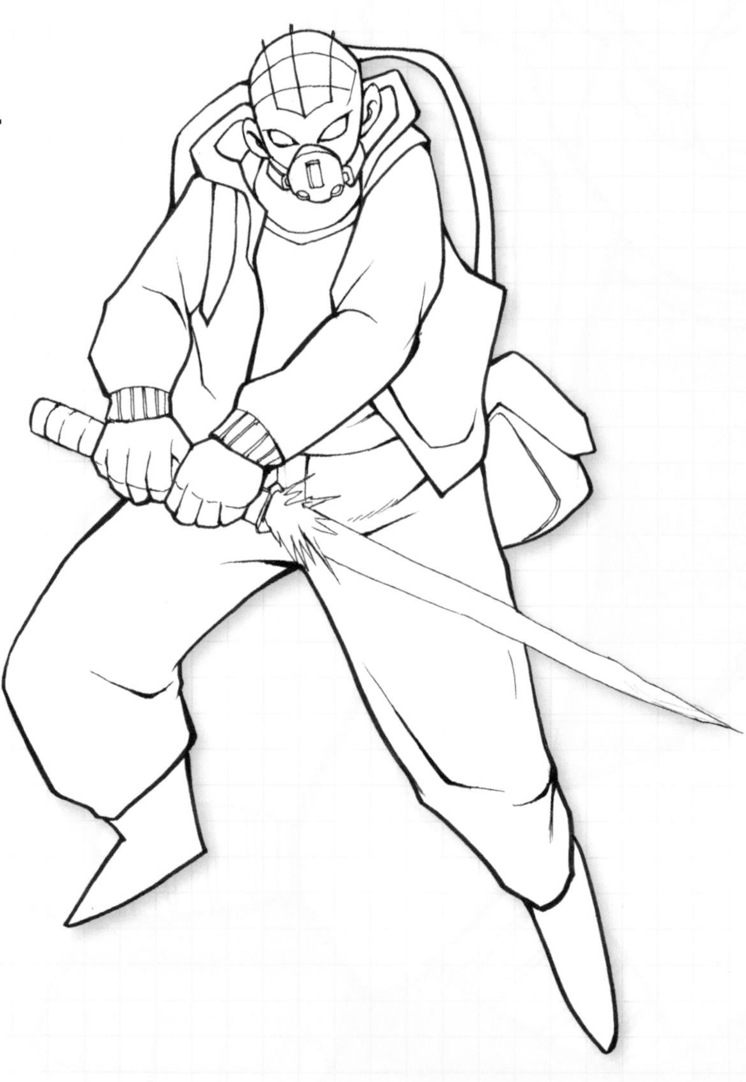

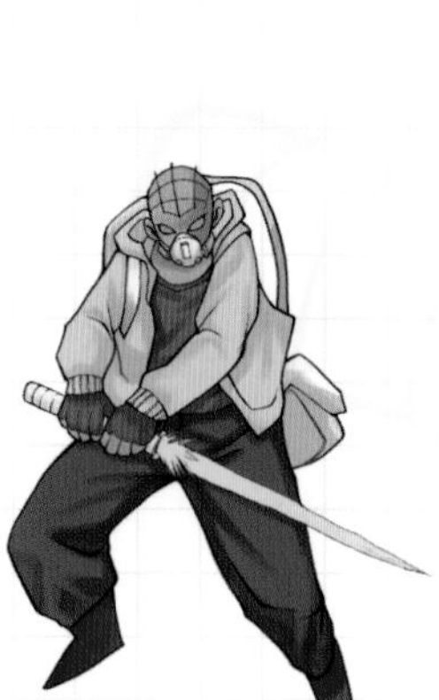

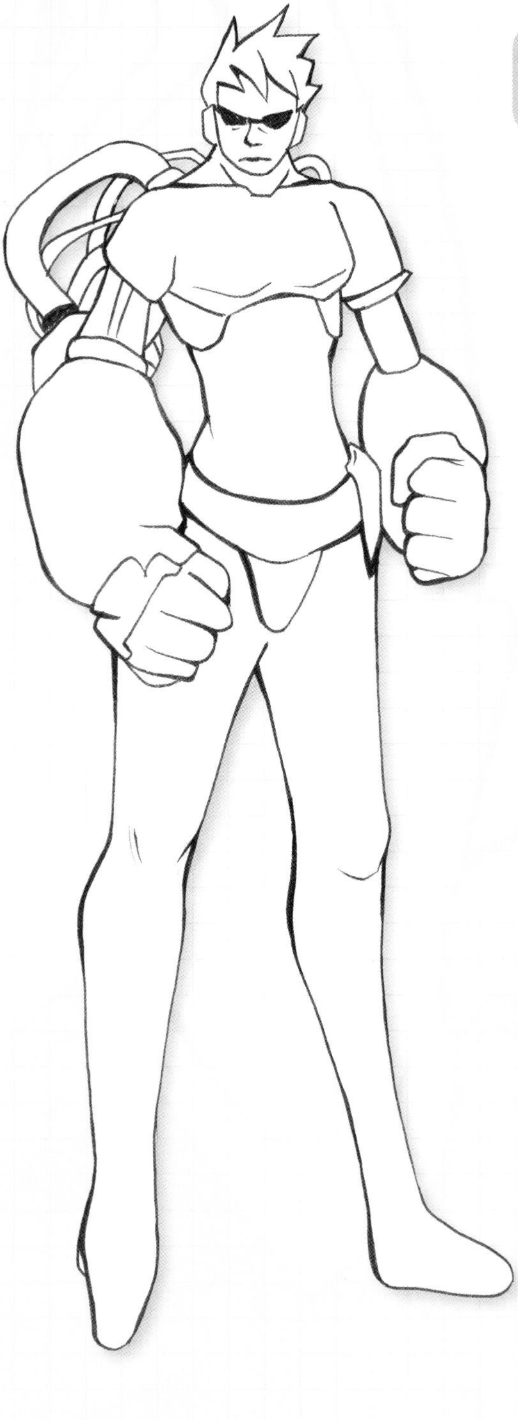

032

sci-fi and cyber punk villains

search criteria

male. standing. cyborg. sunglasses. muscle. fighter.

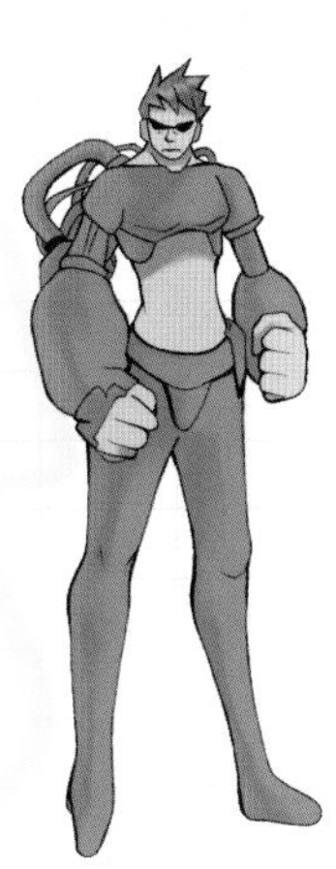

033

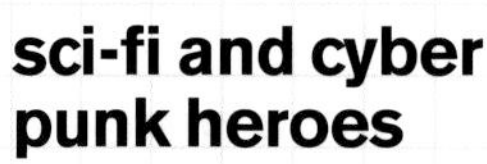

sci-fi and cyber punk heroes

search criteria

female. standing. muscle. stitches. scars. smiling.

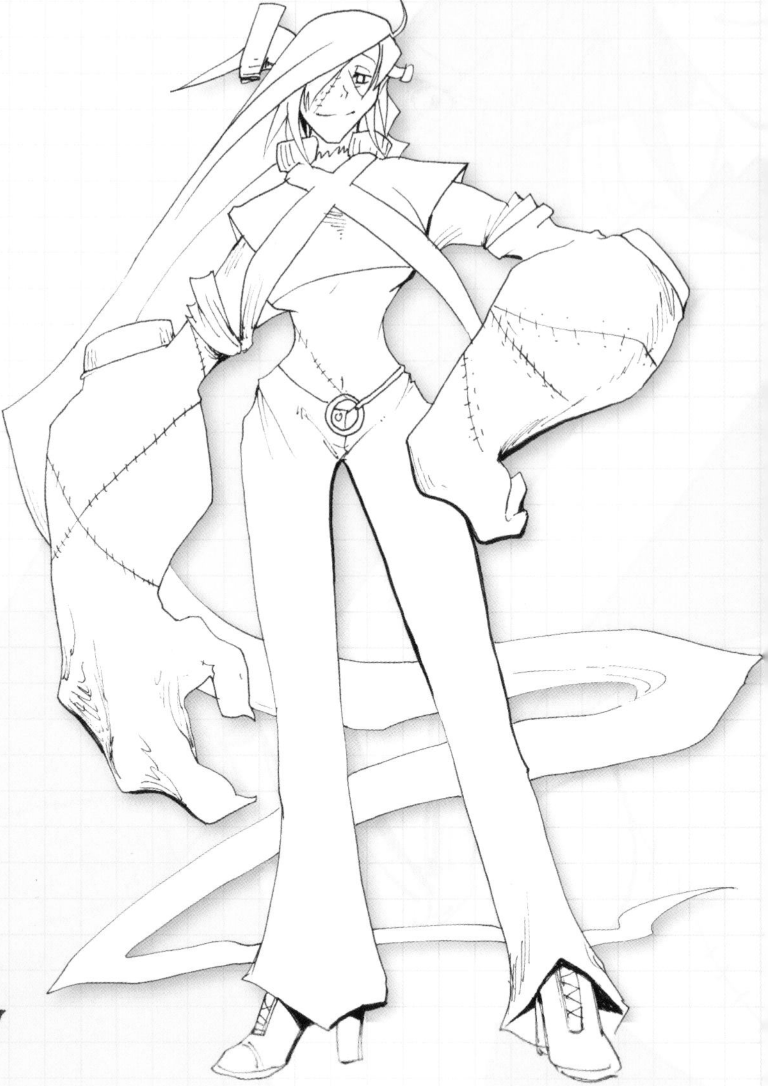

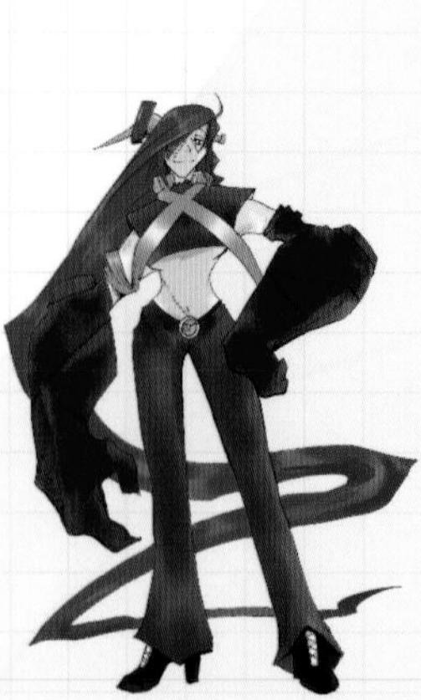

034

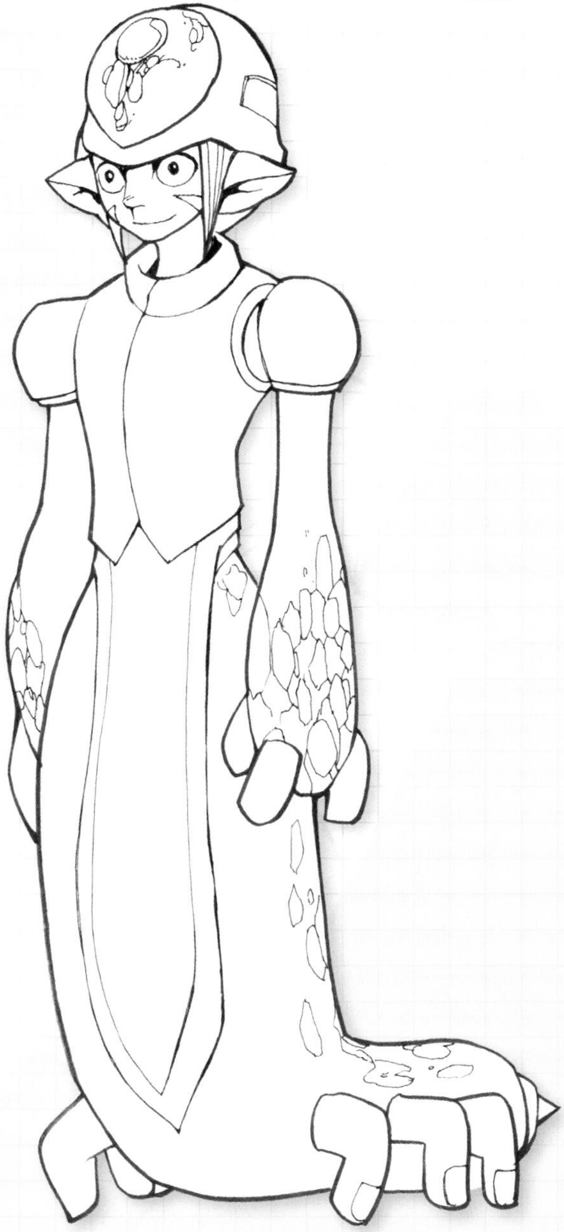

sci-fi and cyber punk heroes

search criteria

male. standing. monster. smiling. happy. helmet. goofy. tail.

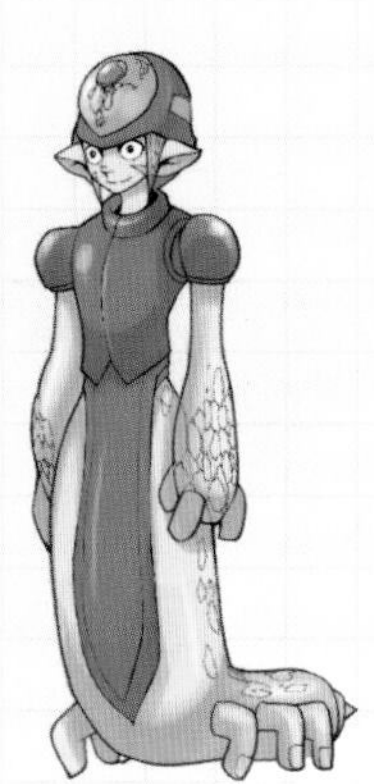

035

sci-fi and cyber punk heroes

search criteria

female. side. robot. jump. android. floating. futuristic.

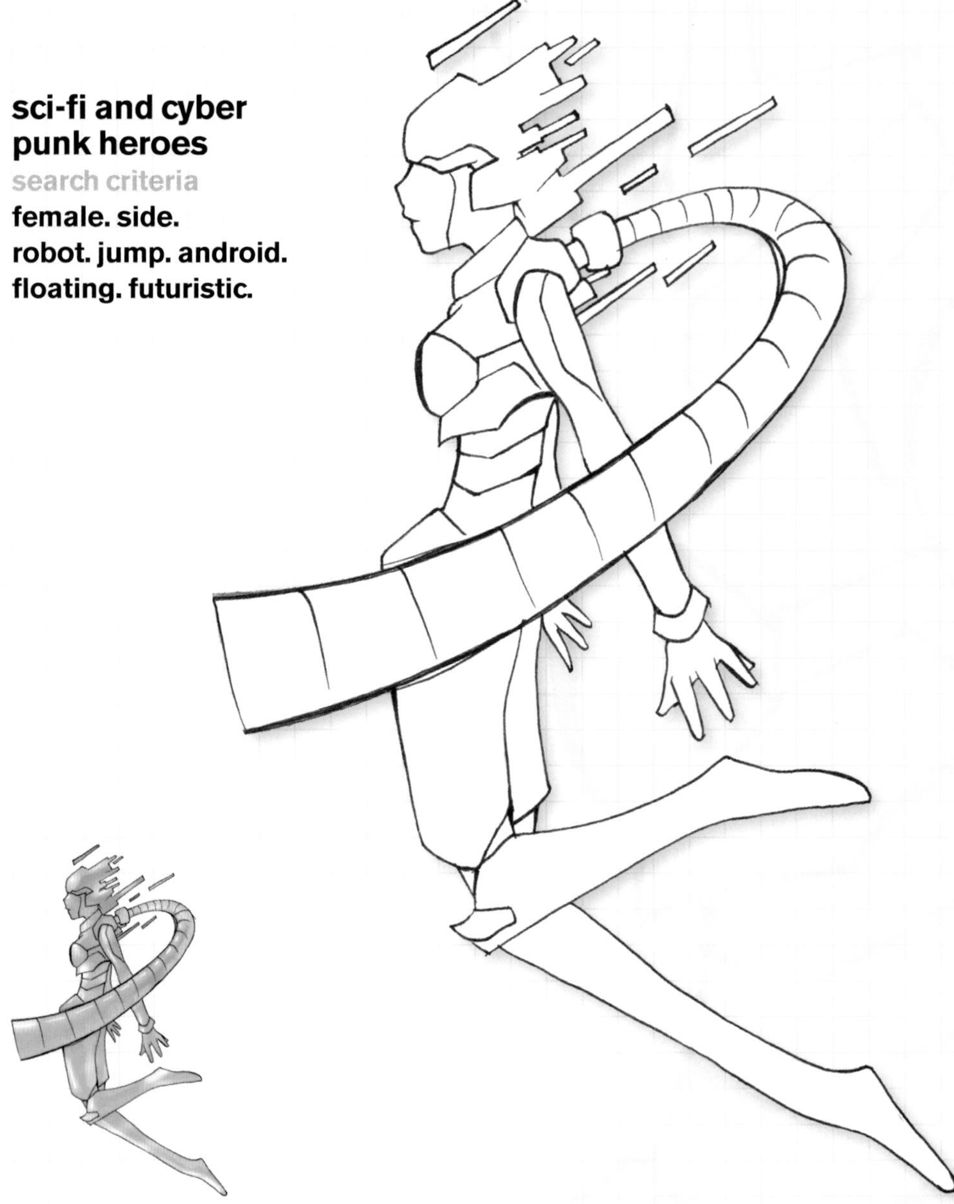

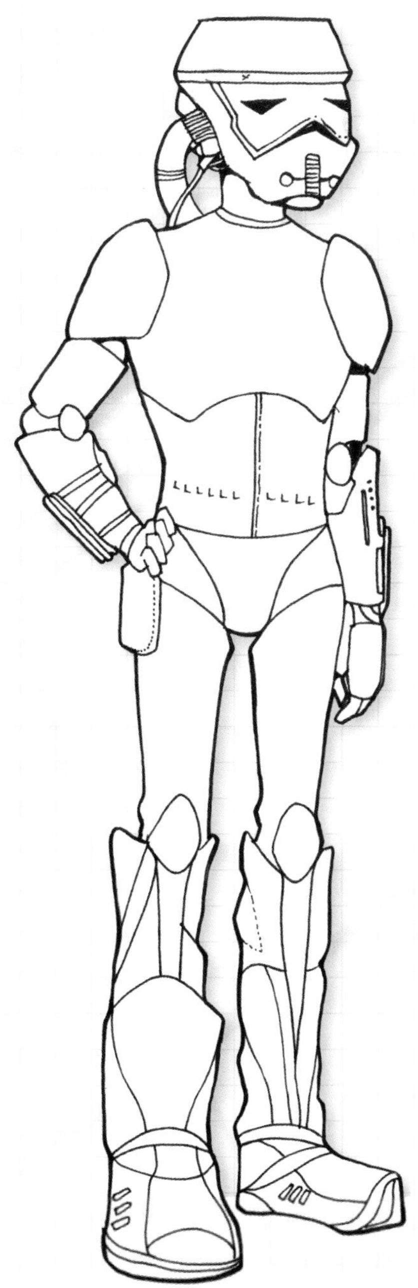

036

sci-fi and cyber punk heroes

search criteria

male. standing. robot. android. mask. futuristic.

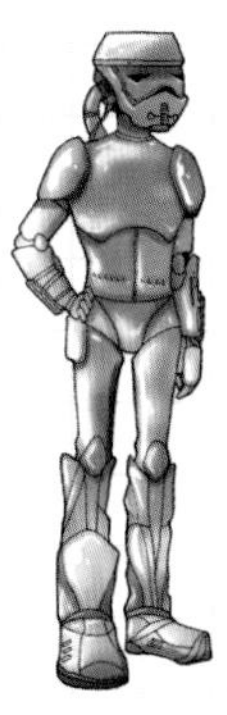

037

sci-fi and cyber punk heroes

search criteria

male. standing. futuristic. monocle. boy.

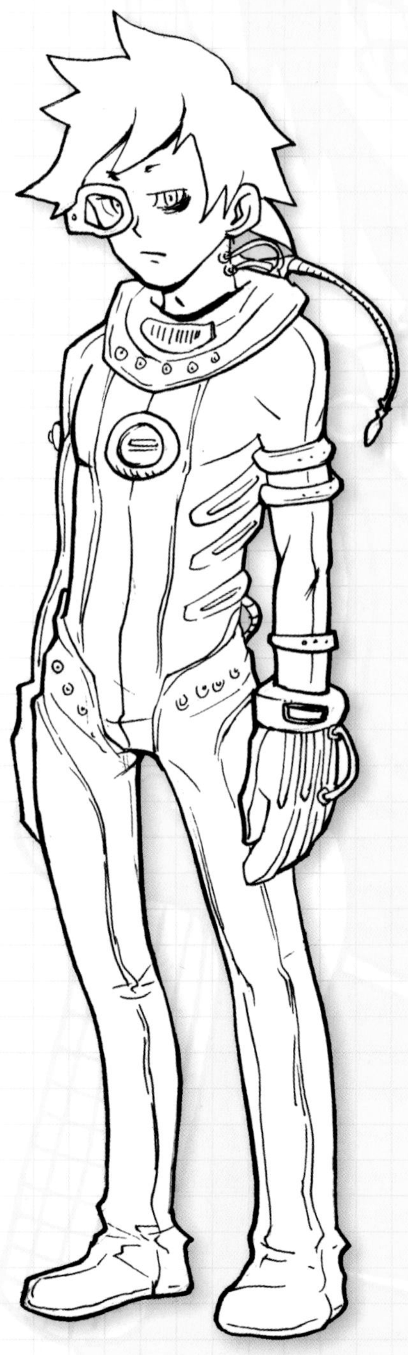

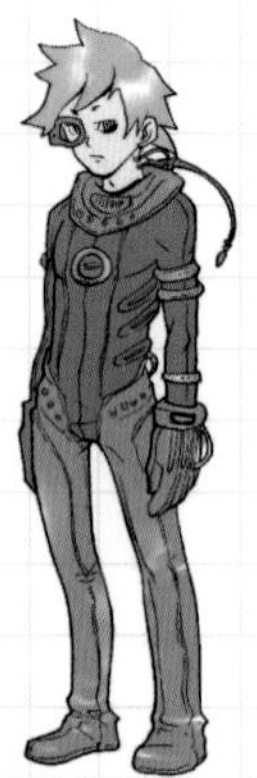

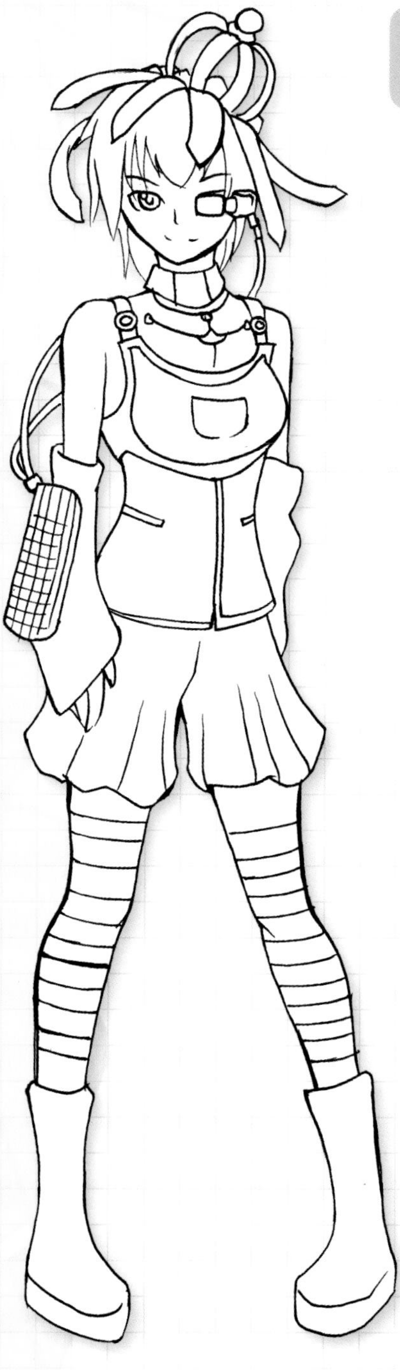

038

sci-fi and cyber punk heroes

search criteria

female. standing. monocle. futuristic. smiling. girl.

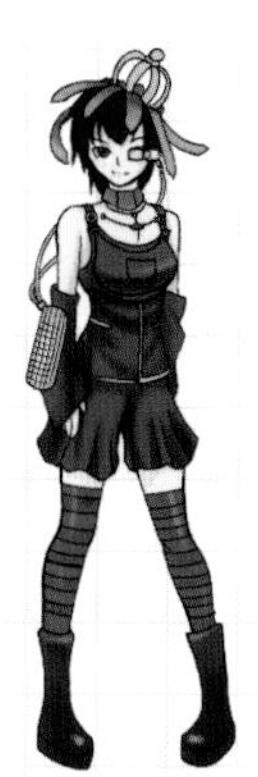

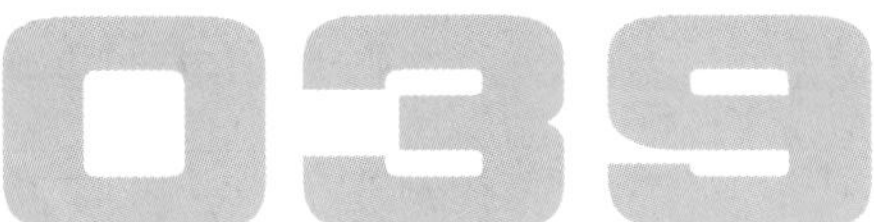

sci-fi and cyber punk heroes

search criteria

male. standing. futuristic. cyborg. mask. boy.

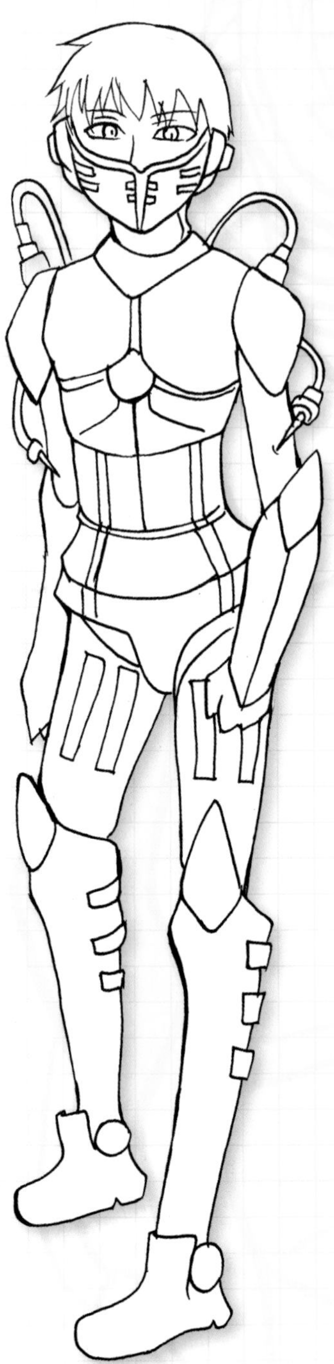

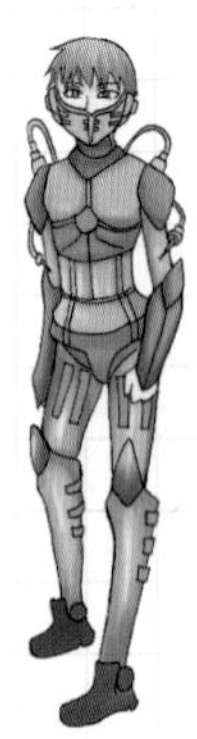

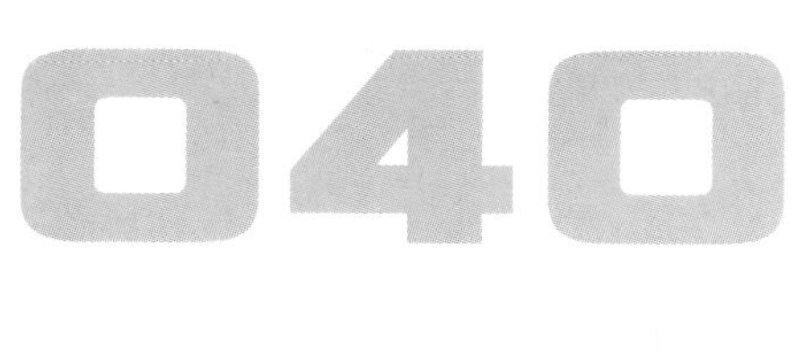

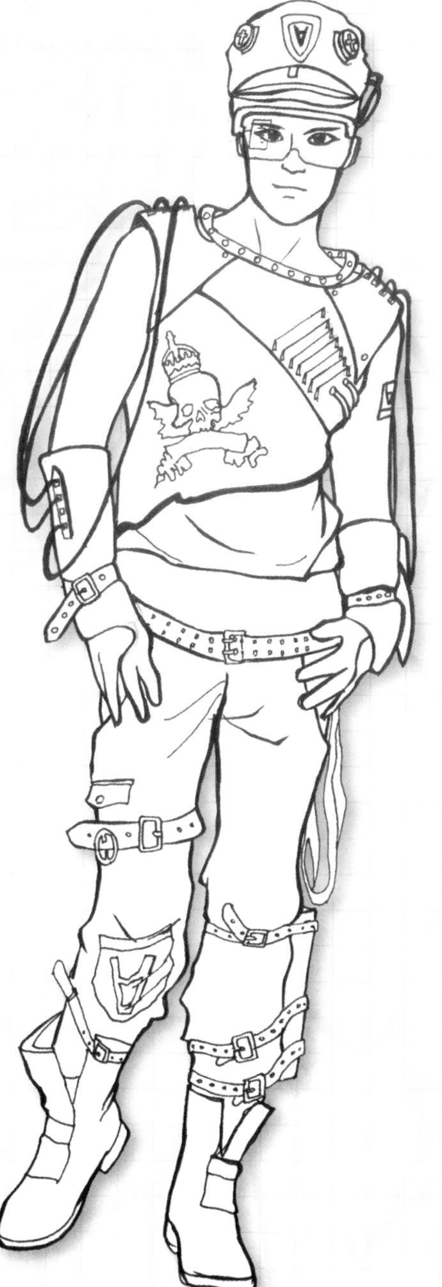

sci-fi and cyber punk heroes

search criteria

male. standing. skull. glasses. belts. hat.

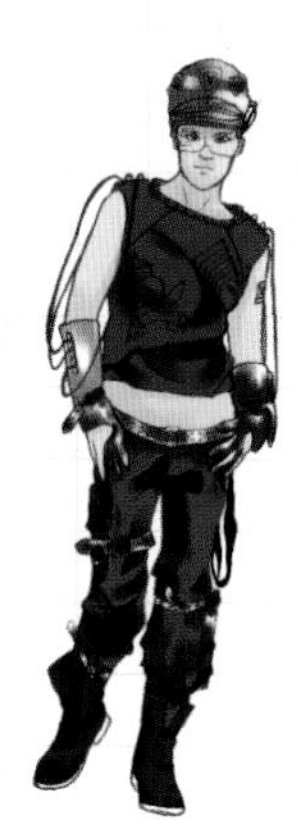

041

sci-fi and cyber punk heroes

search criteria

female. cyborg. futuristic. tentacles. microchip. alien.

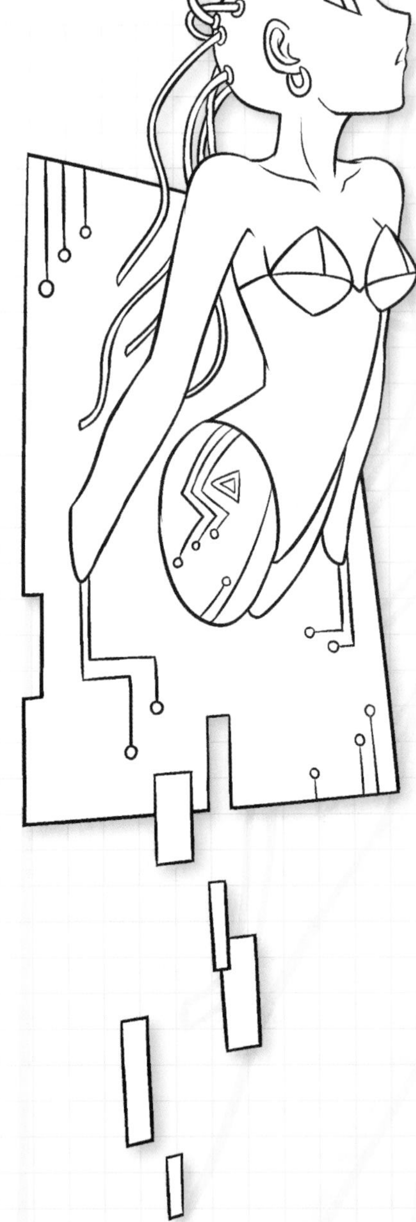

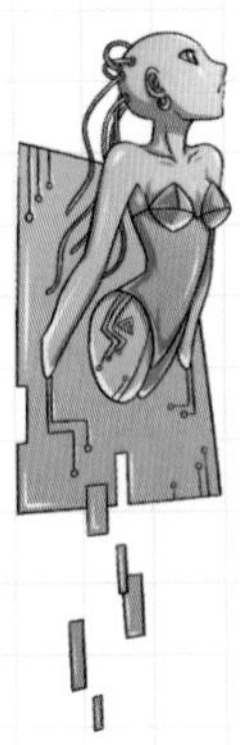

042

sci-fi and cyber punk heroes

search criteria

male. cyborg. futuristic. tentacles. microchip. boy.

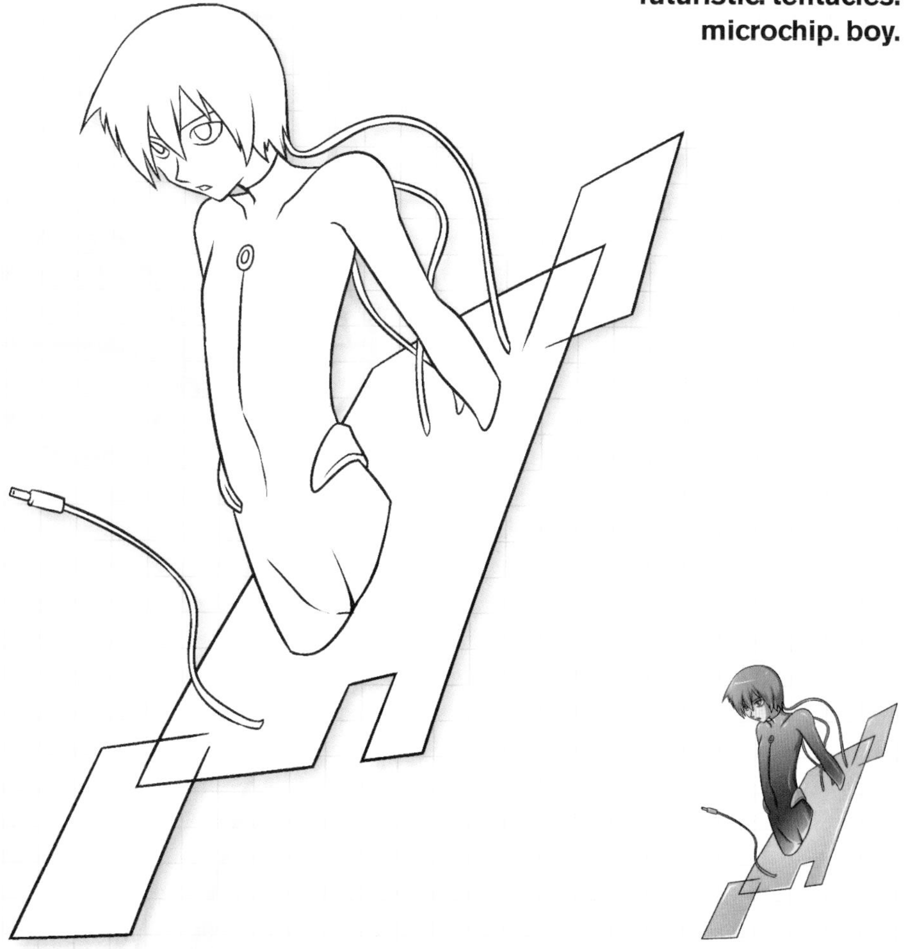

043

sci-fi and cyber punk heroes

search criteria

male. cyborg. microchip. boy. futuristic. sad.

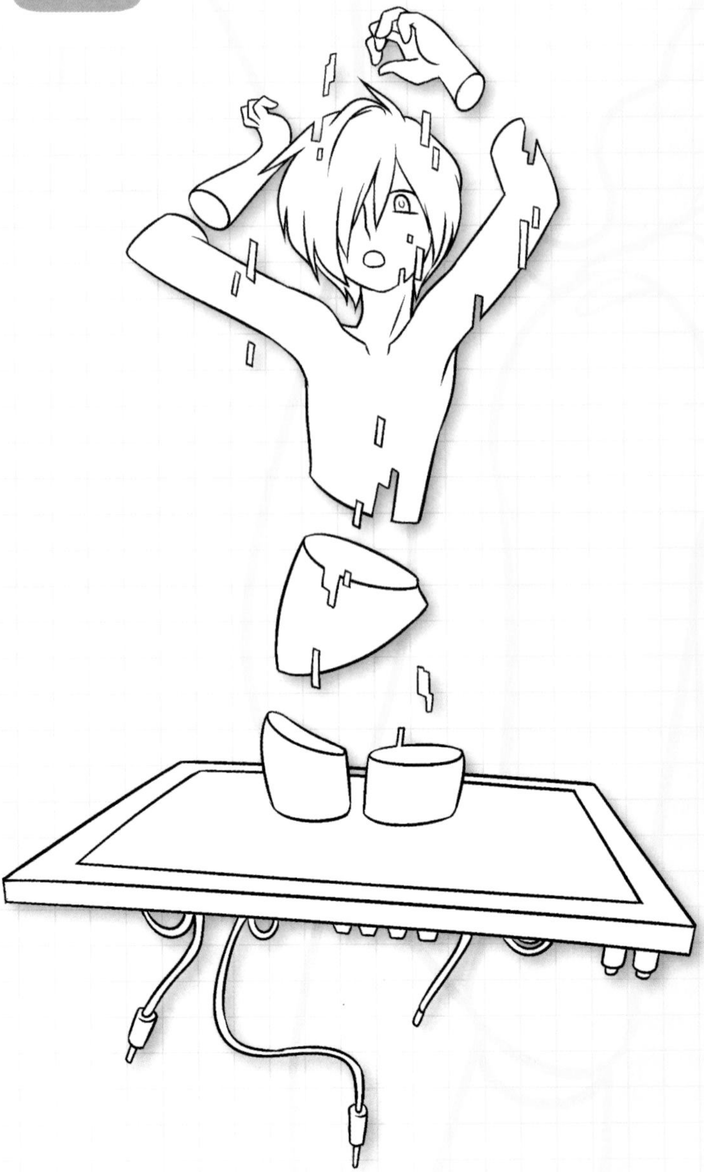

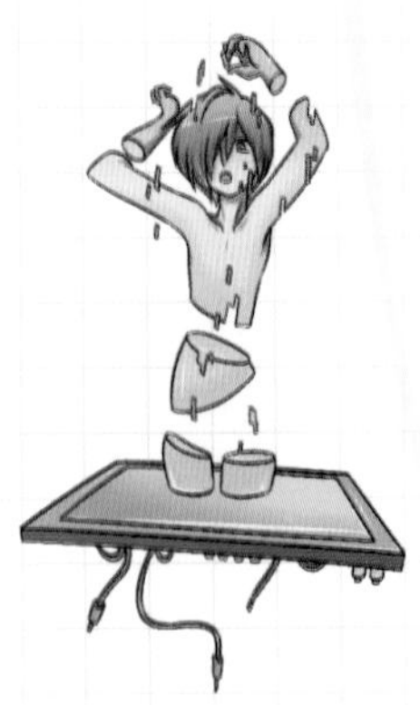

044

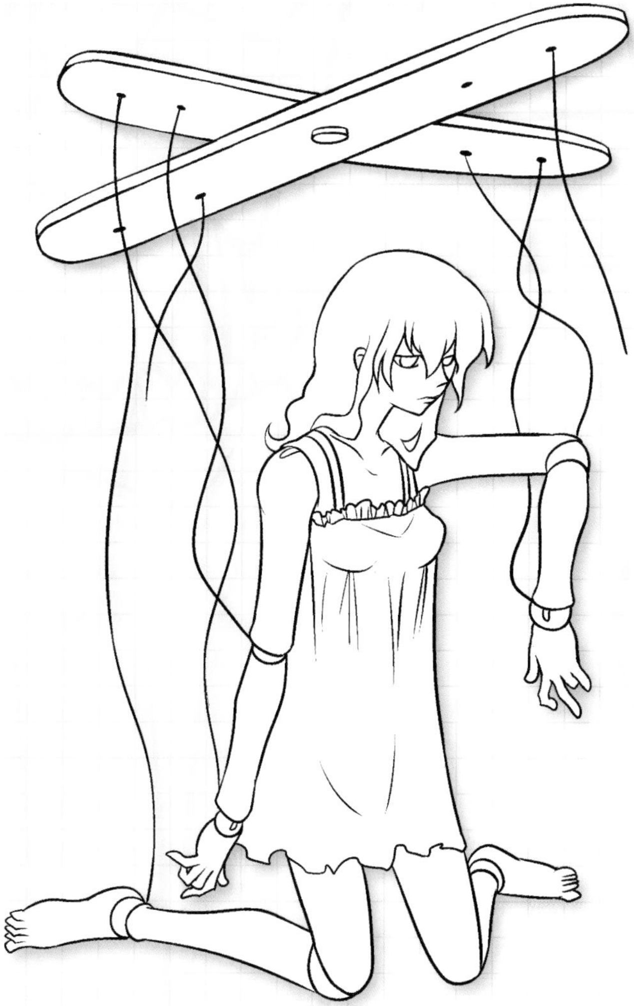

sci-fi and cyber punk heroes

search criteria

female. kneeling. posed. doll. strings. sad. puppet.

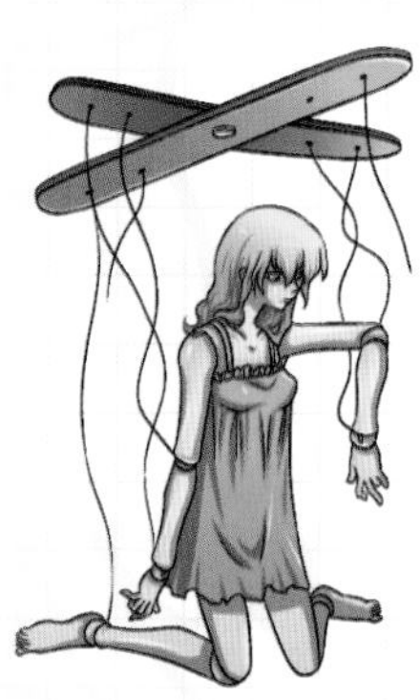

045

sci-fi and cyber punk heroes

search criteria

female. floating. tentacles. sad. cyborg. futuristic.

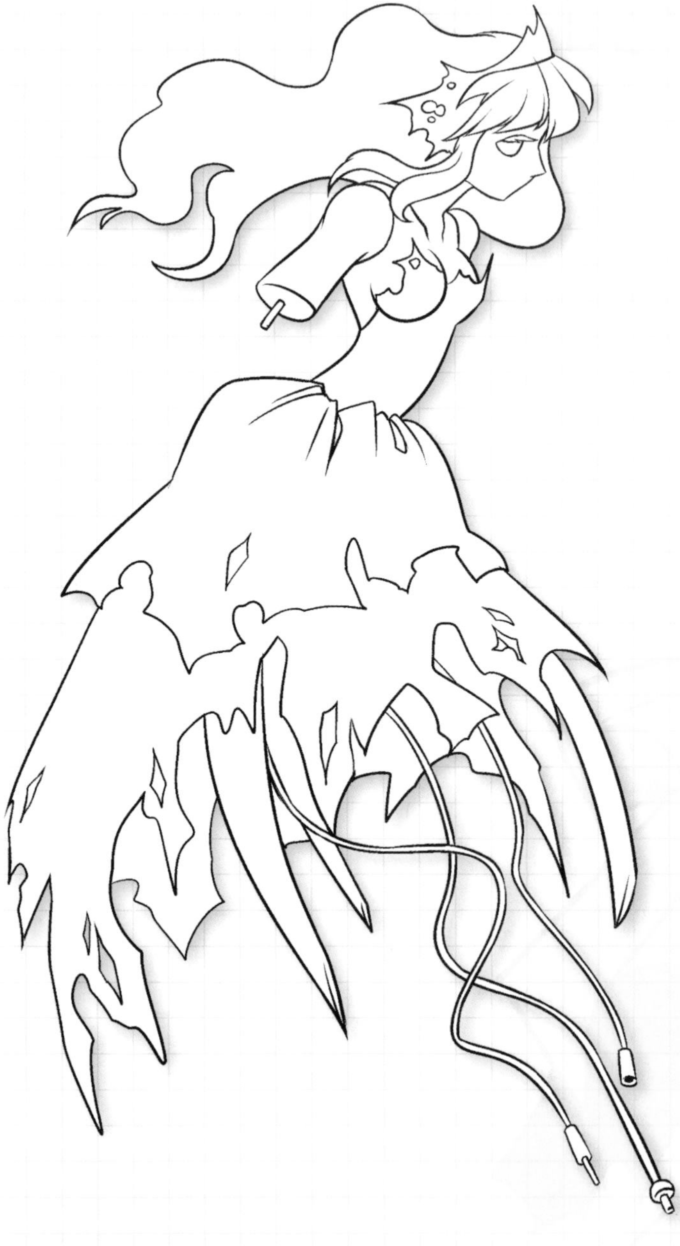

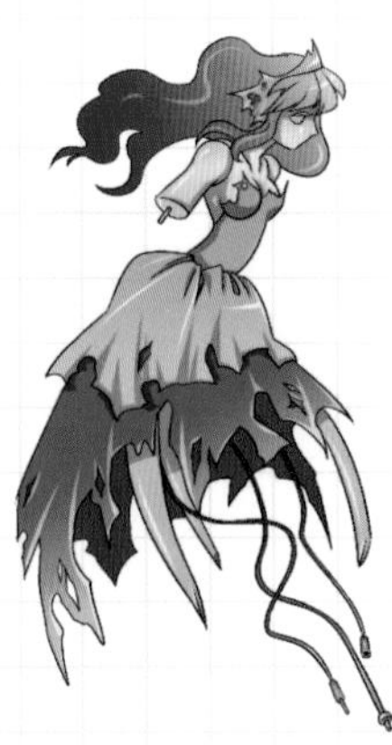

046

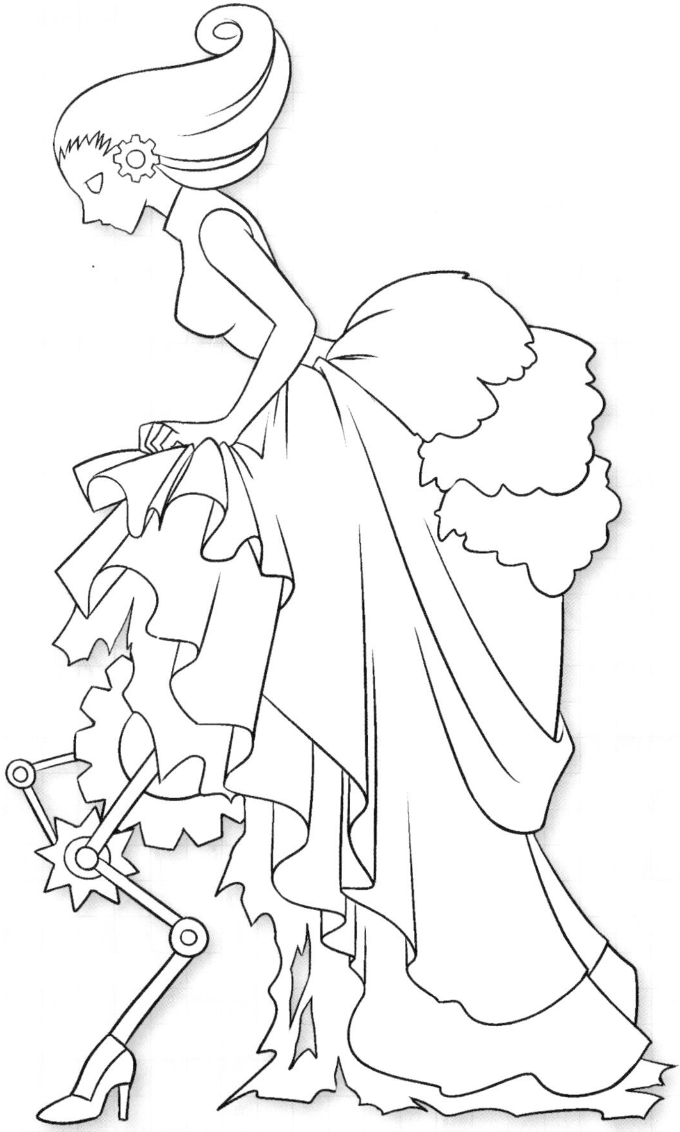

sci-fi and cyber punk heroes

search criteria

female. standing. side. cyborg. mechanical. cogs.

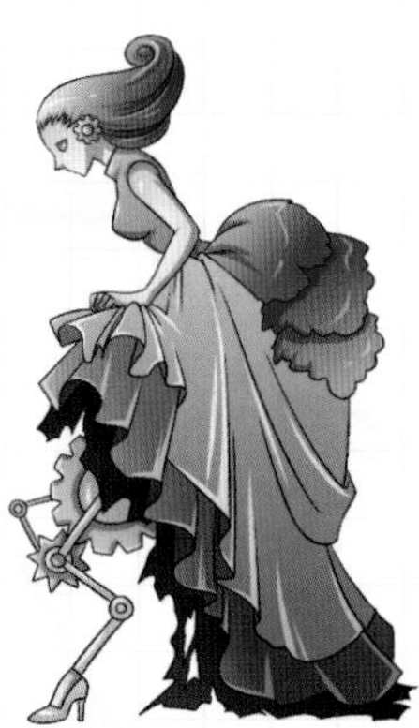

047

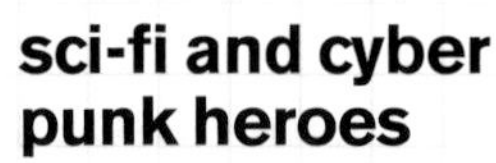

sci-fi and cyber punk heroes

search criteria

male. sitting. computer. futuristic. boy.

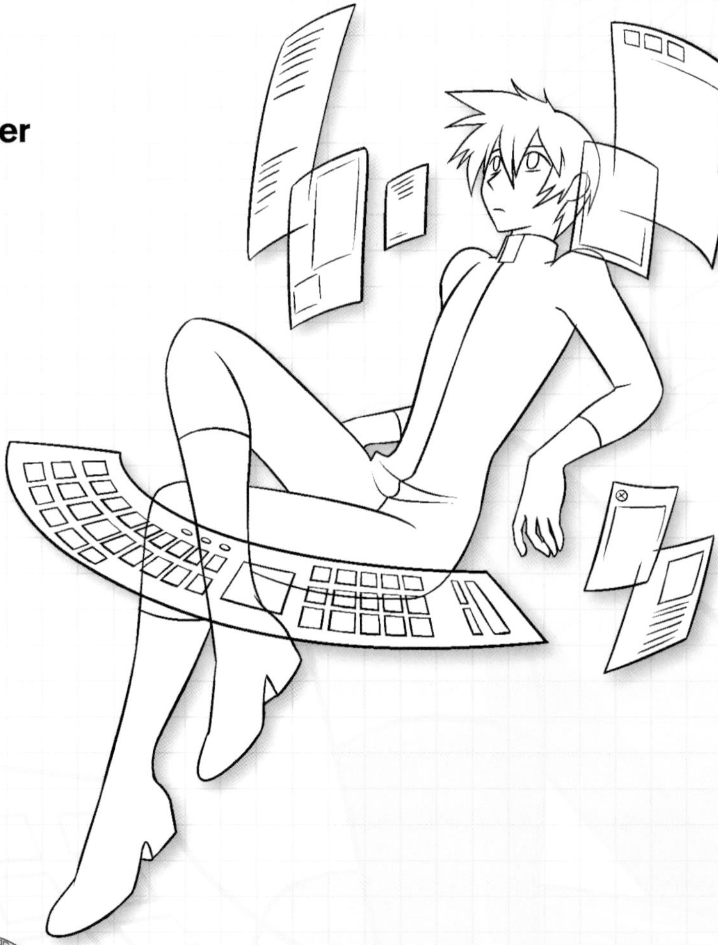

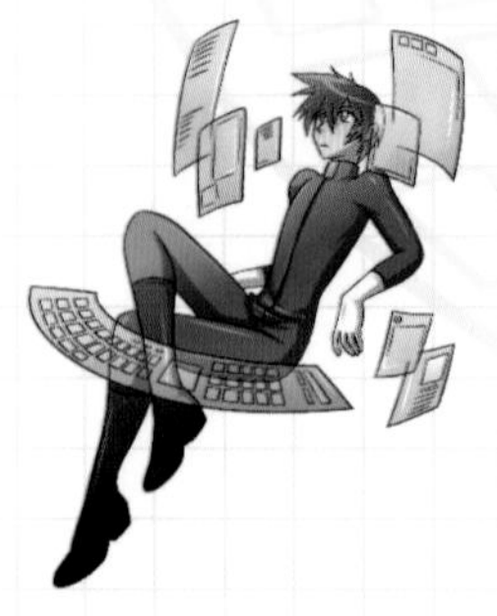

048

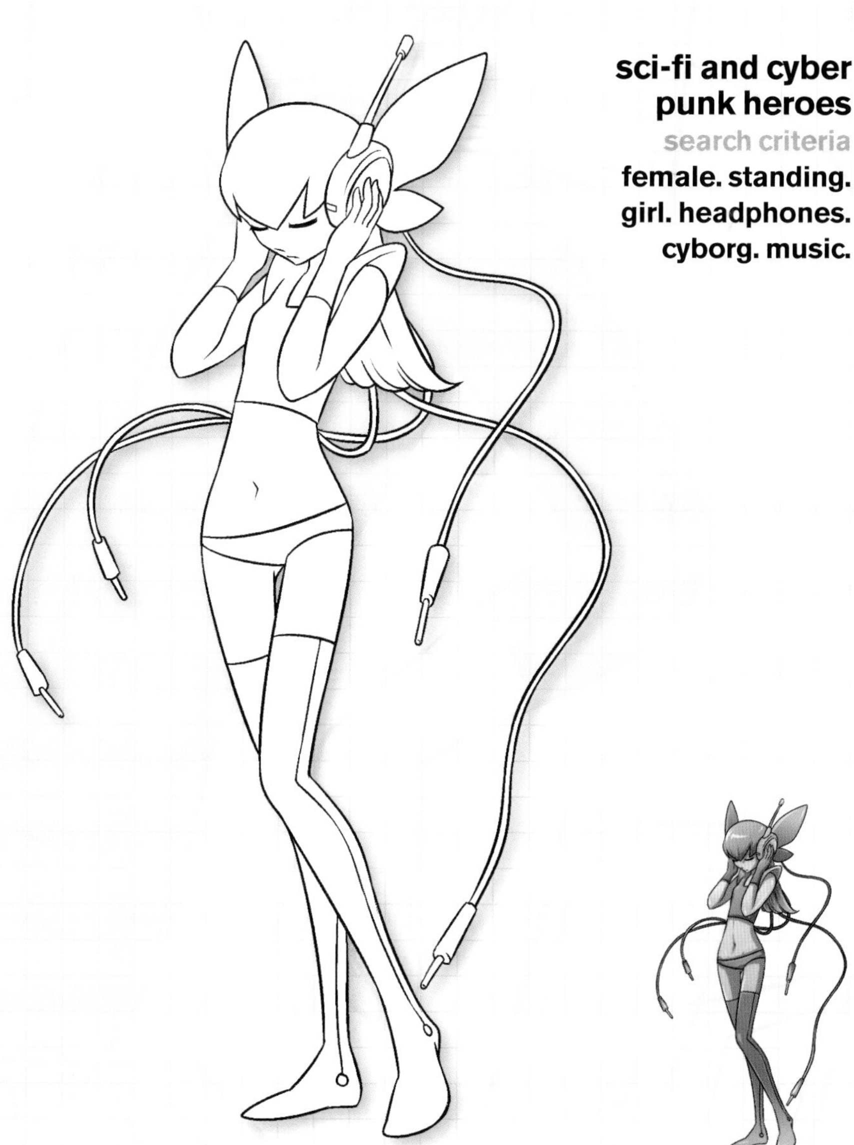

sci-fi and cyber punk heroes

search criteria

female. standing. girl. headphones. cyborg. music.

049

sci-fi and cyber punk heroes

search criteria

male. jump. moving. cyborg. futuristic. boy.

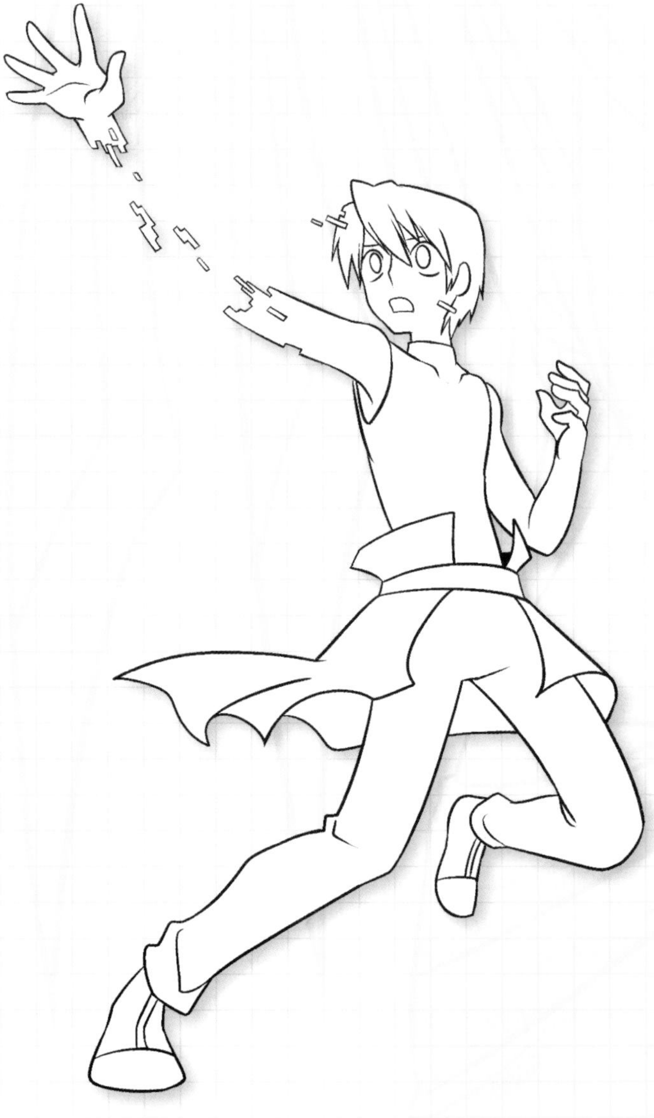

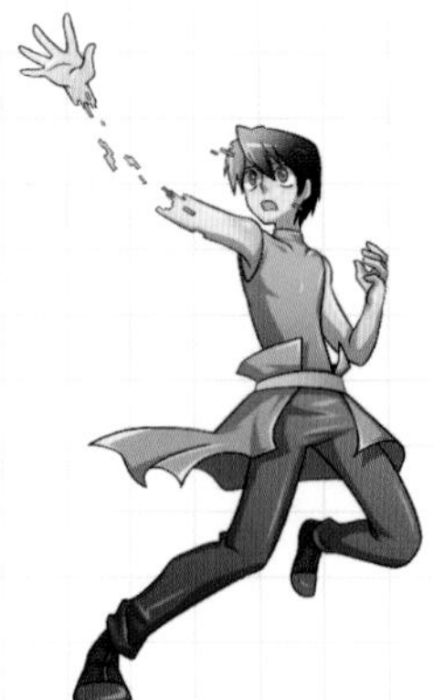

050

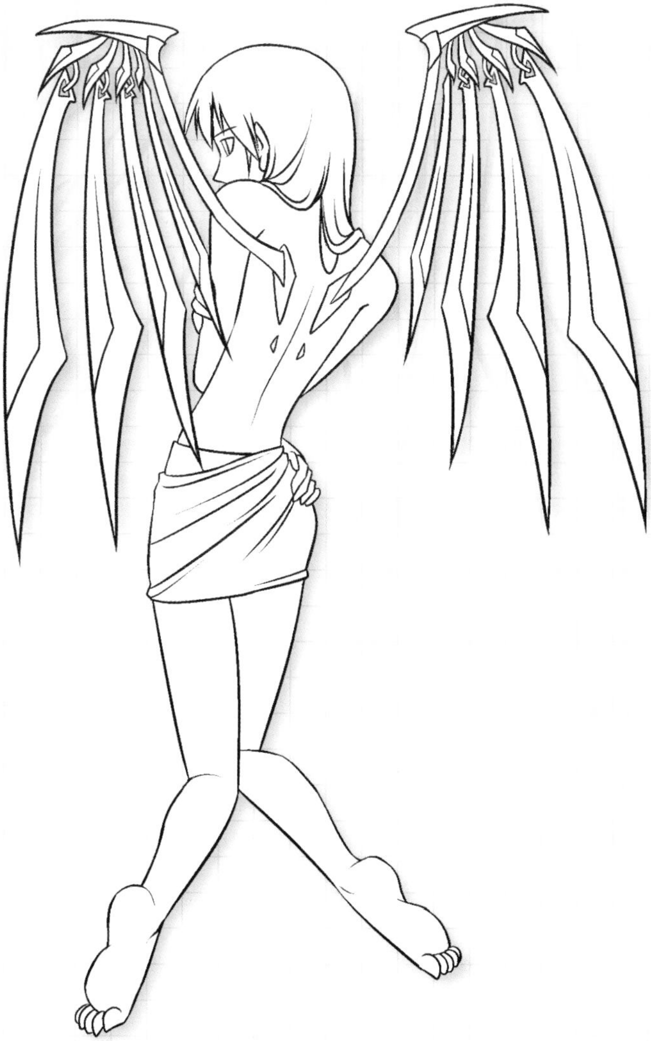

sci-fi and cyber punk heroes

search criteria

female. floating. wings. futuristic. girl. cyborg.

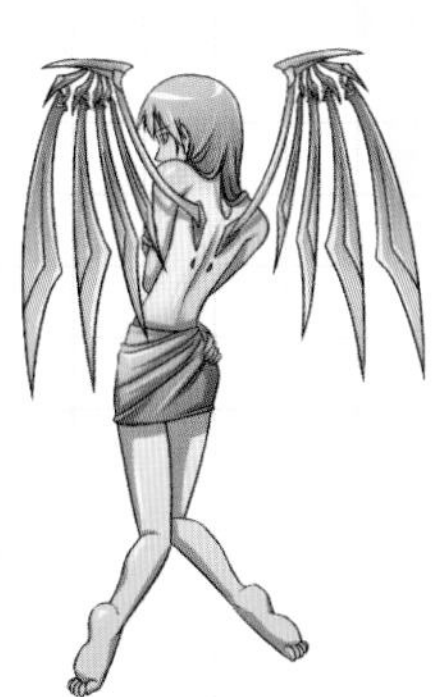

051

sci-fi and cyber punk heroes

search criteria

male. jump. mask. moving. flying. superhuman.

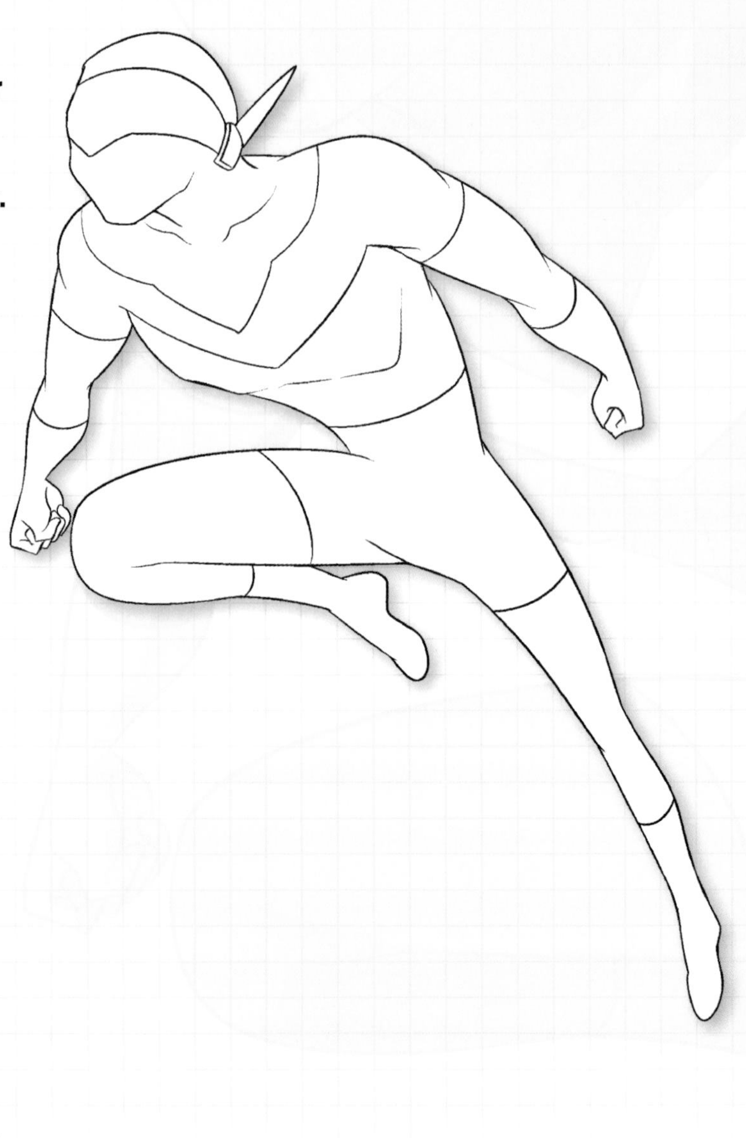

052

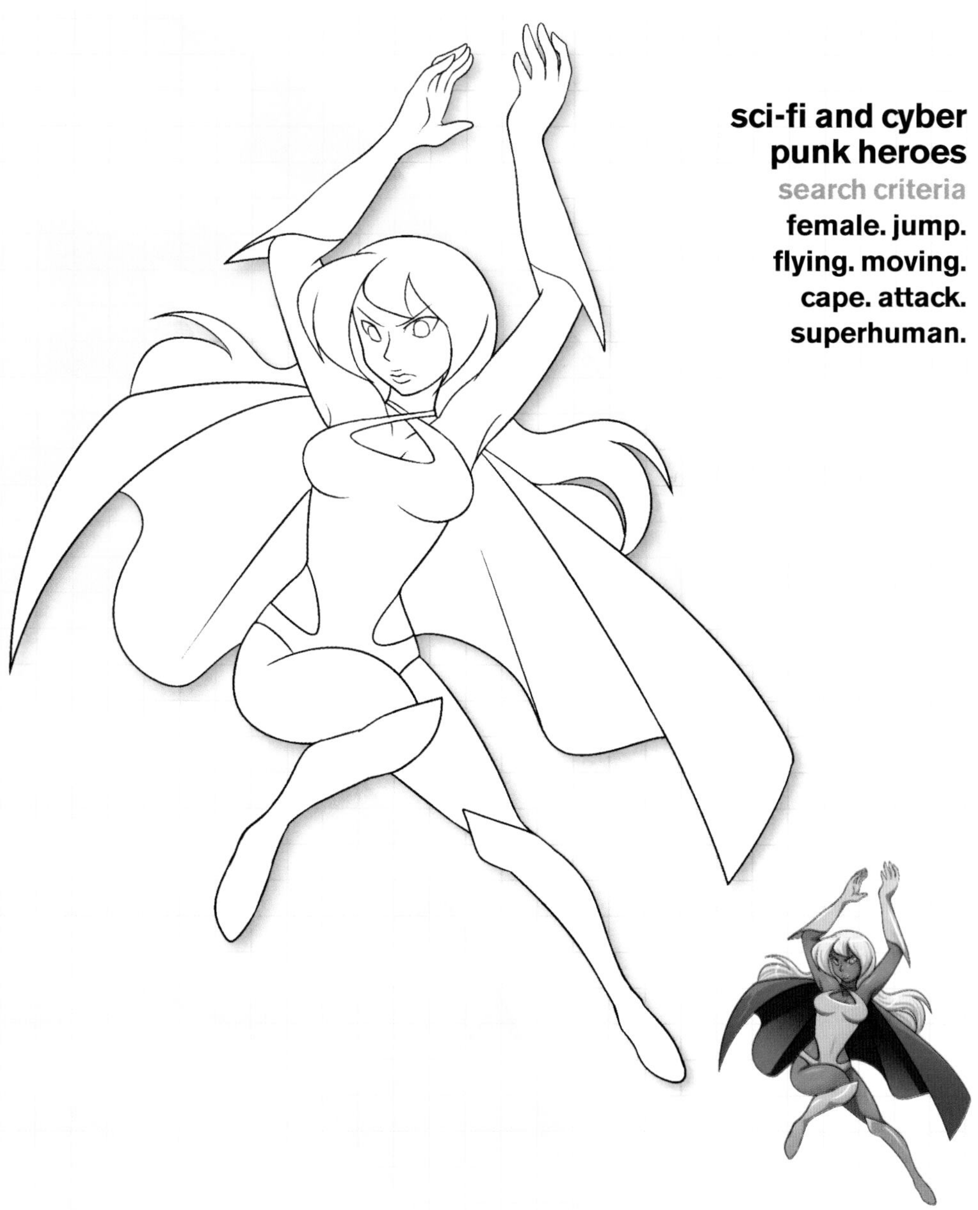

sci-fi and cyber punk heroes

search criteria

female. jump. flying. moving. cape. attack. superhuman.

053

sci-fi and cyber punk heroes

search criteria

male. flying. mask. superhuman. cape. moving.

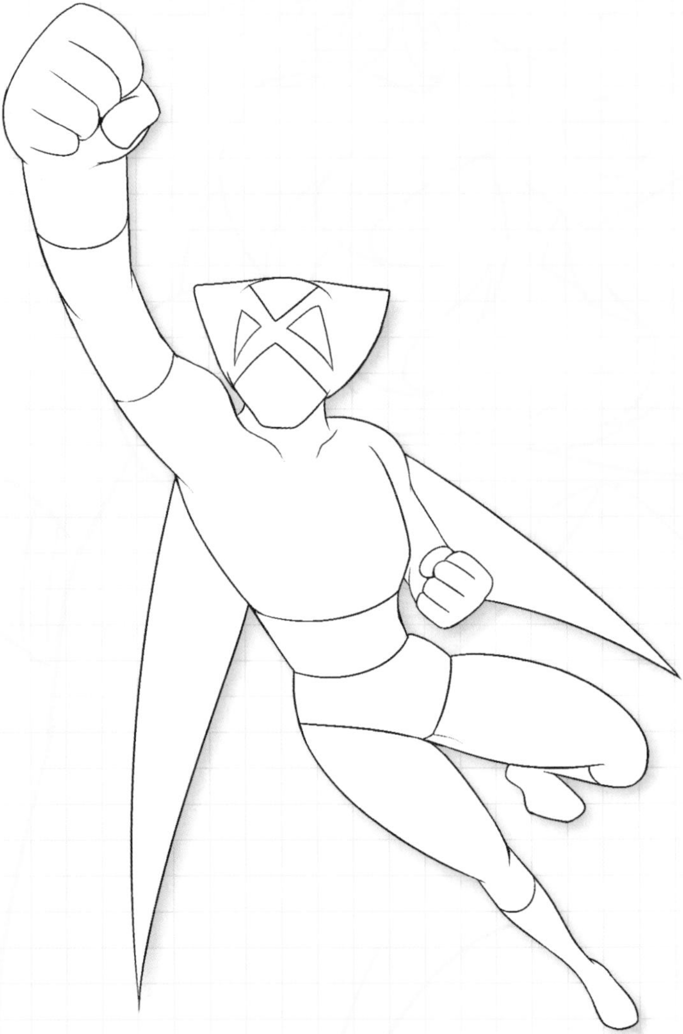

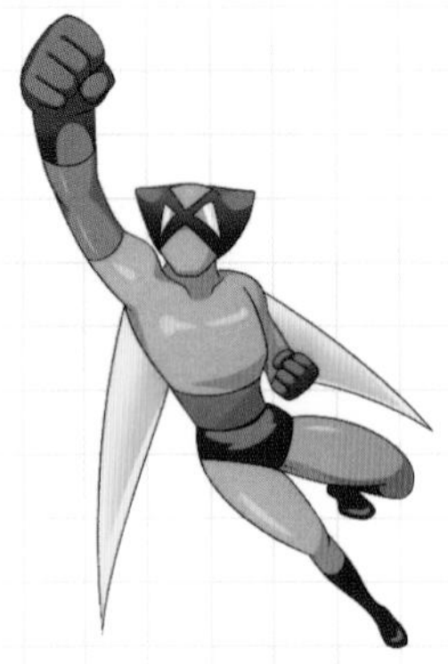

054

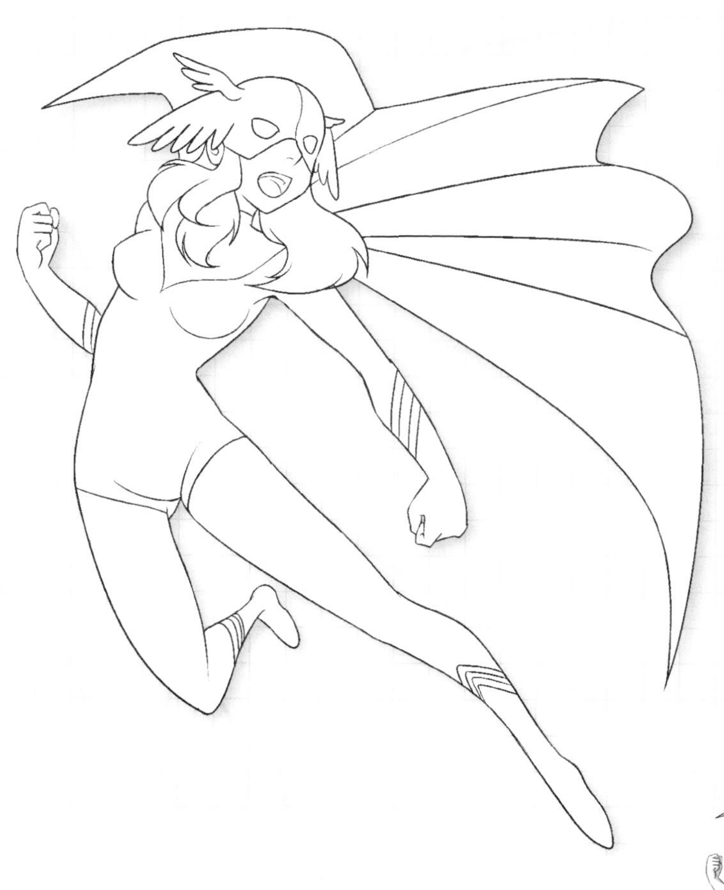

sci-fi and cyber punk heroes

search criteria

female. flying. jump. cape. mask. superhuman.

055

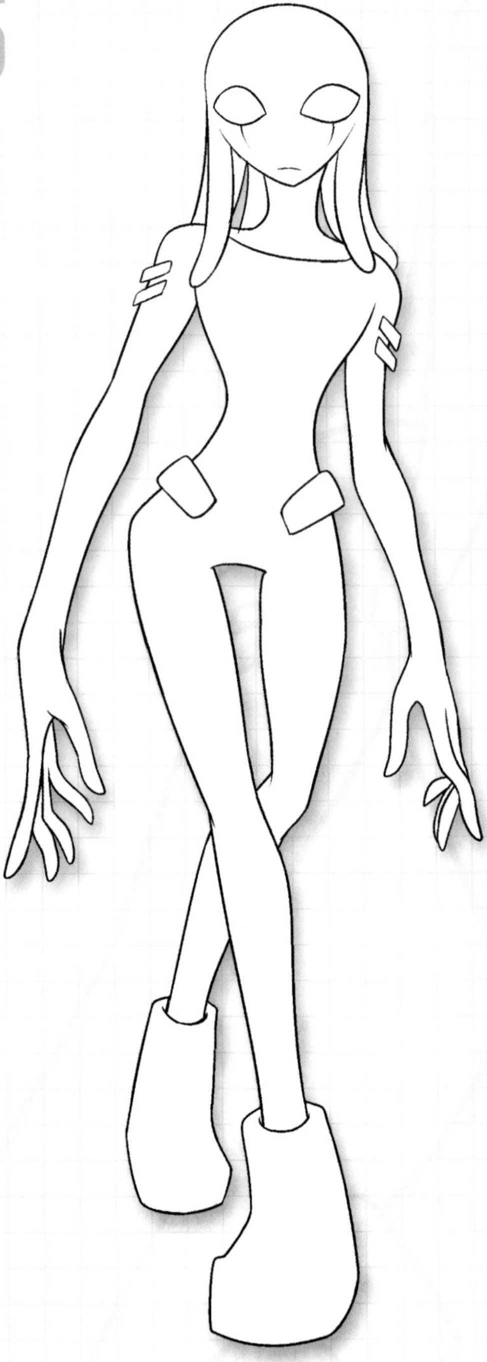

sci-fi and cyber punk heroes

search criteria

female. standing. walking. alien. sad. futuristic.

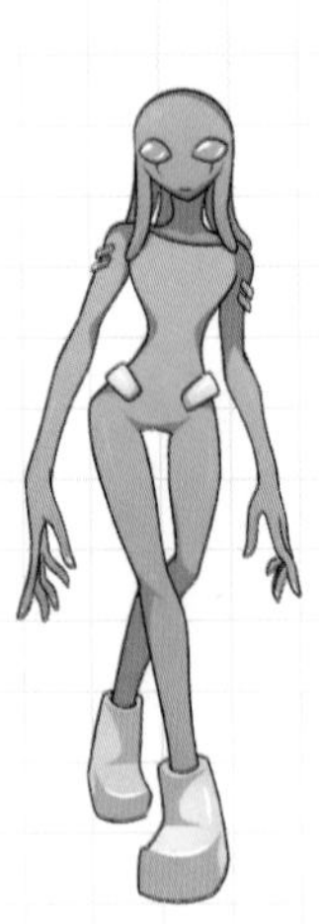

056

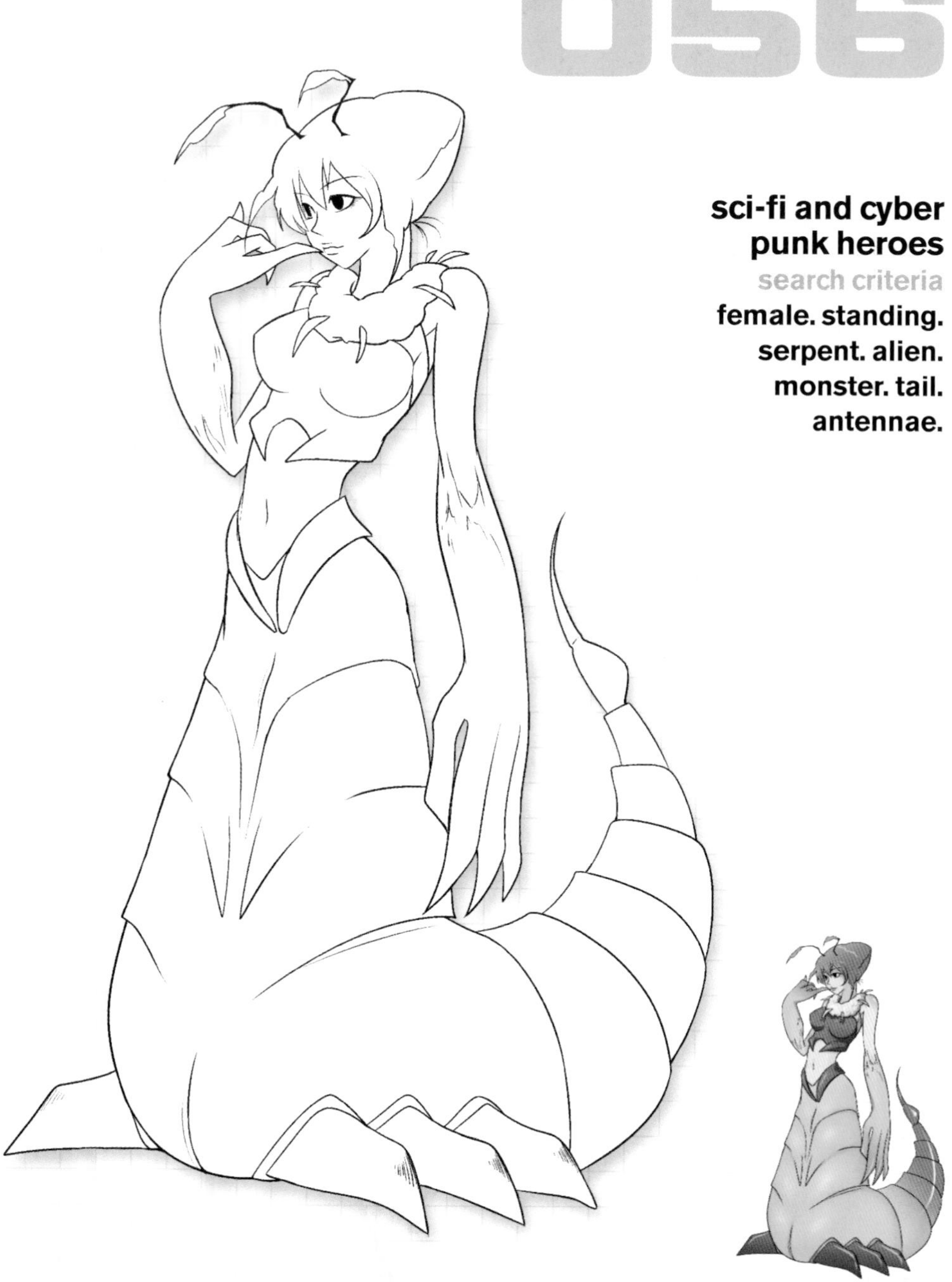

sci-fi and cyber punk heroes

search criteria

female. standing. serpent. alien. monster. tail. antennae.

057

sci-fi and cyber punk heroes

search criteria

monster. standing. smiling. fur. eyes. happy.

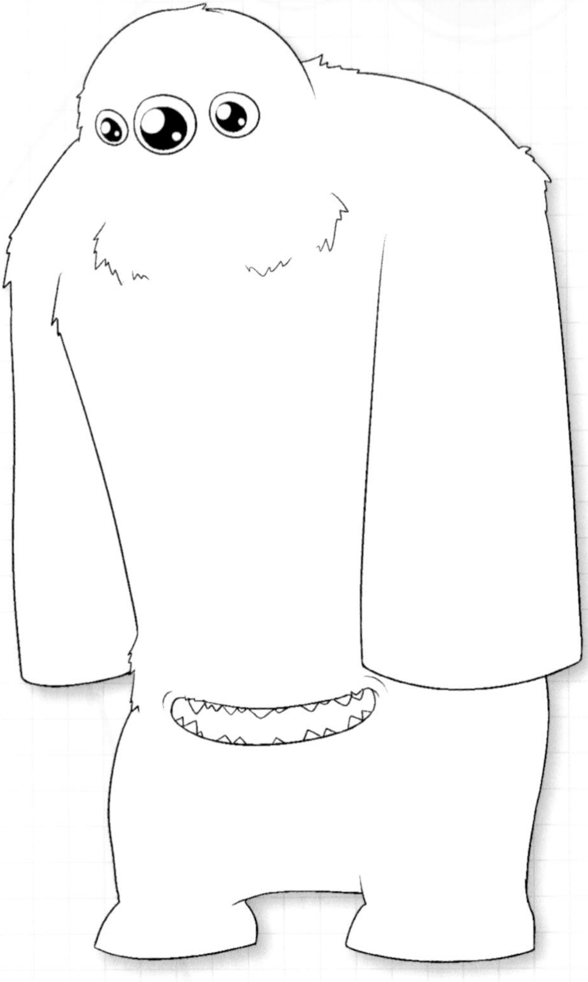

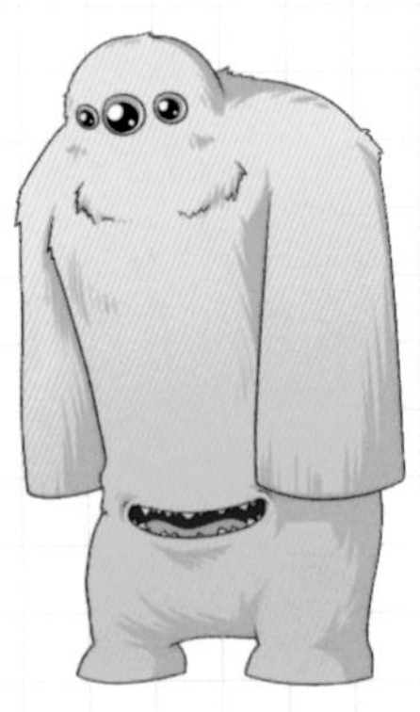

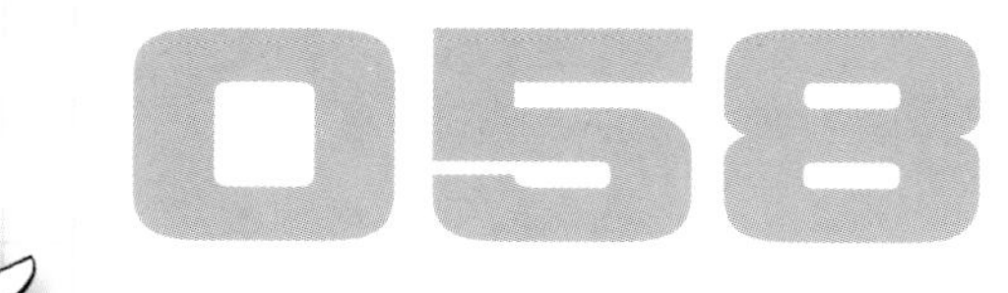

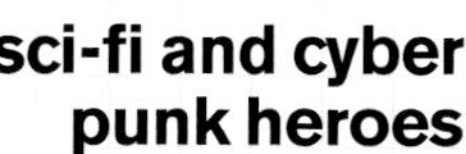

sci-fi and cyber punk heroes

search criteria

female. standing. cyborg. futuristic.

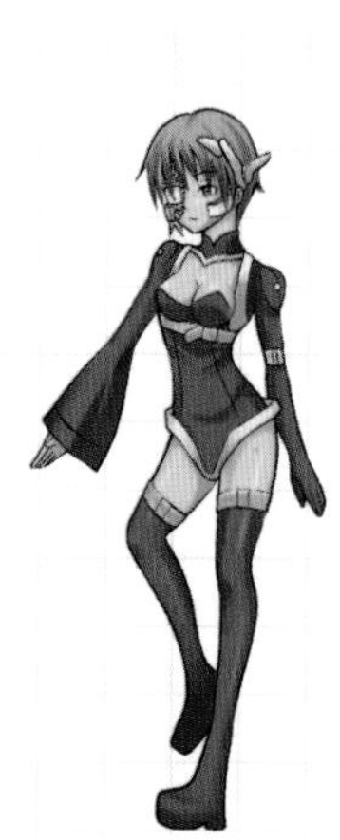

059

mecha villains

search criteria

male. standing.
side. robot.

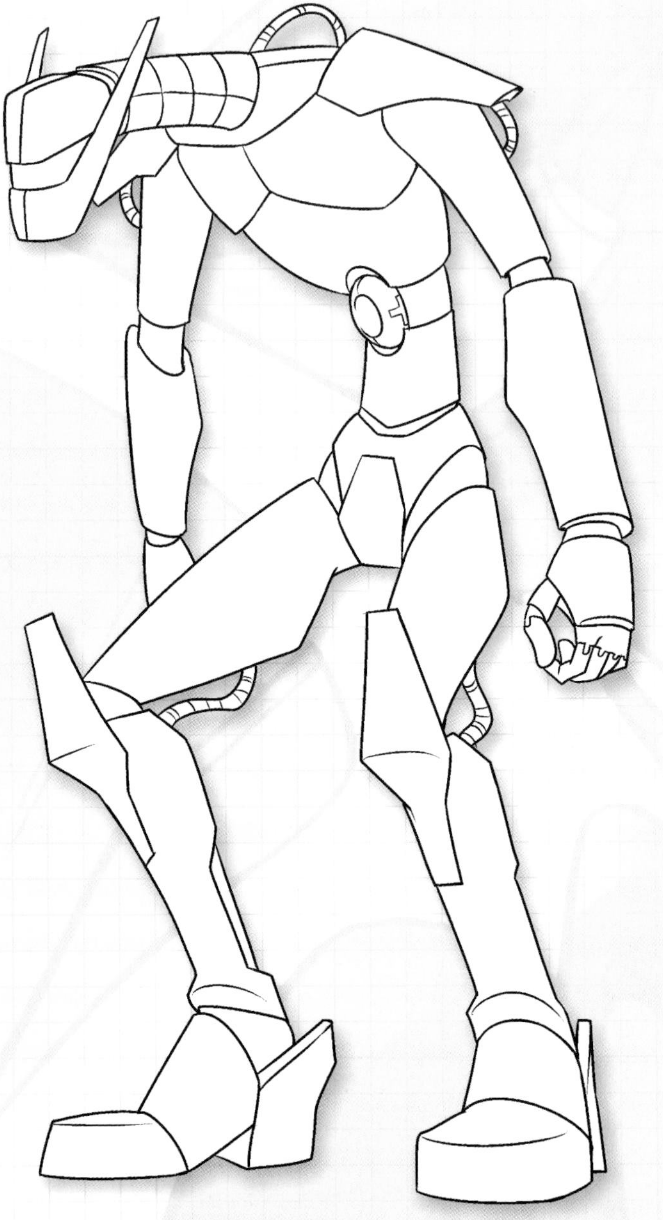

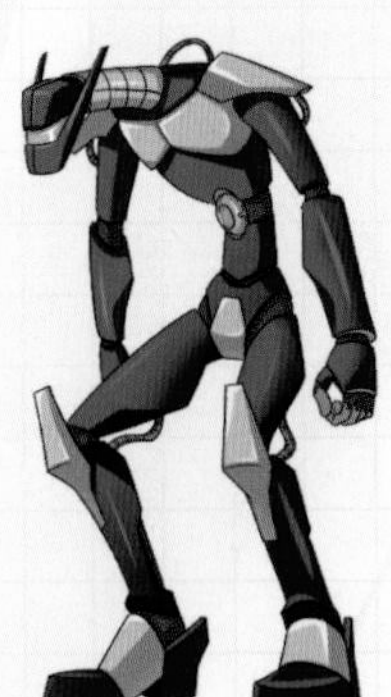

060

mecha villains

search criteria

floating. futuristic. drone. sci-fi.

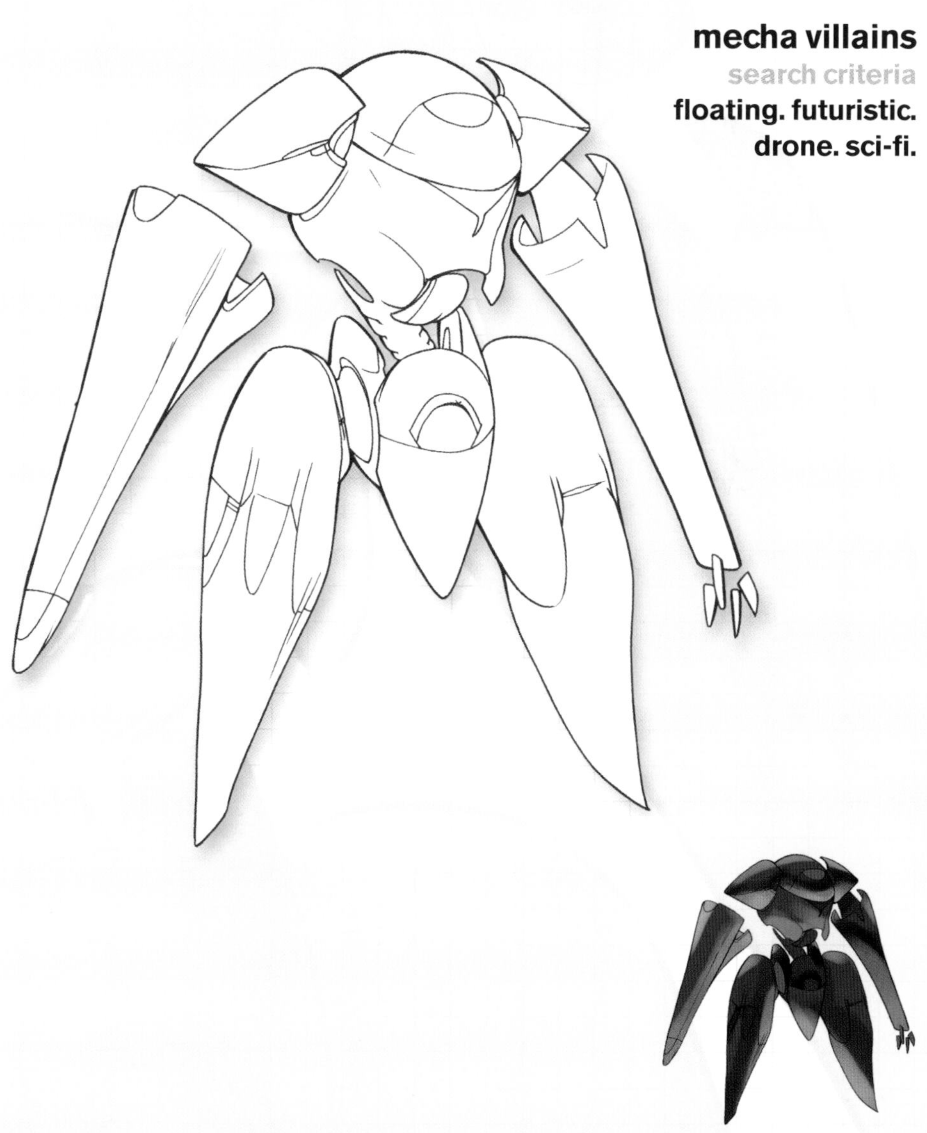

061

mecha villains

search criteria

floating. futuristic. drone. sci-fi.

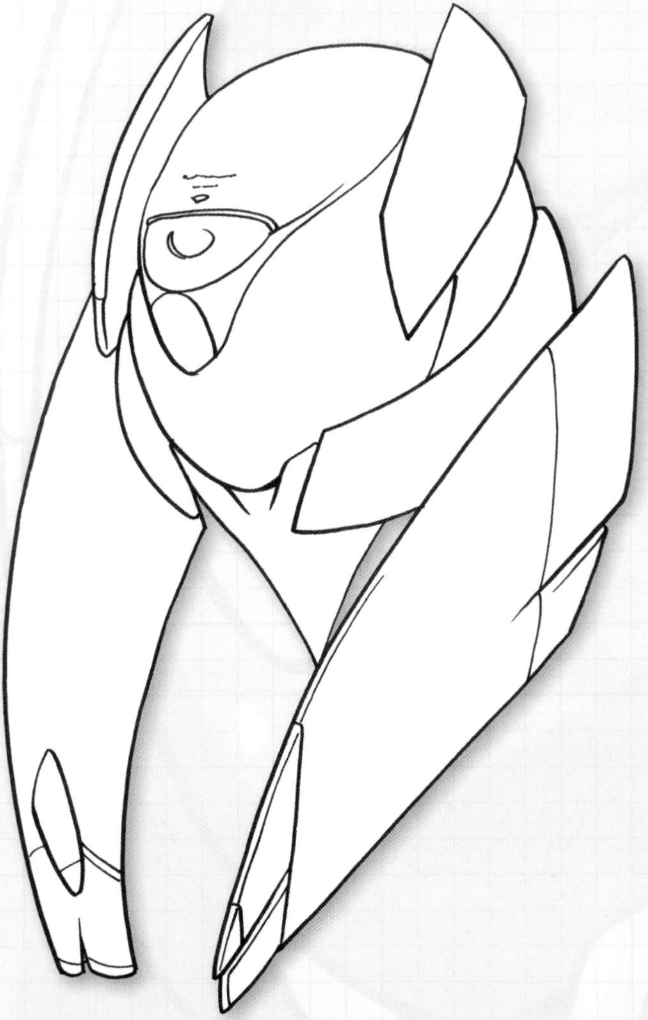

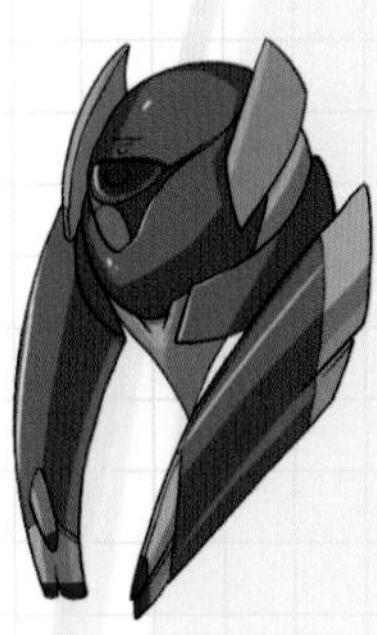

062

mecha villains

search criteria

floating. futuristic. drone. sci-fi.

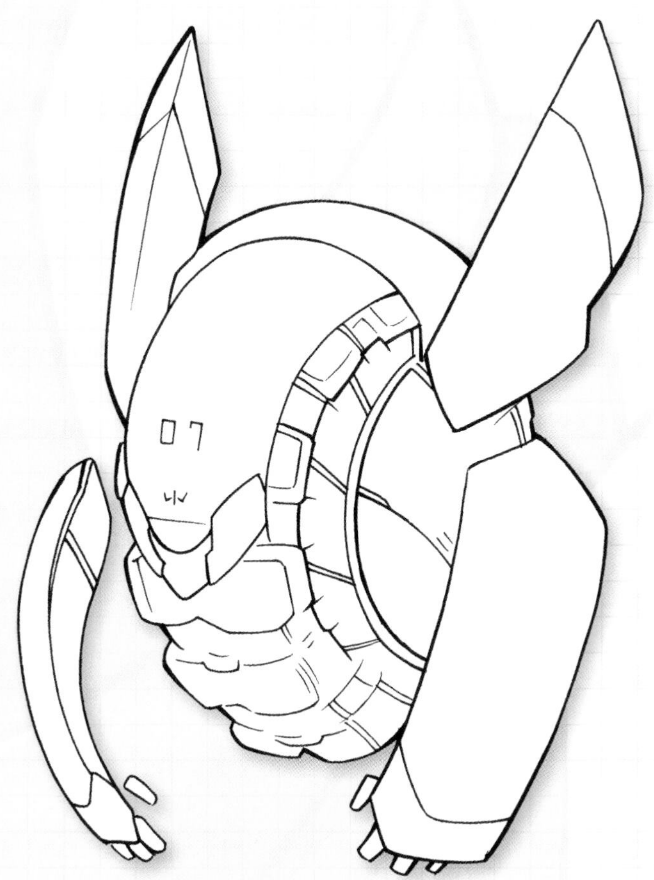

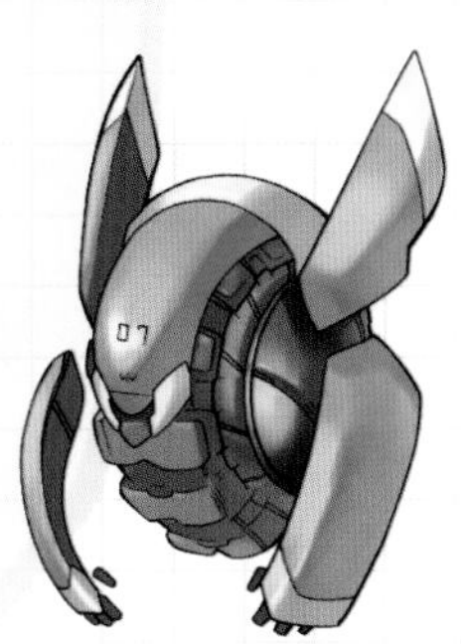

063

mecha villains

search criteria

robot. standing. futuristic.

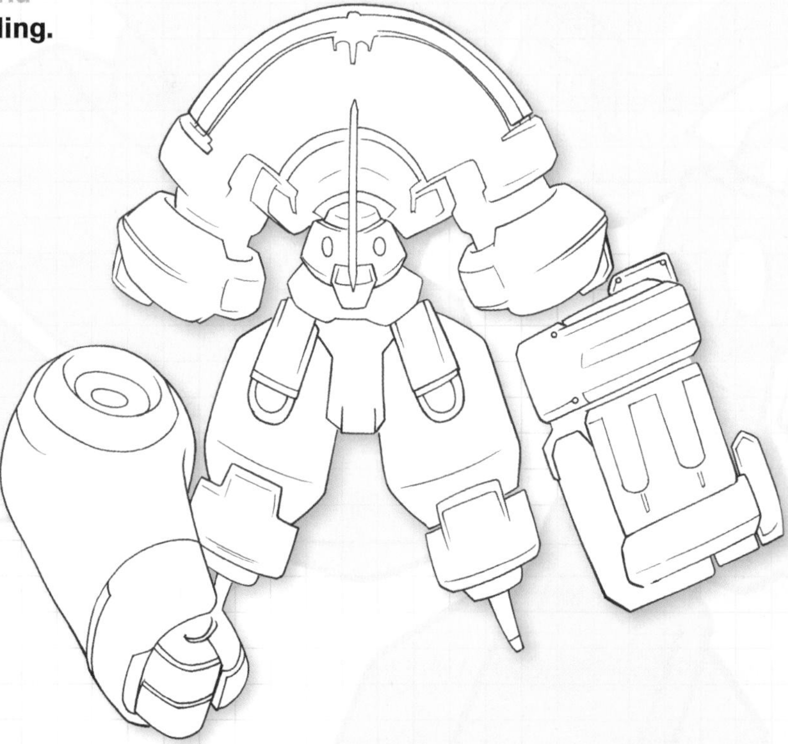

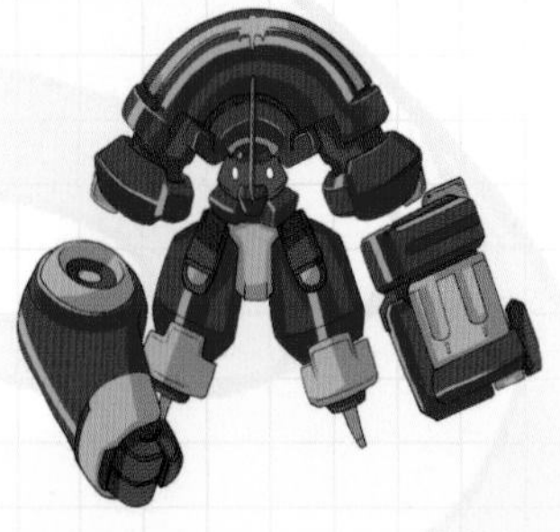

064

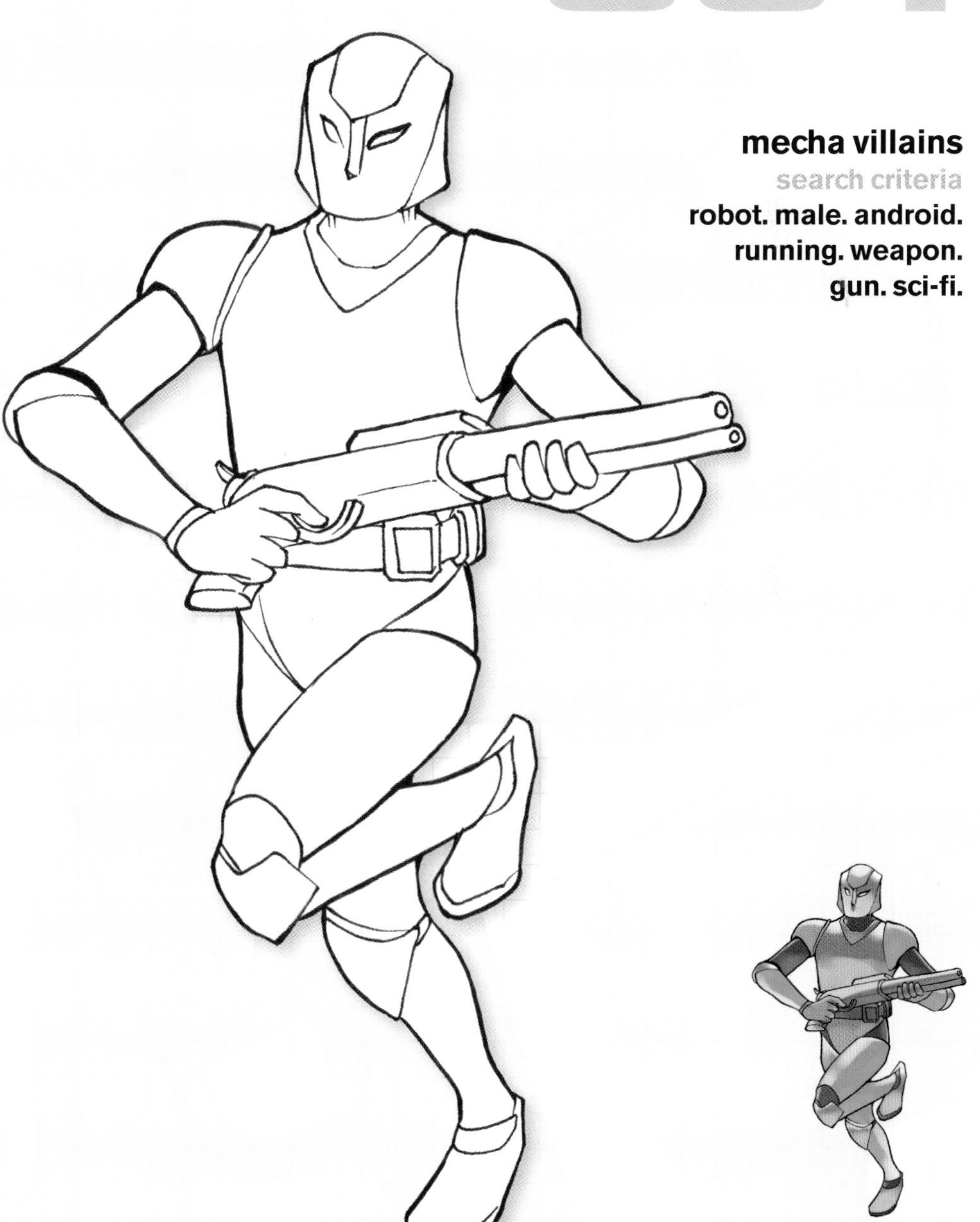

mecha villains

search criteria

robot. male. android. running. weapon. gun. sci-fi.

065

mecha villains

search criteria

robot. male. android. standing. breastplate. sci-fi.

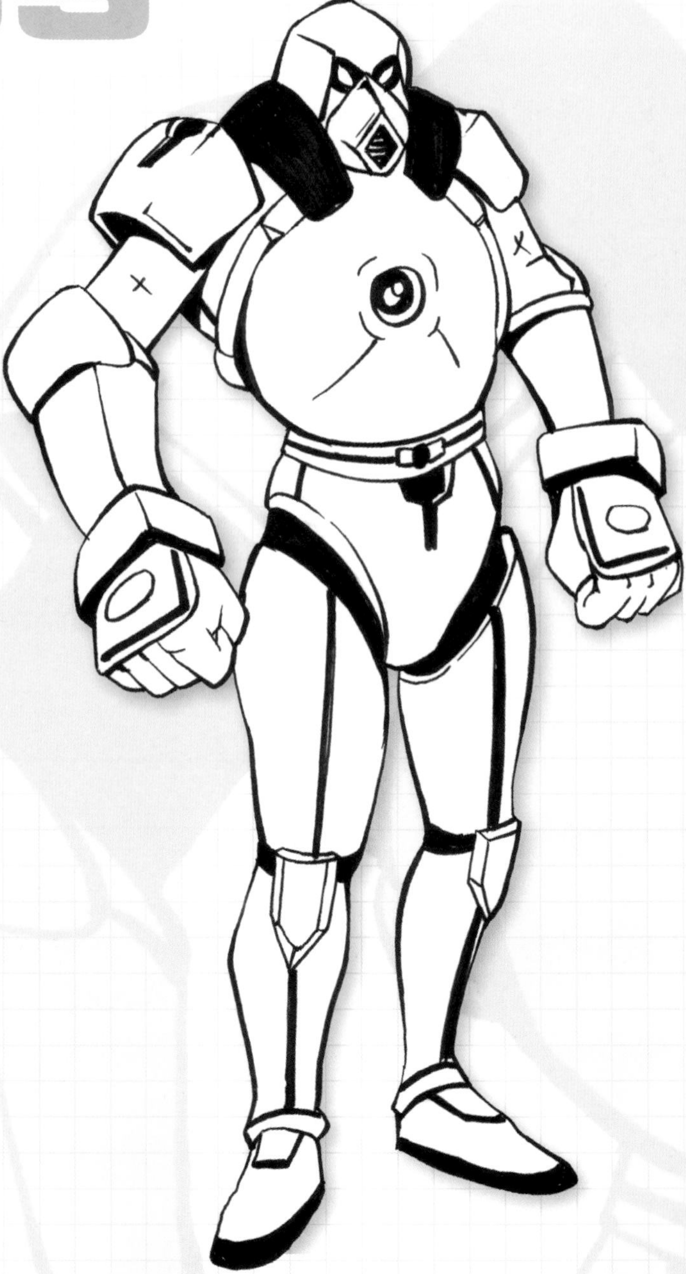

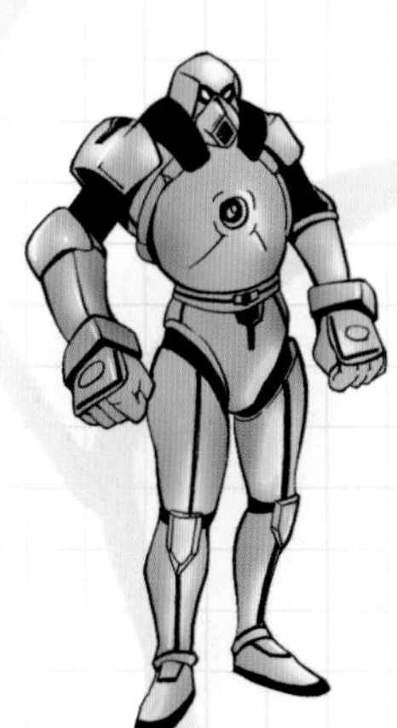

066

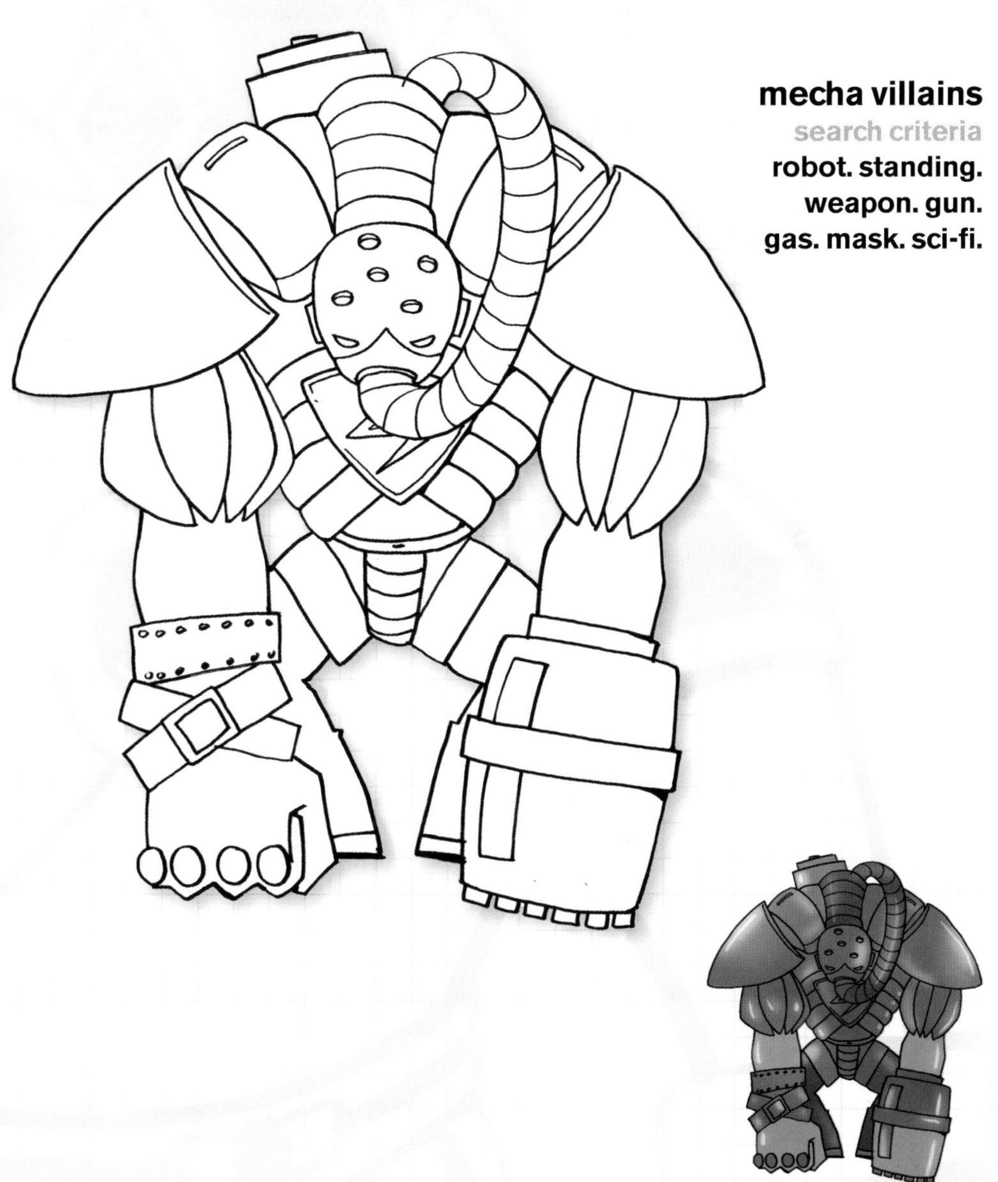

mecha villains

search criteria

robot. standing. weapon. gun. gas. mask. sci-fi.

067

mecha villains

search criteria

robot. standing. claws. mask. sci-fi.

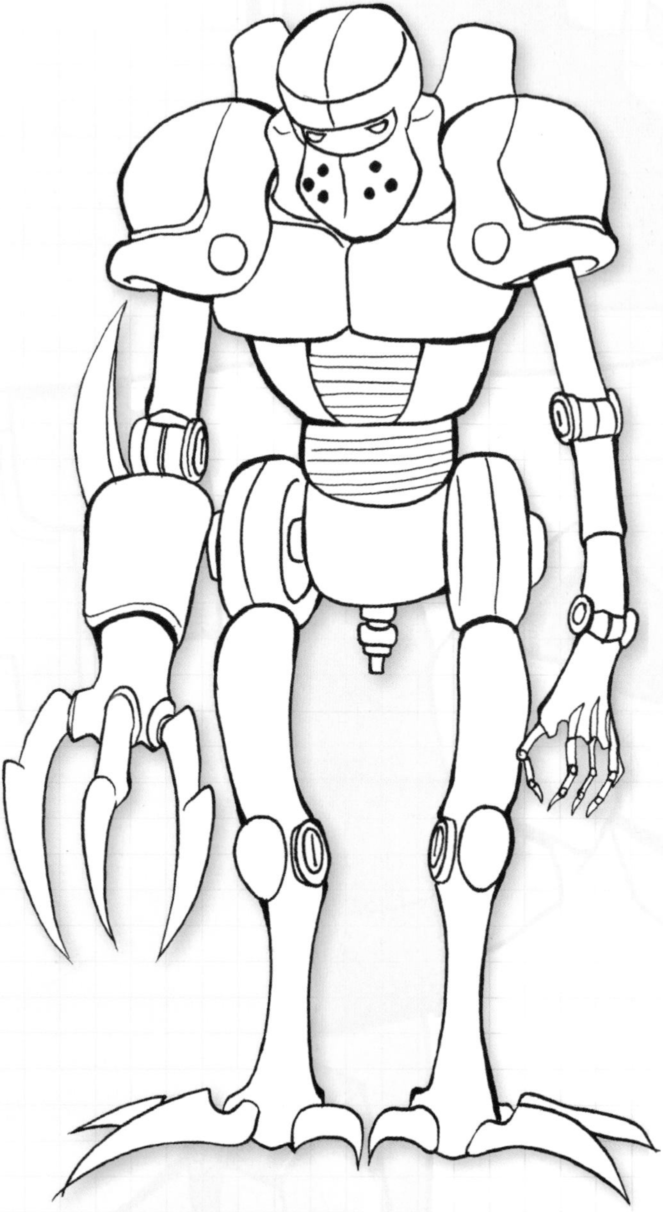

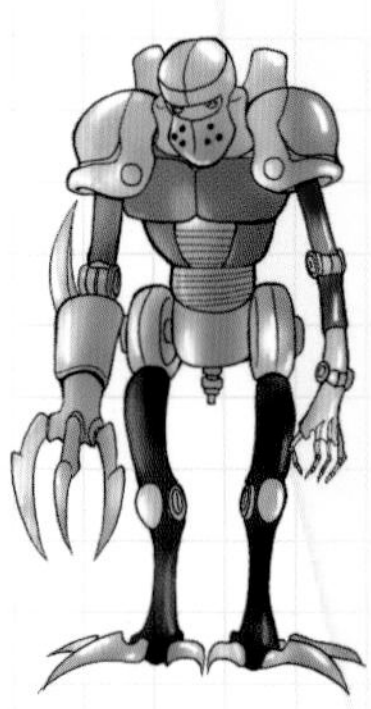

068

mecha villains

search criteria

robot. standing. futuristic. sci-fi.

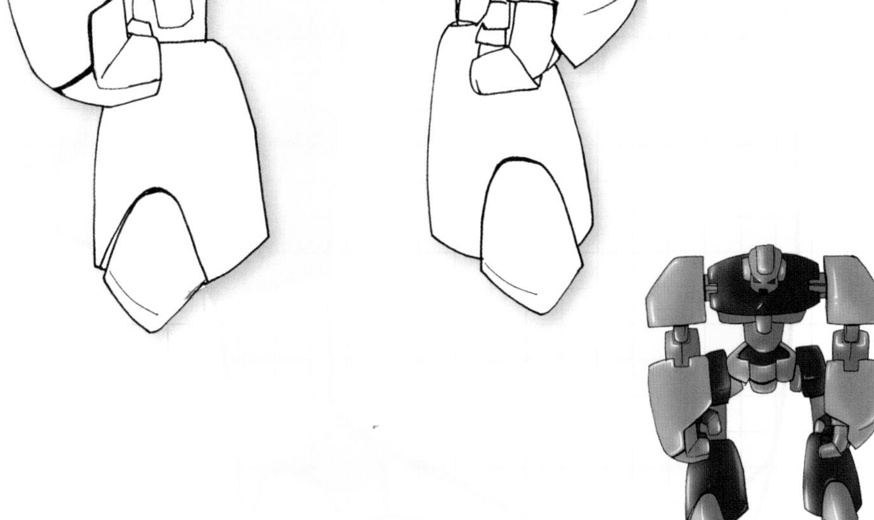

069

mecha villains

search criteria

**robot. standing.
sci-fi. side. futuristic.**

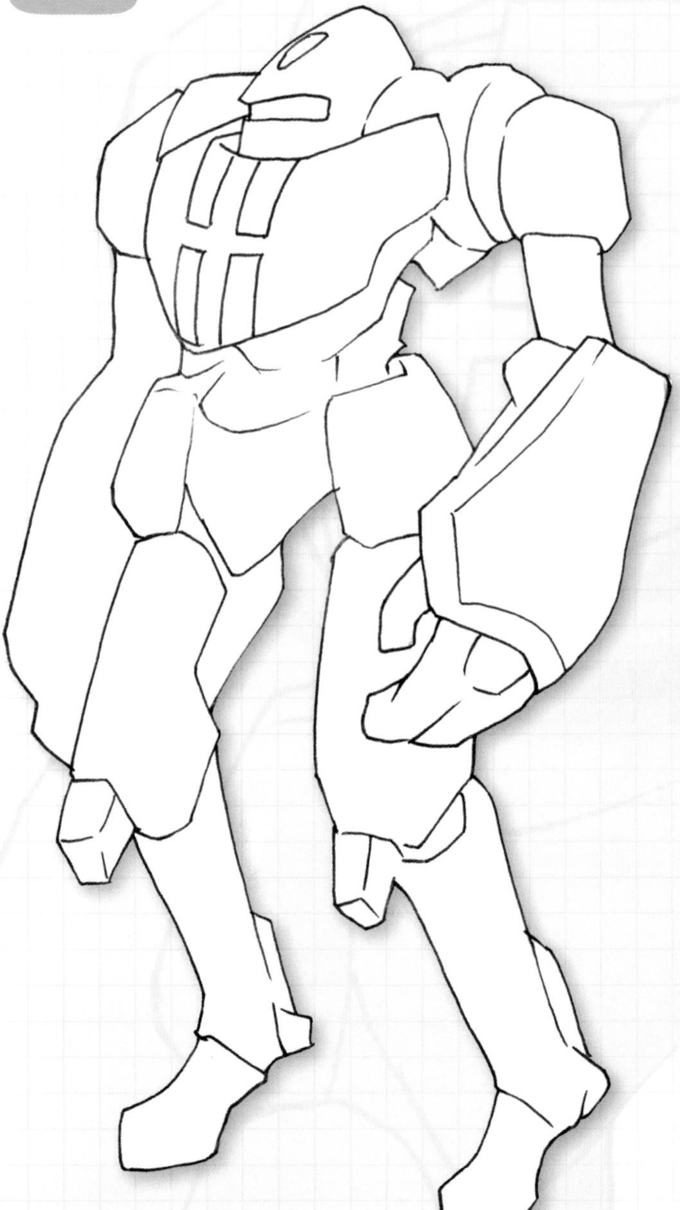

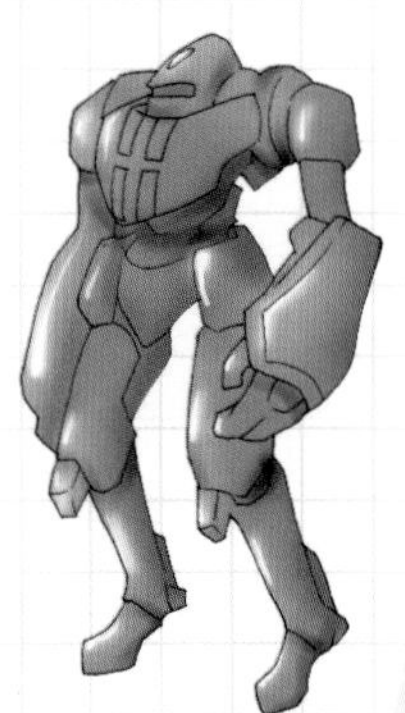

070

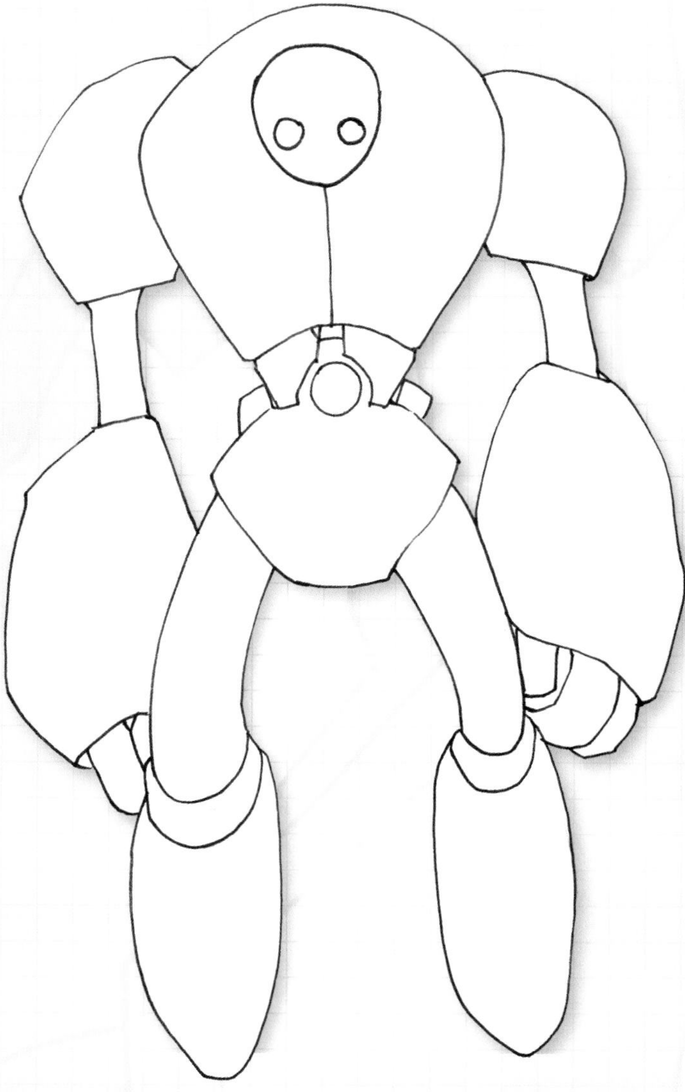

mecha villains

search criteria

robot. standing. futuristic. floating. goofy. sci-fi.

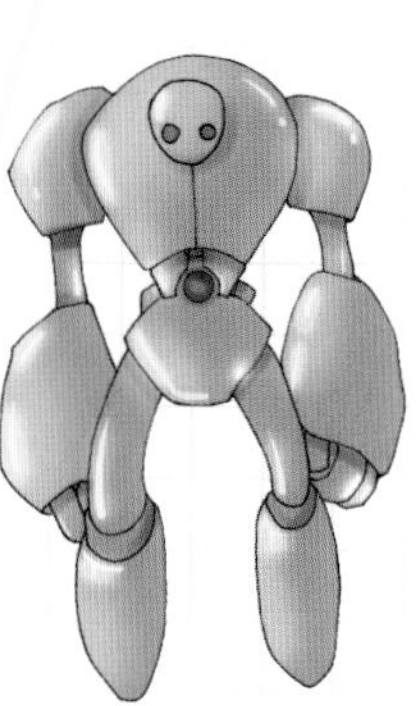

071

mecha villains
search criteria
robot. standing.
side. rocket. sci-fi.

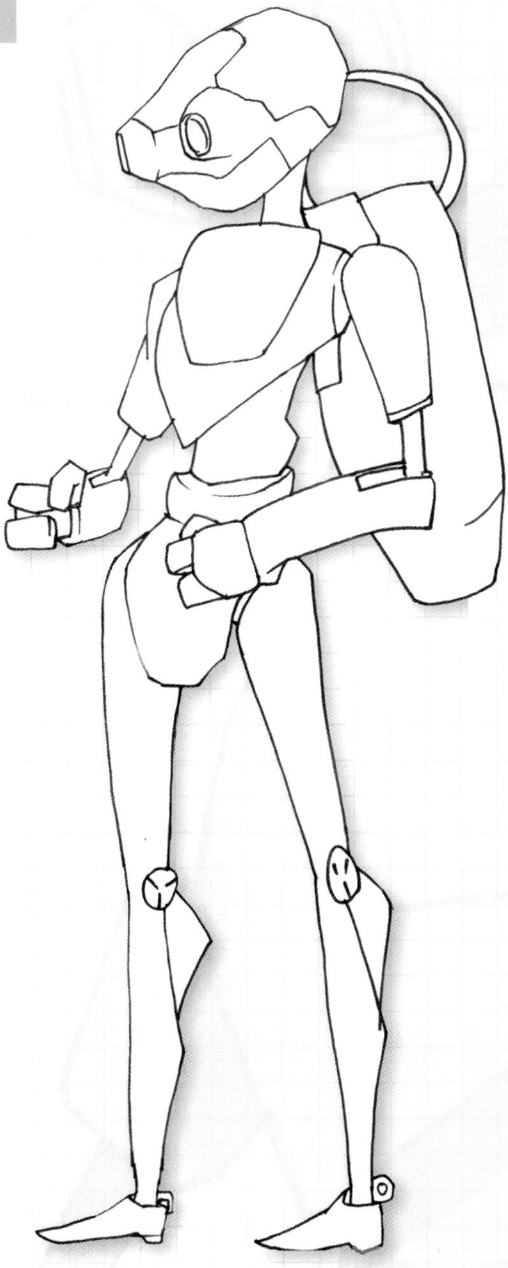

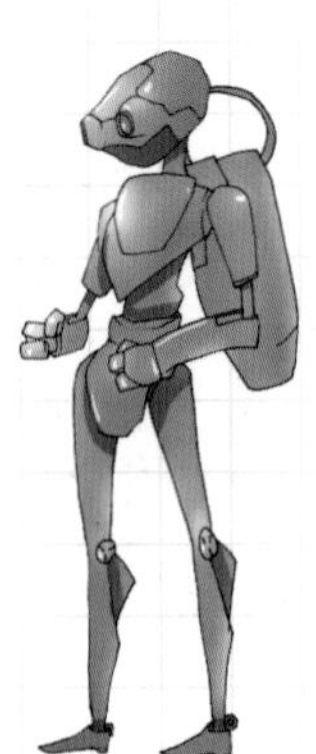

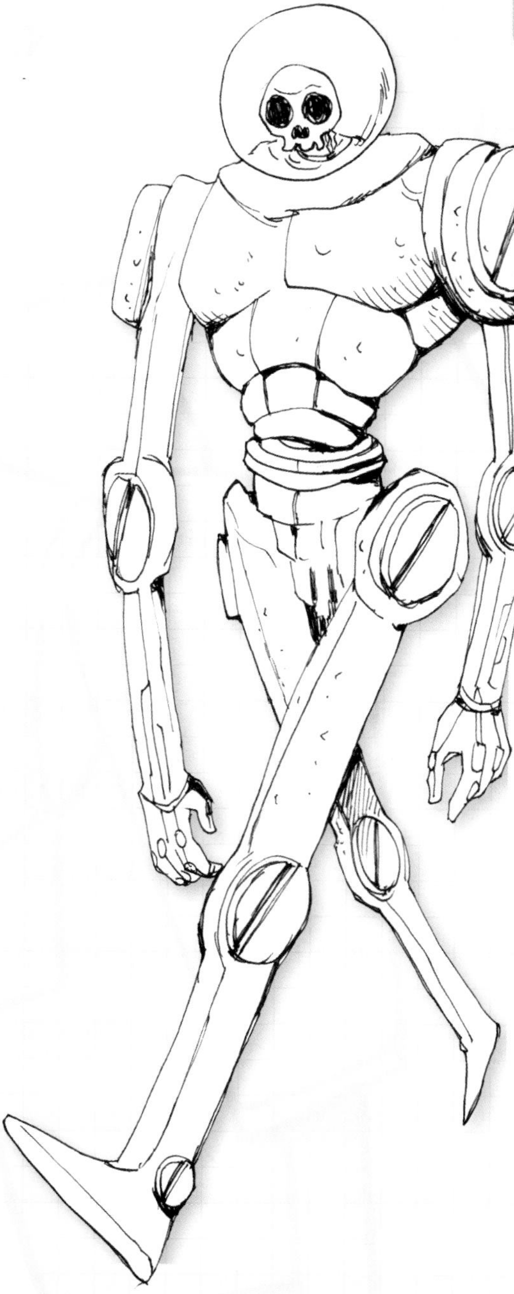

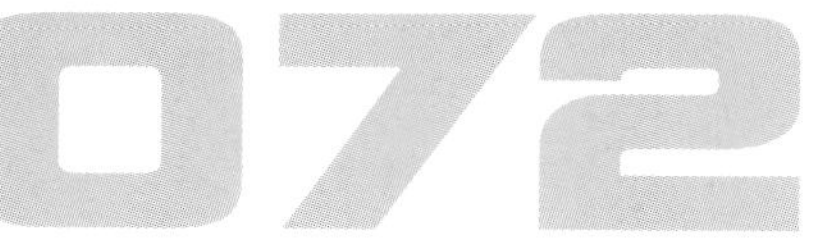

mecha villains

search criteria

robot. walking. muscle. skull. bones. helmet. sci-fi.

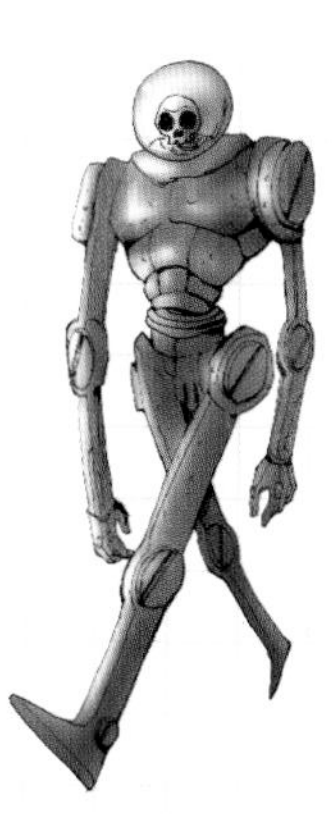

073

mecha villains

search criteria

robot. walking. tin. sci-fi. helmet.

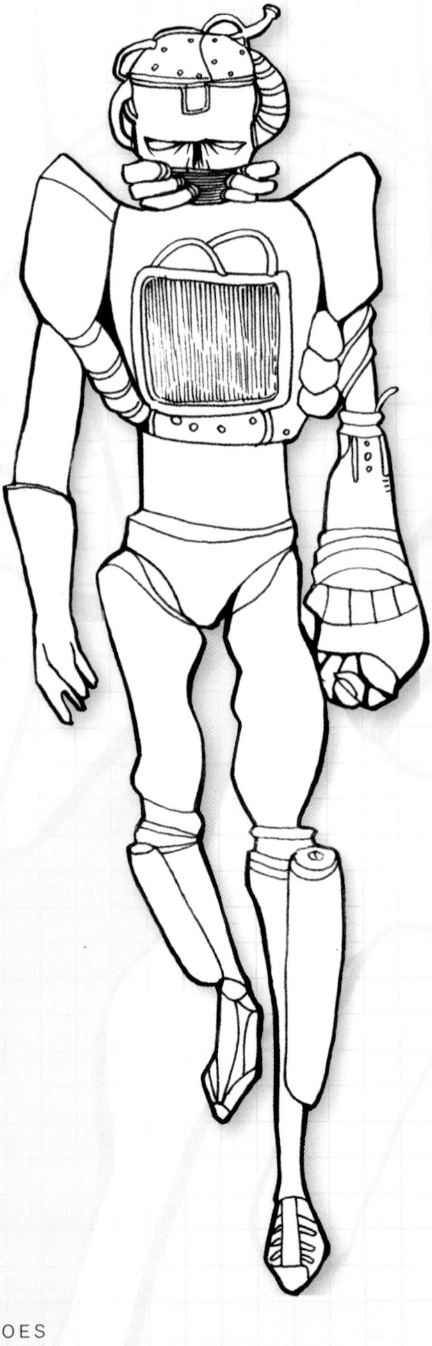

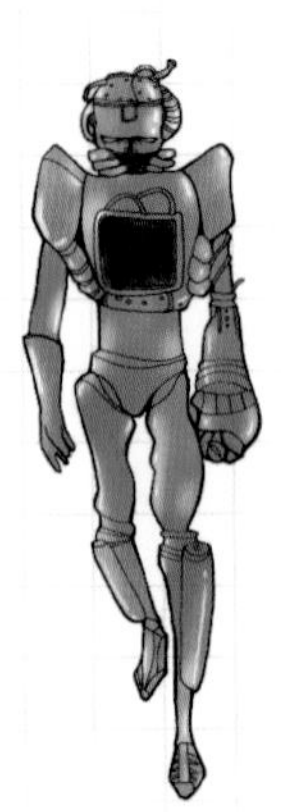

074

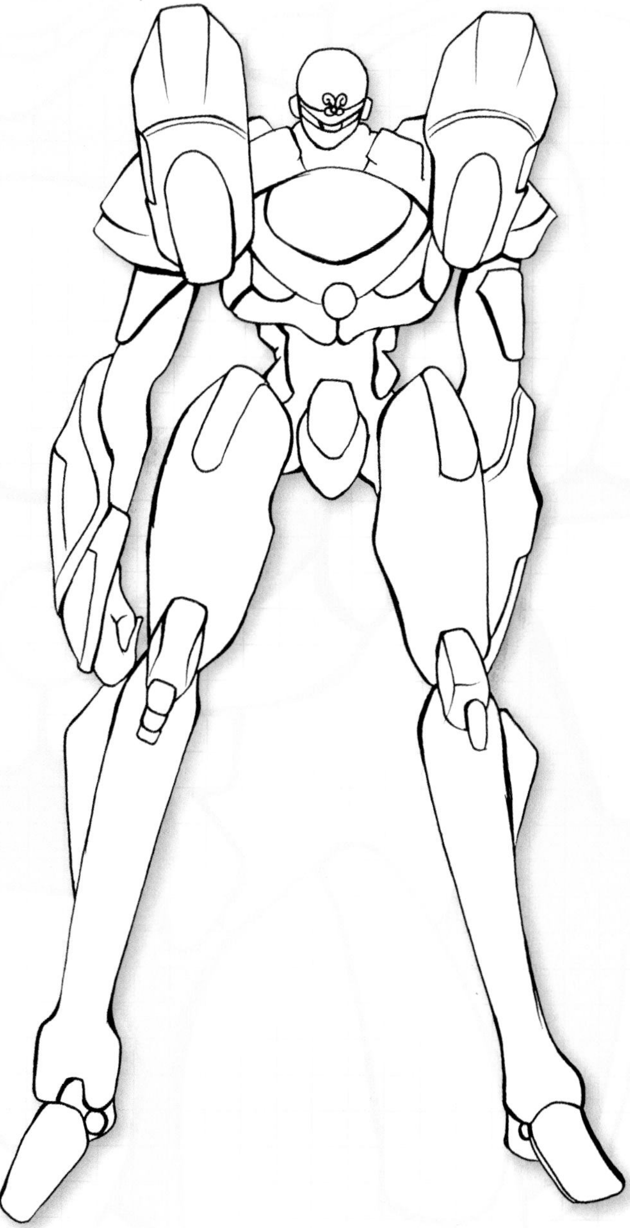

mecha villains

search criteria

robot. standing.
sci-fi. futuristic.

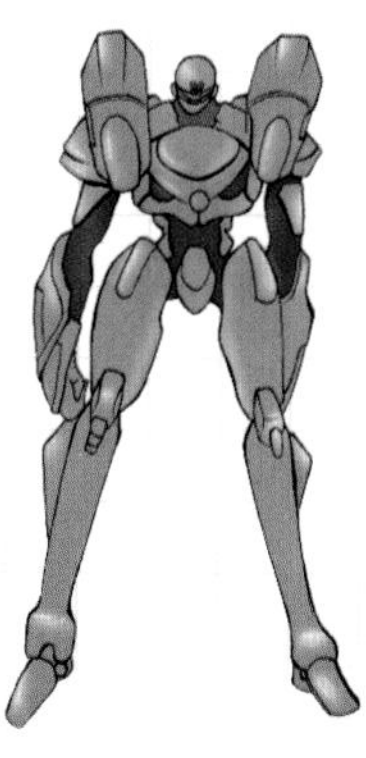

075

mecha villains

search criteria

male. standing.
sci-fi. futuristic.

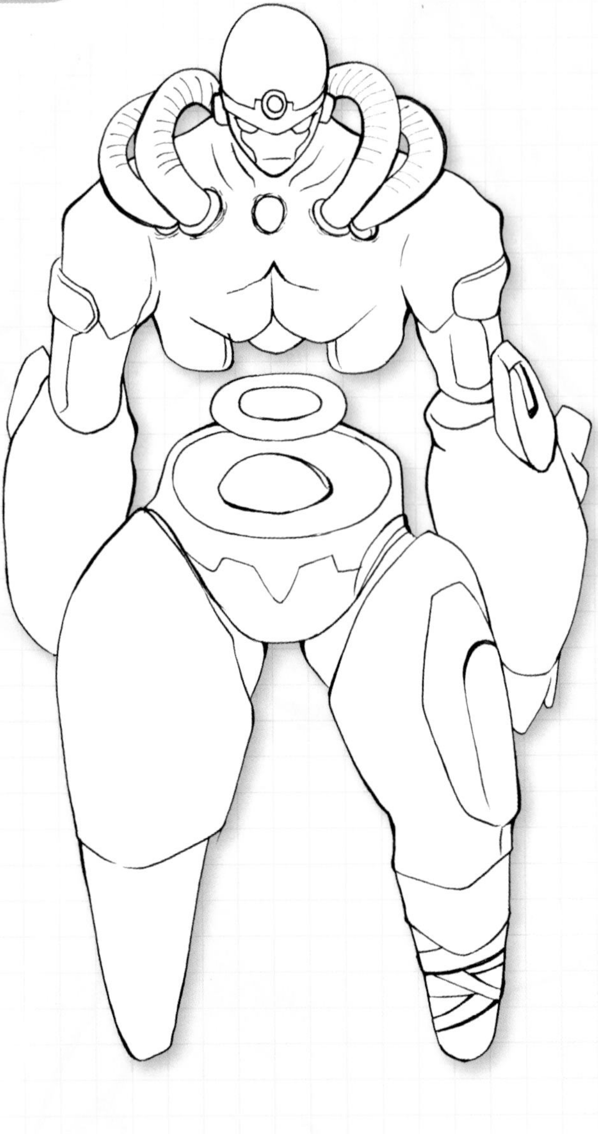

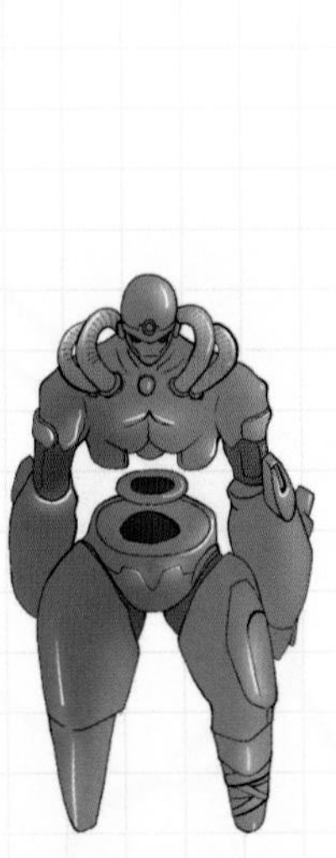

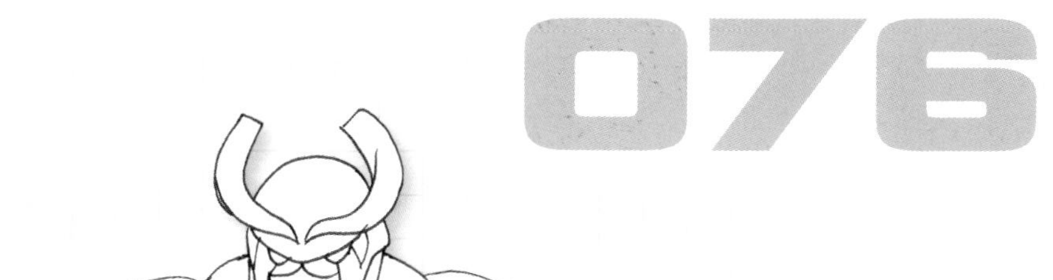

mecha villains

search criteria

robot. standing. futuristic. sci-fi.

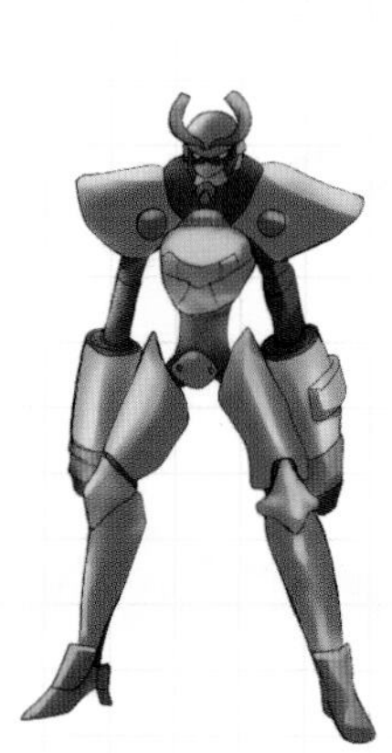

077

mecha villains

search criteria

robot. standing. futuristic. sci-fi.

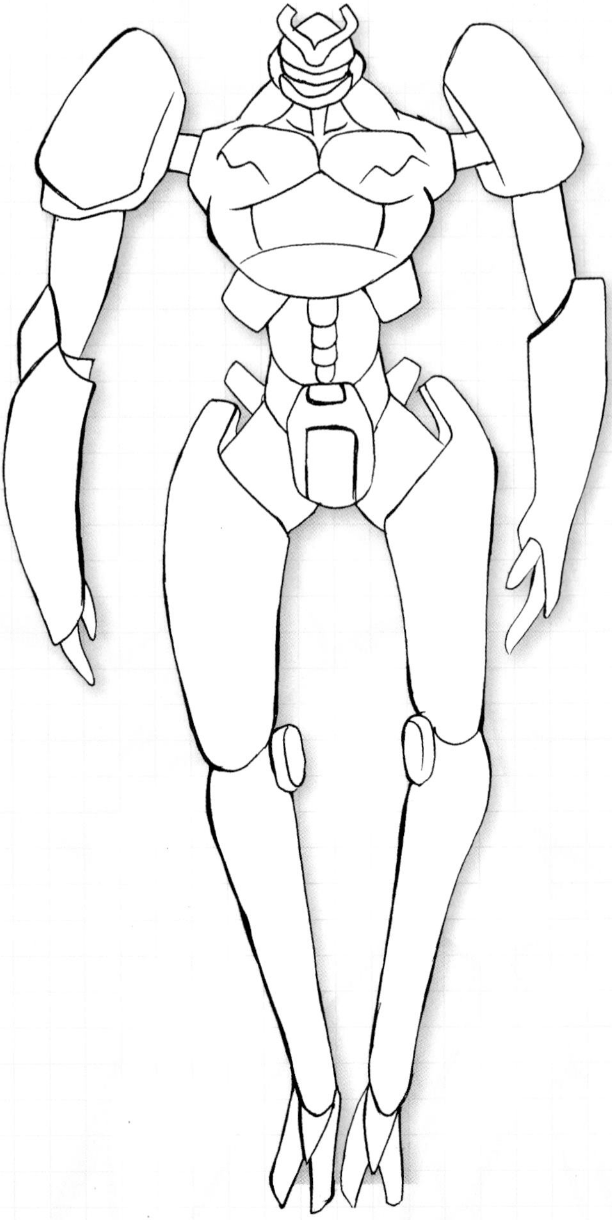

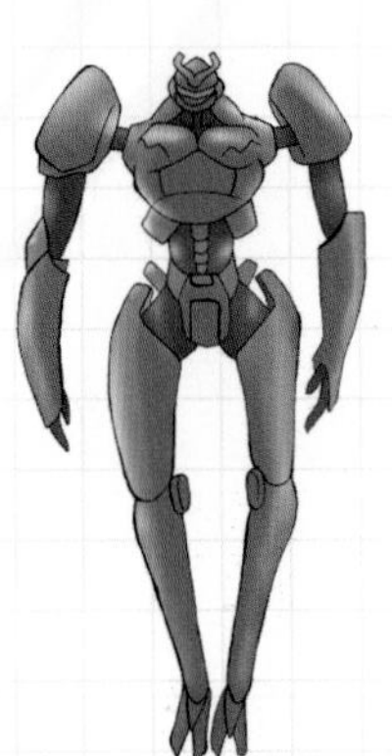

078

mecha villains

search criteria

robot. standing. angry. futuristic.

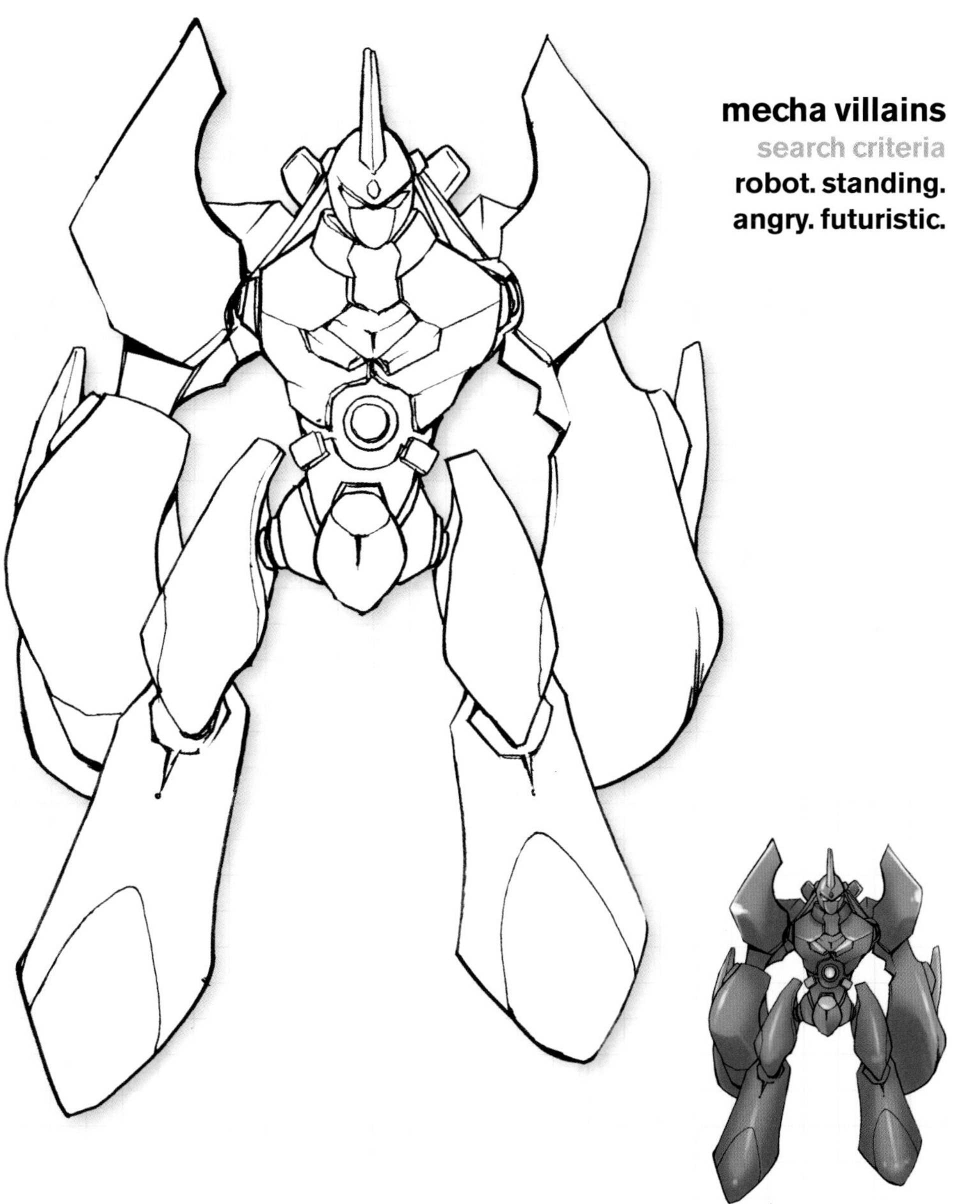

079

mecha heroes

search criteria

female. floating. robot. broomstick. petticoat. hover. cleaner. heart.

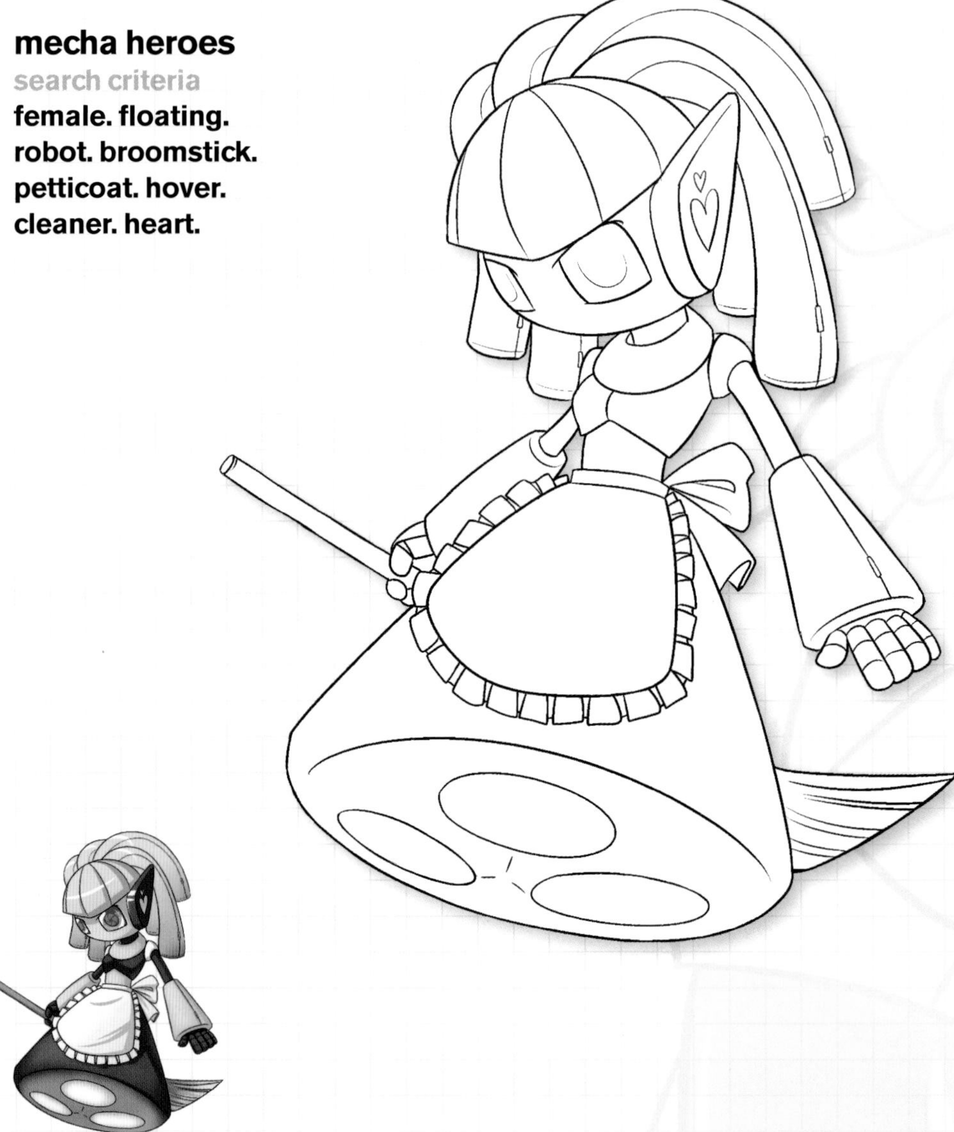

080

mecha heroes

search criteria

female. robot. android. kneeling. computer. side. sci-fi. futuristic.

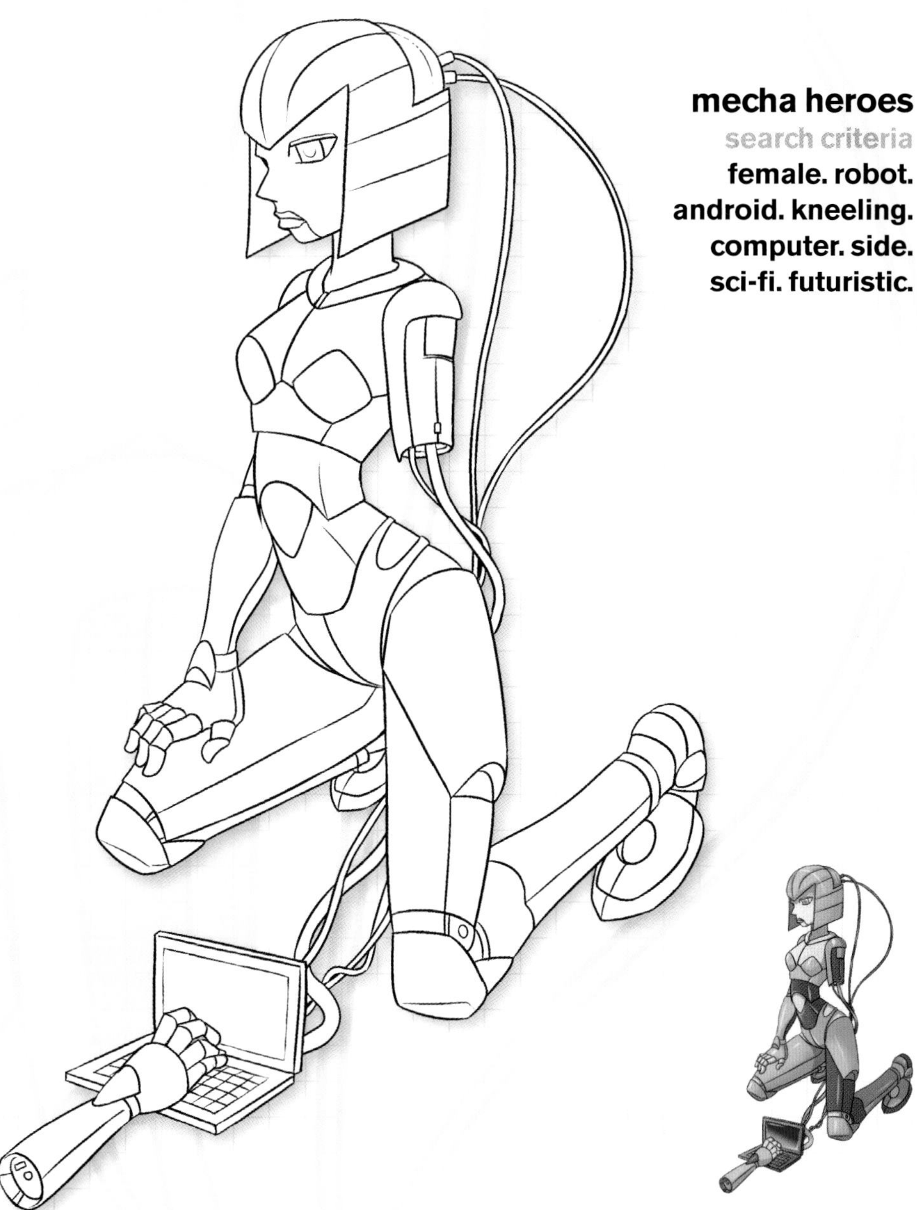

081

mecha heroes

search criteria

robot. standing. male. weapons.

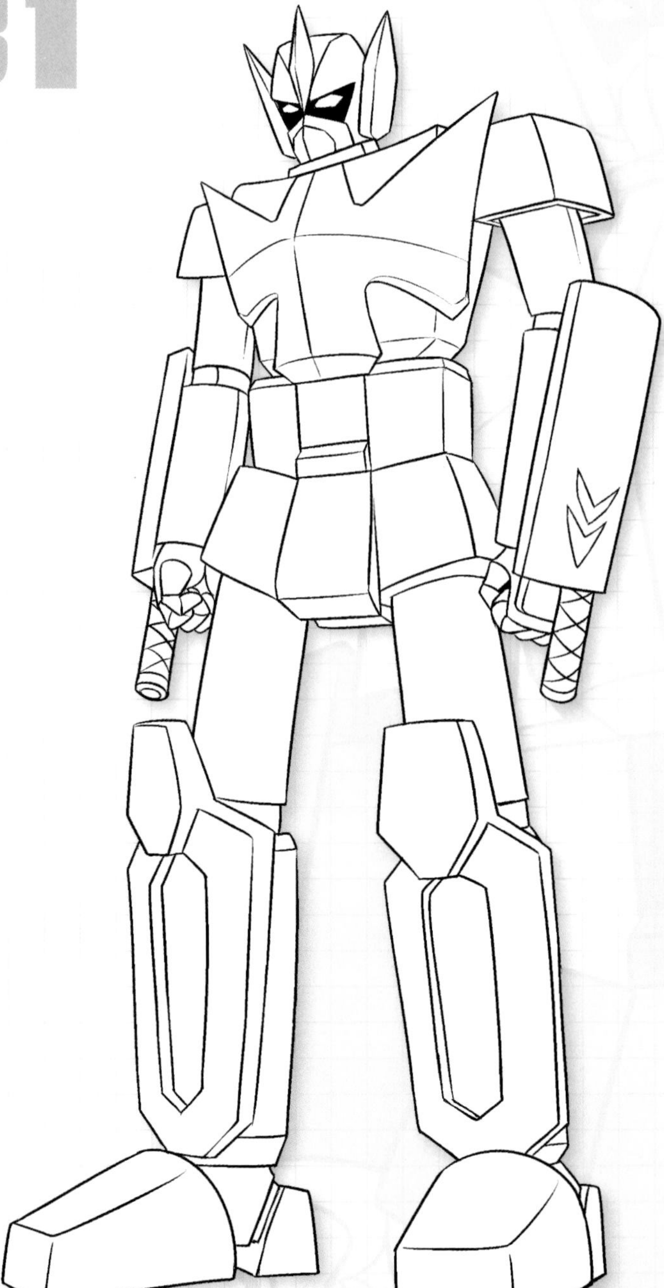

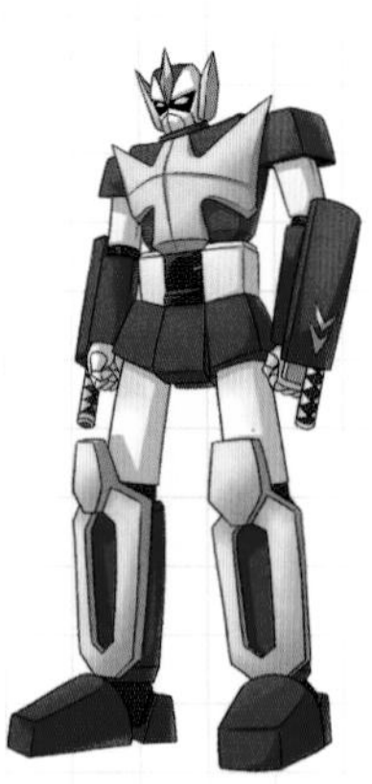

082

mecha heroes

search criteria

robot. standing. claw. wheels. sci-fi. antenna. screwdriver.

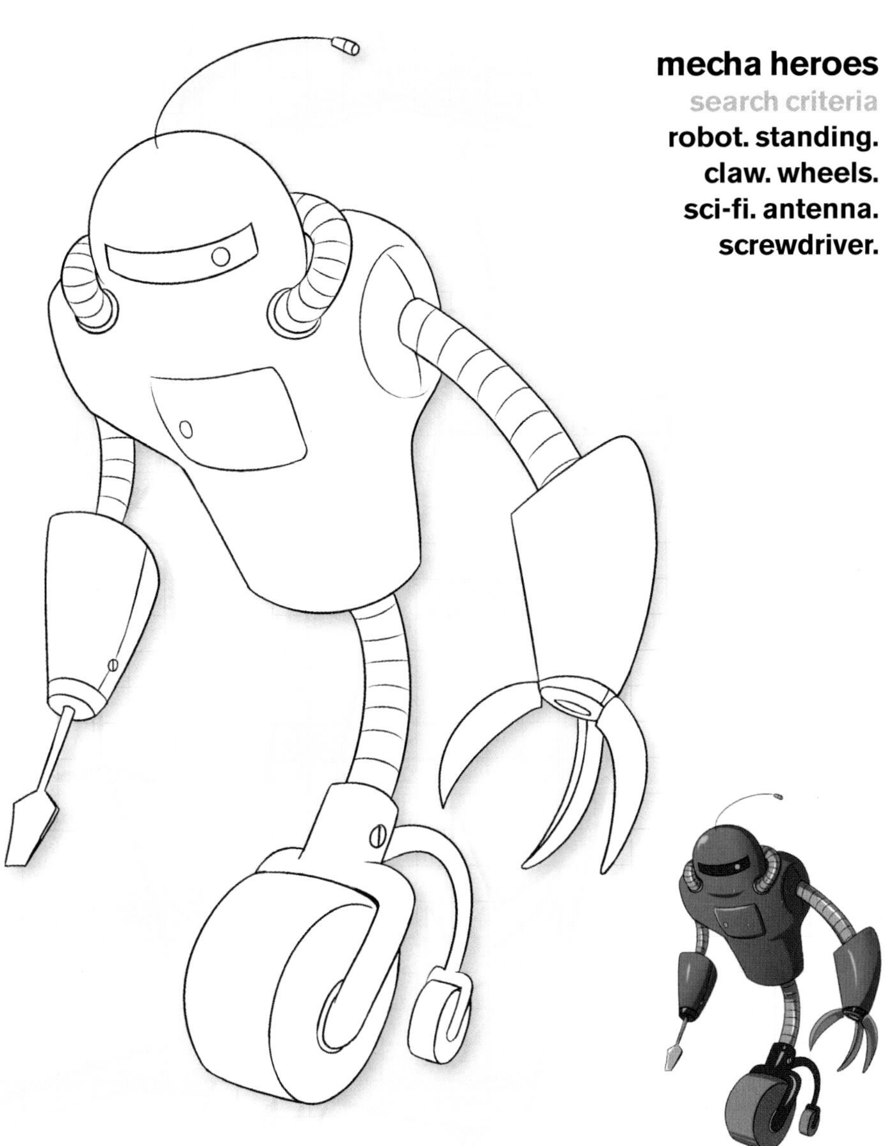

083

mecha heroes

search criteria

robot. floating. flying. kawaii. smiling.

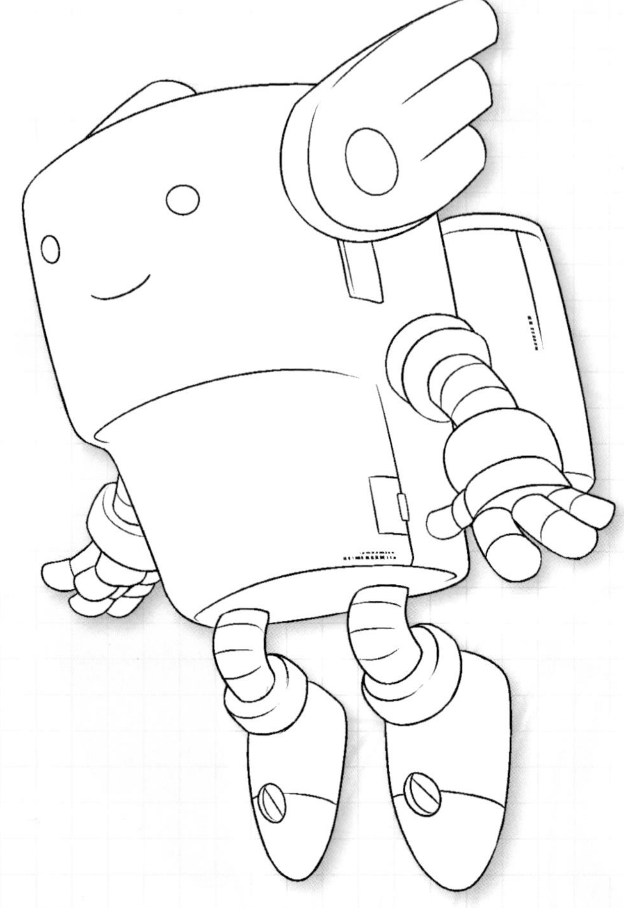

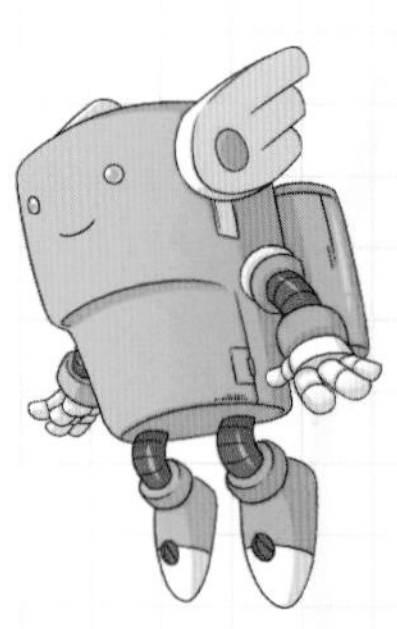

084

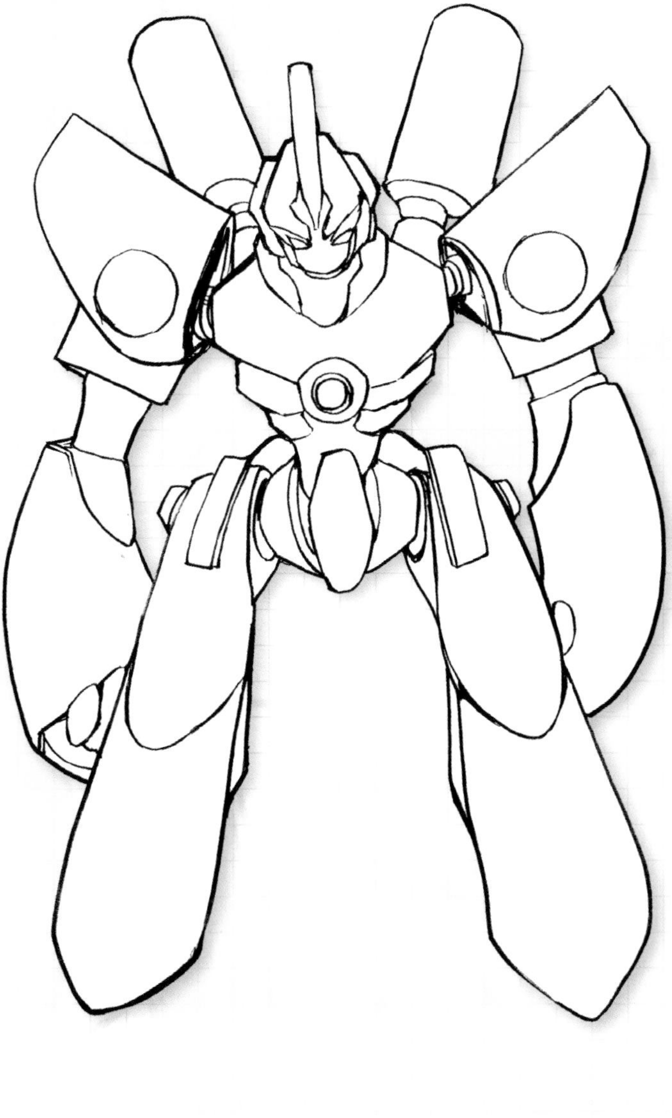

mecha heroes

search criteria

robot. standing. fighter. rockets.

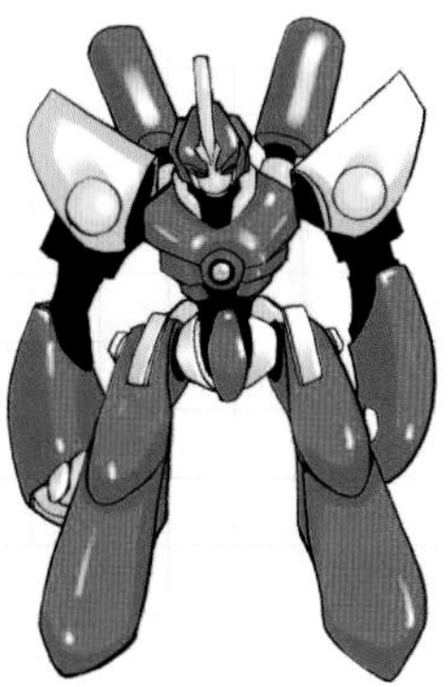

085

mecha heroes

search criteria

**robot. standing.
bunny. kawaii.**

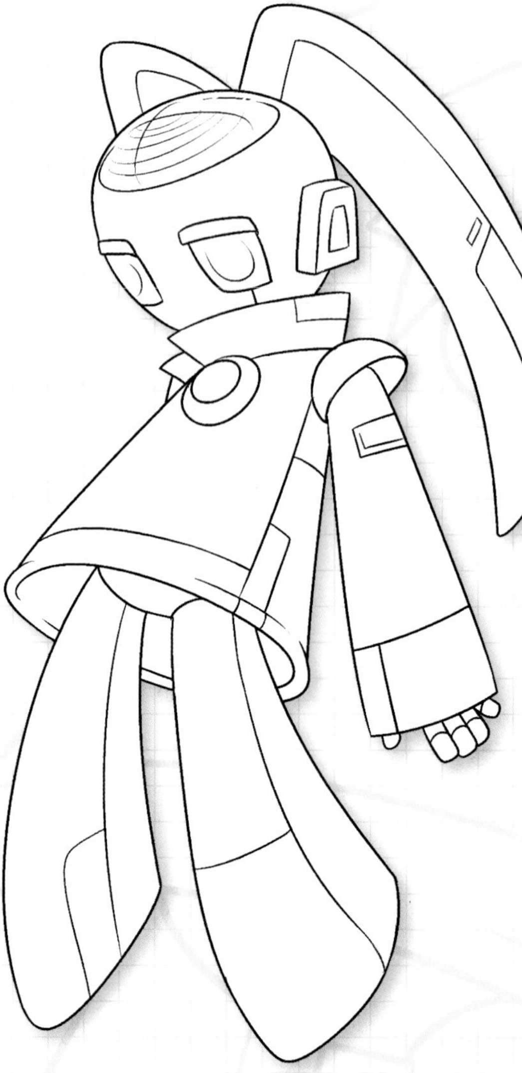

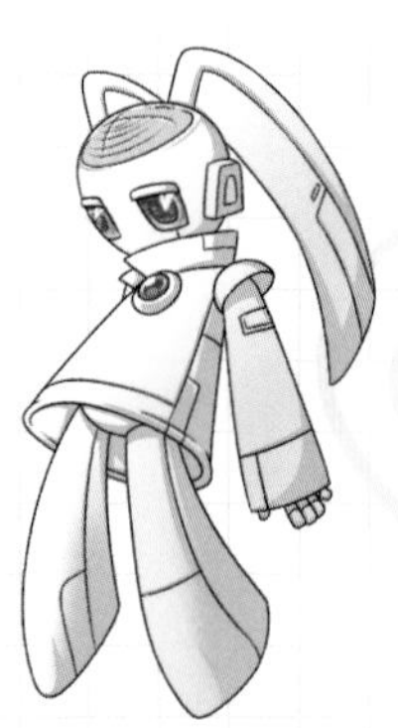

086

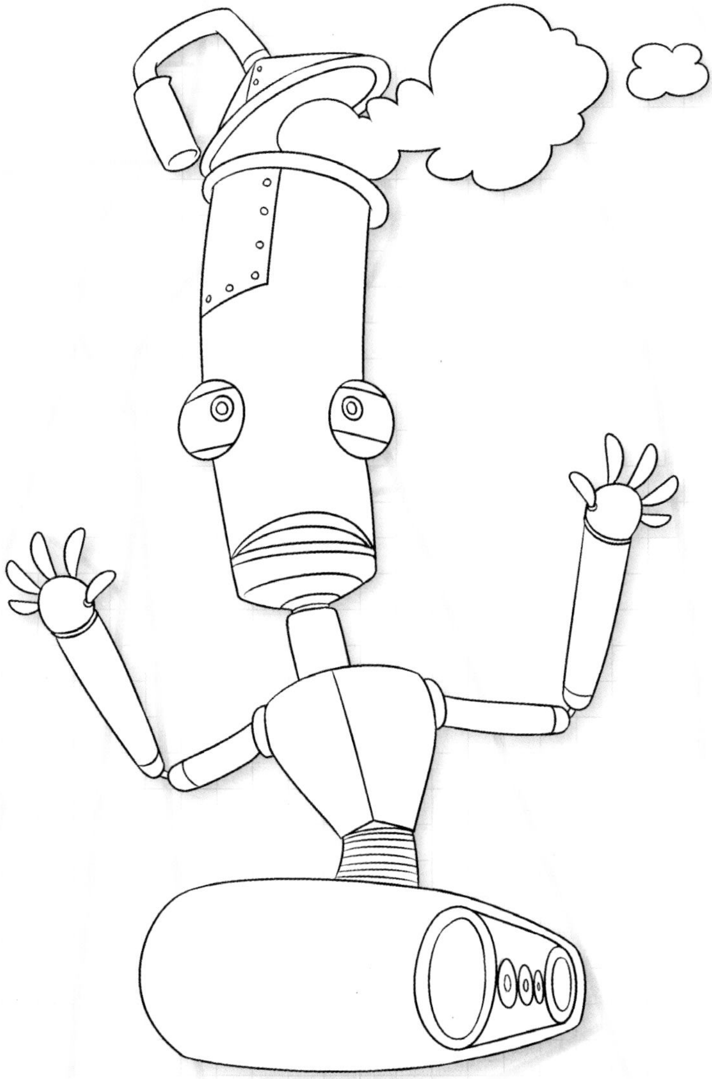

mecha heroes

search criteria

robot. standing. goofy. humor. tin. smoke.

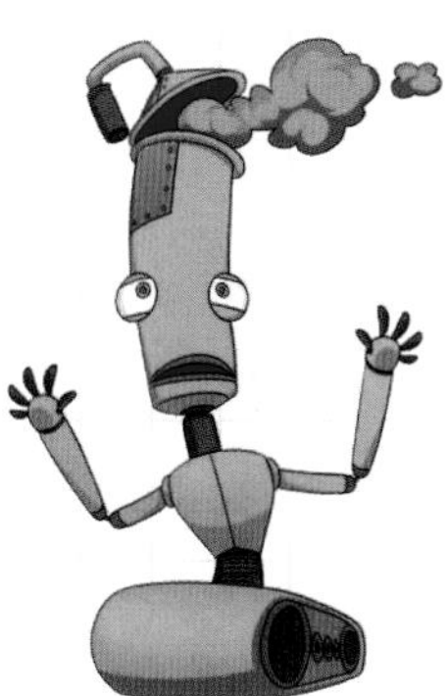

087

mecha heroes
search criteria
robot. standing. antenna. bolt. sad. music. humor.

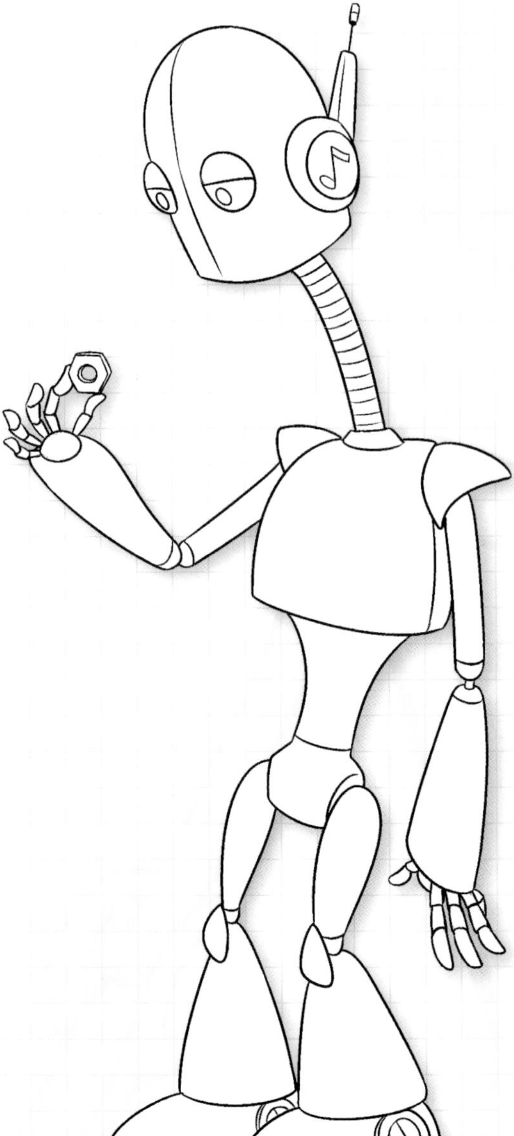

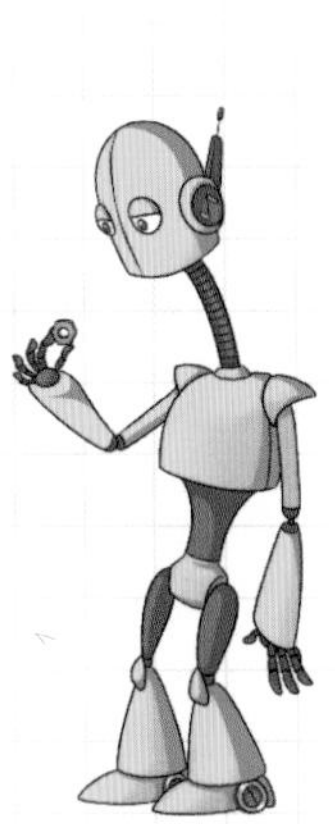

088

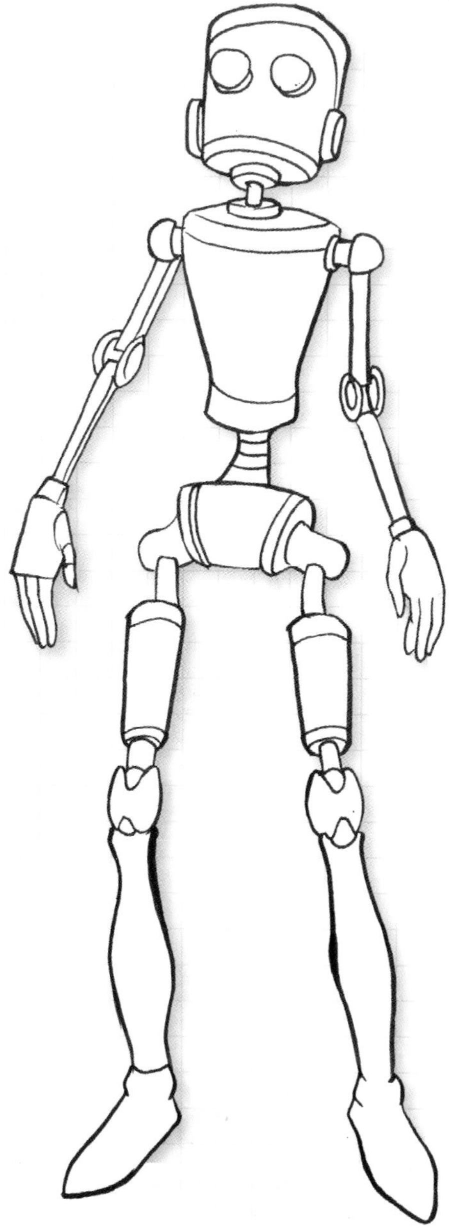

mecha heroes

search criteria

robot. standing. looking. humor. tin. sci-fi.

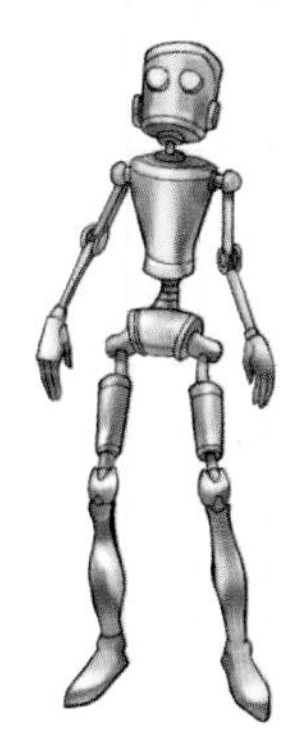

089

mecha heroes

search criteria

robot. standing. futuristic. sci-fi.

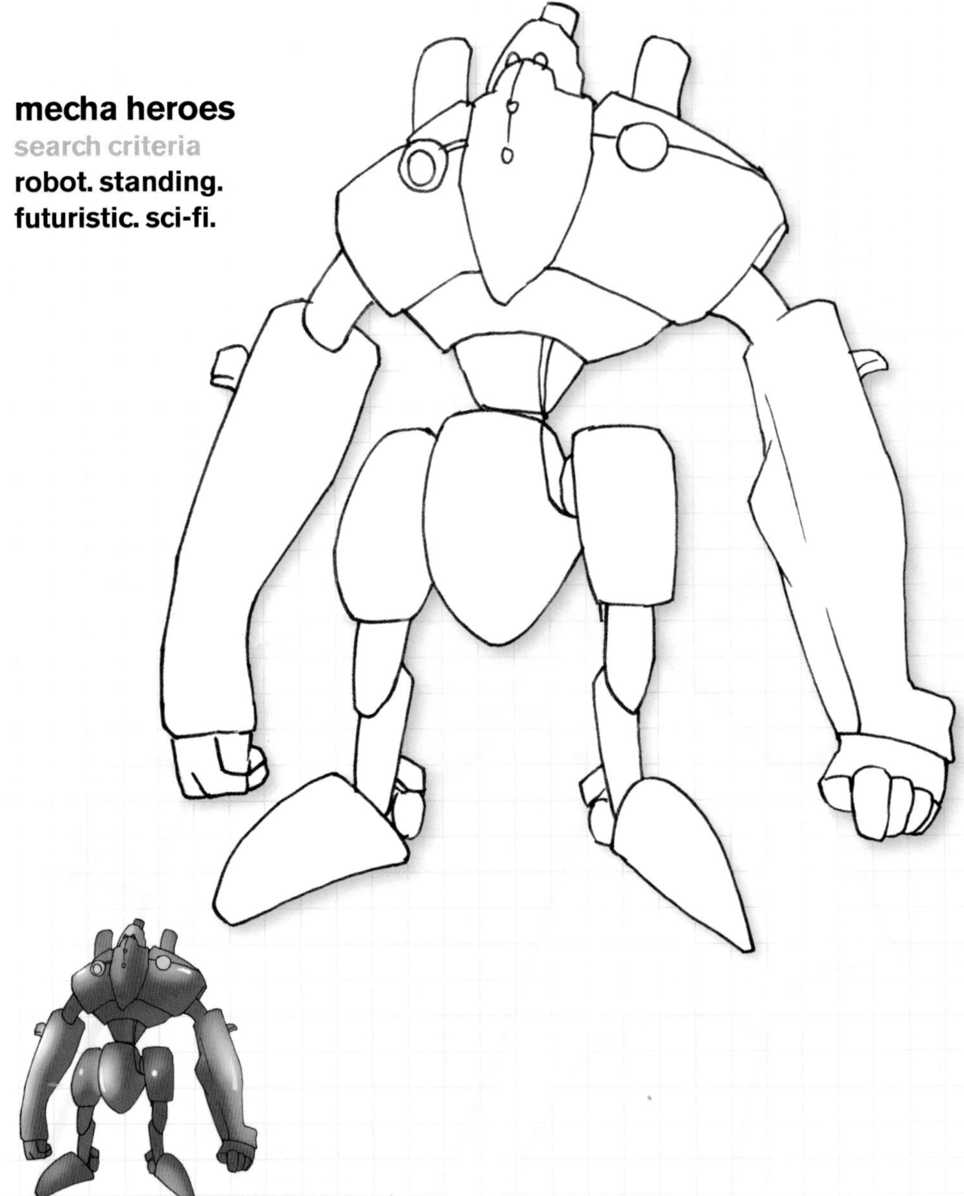

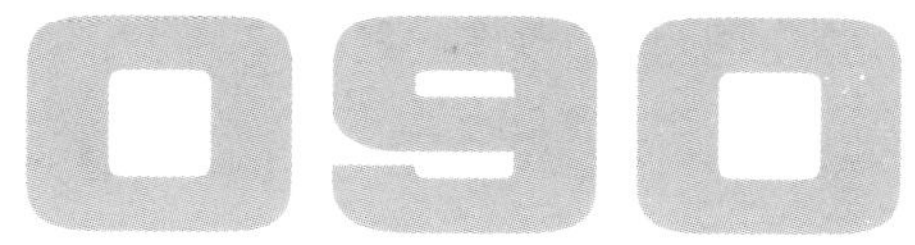

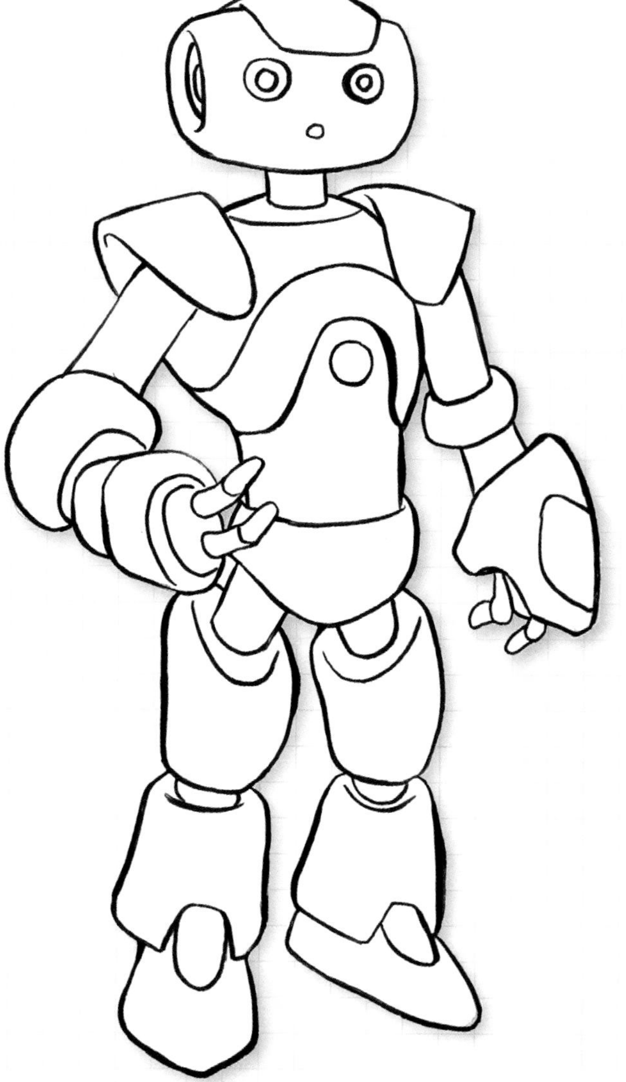

mecha heroes

search criteria

robot. standing.
cute. sci-fi.

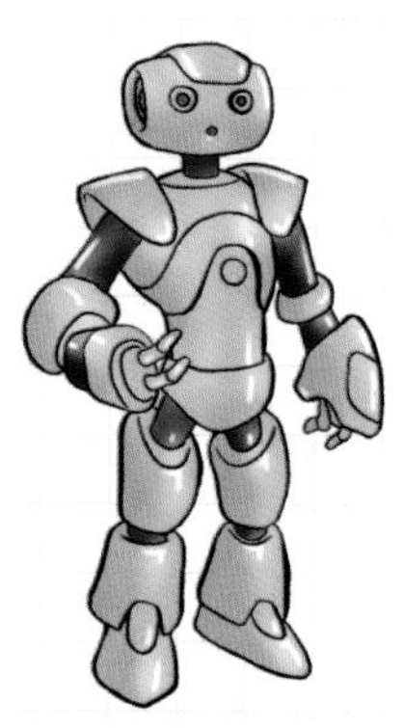

091

mecha heroes

search criteria

female. standing. robot. cyborg. sci-fi.

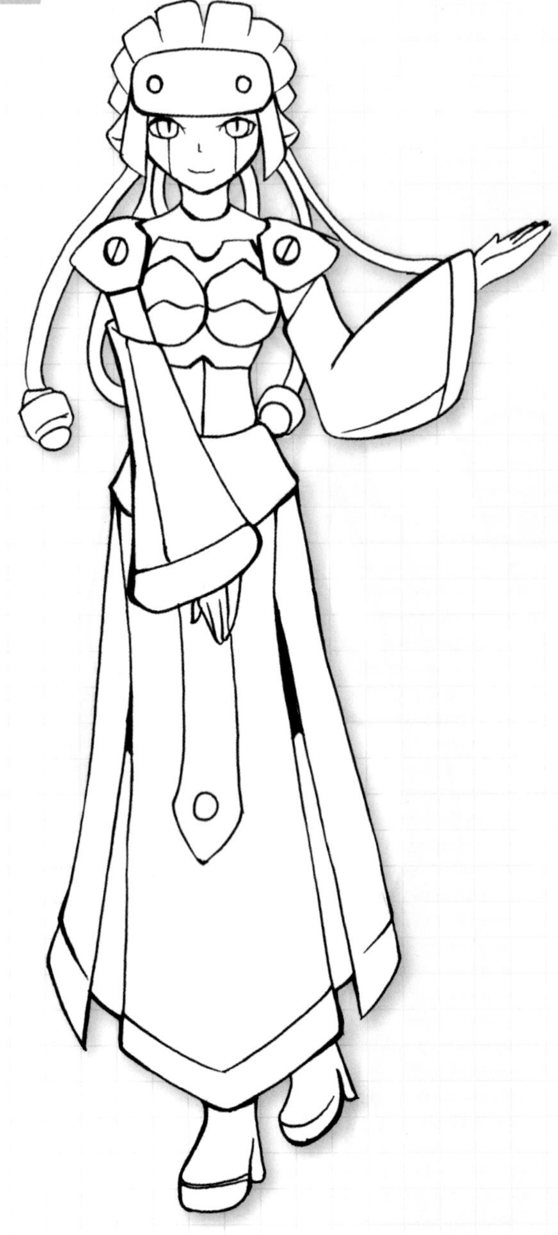

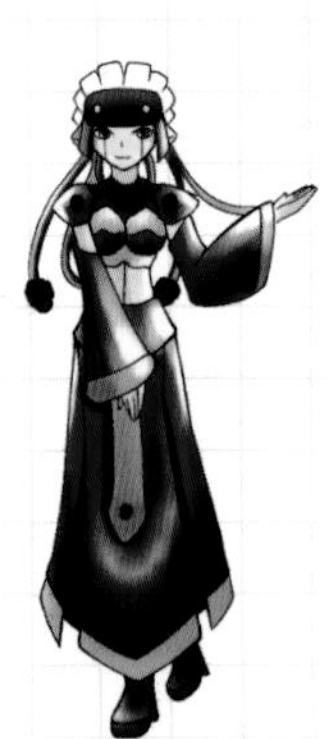

092

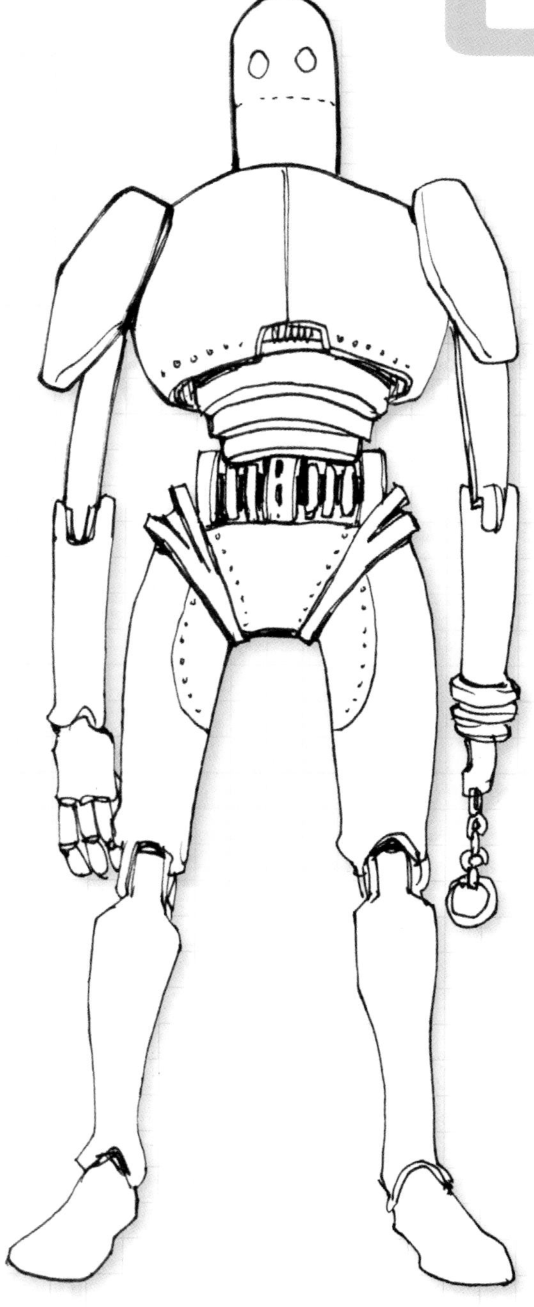

mecha heroes

search criteria

robot. standing. tool. sci-fi.

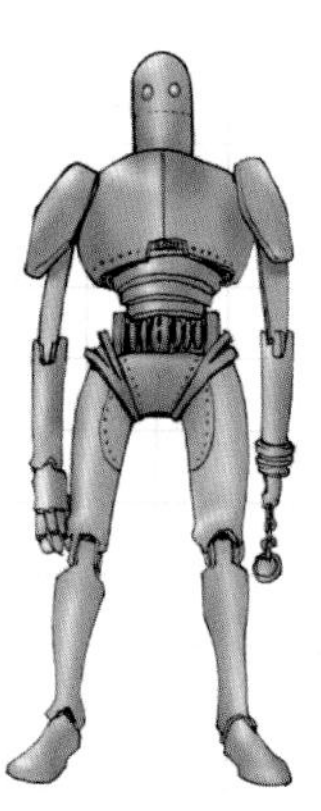

093

mecha heroes

search criteria

robot. standing. utensils. cleaner. goofy. wheels. humor.

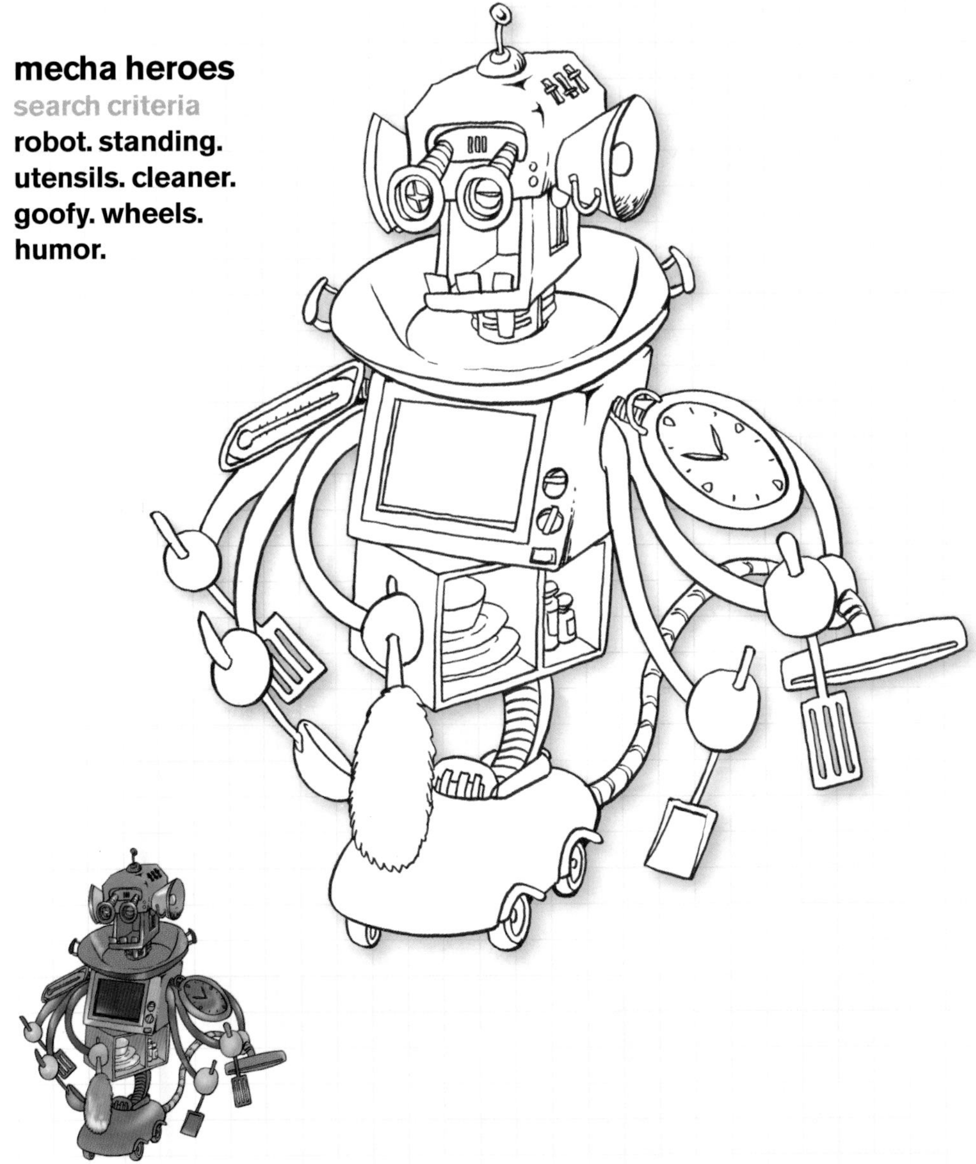

094

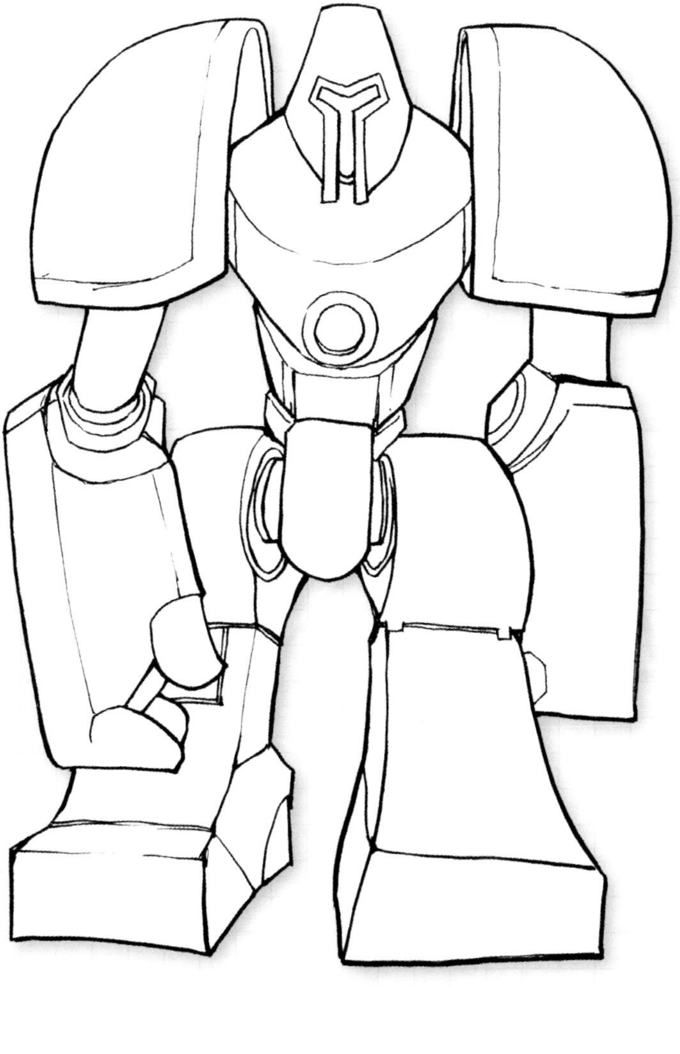

mecha heroes

search criteria

robot. standing. giant. sci-fi.

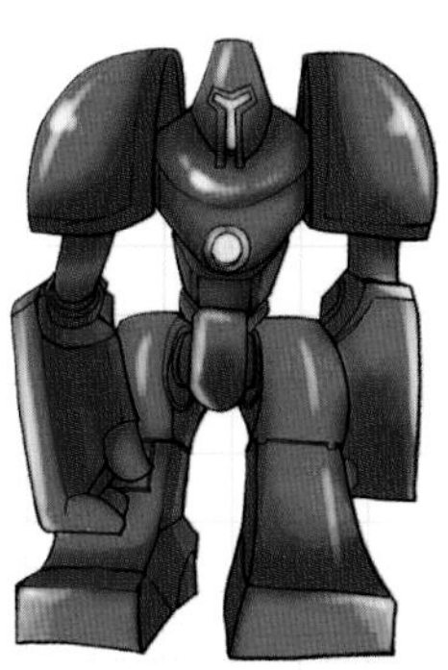

095

mecha heroes

search criteria

female. floating. cyborg. jump. sci-fi. weapons. gun. blade.

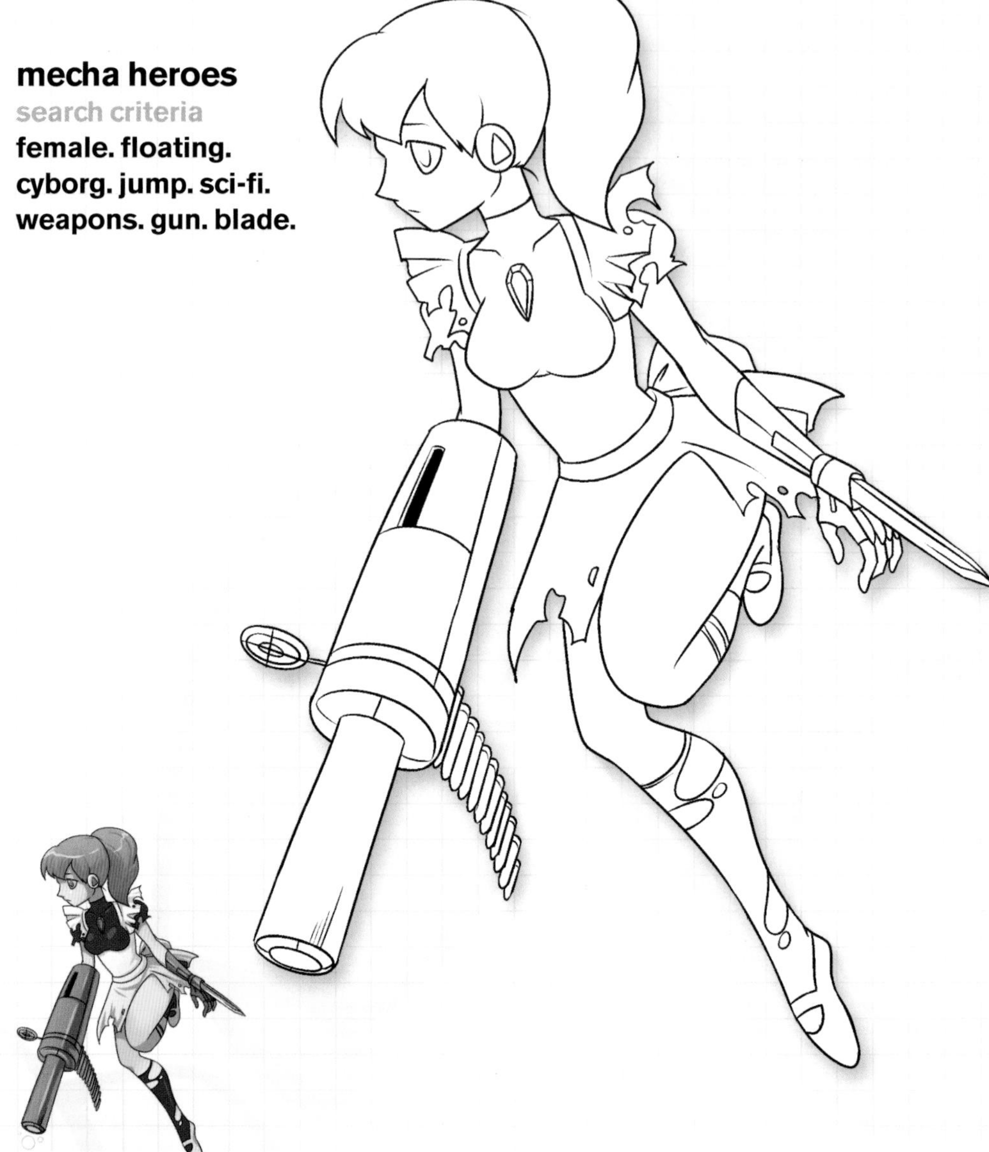

096

mecha heroes

search criteria

robot. standing. floating. bug.

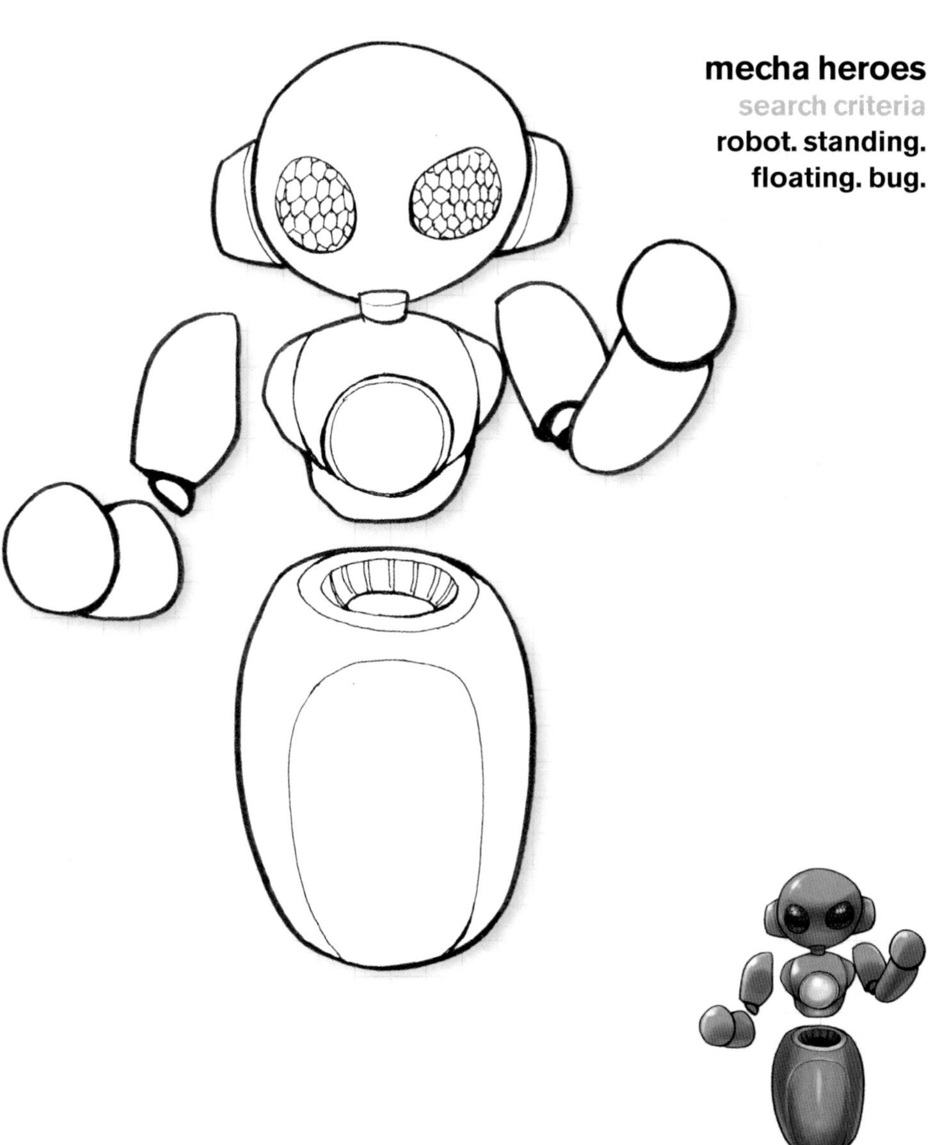

097

mecha heroes

search criteria

robot. standing. android. sci-fi.

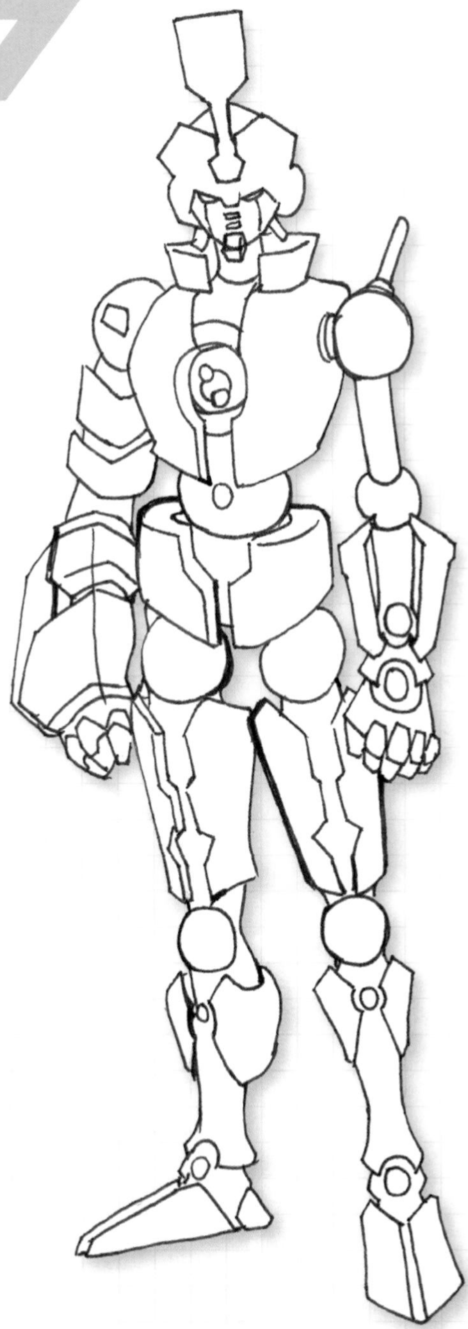

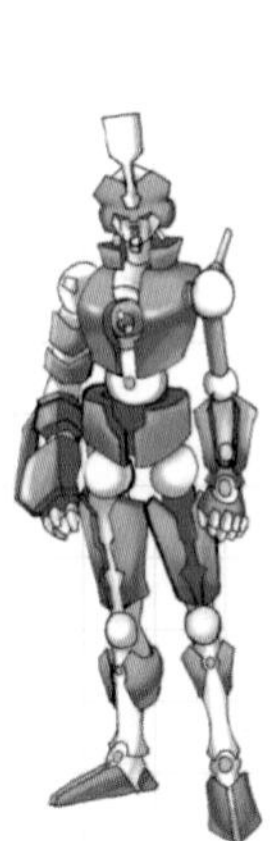

mecha heroes

search criteria

robot. standing. angry. weapon. sword. fighter.

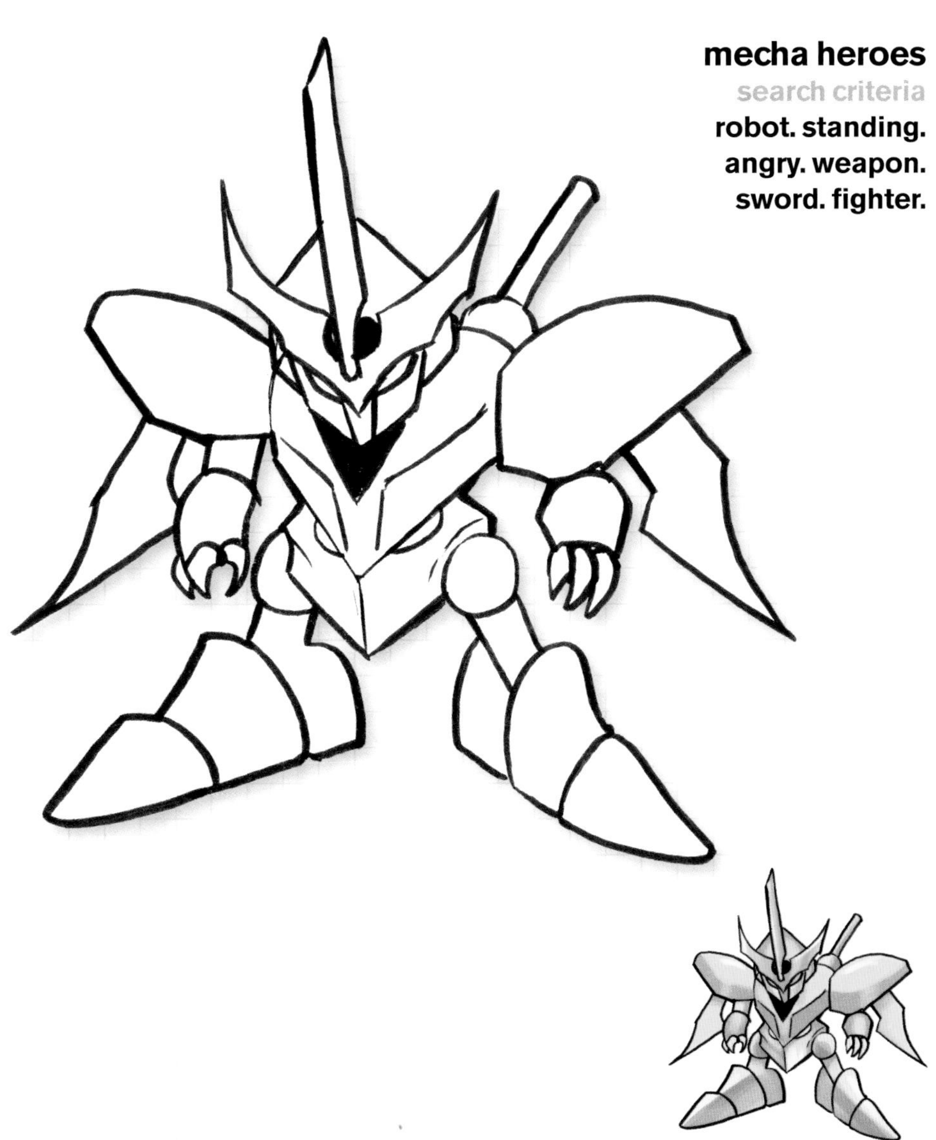

099

ninja villains

search criteria

male. jump. kick. contemporary. attack. shout.

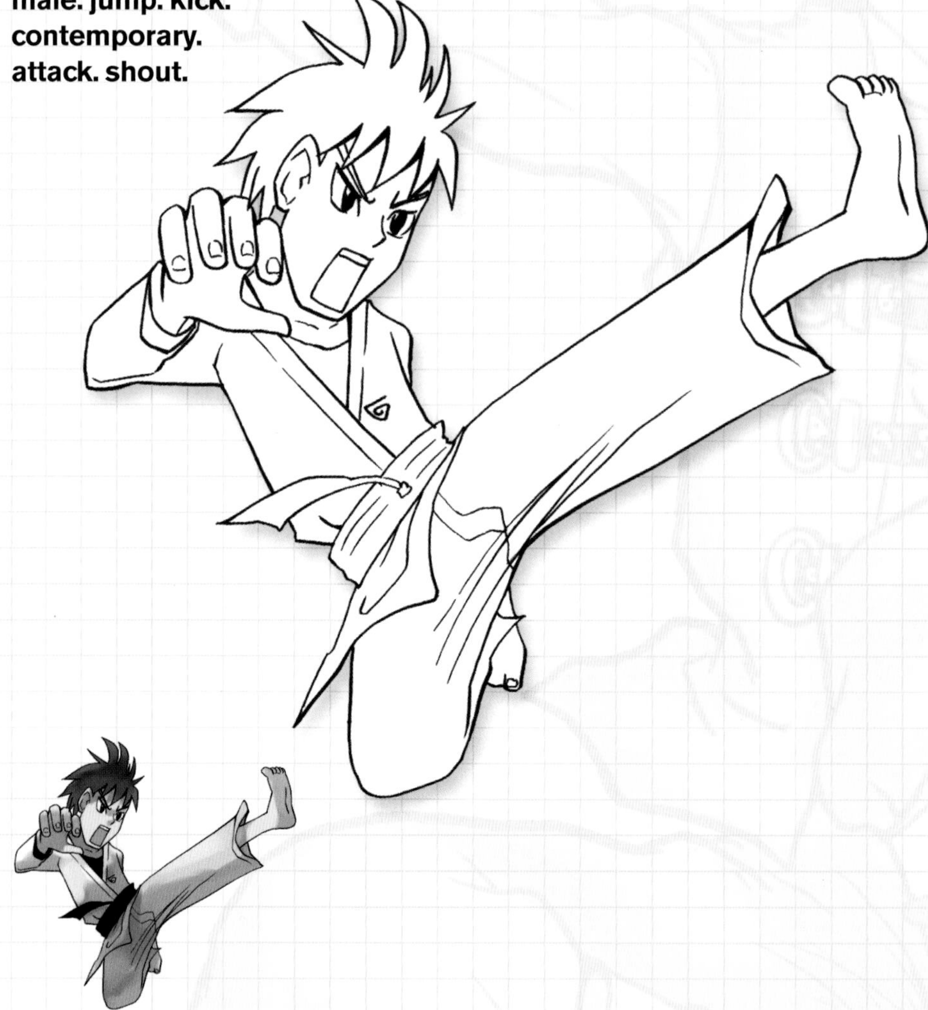

100

ninja villains

search criteria

male. sitting. crouch. weapon. sword. historical.

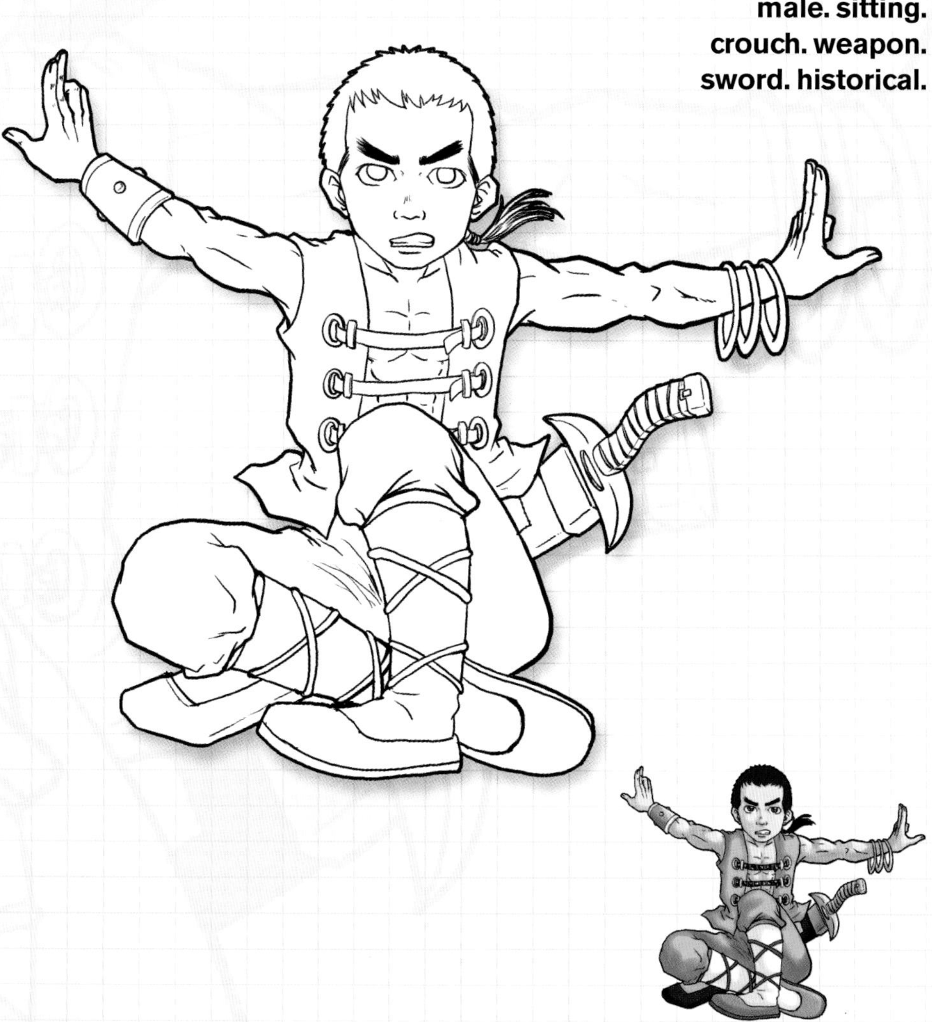

101

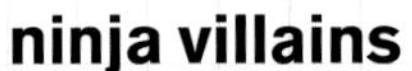

ninja villains

search criteria

male. side. jump. gesture. scarf. spy.

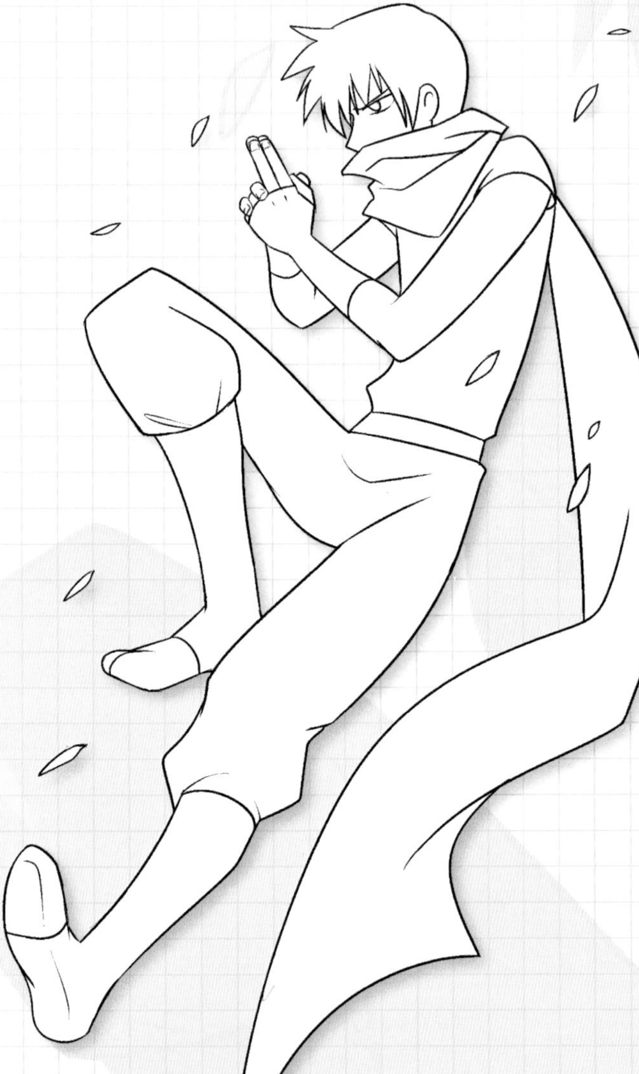

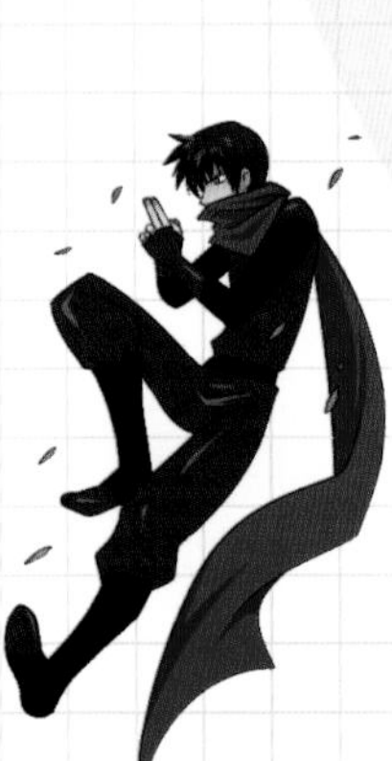

102

ninja villains

search criteria

male. jump. pounce. attack. weapon. blades. scarf. assassin.

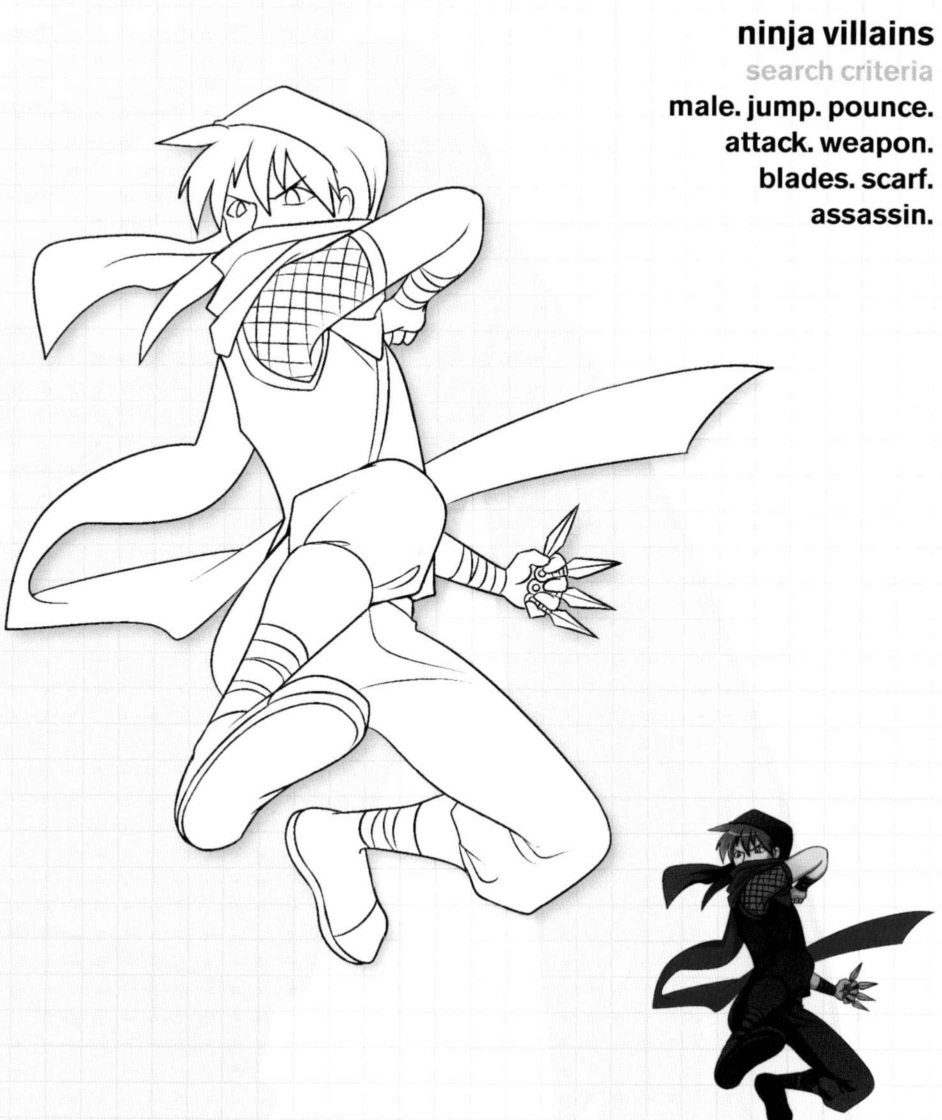

103

ninja villains

search criteria

male. crouched. weapons. crutches. contemporary. sinister. biker.

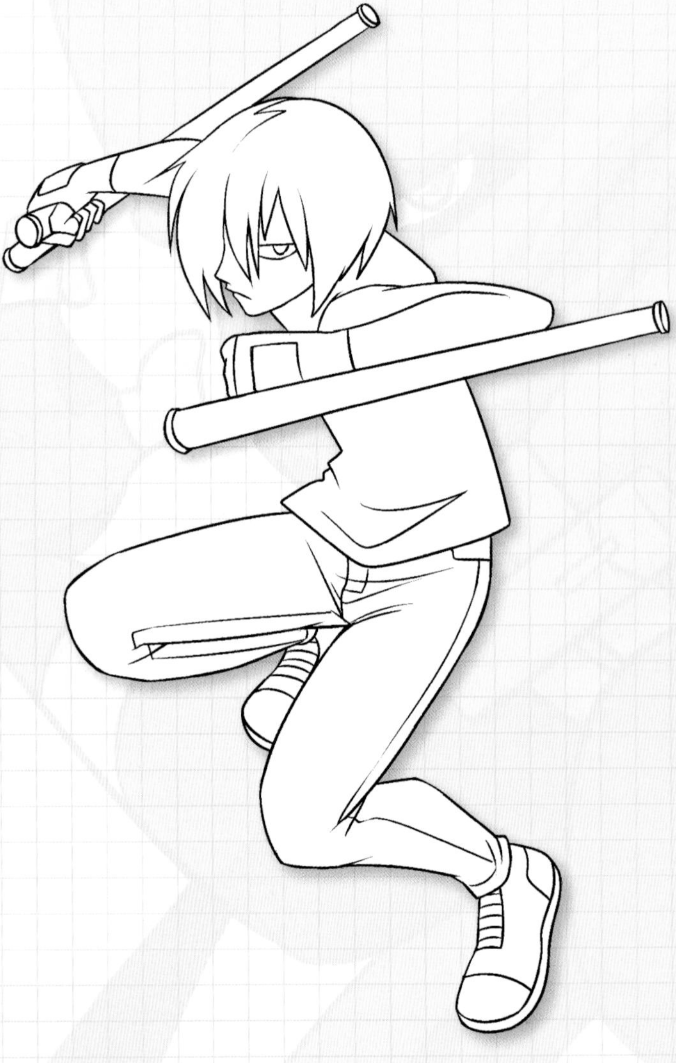

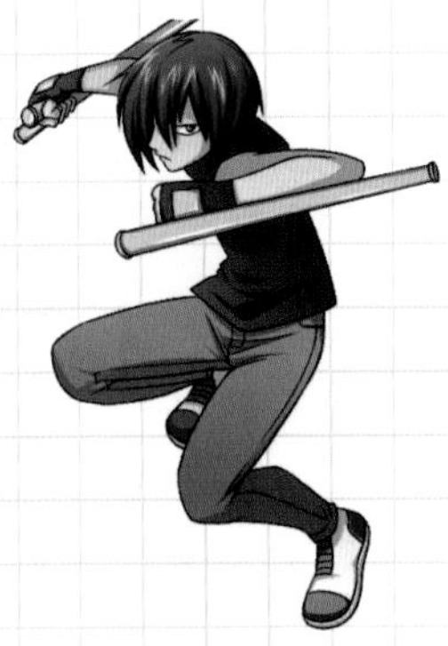

104

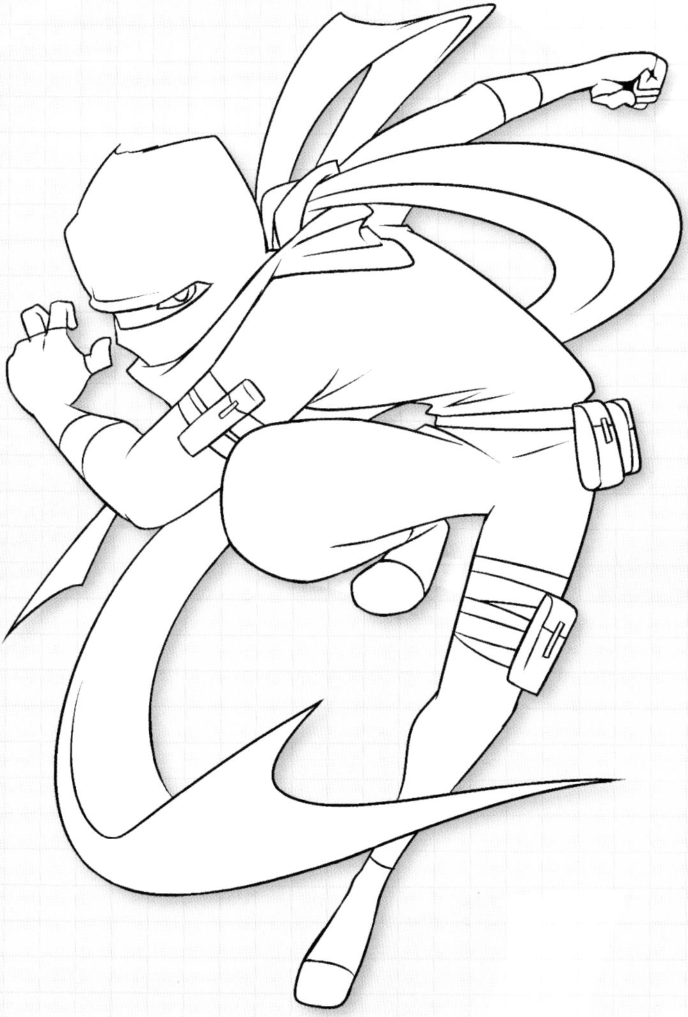

ninja villains

search criteria

male. jump. pounce. mask. assassin. spy. sinister.

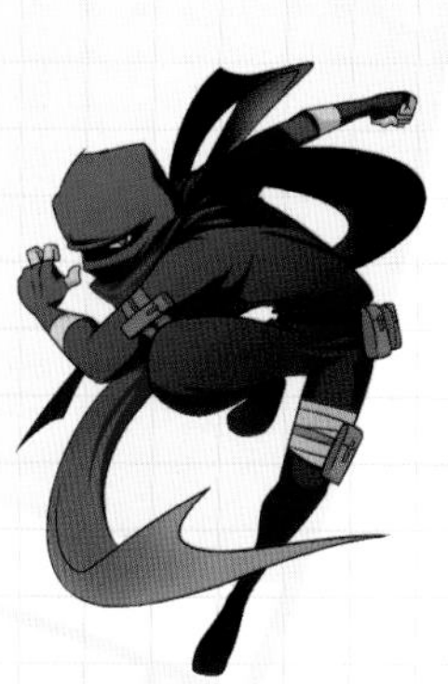

105

ninja villains

search criteria

male. attack. angry. pounce. headband. weapon. sword. contemporary.

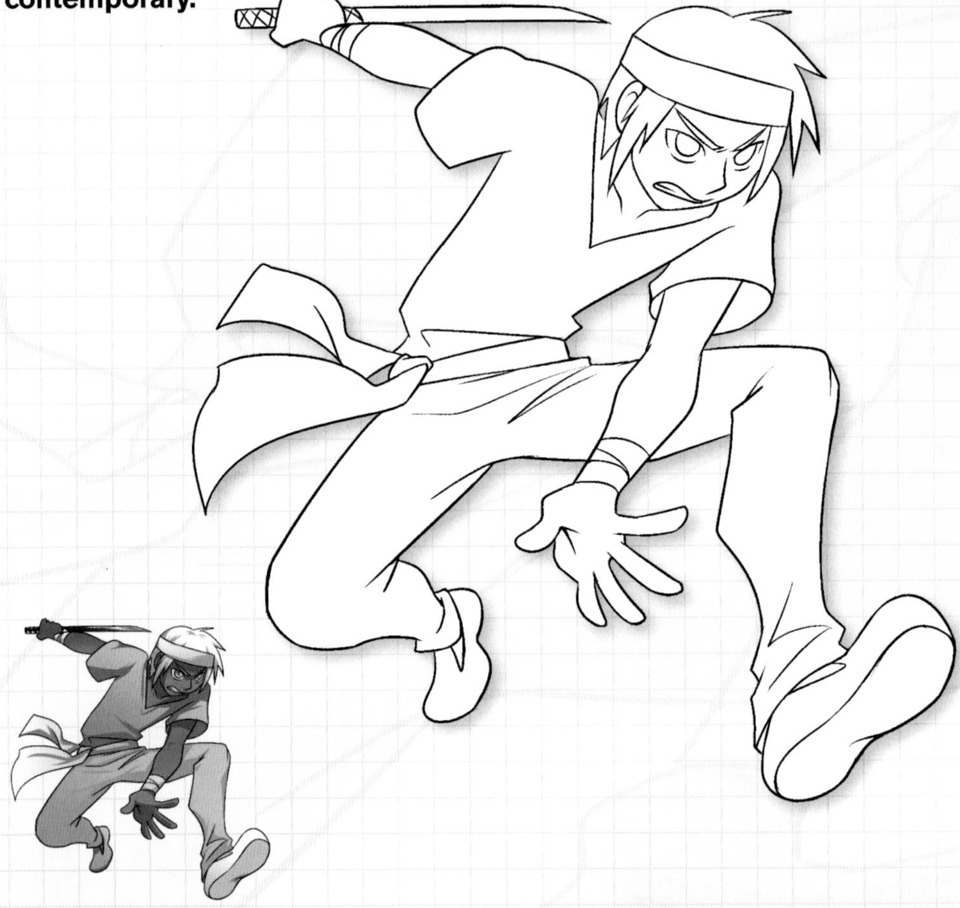

106

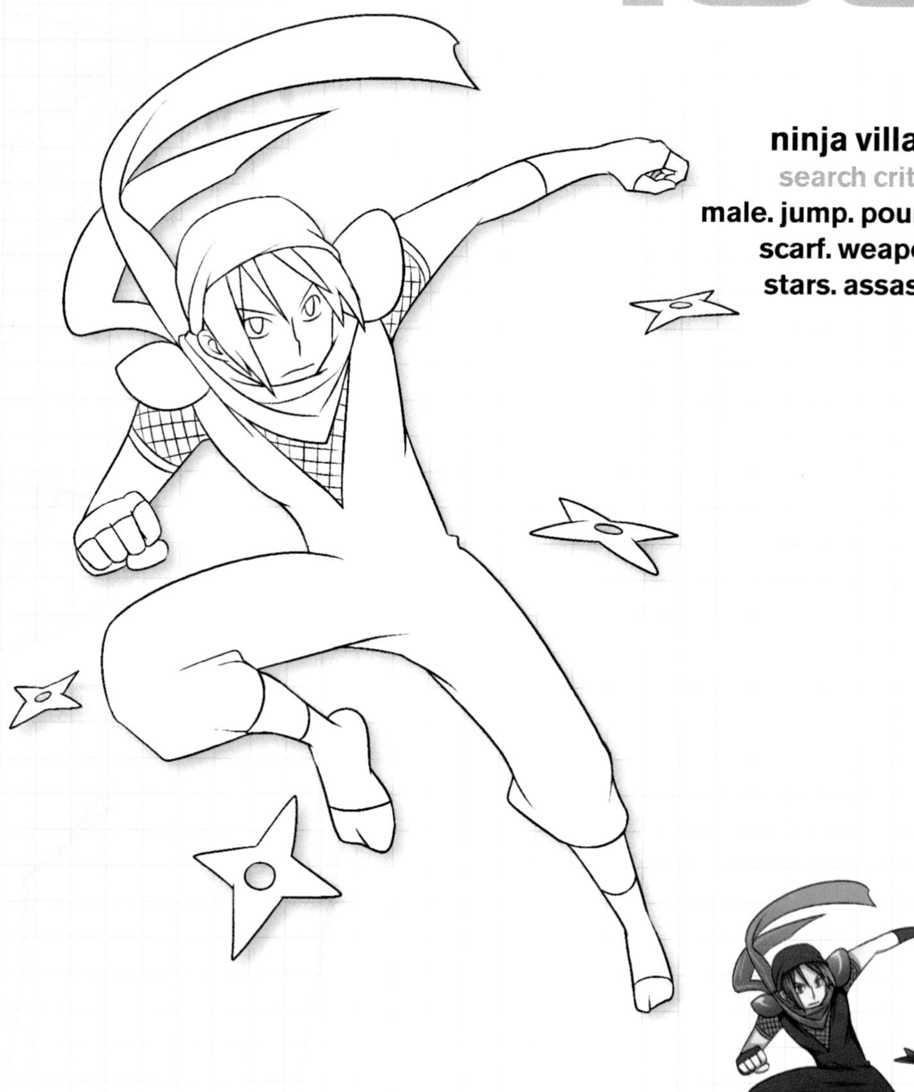

ninja villains

search criteria

male. jump. pounce. scarf. weapons. stars. assassin.

107

ninja villains

search criteria

male. side. crouched. bandages. scarf. weapons. swords. assassin.

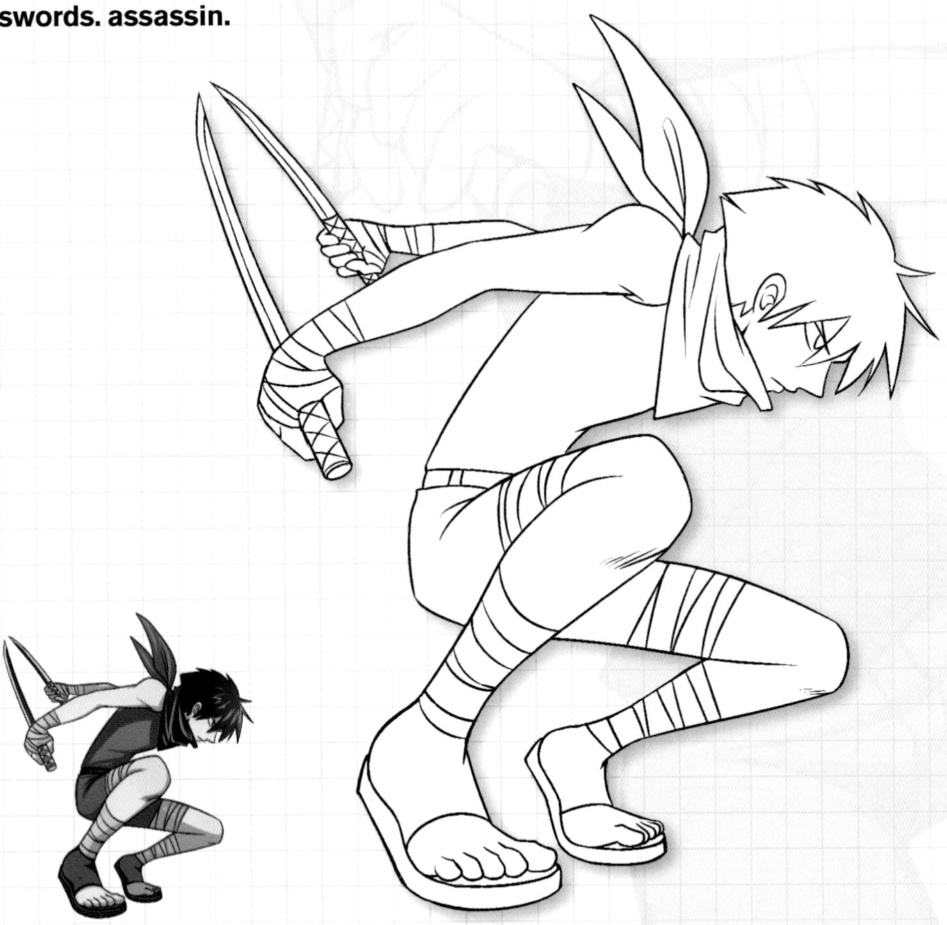

108

ninja villains

search criteria

male. crouched. bandages. scarf. weapons. swords. spy. assassin.

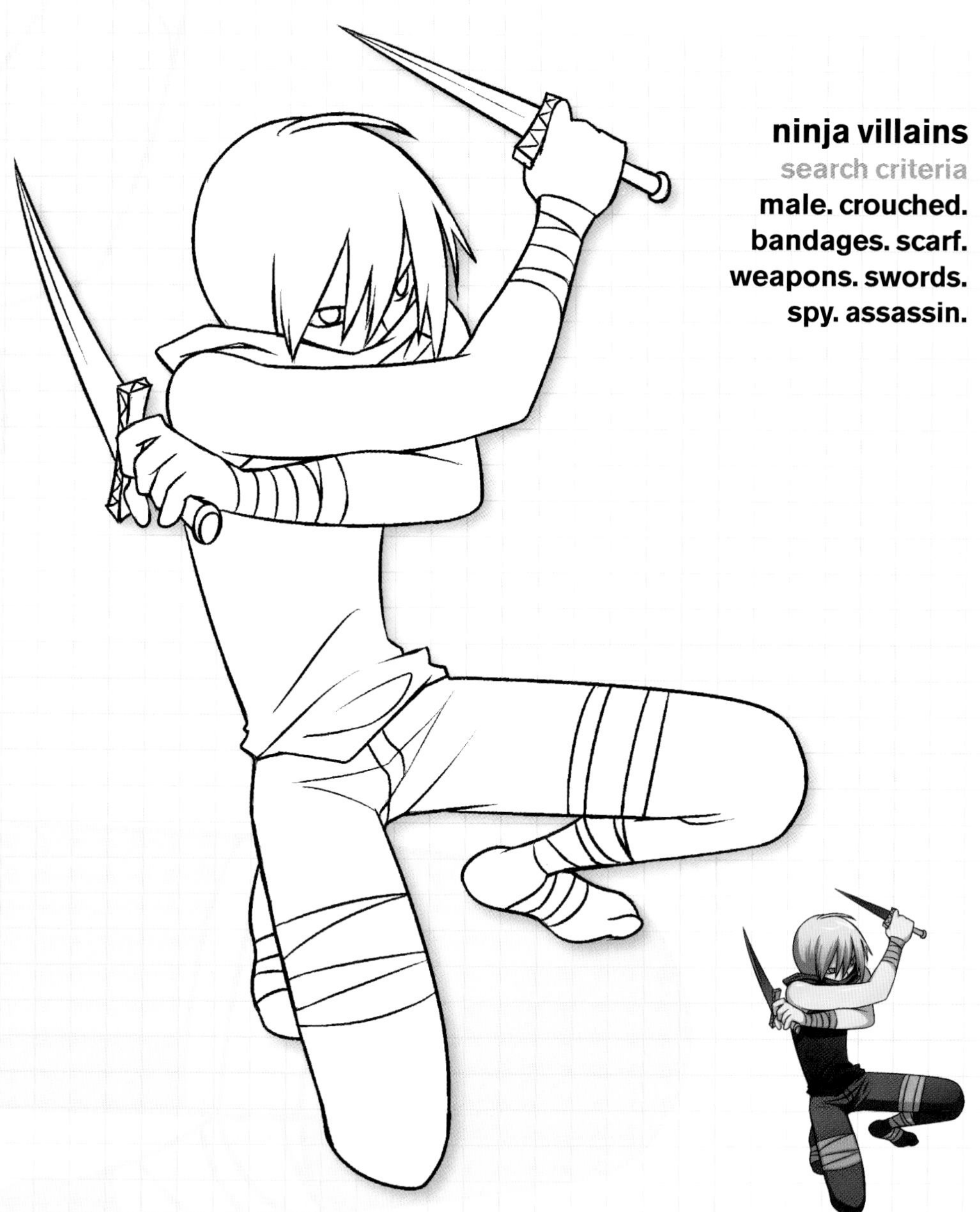

109

ninja villains

search criteria

male. standing.
angry. contemporary.

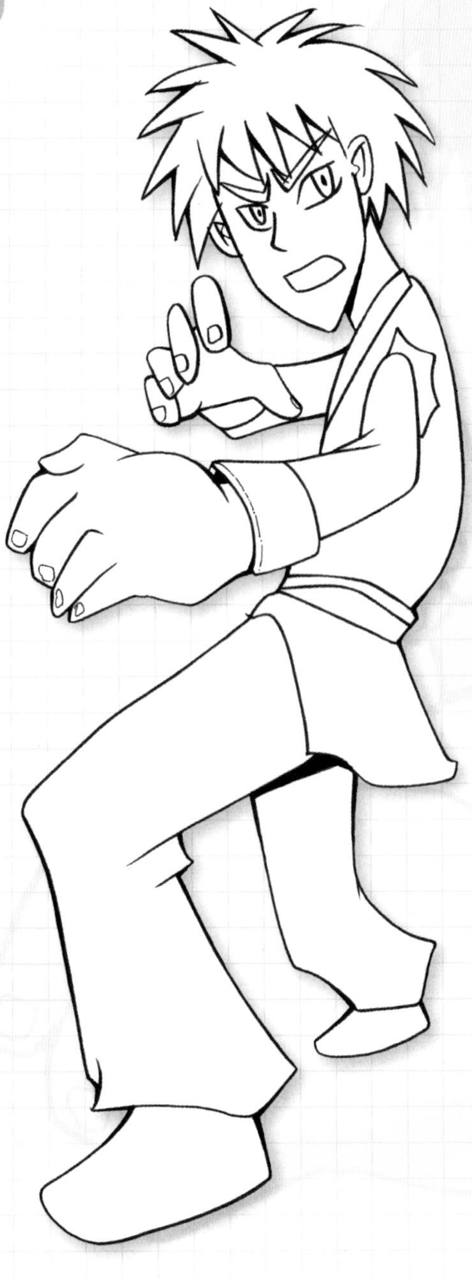

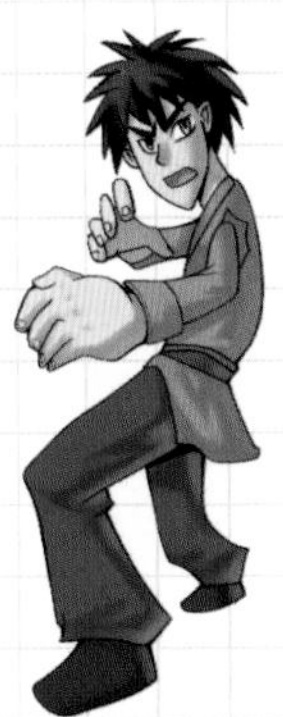

110

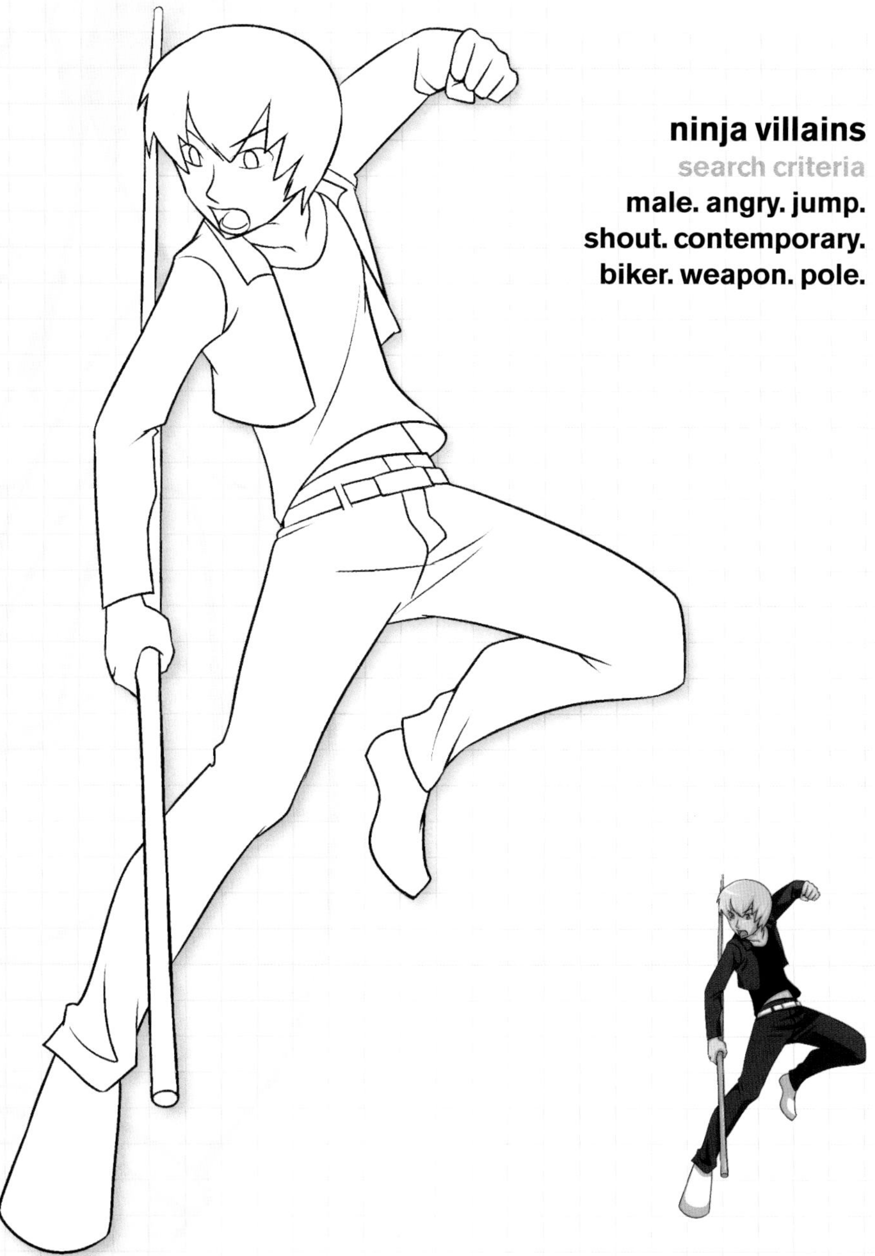

ninja villains

search criteria

male. angry. jump. shout. contemporary. biker. weapon. pole.

111

ninja villains

search criteria

male. kick. crouched. bandages. contemporary.

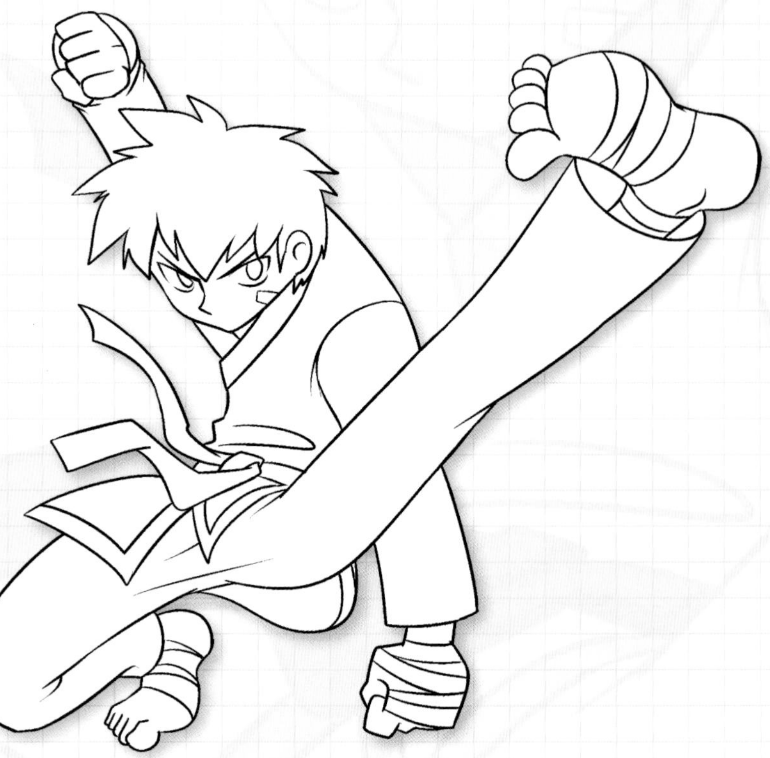

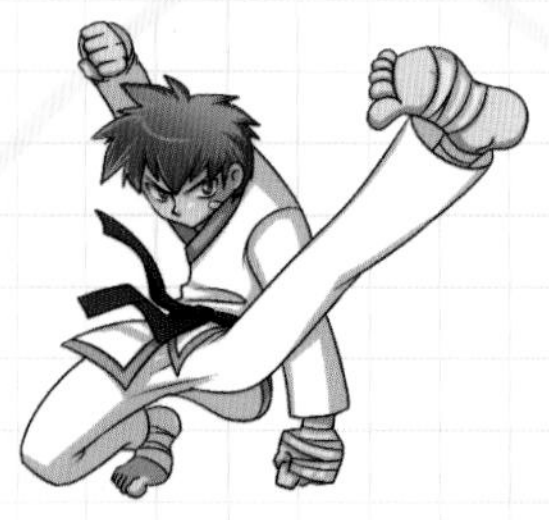

112

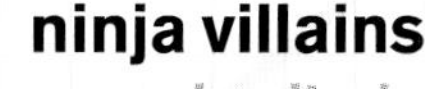

ninja villains

search criteria

male. crouched. scarf. bandages. spy. assassin. sinister.

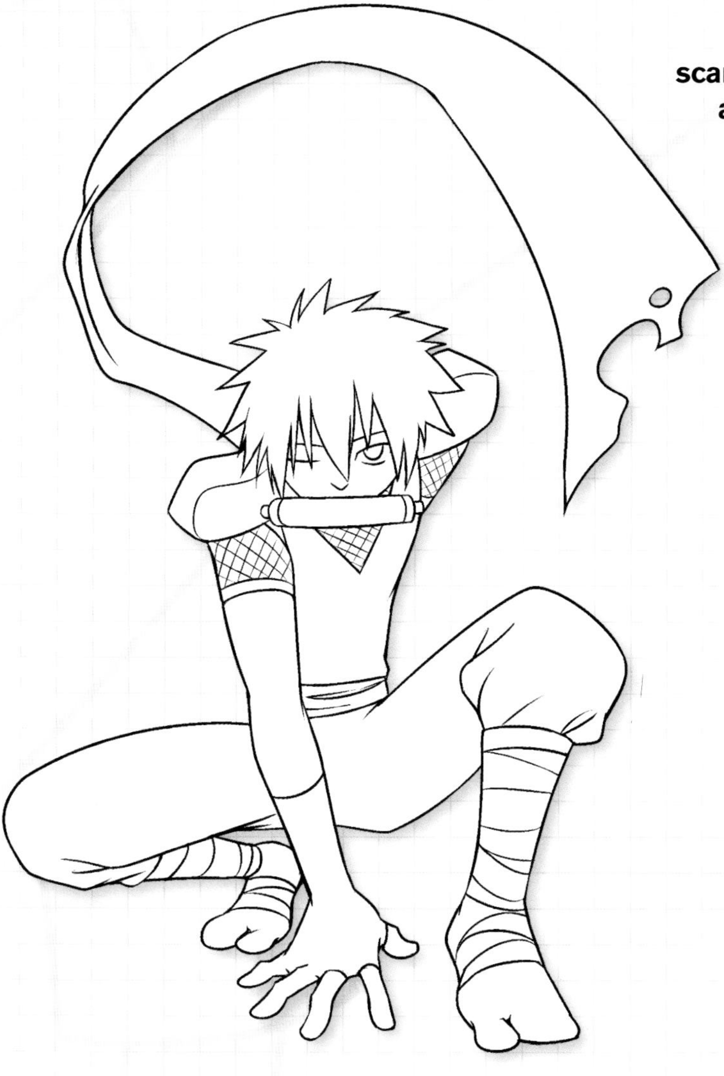

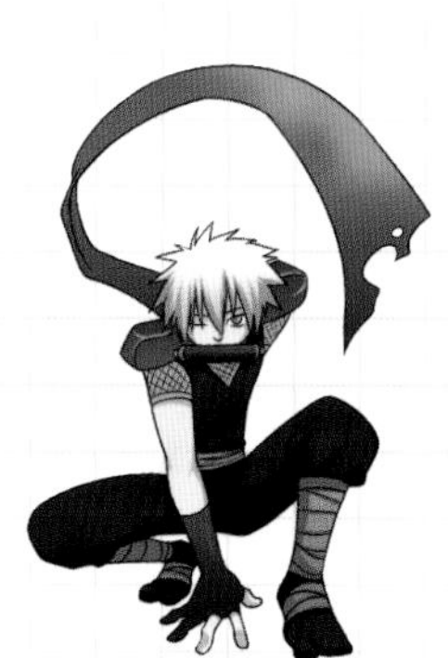

113

ninja villains

search criteria

female. crouched. scarf. bandages. spy. assassin. sinister.

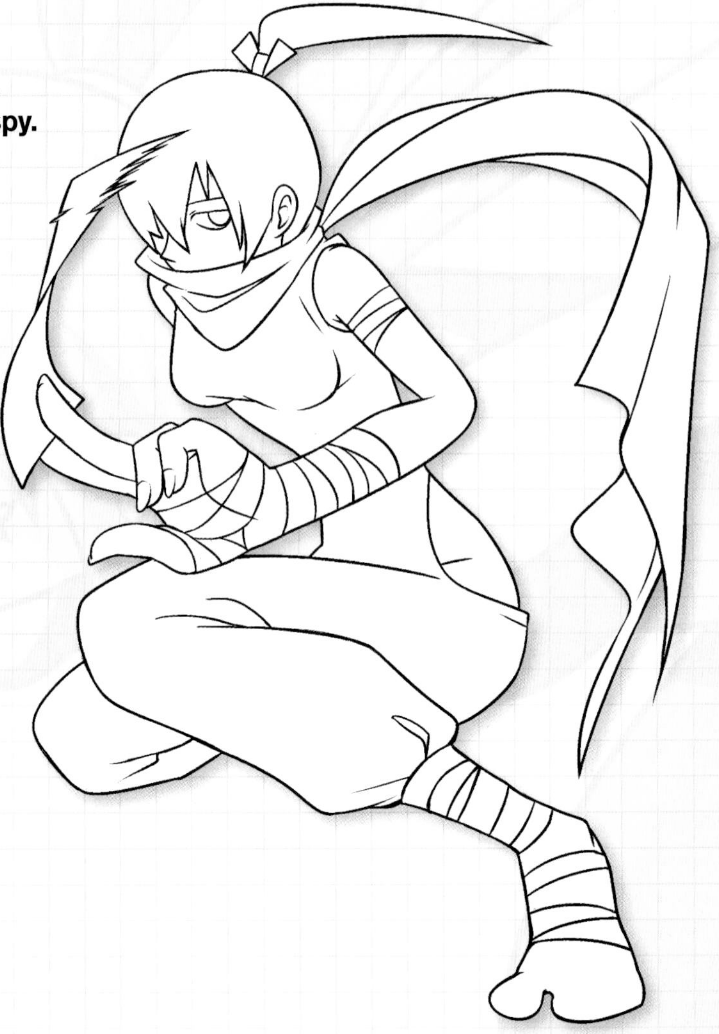

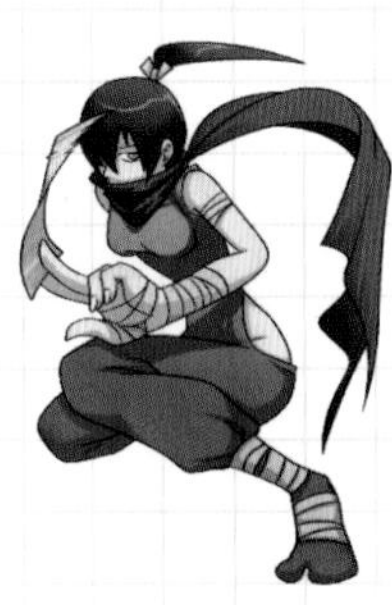

114

ninja villains

search criteria

female. attack. jump. pounce. weapons. blades. spy. assassin.

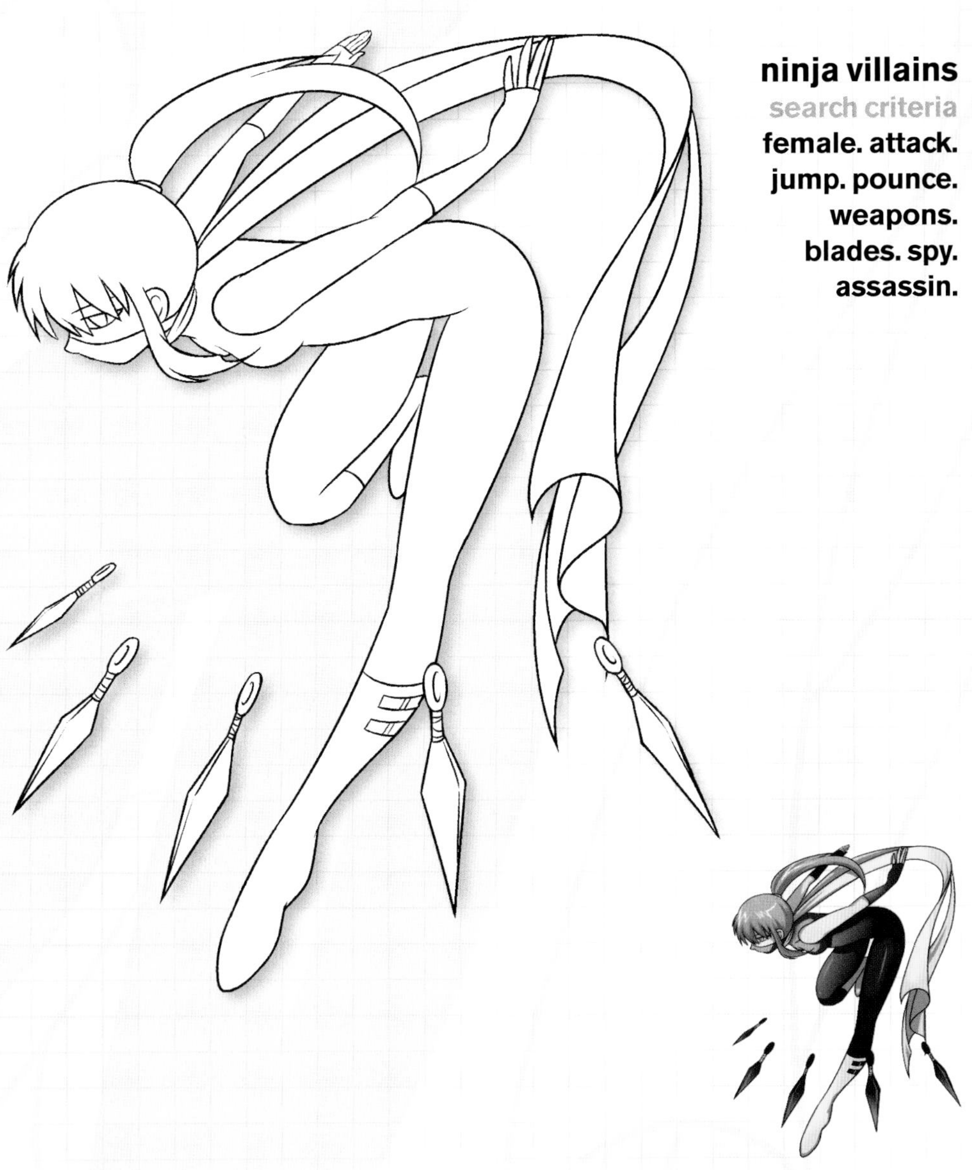

115

ninja villains

search criteria

male. standing. weapons. swords. mask. samurai. historical. armor.

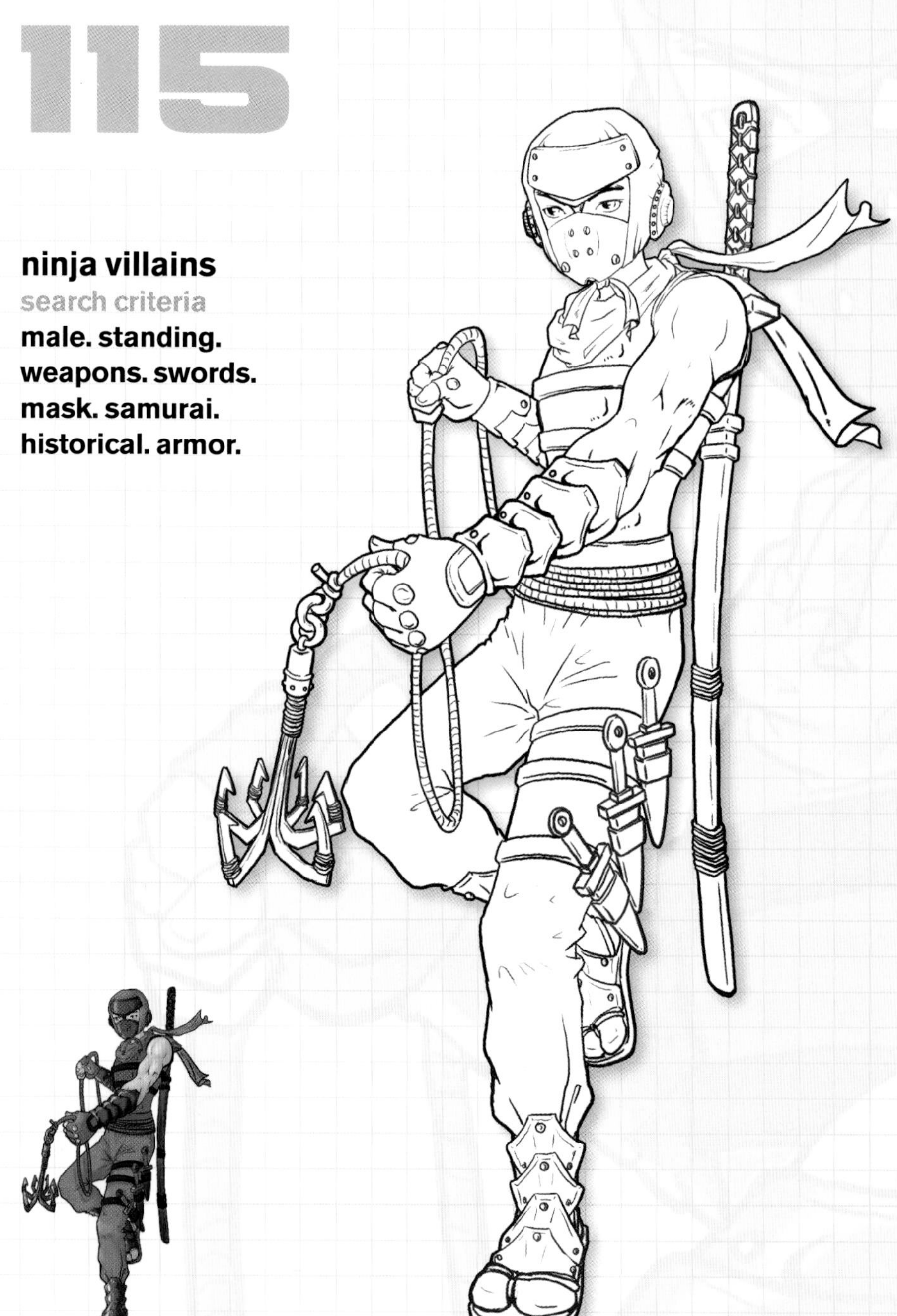

116

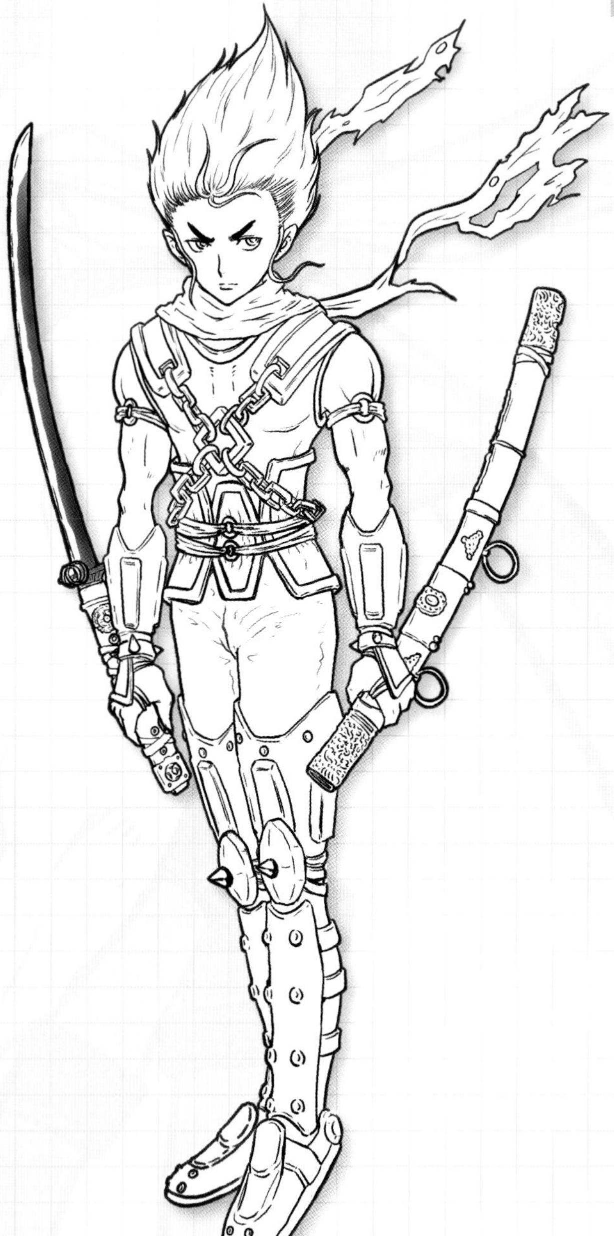

ninja villains

search criteria

male. standing. weapons. swords. scarf. samurai. historical. armor.

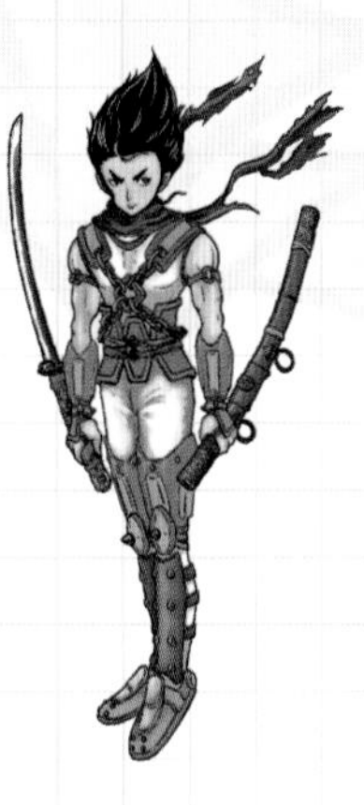

117

ninja heroes

search criteria

male. weapon. nunchucks. contemporary. headband.

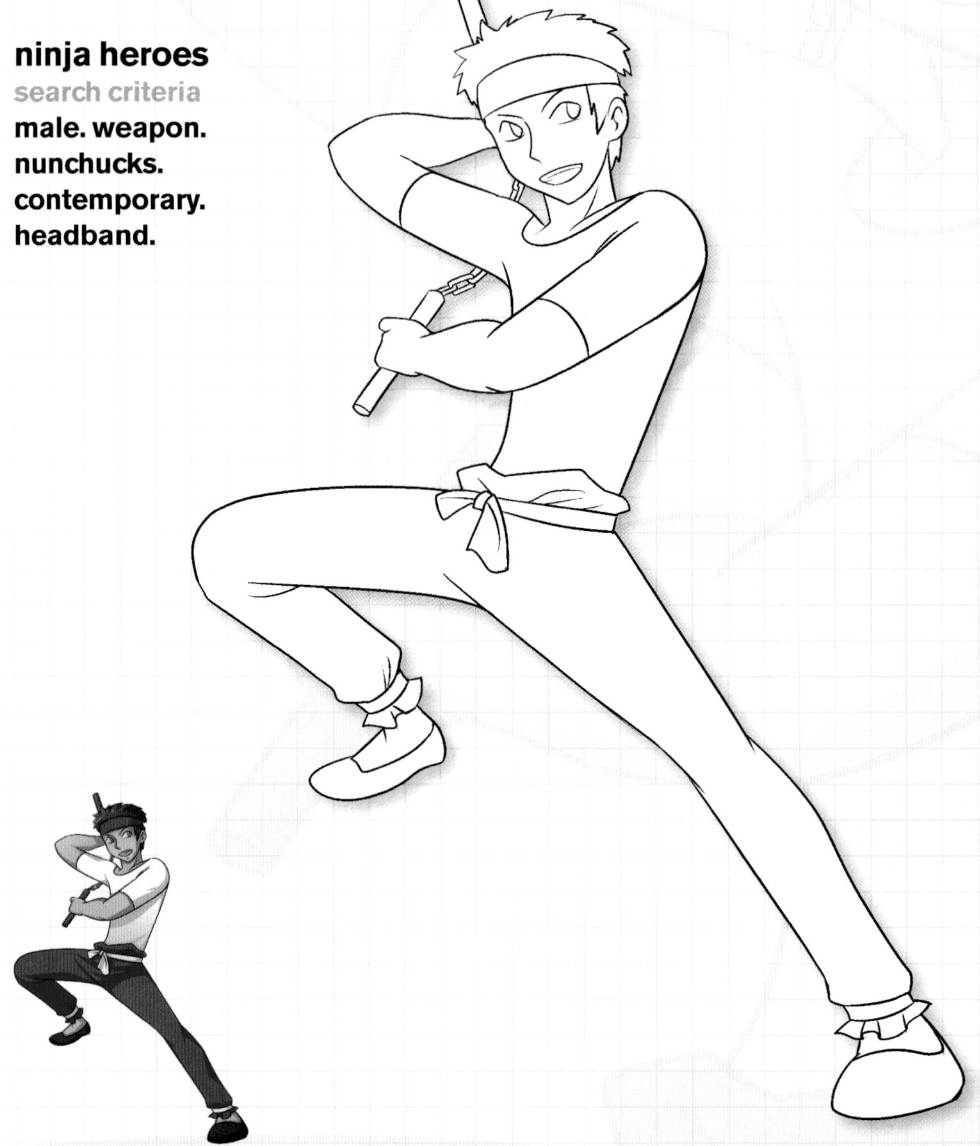

118

ninja heroes

search criteria

male. standing. contemporary.

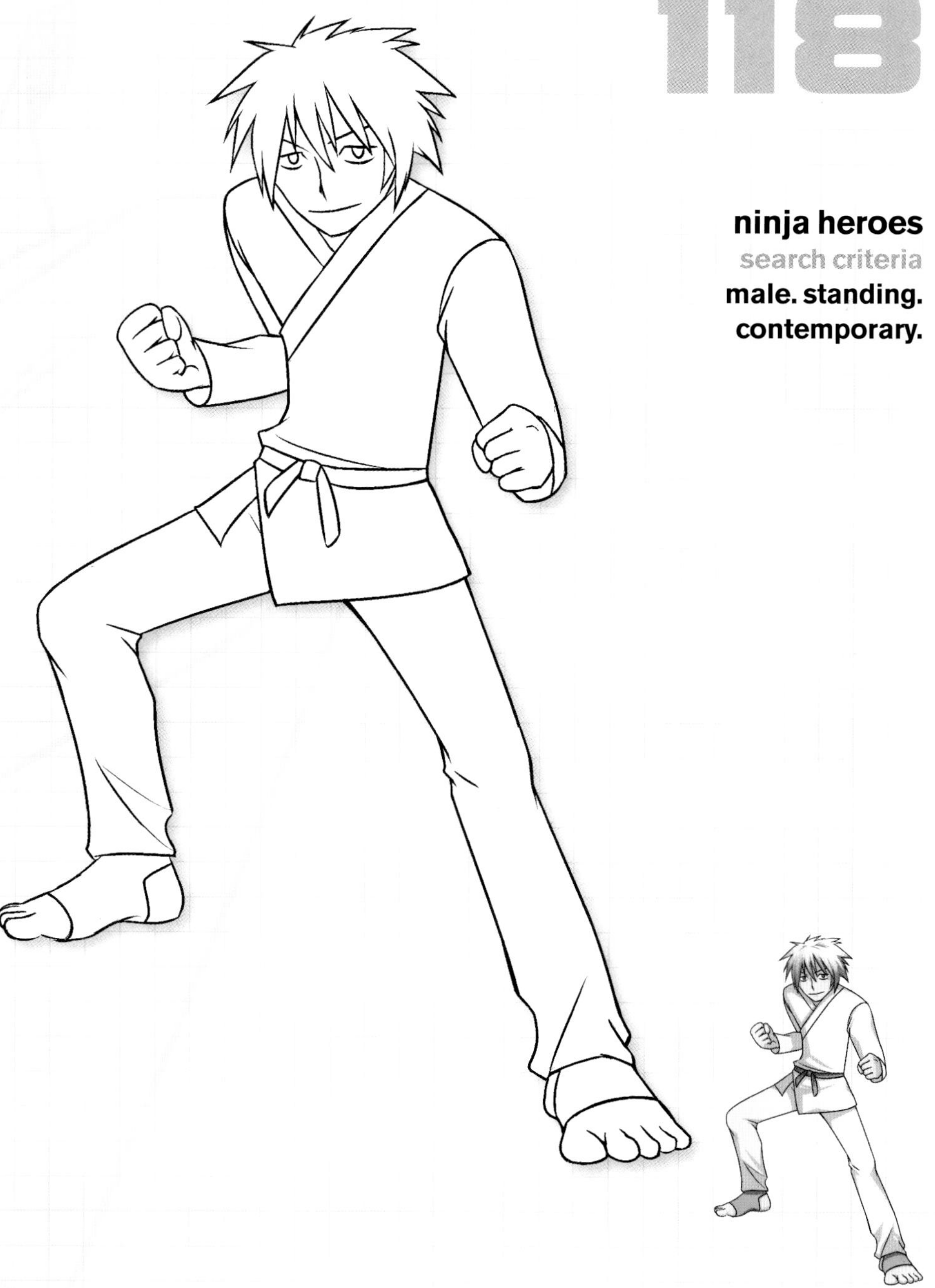

119

ninja heroes
search criteria
female. sitting. side. book. paper. contemporary.

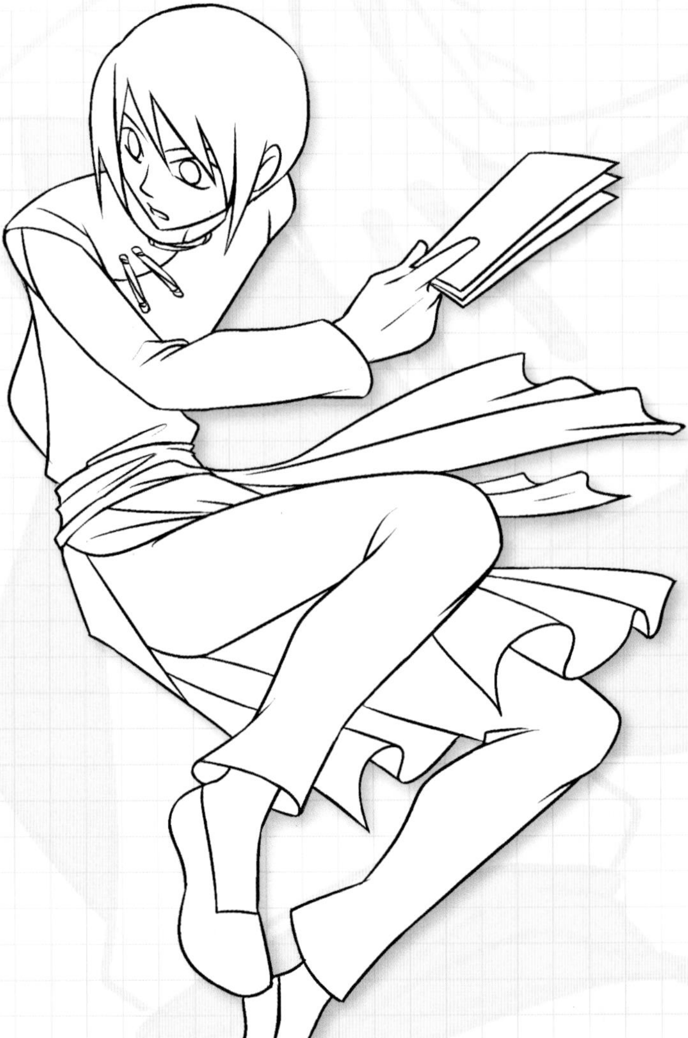

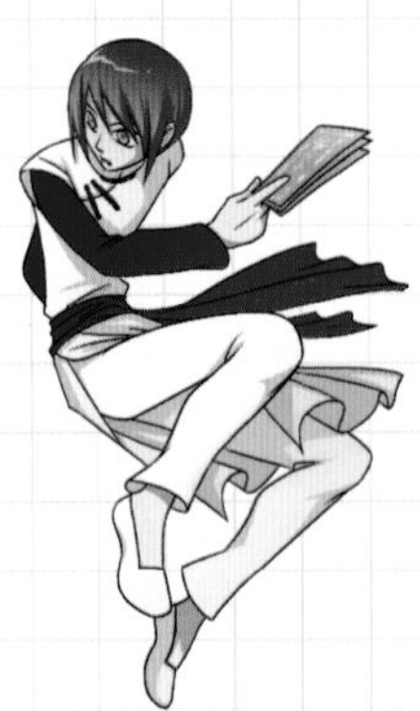

120

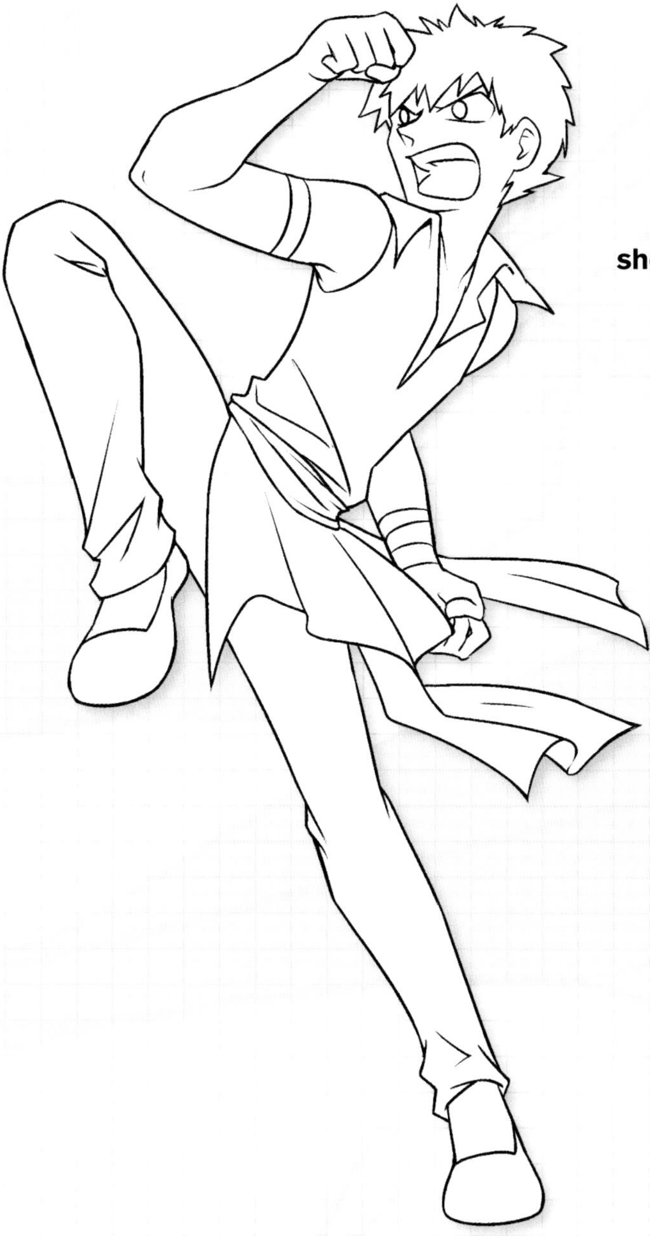

ninja heroes

search criteria

male. standing. attack. kick. side. shout. contemporary.

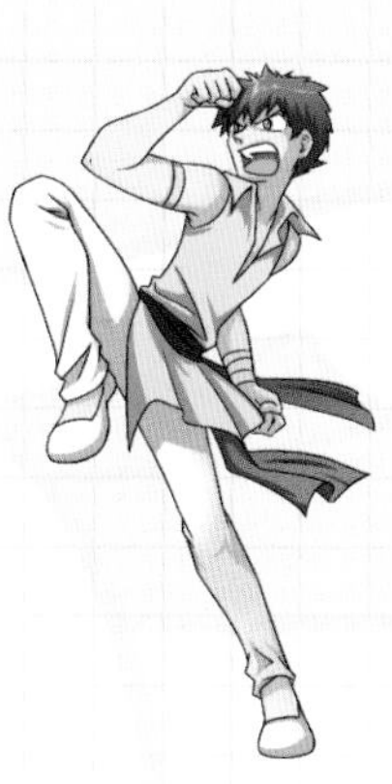

121

ninja heroes
search criteria
female. attack. jump. kick. side. shout. contemporary.

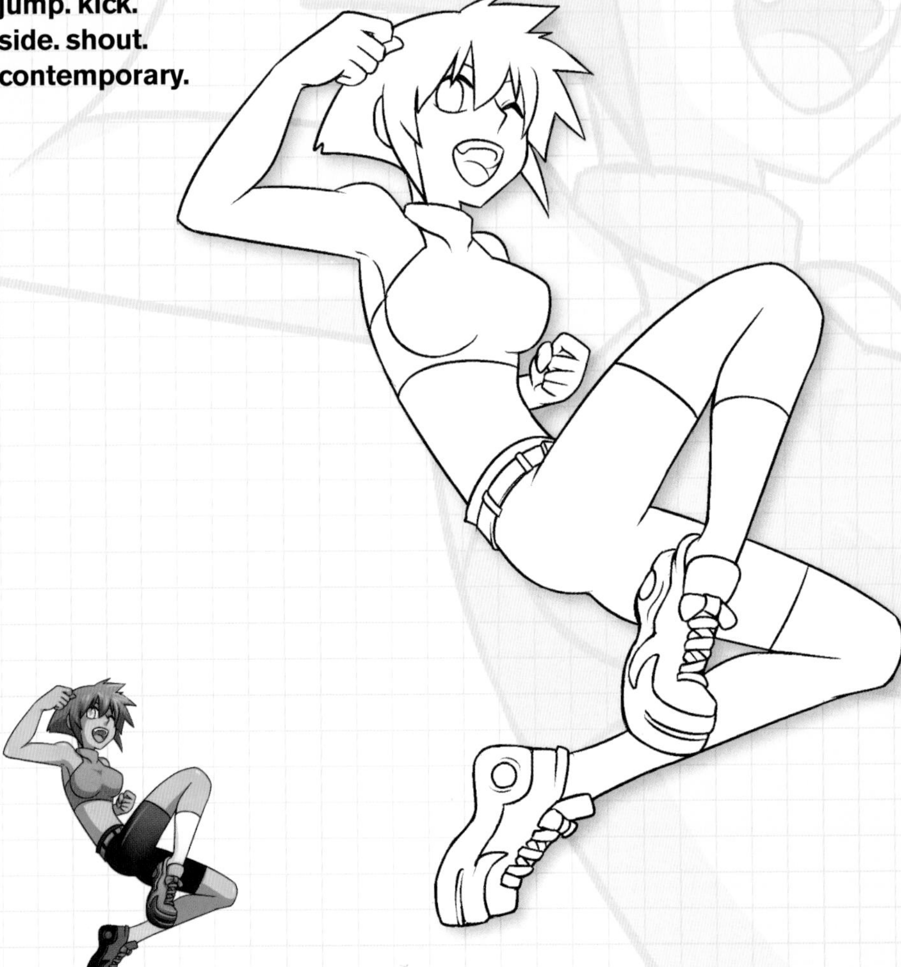

122

ninja heroes

search criteria

female. attack. kick. handstand. side. acrobat. contemporary.

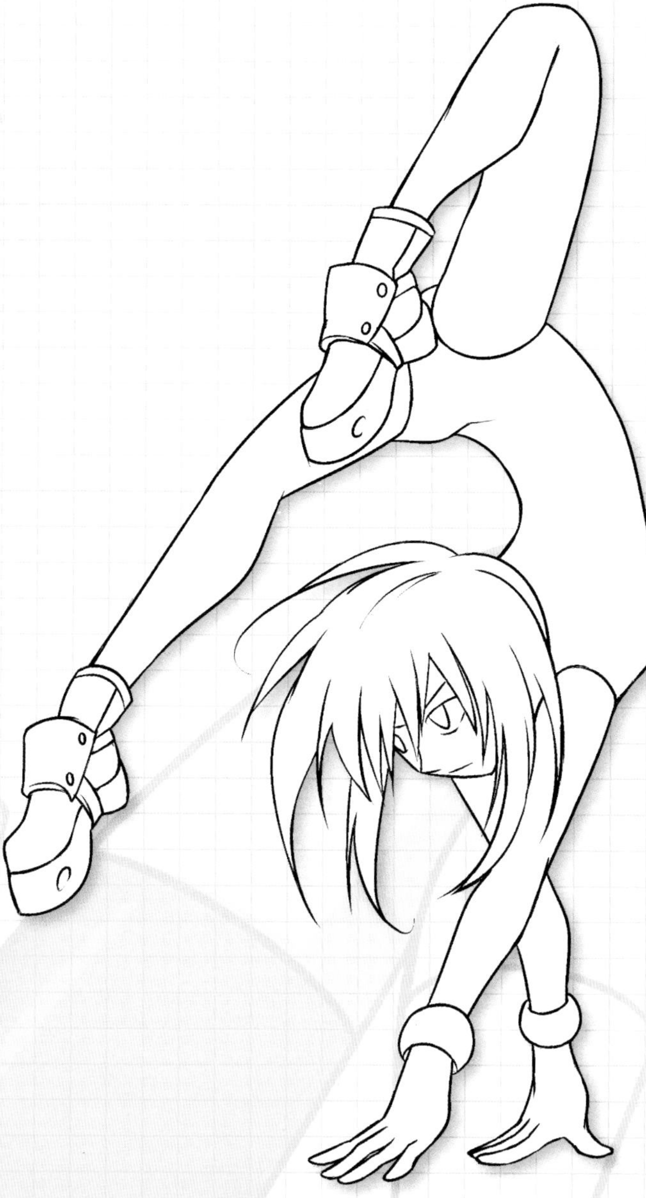

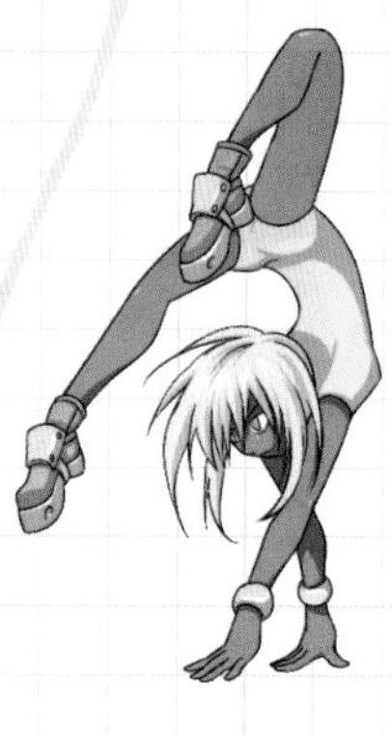

123

ninja heroes

search criteria

female. attack. side. kick. acrobat. contemporary. bunny.

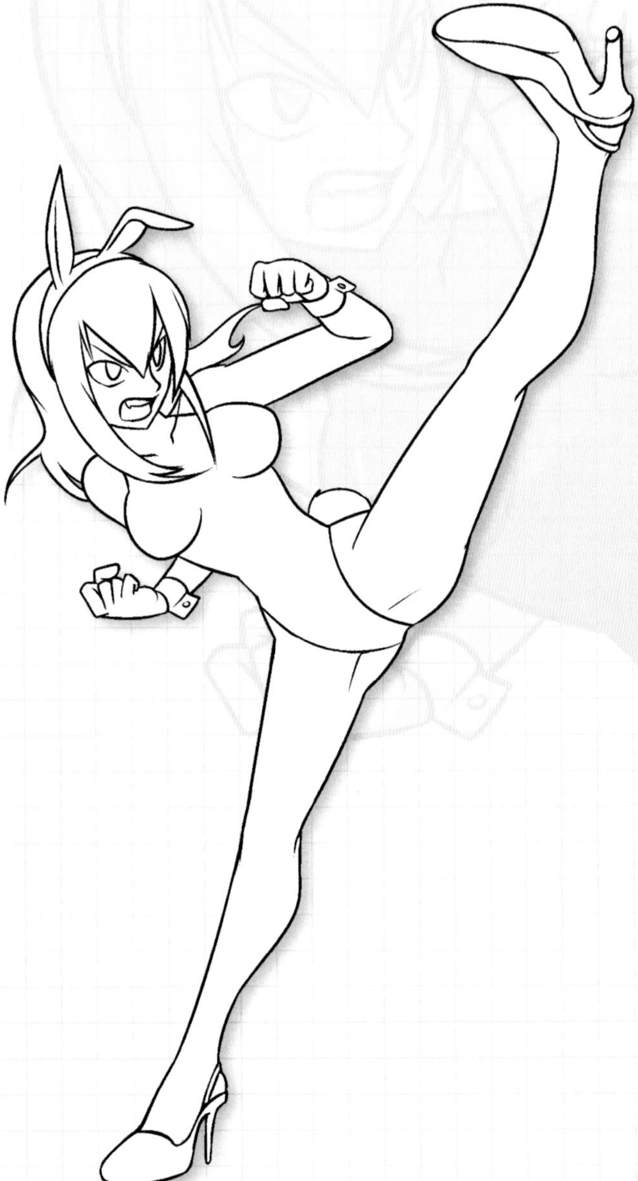

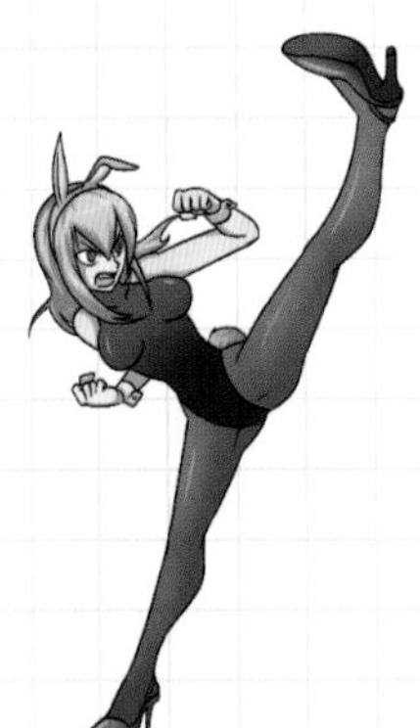

124

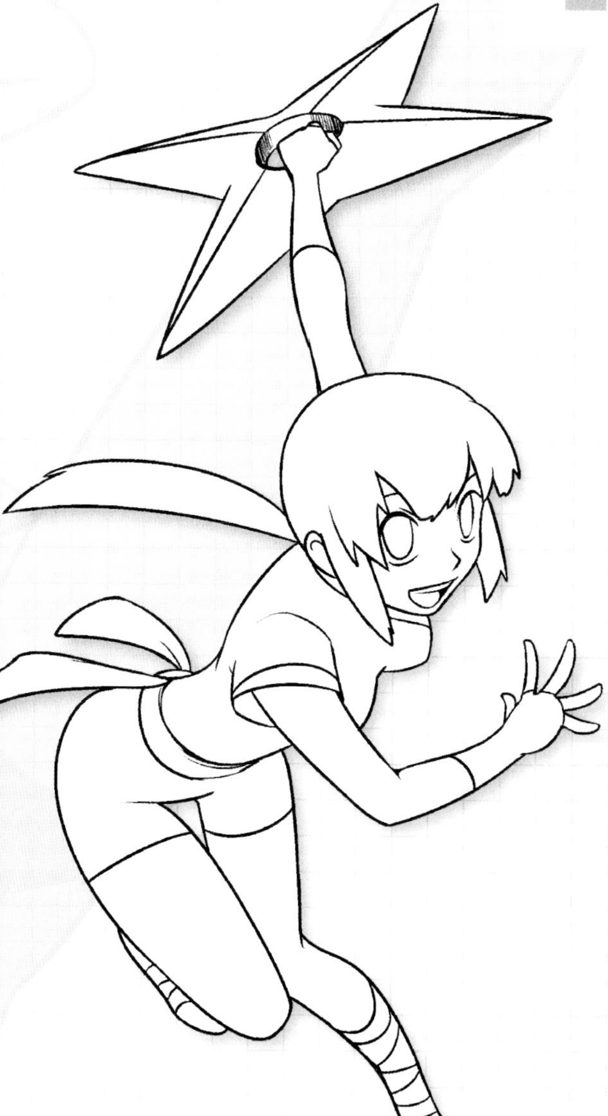

ninja heroes

search criteria

female. attack. pounce. smiling. bandages. weapon. star. contemporary.

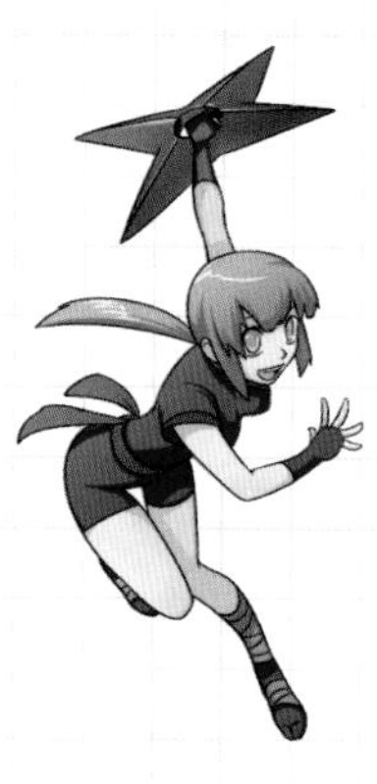

125

ninja heroes

search criteria

female. attack. jump. smiling. historical. pigtails. acrobat.

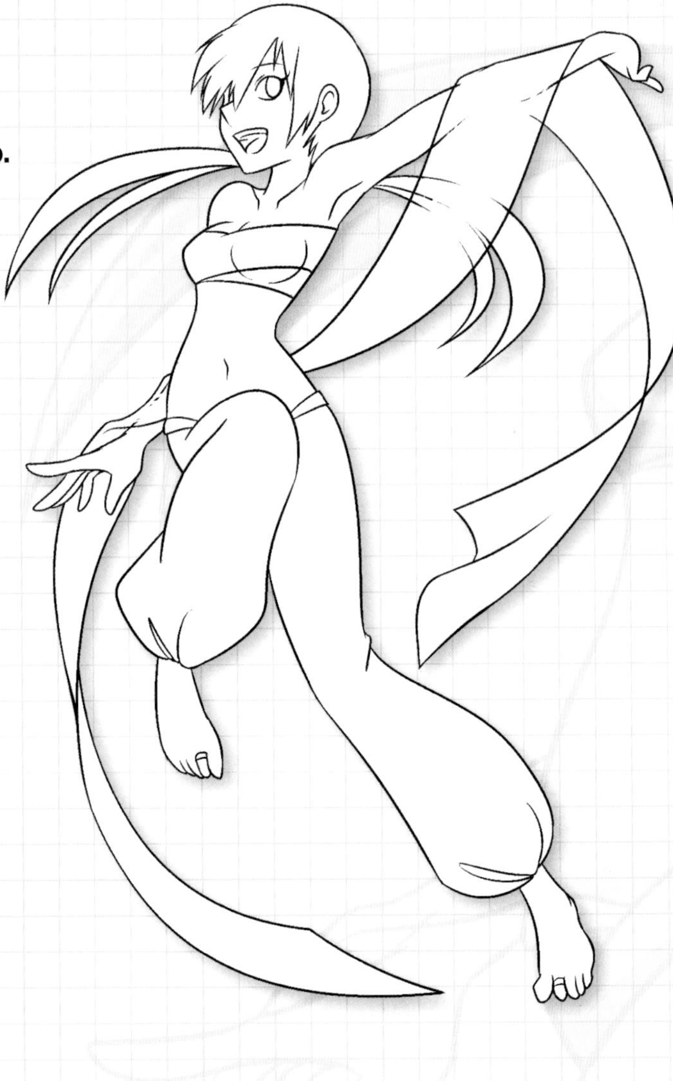

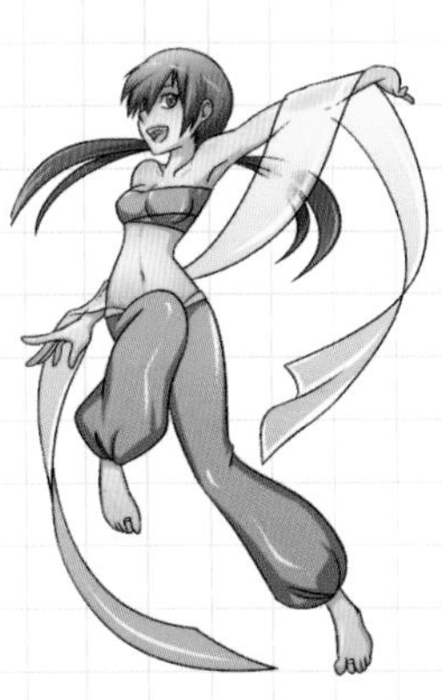

126

ninja heroes

search criteria

male. attack. kick. shout. contemporary.

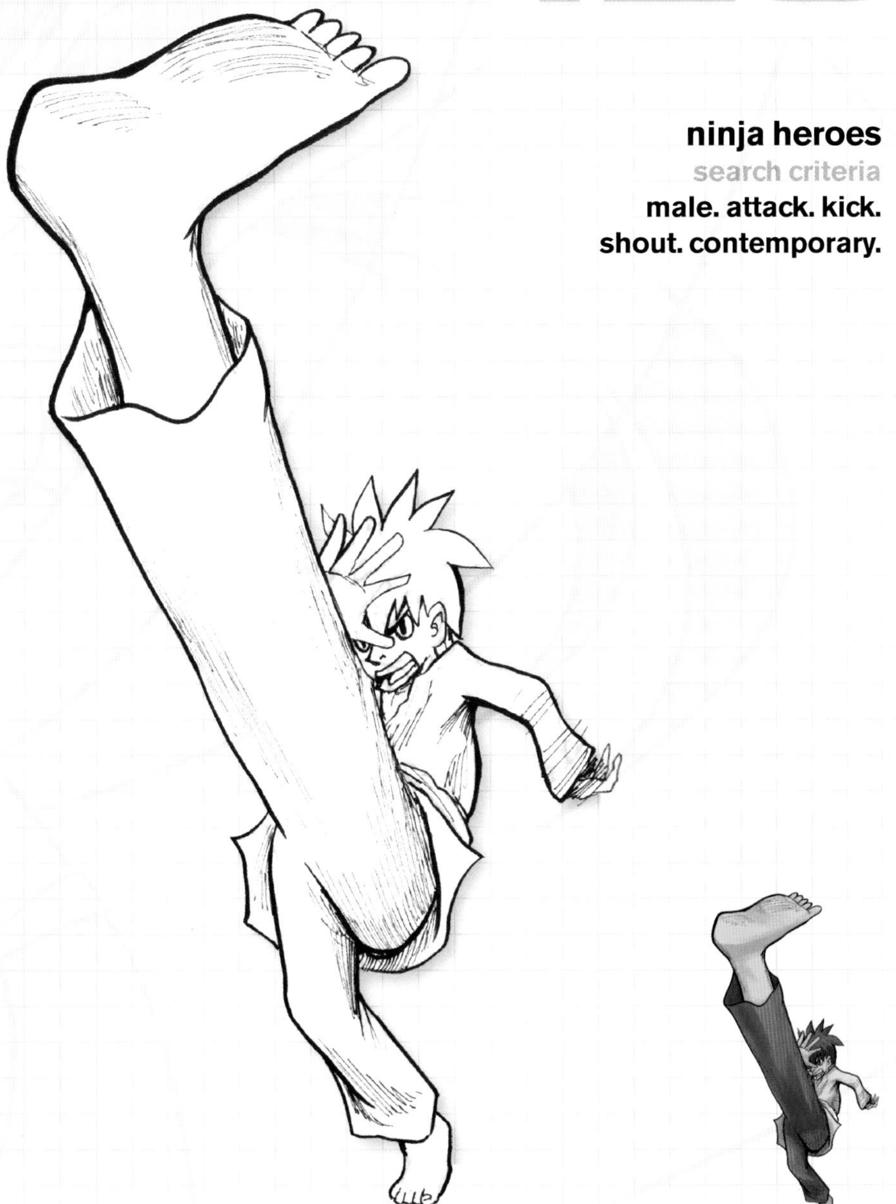

127

ninja heroes

search criteria

female. standing. side. biker. contemporary.

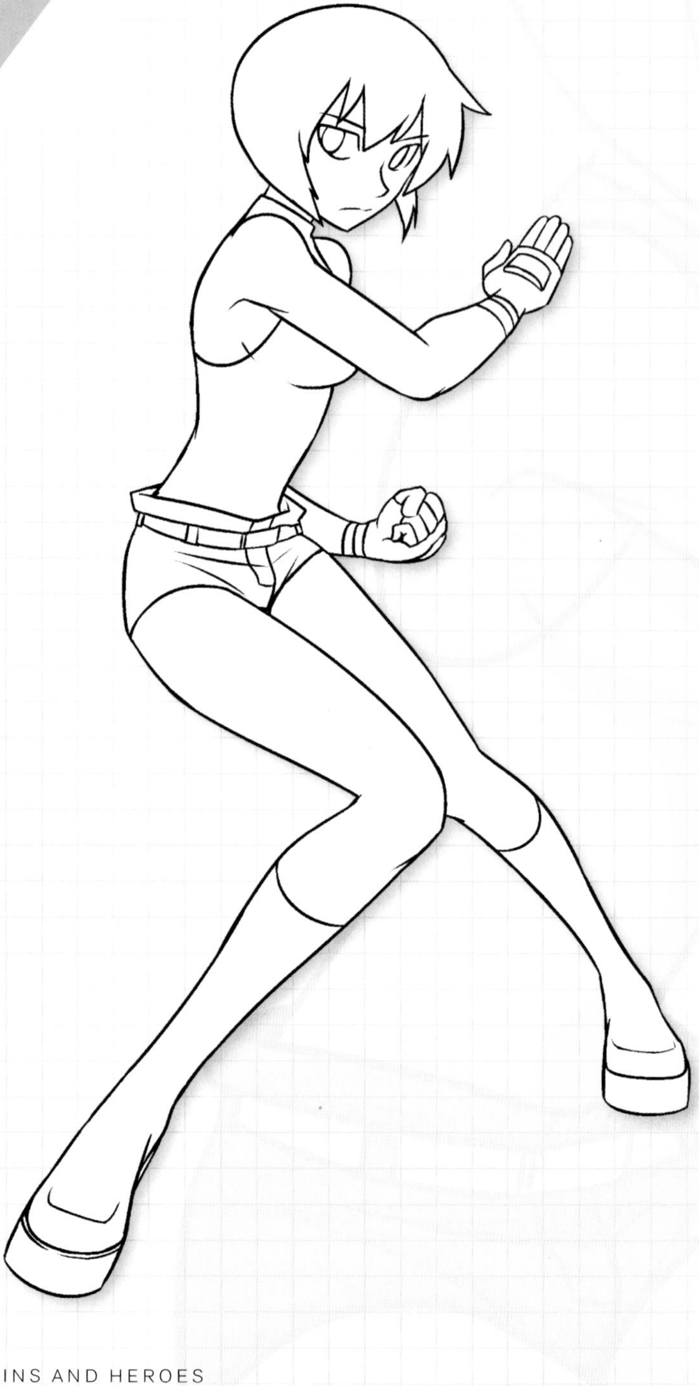

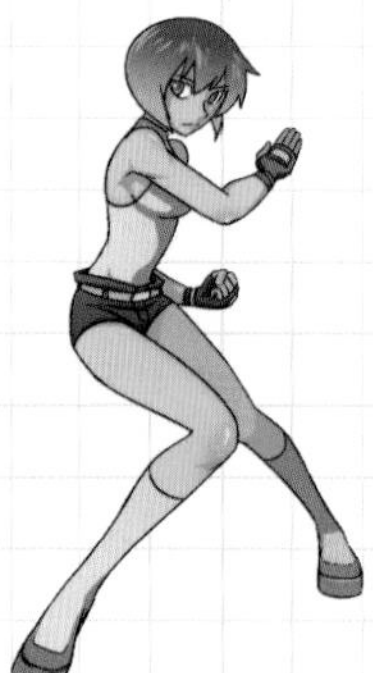

128

ninja heroes

search criteria

female. side. crouched. bow. weapons. stars. assassin. spy.

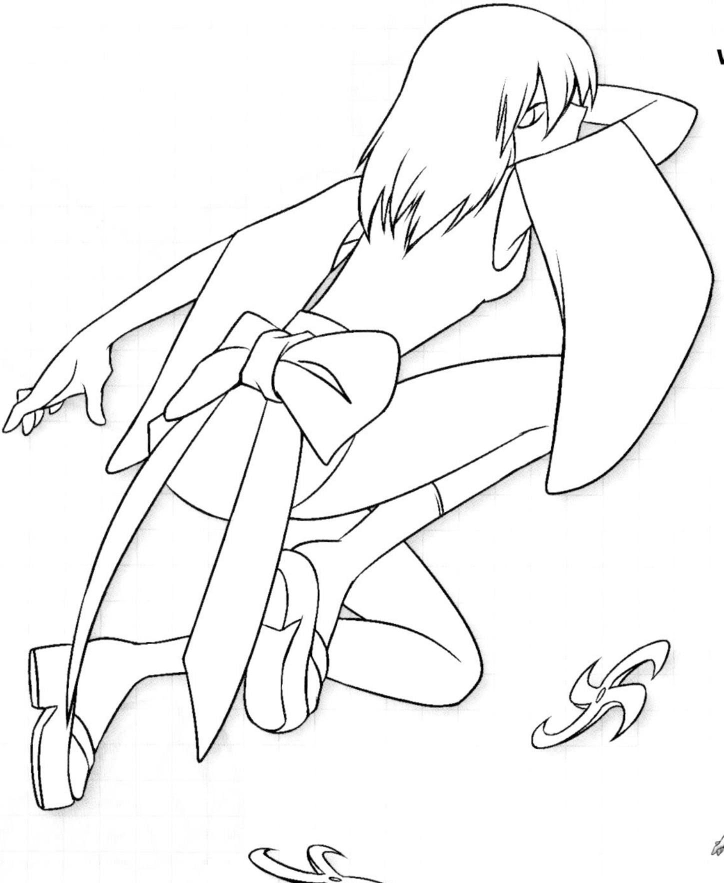

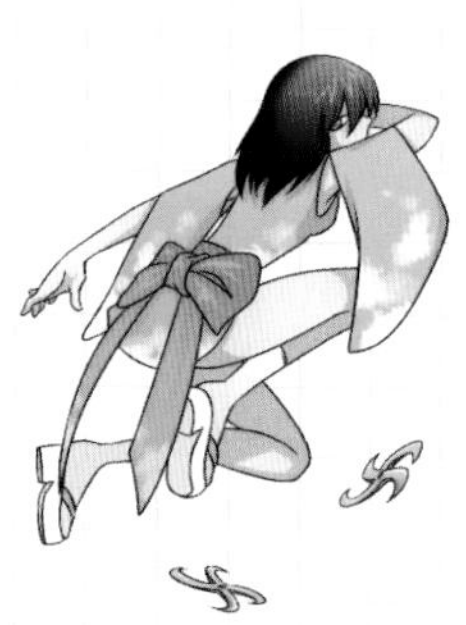

129

ninja heroes

search criteria

female. jump. attack. kick. pounce. shout. pigtails. contemporary.

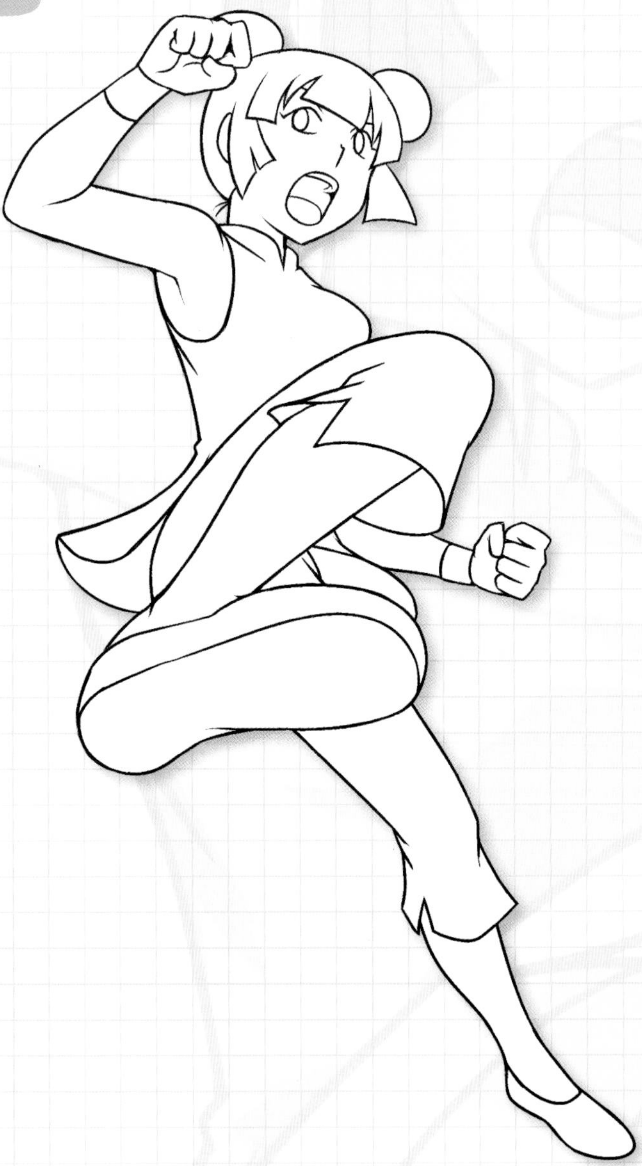

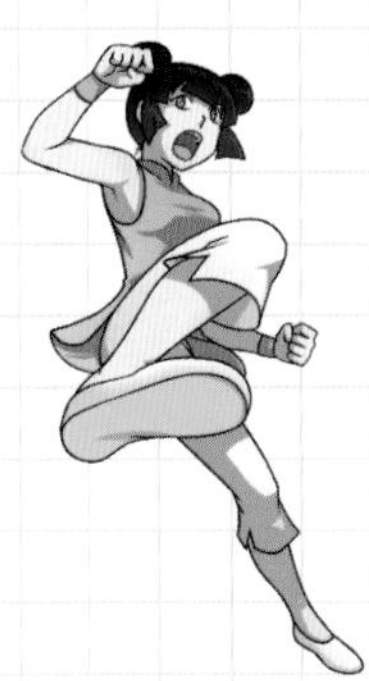

130

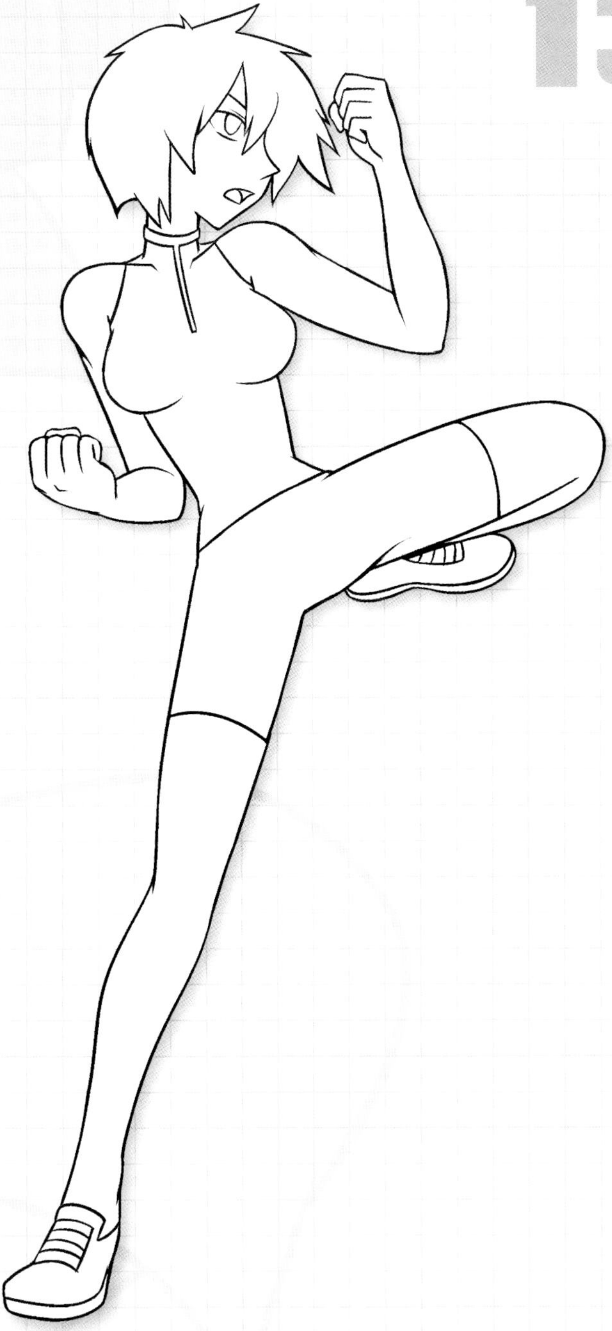

ninja heroes
search criteria
female. side. box. kick. contemporary.

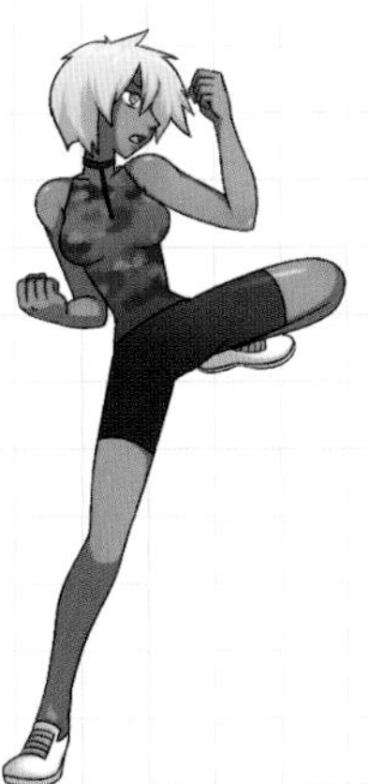

131

ninja heroes

search criteria

male. claw. weapon. sword. historical. samurai. bandages.

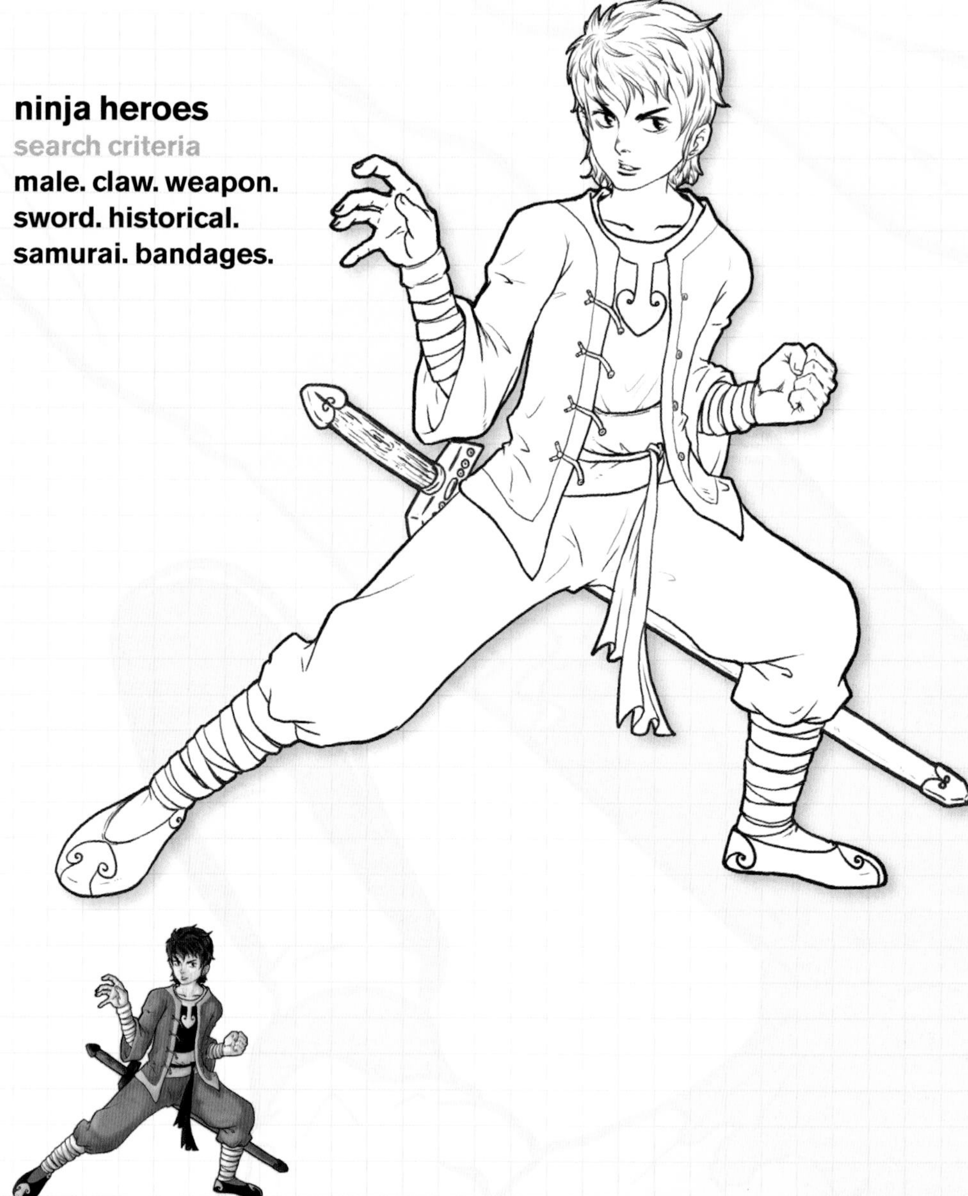

132

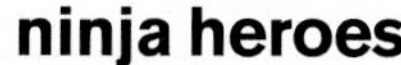

ninja heroes

search criteria

male. side. jump. kick. box. weapon. nunchucks. contemporary.

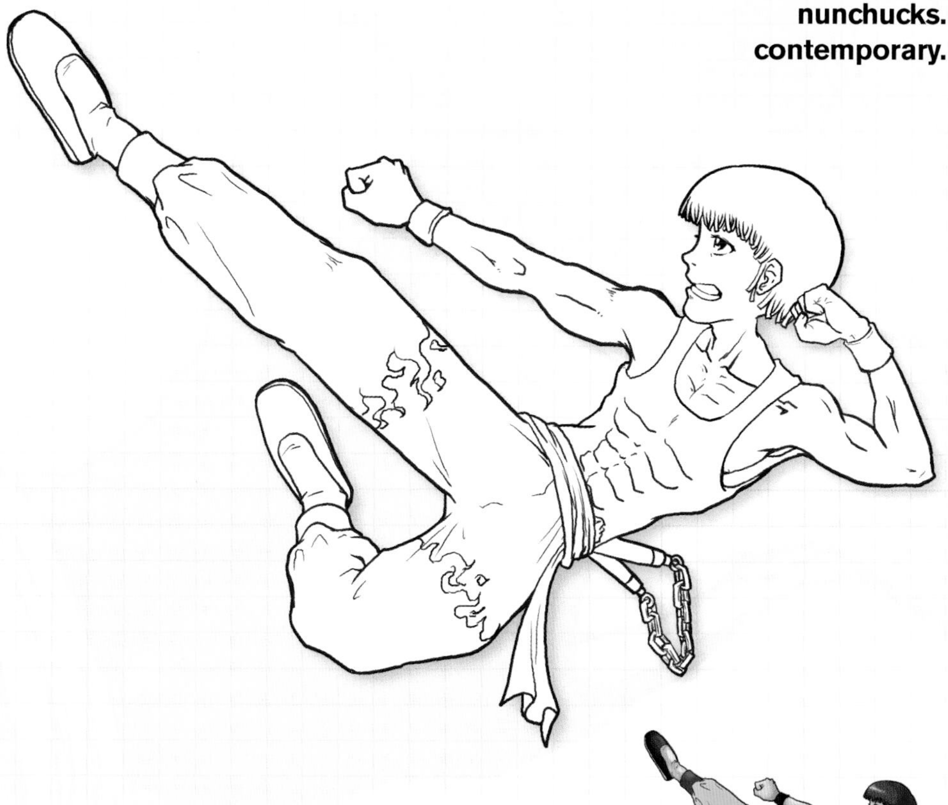

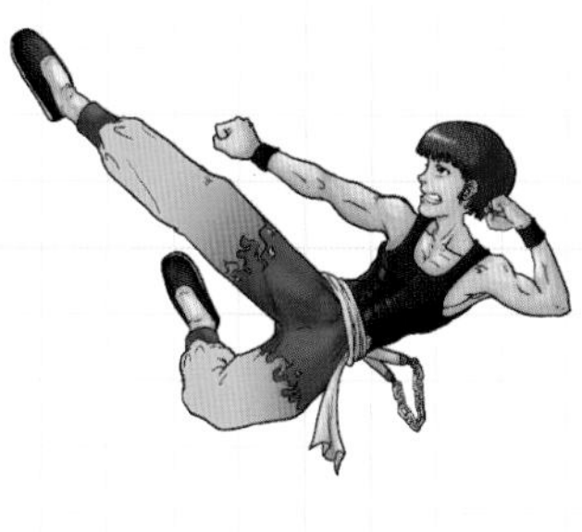

133

ninja heroes

search criteria

male. standing. weapons. swords. historical. samurai. armor. bandages.

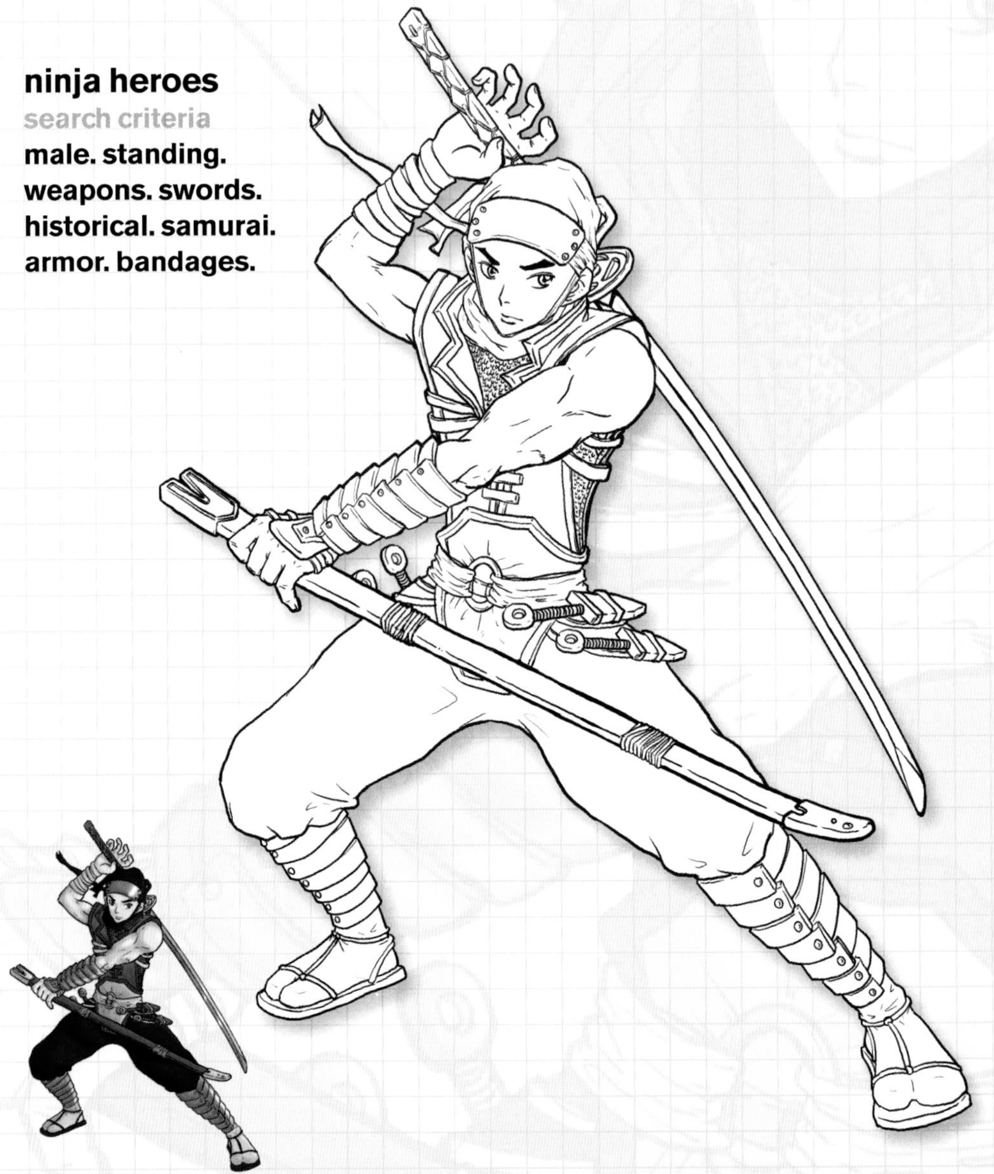

134

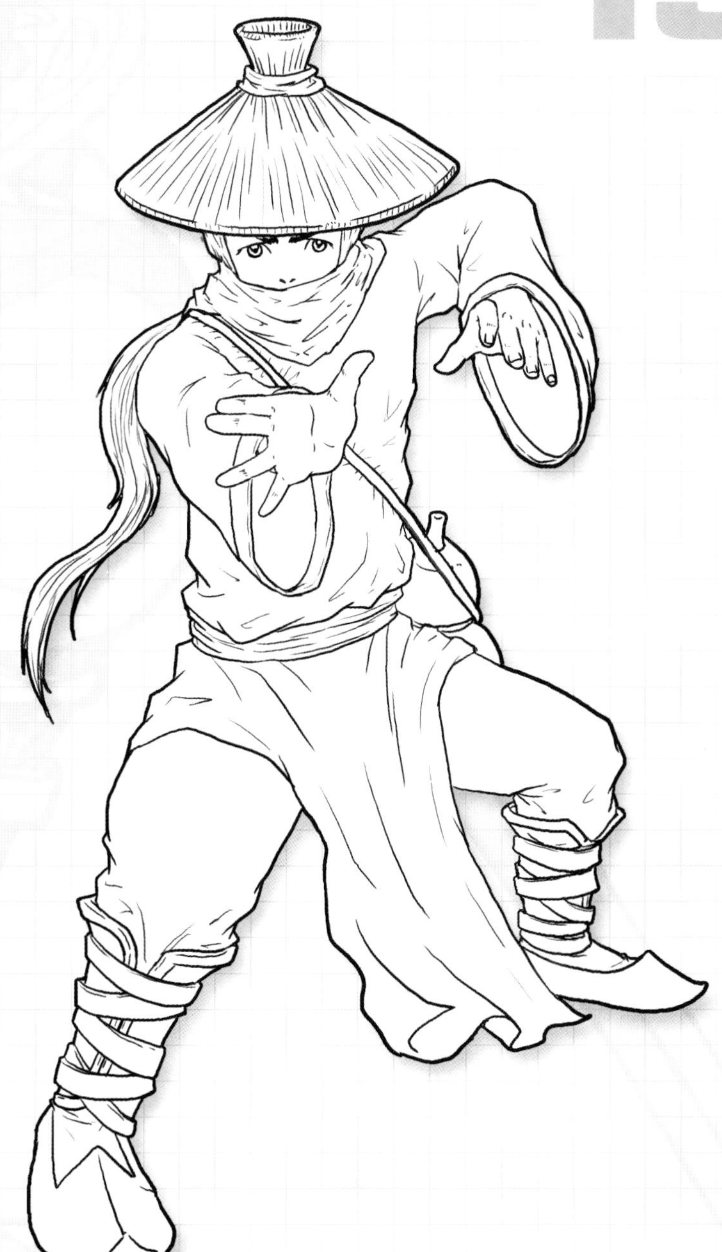

ninja heroes

search criteria

male. standing. scarf. bottle. hat. historical.

135

ninja heroes

search criteria

male. crouched. weapons. swords. mask. historical. samurai.

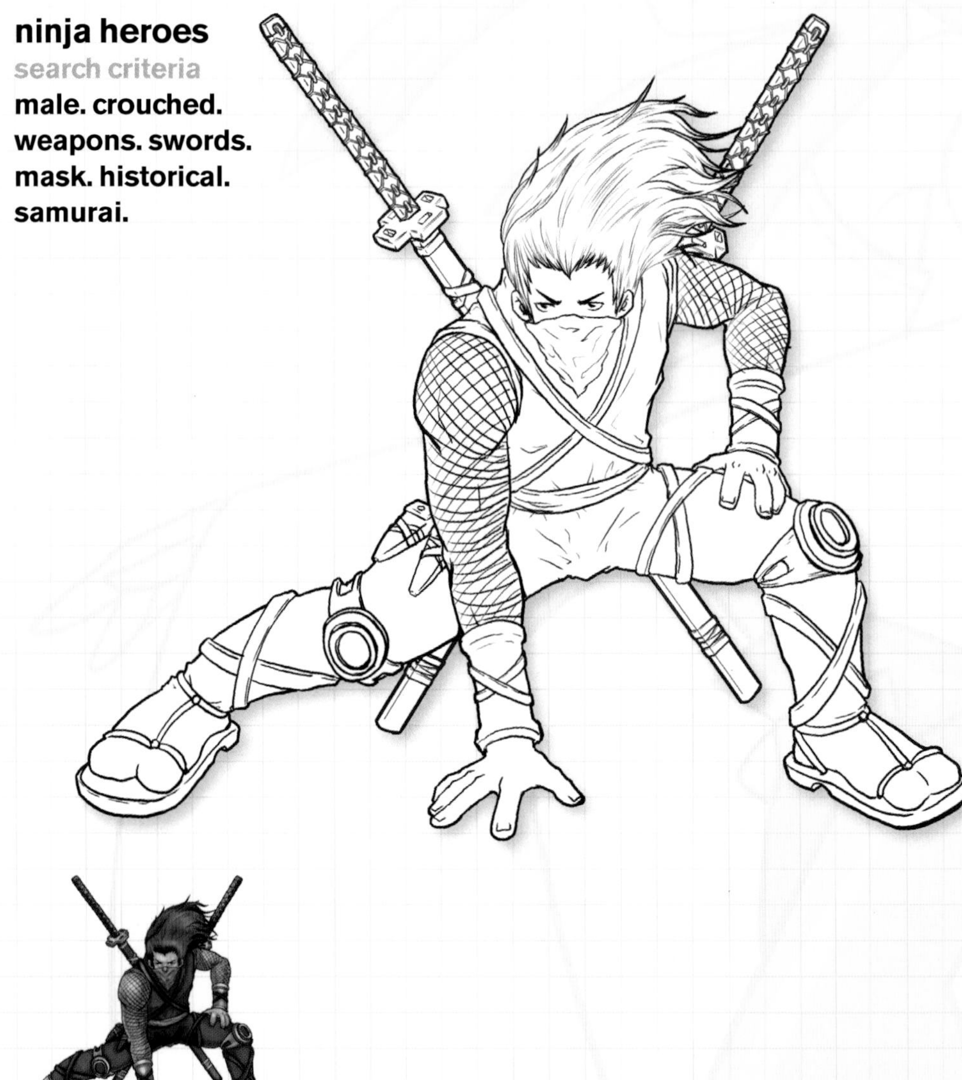

136

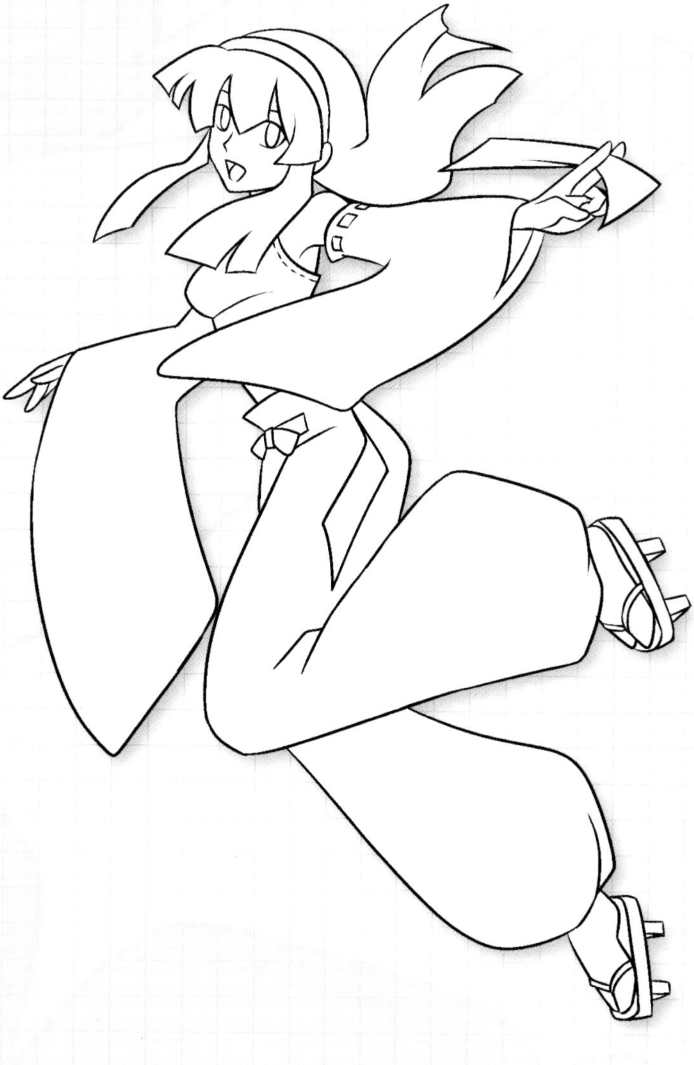

ninja heroes
search criteria
**female. side.
jump. smiling.
historical.**

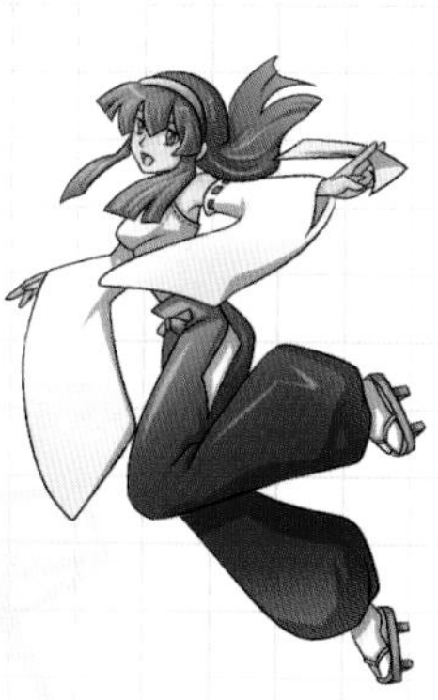

137

mythical and fantasy villains

search criteria

female. standing. side. witch. magic. cat. staff. smiling.

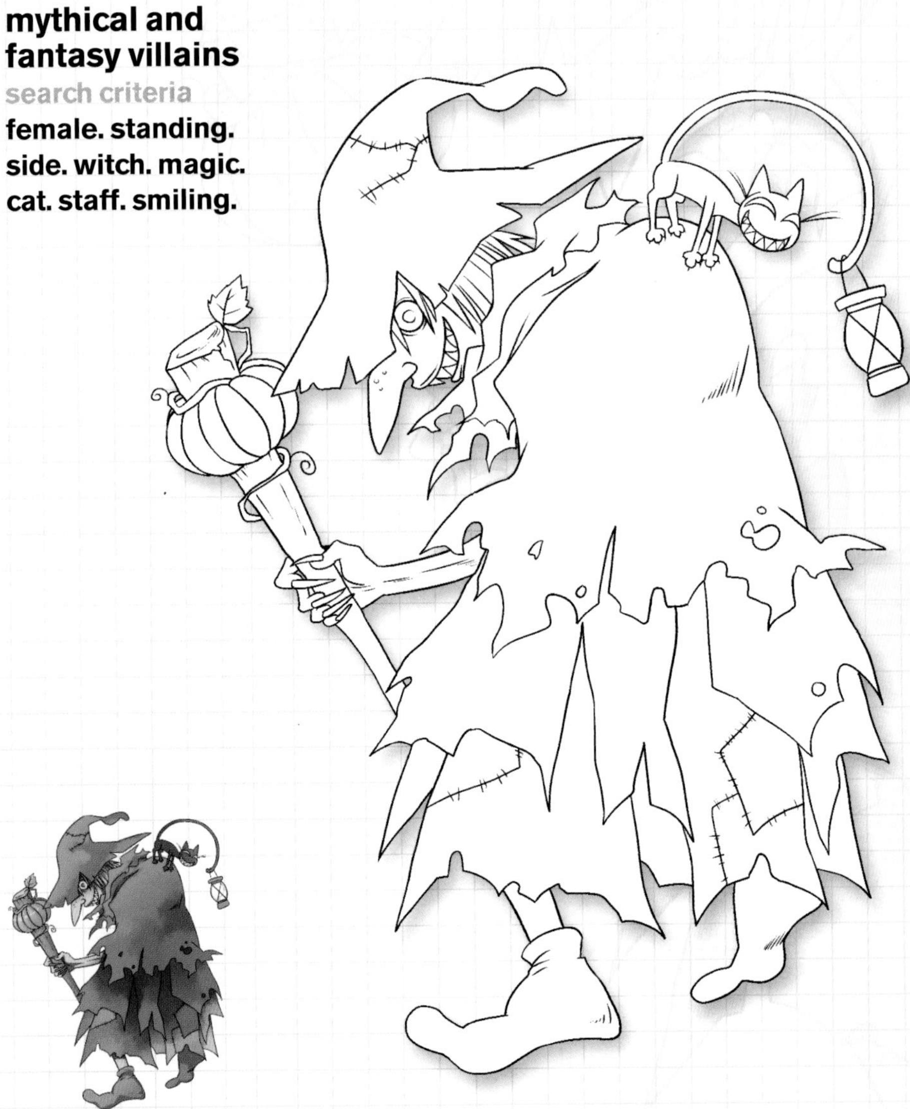

mythical and fantasy villains

search criteria

male. standing. magic. staff. sorcerer. boy.

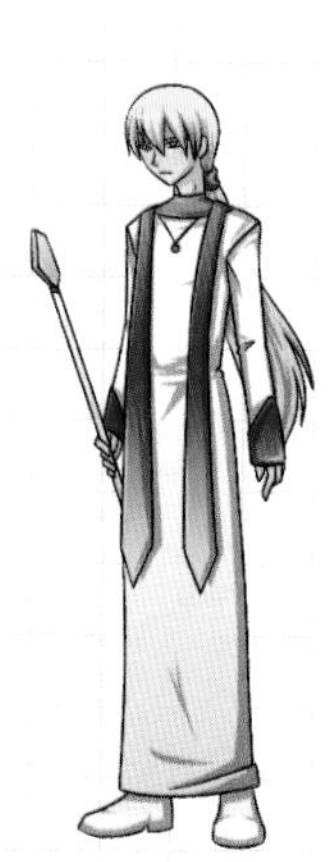

139

mythical and fantasy villains

search criteria

male. standing. wizard. magic. staff. hat.

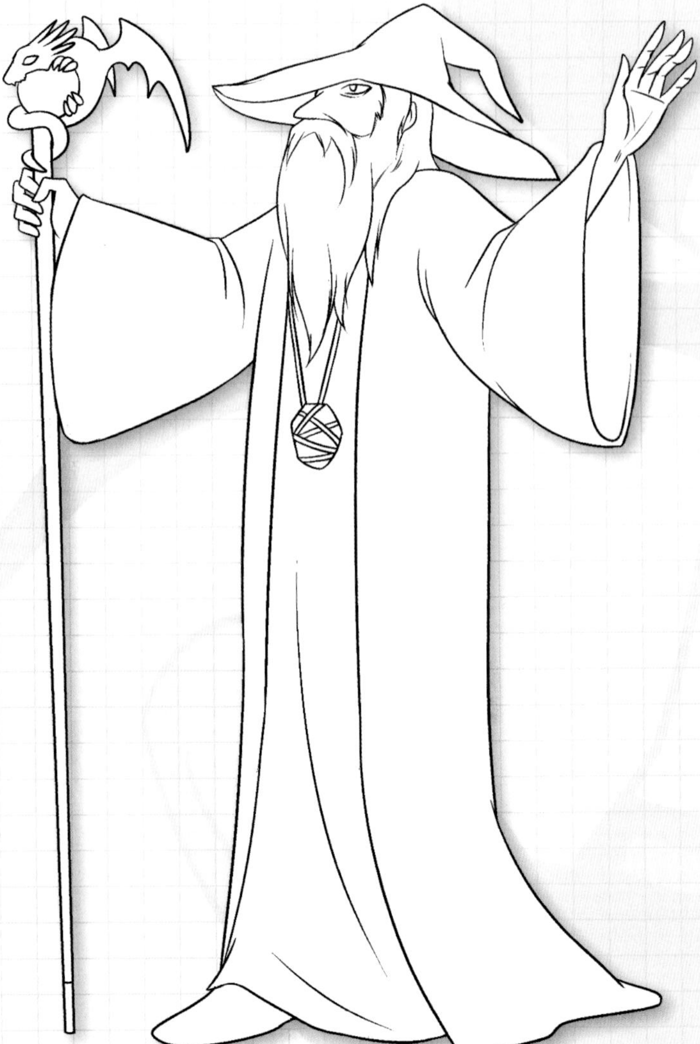

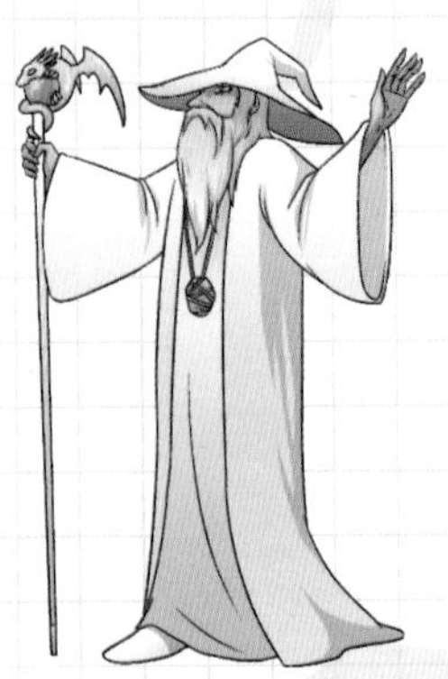

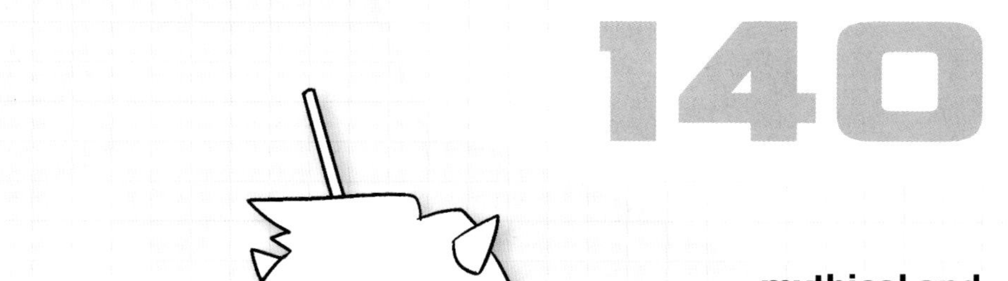

140

mythical and fantasy villains

search criteria

male. sitting. devil. boy. wings. tail. horns. fork.

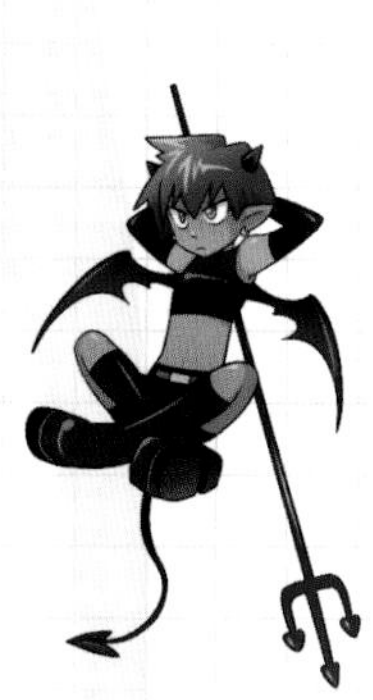

141

mythical and fantasy villains

search criteria

male. jump. flying. devil. horns. wings. tail. piercings. gothic.

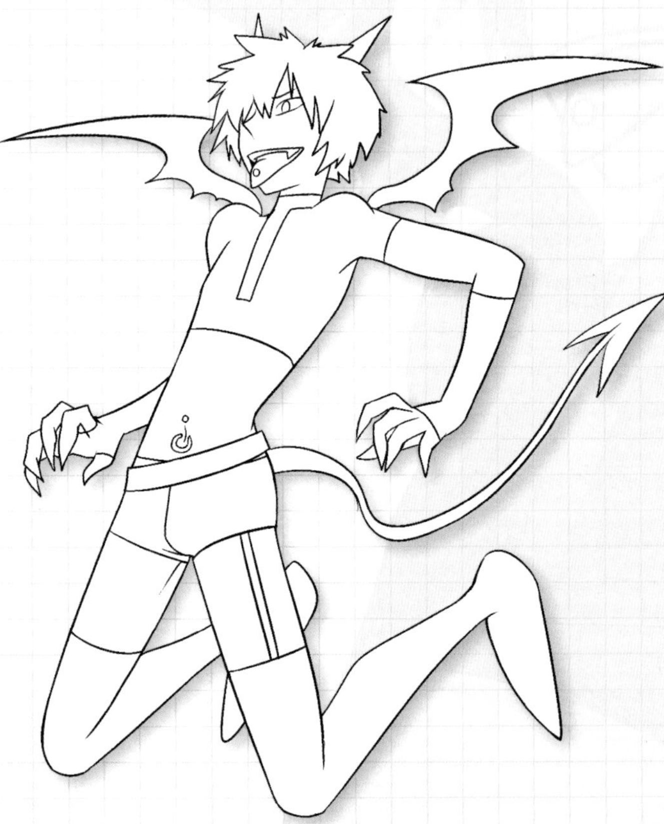

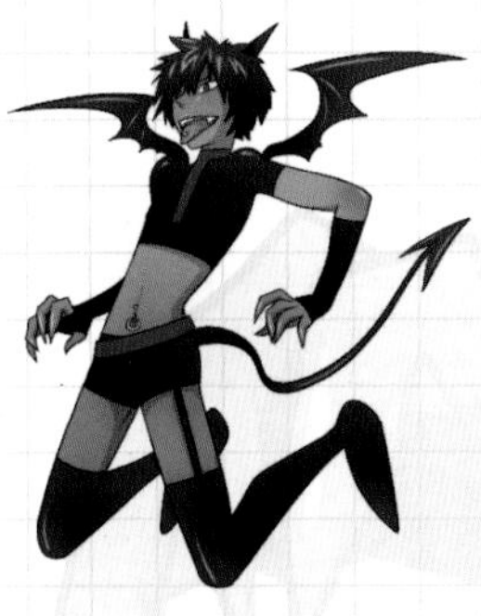

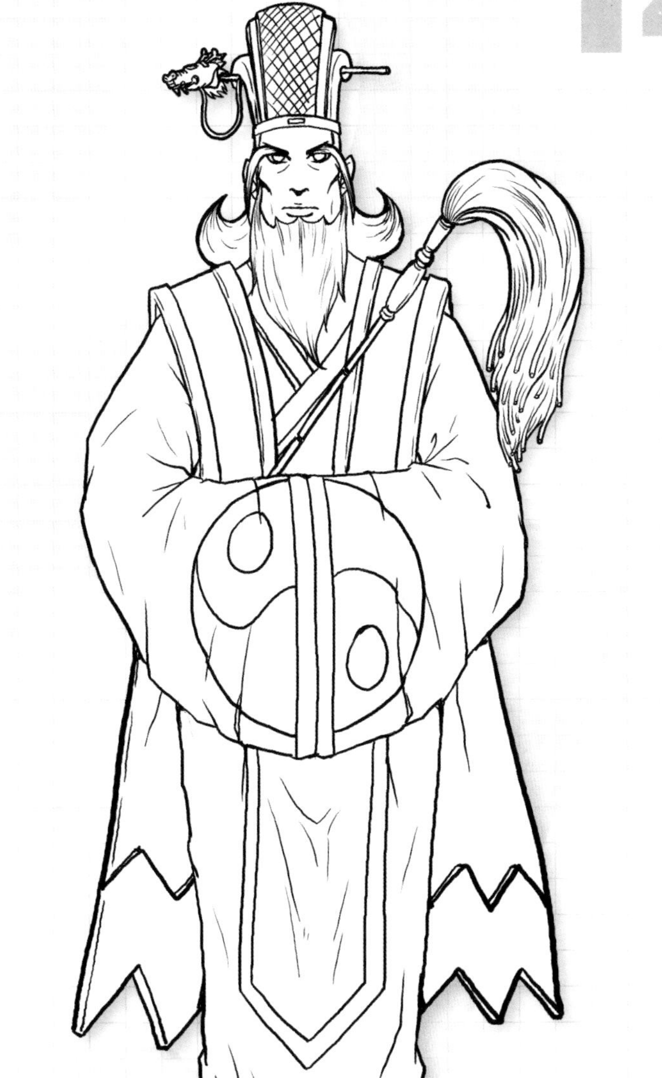

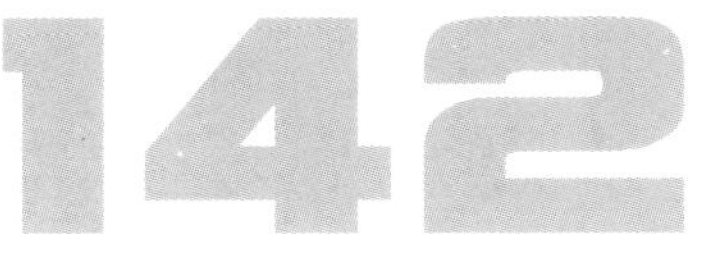

mythical and fantasy villains

search criteria

male. standing. magic. historical. emperor. staff.

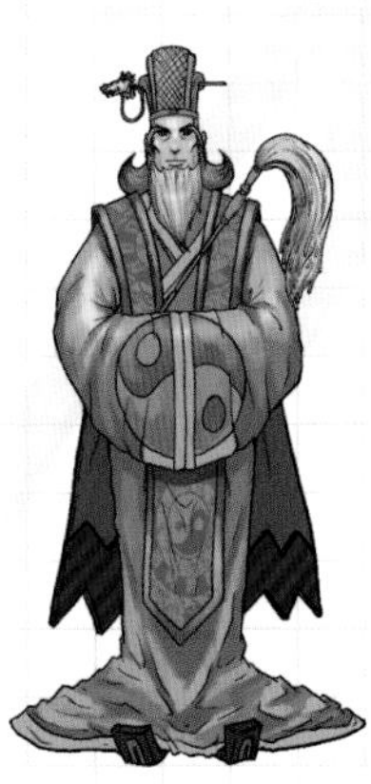

143

mythical and fantasy villains

search criteria

female. sitting. fairy. wings. antennae. bandages. magic.

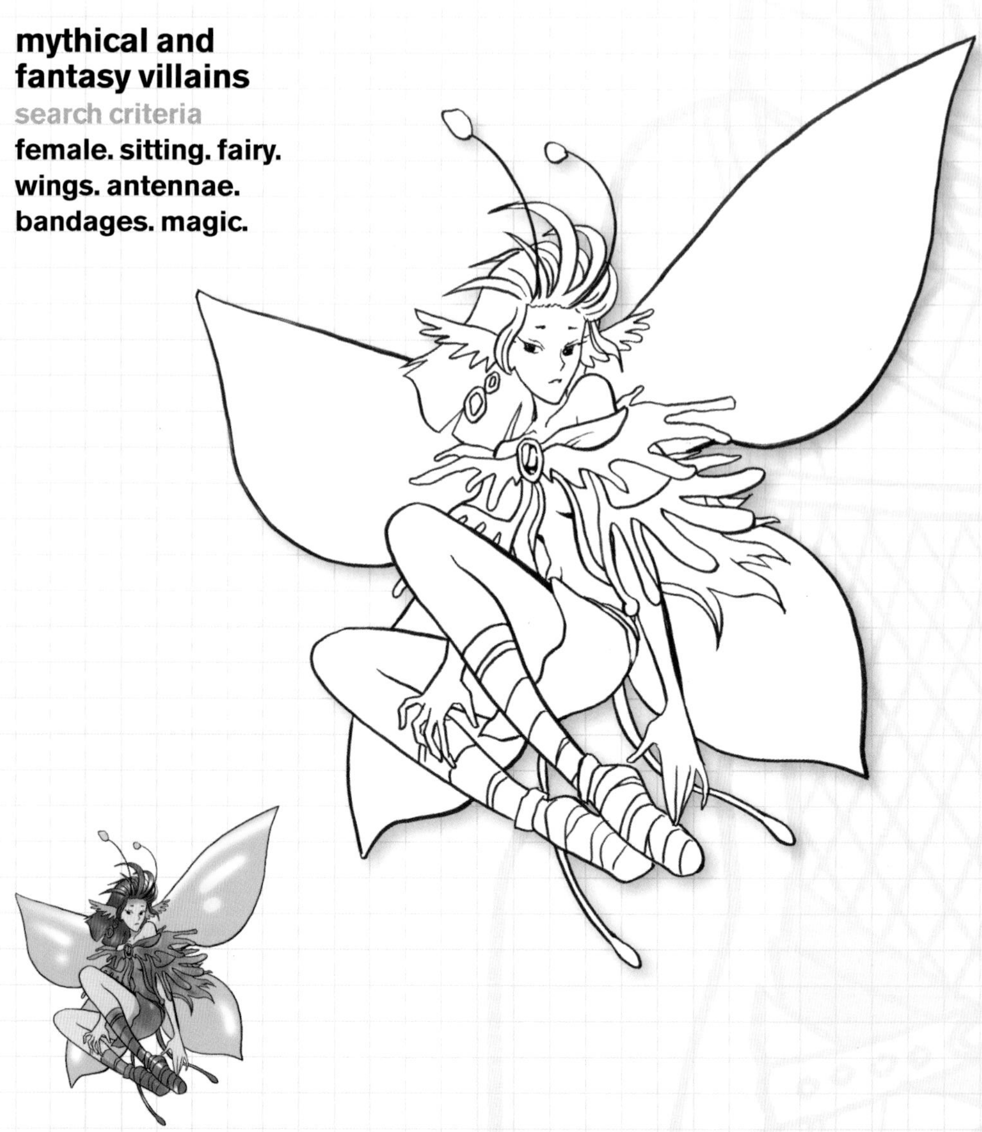

144

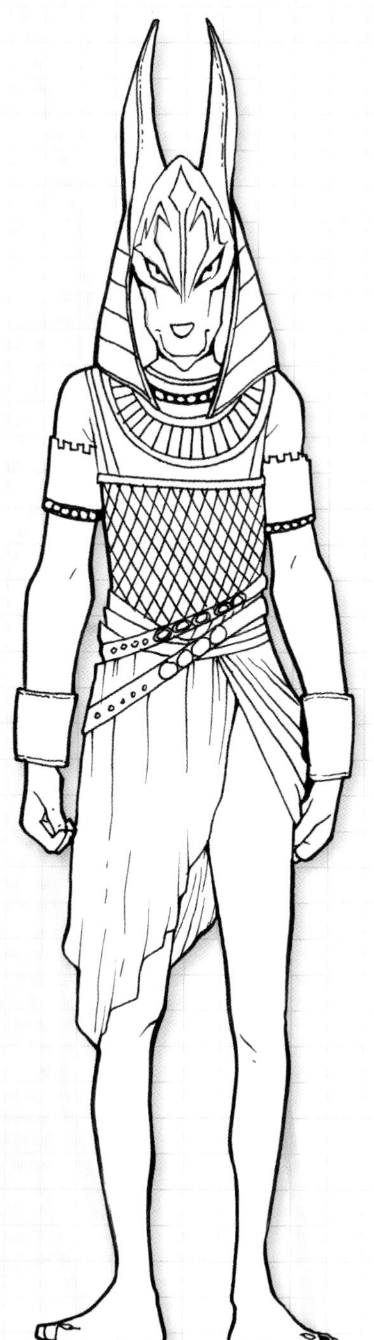

mythical and fantasy villains

search criteria

male. standing. sphinx. egyptian. armor. warrior.

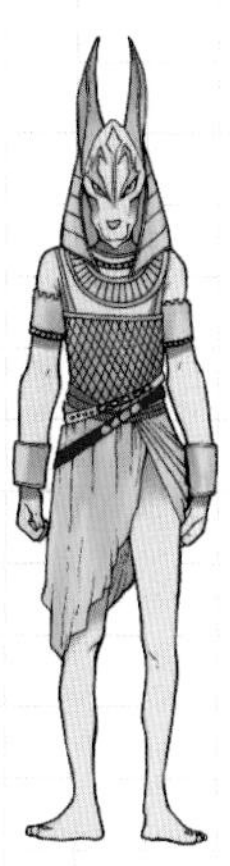

145

mythical and fantasy villains

search criteria

female. standing. serpent. medusa. snakes. tail.

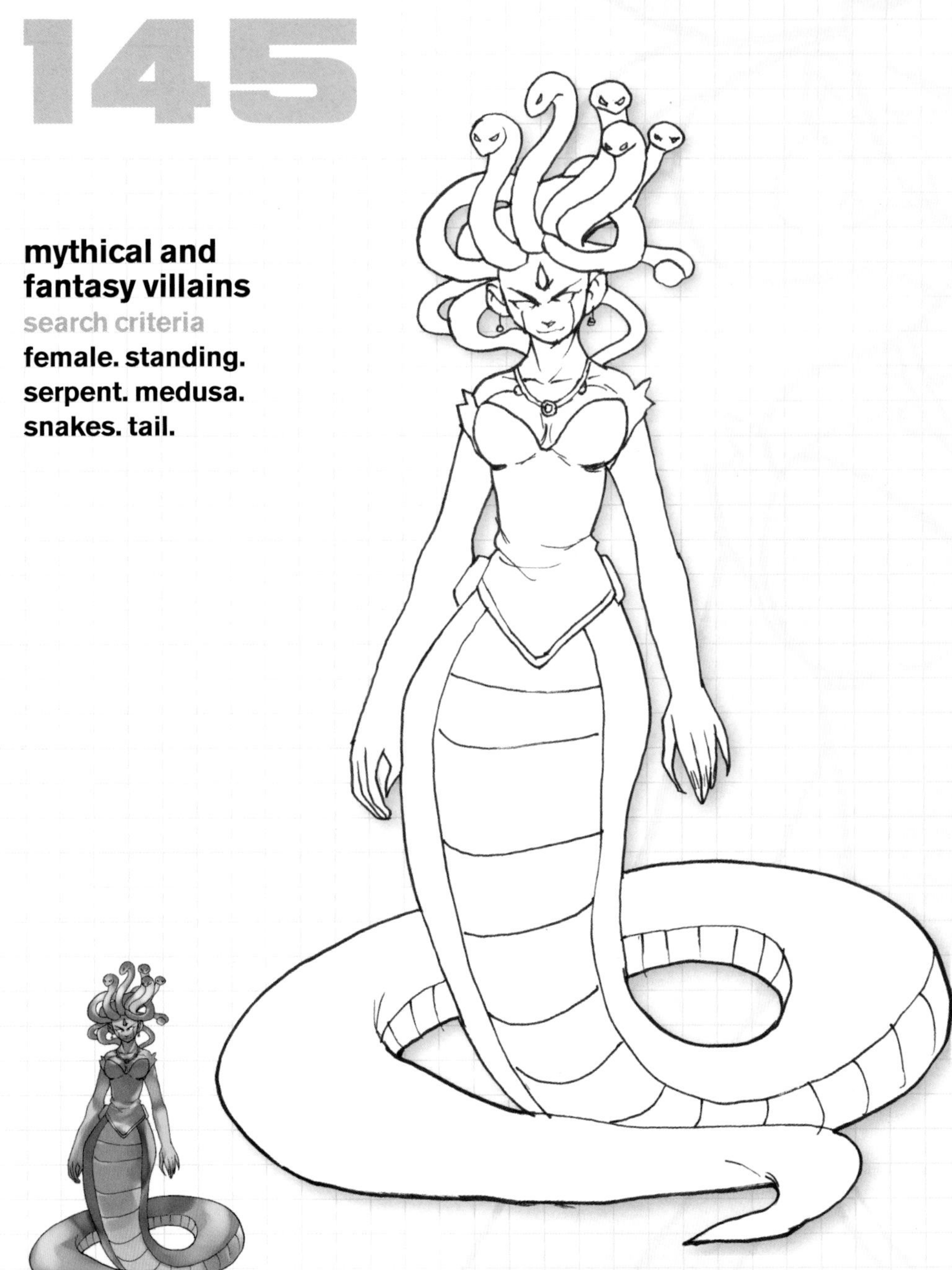

146

mythical and fantasy villains

search criteria

male. standing. floating. god. greek. thor. lightning.

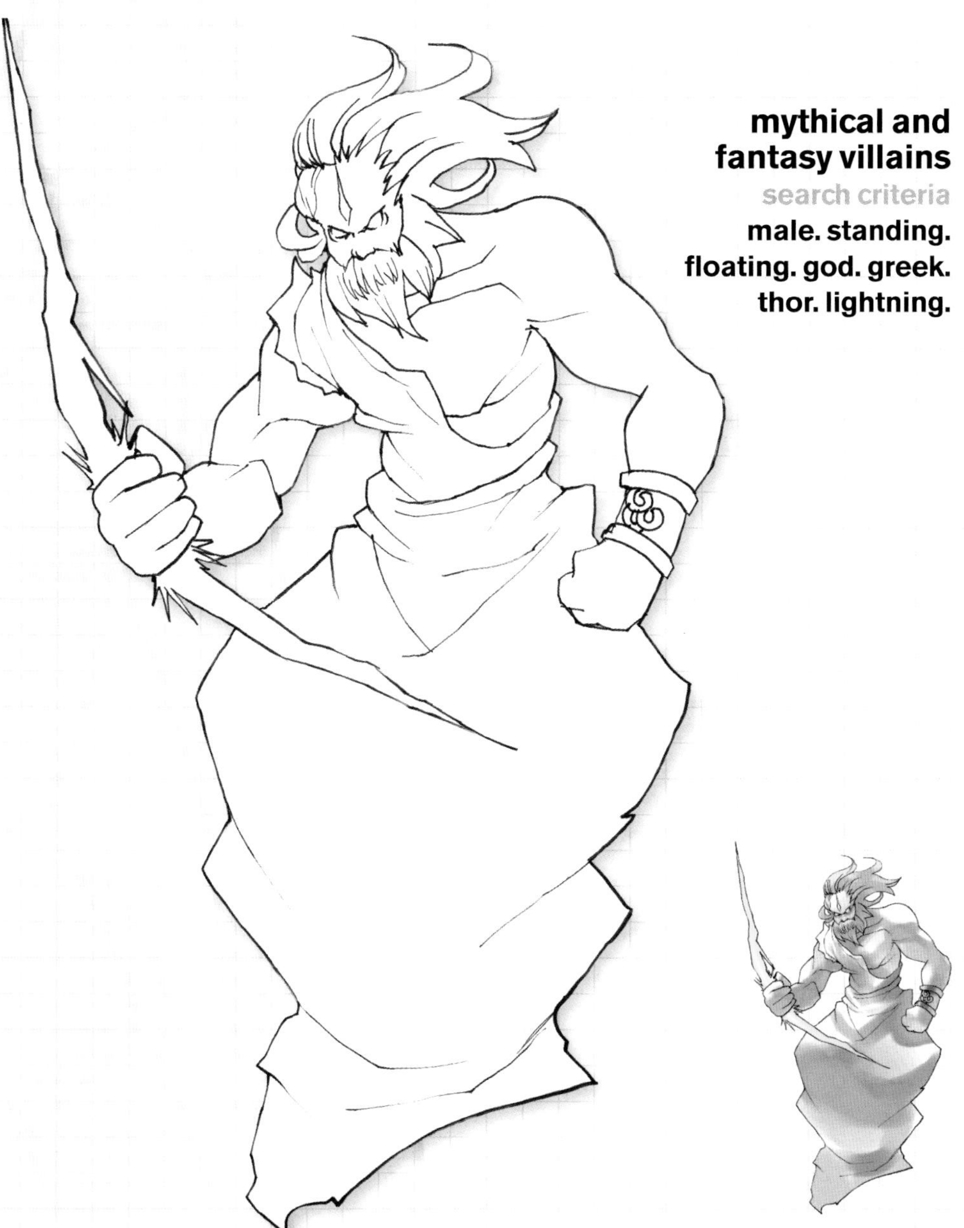

147

mythical and fantasy villains

search criteria

male. standing. side. archer. weapon. arrows. bow. bandages.

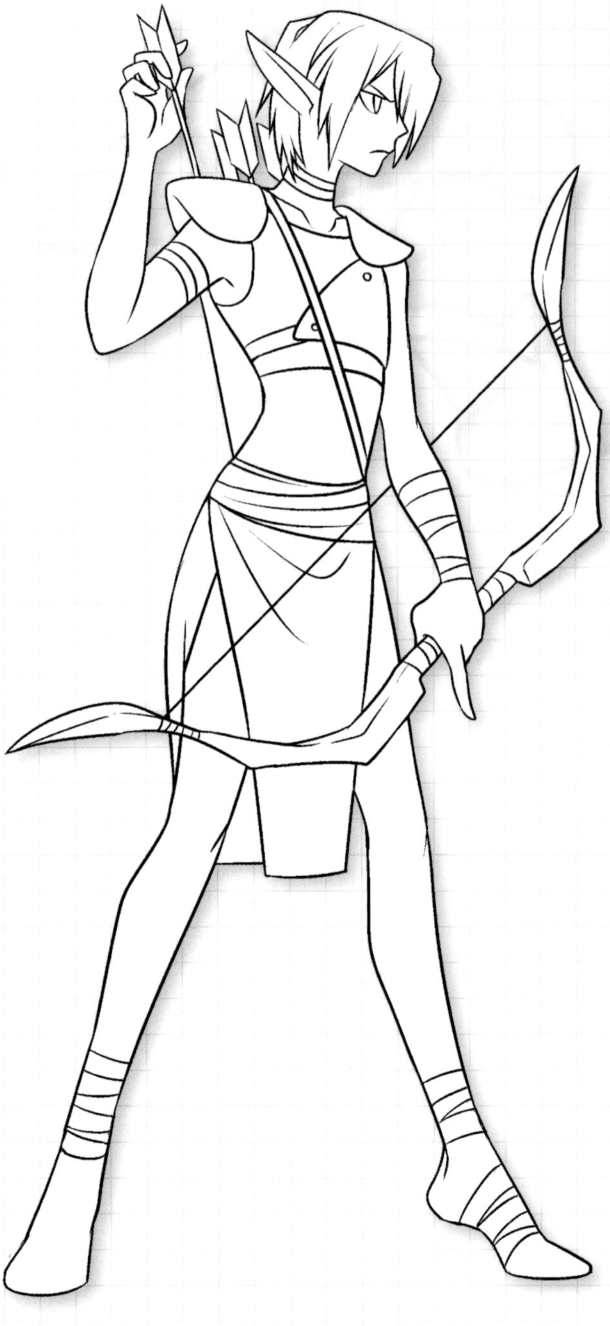

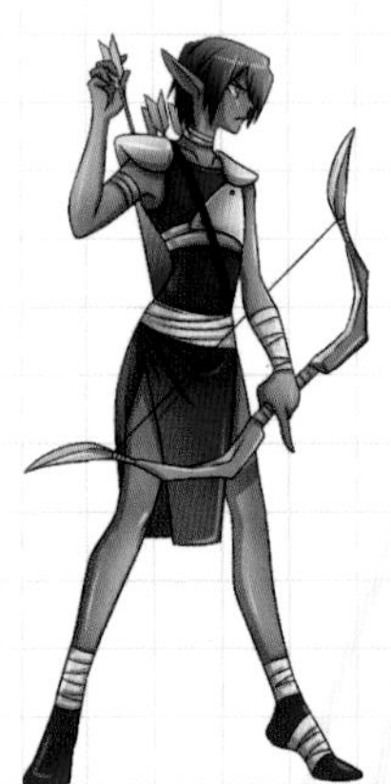

148

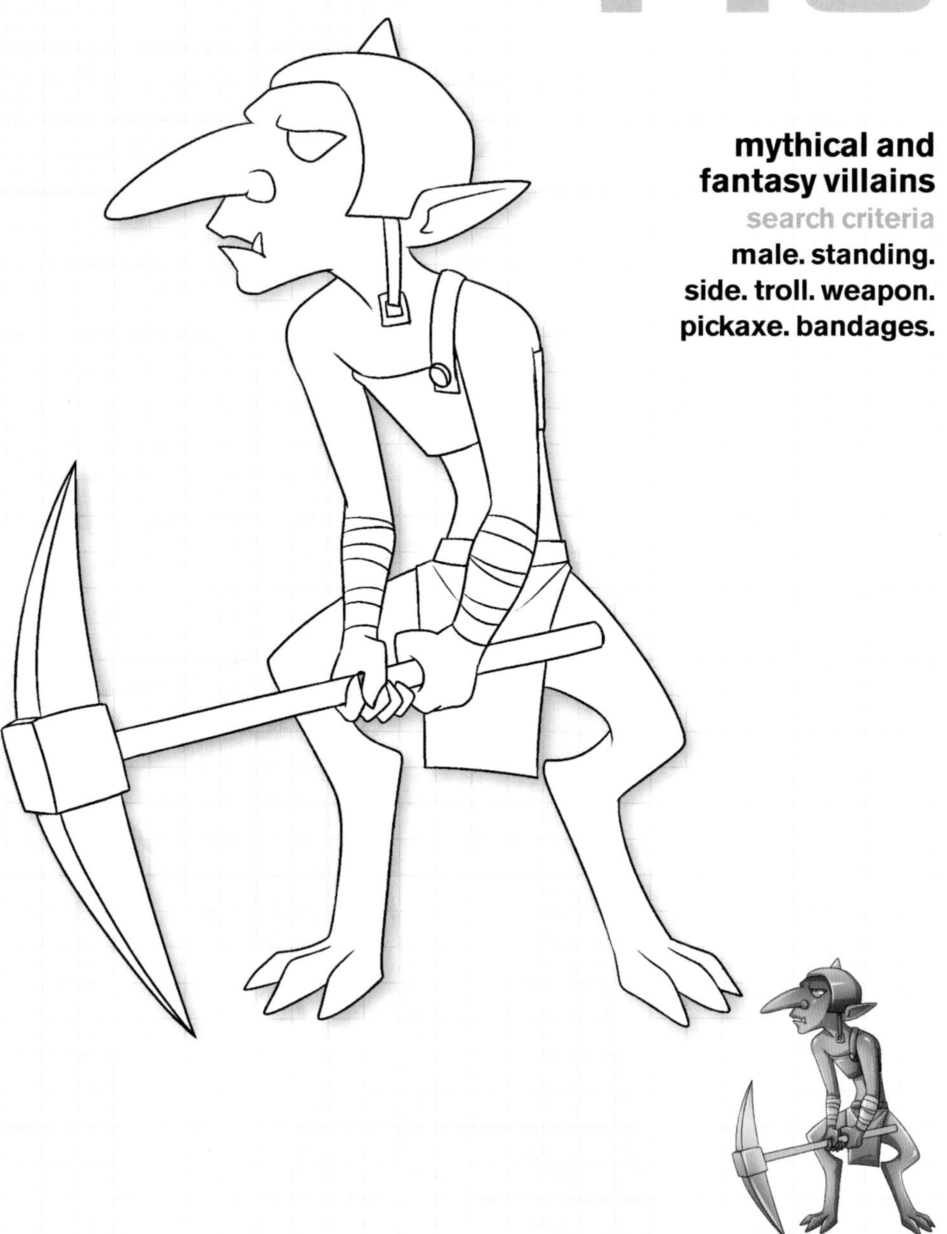

mythical and fantasy villains

search criteria

male. standing. side. troll. weapon. pickaxe. bandages.

149

mythical and fantasy villains

search criteria

male. standing. troll. tools. helmet. mallet. sad. light.

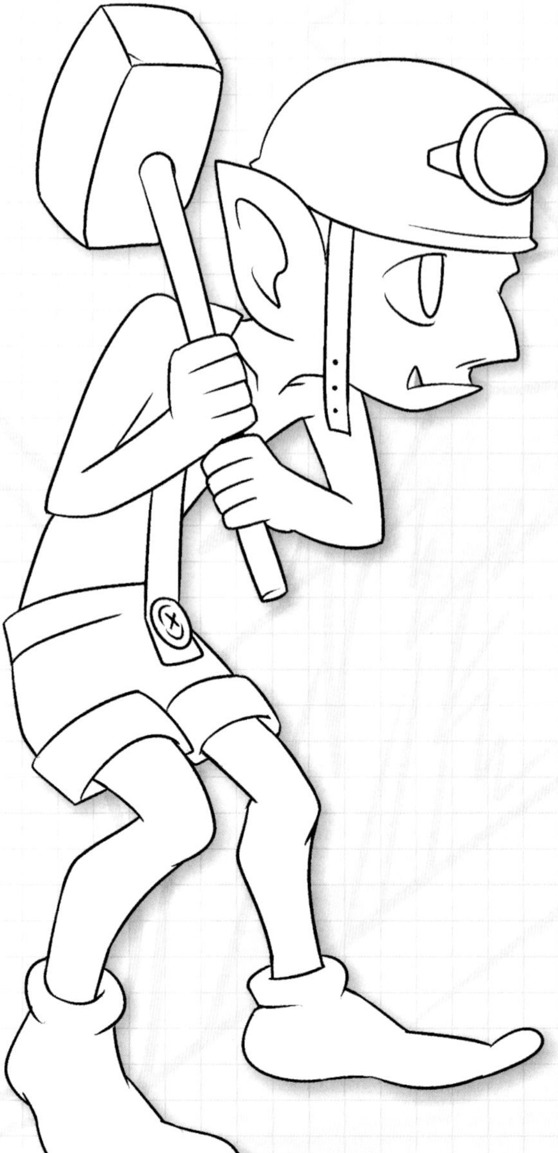

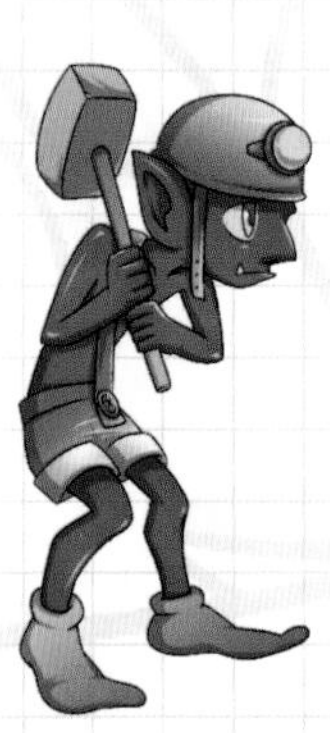

150

mythical and fantasy villains

search criteria

male. standing. lion. claws. tail. beast. fur. lightning.

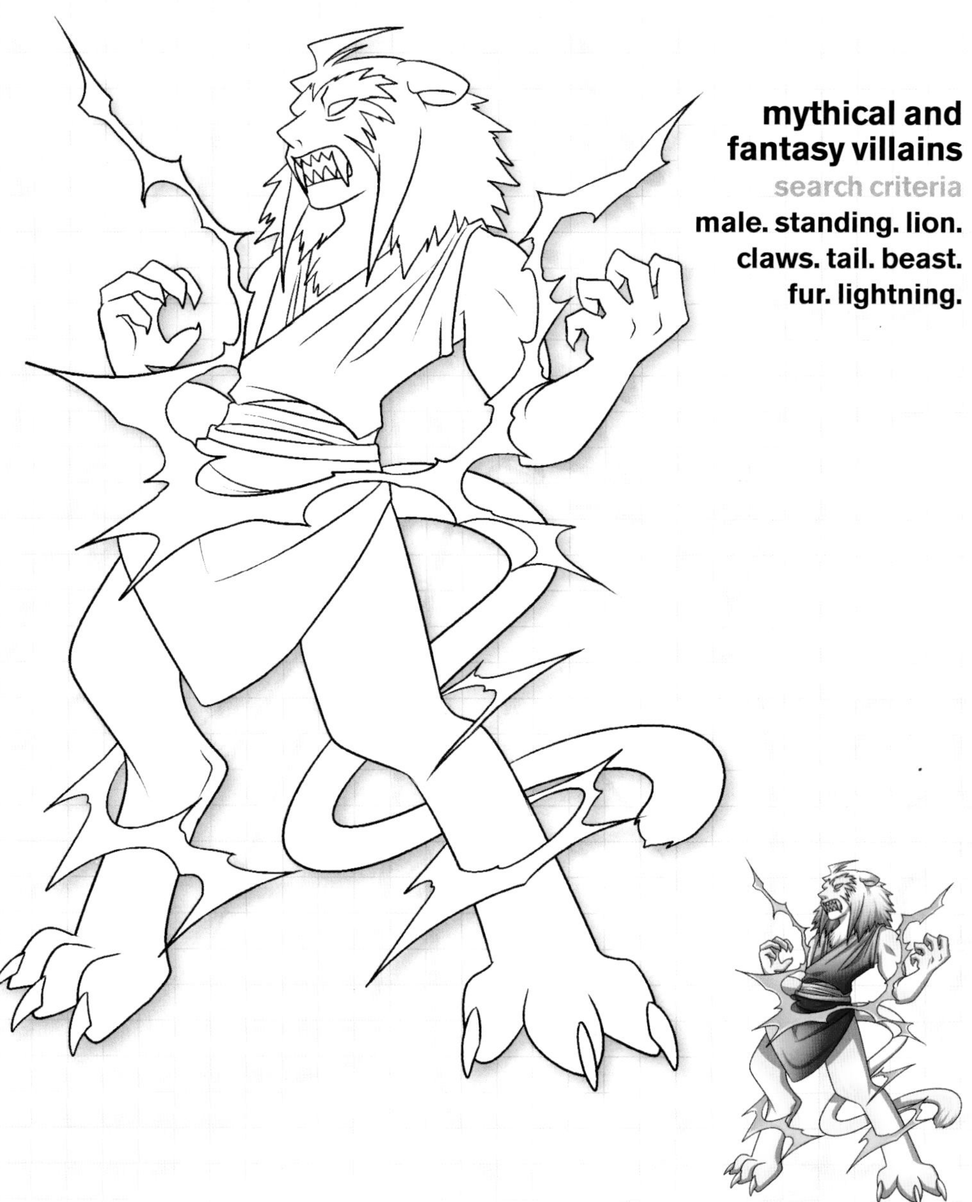

151

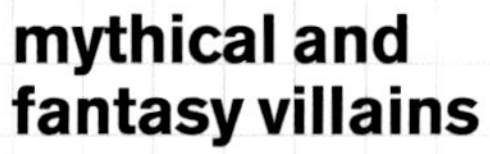

mythical and fantasy villains

search criteria

female. flying. witch. magic. hat. broomstick. bunny.

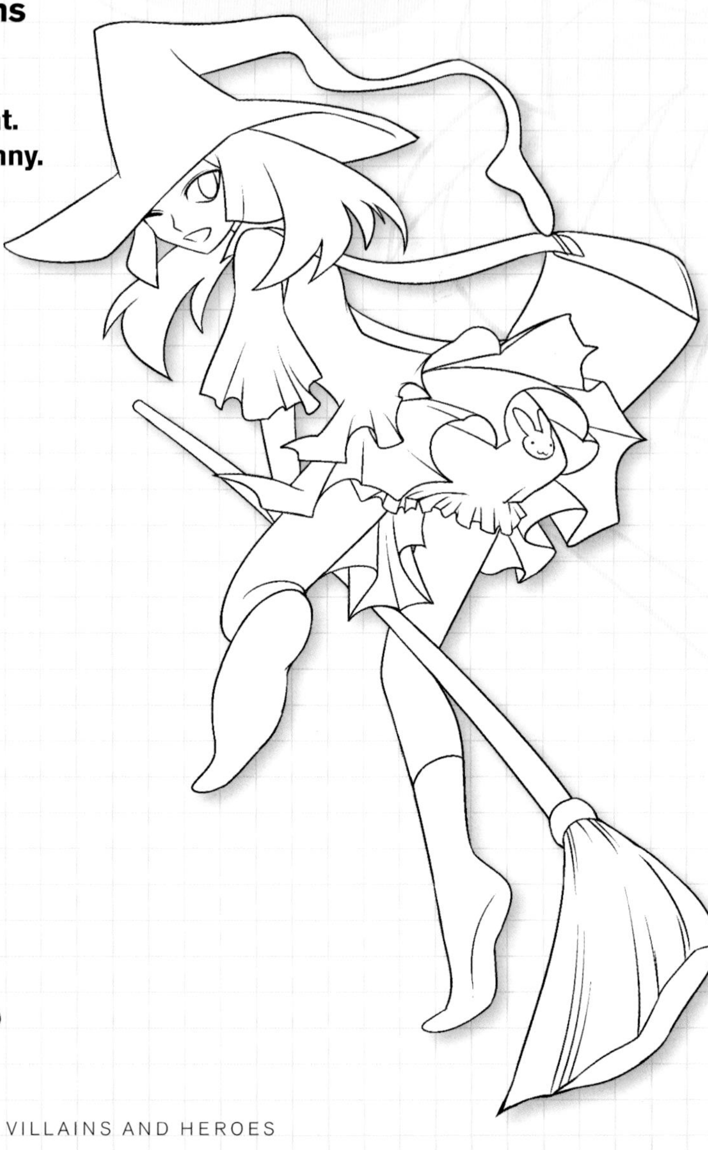

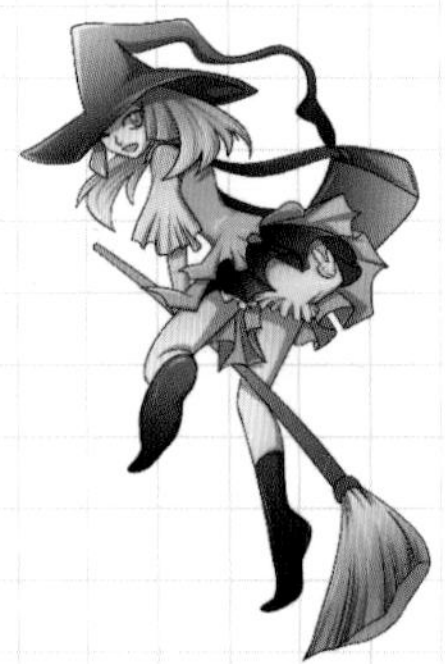

152

mythical and fantasy villains

search criteria

female. sitting. beast. horns. wings. gothic.

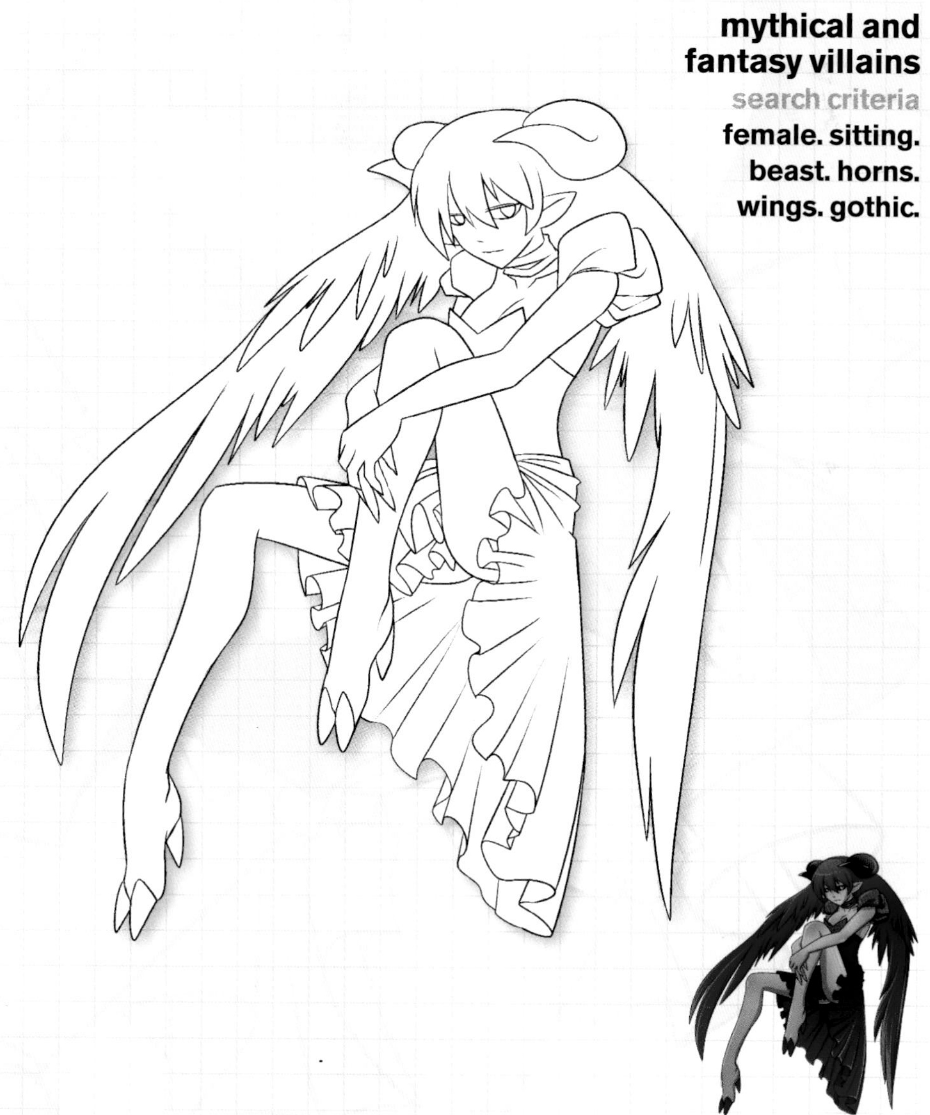

153

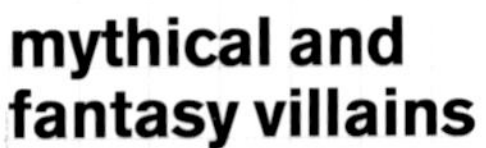

mythical and fantasy villains

search criteria

male. flying. side. wings. dragon. claws. tail. boy.

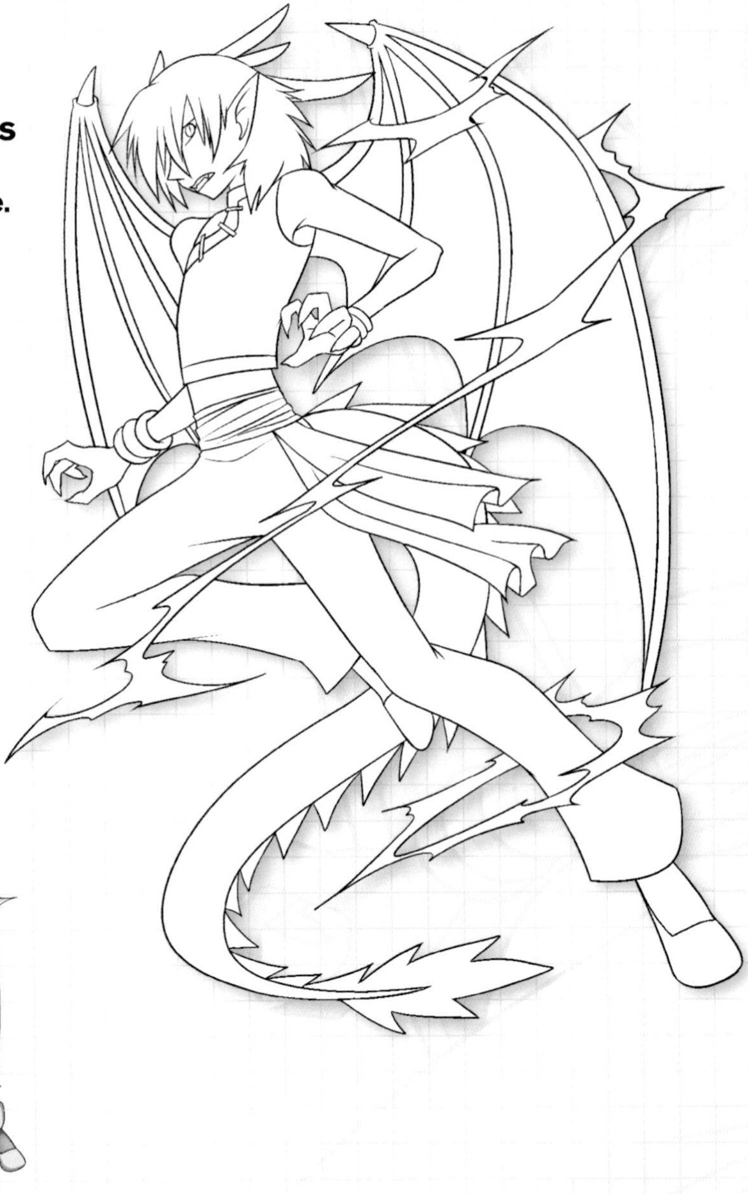

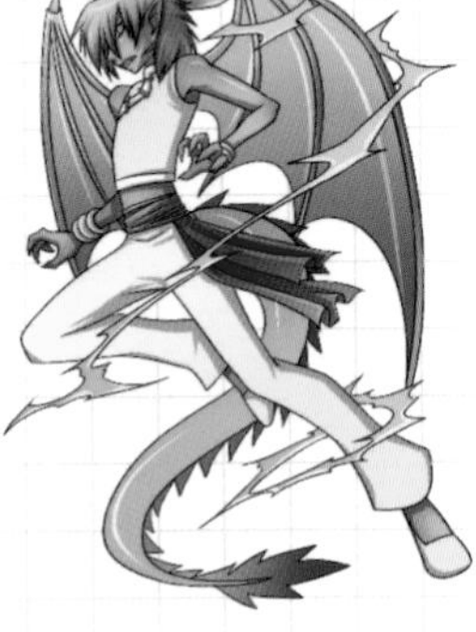

154

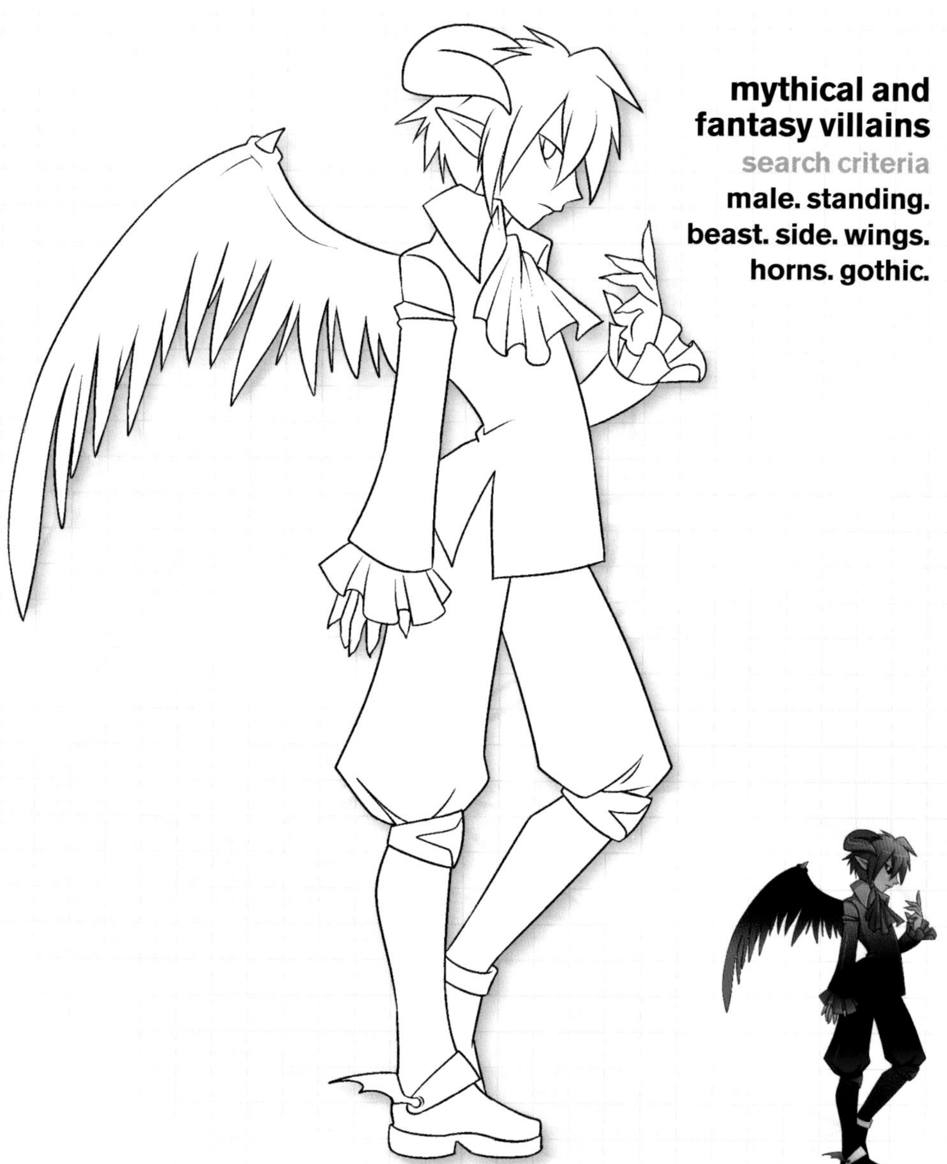

mythical and fantasy villains

search criteria

male. standing. beast. side. wings. horns. gothic.

155

mythical and fantasy heroes

search criteria

female. floating. flying. fairy. wings. magic. antennae.

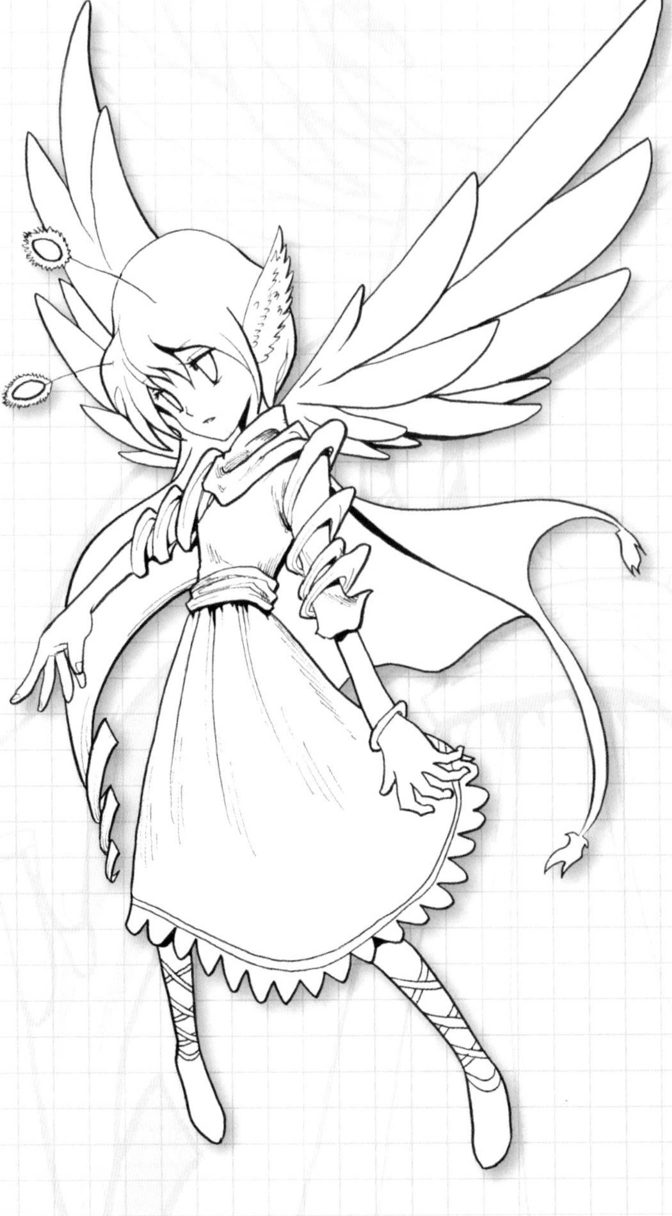

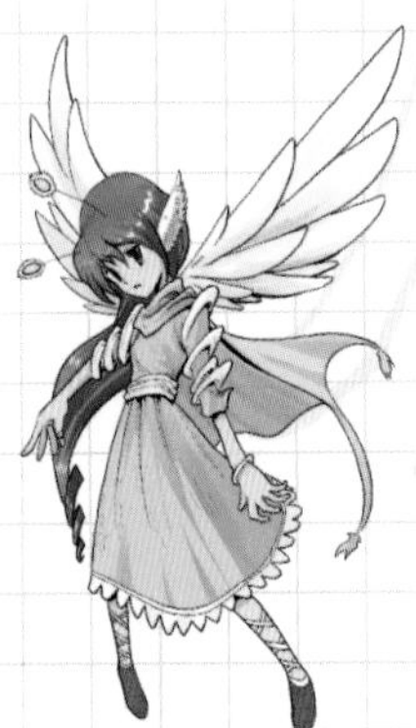

156

mythical and fantasy heroes

search criteria

male. sitting. greek. god. zeus. throne. king. staff.

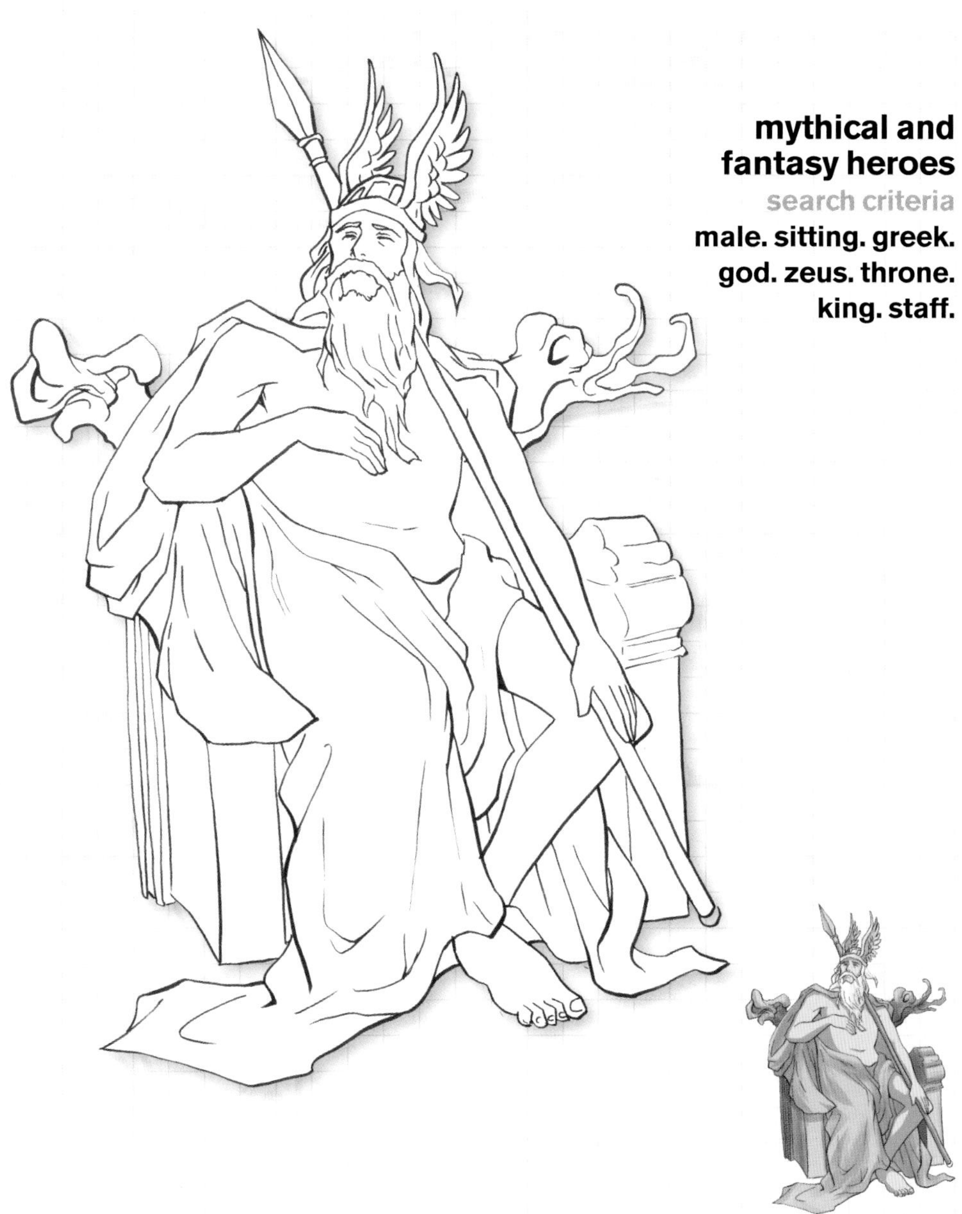

157

mythical and fantasy heroes

search criteria

female. flying. fairy. wings. smiling. magic.

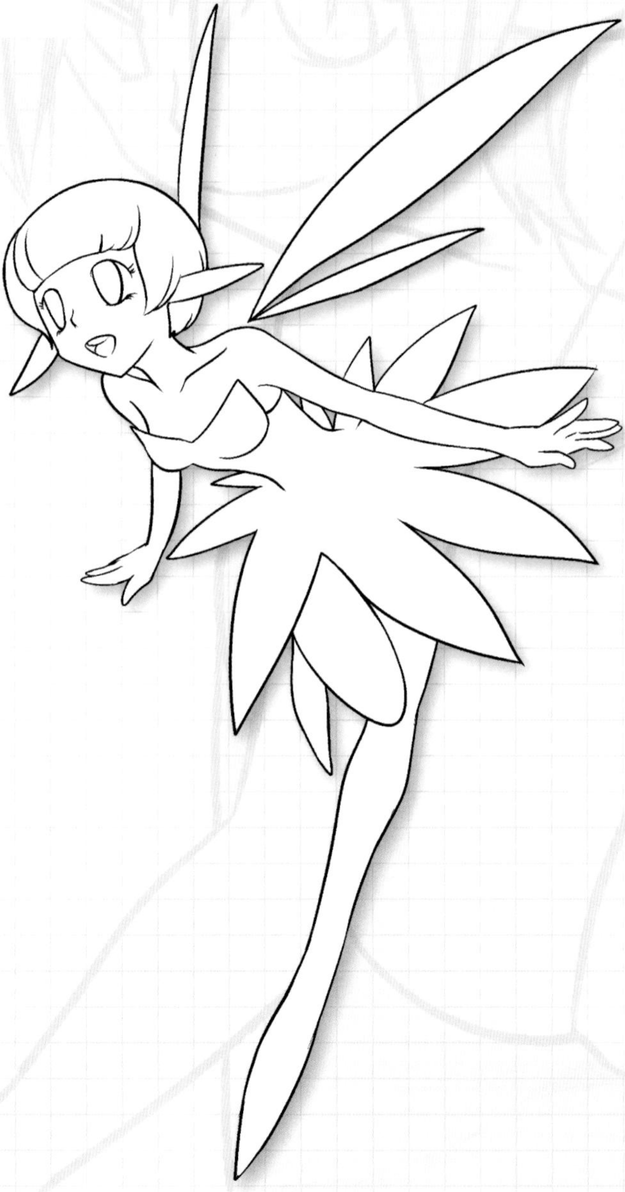

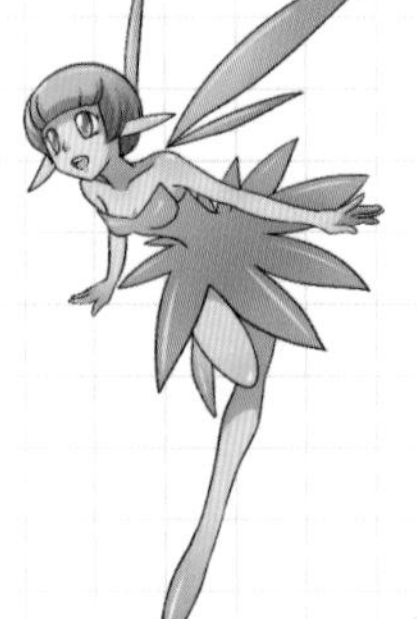

158

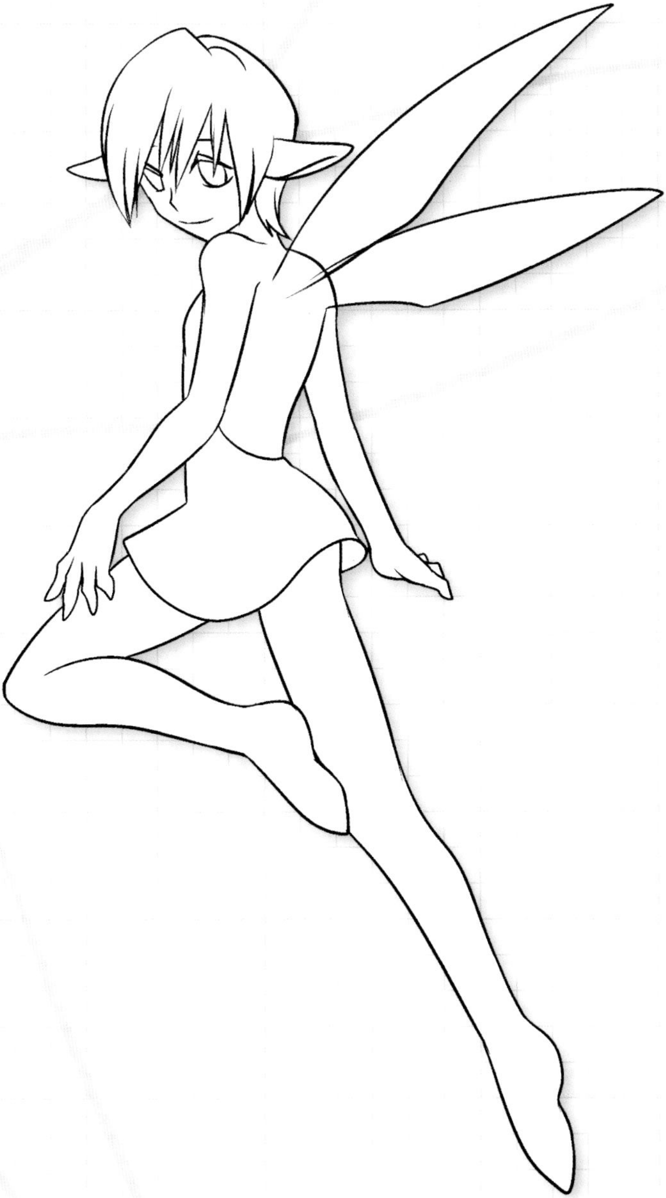

mythical and fantasy heroes

search criteria

female. flying. side. fairy. wings. magic. smiling.

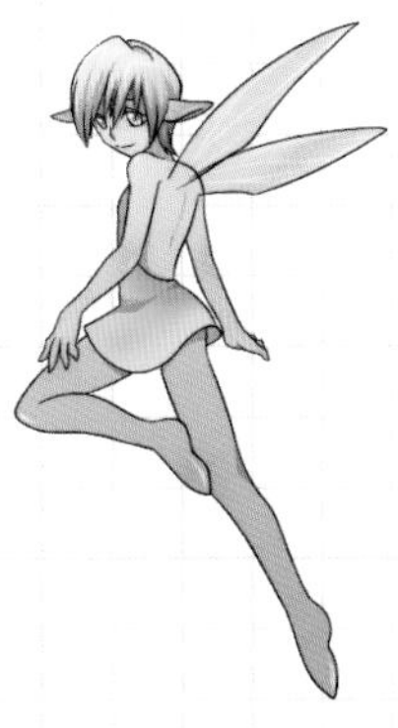

159

mythical and fantasy heroes

search criteria

female. standing. beast. centaur. greek. sad.

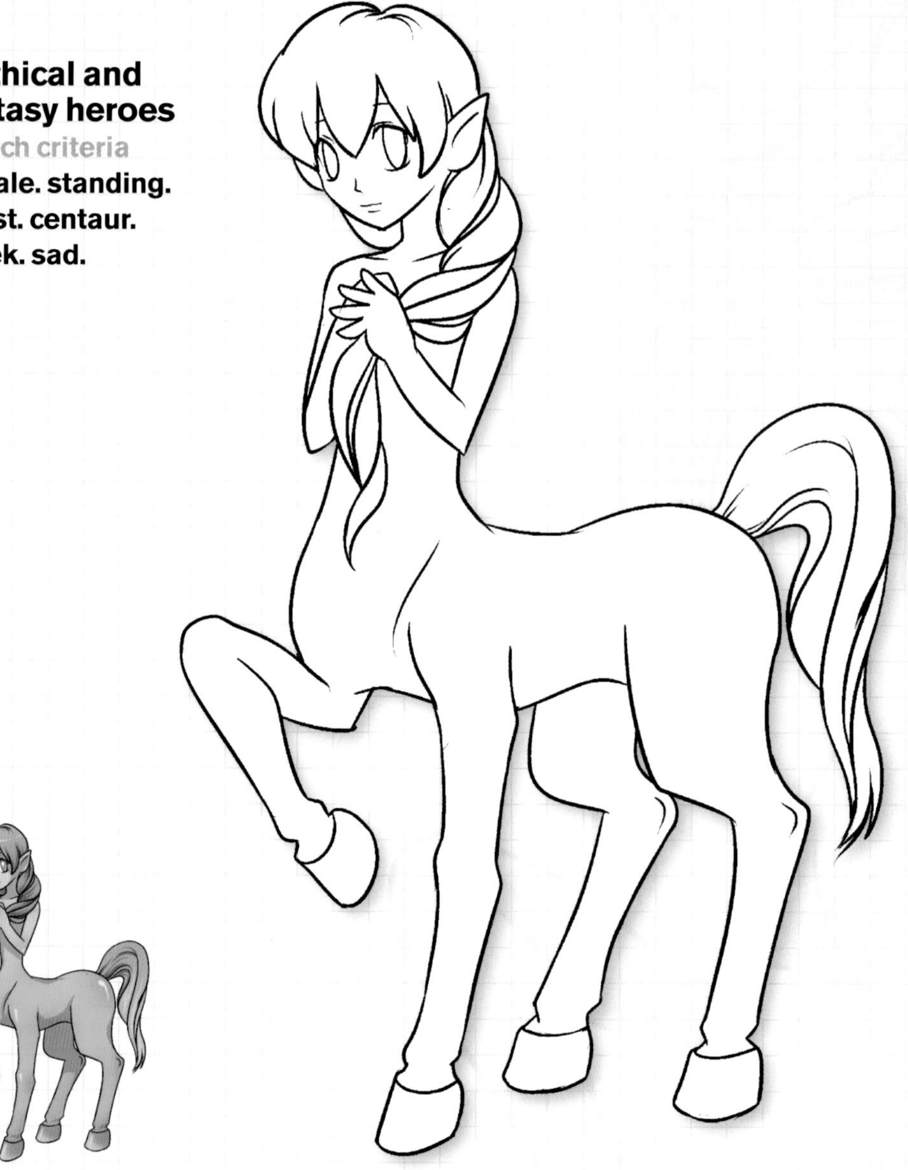

160

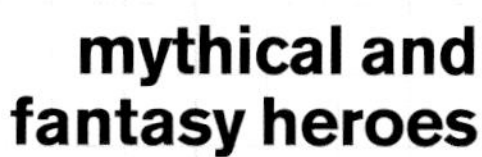

mythical and fantasy heroes

search criteria

female. floating. flying. fairy. angel. halo. wings.

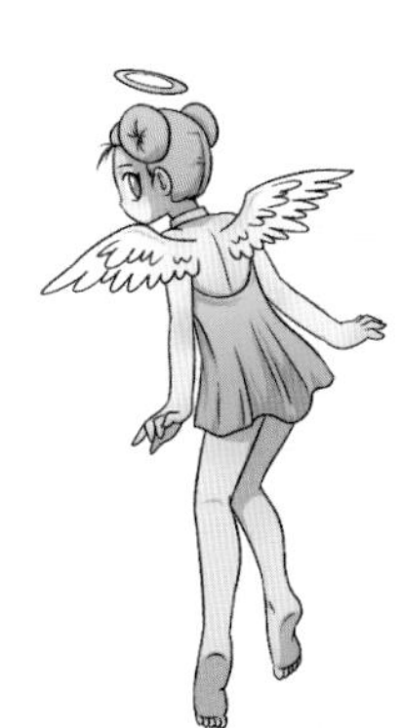

161

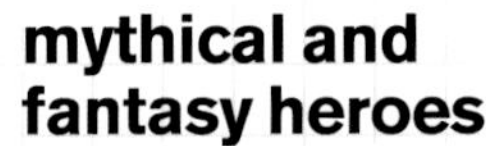

mythical and fantasy heroes

search criteria

male. sitting. fairy. wings. feathers.

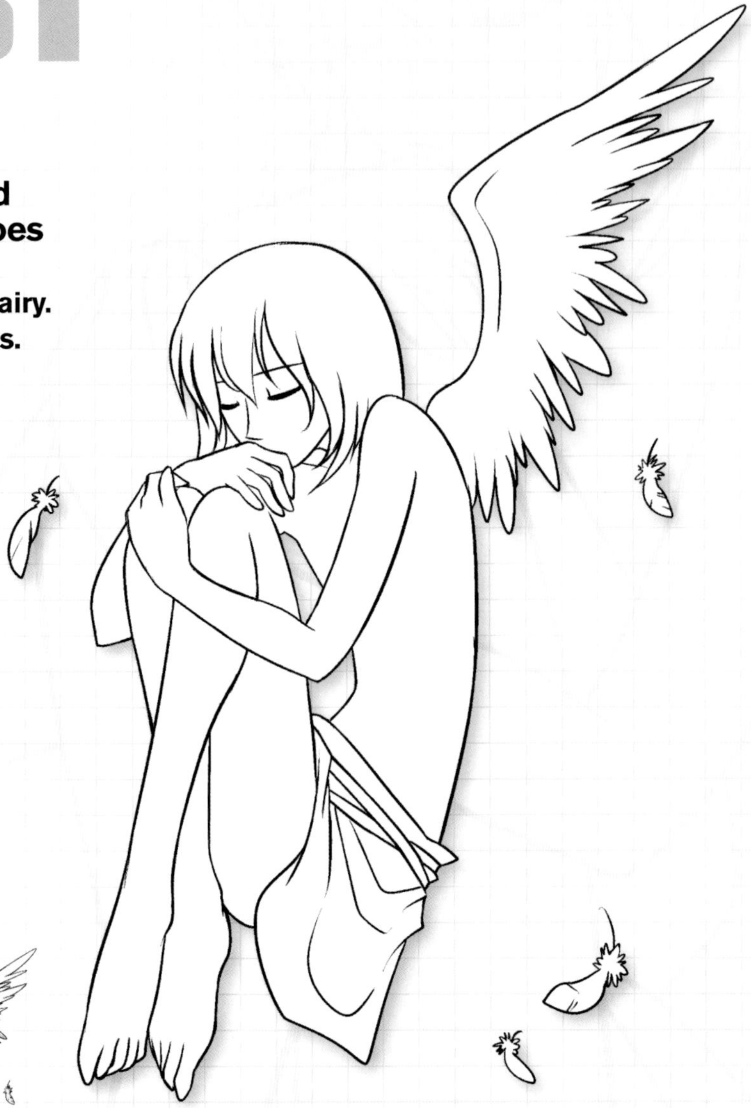

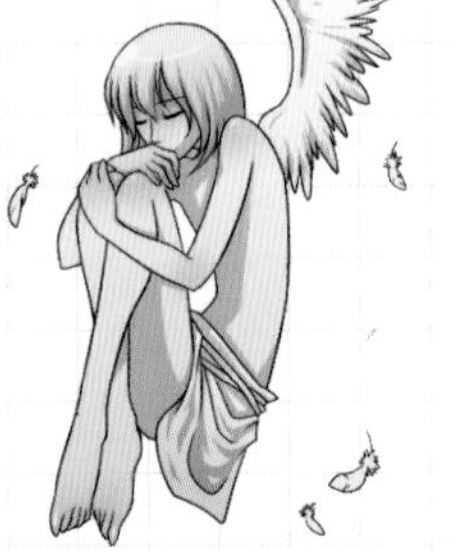

162

mythical and fantasy heroes

search criteria

male. side. jump. archer. weapon. bow. arrows. attack.

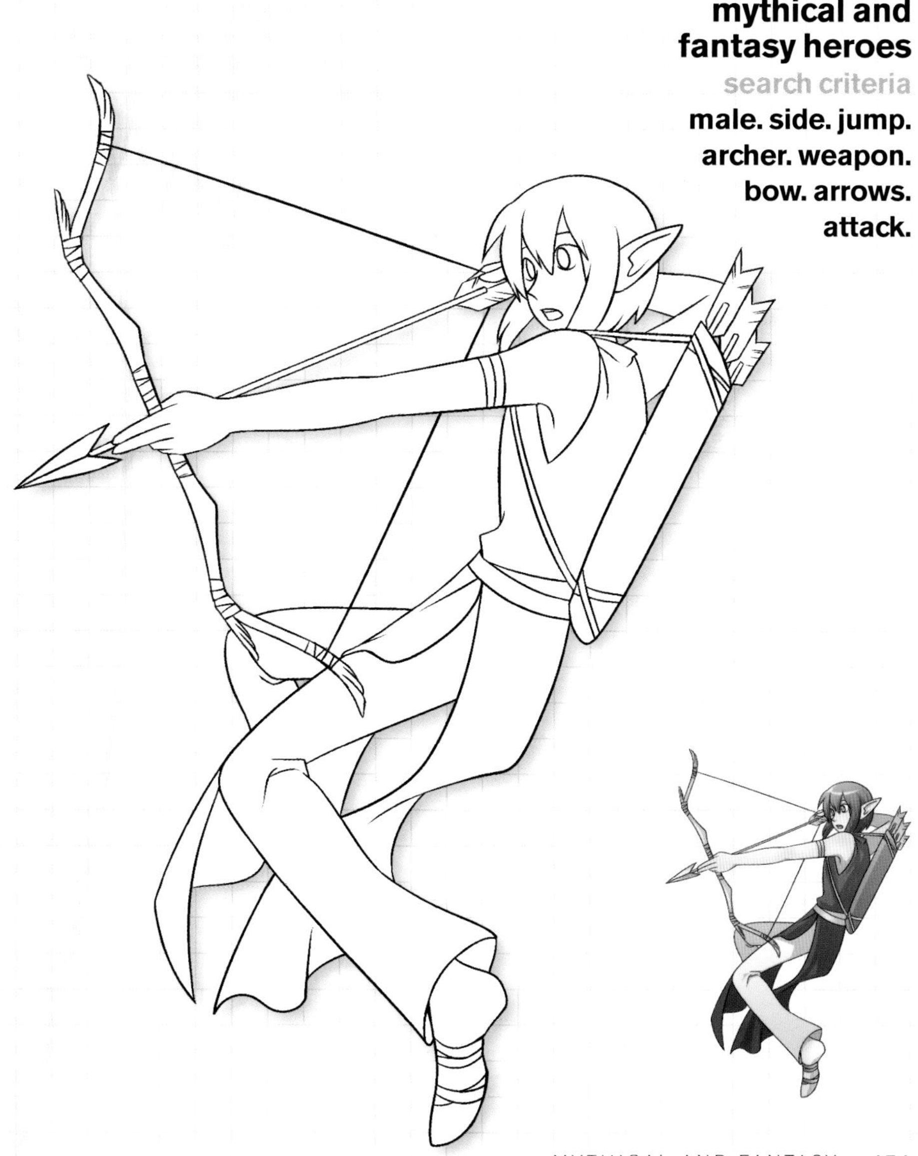

163

mythical and fantasy villains

search criteria

female. standing. warrior. shield. weapon. spear.

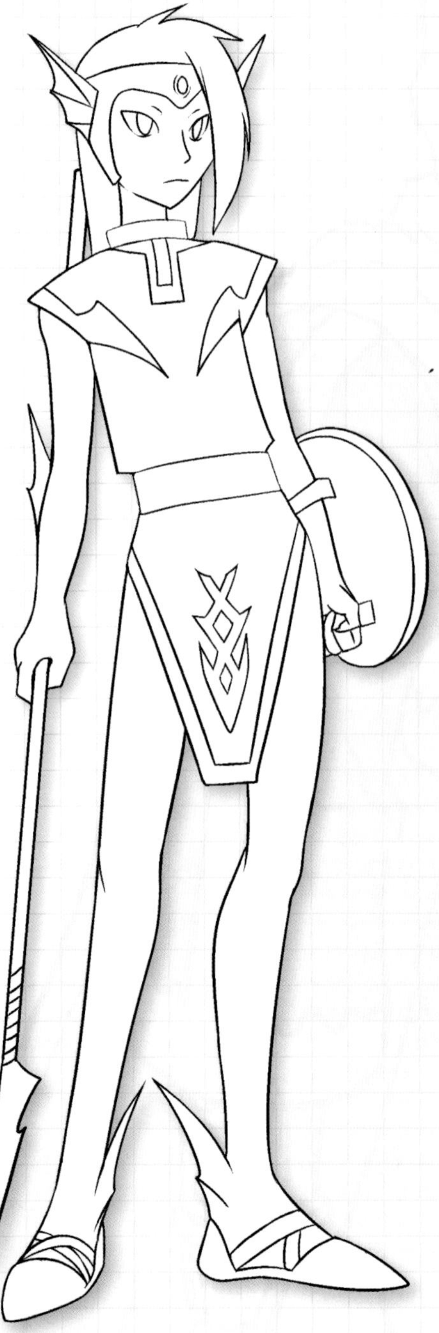

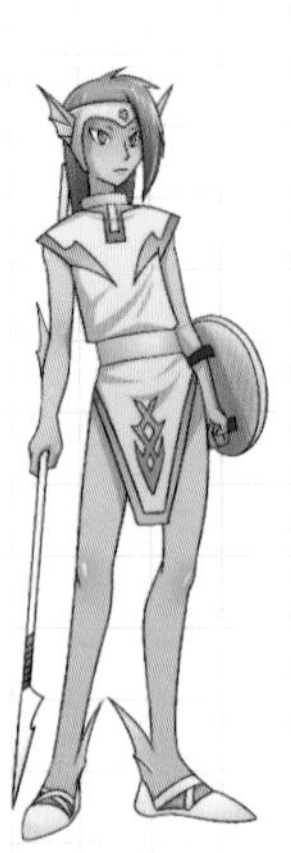

164

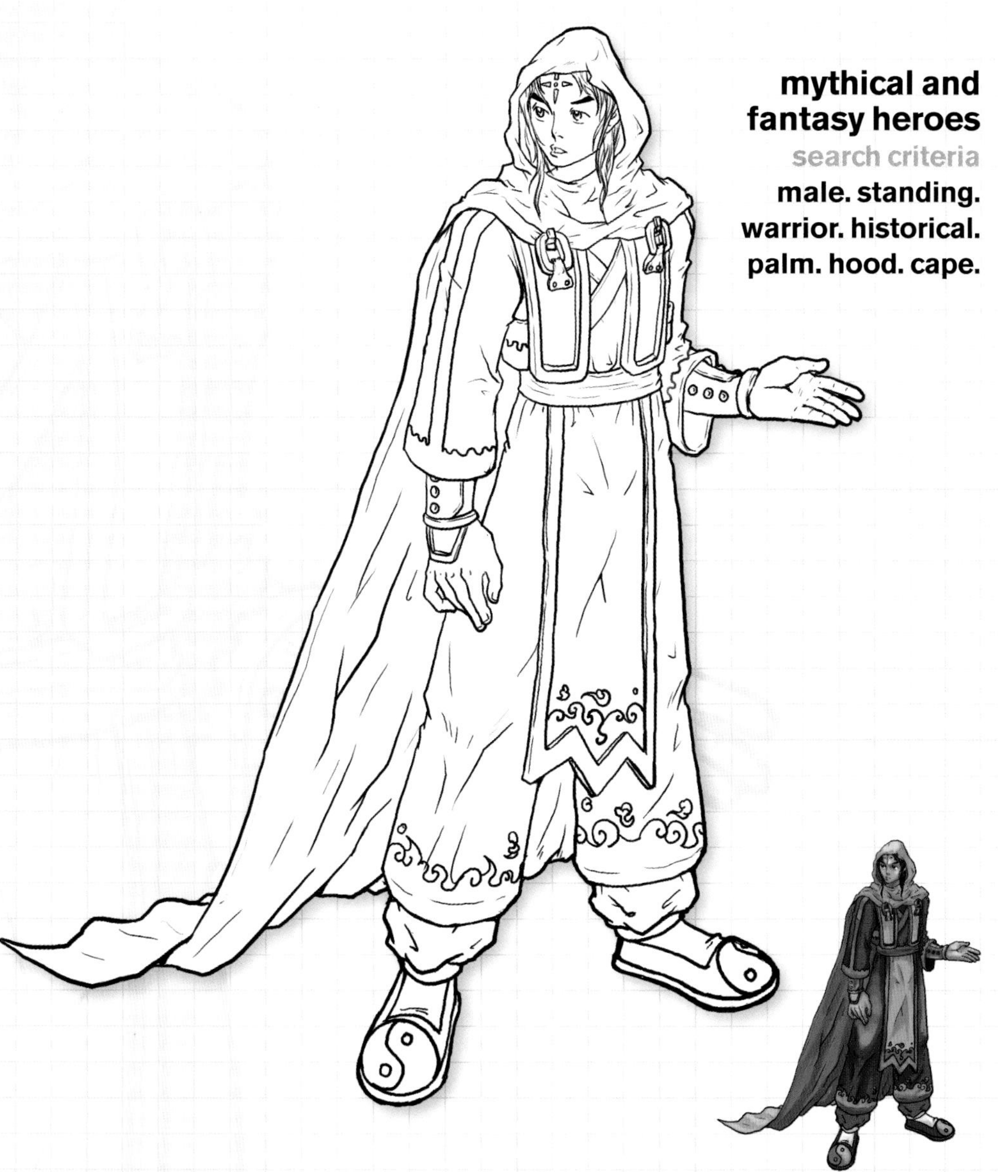

mythical and fantasy heroes

search criteria

male. standing. warrior. historical. palm. hood. cape.

165

mythical and fantasy heroes

search criteria

female. standing. greek. goddess. historical.

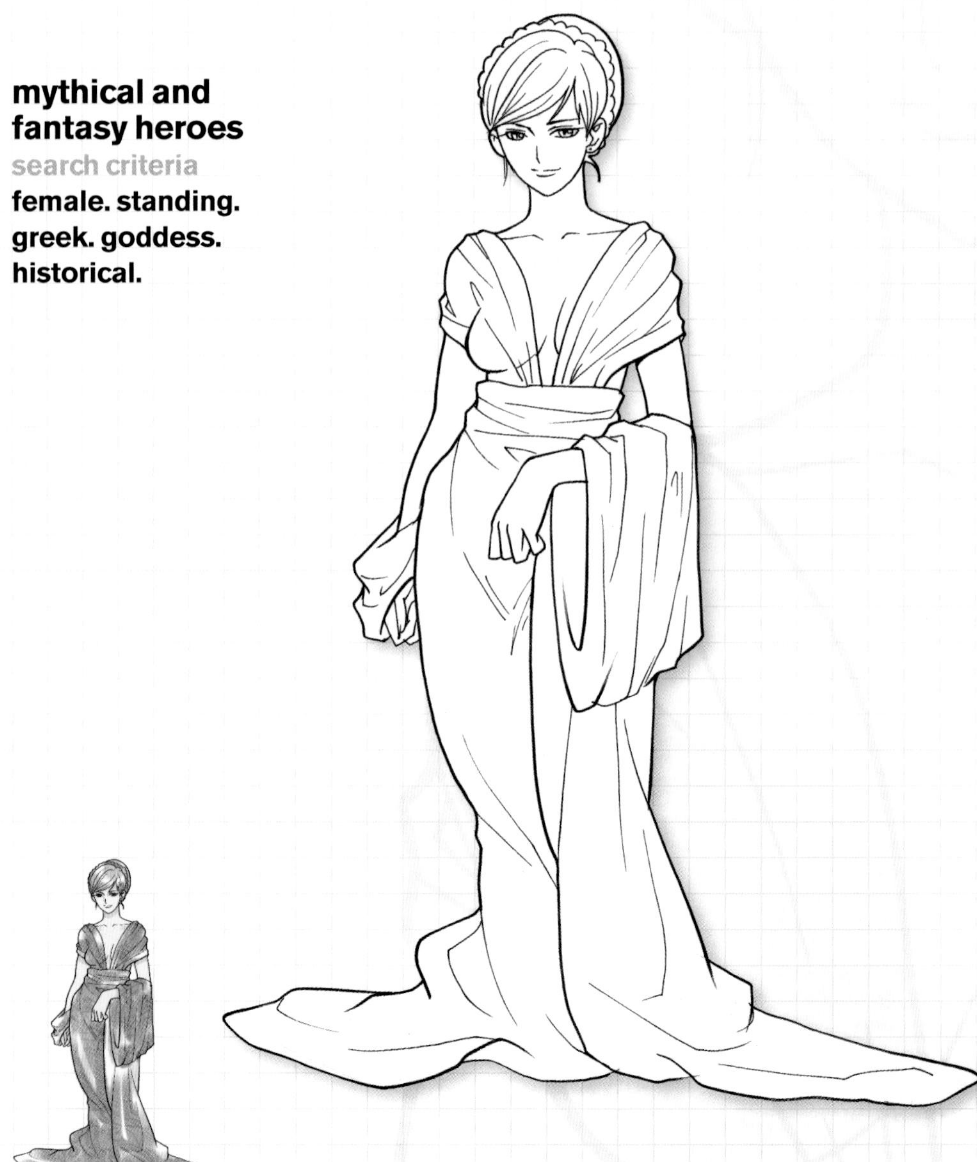

166

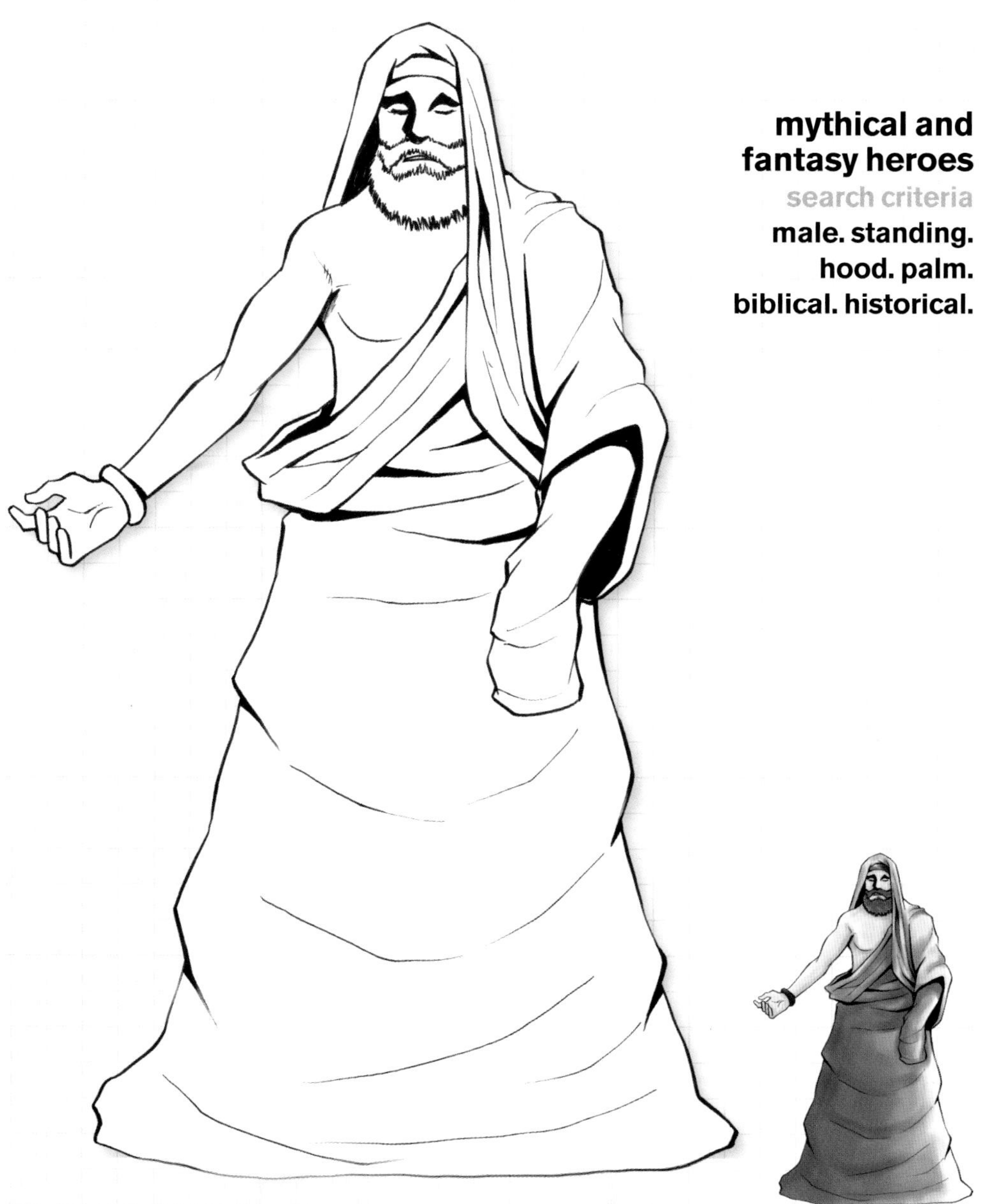

mythical and fantasy heroes

search criteria

male. standing. hood. palm. biblical. historical.

167

mythical and fantasy heroes

search criteria

male. standing. beast. centaur. weapon. spear.

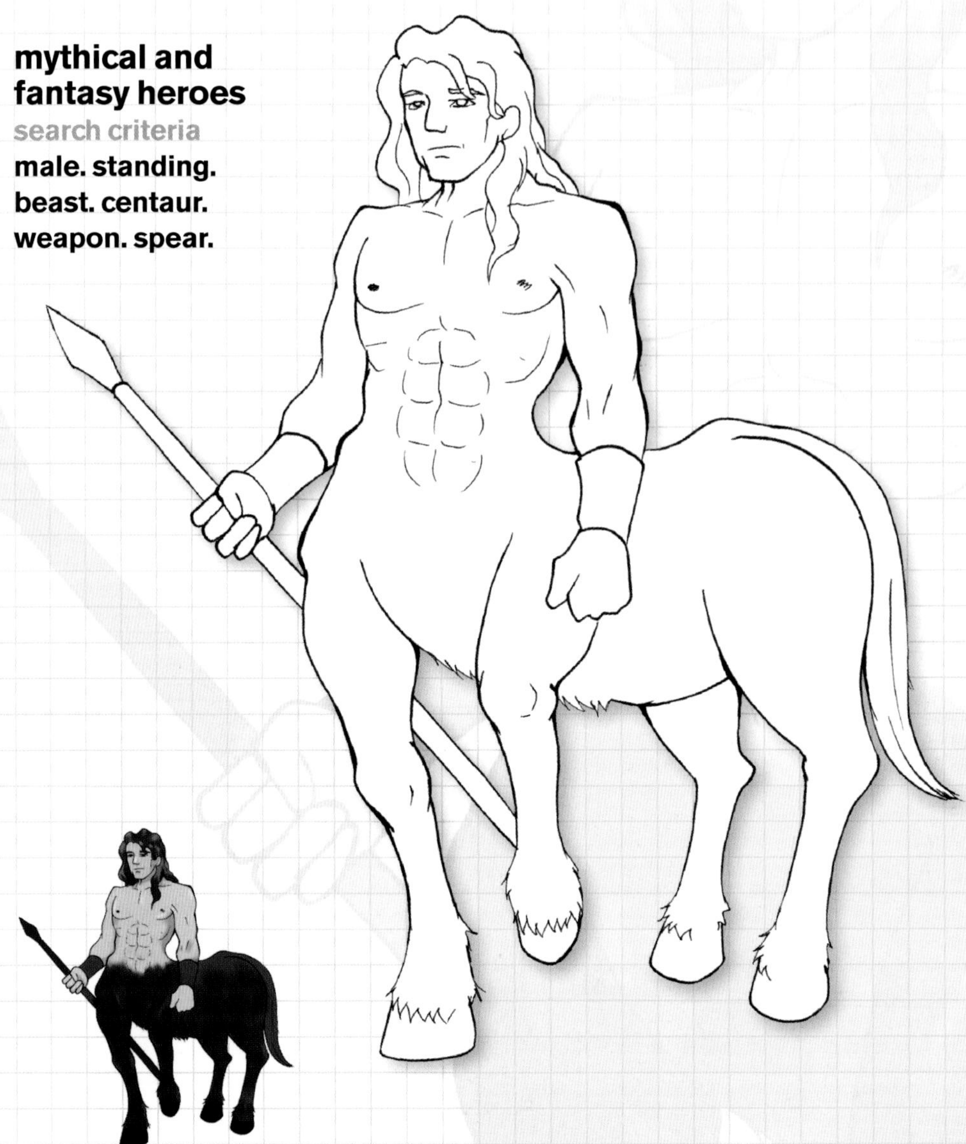

168

mythical and fantasy heroes

search criteria

female. sitting. beast. serpent. tail. snake. rock.

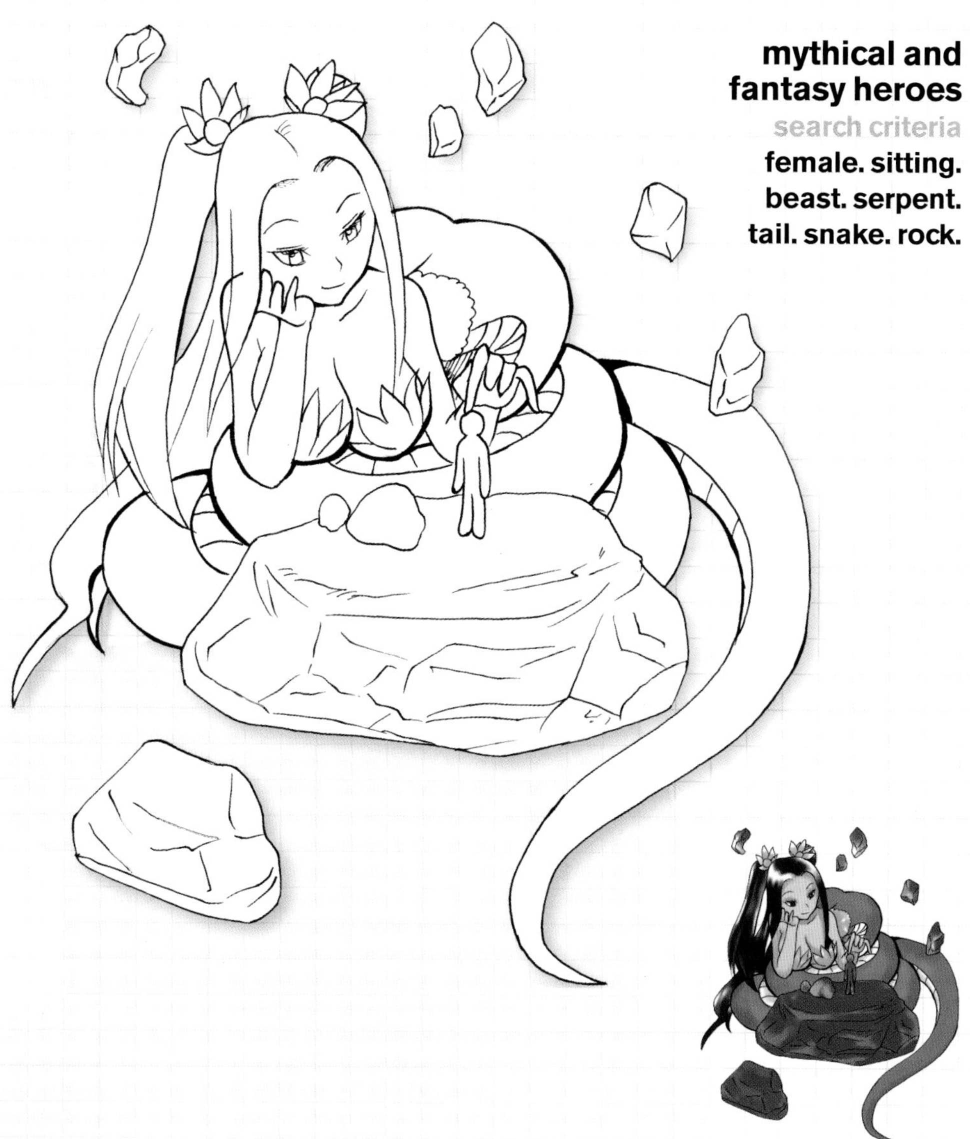

169

mythical and fantasy heroes

search criteria

female. standing. walking. goddess. arabian. headband.

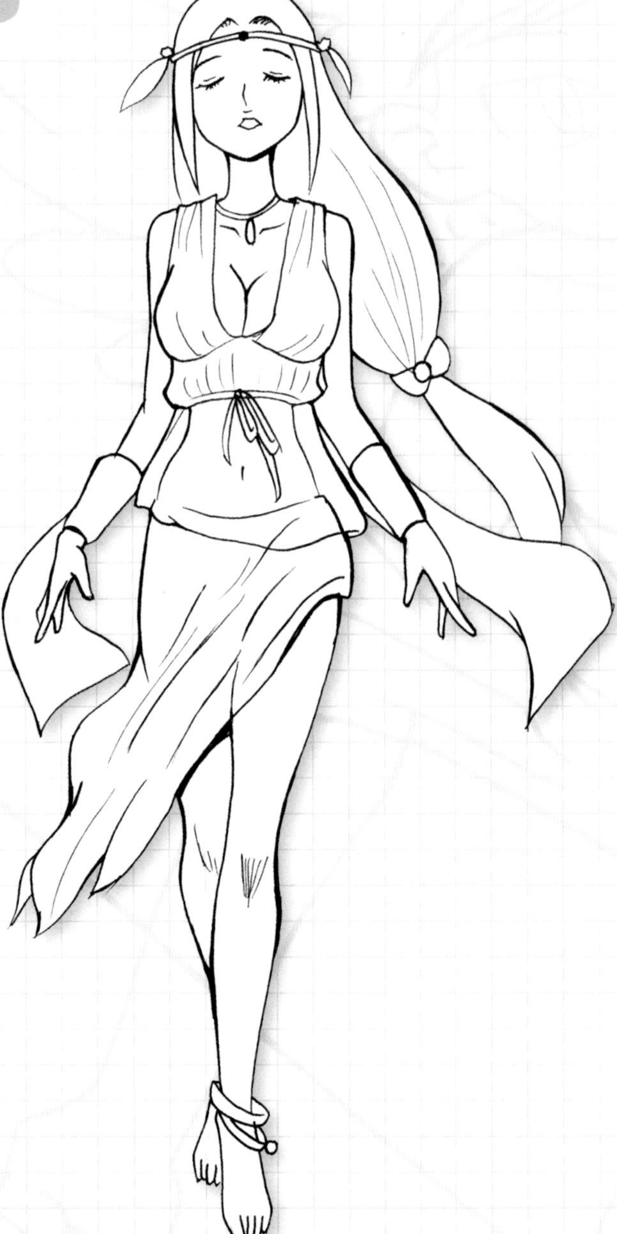

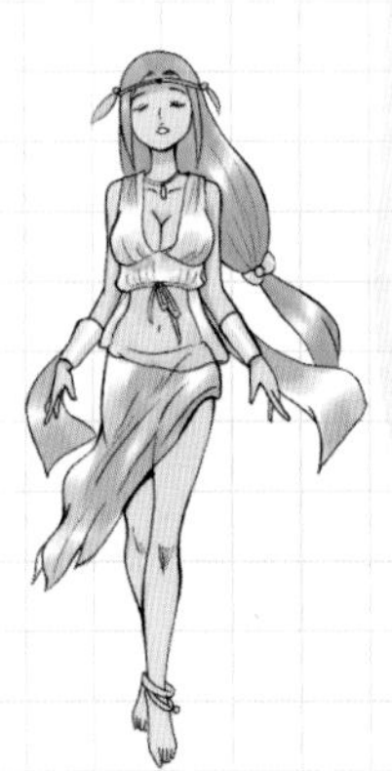

170

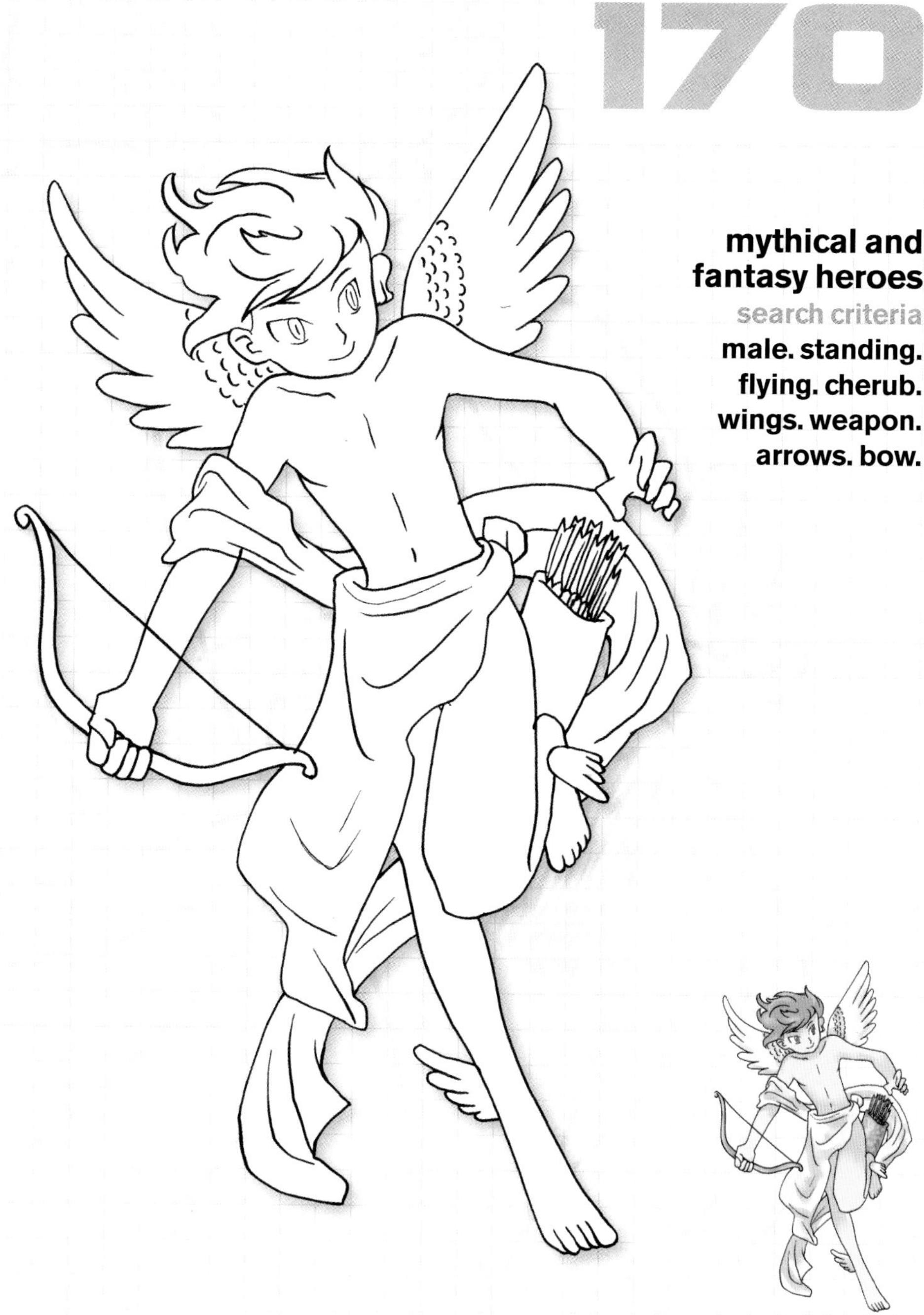

mythical and fantasy heroes

search criteria

male. standing. flying. cherub. wings. weapon. arrows. bow.

171

mythical and fantasy heroes

search criteria

male. standing. magic. cape. hood. ball. nomad. spy.

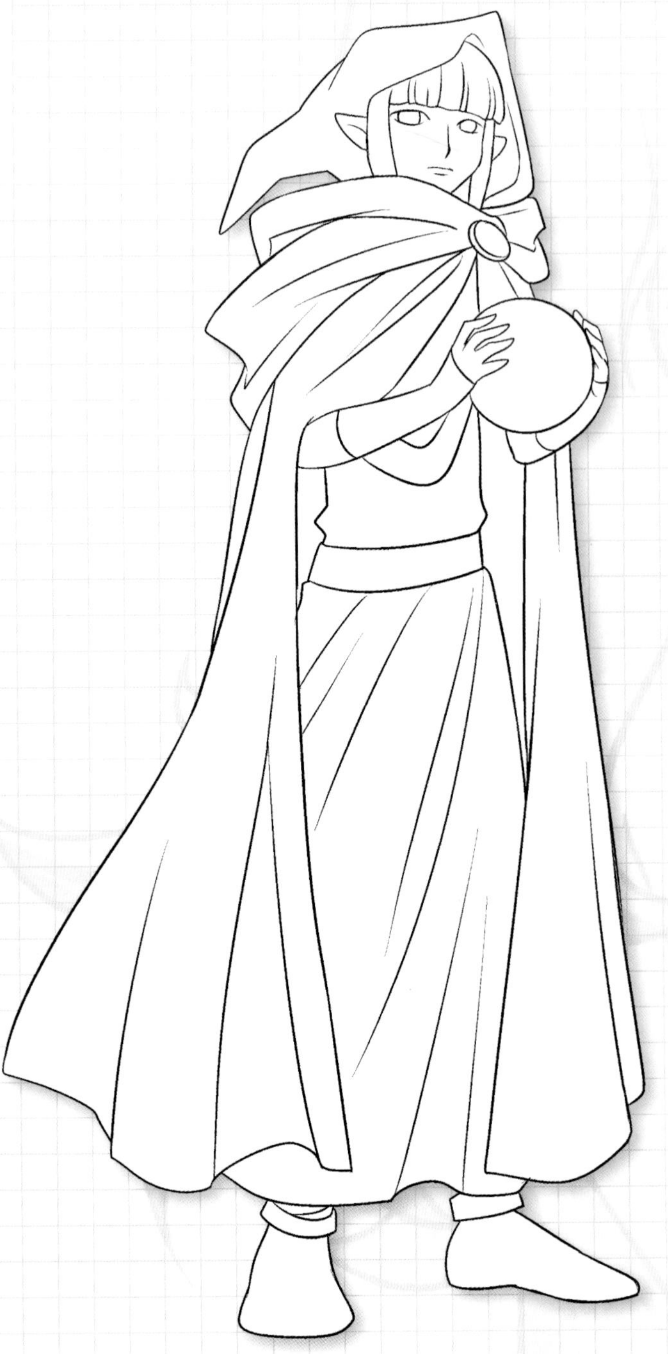

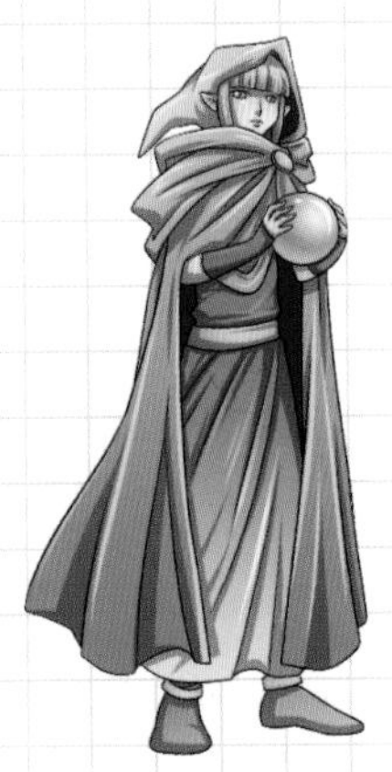

172

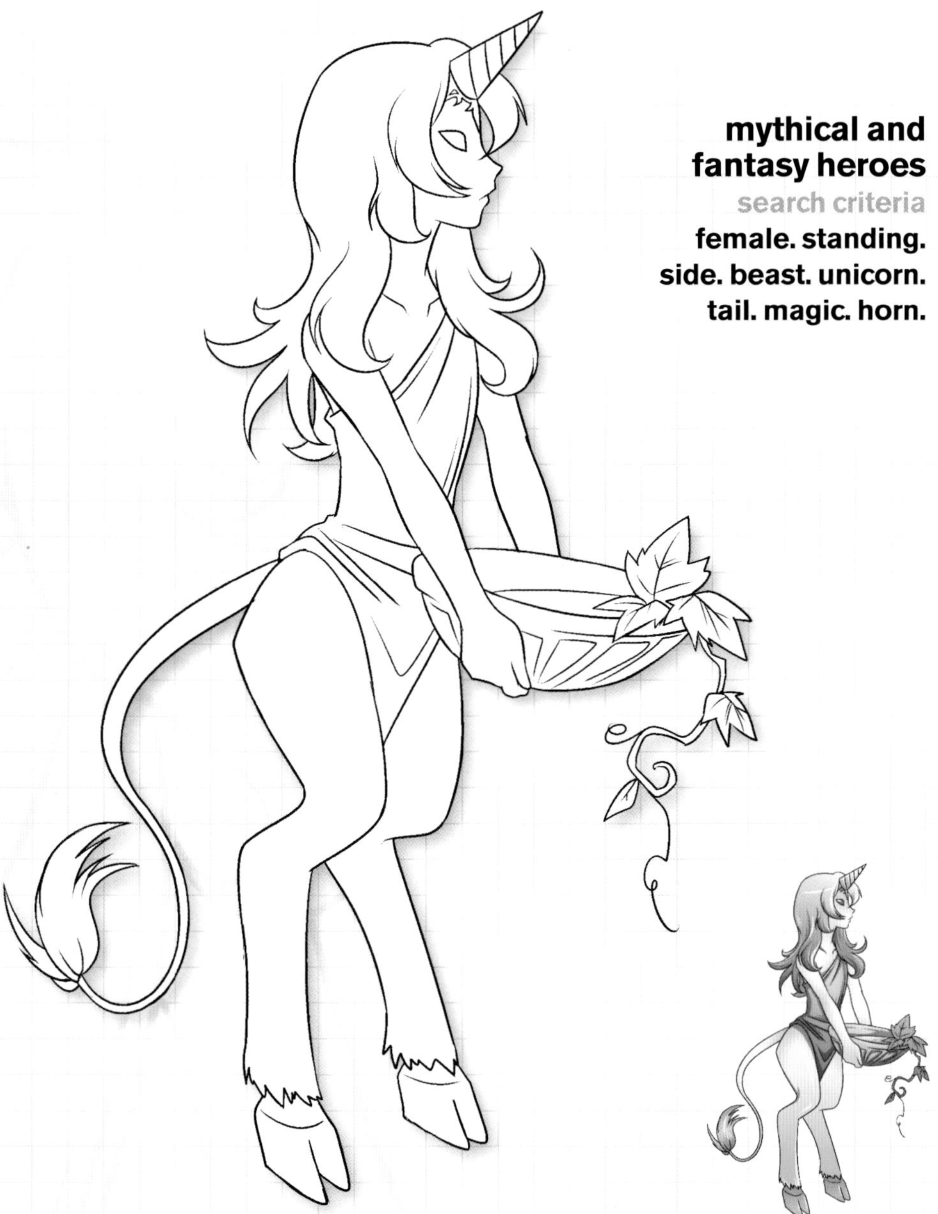

mythical and fantasy heroes

search criteria

female. standing. side. beast. unicorn. tail. magic. horn.

173

mythical and fantasy heroes

search criteria

male. jump. side. beast. horns. music. flute. faun.

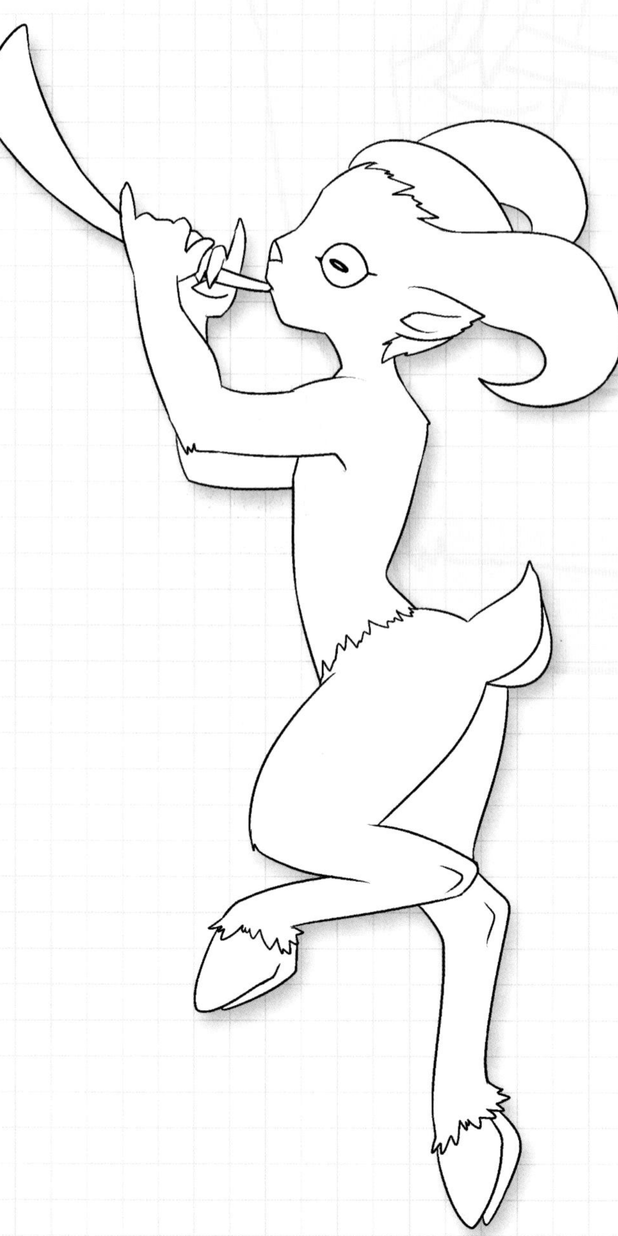

174

mythical and fantasy heroes

search criteria

female. floating. side. mermaid. sea. tail.

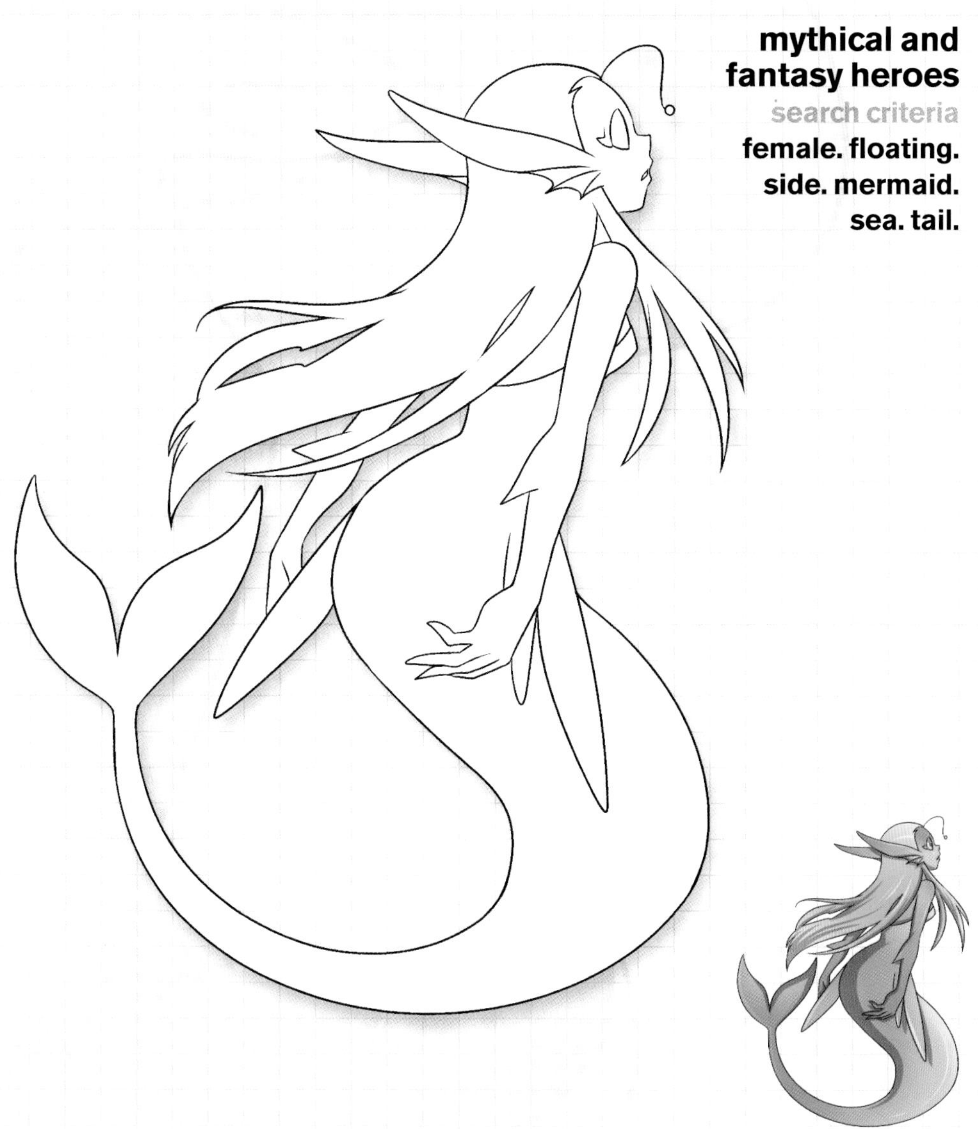

175

mythical and fantasy heroes

search criteria

male. sitting. scarf. hat. boy. kawaii. star. wand. magic.

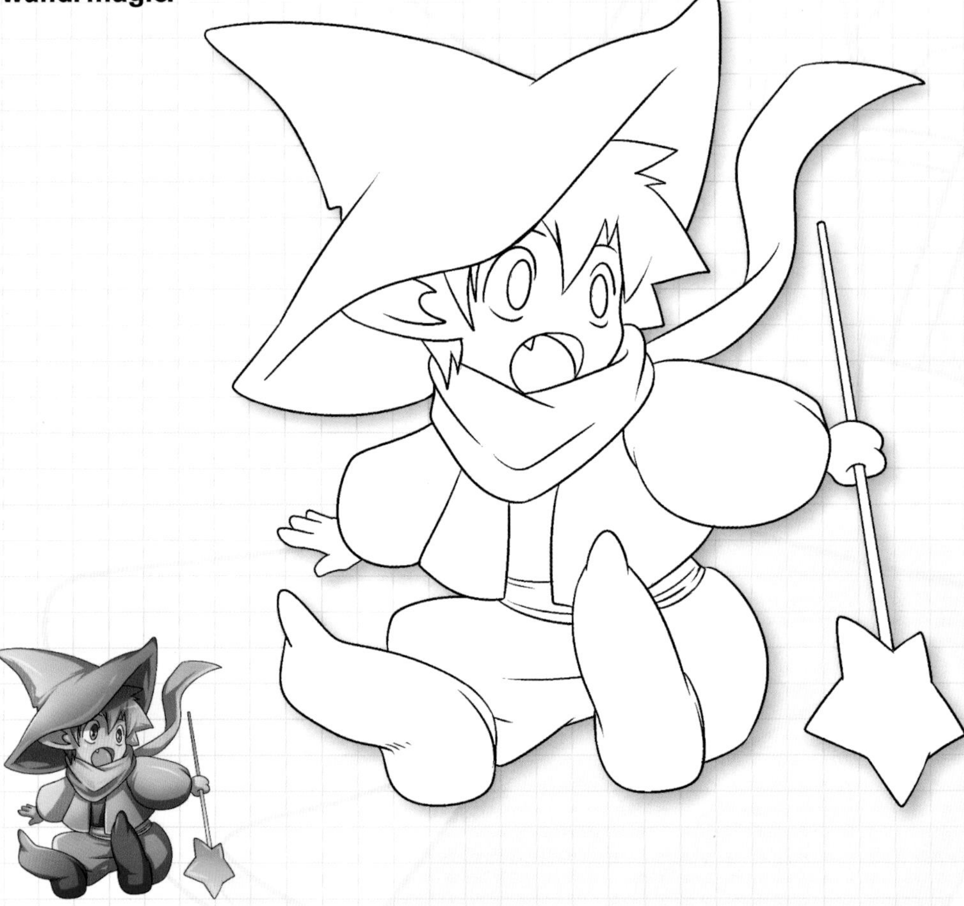

176

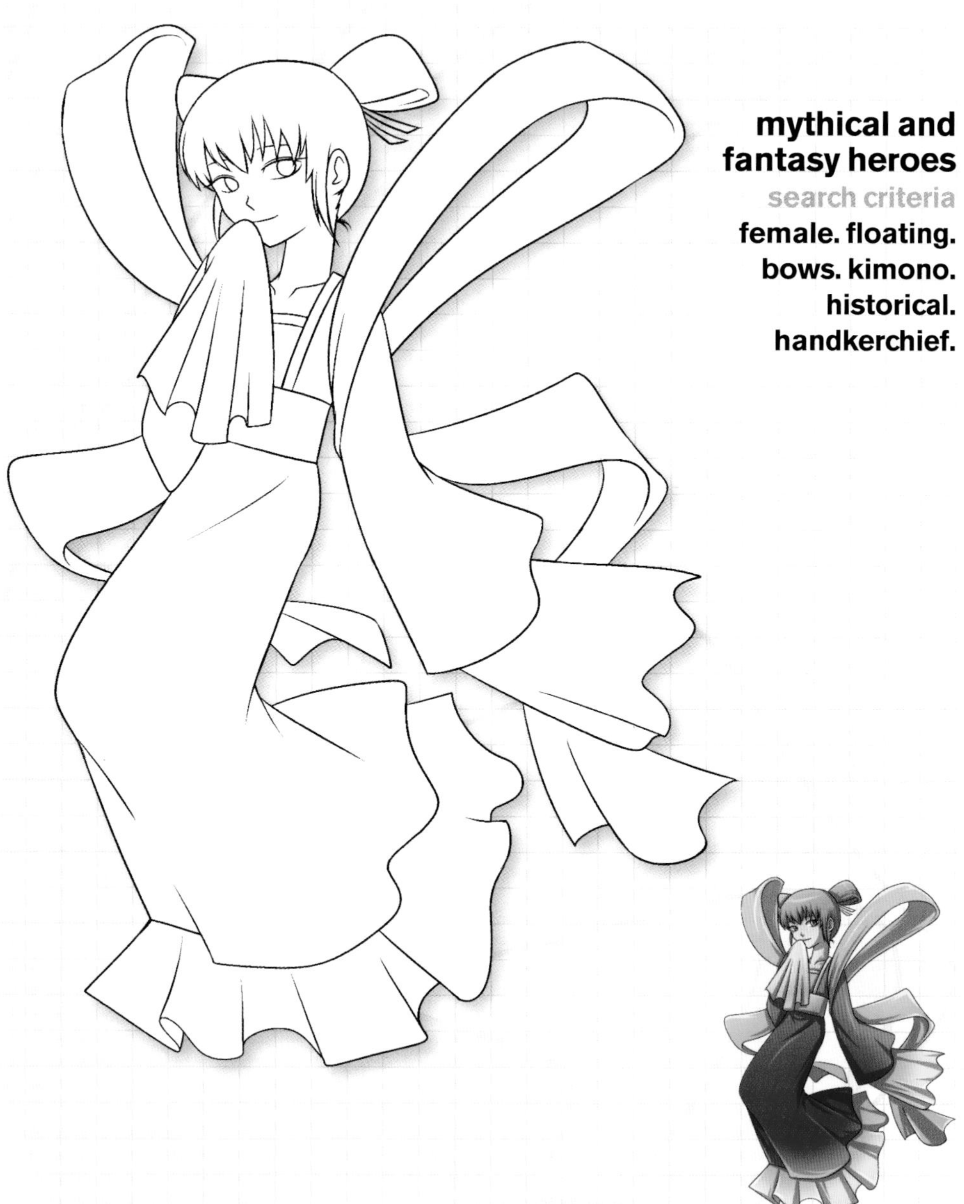

mythical and fantasy heroes

search criteria

female. floating. bows. kimono. historical. handkerchief.

177

pirate villains

search criteria

male. standing. hat. hook. pegleg. bones. captain. scar. skull.

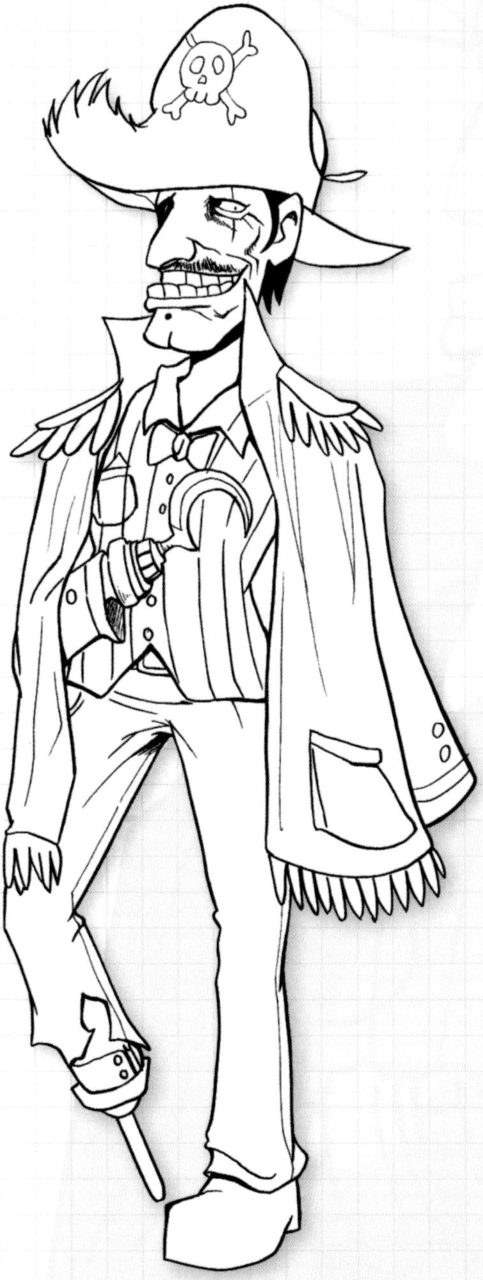

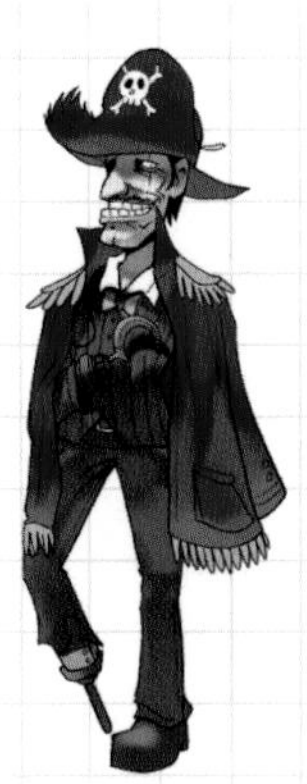

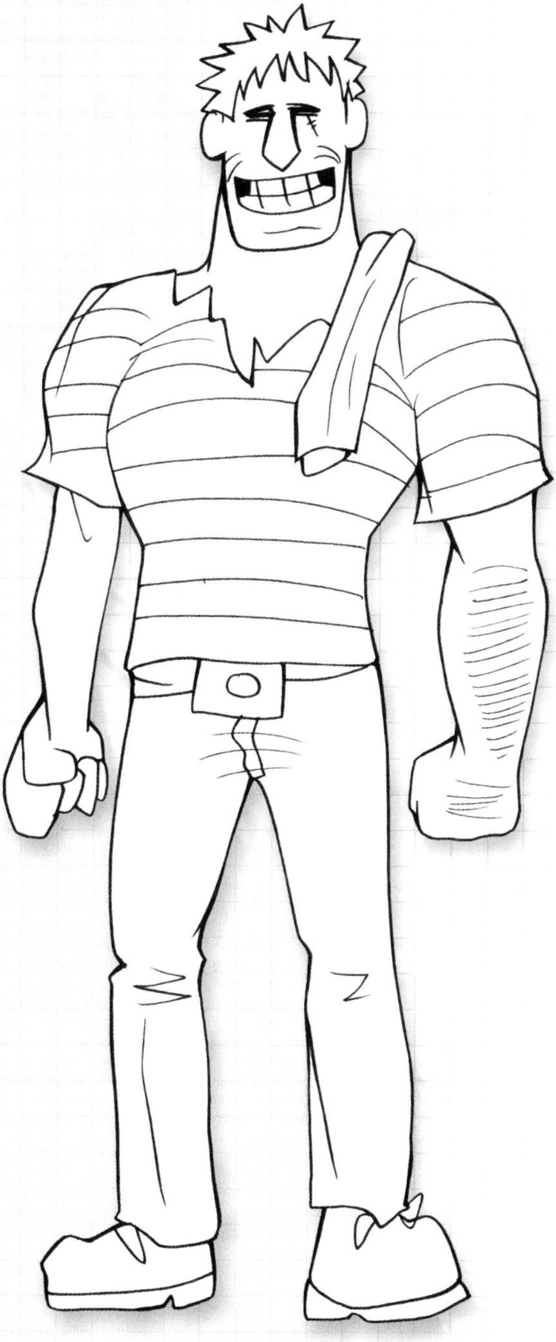

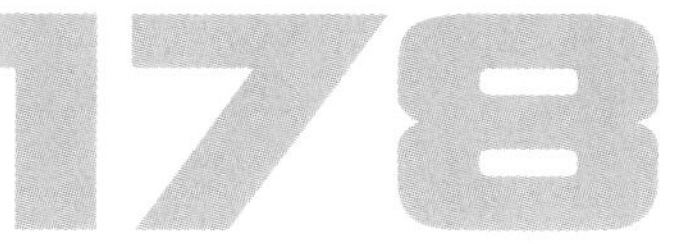

pirate villains

search criteria

male. standing. smiling. deckhand. scar. stripes. goofy.

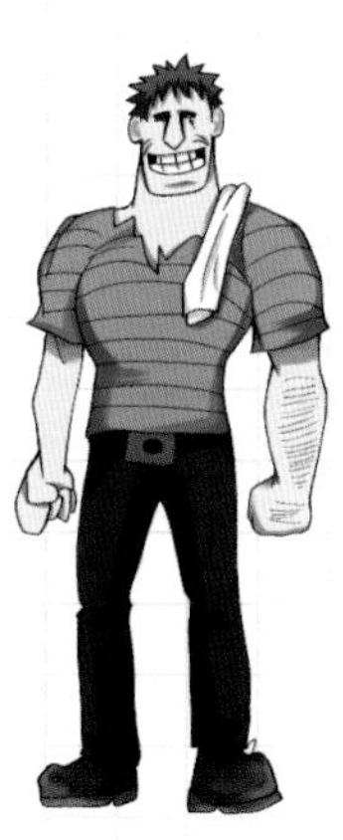

179

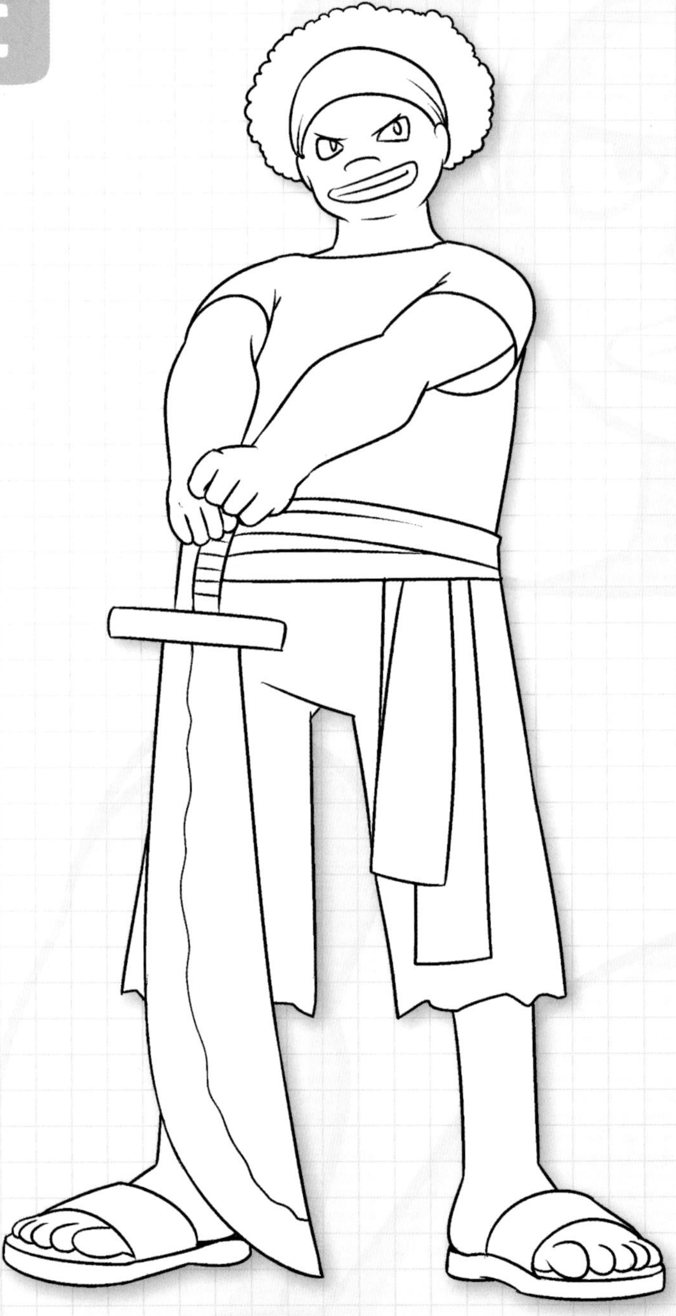

pirate villains

search criteria

male. standing. smiling. weapon. sword. deckhand.

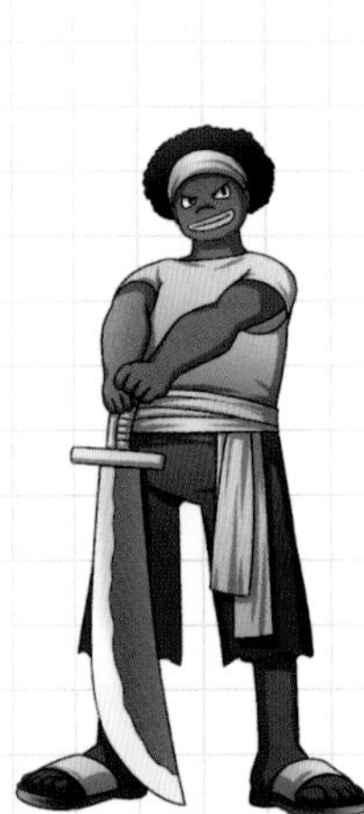

180

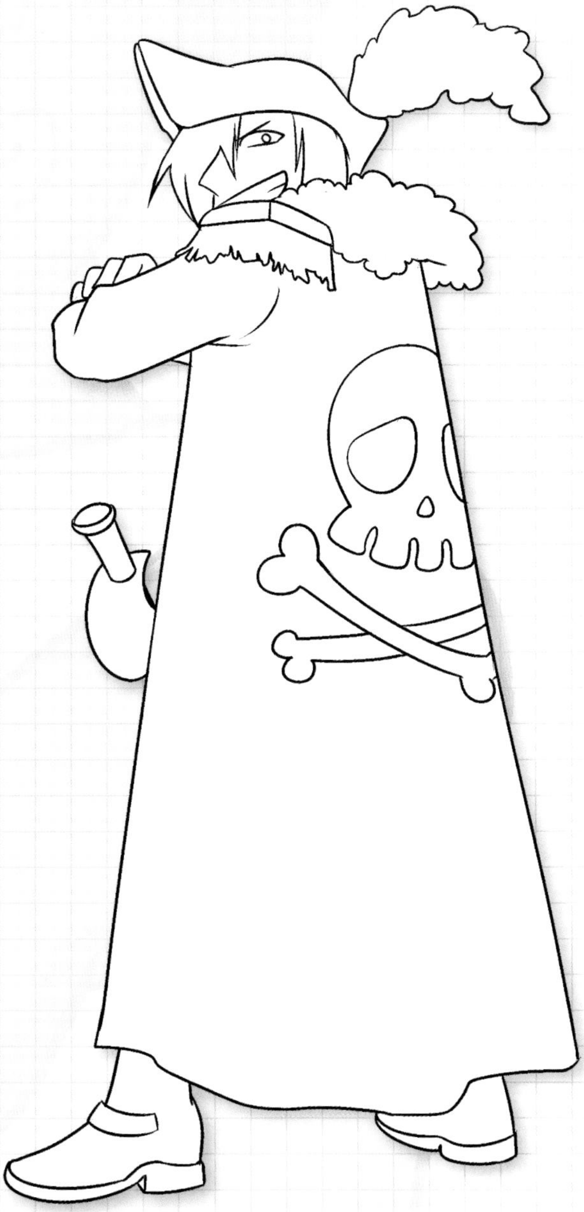

pirate villains

search criteria

male. standing. smiling. captain. hat. bones. skull. weapon. sword.

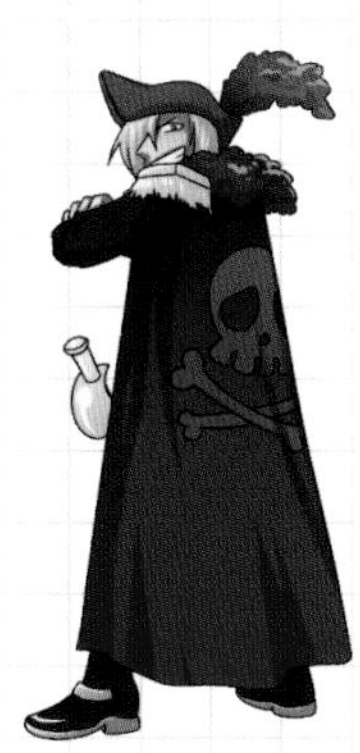

181

pirate villains

search criteria

male. standing. smiling. deckhand. stripes. weapon. sword. drink. eyepatch. beer.

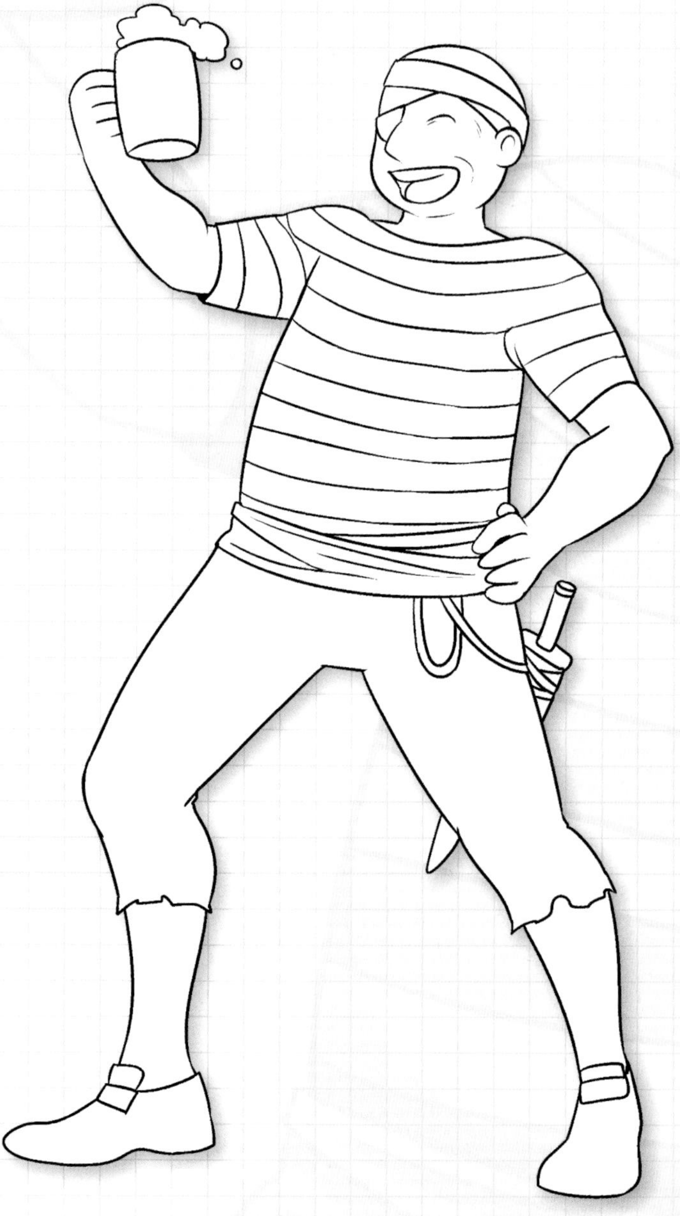

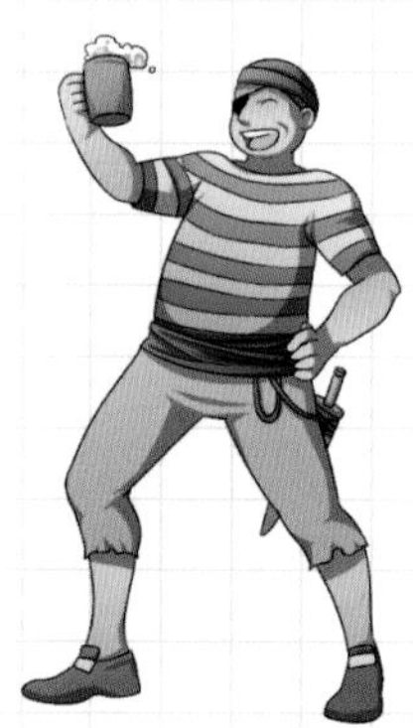

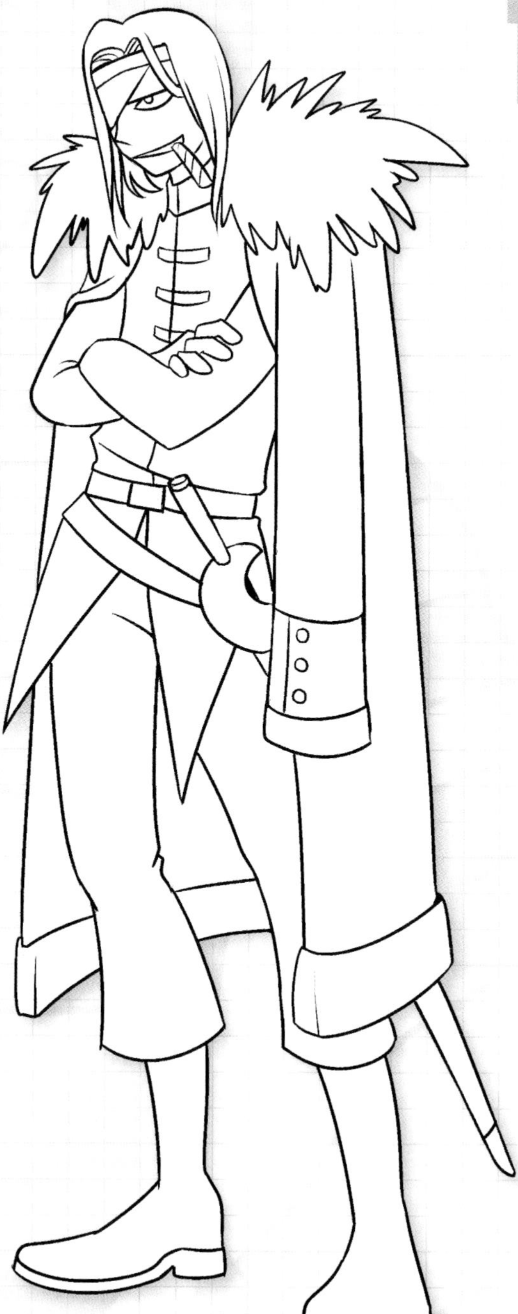

182

pirate villains

search criteria

male. standing. side. captain. smoking. cigar. weapon. sword.

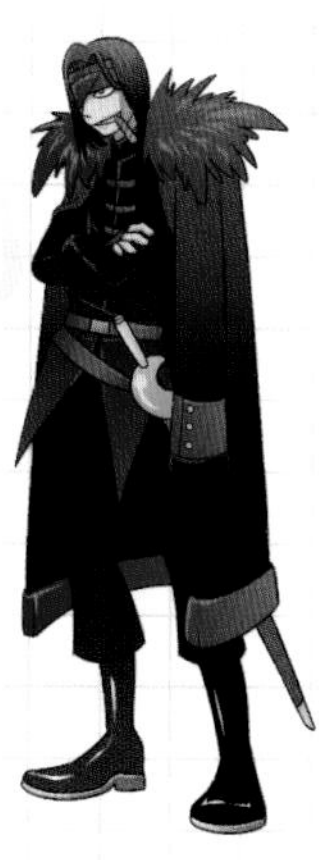

183

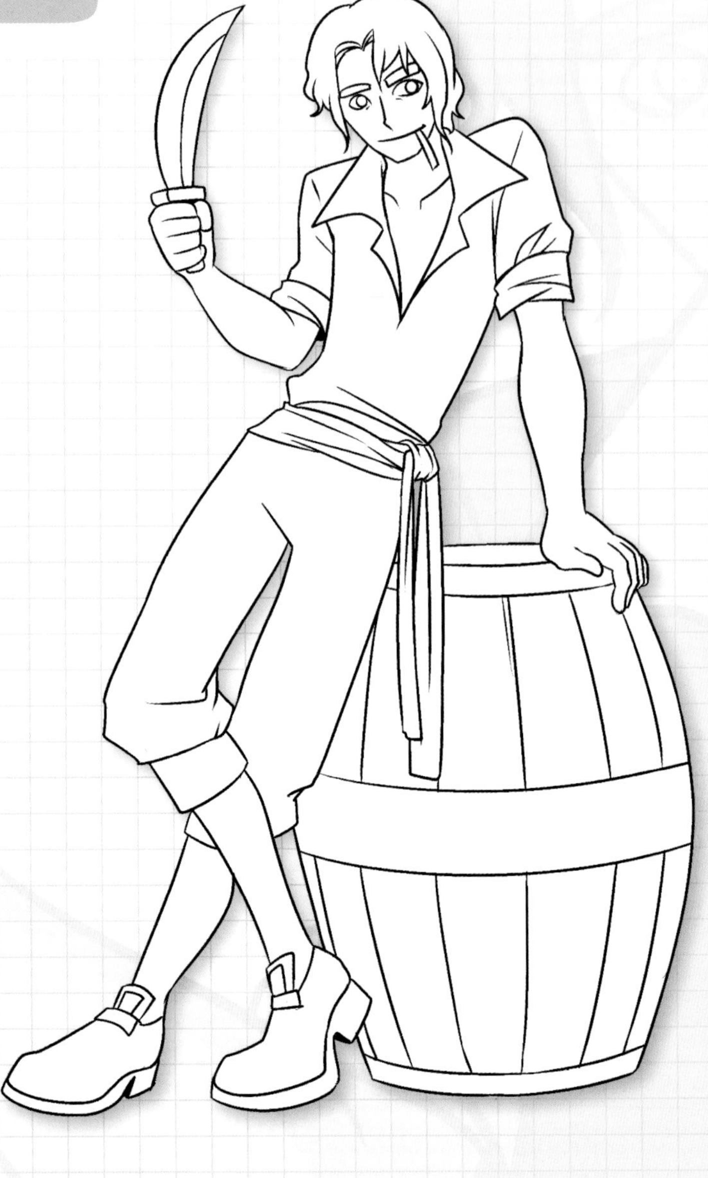

pirate villains

search criteria

male. leaning. smoking. cigarette. weapon. sword. barrel. lothario.

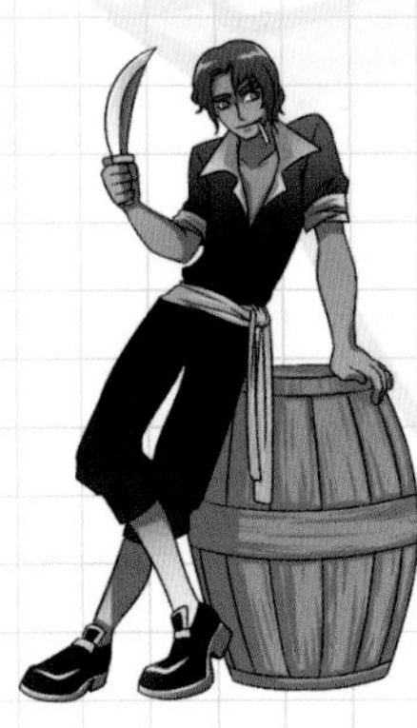

186

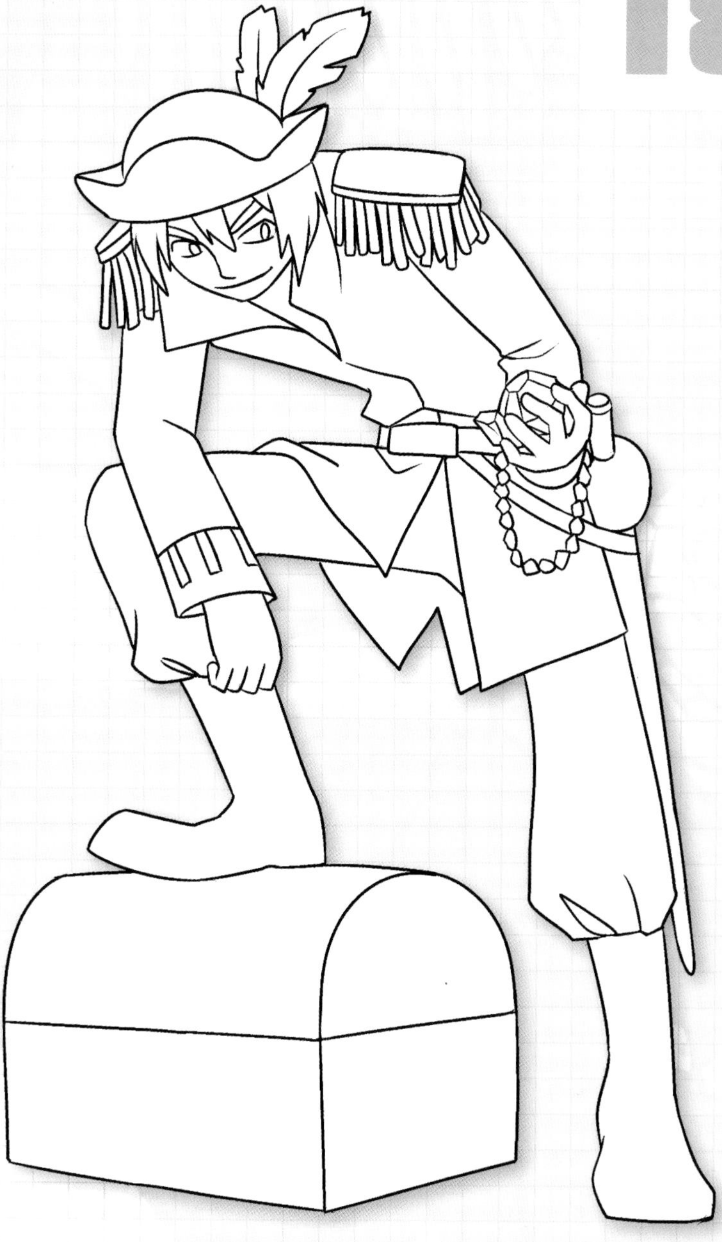

pirate villains

search criteria

male. leaning. captain. hat. treasure. chest. weapon. sword.

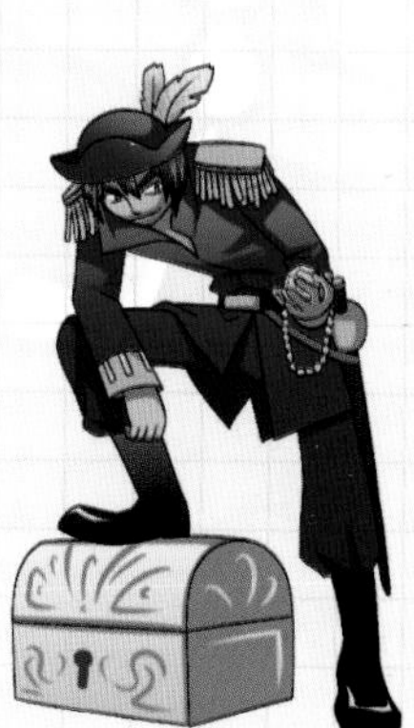

187

pirate villains

search criteria

male. standing. muscle. bones. skull. tattoo. weapon. sword.

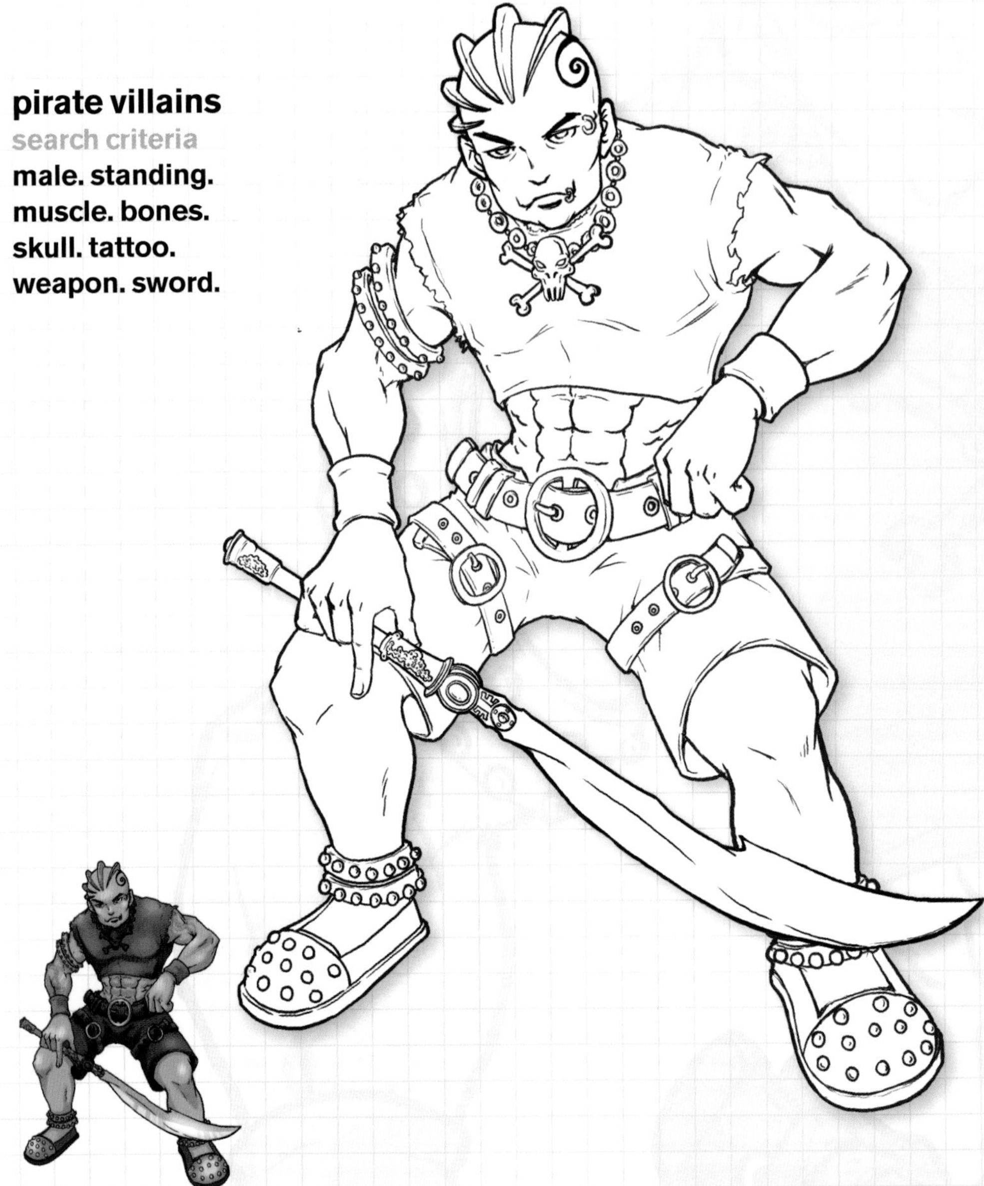

188

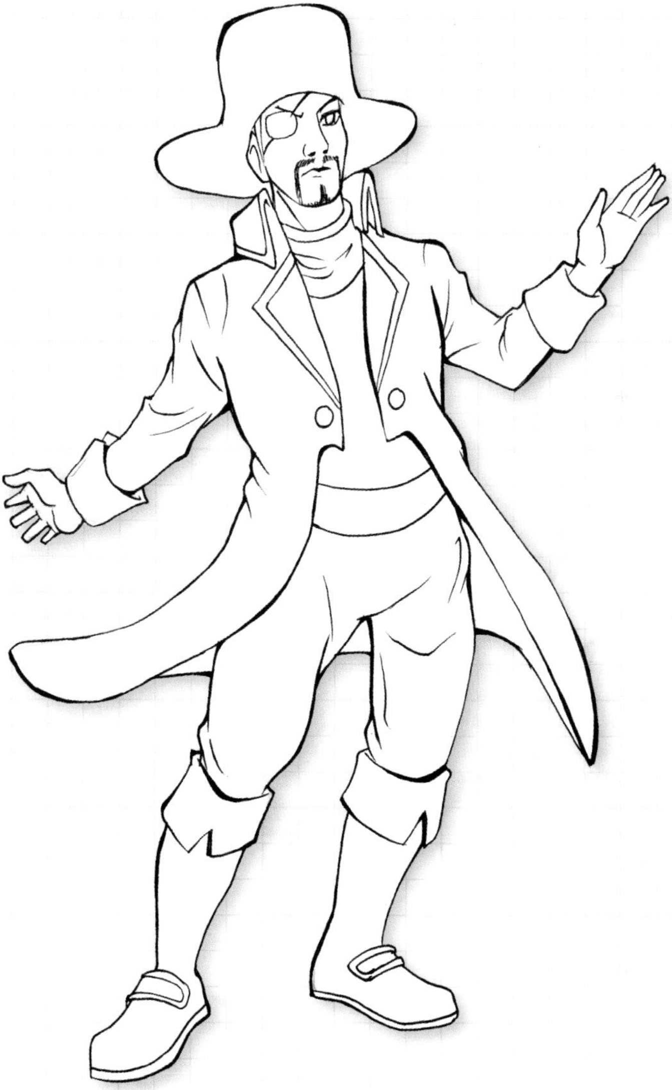

pirate villains

search criteria

male. standing. hat. eyepatch. captain.

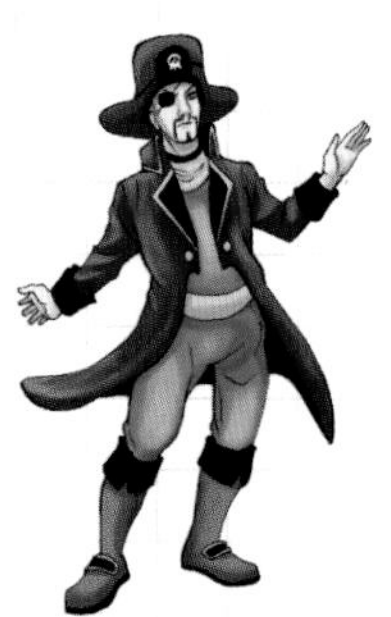

189

pirate villains

search criteria

male. standing.
headband. eyepatch.
weapon. sword.

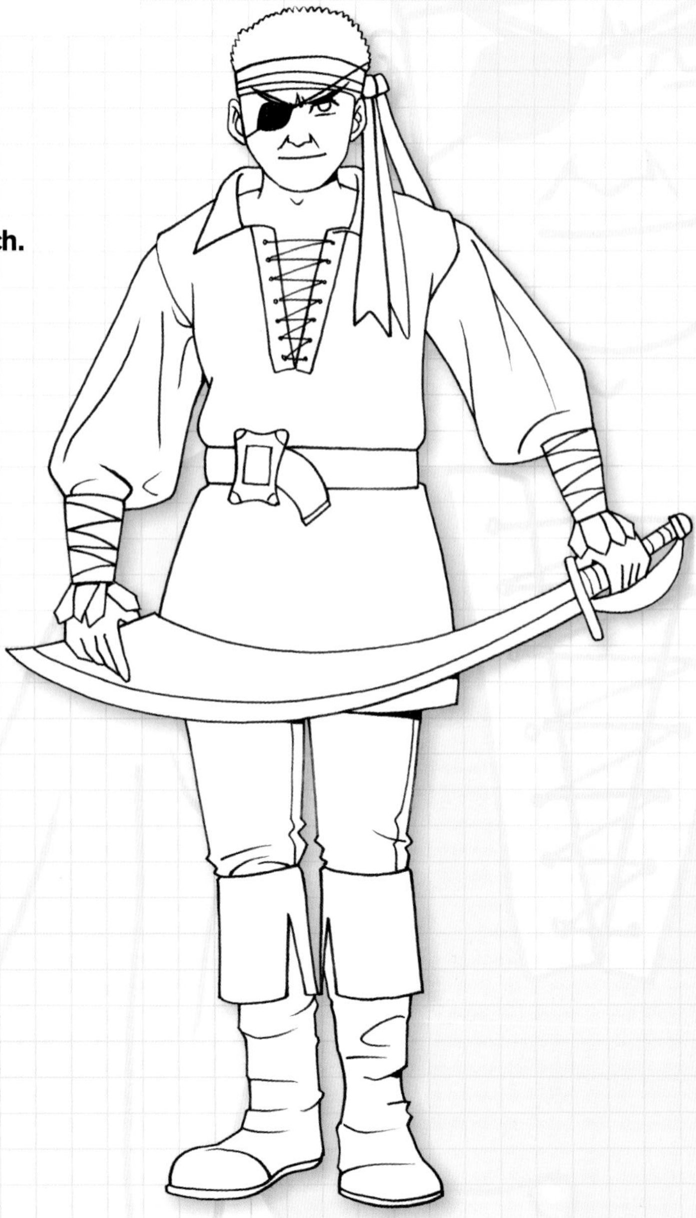

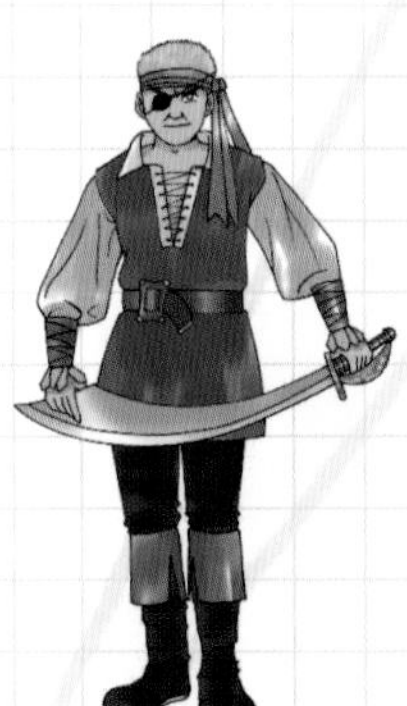

190

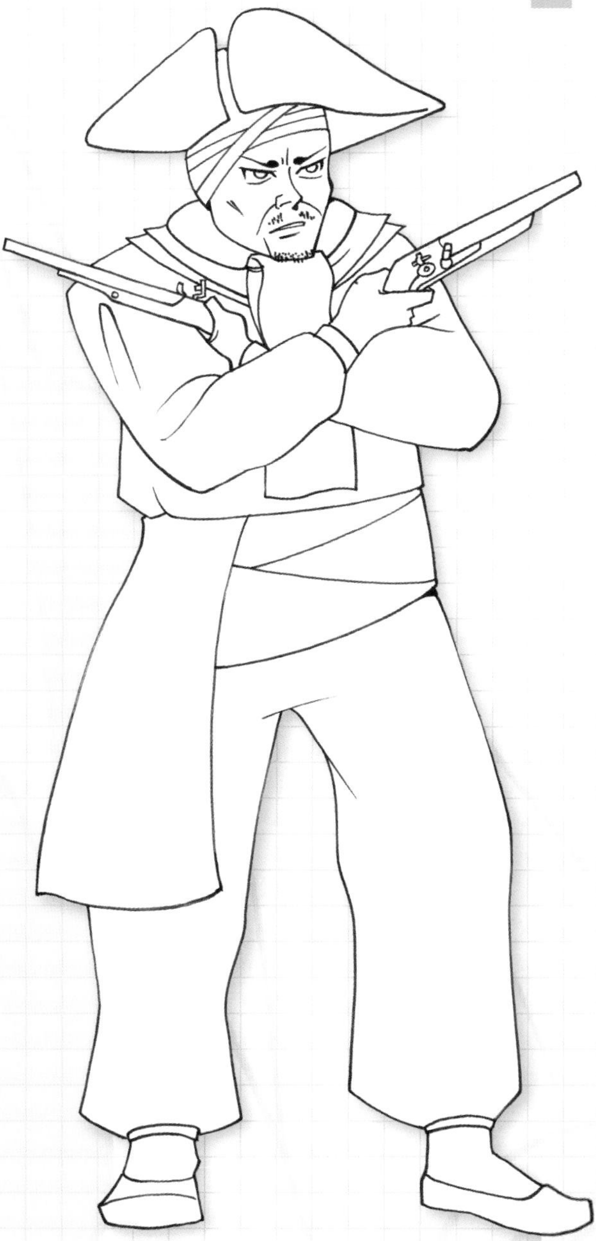

pirate villains

search criteria

male. standing. hat. weapons. guns. bandages. scarf.

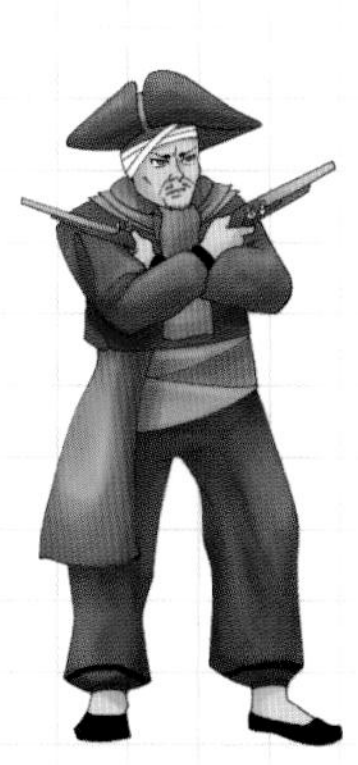

191

pirate villains

search criteria

male. standing. hat. skull. bones. hook. pegleg. staff.

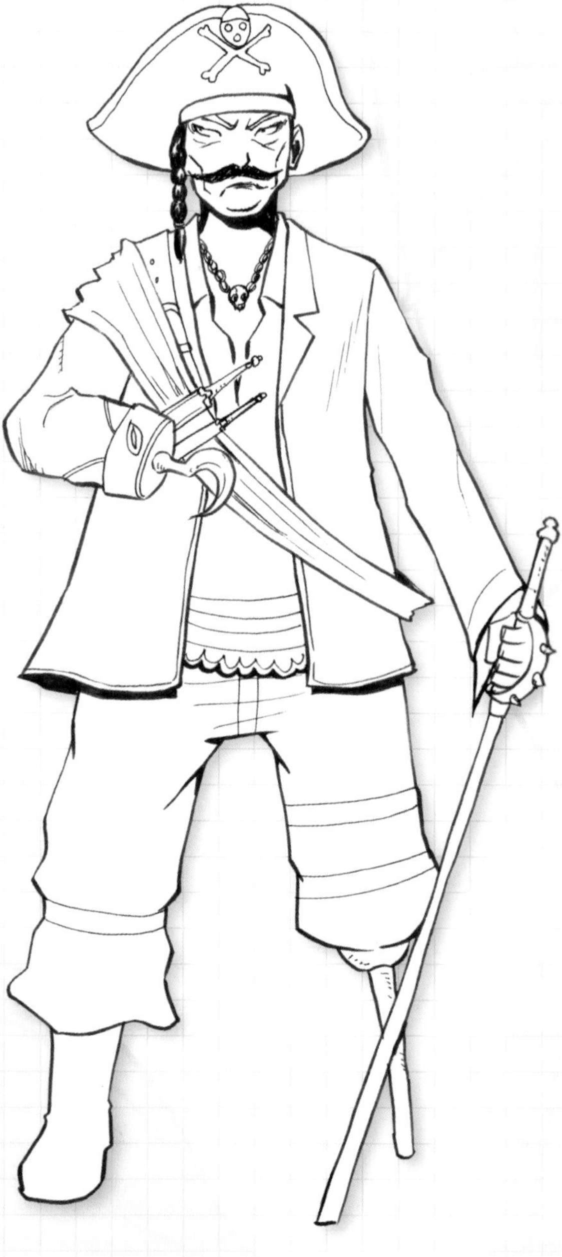

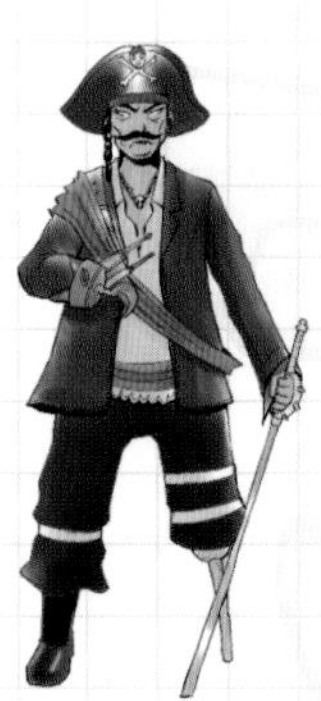

192

pirate villains

search criteria

male. jump. shout. flag. boy. skull. bones.

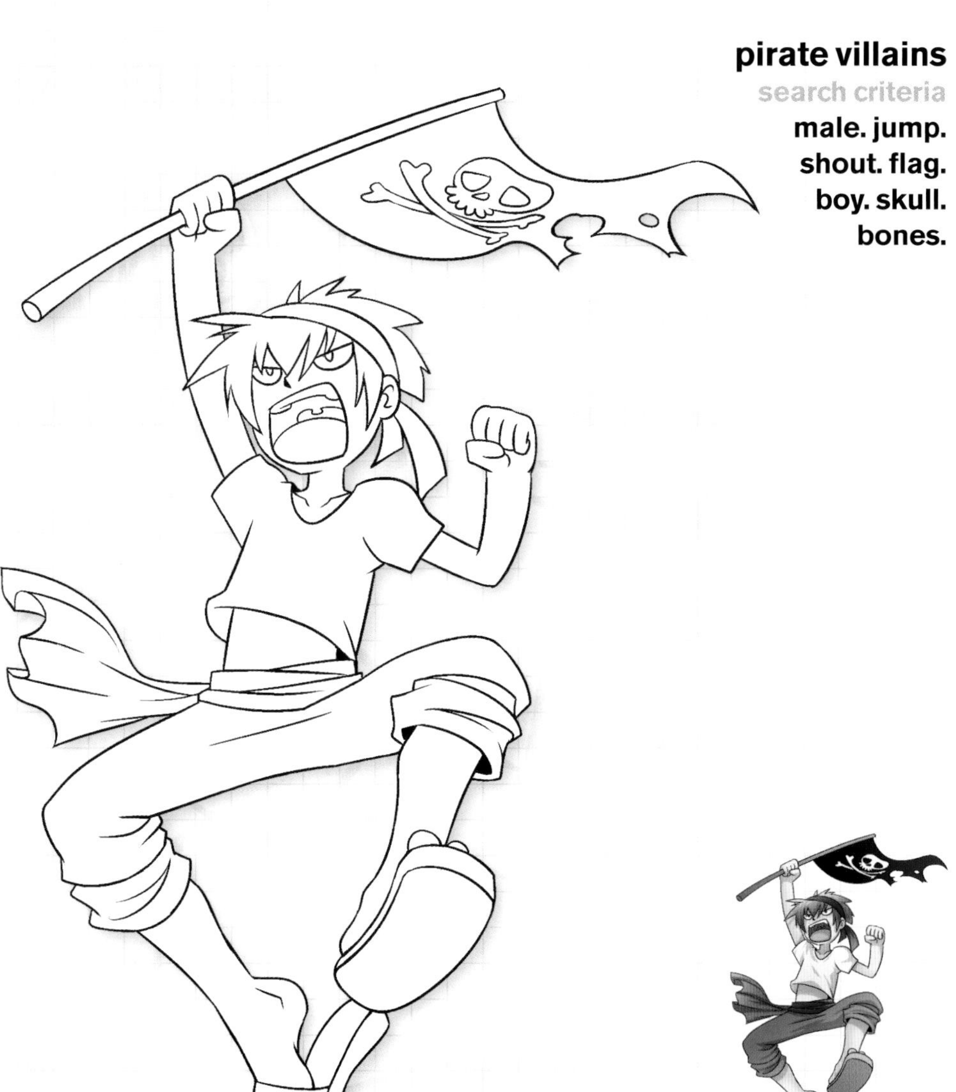

193

pirate villains

search criteria

male. sitting. side. hat. skull. parrot. coins. captain.

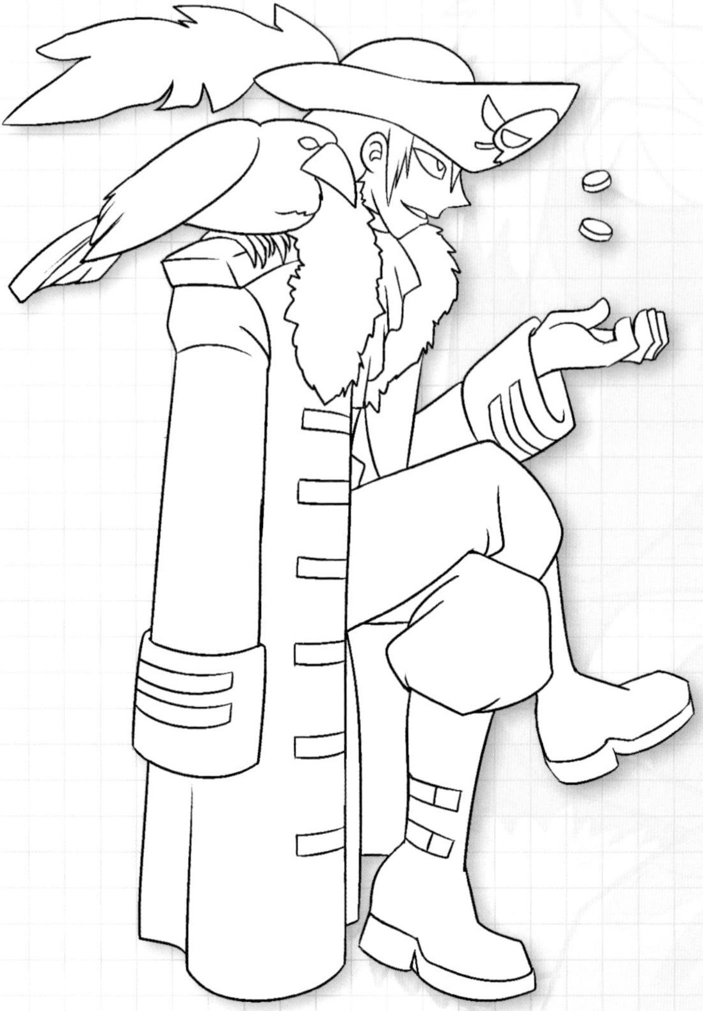

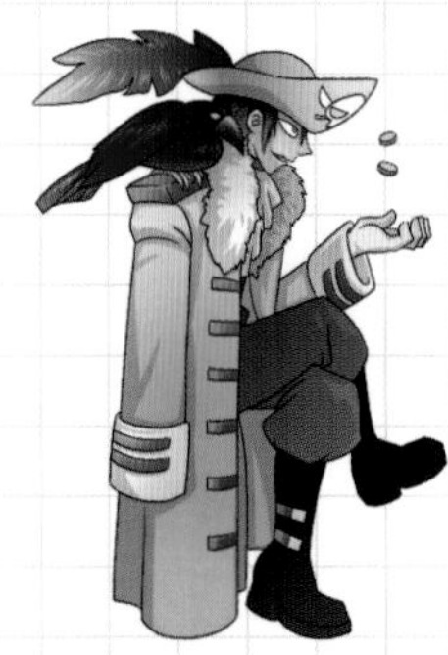

194

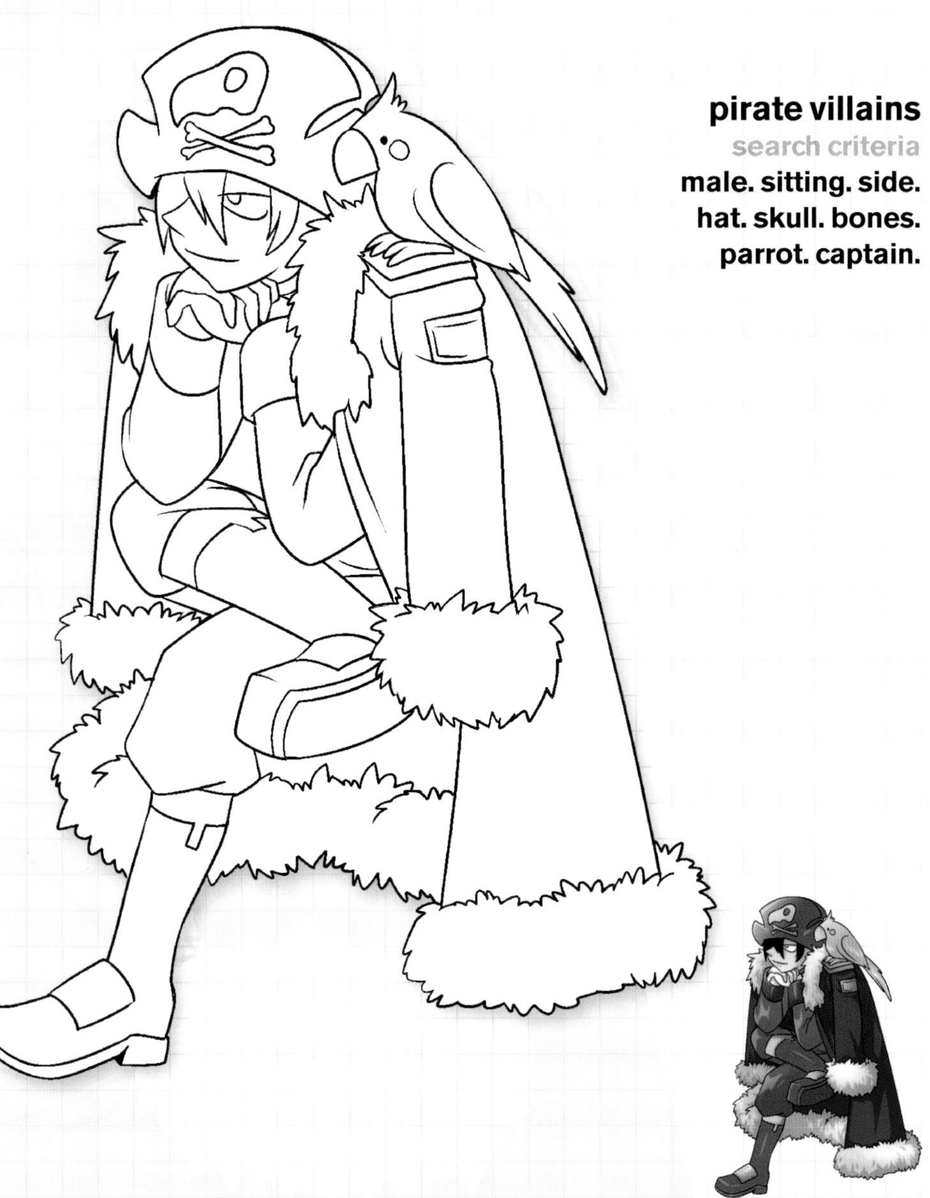

pirate villains

search criteria

male. sitting. side. hat. skull. bones. parrot. captain.

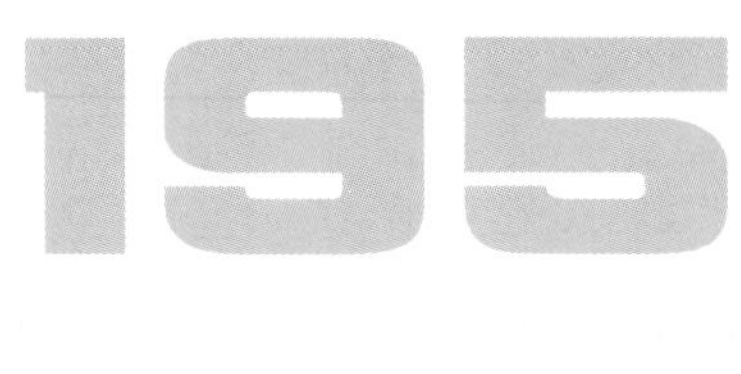

pirate villains

search criteria

male. standing. eyepatch. weapon. sword. deckhand.

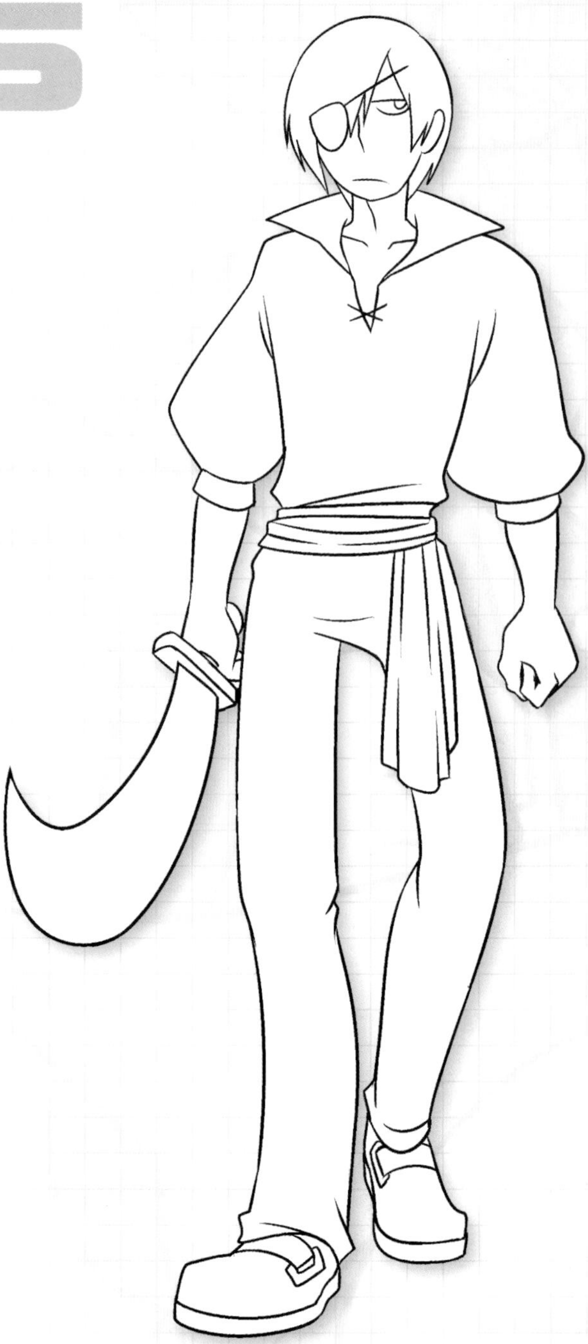

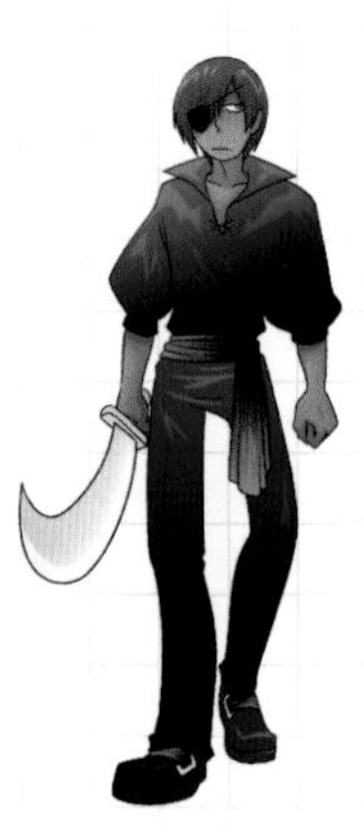

196

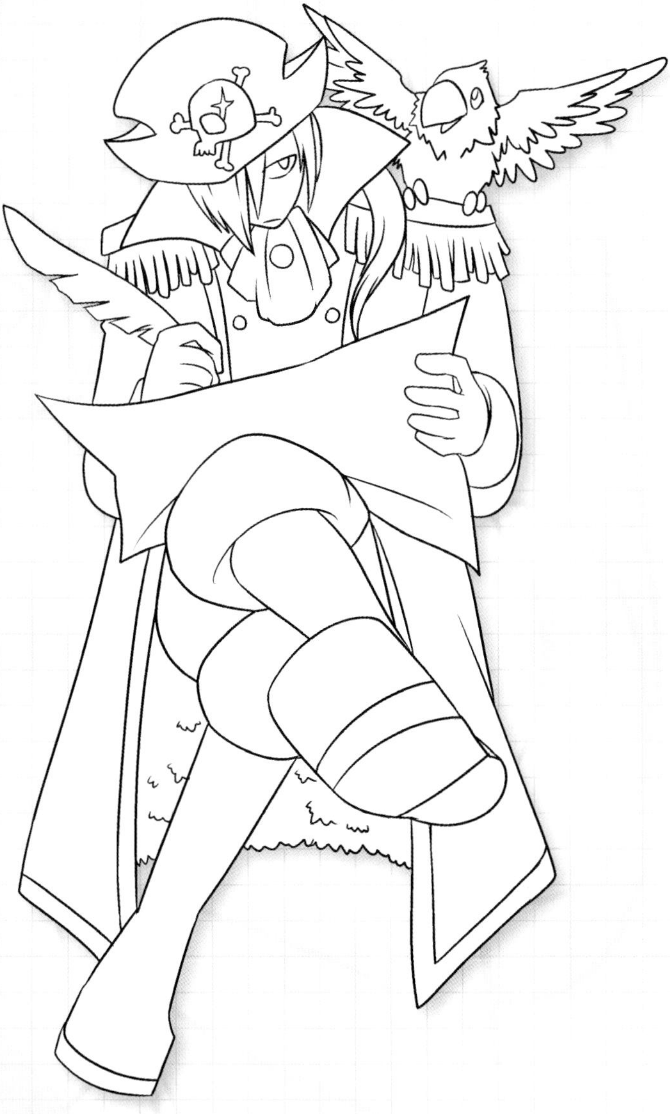

pirate villains

search criteria

male. sitting. captain. hat. quill. parrot. skull. bones. writing.

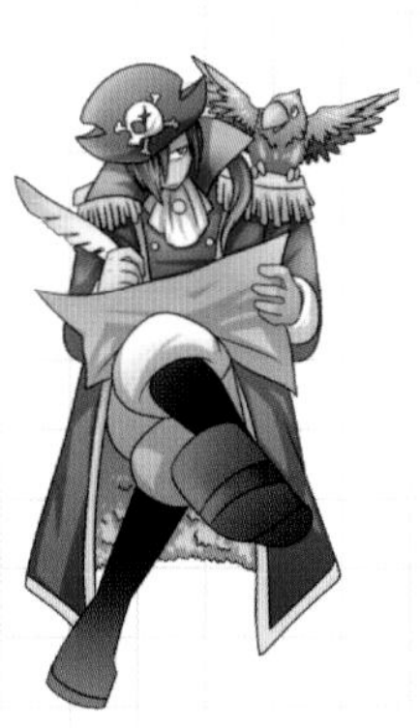

197

pirate heroes

search criteria

male. side. punch. attack. deckhand. ninja. angry.

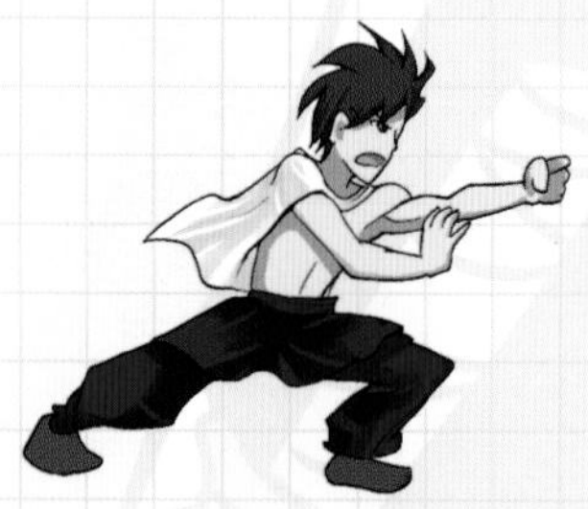

198

pirate heroes

search criteria

male. standing. side. shout. weapon. sword. deckhand.

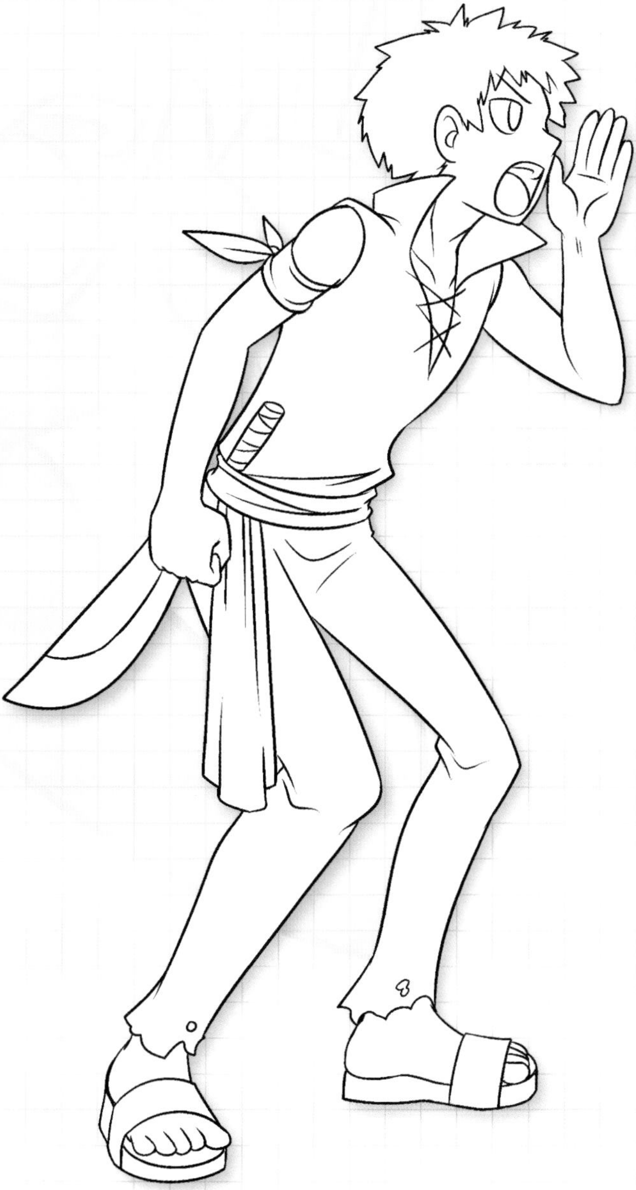

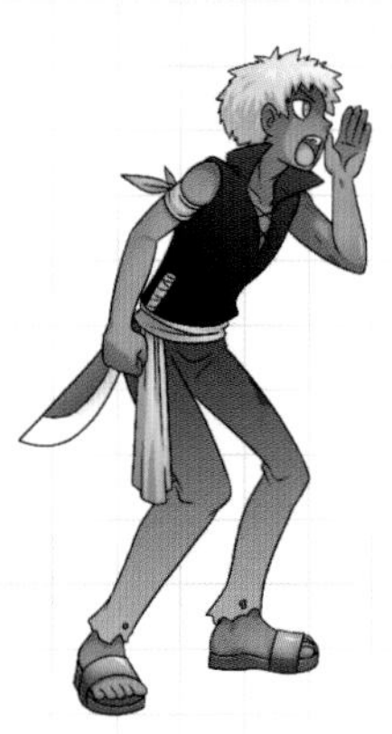

199

pirate heroes

search criteria

male. standing. struggle. shark. deckhand. lifeguard. necklace. rescue.

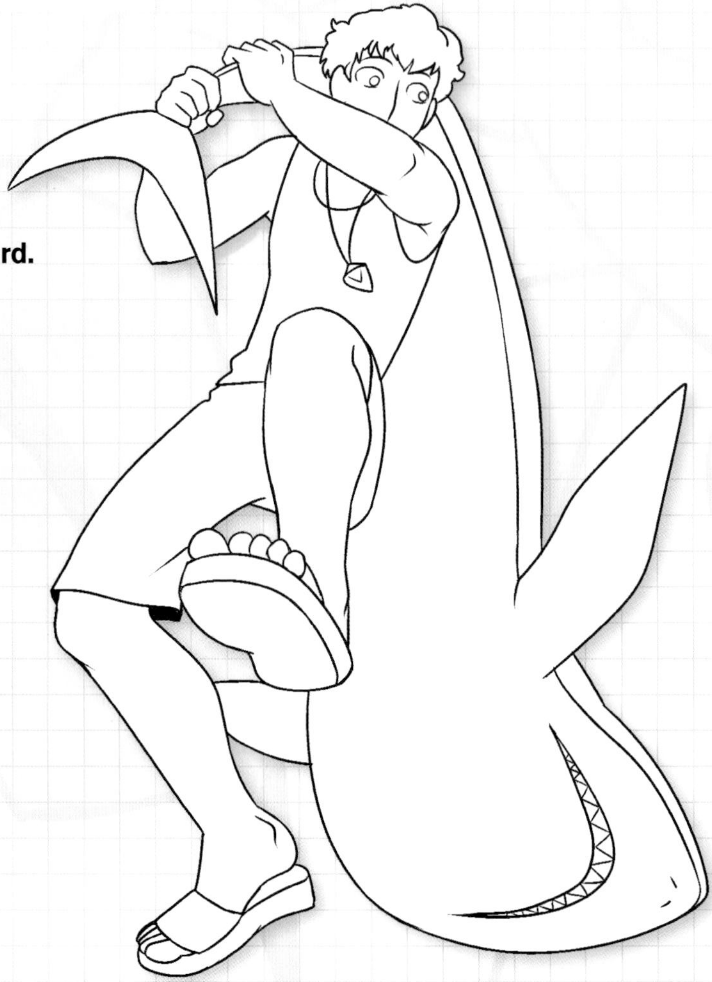

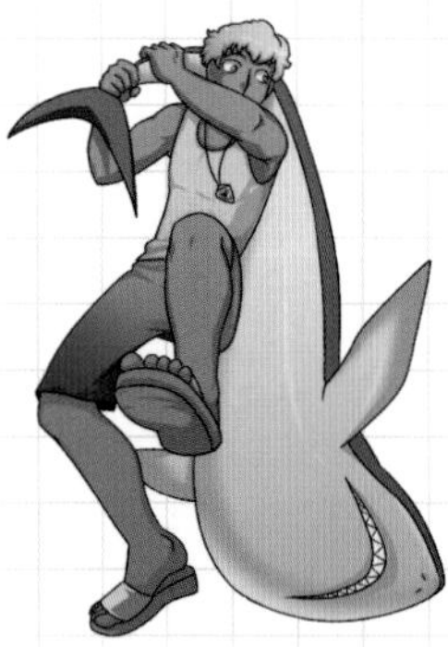

200

pirate heroes

search criteria

male. jump. attack. smiling. teeth. weapon. sword.

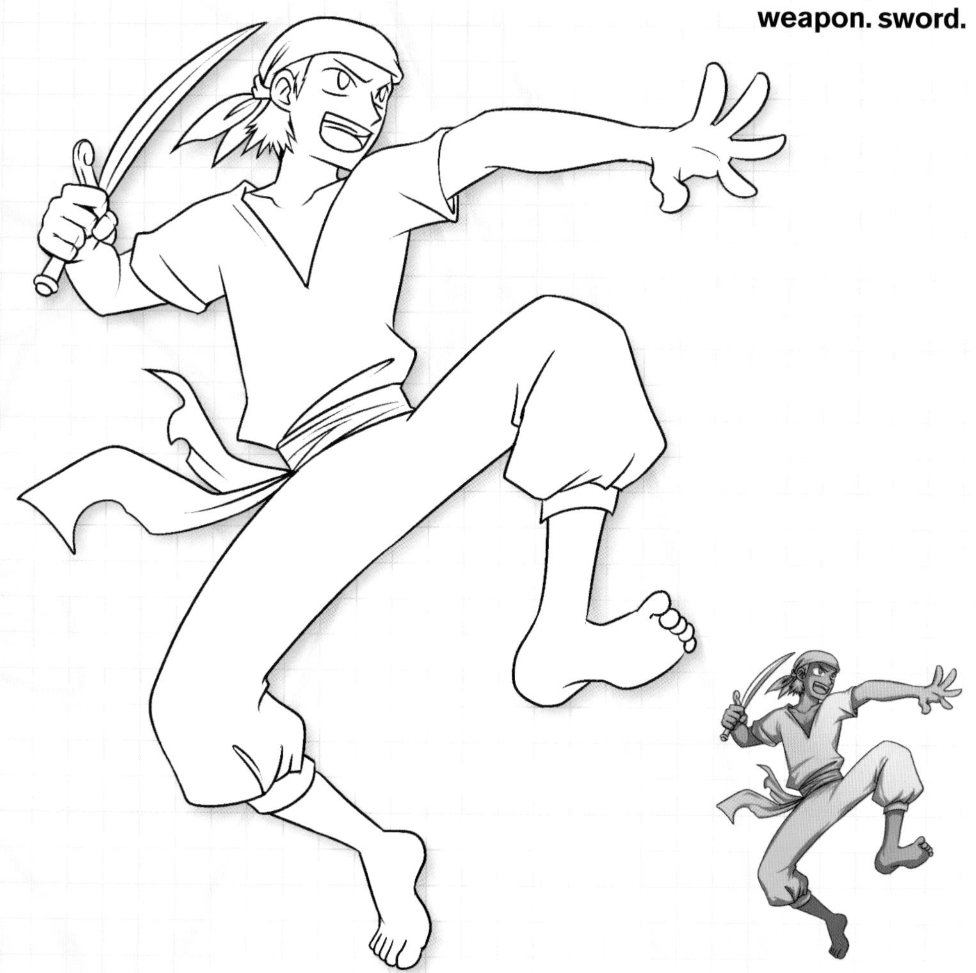

pirate heroes

search criteria

male. standing.
compass. weapon.
sword. captain.

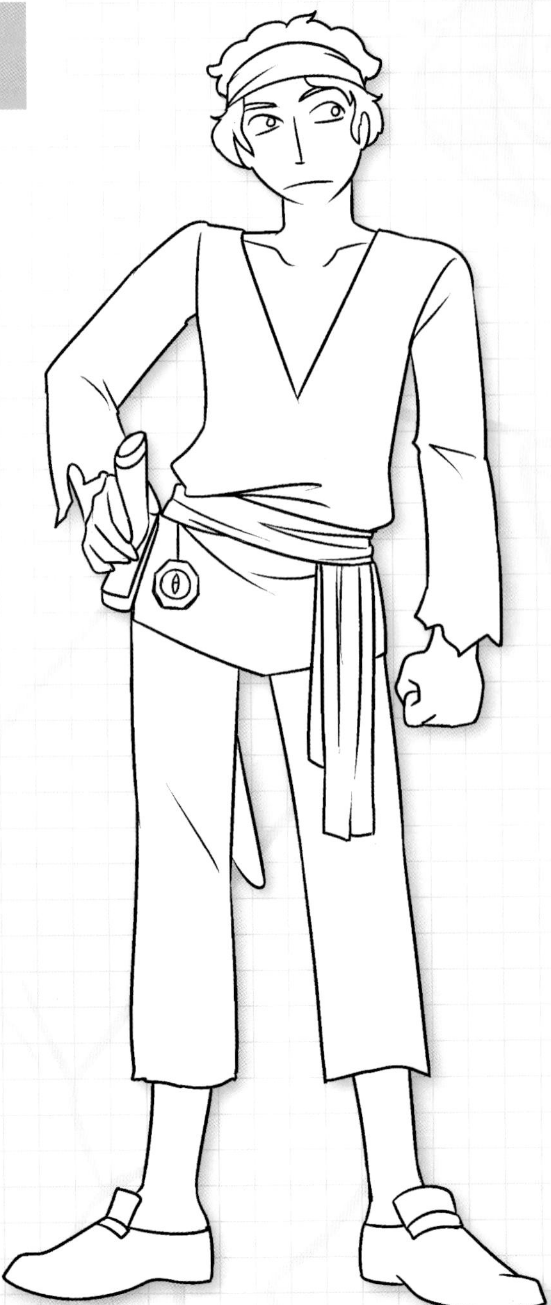

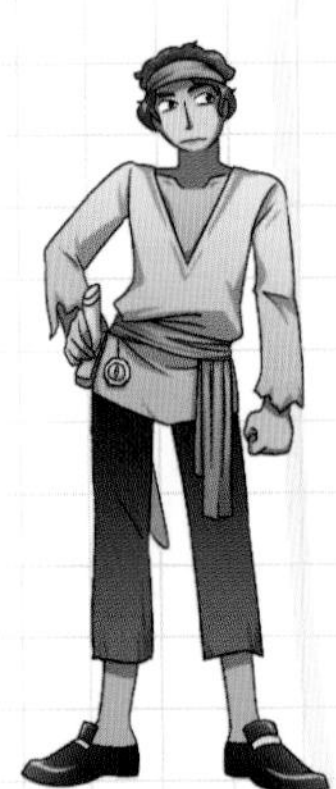

202

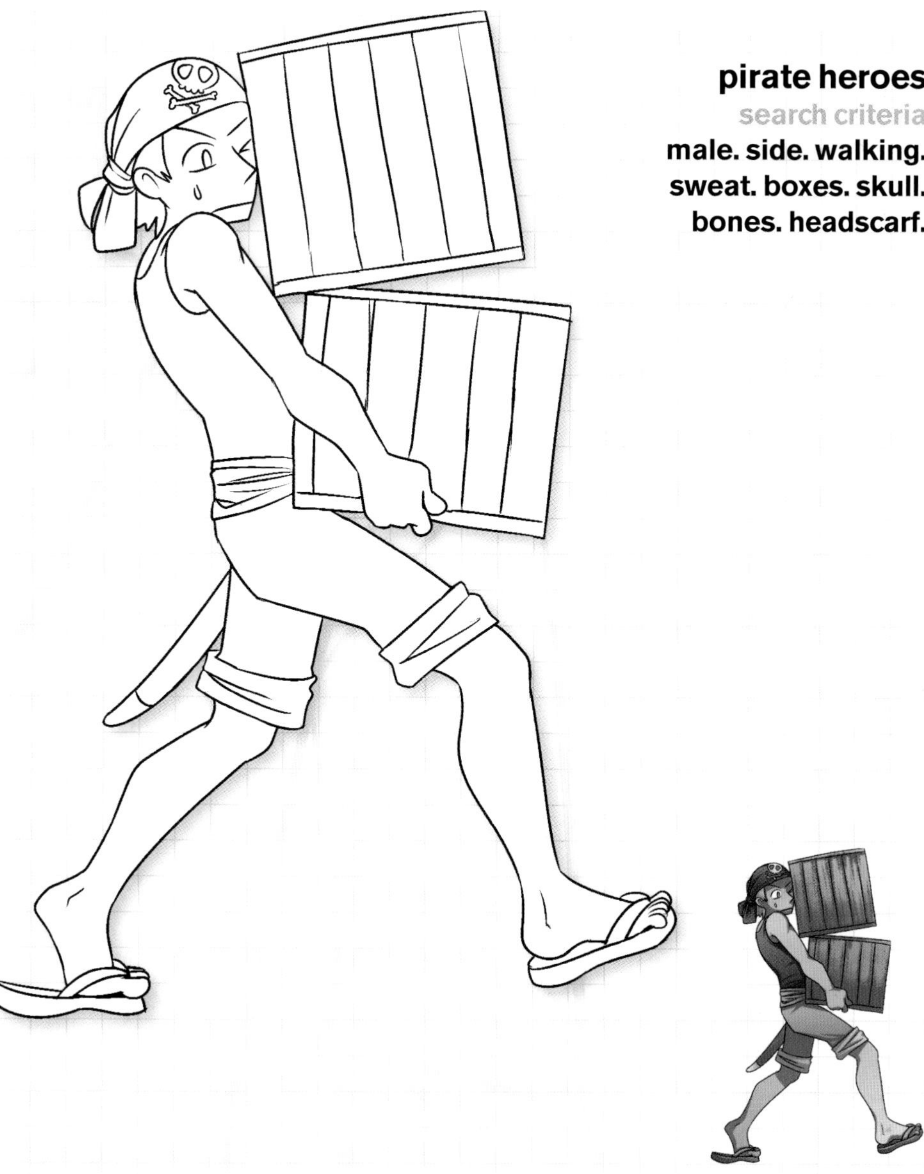

pirate heroes

search criteria

male. side. walking. sweat. boxes. skull. bones. headscarf.

203

pirate heroes
search criteria
male. smiling.
cleaning. mop.
bucket. headscarf.
deckhand.

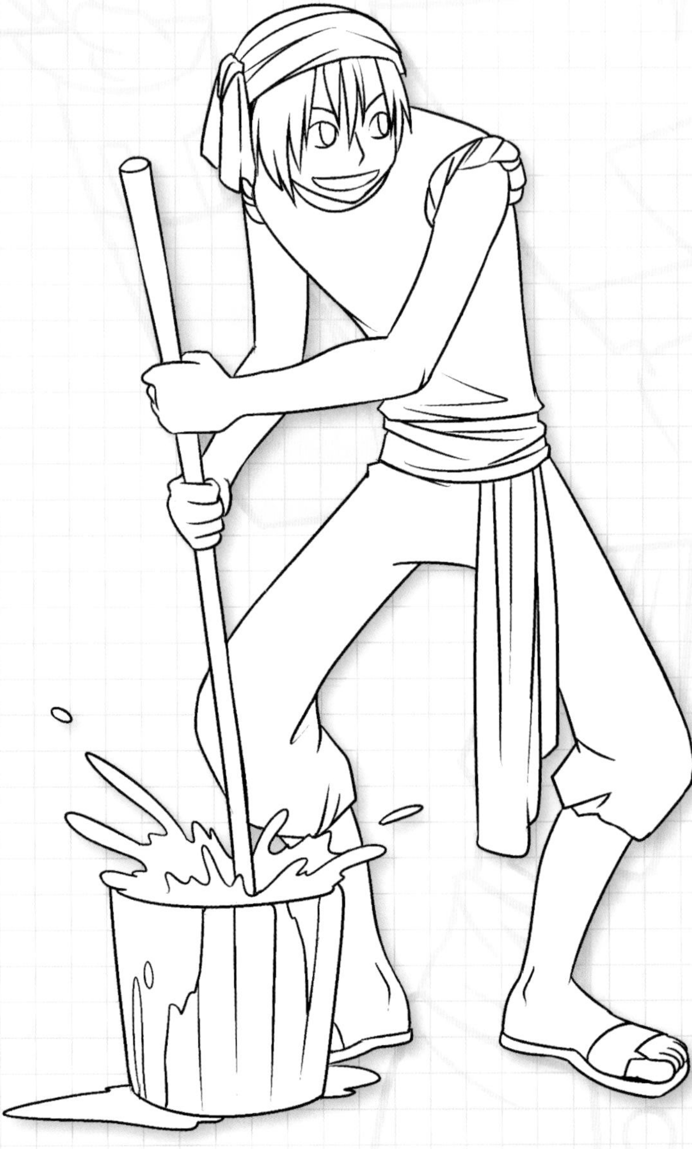

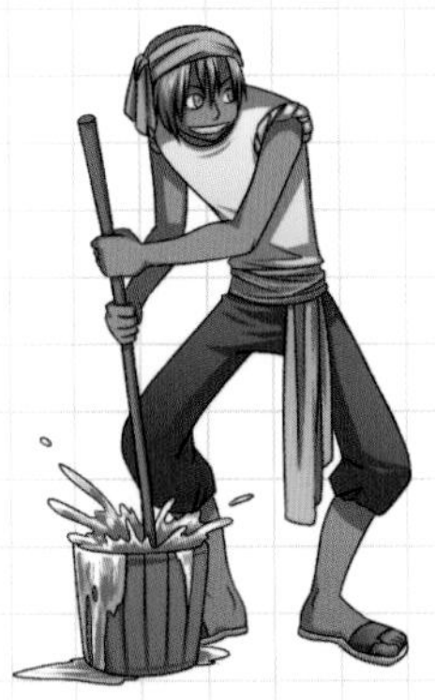

204

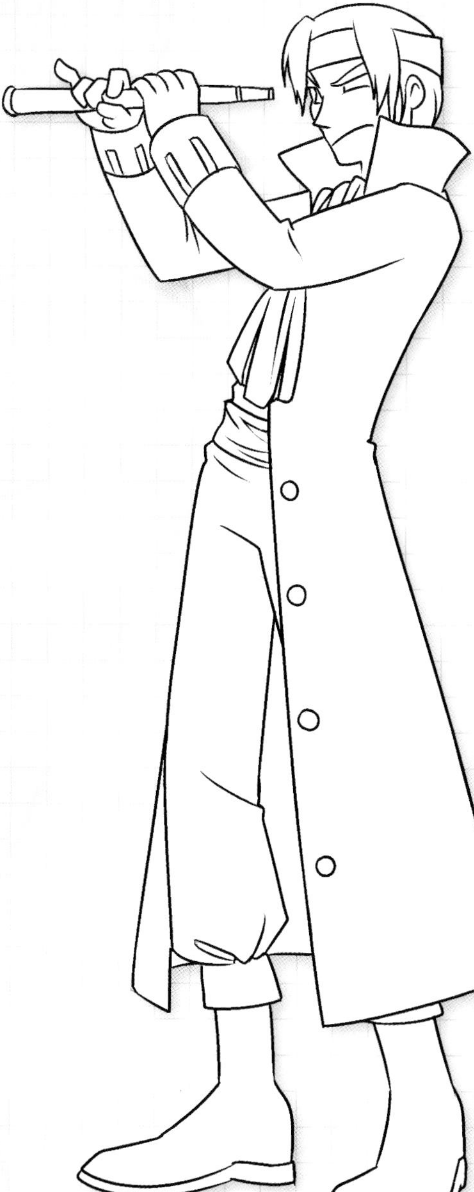

pirate heroes

search criteria

**male. standing.
side. looking.
captain. spyglass.**

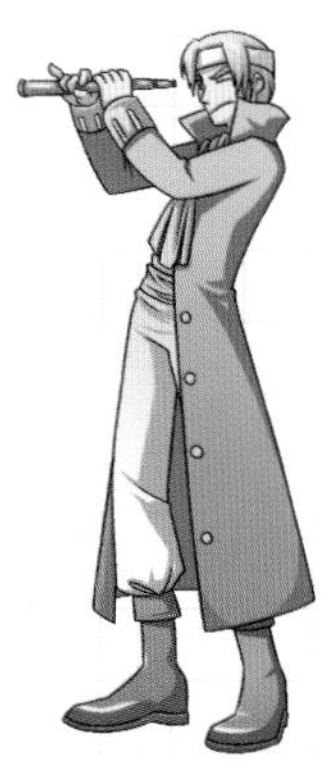

205

pirate heroes

search criteria

male. standing. side. smiling. weapon. sword. deckhand.

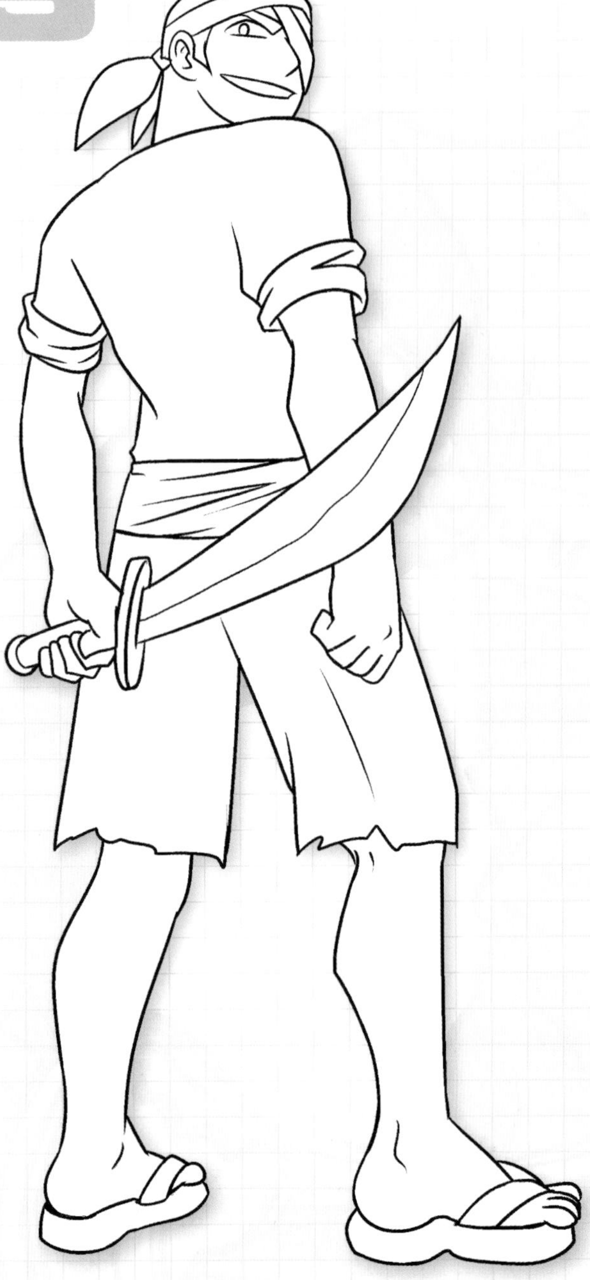

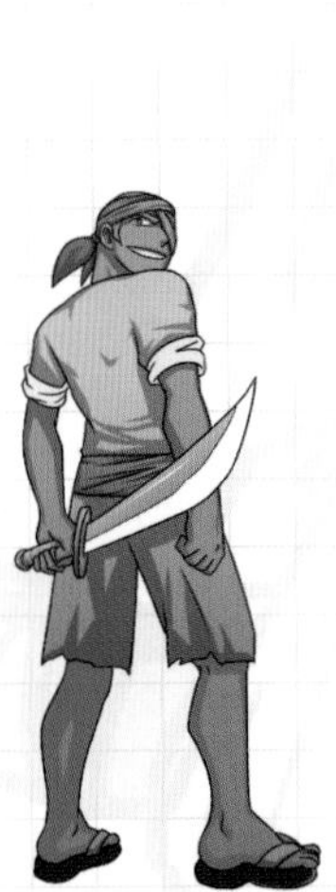

206

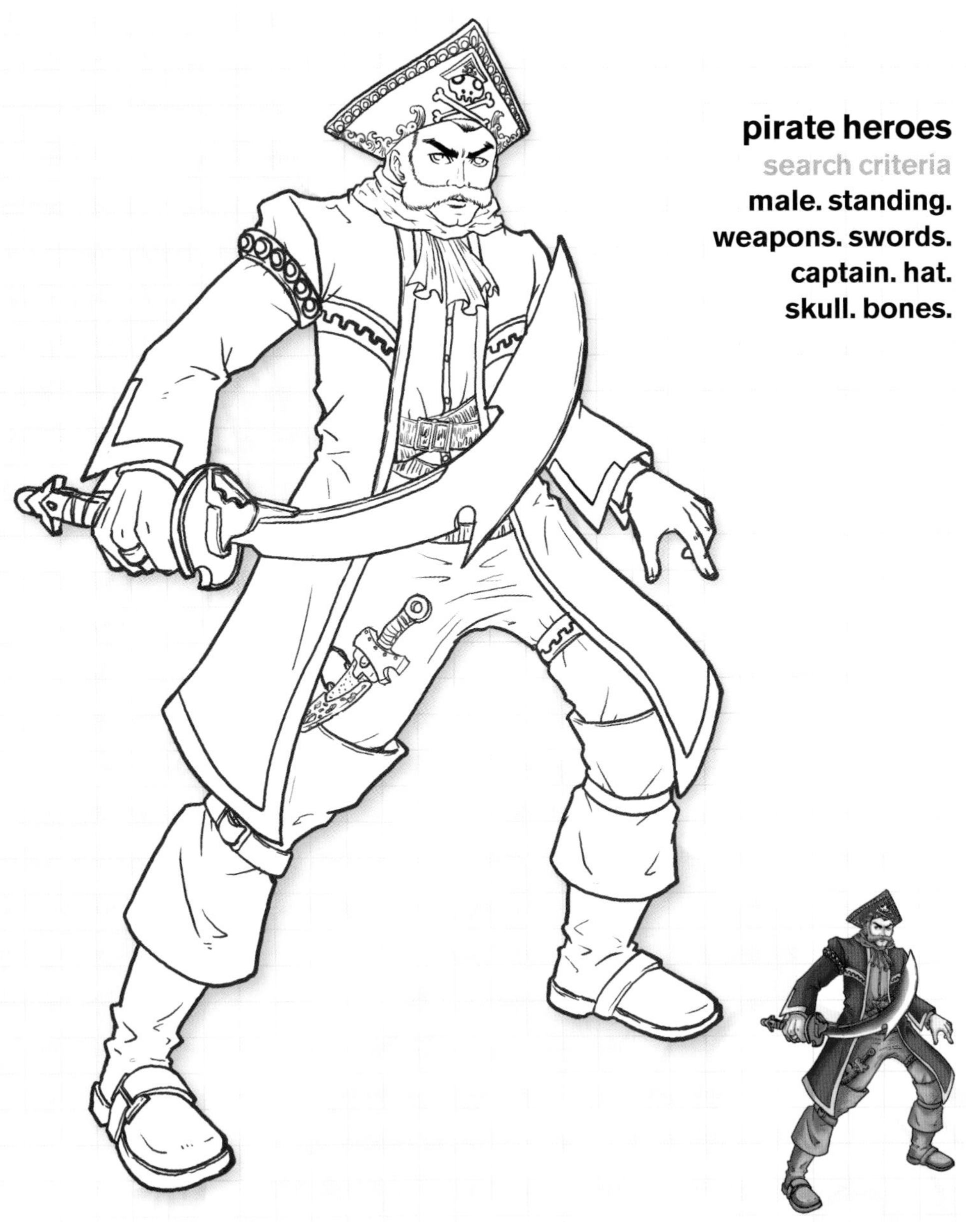

pirate heroes

search criteria

male. standing. weapons. swords. captain. hat. skull. bones.

207

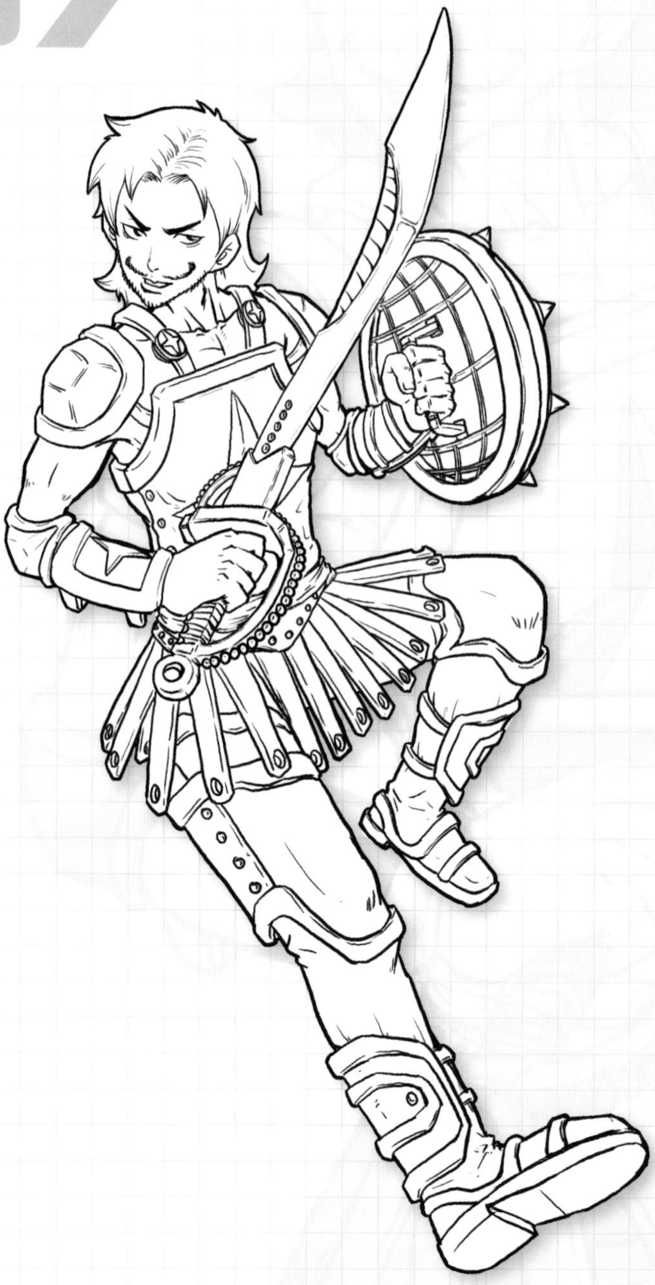

pirate heroes

search criteria

male. jump. armor. shield. weapon. sword. sinister.

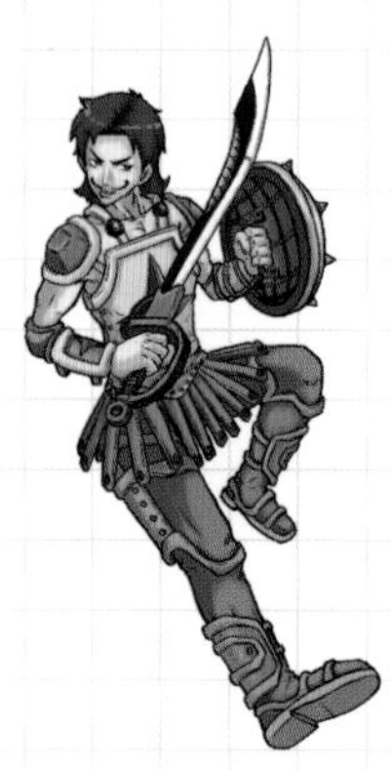

208

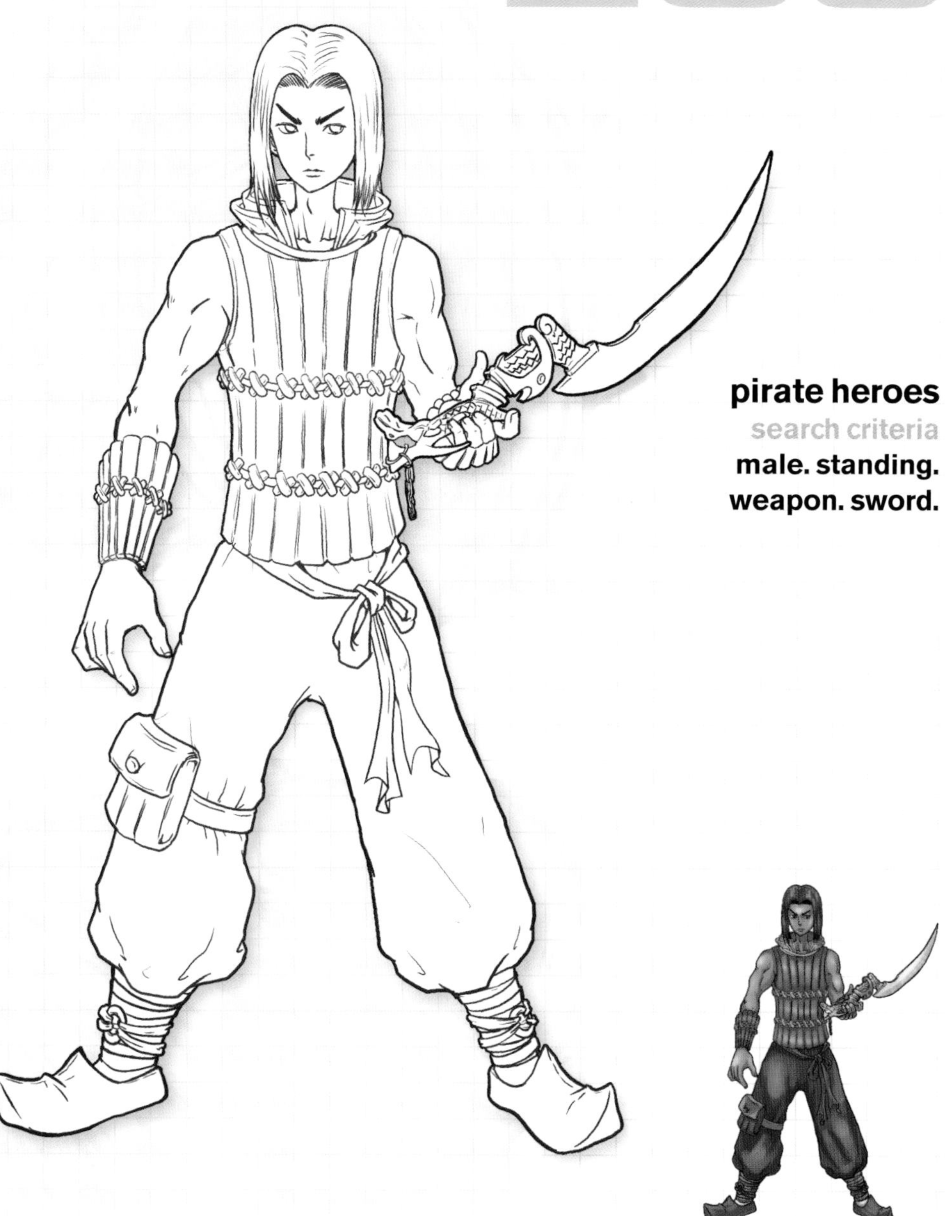

pirate heroes

search criteria

male. standing. weapon. sword.

209

pirate heroes

search criteria

female. standing. hat. deckhand.

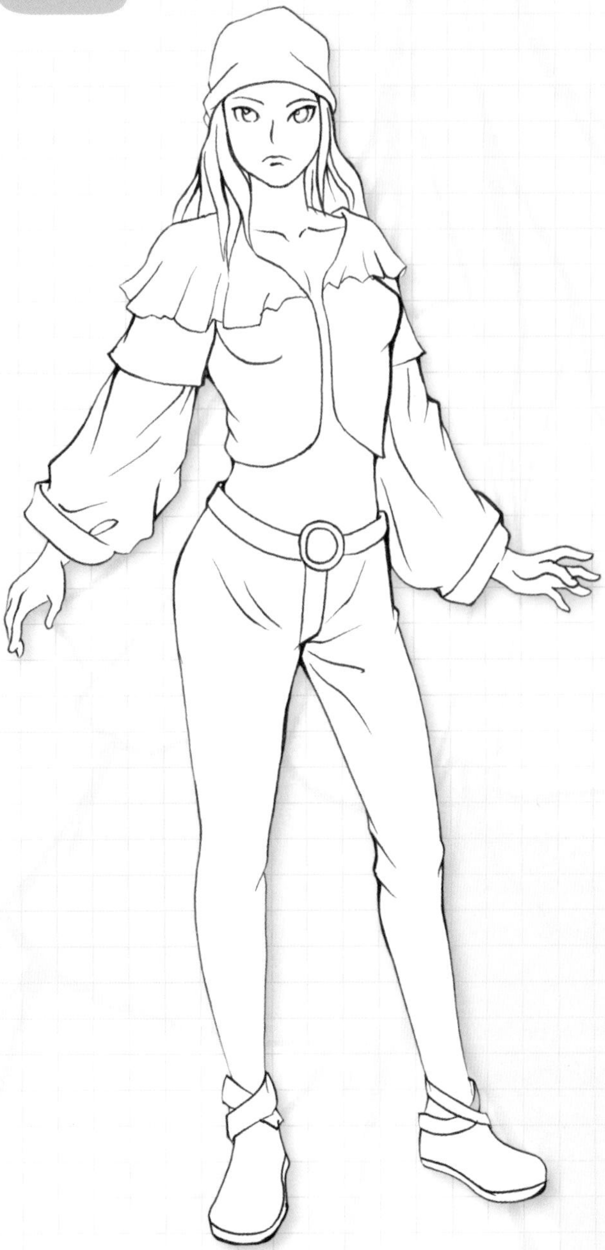

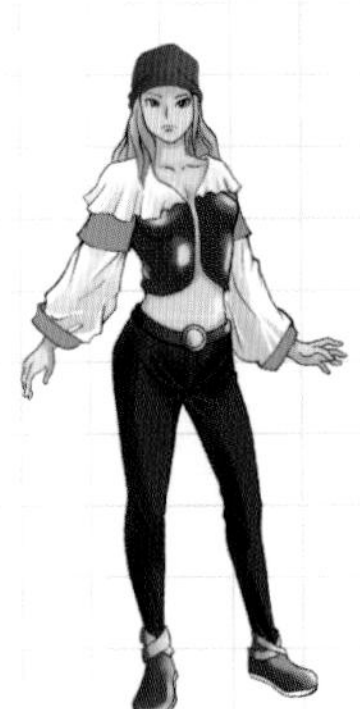

210

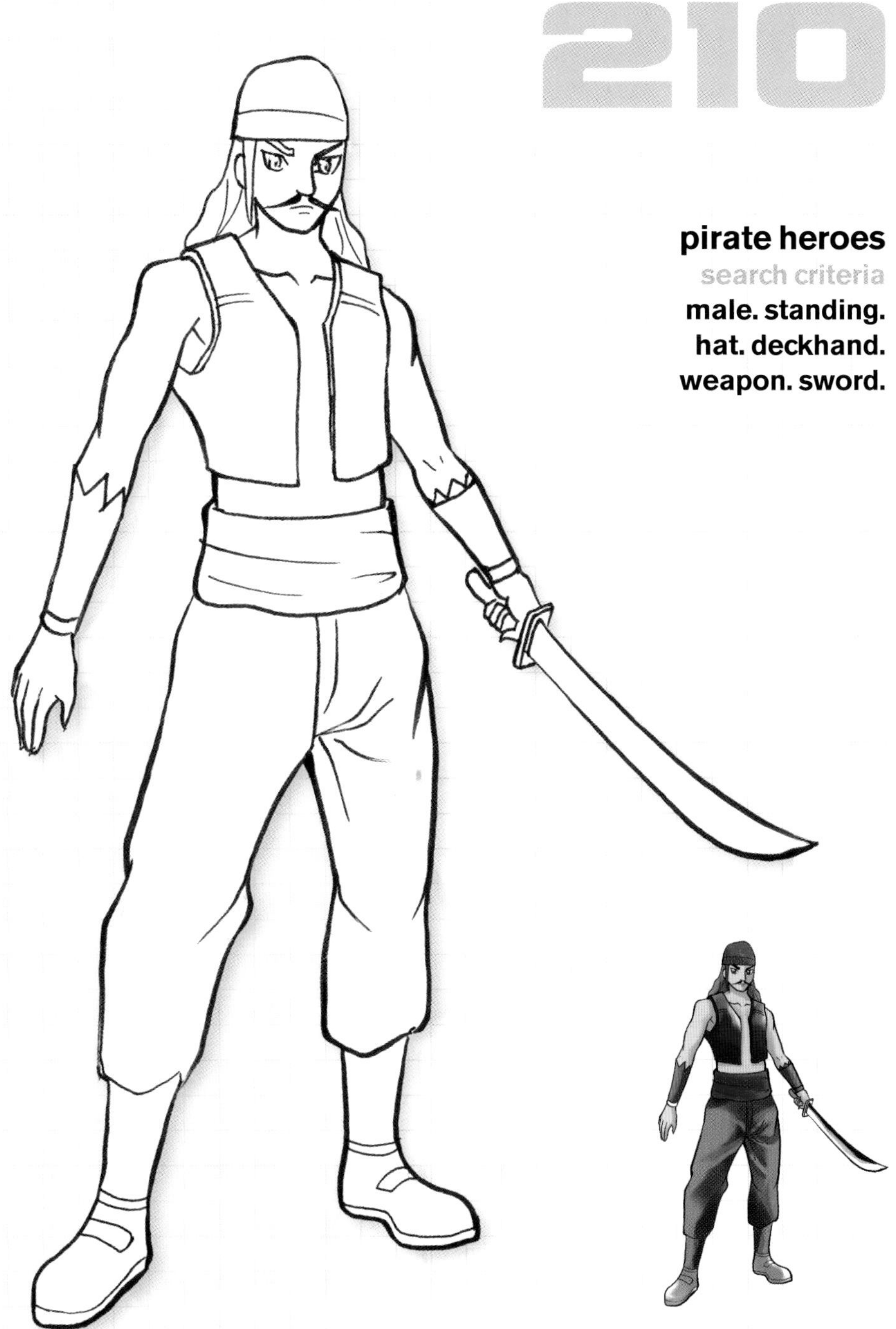

pirate heroes

search criteria

male. standing. hat. deckhand. weapon. sword.

211

pirate heroes

search criteria

male. standing. deckhand. old. weapon. sword.

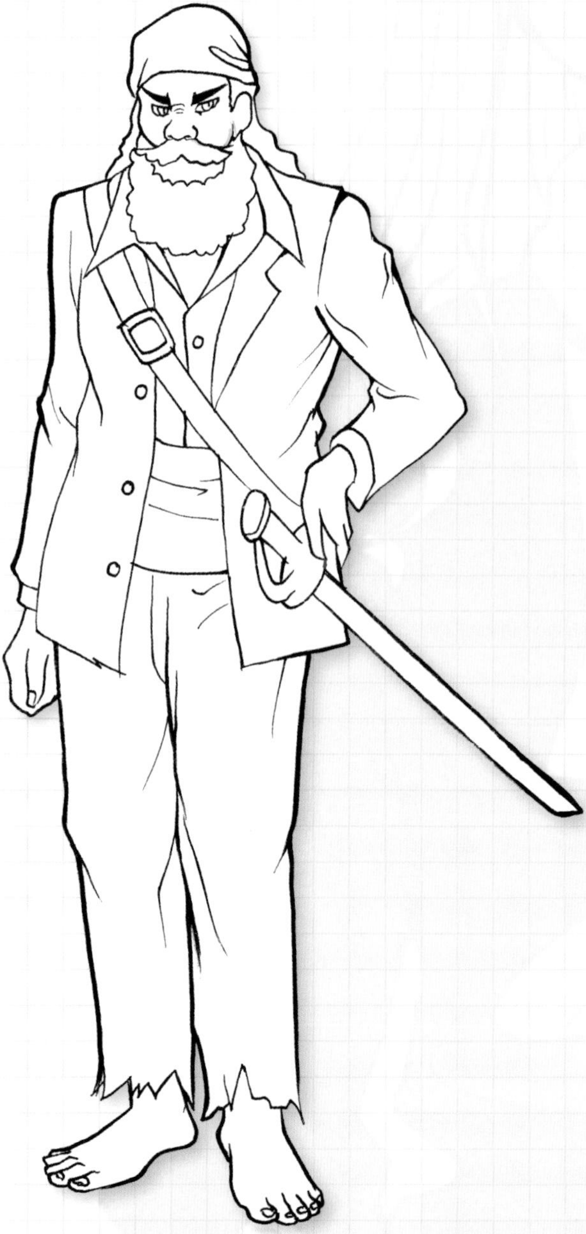

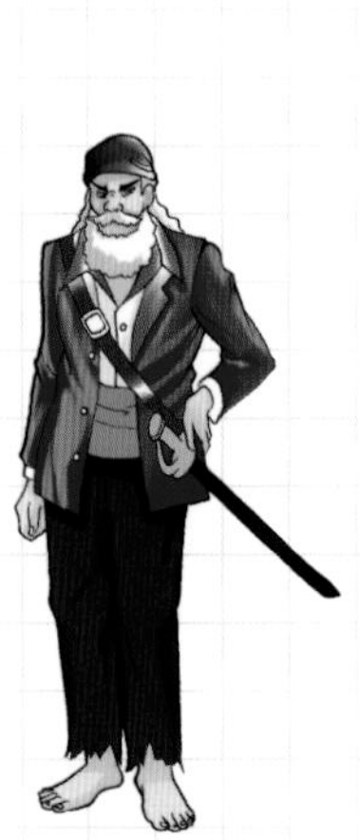

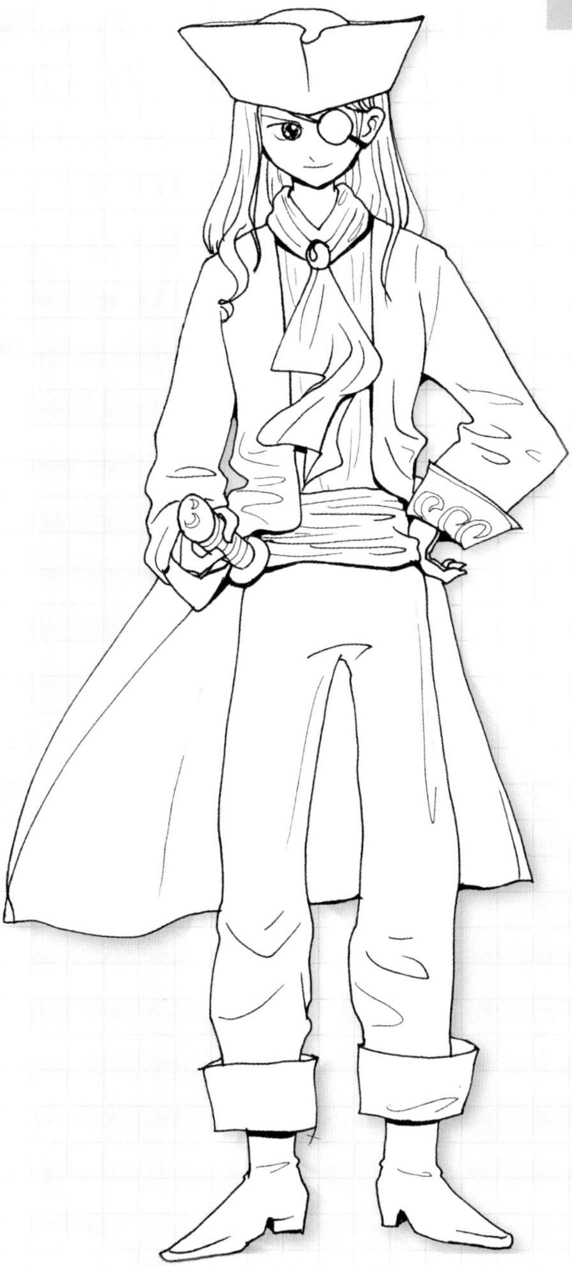

pirate heroes

search criteria

male. standing. hat. eyepatch. scarf. weapon. sword.

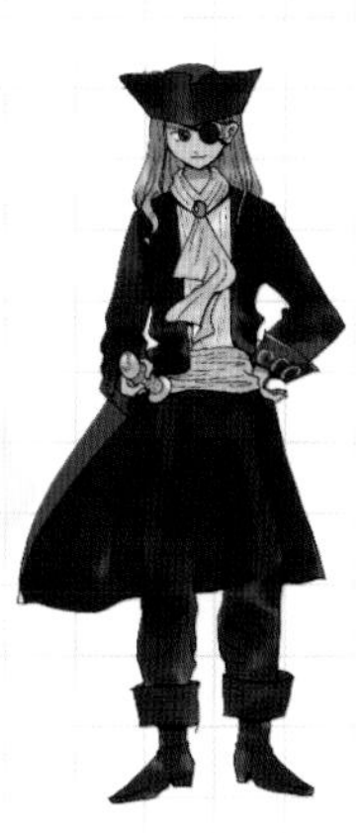

213

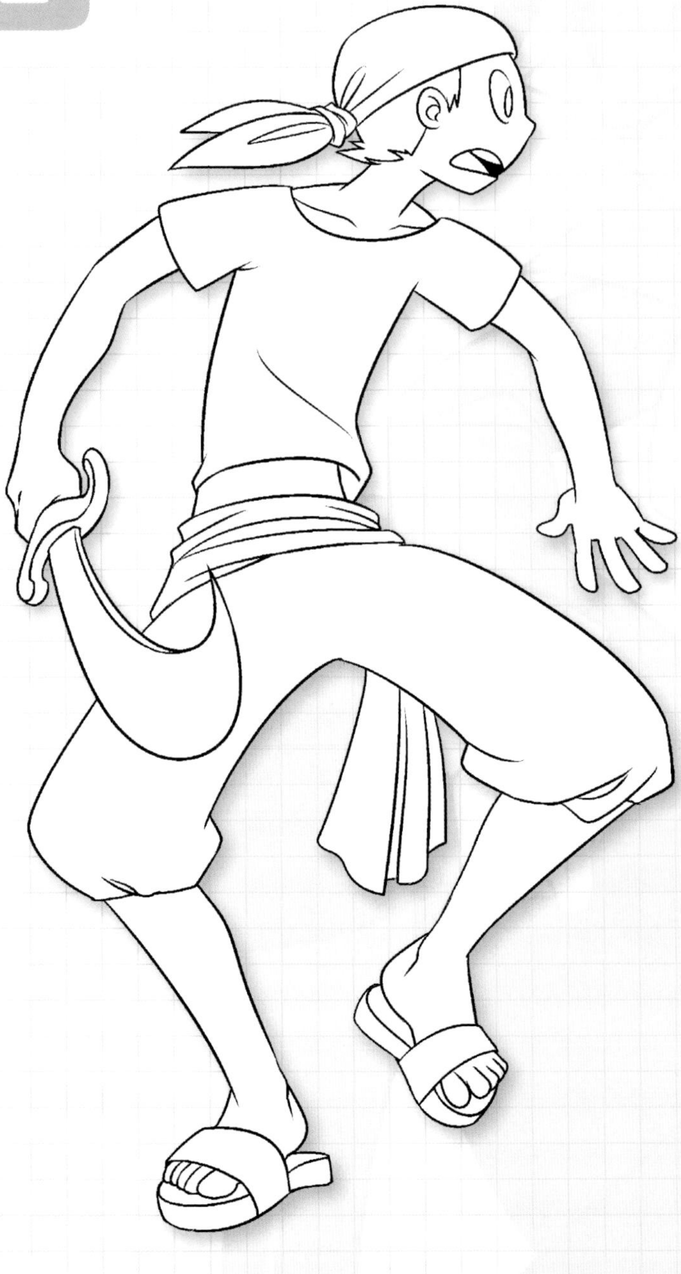

pirate heroes

search criteria

male. standing. side. headscarf. surprise. weapon. sword. deckhand.

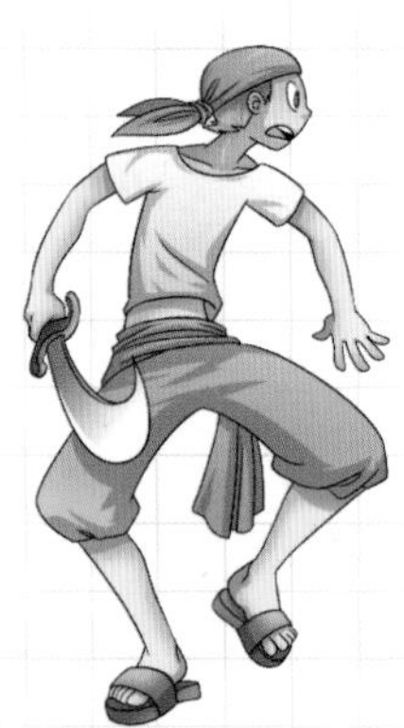

214

pirate heroes

search criteria

male. sitting. side. hat. feather. captain. weapon. sword. smiling.

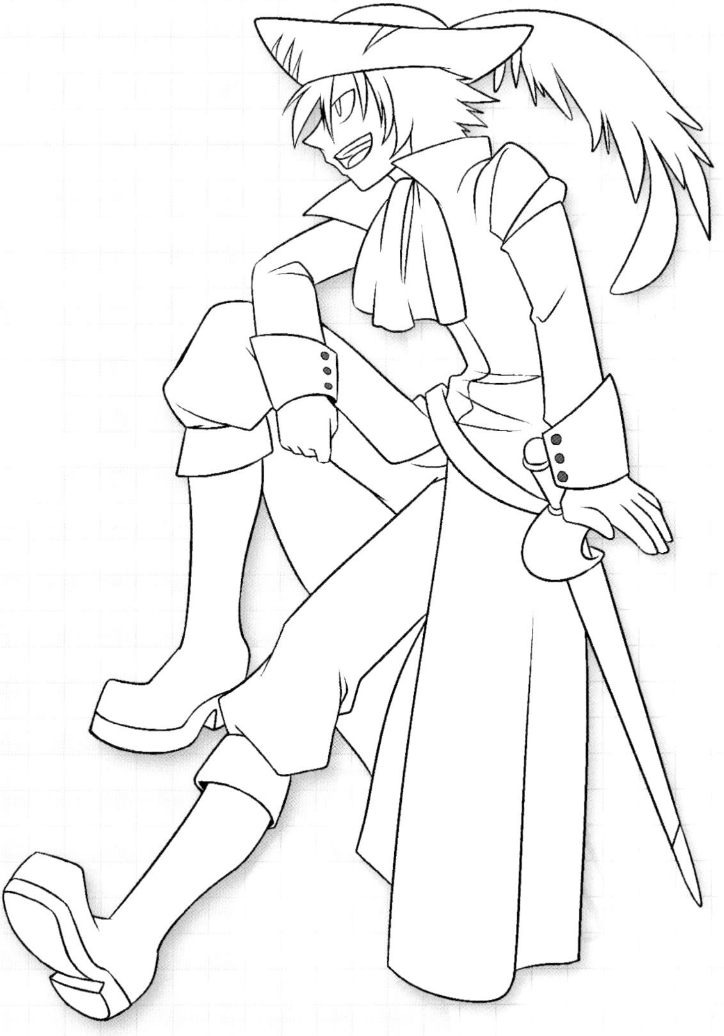

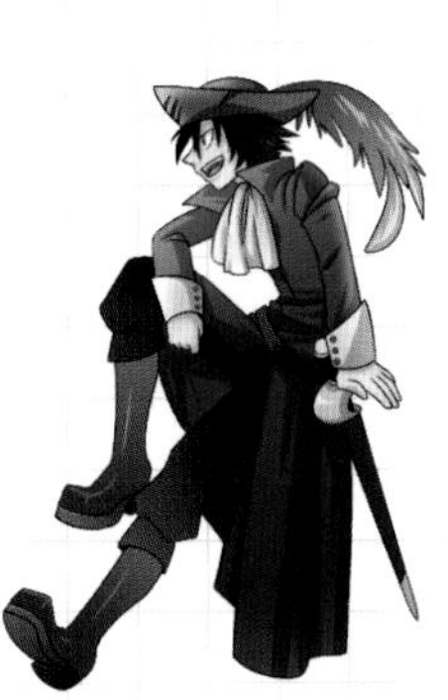

215

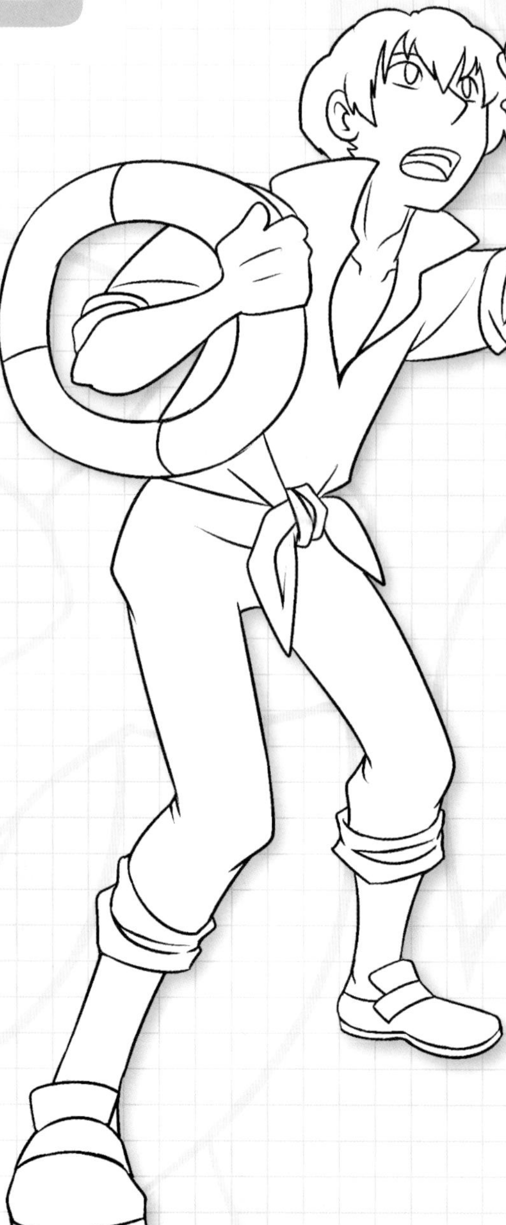

pirate heroes

search criteria

male. standing. looking. life. ring. rescue.

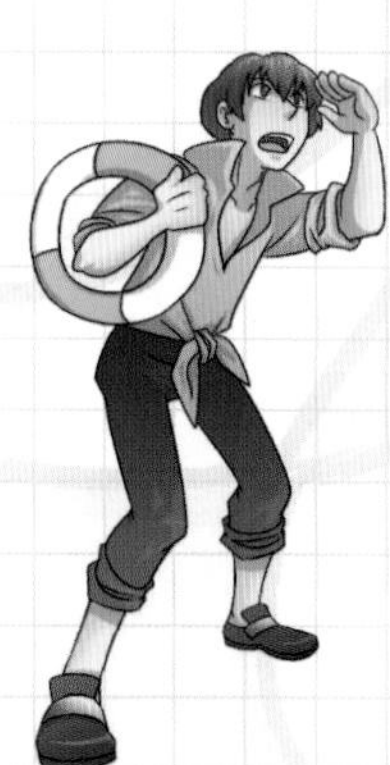

216

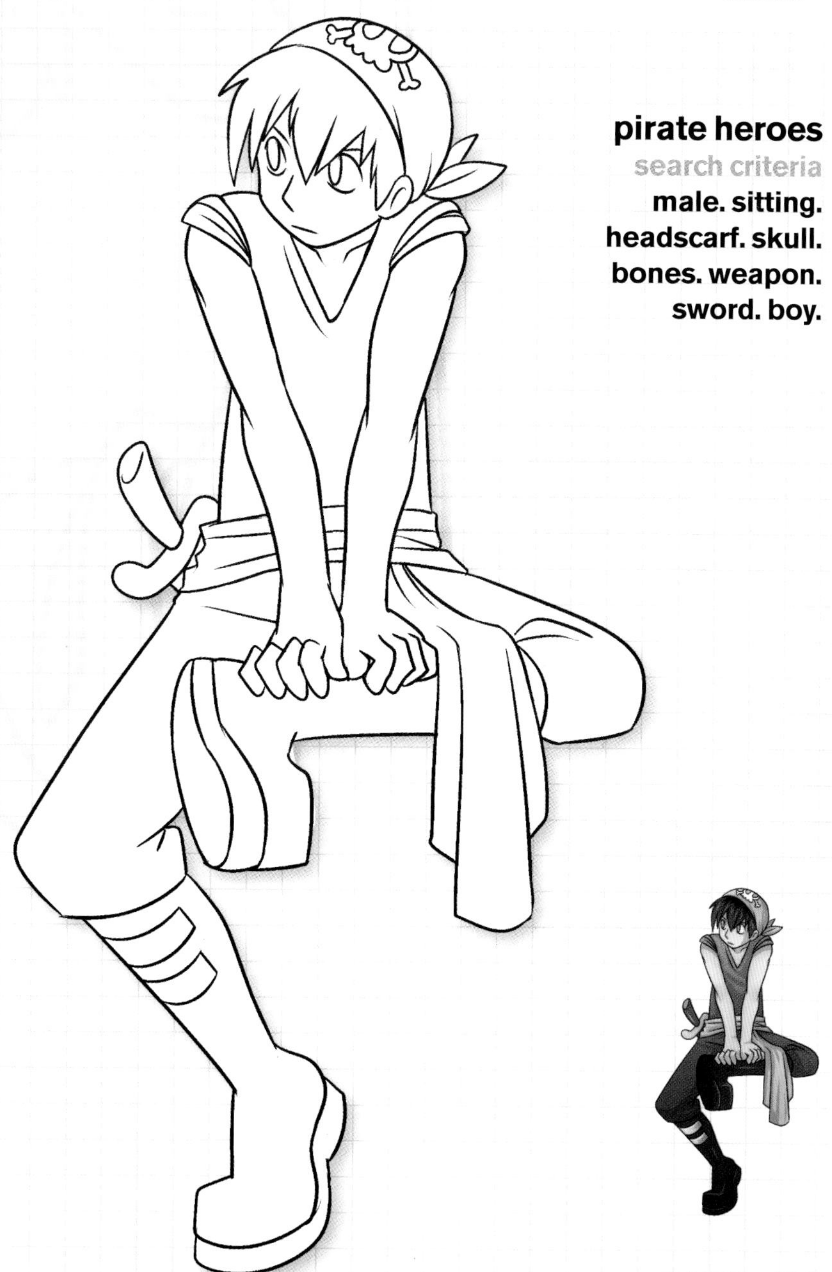

pirate heroes

search criteria

male. sitting. headscarf. skull. bones. weapon. sword. boy.

217

beast villains

search criteria

female. standing. cat. hat. assassin. spy.

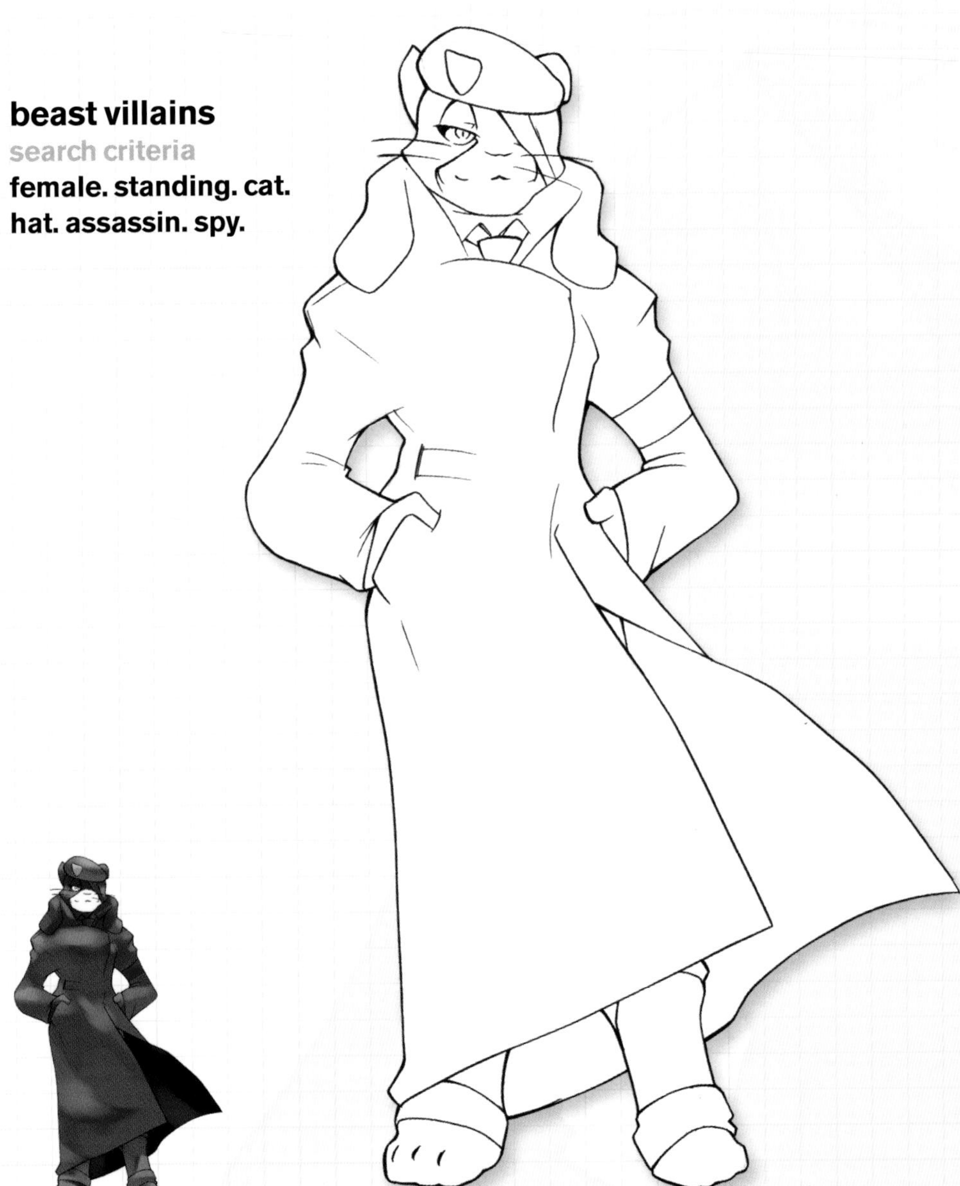

218

beast villains

search criteria

male. standing. wolf. claws. growl. fur. tail.

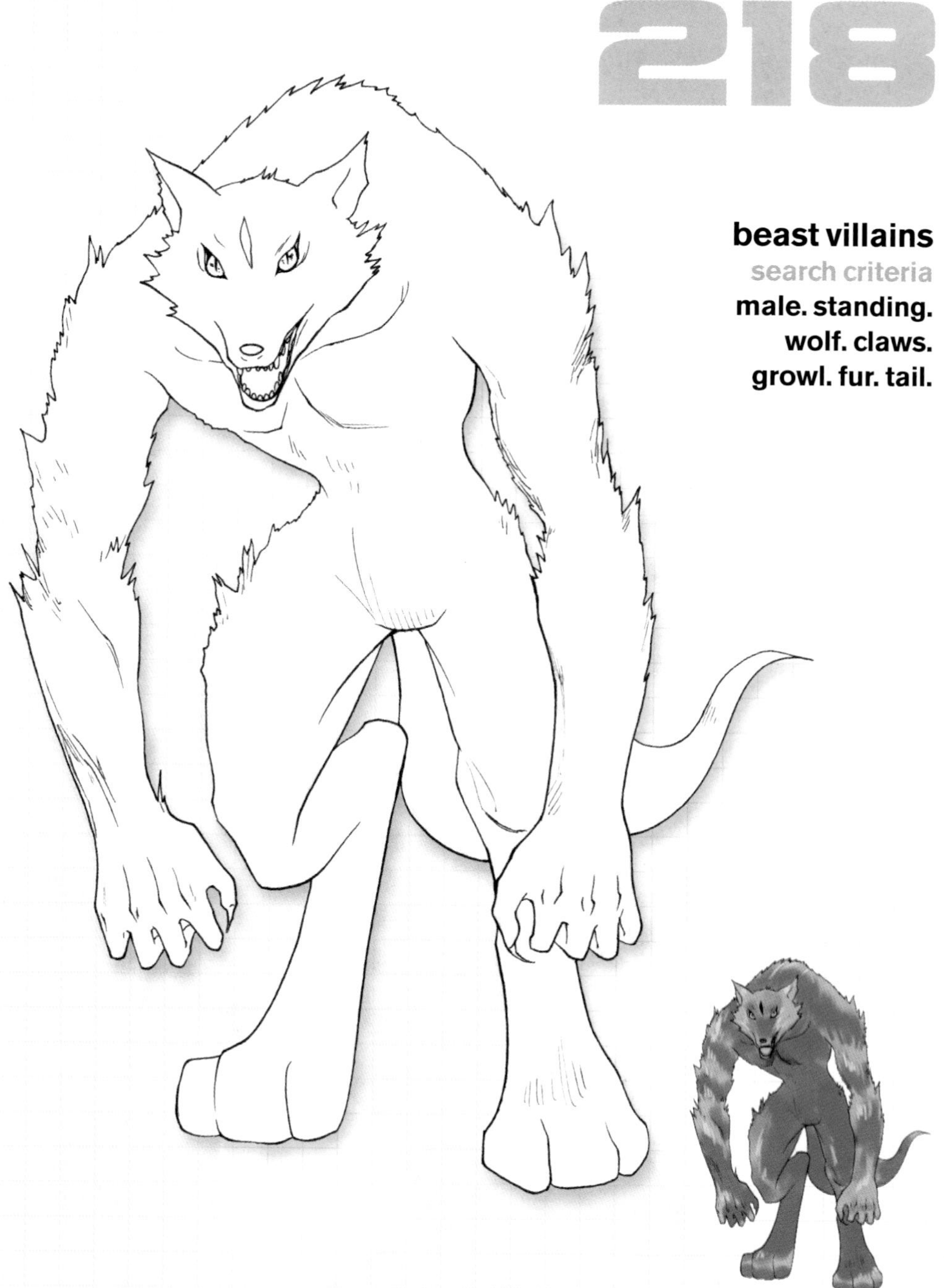

219

beast villains

search criteria

male. horns. shield. weapon. spear. armor. warrior.

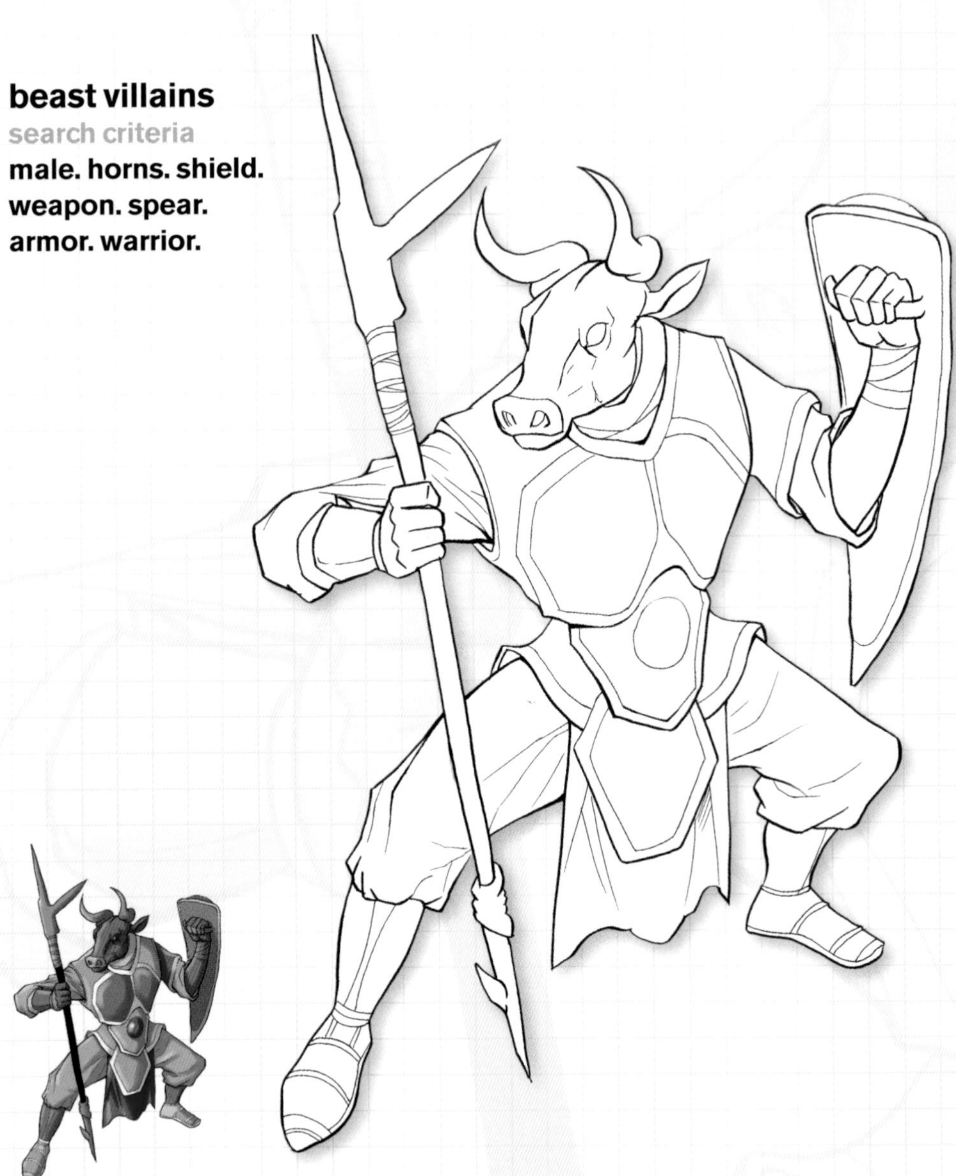

220

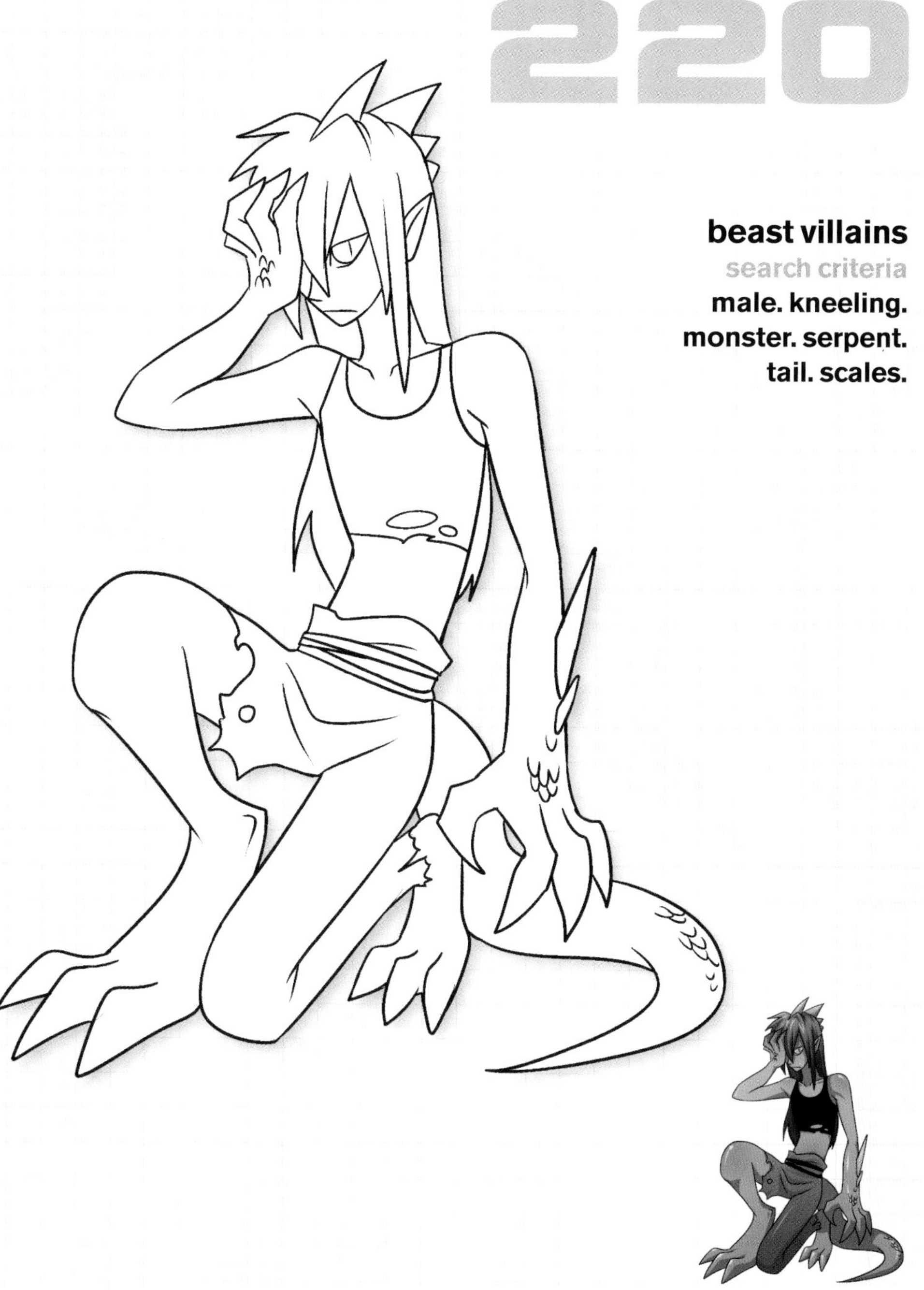

beast villains

search criteria

male. kneeling. monster. serpent. tail. scales.

221

beast villains

search criteria

male. standing. armor. fur. lion. growl. weapon. warrior. angry.

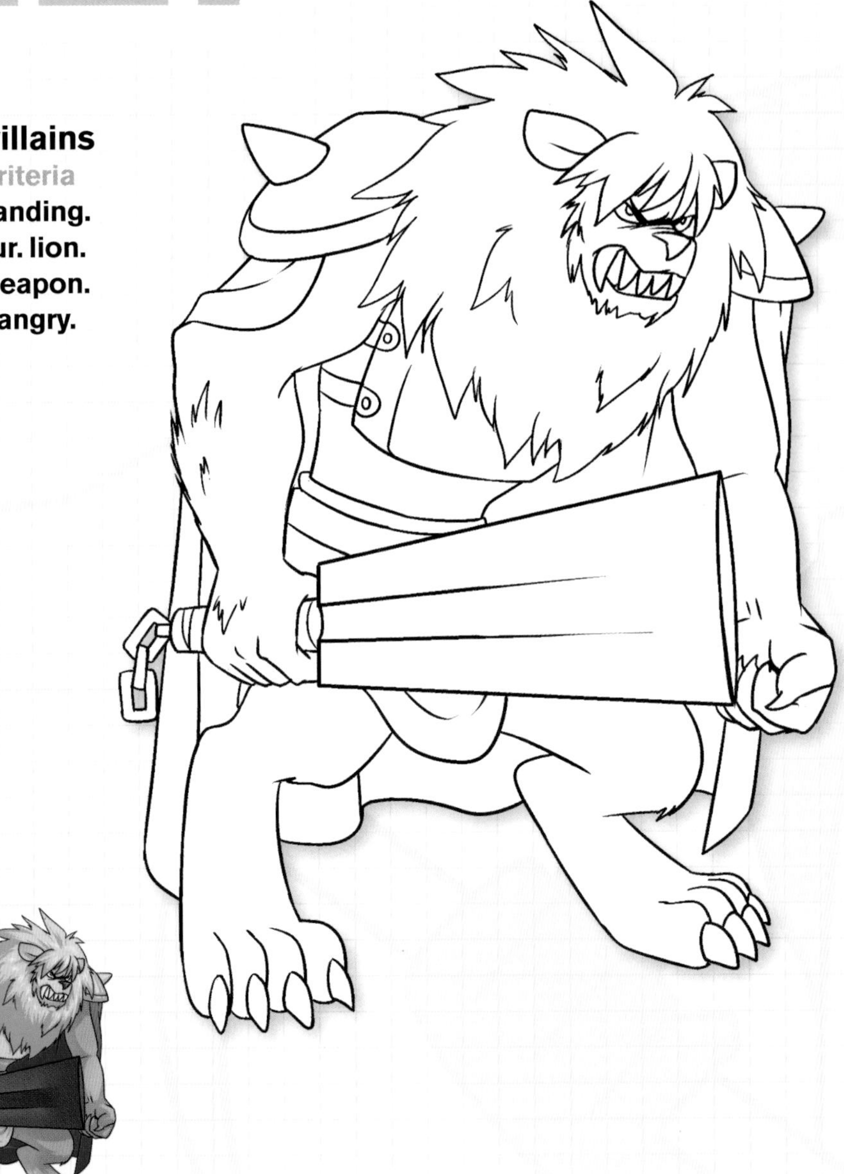

222

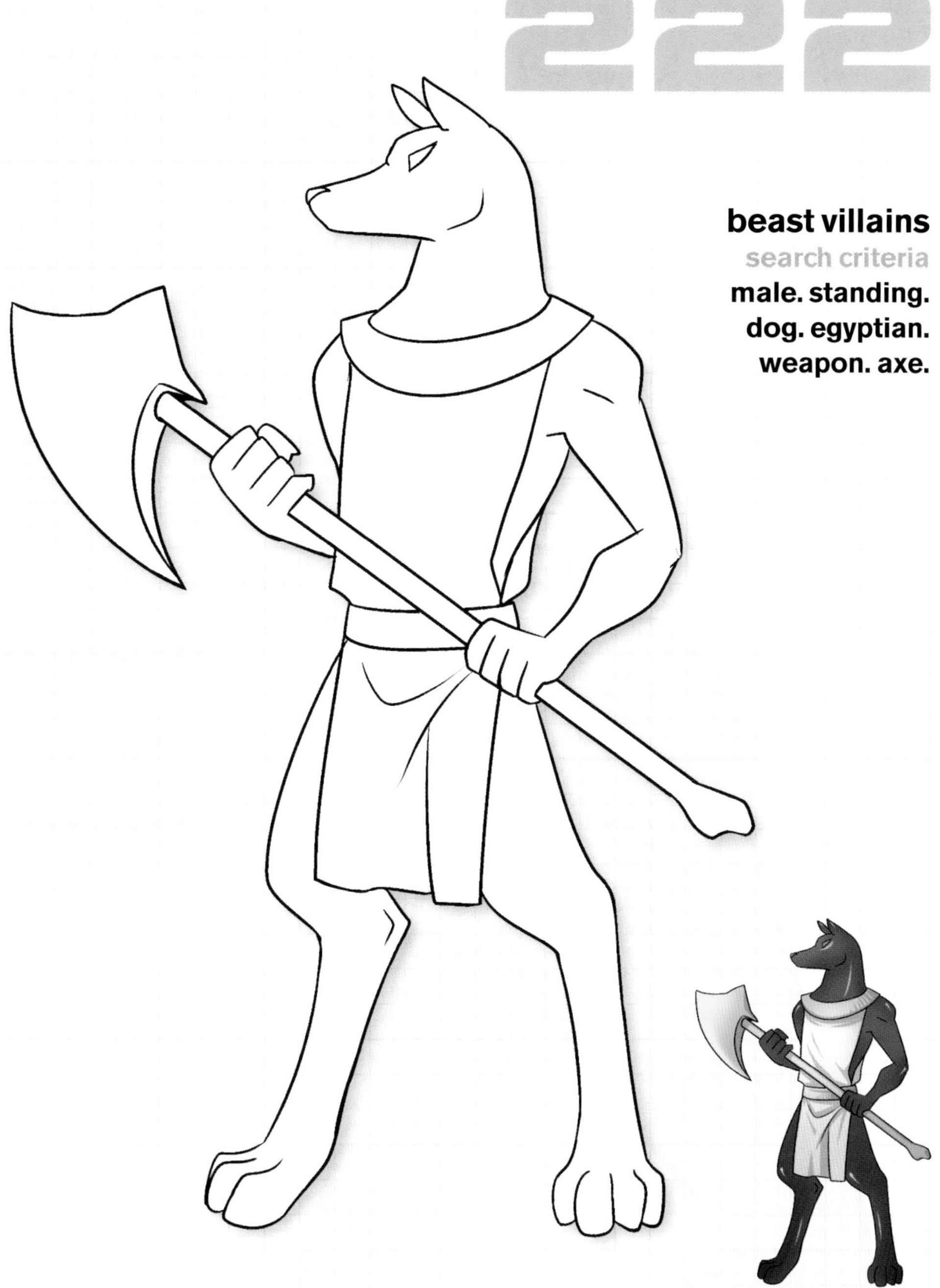

beast villains

search criteria

male. standing. dog. egyptian. weapon. axe.

223

beast villains

search criteria

male. standing. egyptian. armor. weapon. spear. bird. mythical.

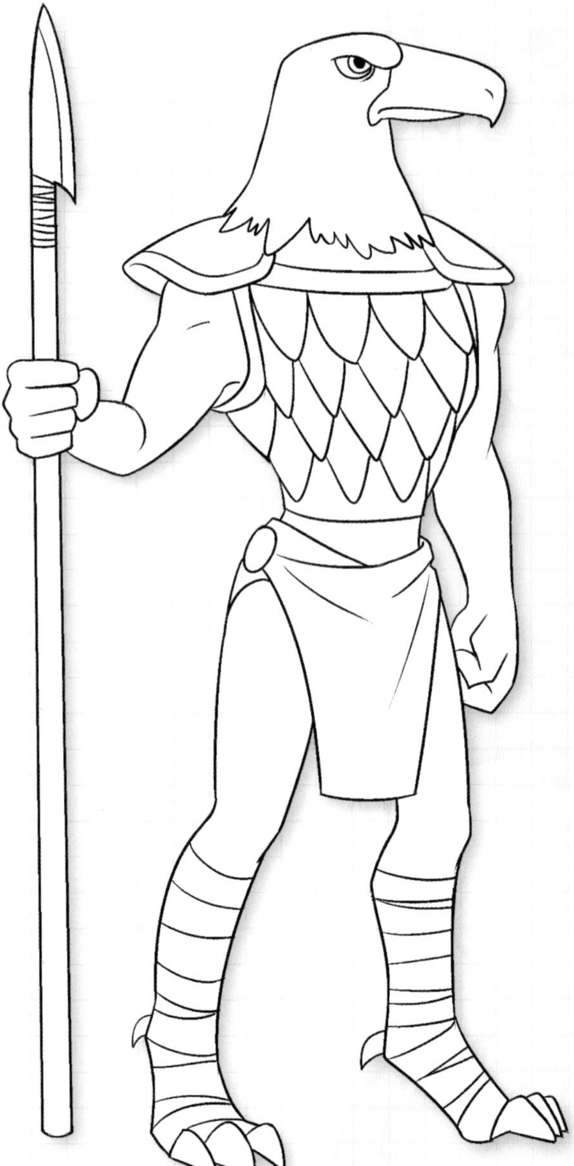

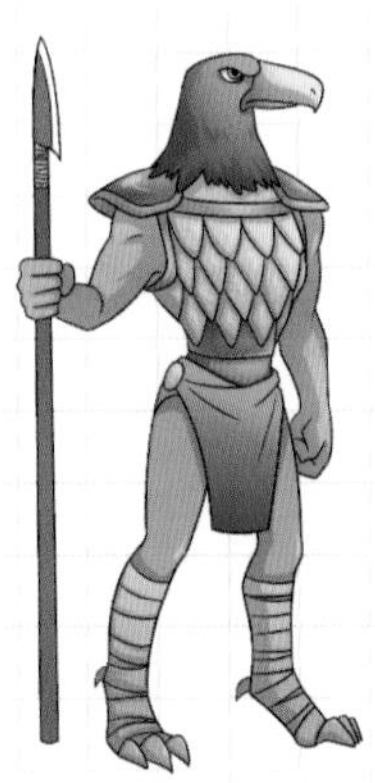

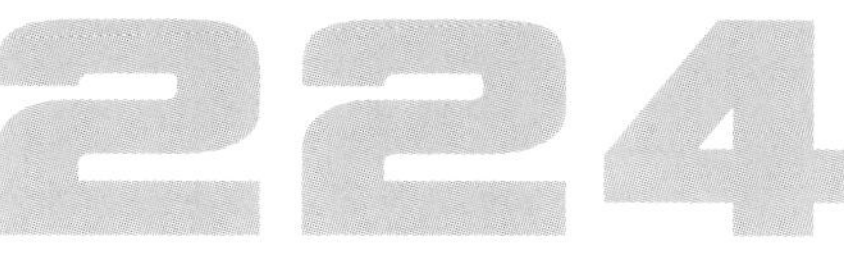

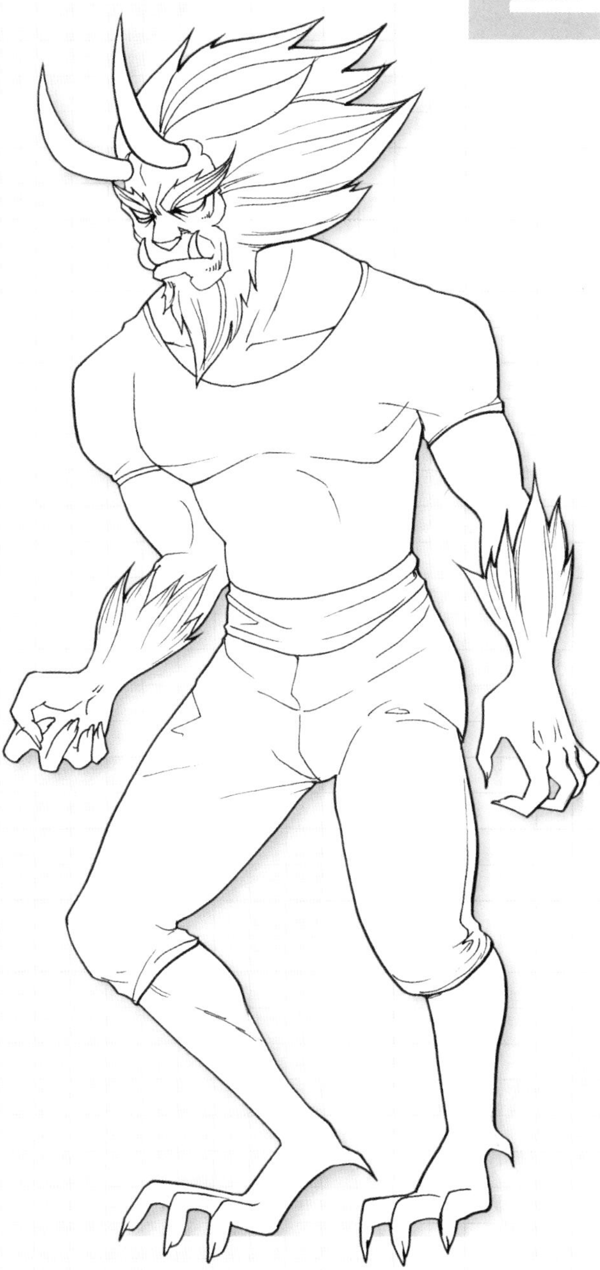

beast villains

search criteria

male. standing. horns. fur. demon. muscle. lion.

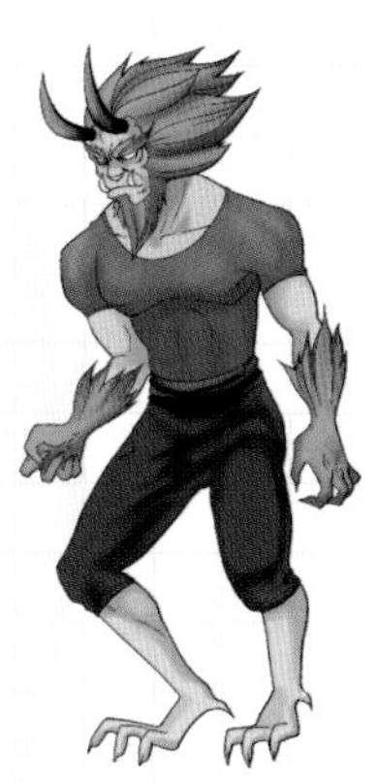

225

beast villains
search criteria
male. standing.
fur. muscle.
claws. growl.

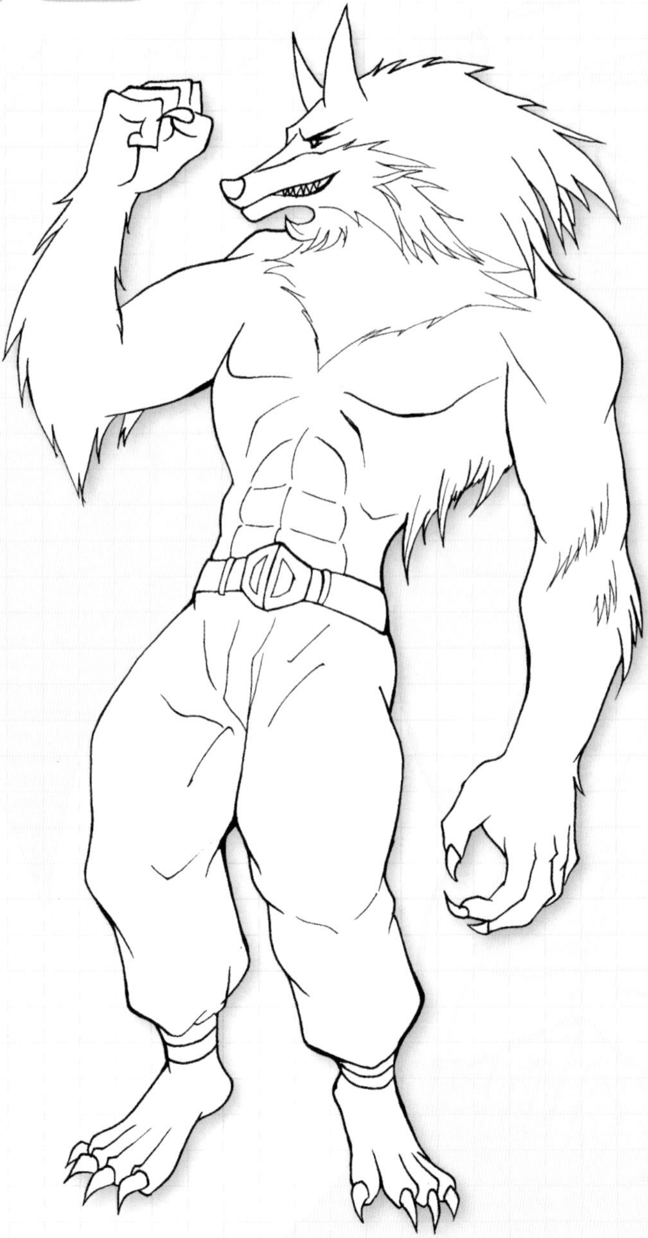

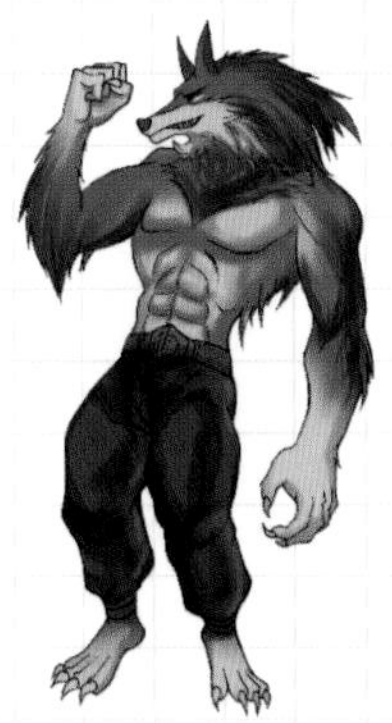

226

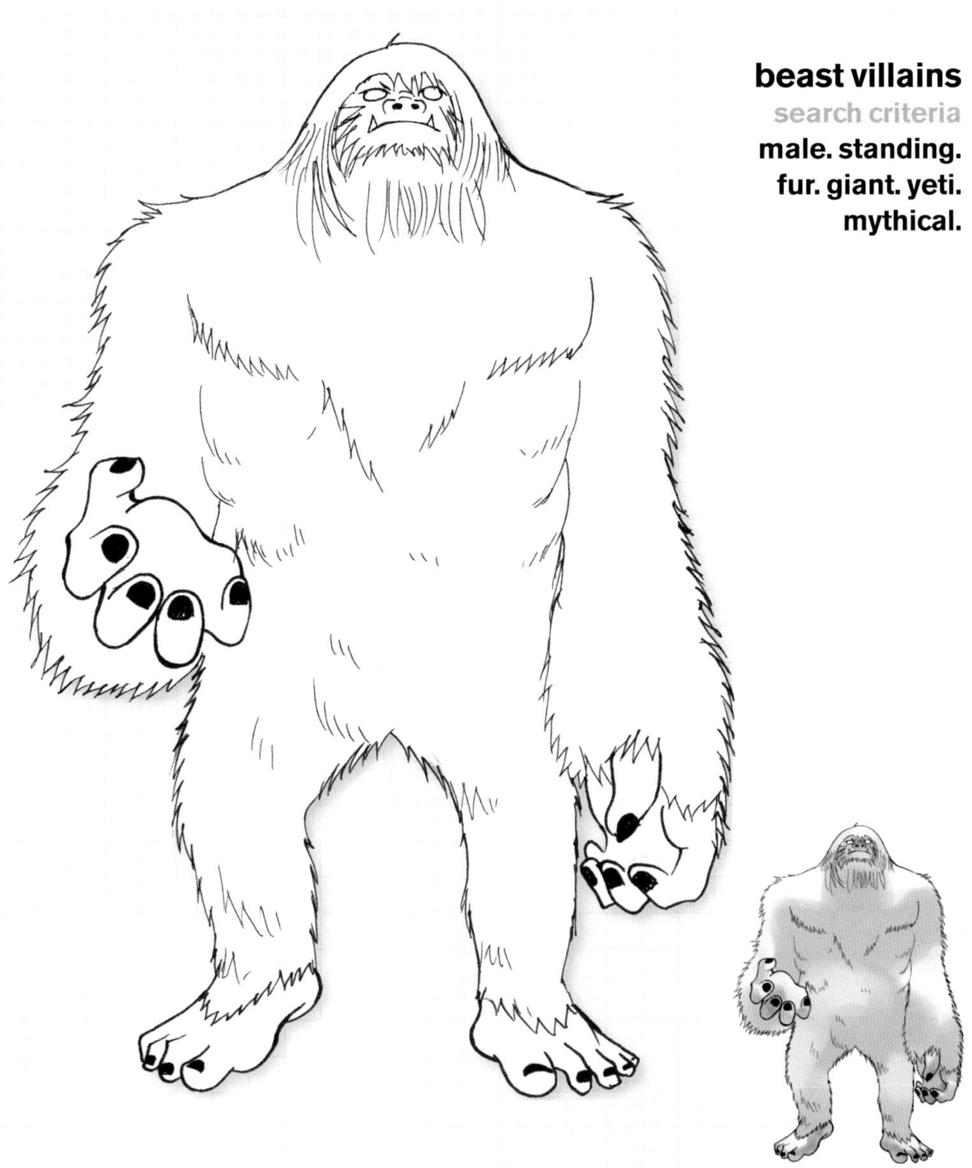

beast villains

search criteria

male. standing. fur. giant. yeti. mythical.

227

beast villains

search criteria

male. standing. shout. growl. muscle. weapon. blades. skull.

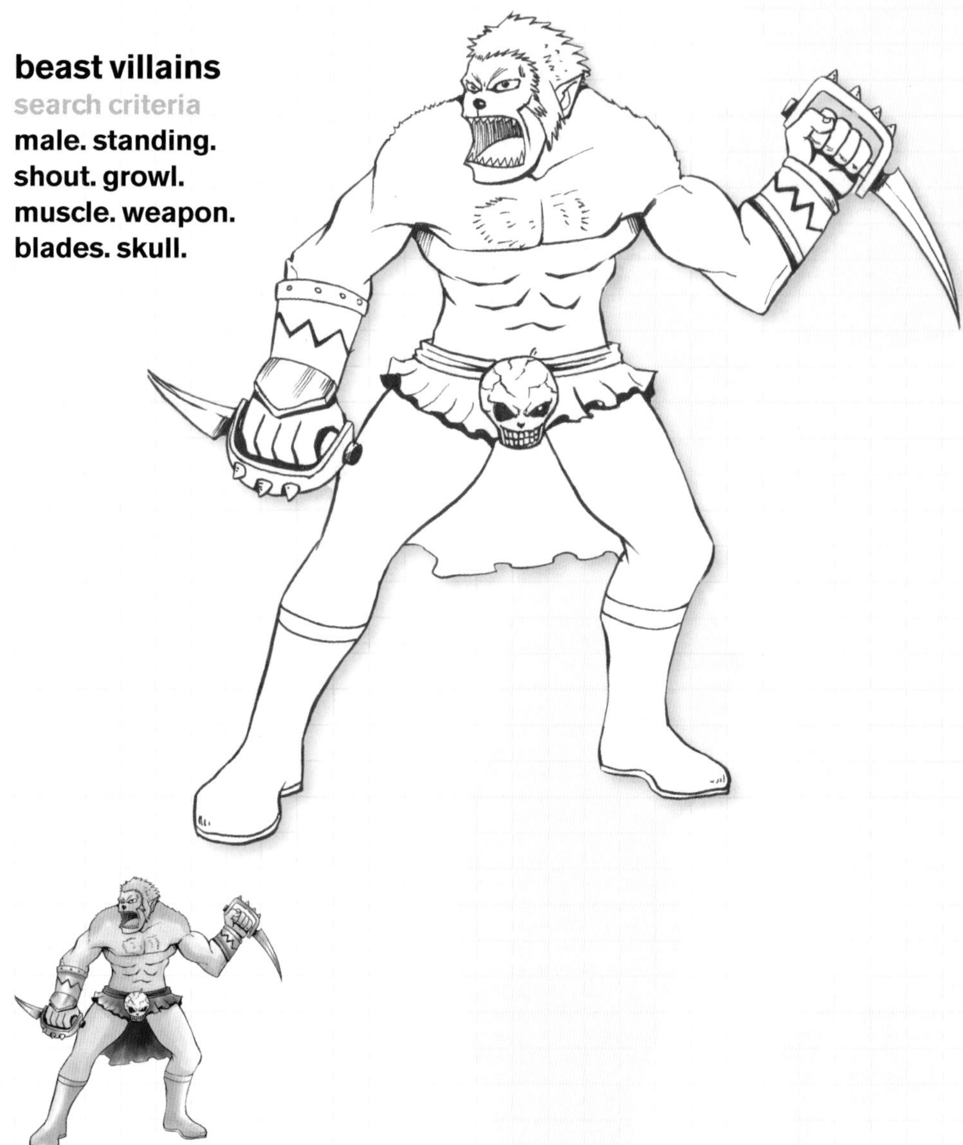

228

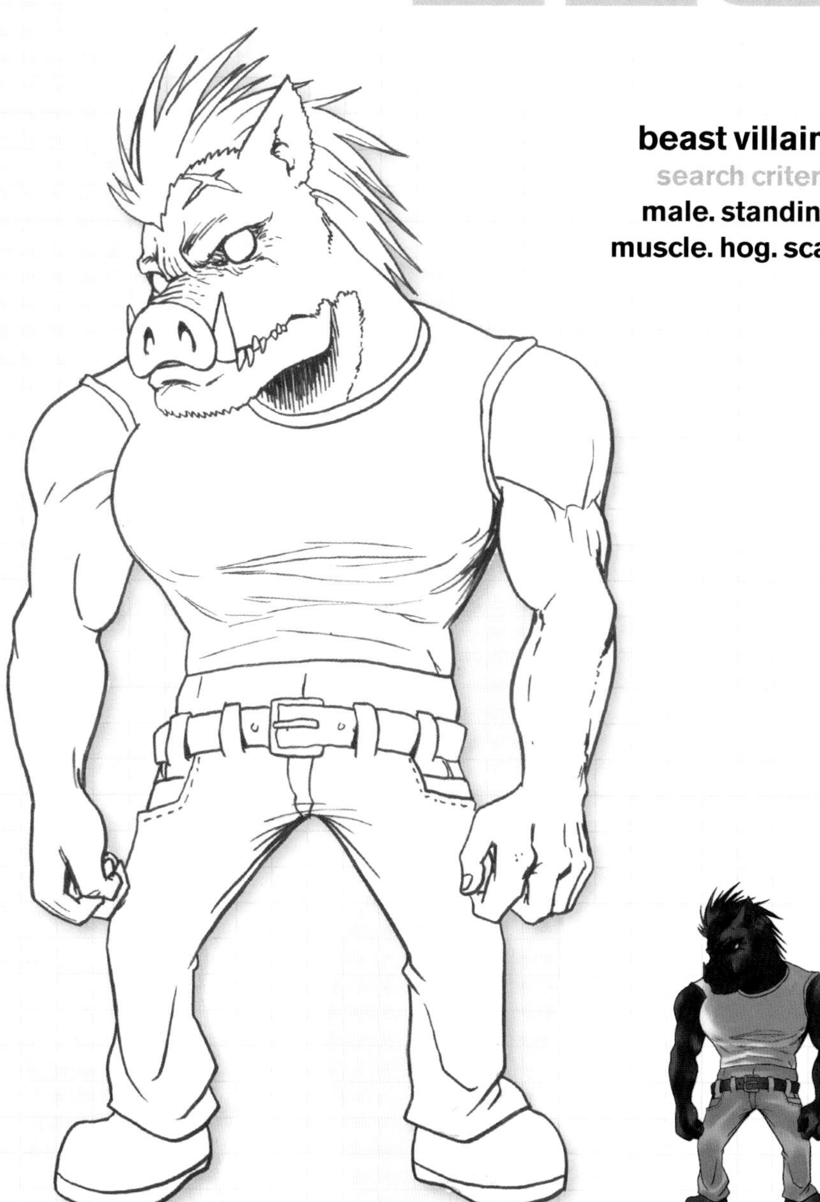

beast villains

search criteria

male. standing. muscle. hog. scar.

229

beast villains

search criteria

male. standing. monster. frog. demon. scales.

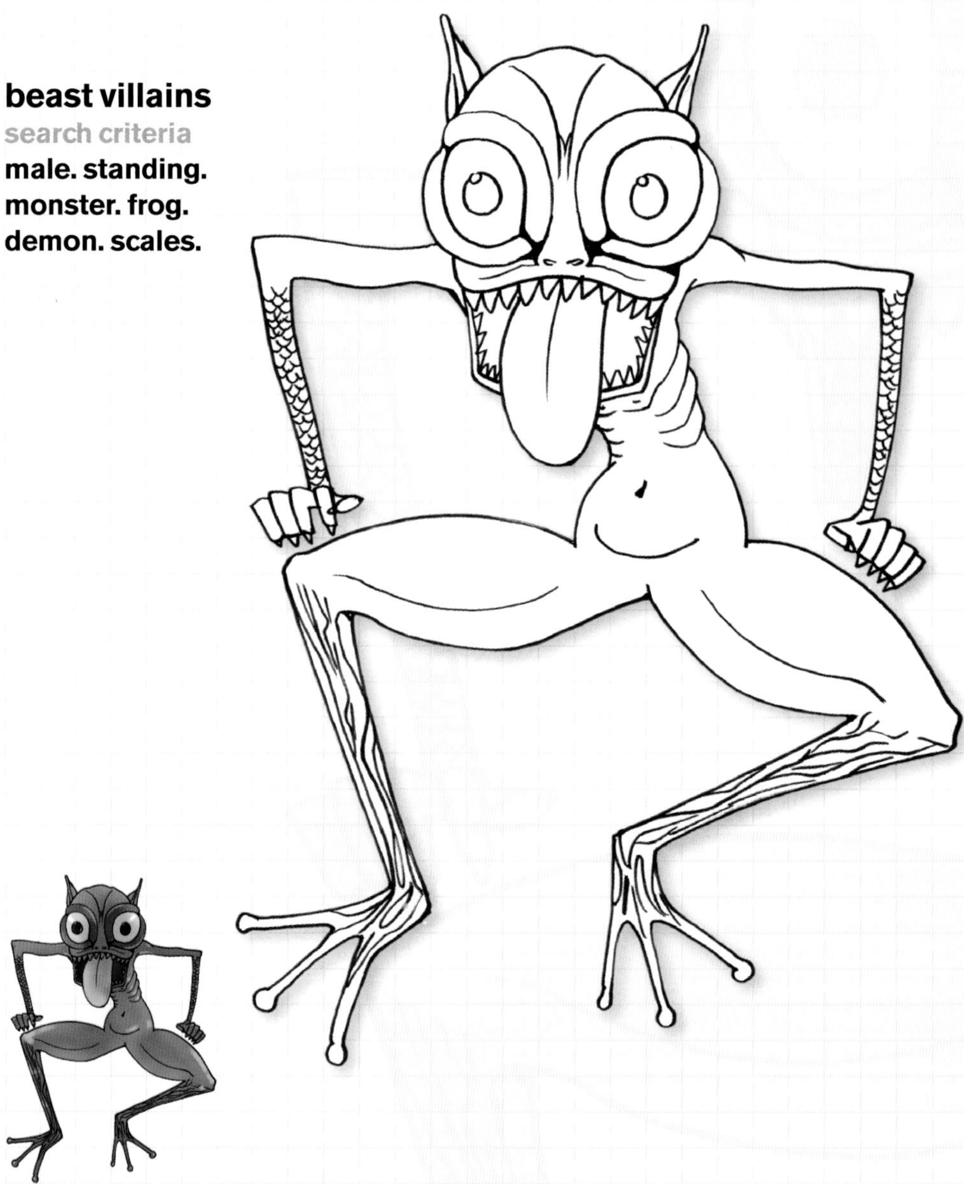

230

beast villains

search criteria

male. standing. side. fur. tail. skull. bones. feline.

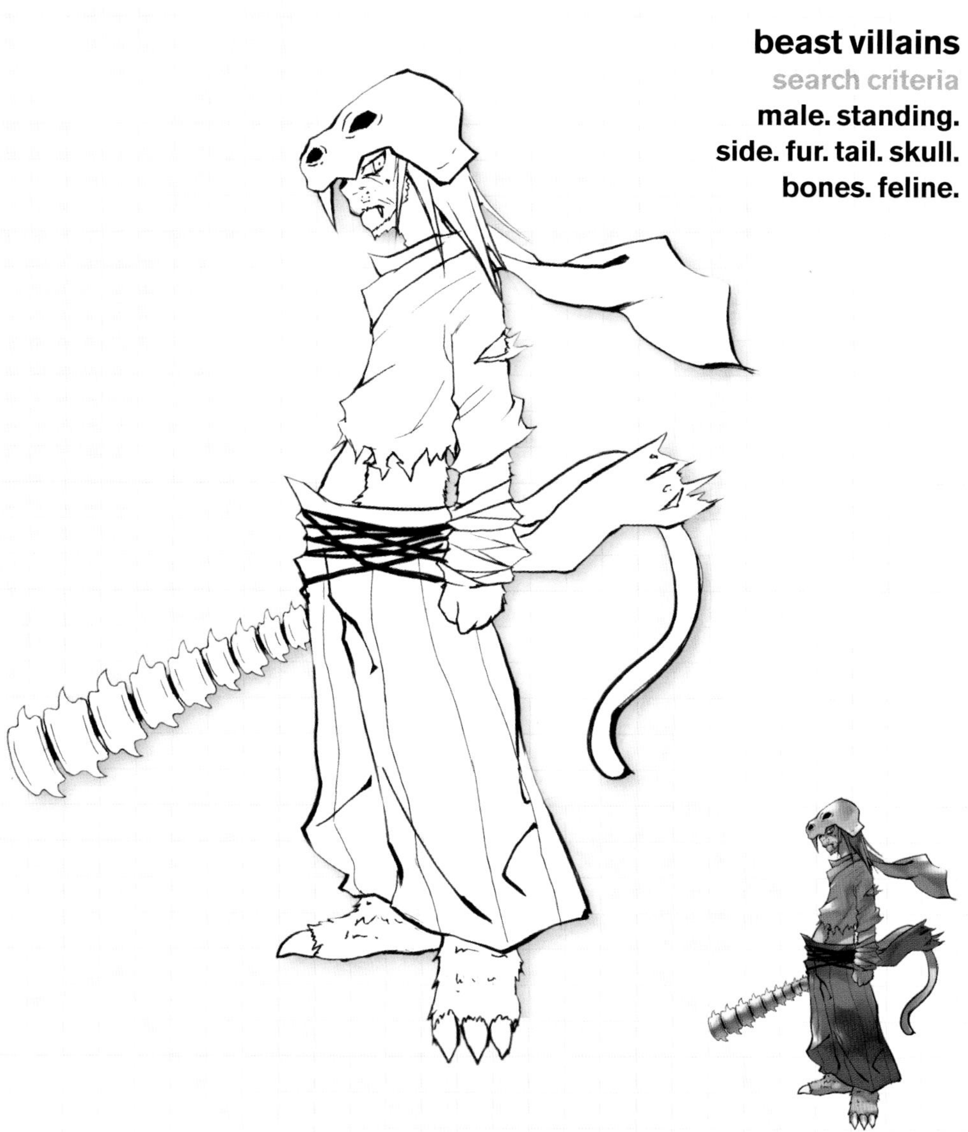

231

beast villains

search criteria

male. monster. crawling. scales. serpent. tail. growl. claws. sinister.

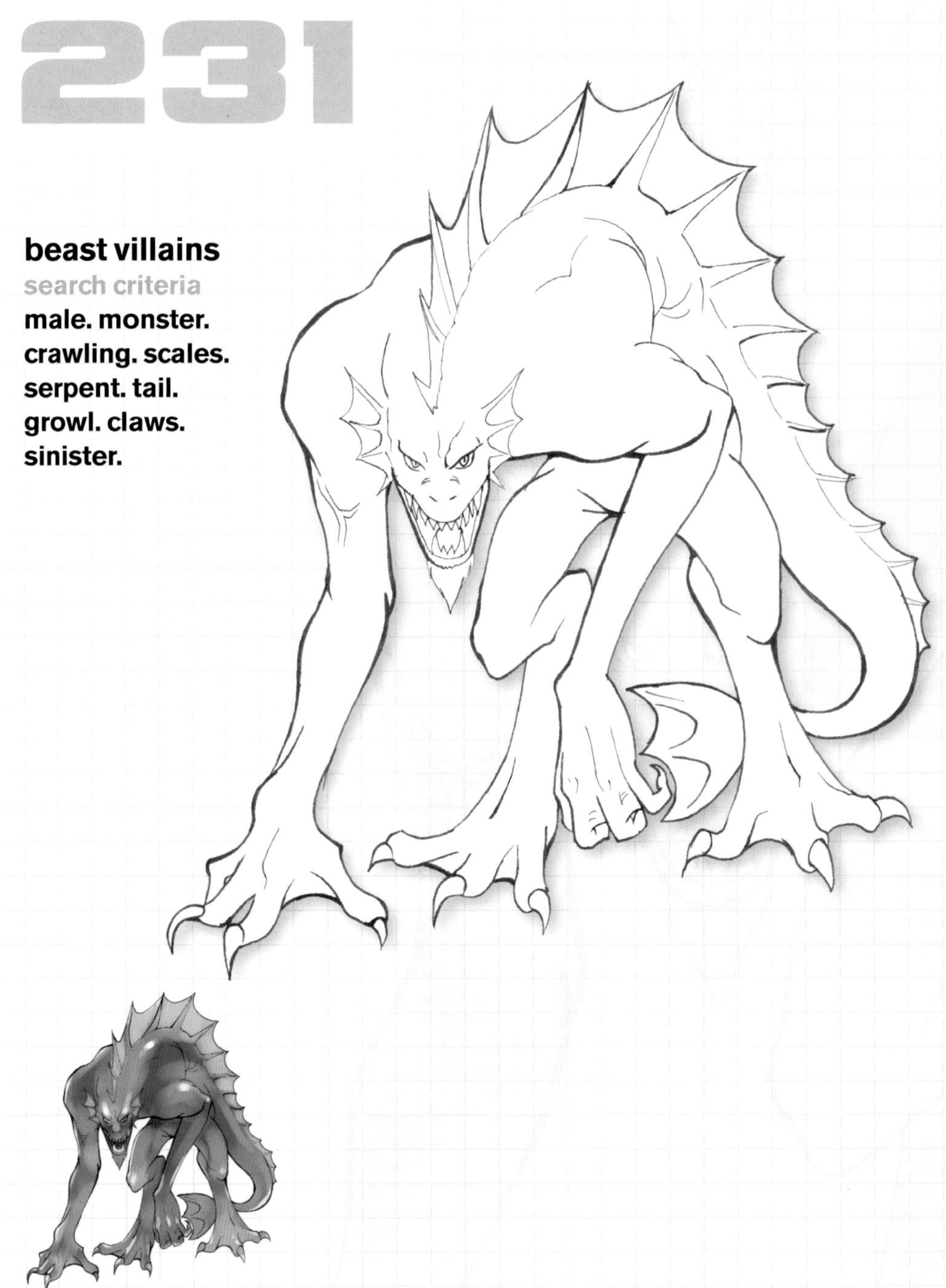

232

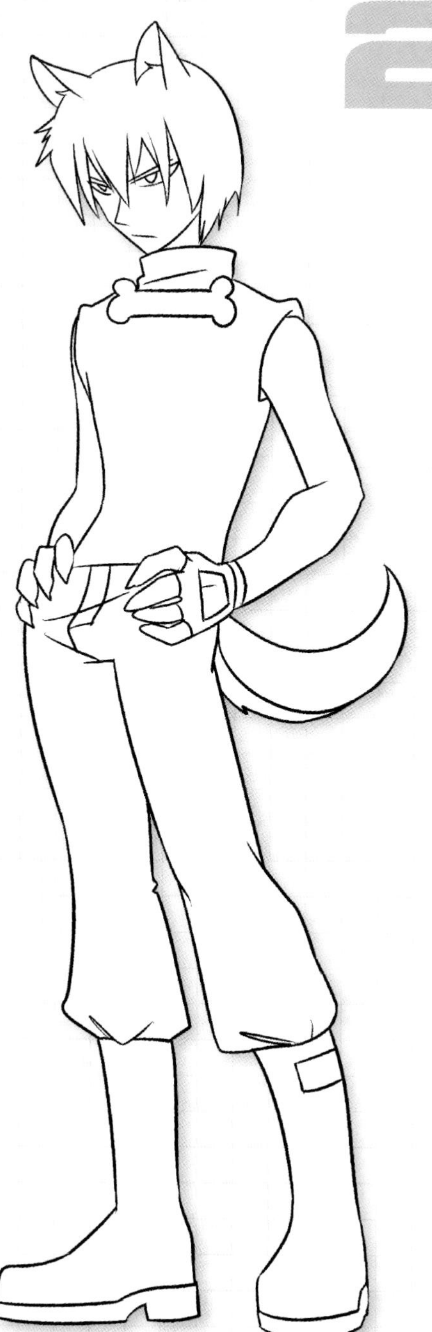

beast villains

search criteria

**male. standing.
wolf. bone.
boy. fur. tail.**

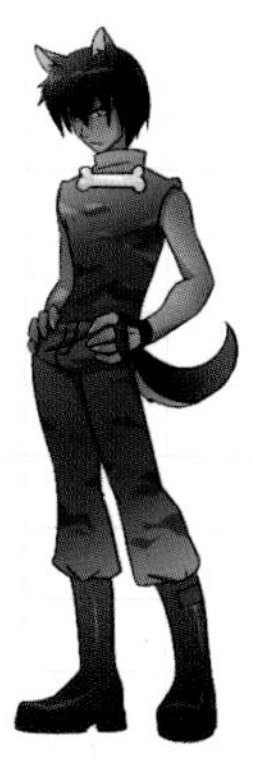

233

beast villains

search criteria

female. kneeling. bandages. siren. wings. feathers. gothic. sad.

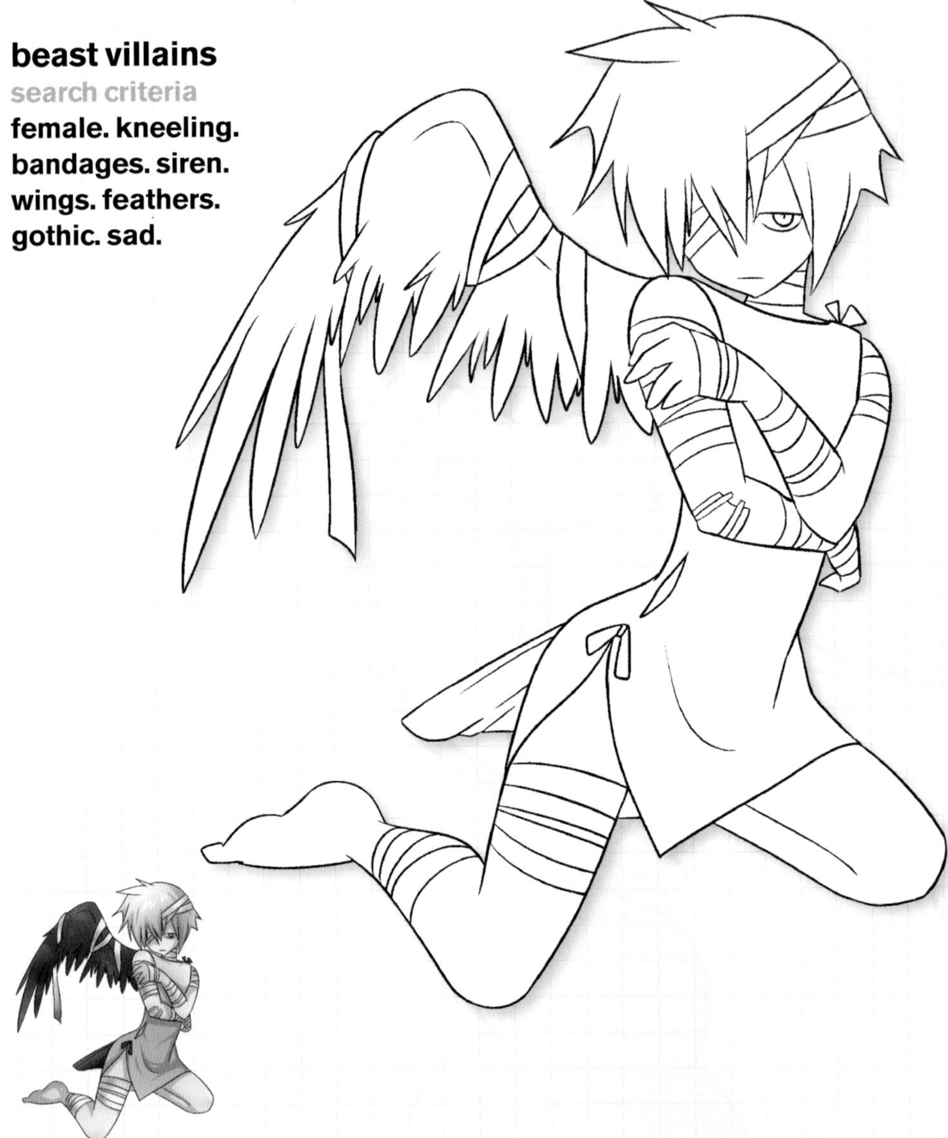

234

beast villains

search criteria

female. jump. side. bunny. tail. bottle. cheeky.

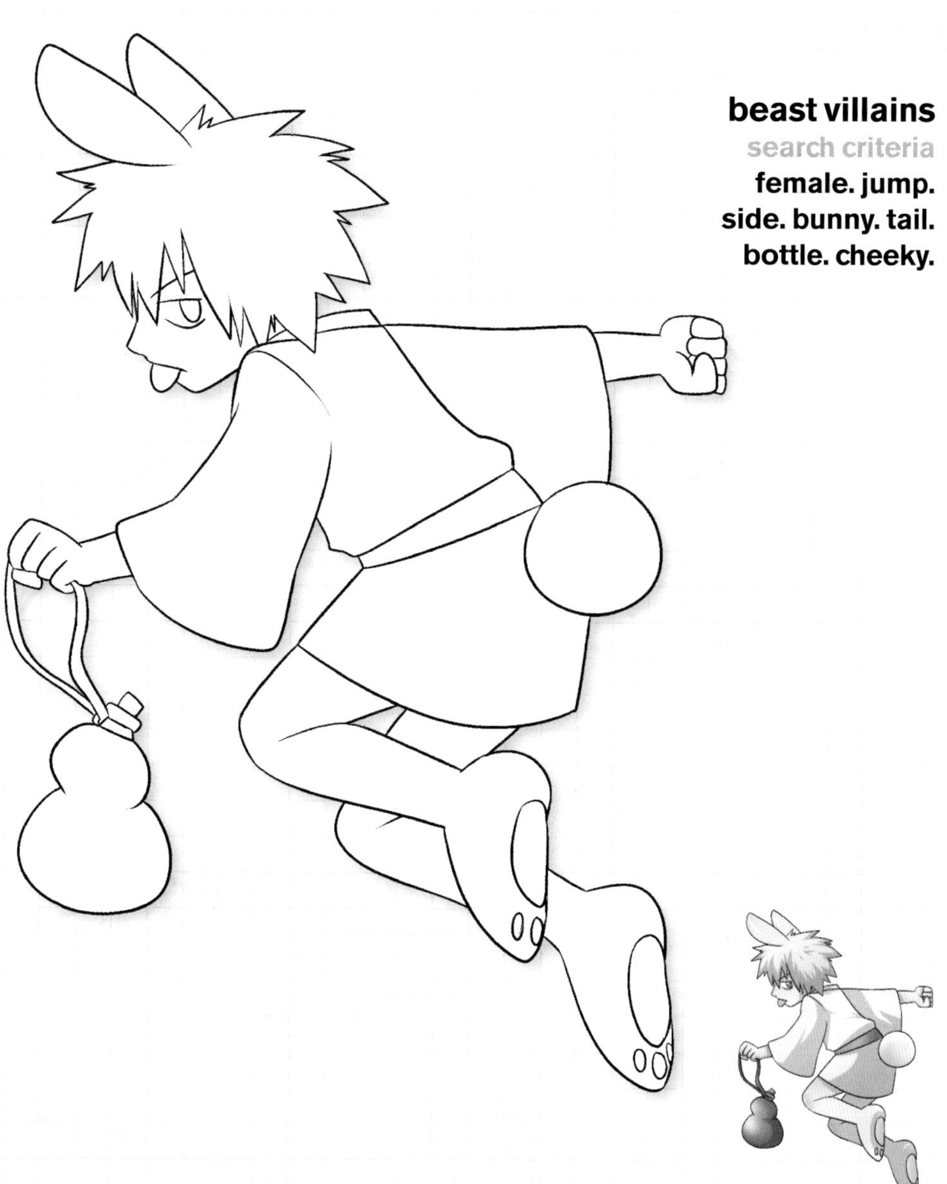

235

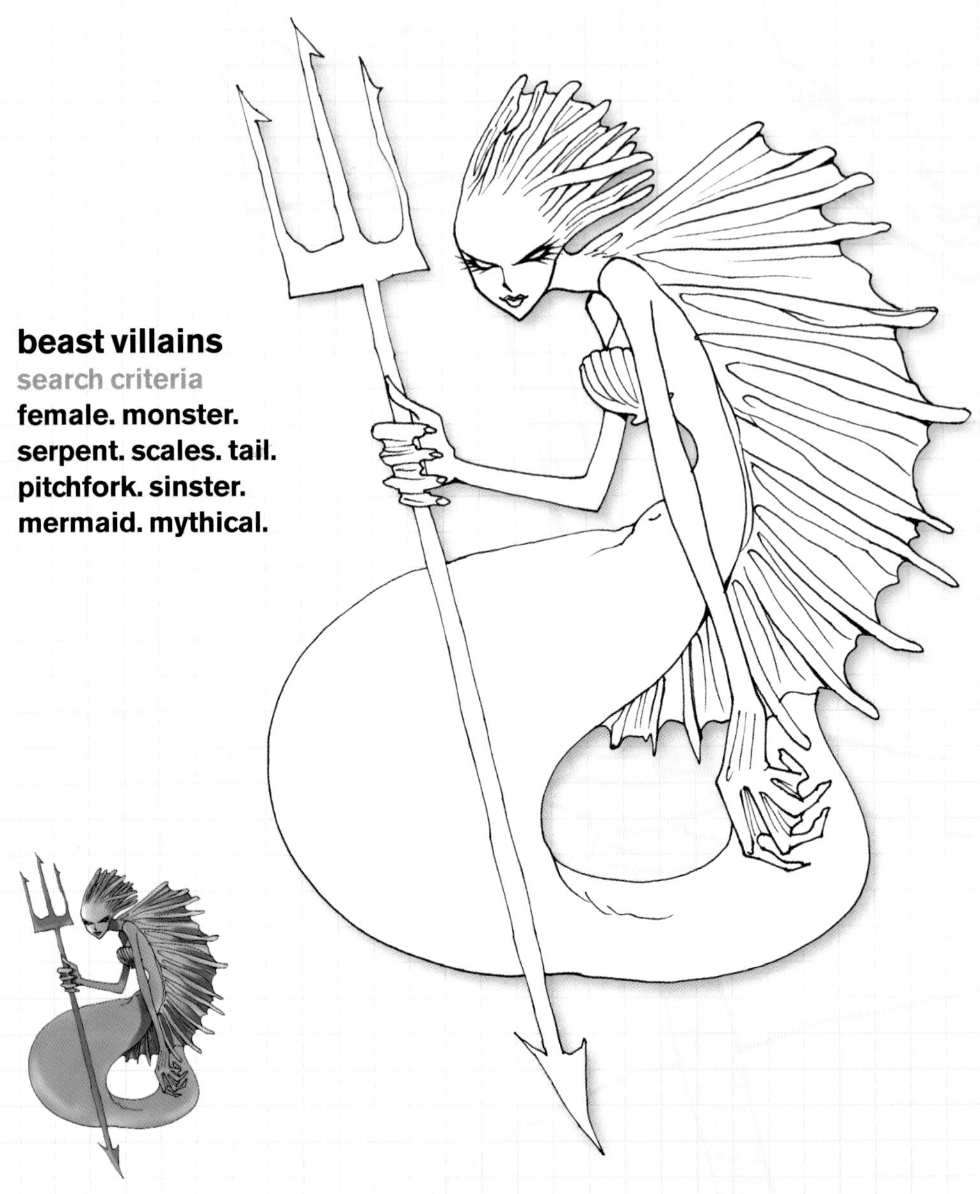

beast villains

search criteria

female. monster. serpent. scales. tail. pitchfork. sinster. mermaid. mythical.

236

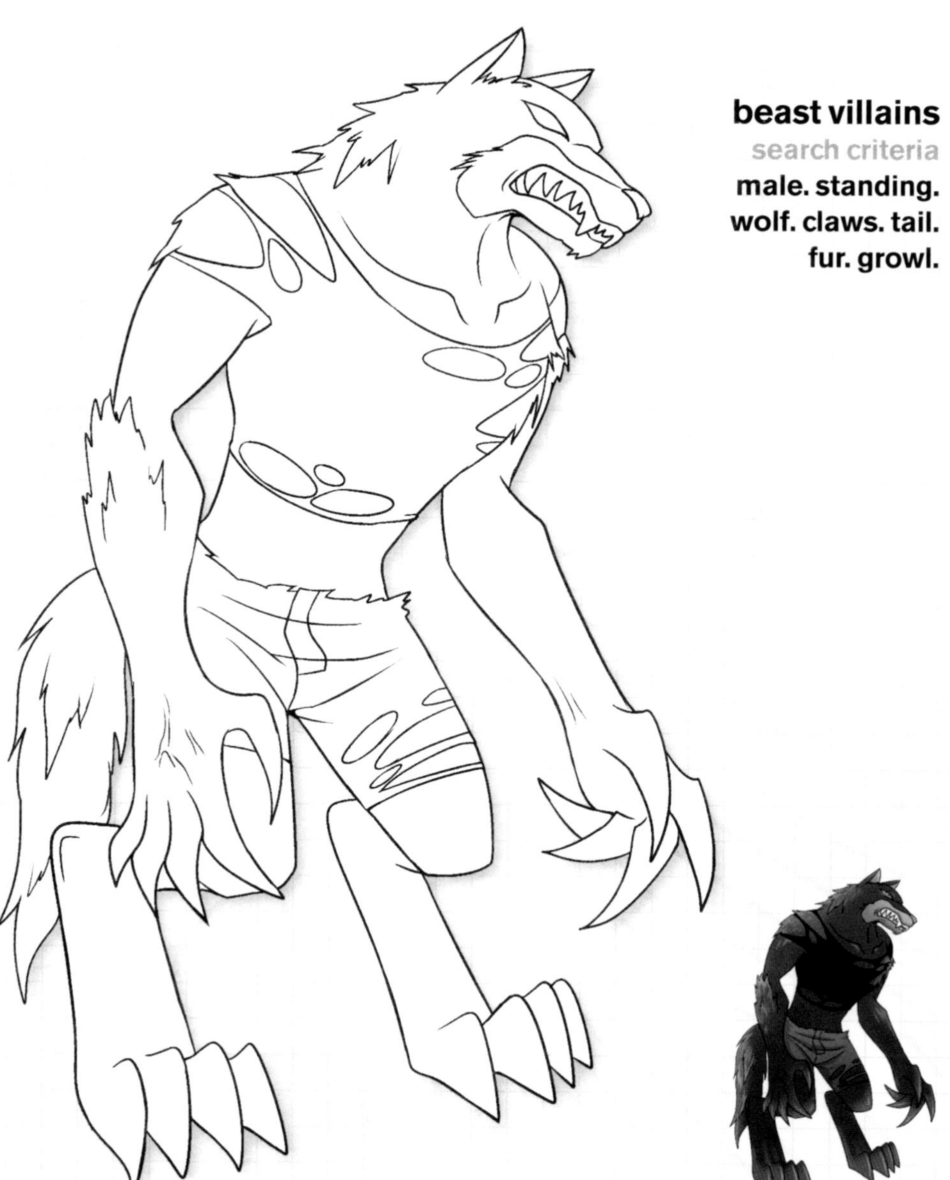

beast villains

search criteria

male. standing. wolf. claws. tail. fur. growl.

237

beast villains

search criteria

male. standing. horse. weapon. club. lantern. tail. kimono. bandages.

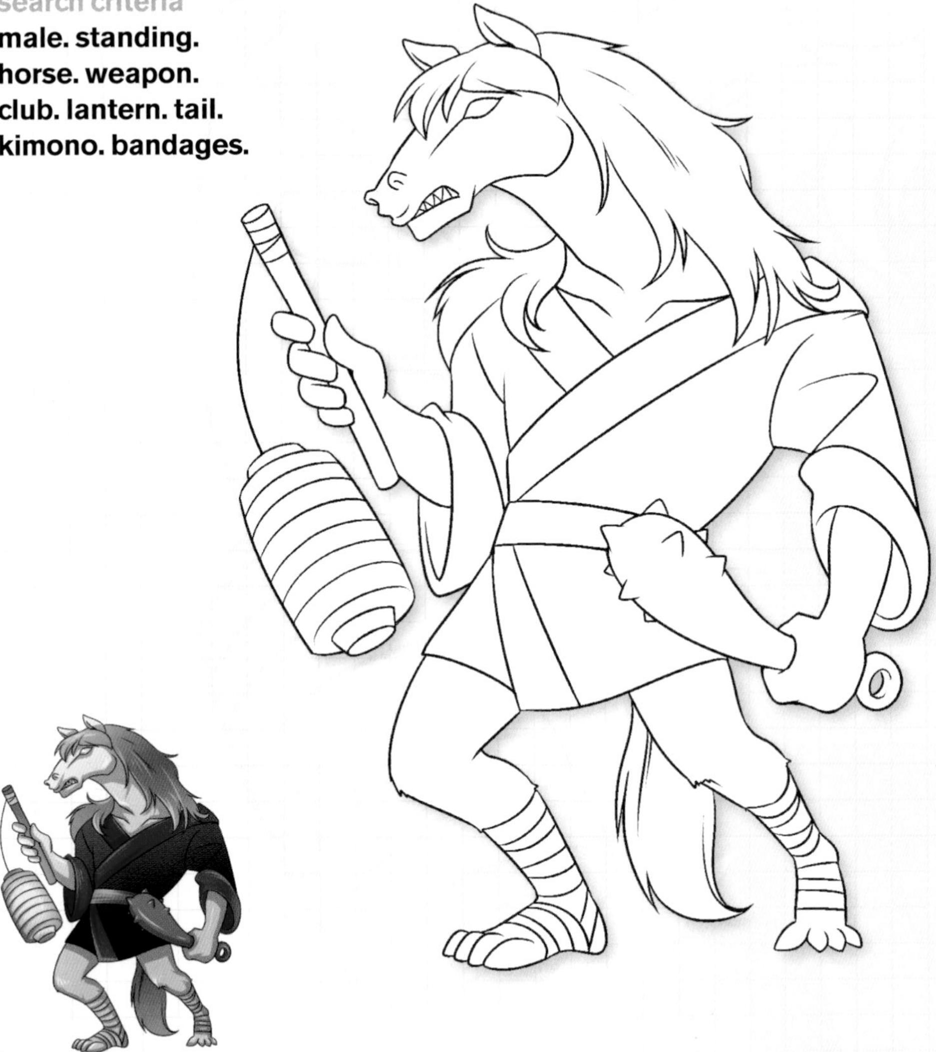

238

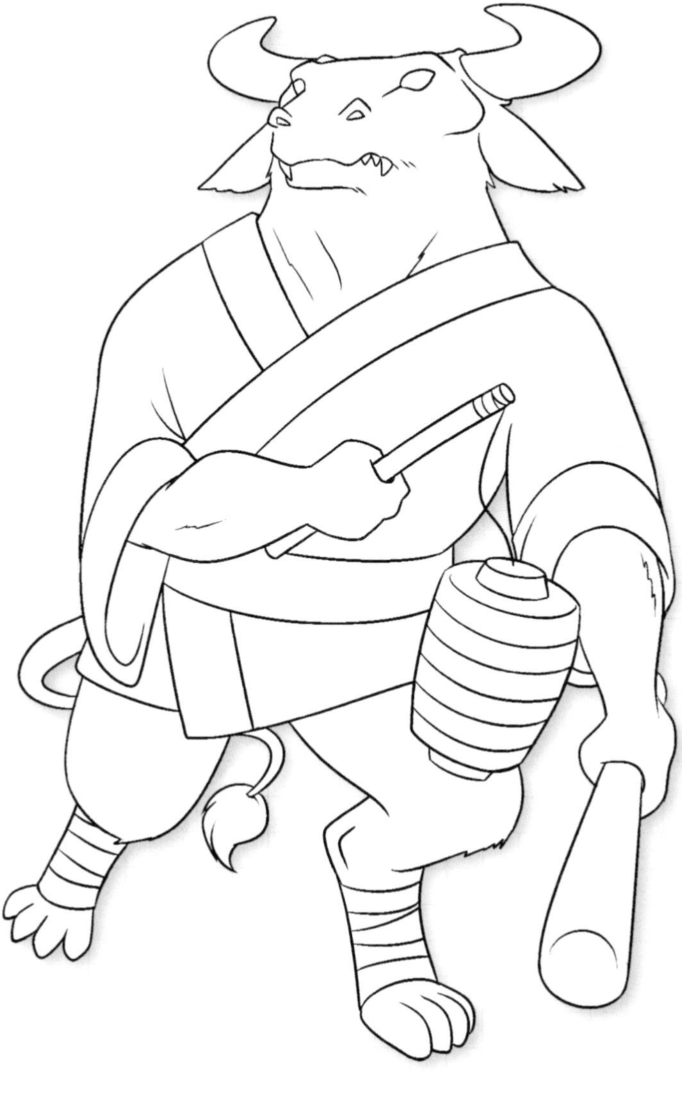

beast villains

search criteria

male. standing. horns. bandages. lantern. weapon. tail. club.

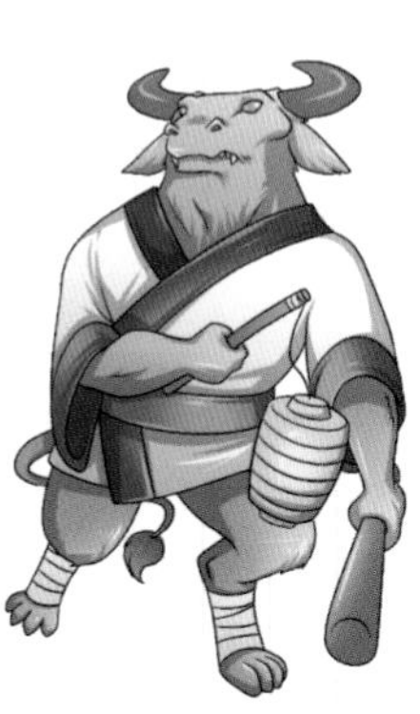

239

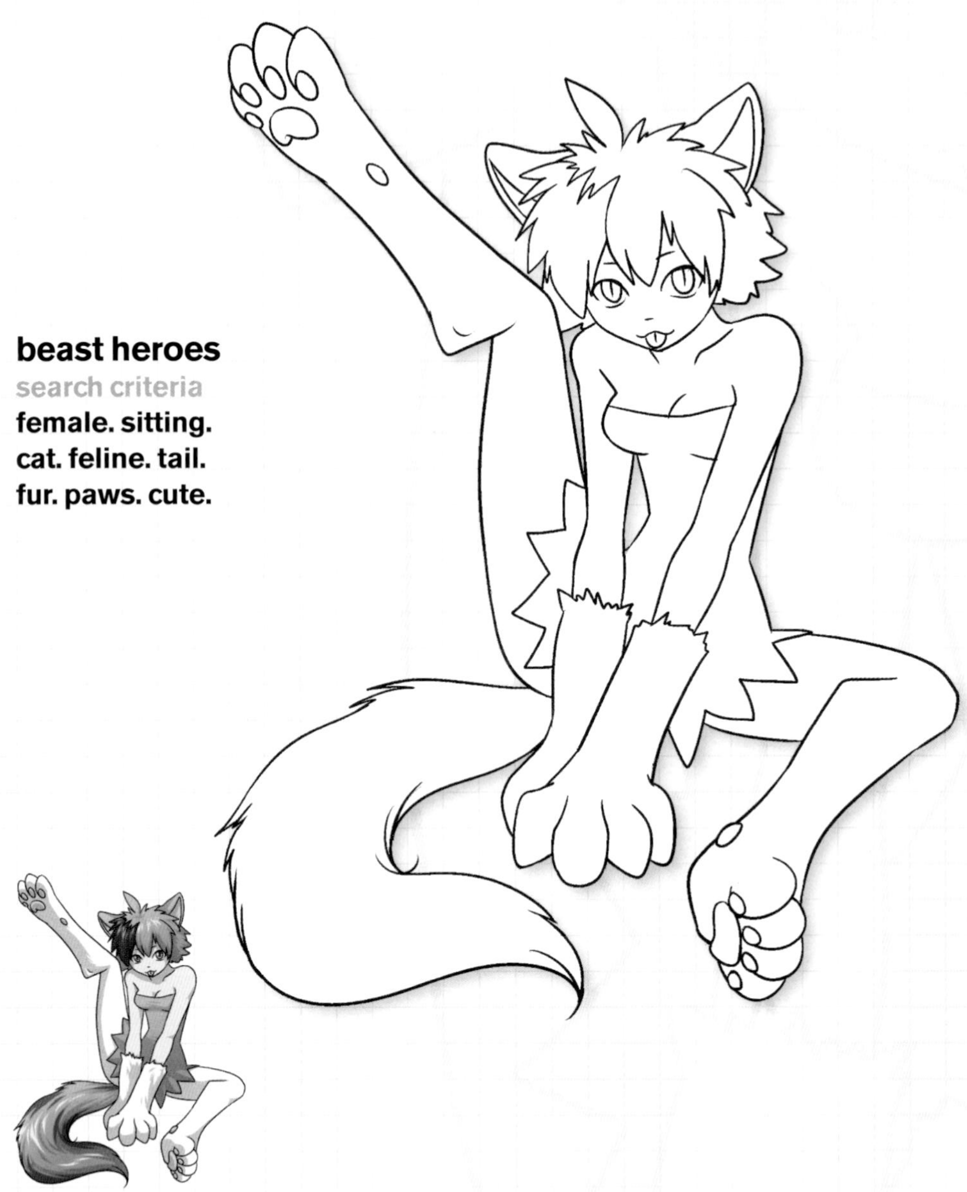

beast heroes

search criteria

female. sitting. cat. feline. tail. fur. paws. cute.

240

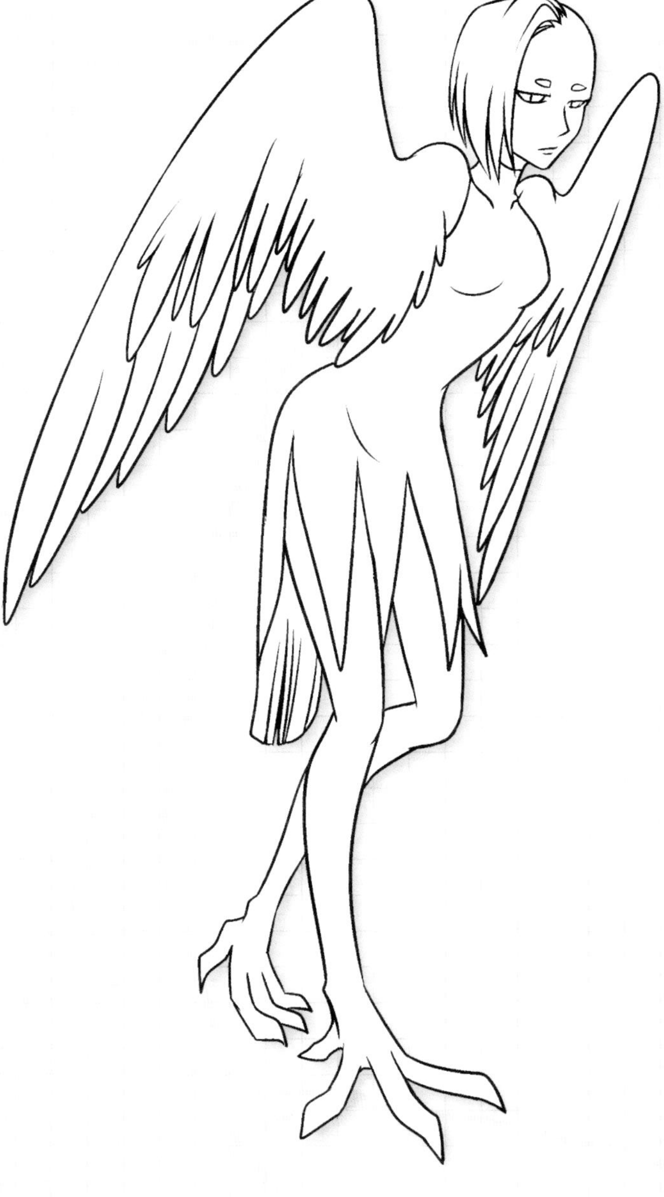

beast heroes

search criteria

female. standing. bird. wings. feathers. sad.

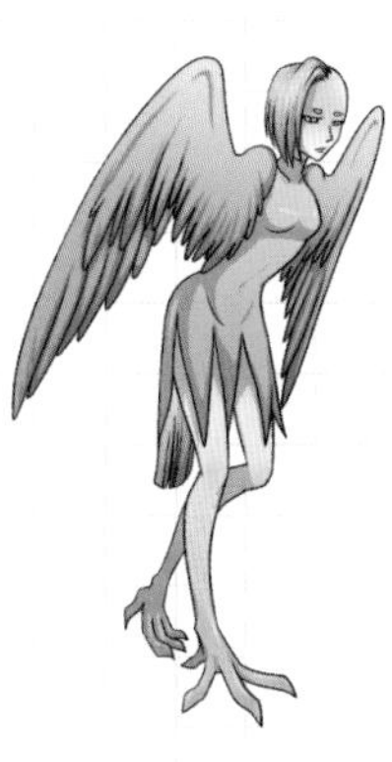

241

beast heroes

search criteria

female. jump. side. horns. faun. tail. flowers. smiling.

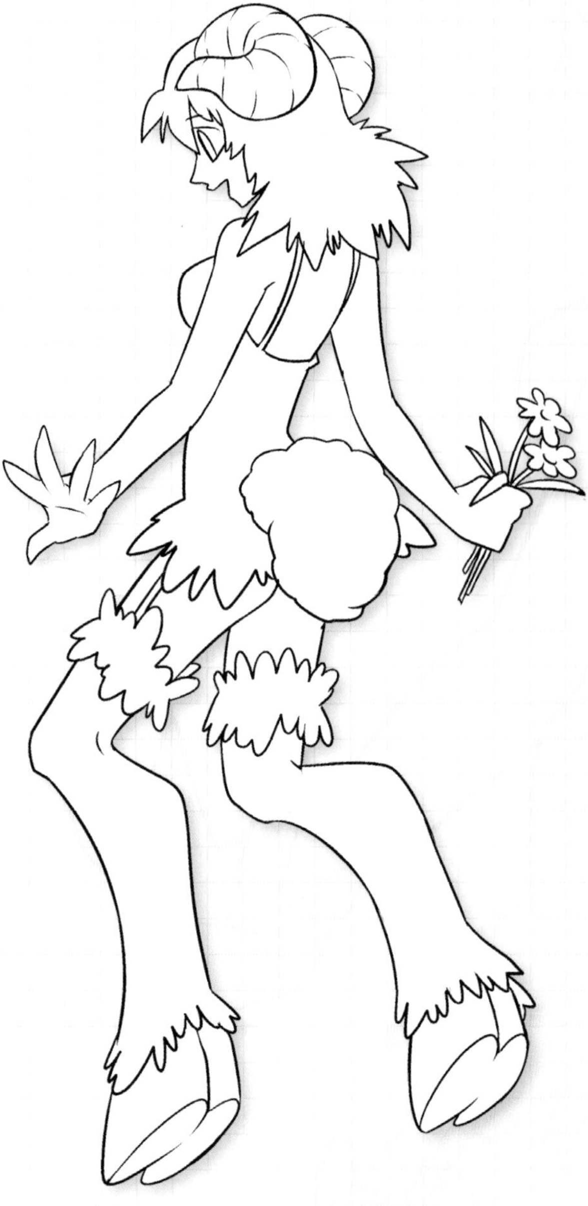

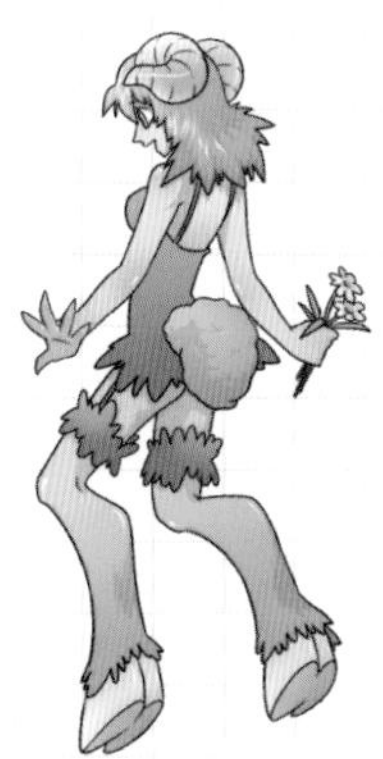

242

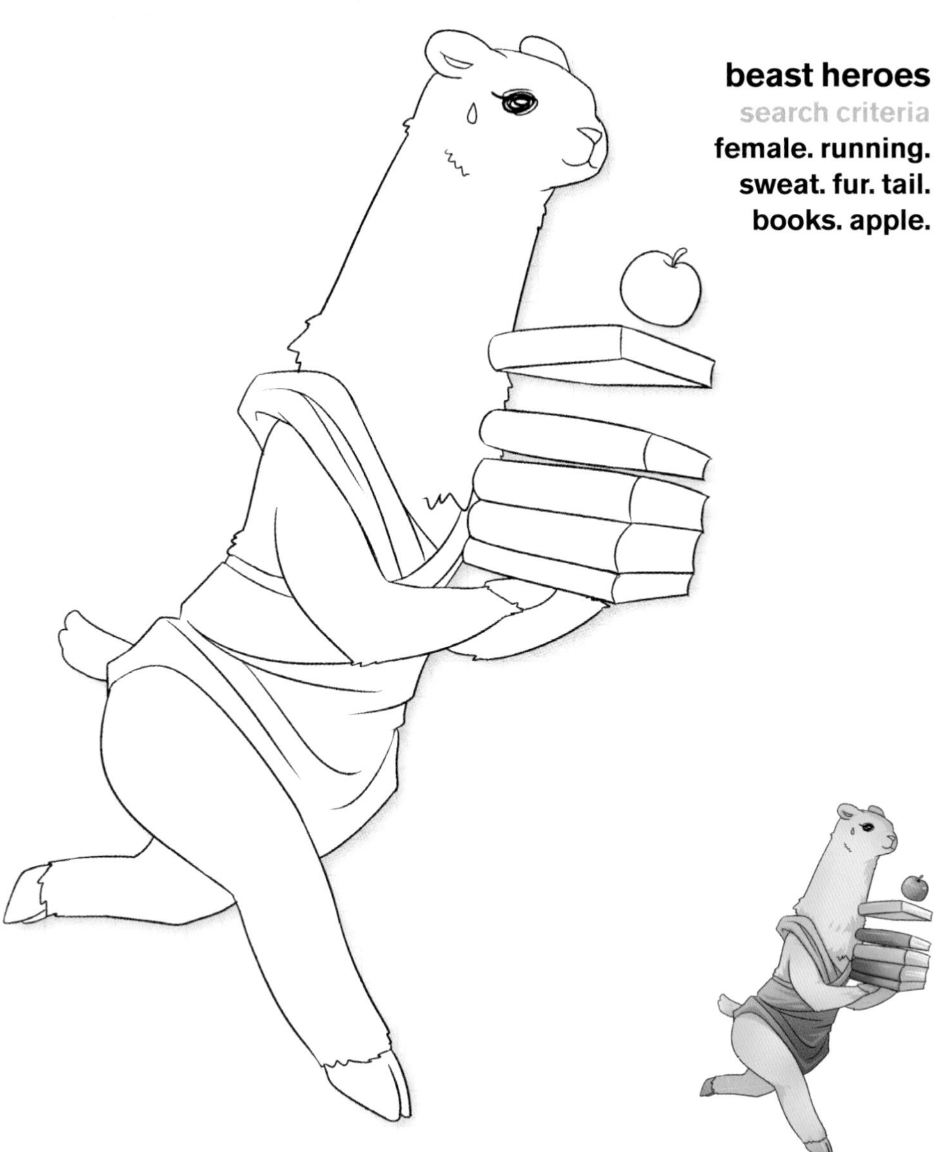

beast heroes

search criteria

female. running. sweat. fur. tail. books. apple.

243

beast heroes

search criteria

female. standing. bird. wings. feathers. armor. beak.

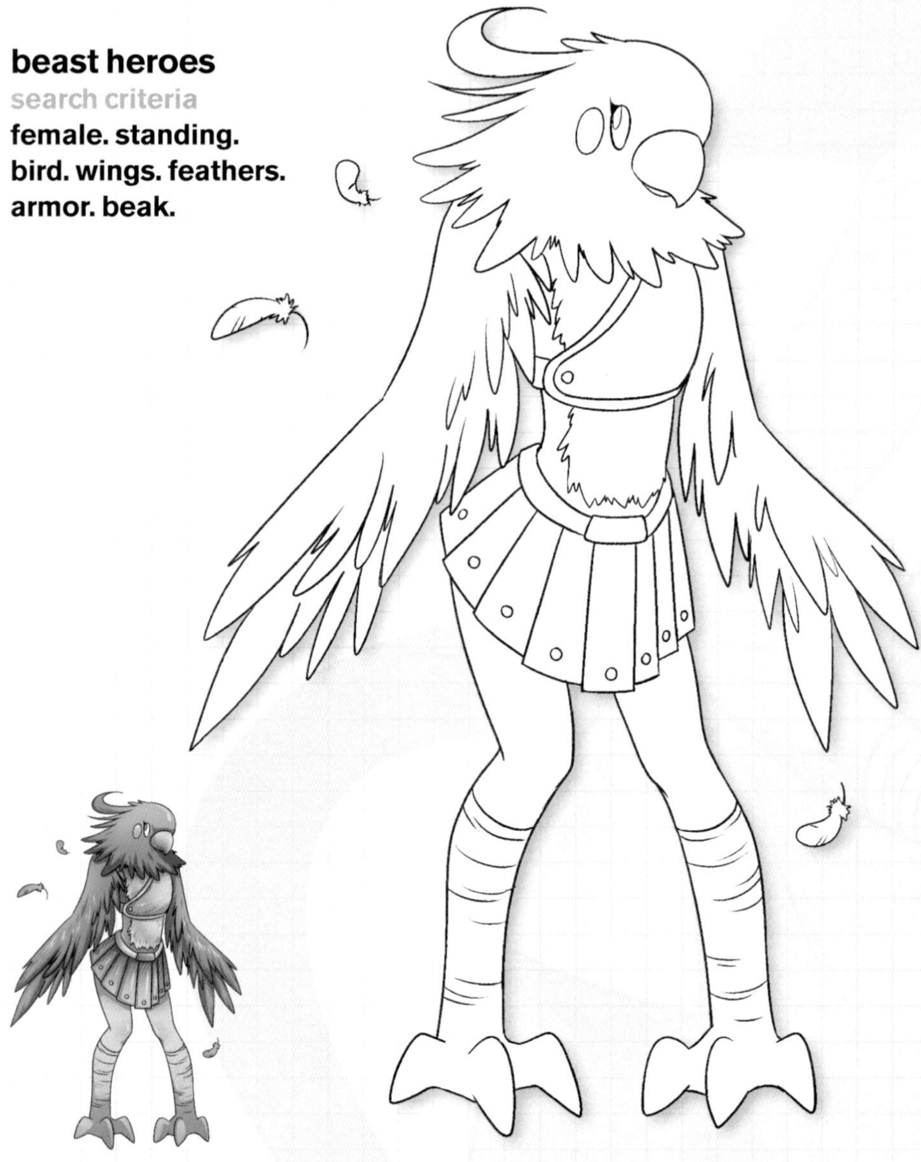

244

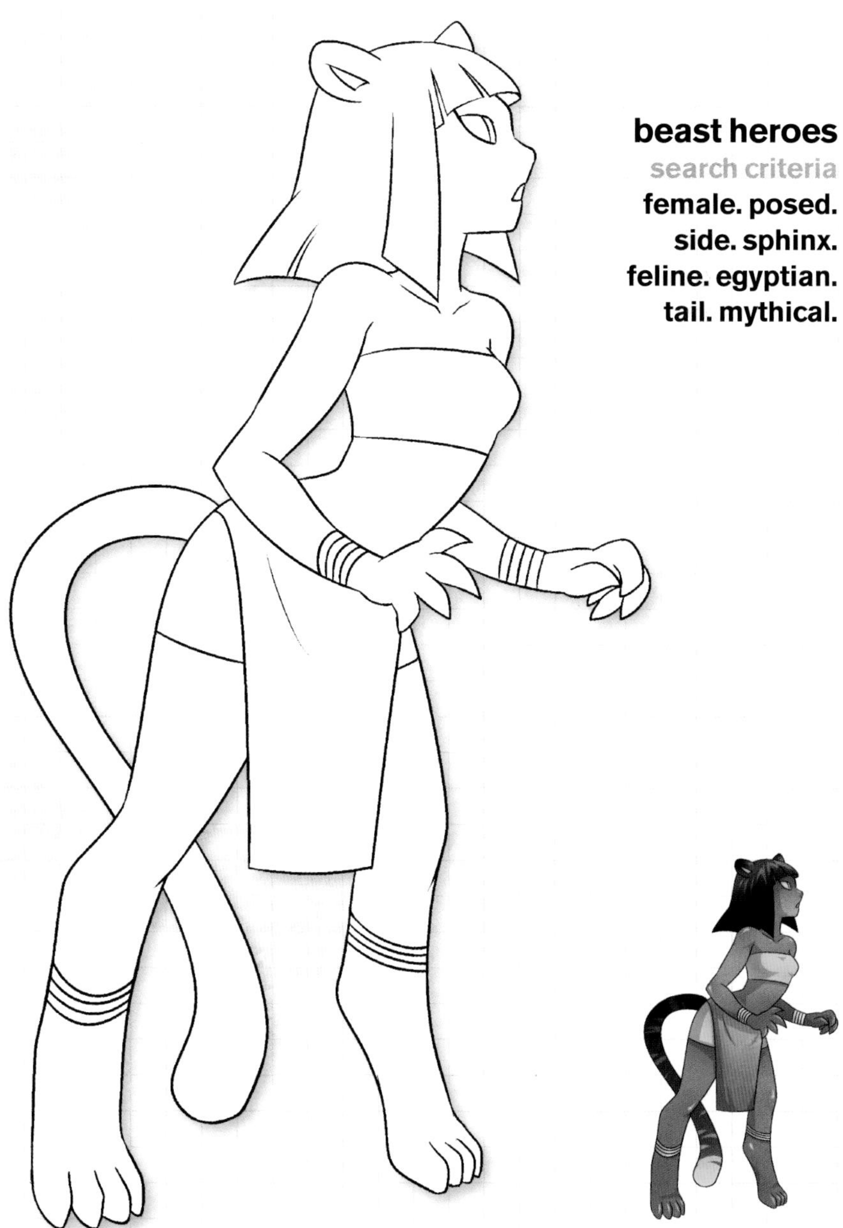

beast heroes

search criteria

female. posed. side. sphinx. feline. egyptian. tail. mythical.

245

beast heroes

search criteria

male. sitting. reading. smoking. pipe. glasses. book. crocodile. scales. tail.

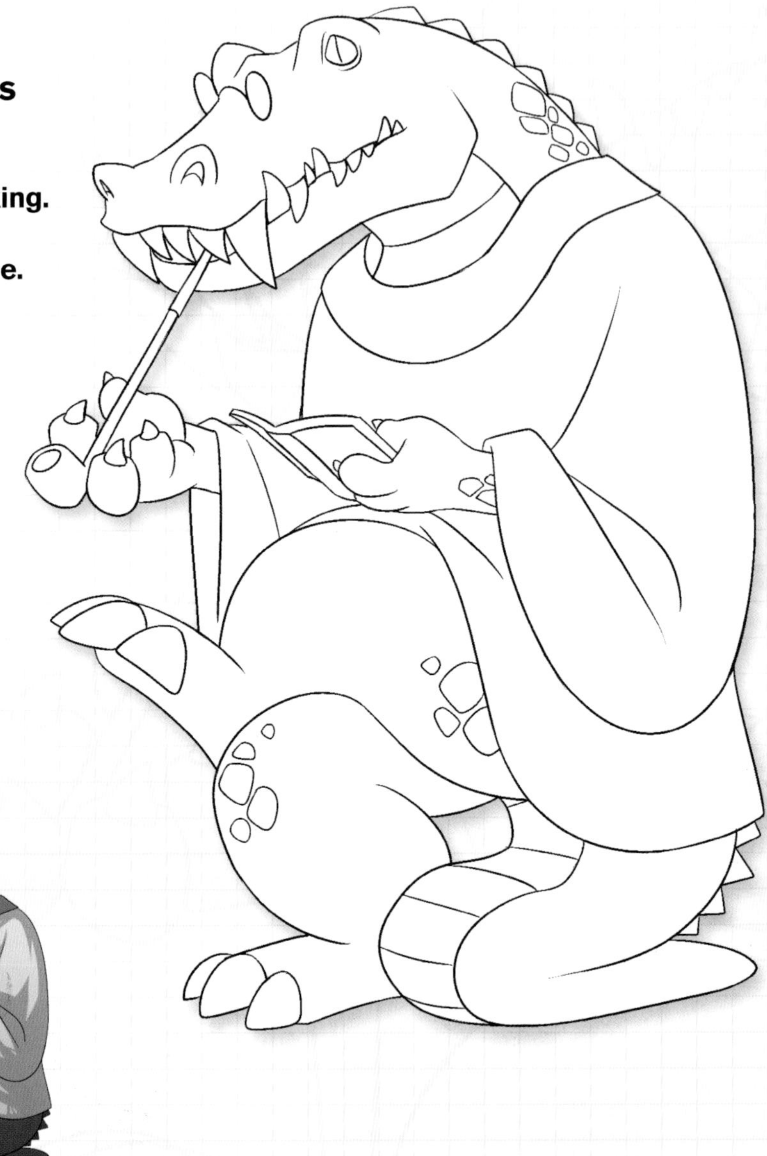

246

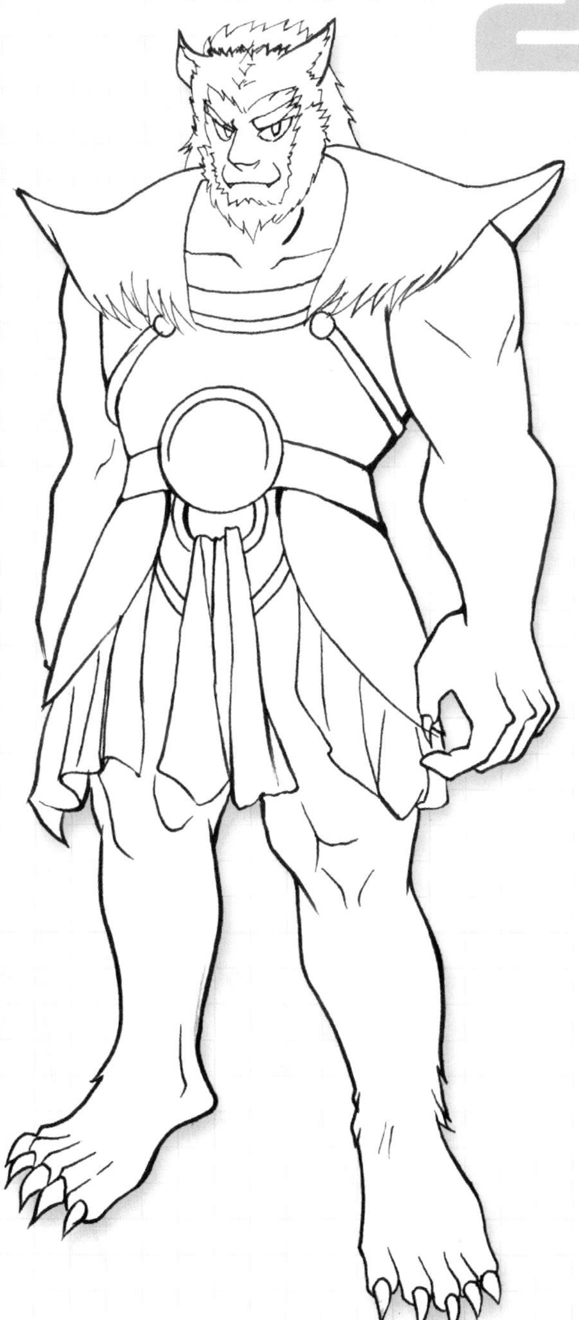

beast heroes

search criteria

male. standing. muscle. fur. wolf. armor. warrior.

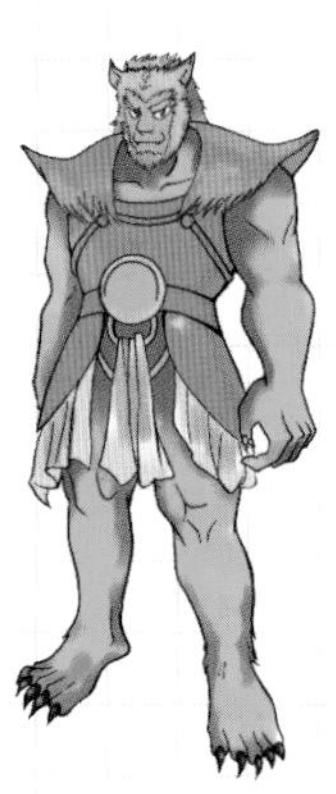

247

beast heroes

search criteria

female. sitting. tail. fur. cute. cat. feline.

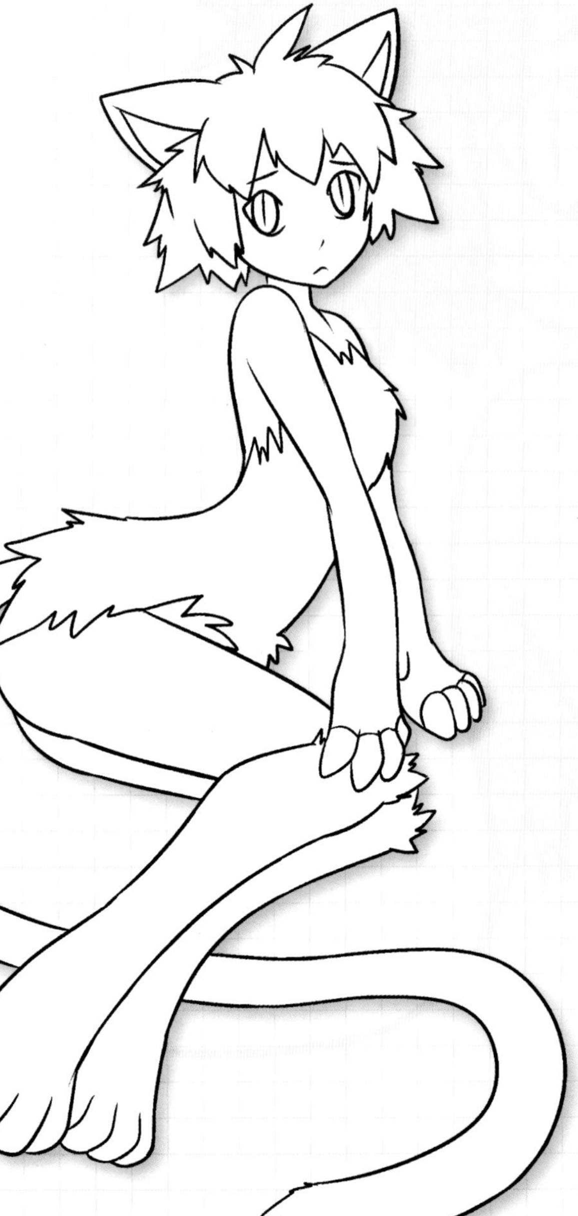

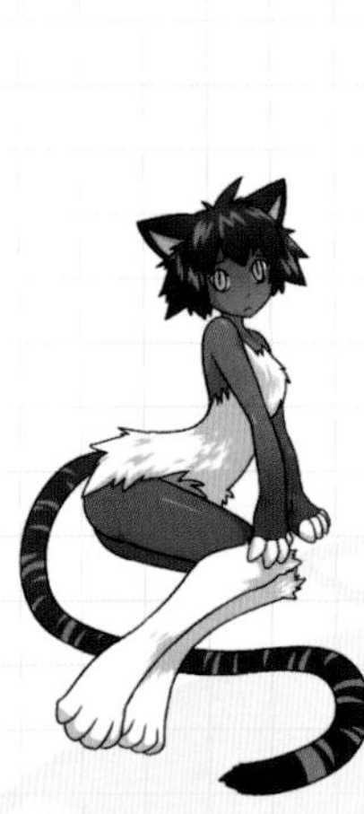

248

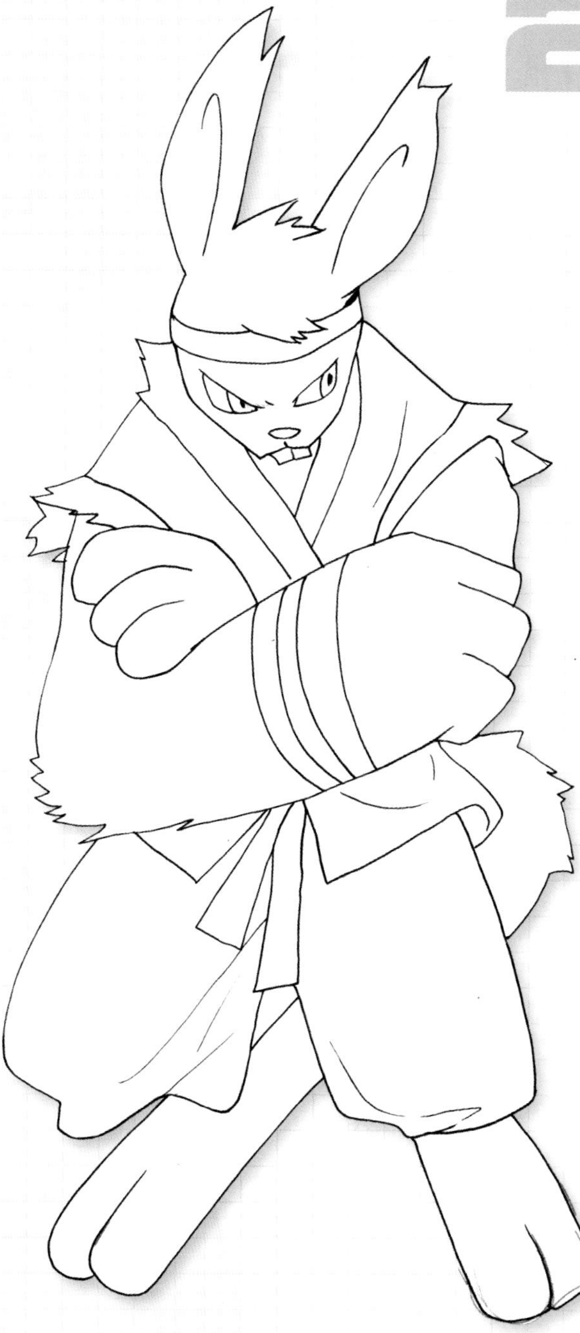

beast heroes

search criteria

male. standing. ninja. bunny. headband. fur. angry. tail.

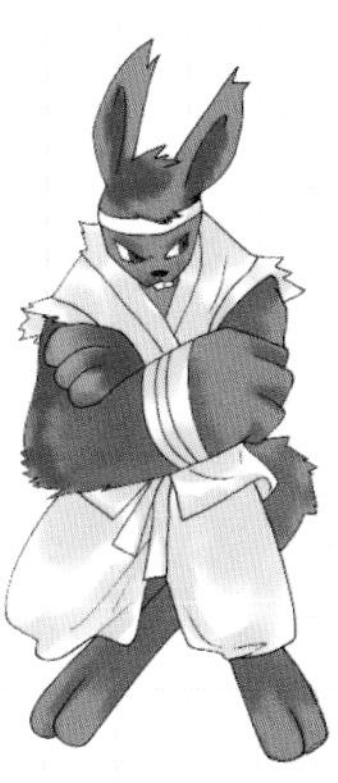

249

beast heroes

search criteria

female. jump. side.
tail. smiling. squirrel.

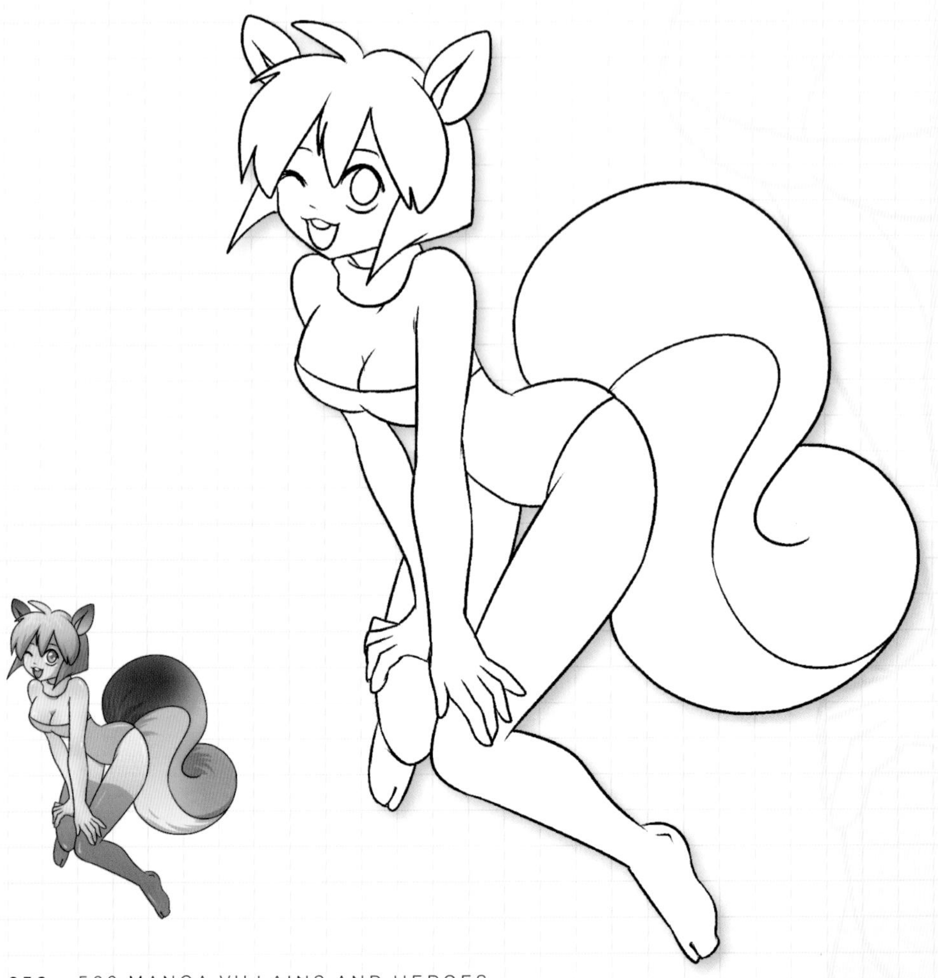

250

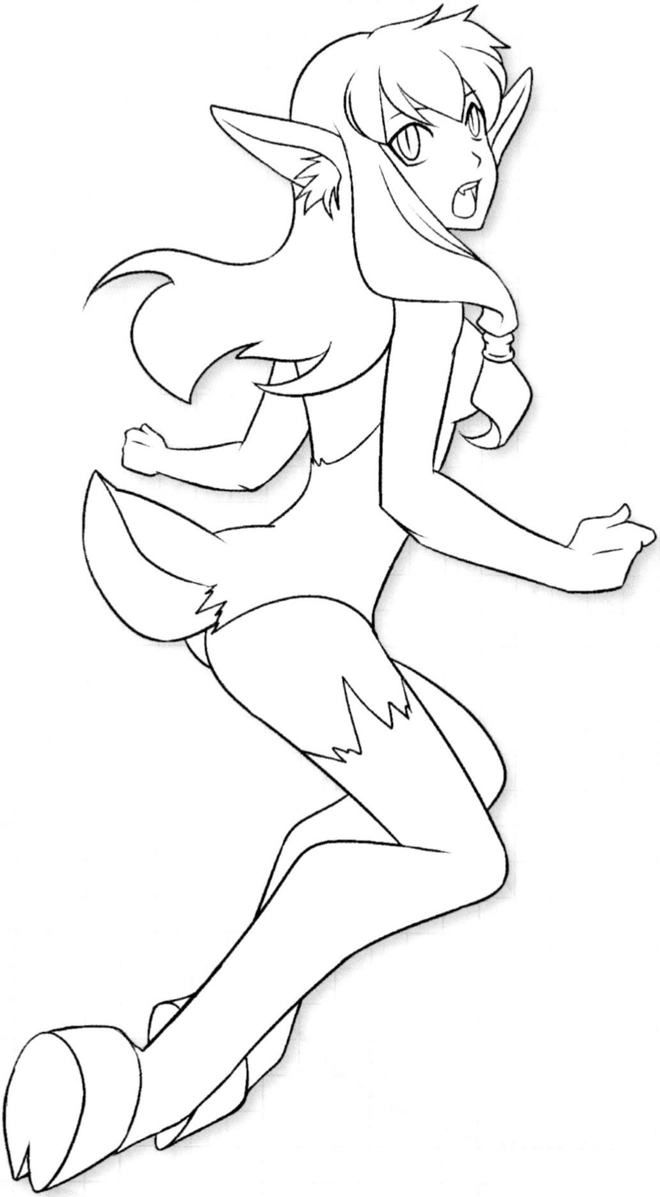

beast heroes

search criteria

**female. jump. side.
fur. tail. faun.**

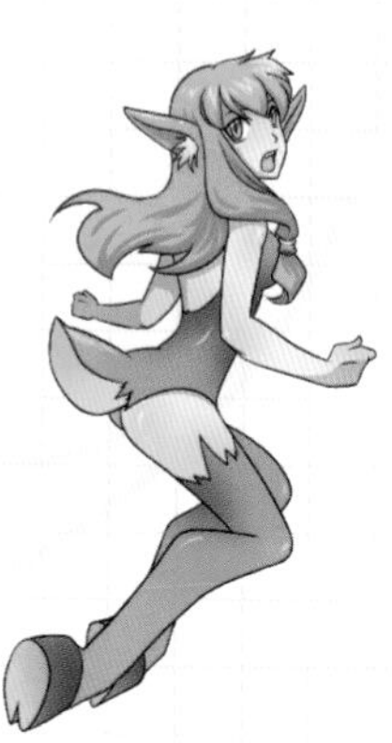

251

beast heroes

search criteria

female. standing.
bunny. tail. whisper.

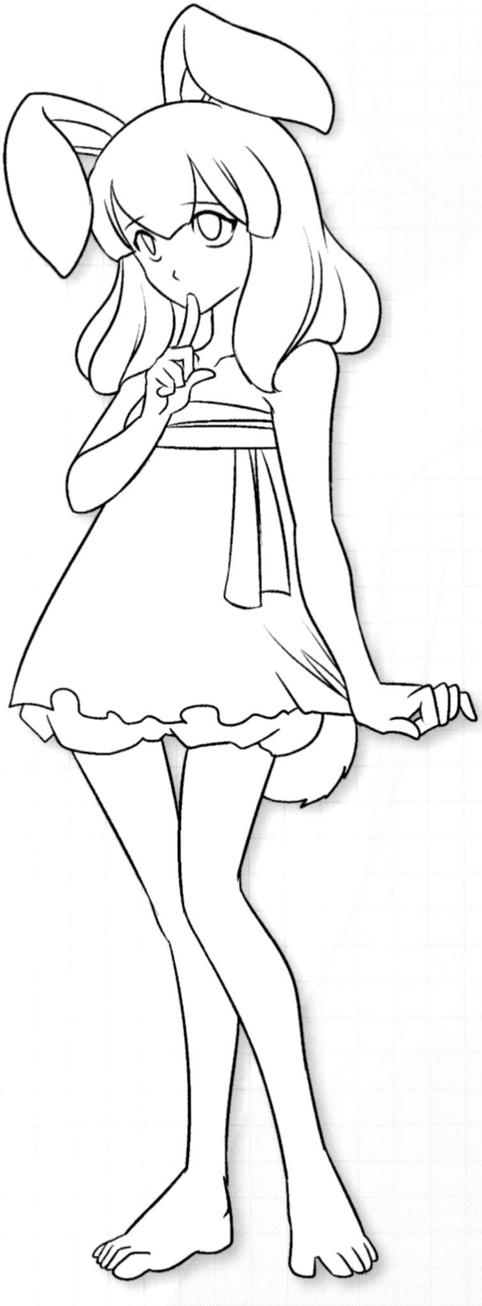

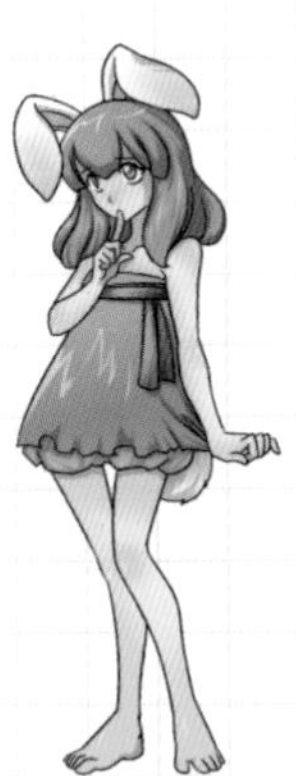

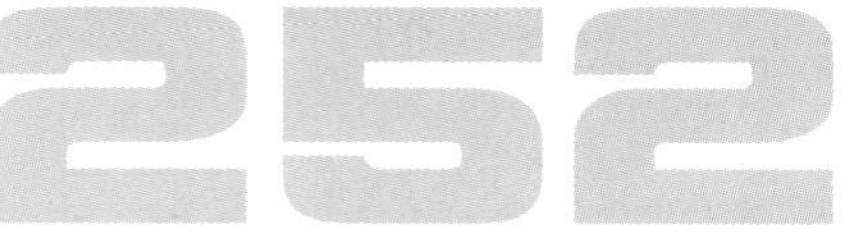

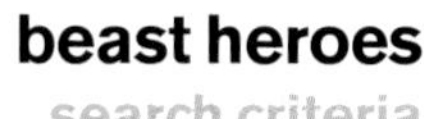

search criteria

female. standing.
tail. sad. bell. heart.

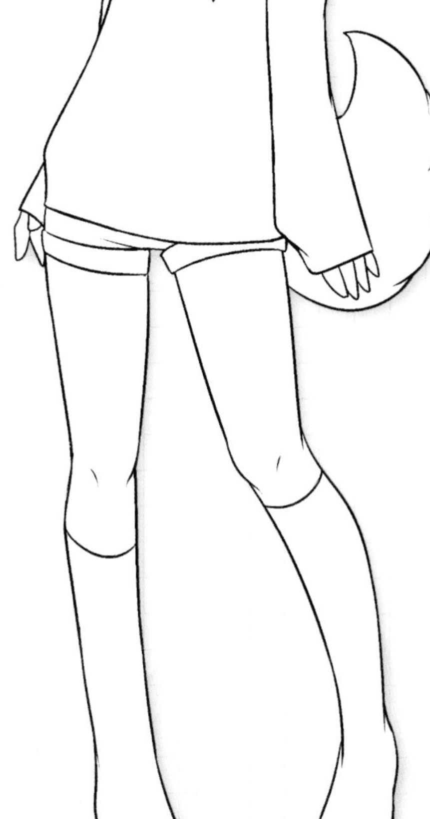

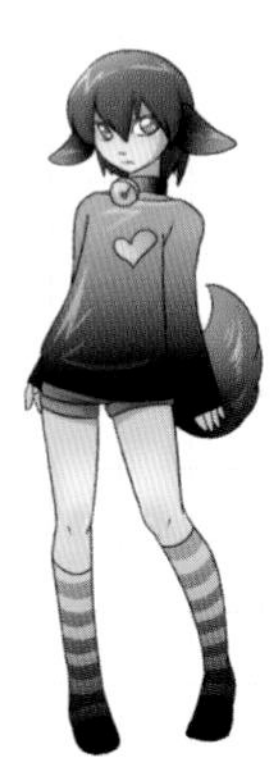

253

beast heroes

search criteria

female. standing.
tail. bell. bone.

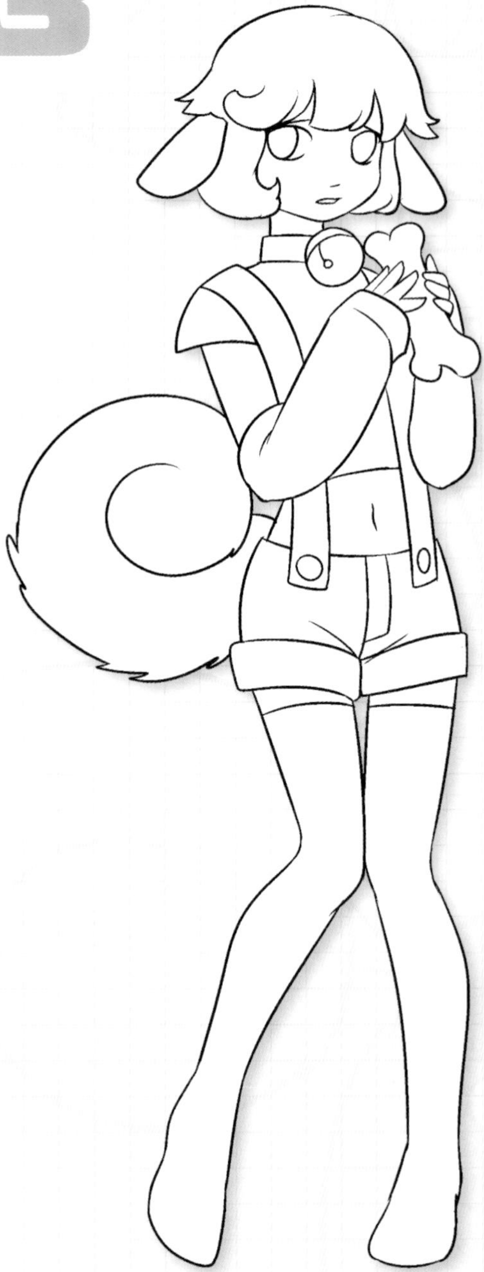

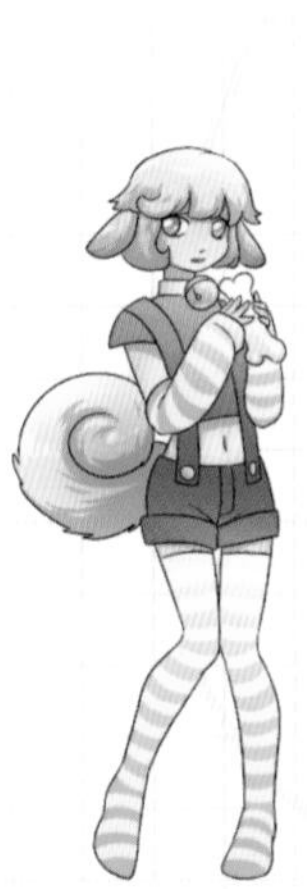

254

beast heroes

search criteria

female. standing. child. tail. apple. smell. cute.

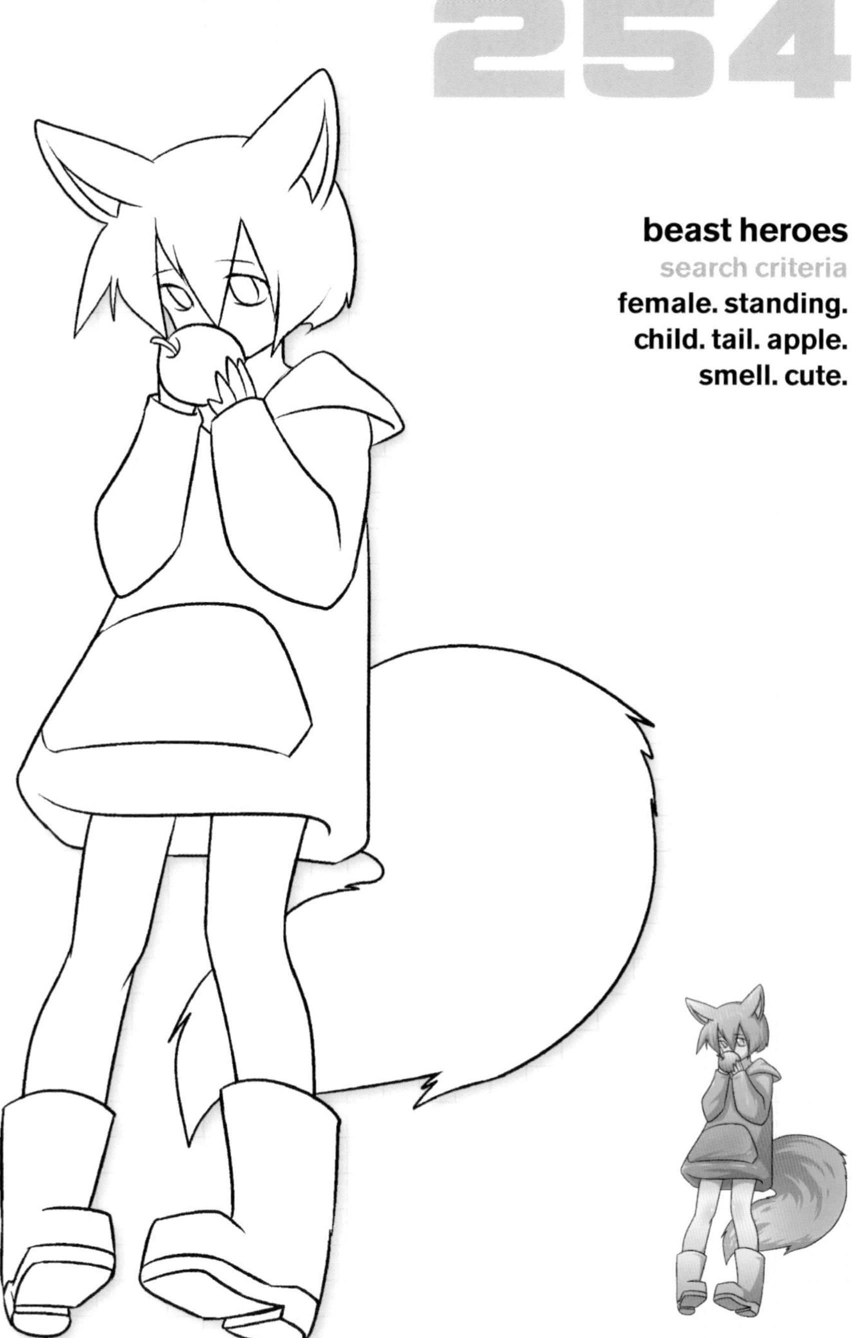

255

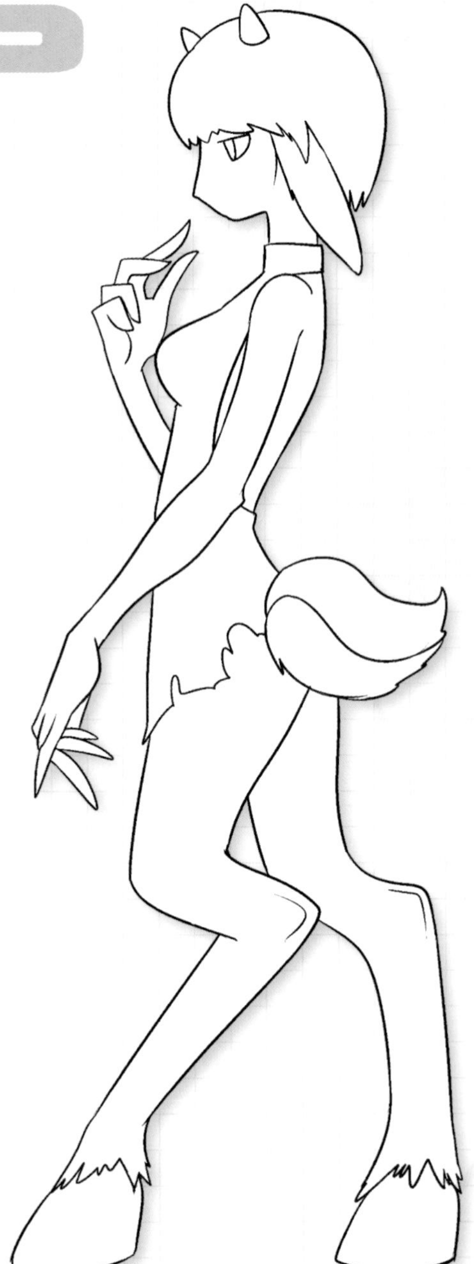

beast heroes

search criteria

female. standing. side. tail. deer. horns. pinch.

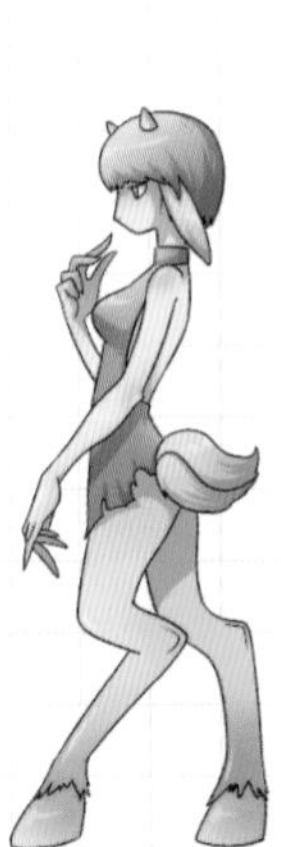

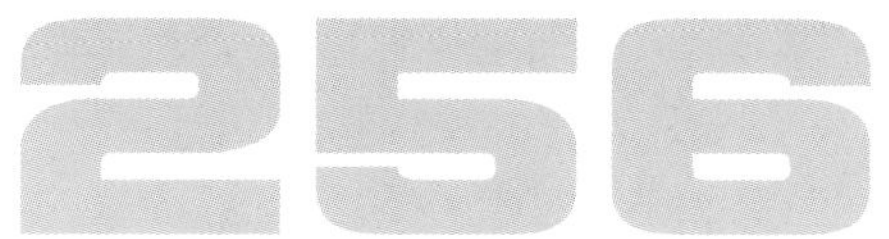

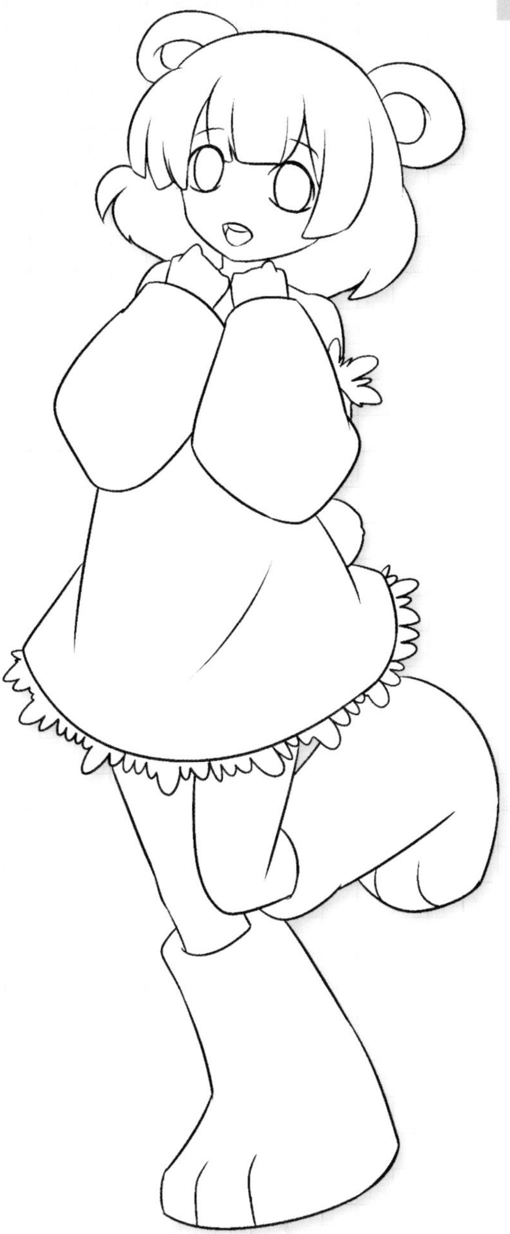

beast heroes

search criteria

female. skipping. smiling. bear. cute.

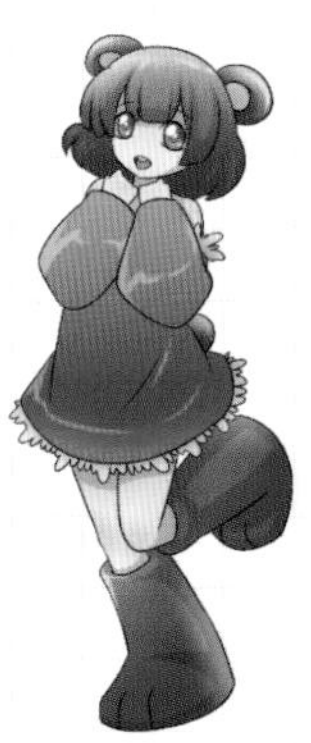

257

beast heroes

search criteria

female. jump.
kimono. bunny.

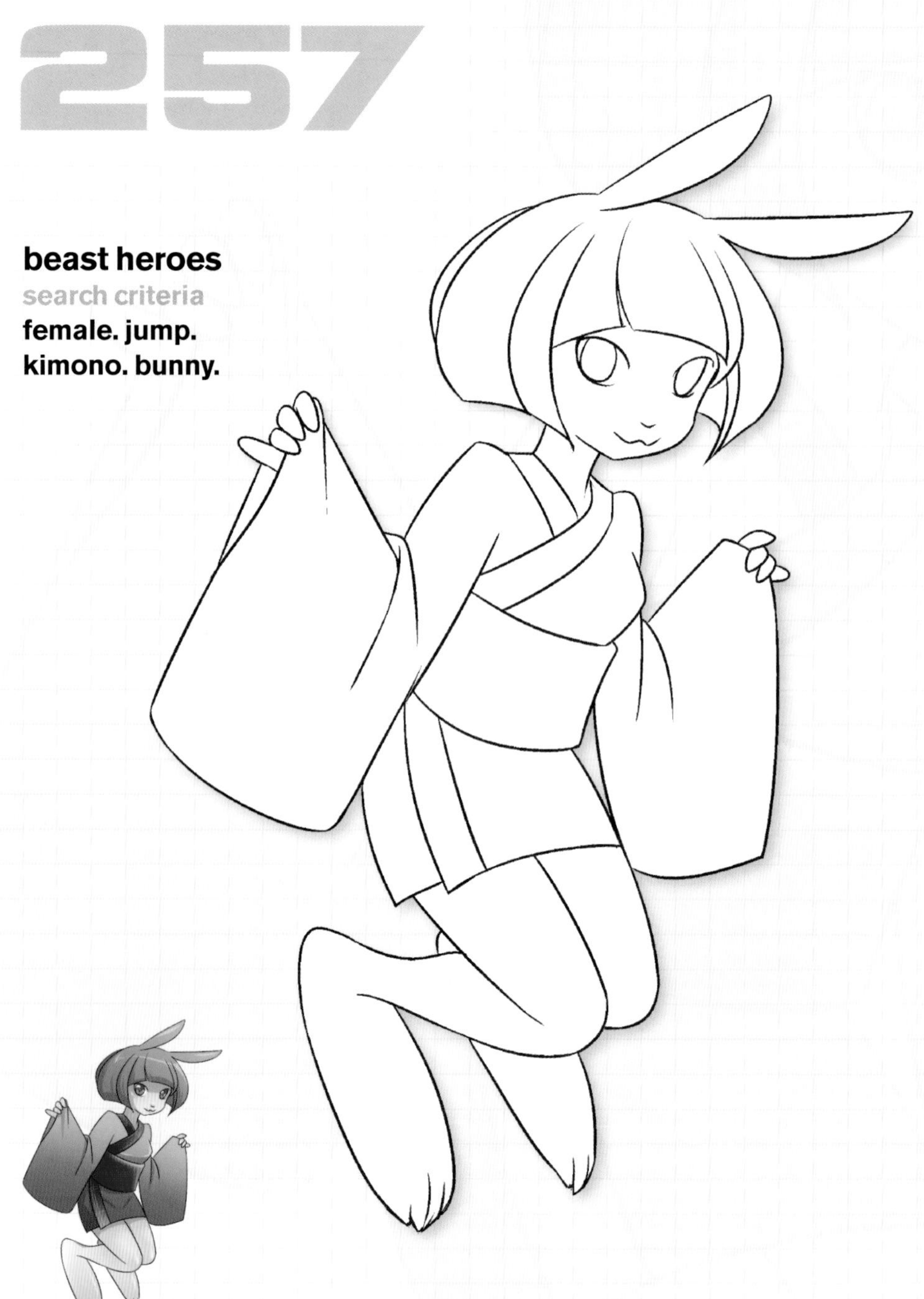

258

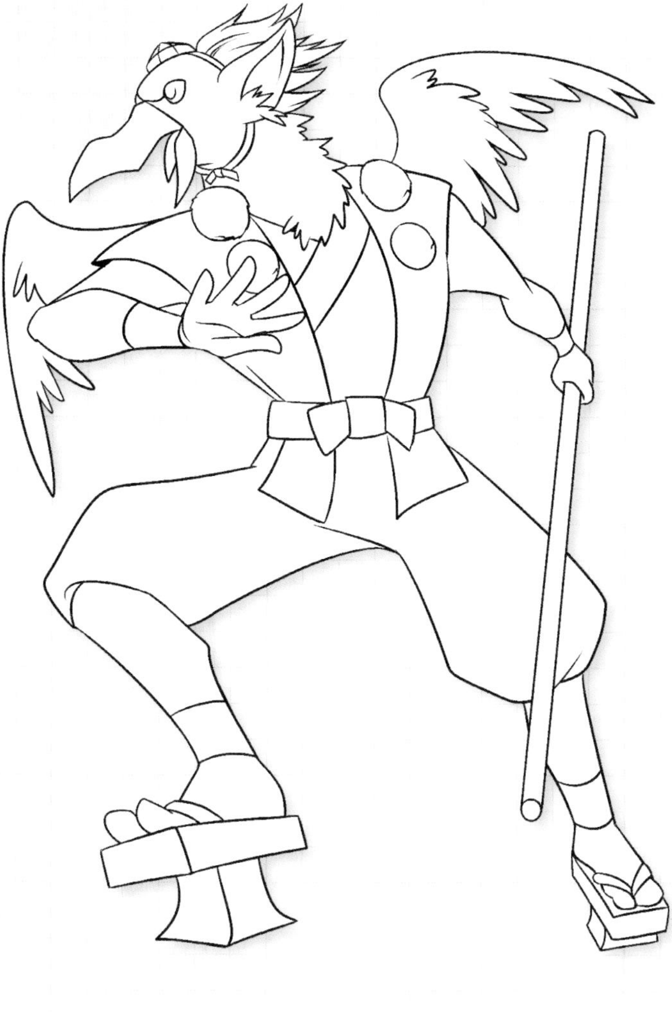

beast heroes

search criteria

male. side. feathers. beak. wings. bird. weapon. stick.

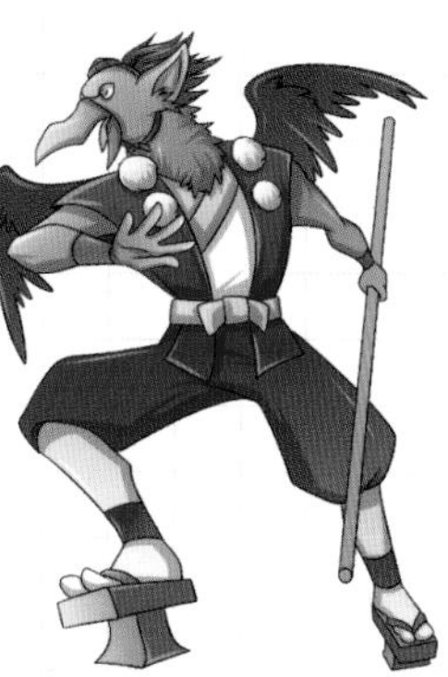

259

elemental villains

search criteria

floating. water.
angry. demon.

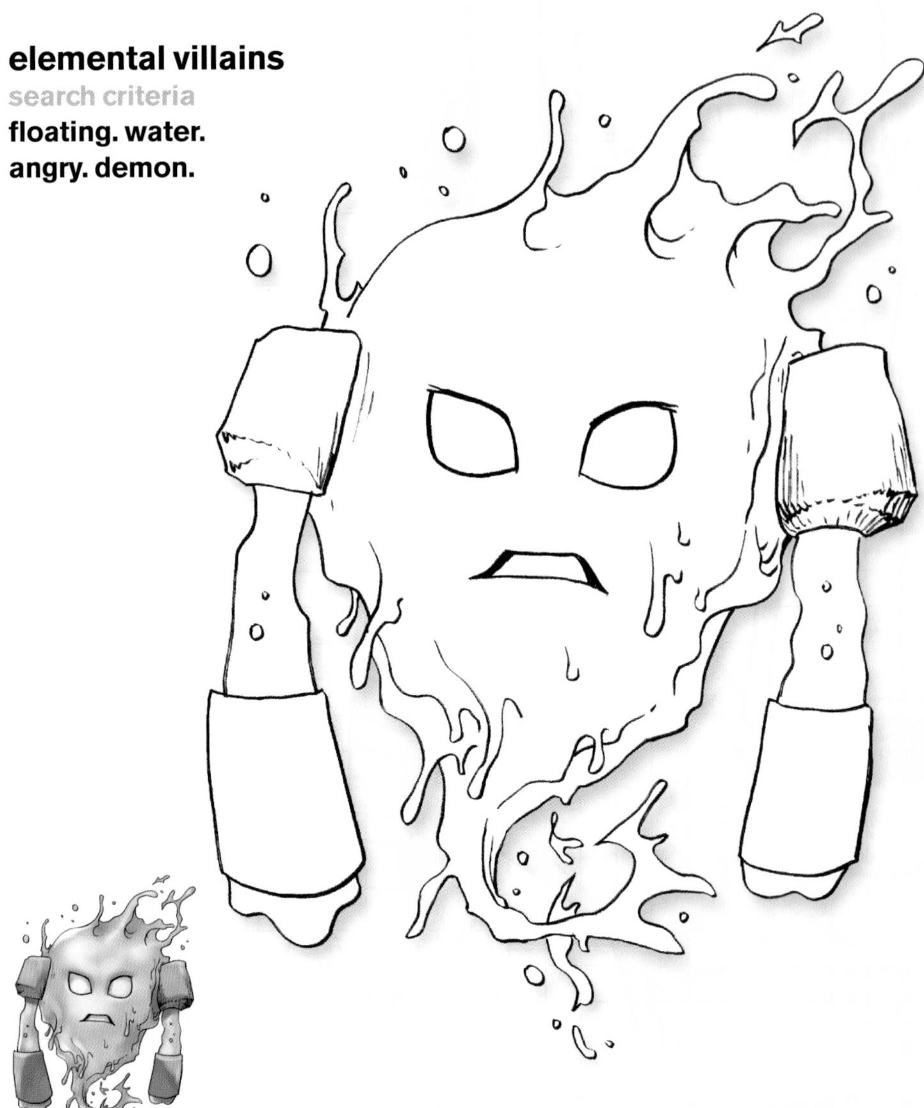

260

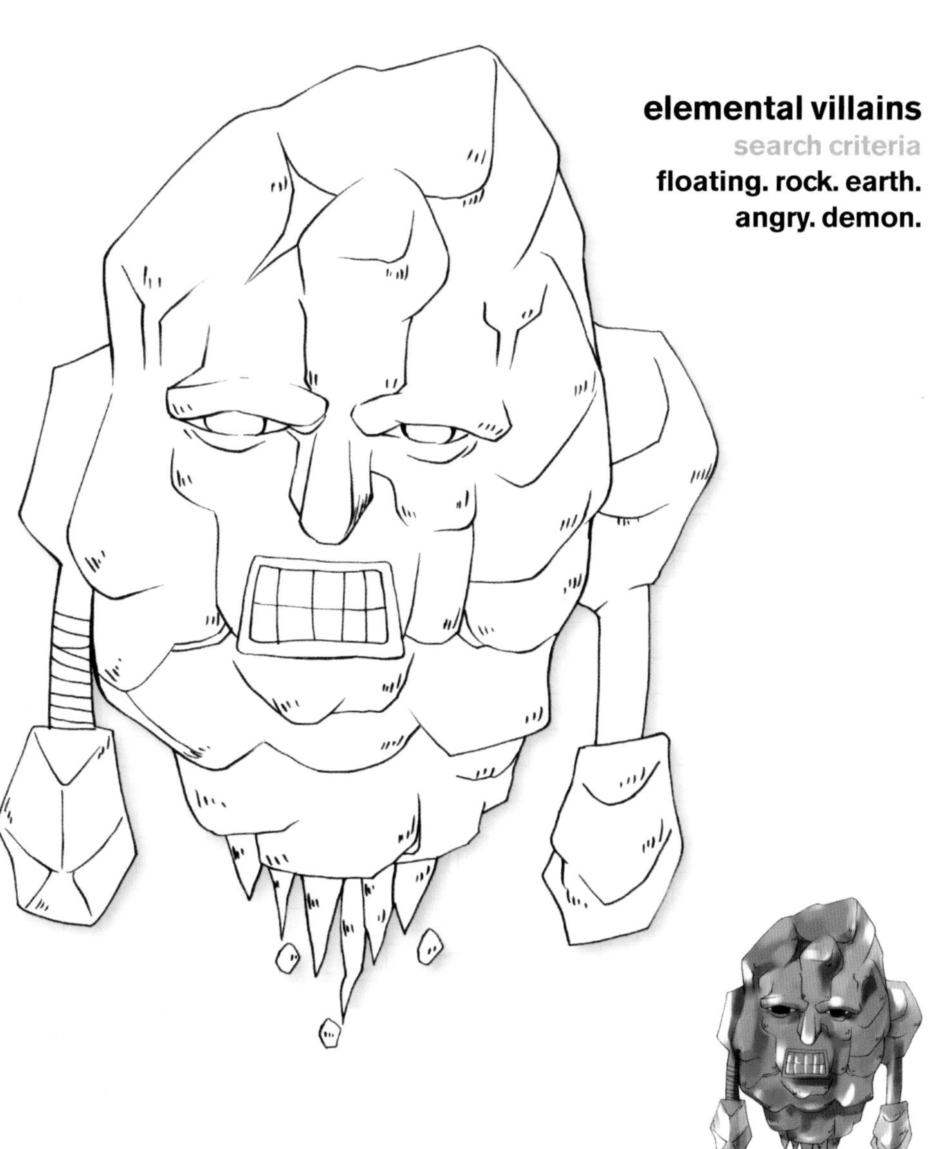

elemental villains

search criteria

floating. rock. earth. angry. demon.

261

elemental villains

search criteria

flying. floating. wind. air. tornado. twister.

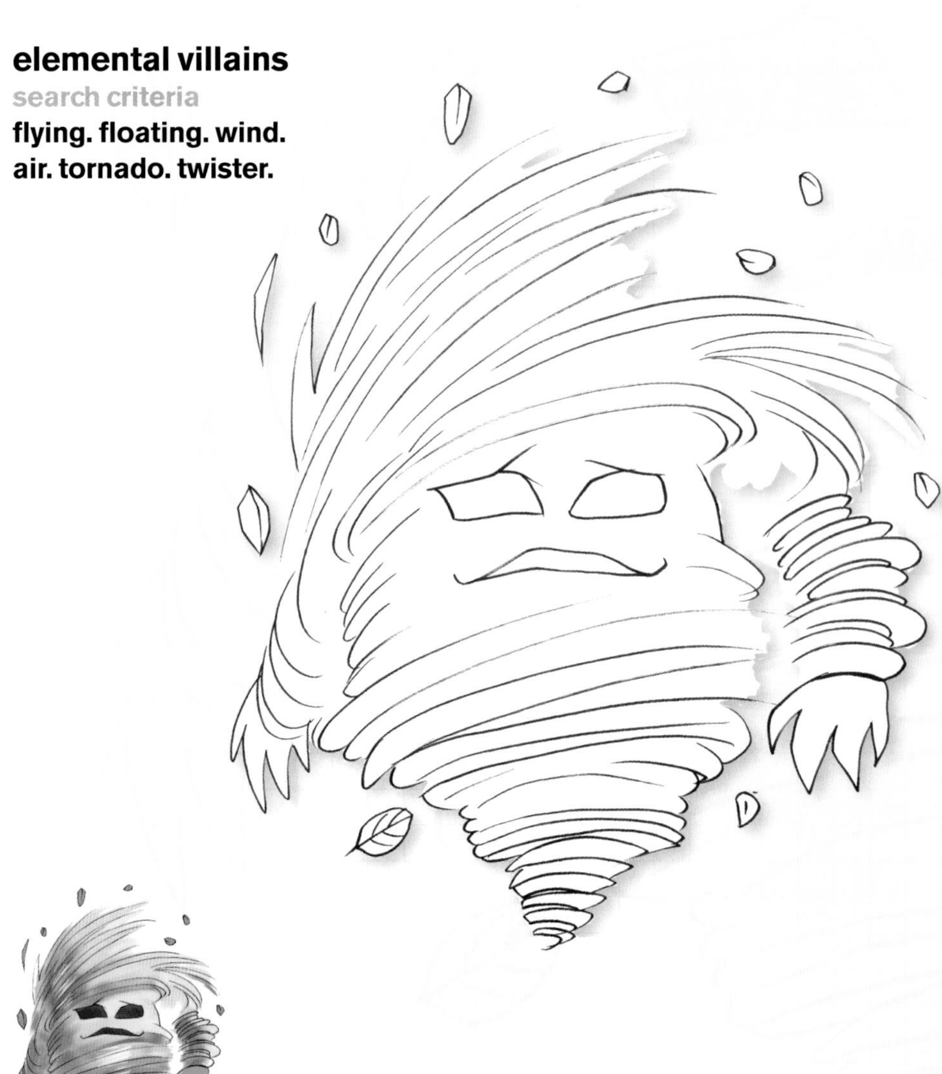

262

elemental villains

search criteria

floating. fire. evil. demon. flames.

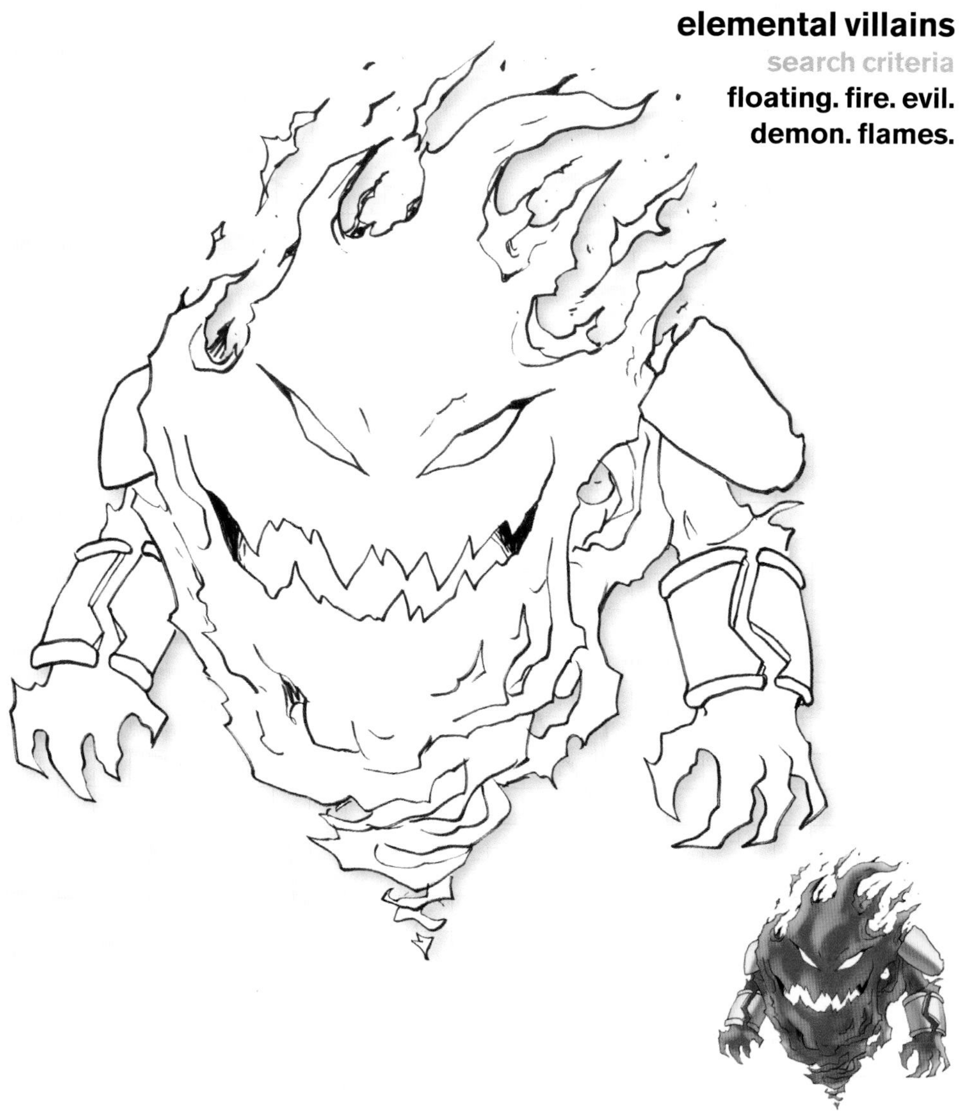

263

elemental villains

search criteria

male. jump.
fire. flames.
mecha. armor.

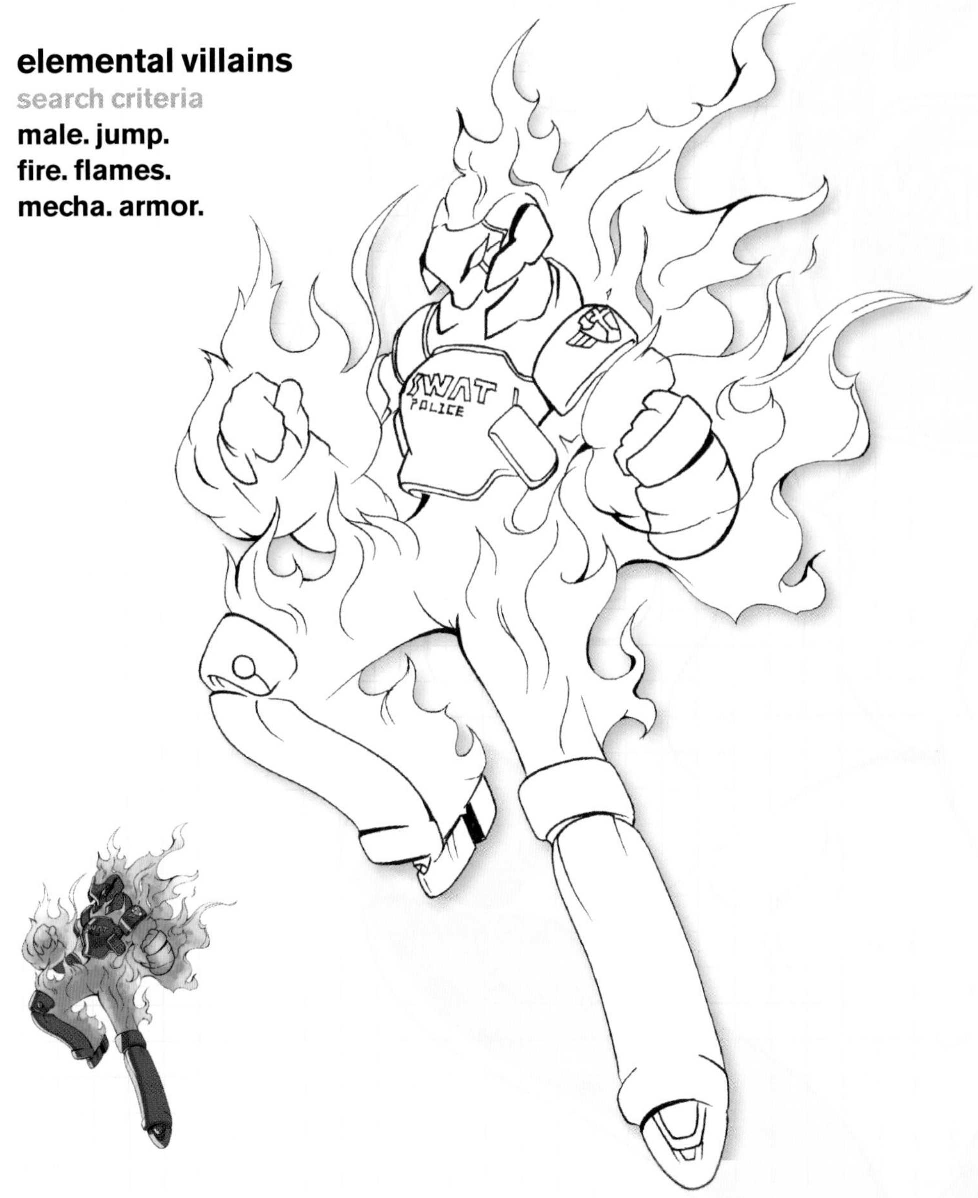

264

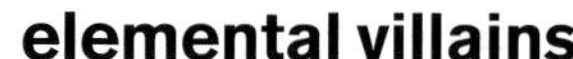

elemental villains

search criteria

male. jump.
fire. flames.
demon. armor.
weapon. scythe.

265

elemental villains

search criteria

female. water. floating. jump.

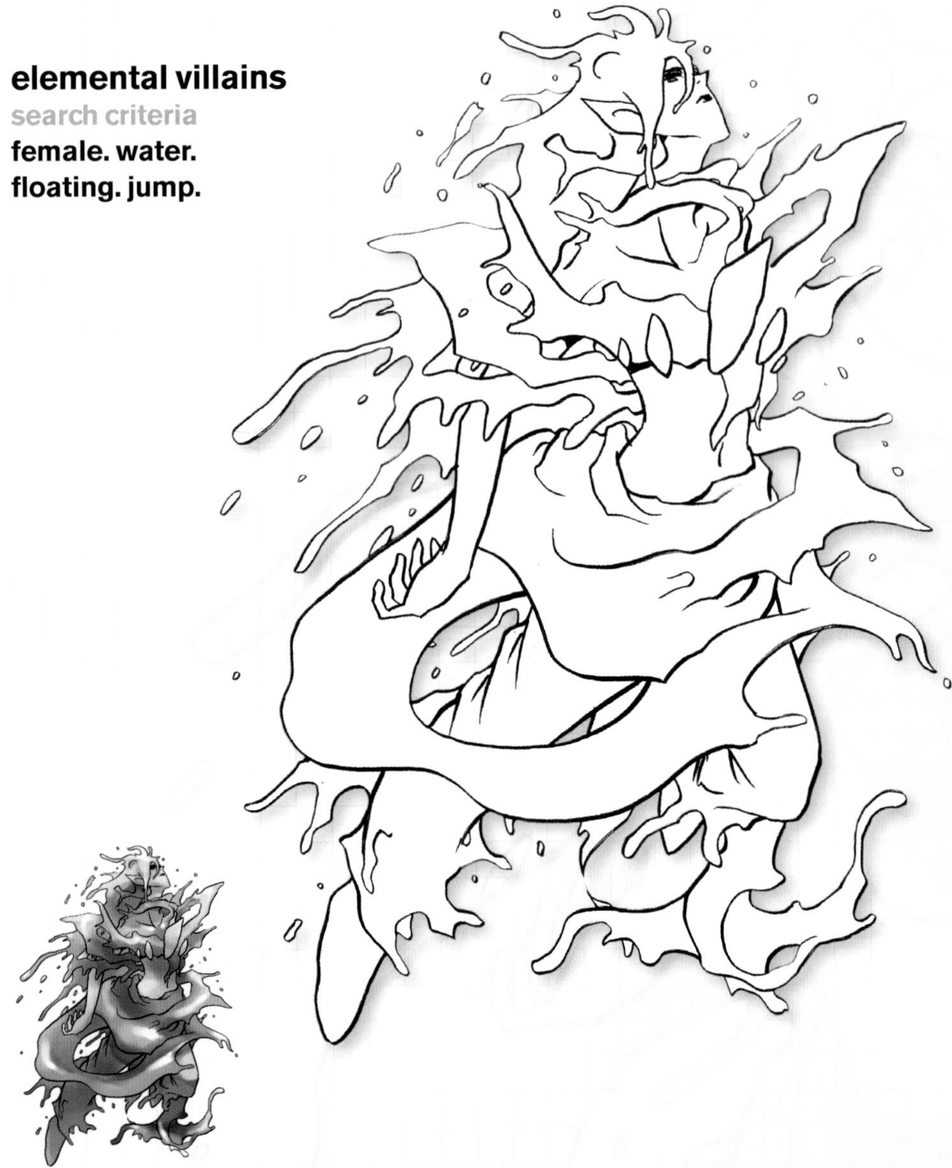

elemental villains

search criteria

female. earth. standing. floating. smell. witch.

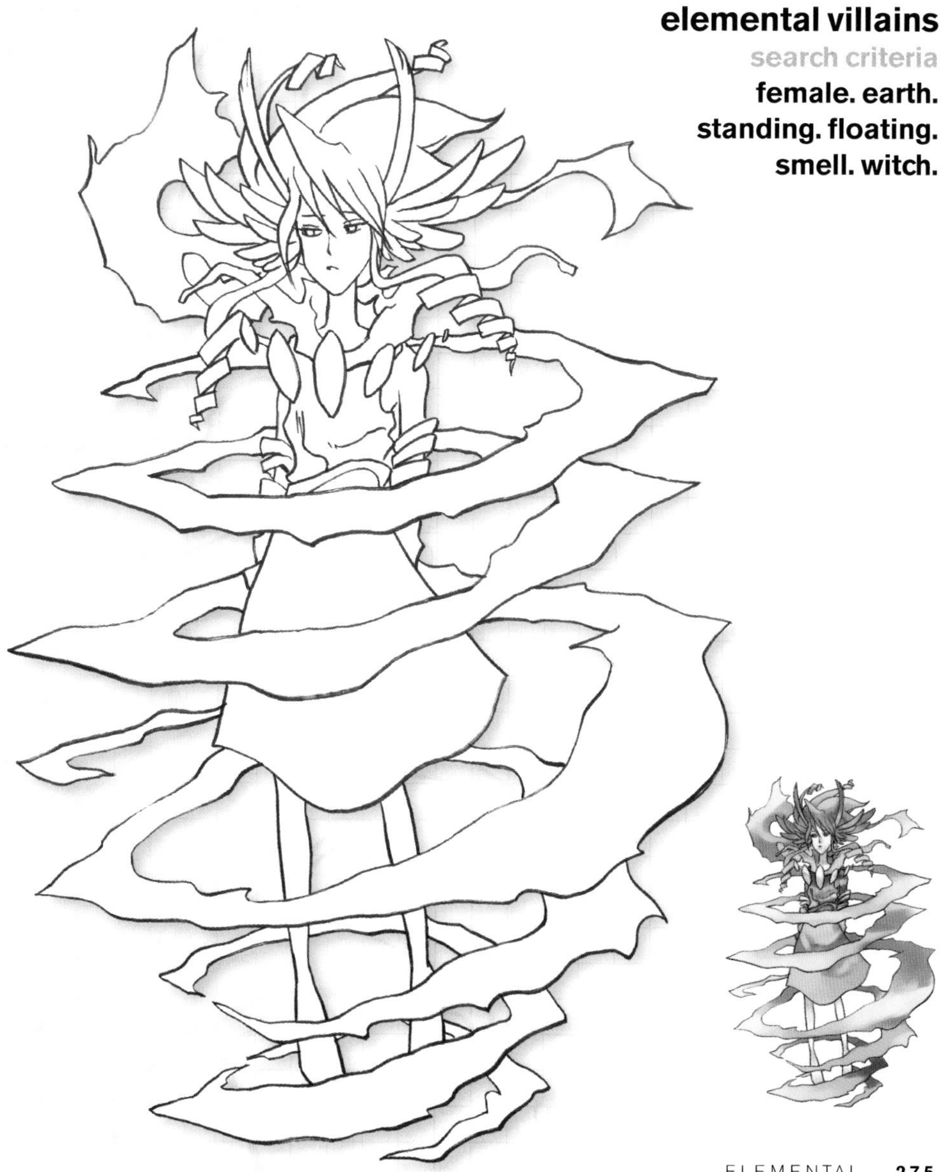

267

elemental villains

search criteria

female. floating. side. flames. fire. clouds.

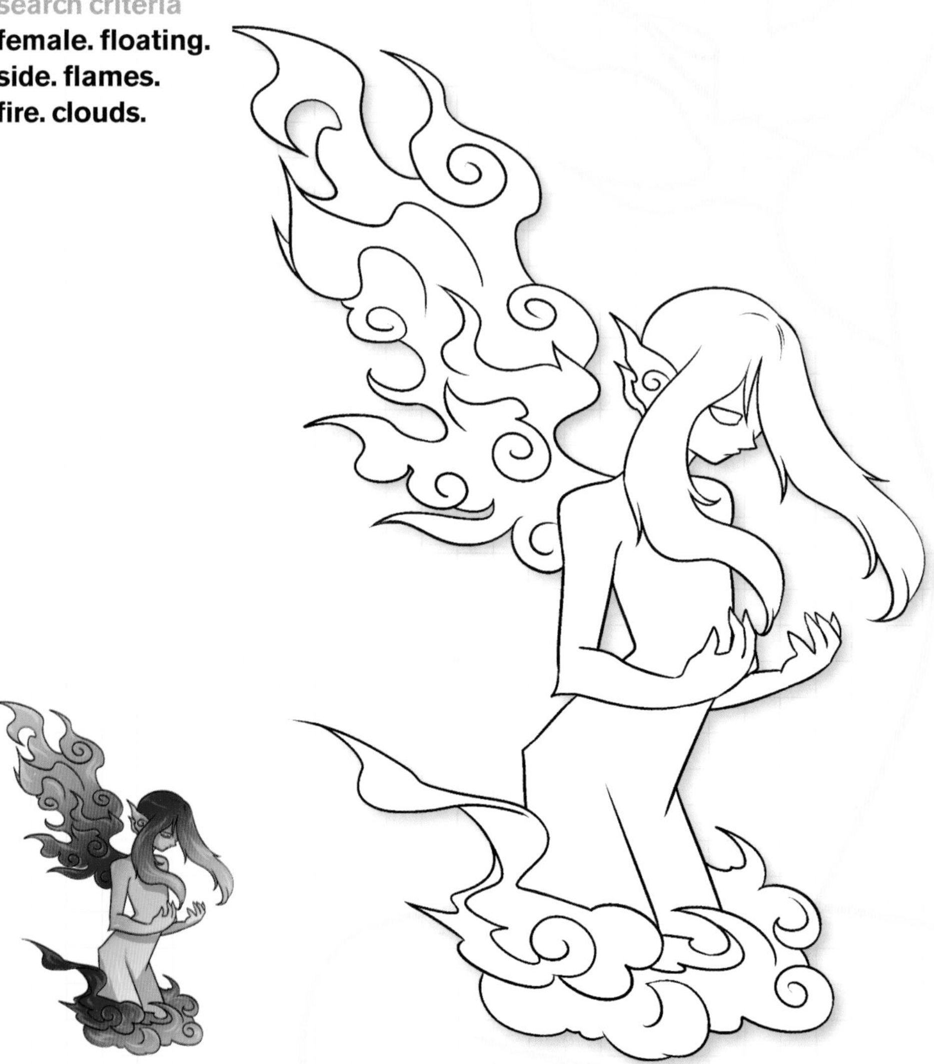

268

elemental villains

search criteria

male. side. wings
flying. diving.
fire. flames.

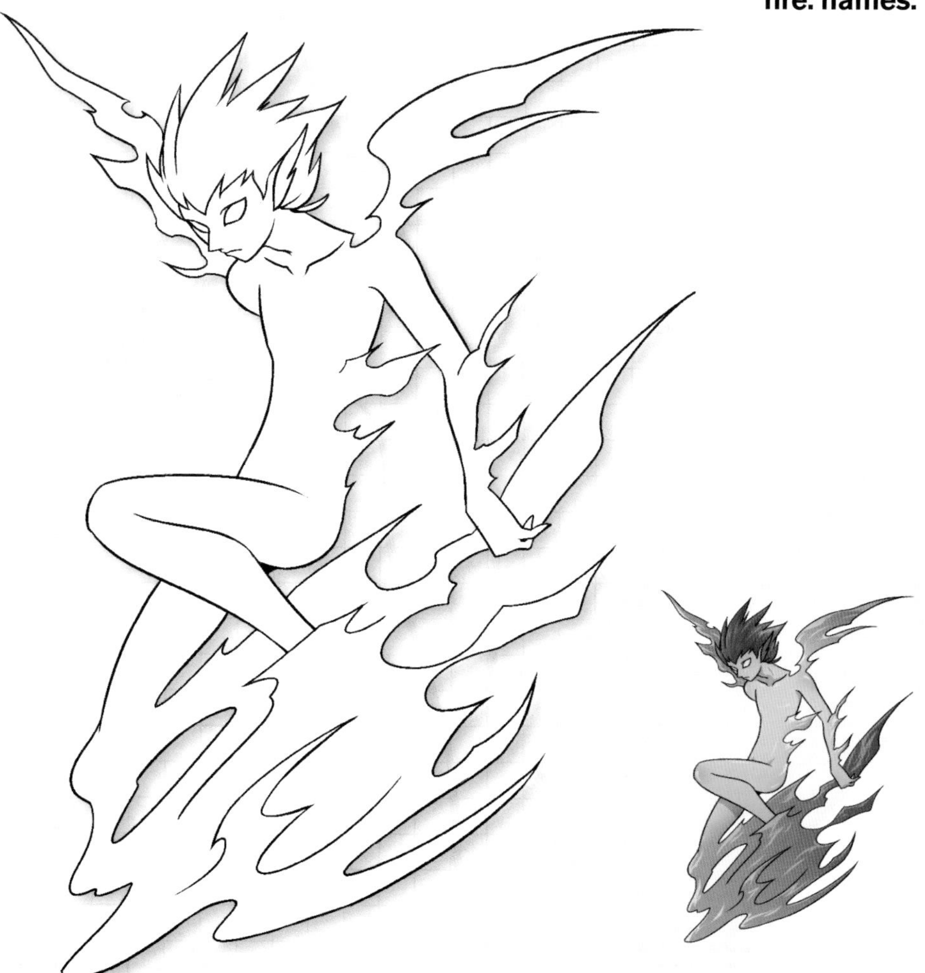

269

elemental villains

search criteria

male. jump. side. floating. water. growl. crystal.

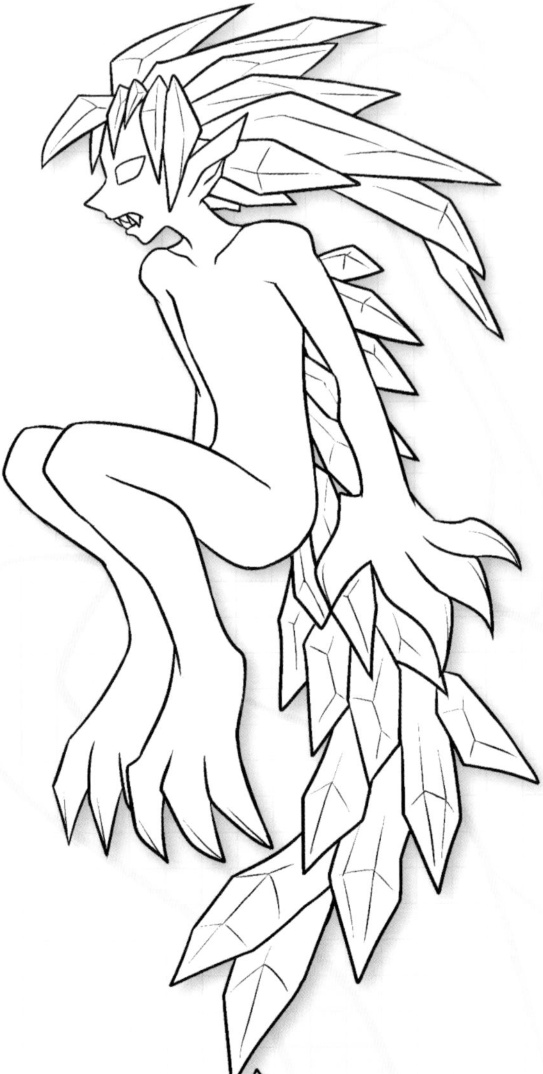

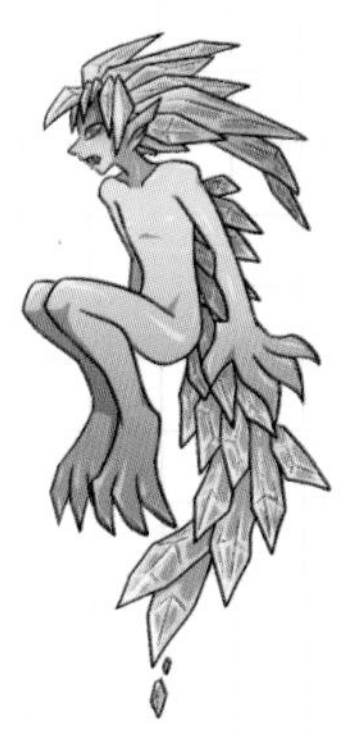

270

elemental villains

search criteria

female. floating. air. smell. smoke. skulls. danger.

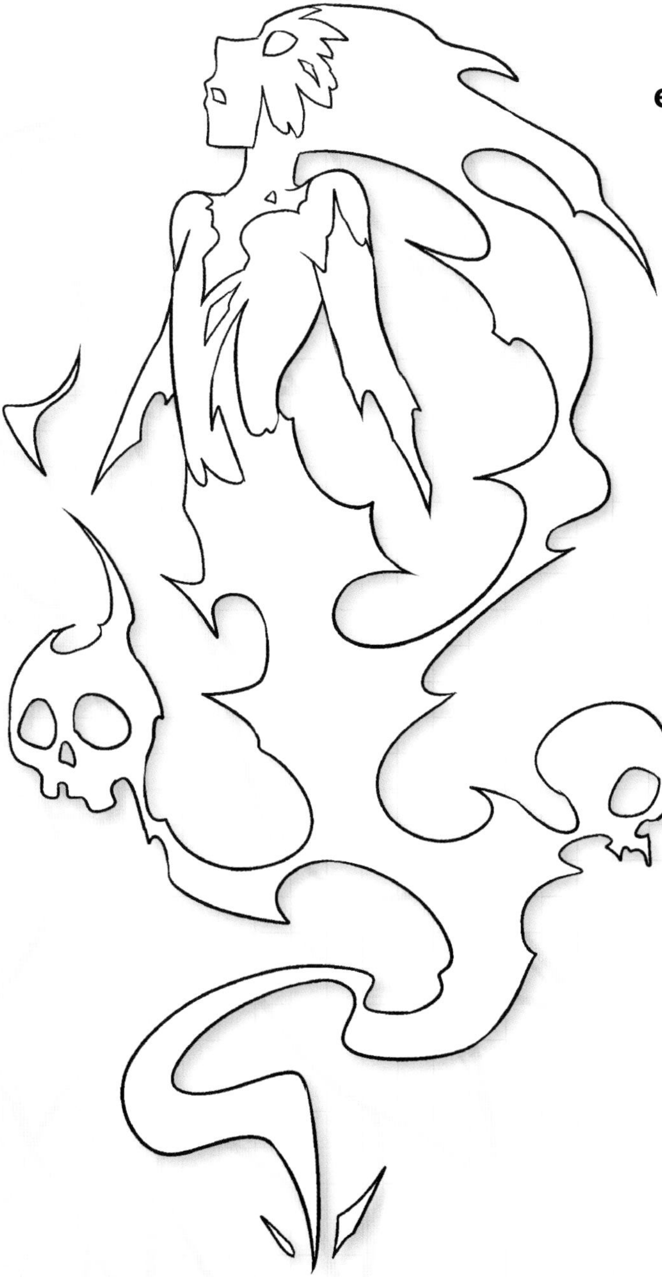

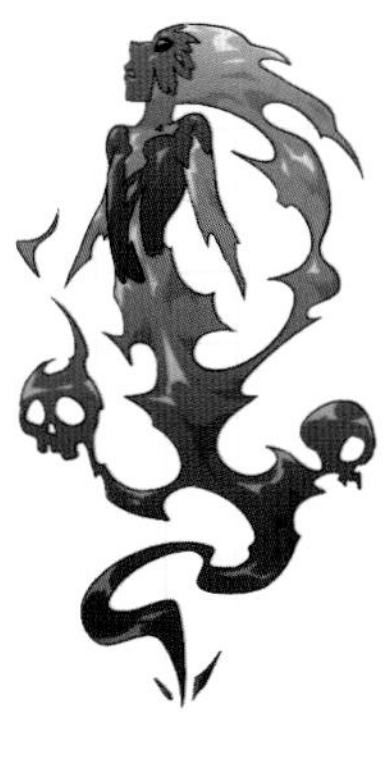

271

elemental heroes

search criteria

male. standing. side. water. tail.

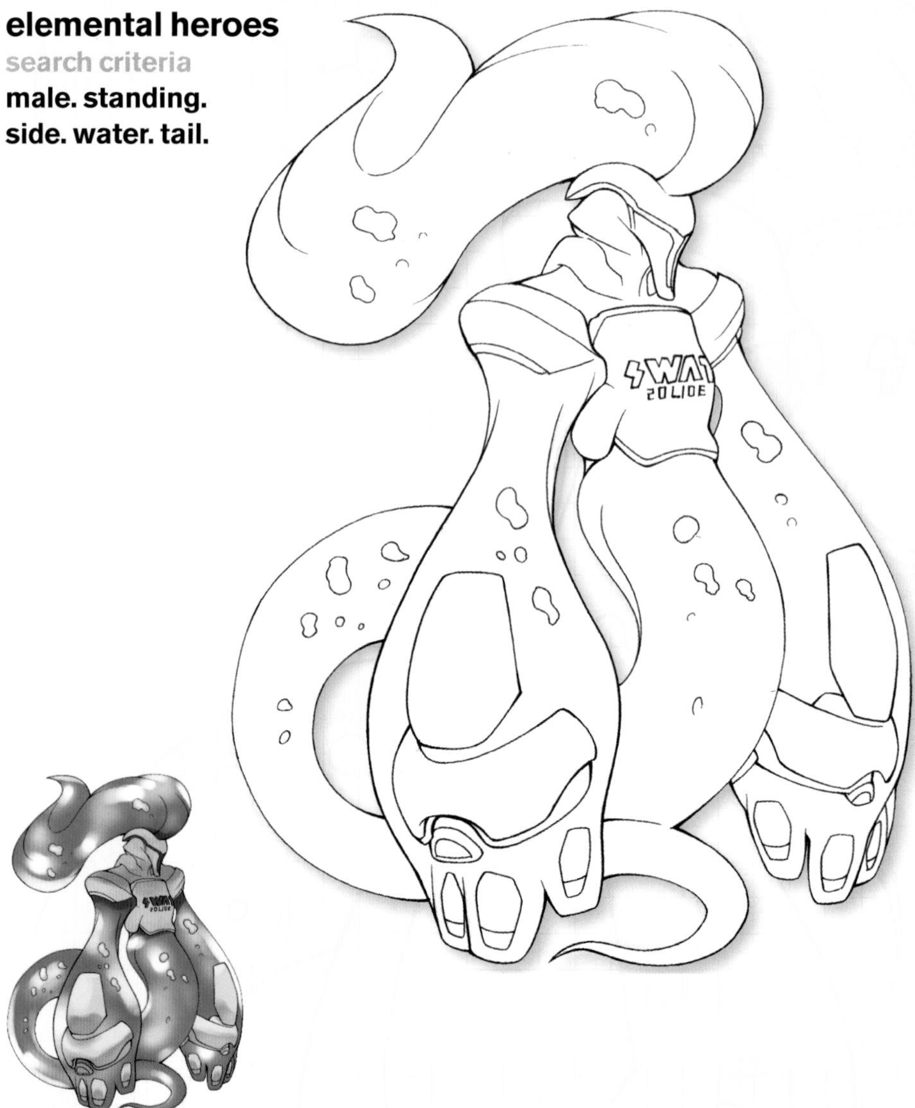

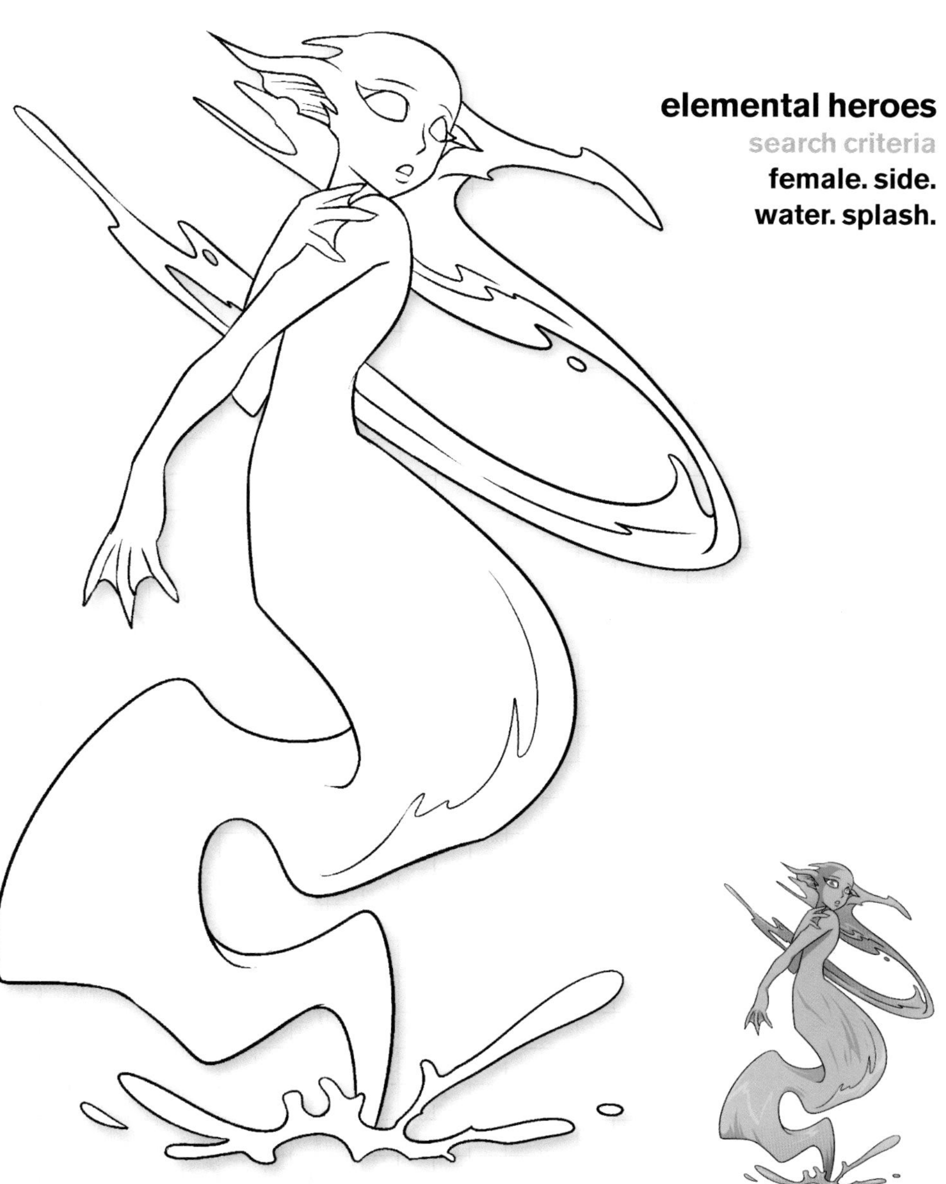

elemental heroes

search criteria

female. side.
water. splash.

273

elemental heroes

search criteria

female. side. earth. nature. tree. leaves.

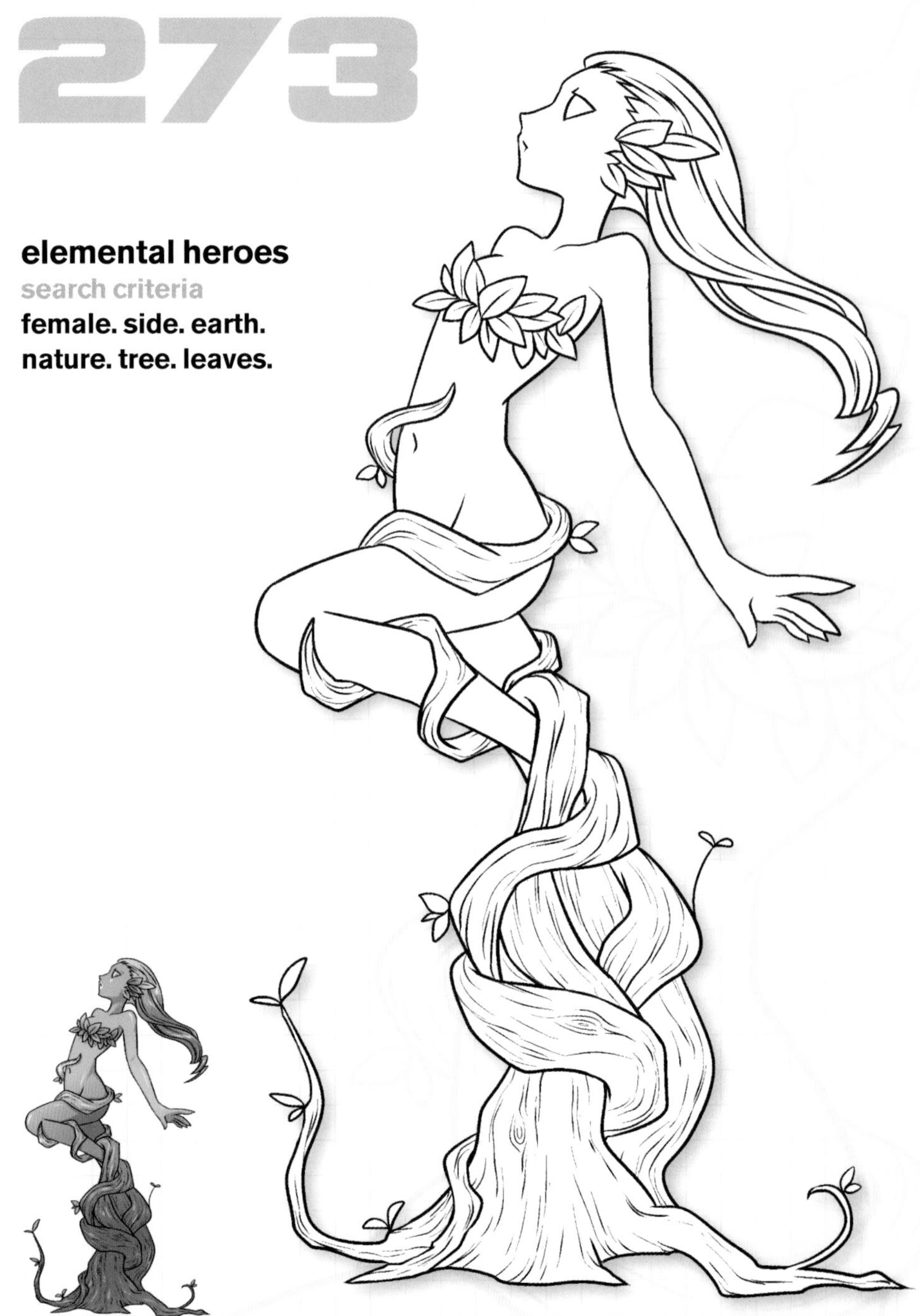

274

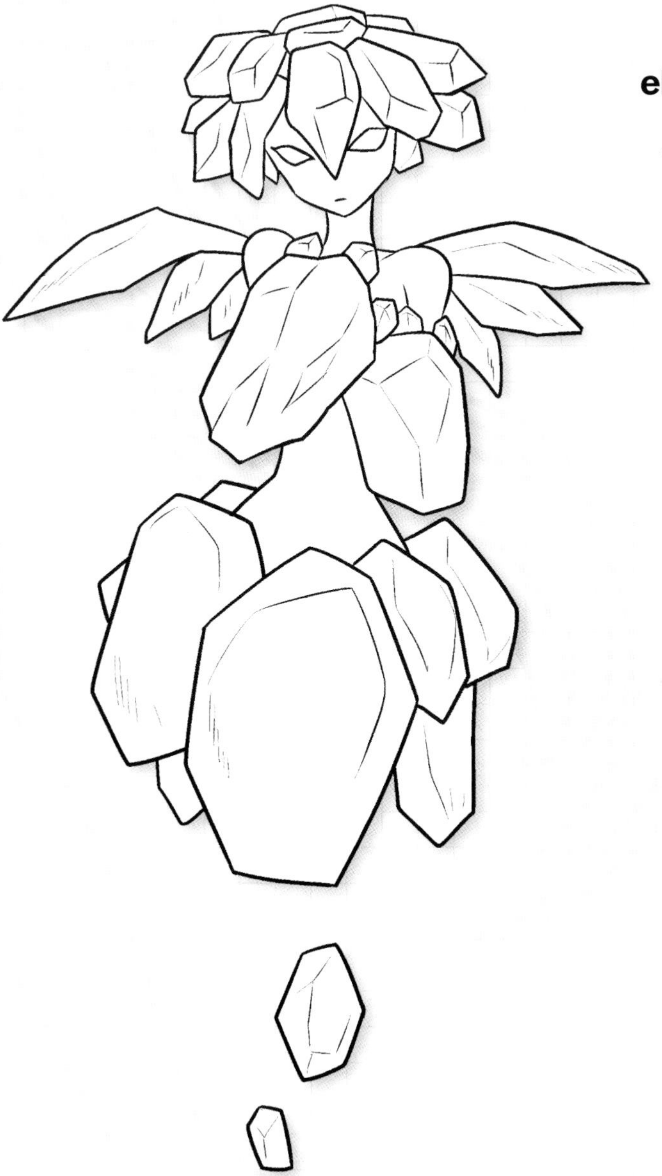

elemental heroes

search criteria

female. earth. rock. floating. wings.

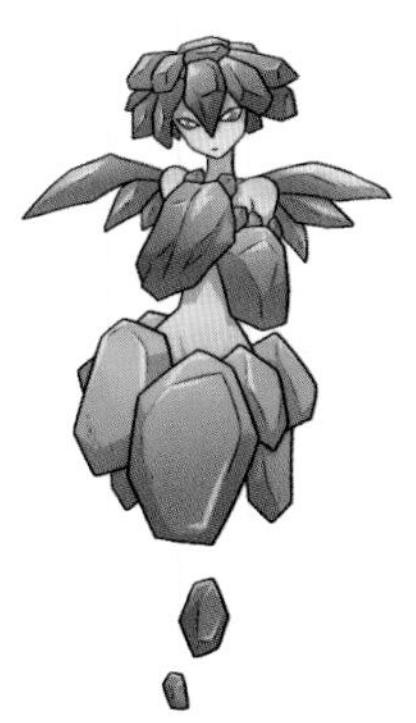

275

elemental heroes

search criteria

female. floating. side. flower. fairy. petals. wings. nature.

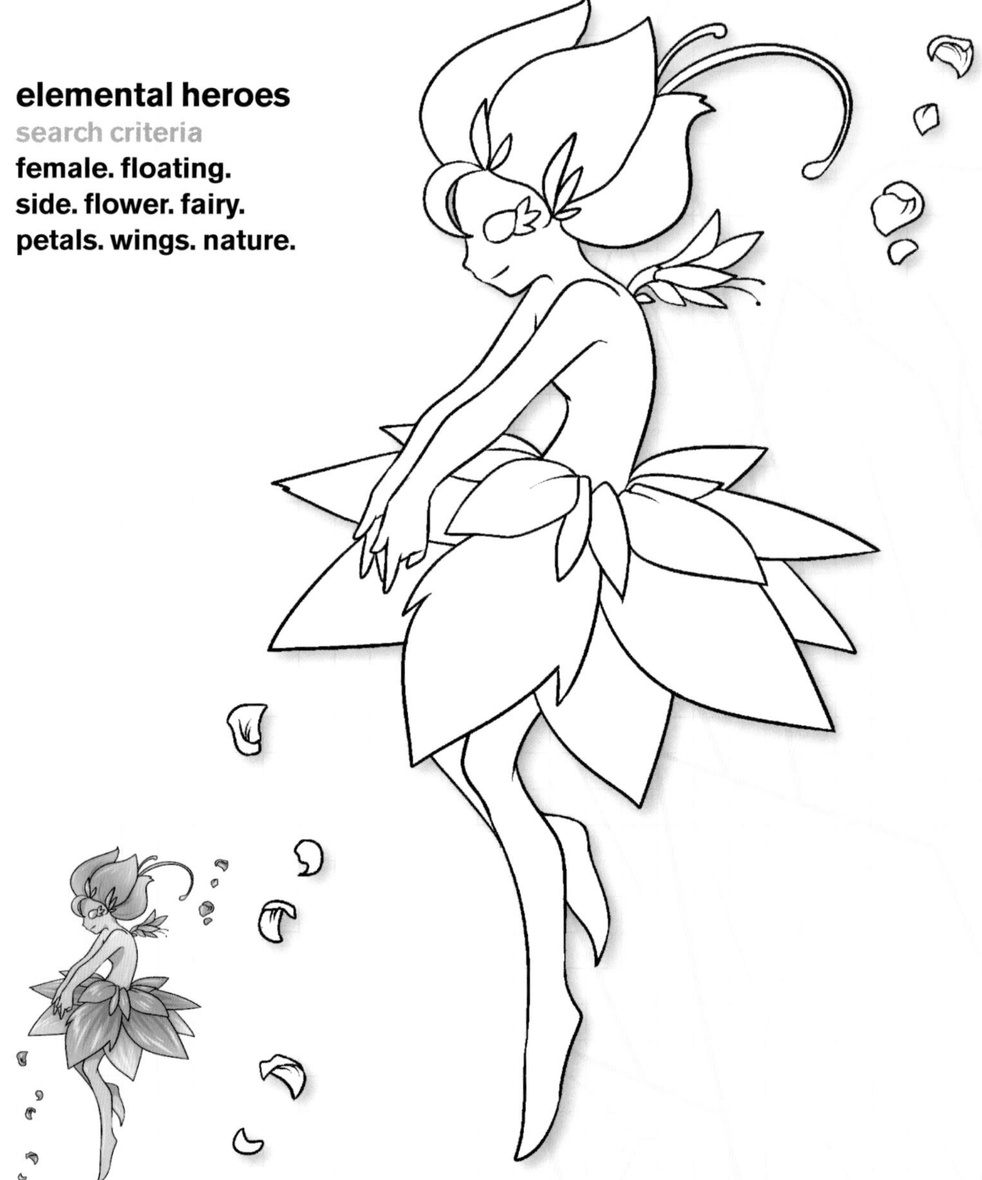

276

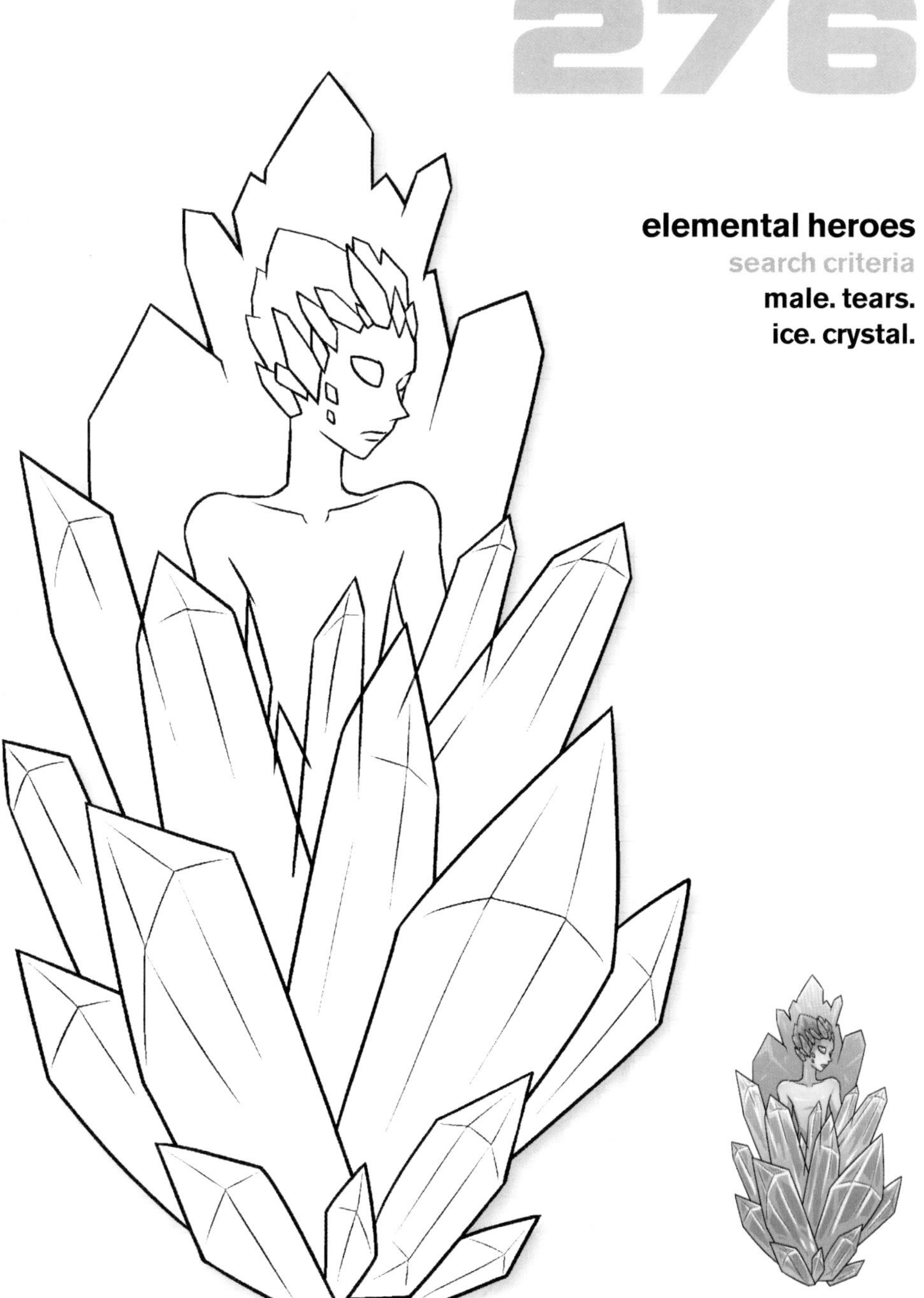

elemental heroes

search criteria

male. tears. ice. crystal.

277

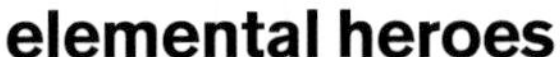

elemental heroes

search criteria

male. water. surfing. wave. splash.

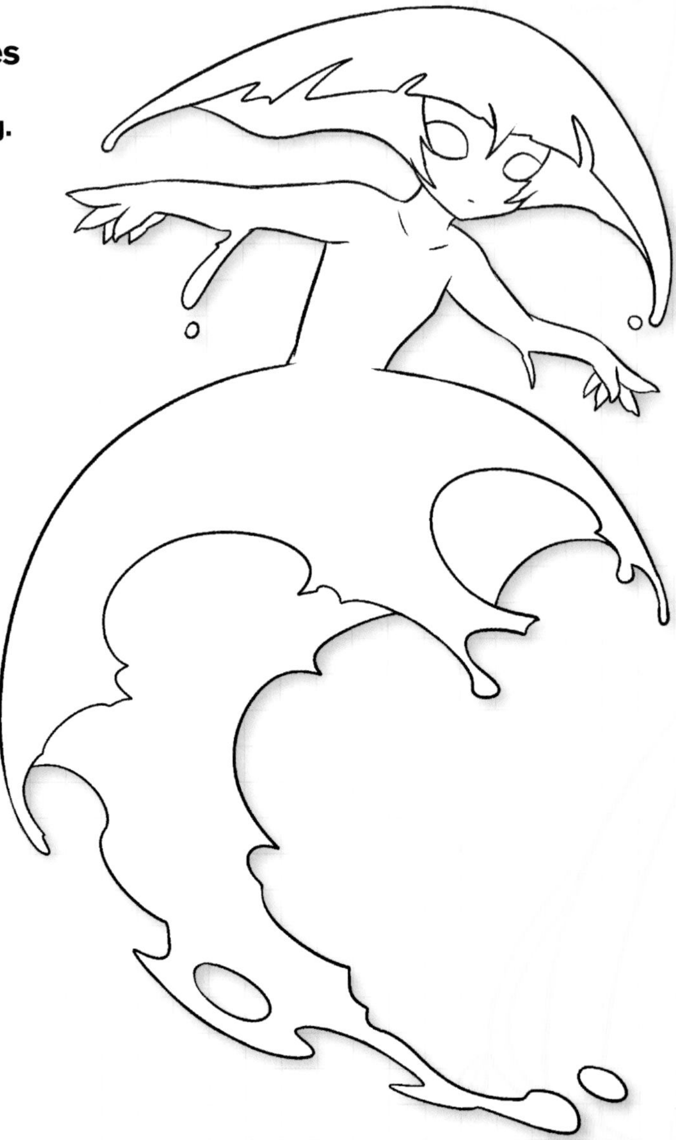

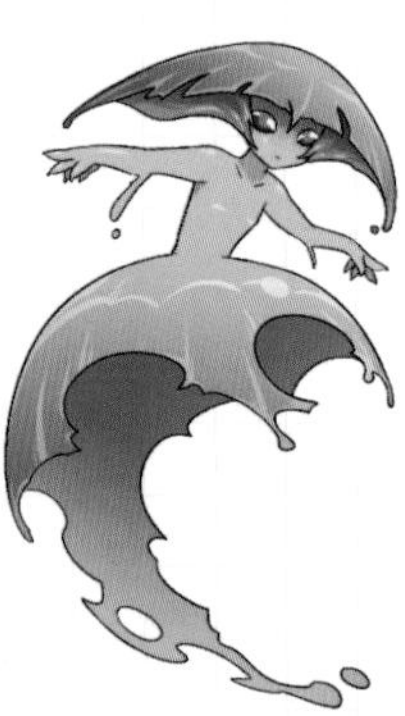

278

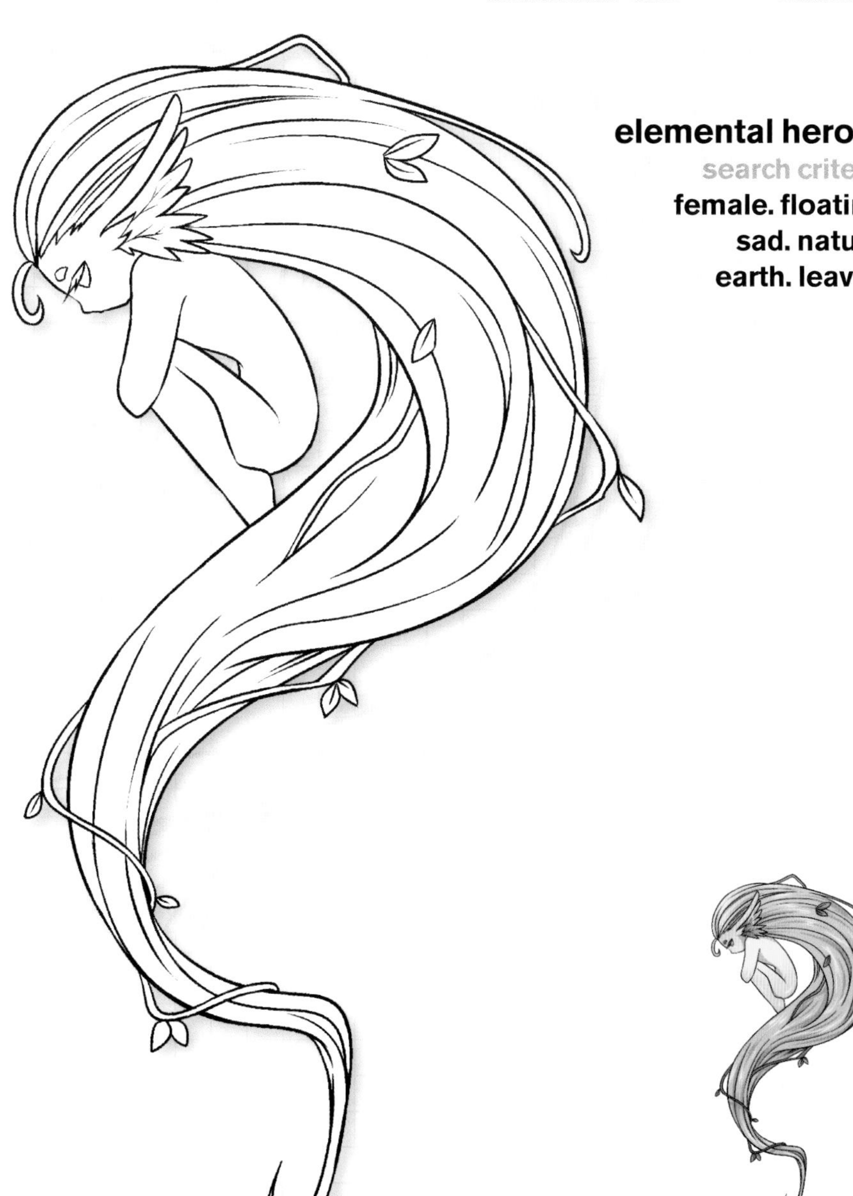

elemental heroes

search criteria

female. floating. sad. nature. earth. leaves.

279

elemental heroes

search criteria

male. side. sitting. shout. lightning. fire.

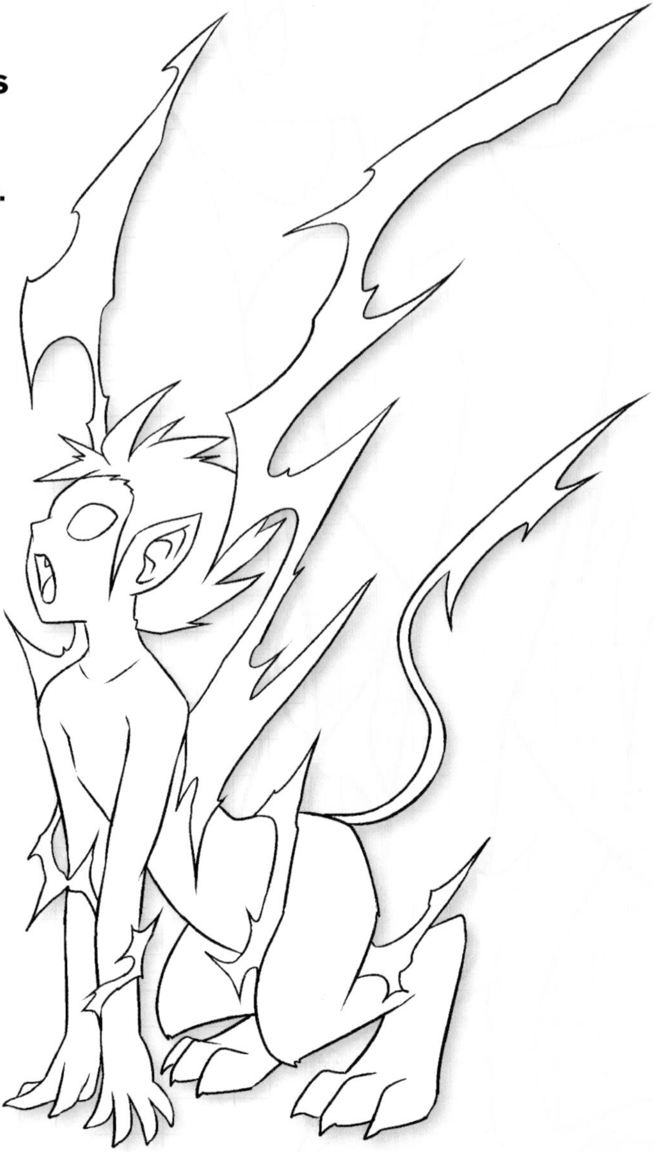

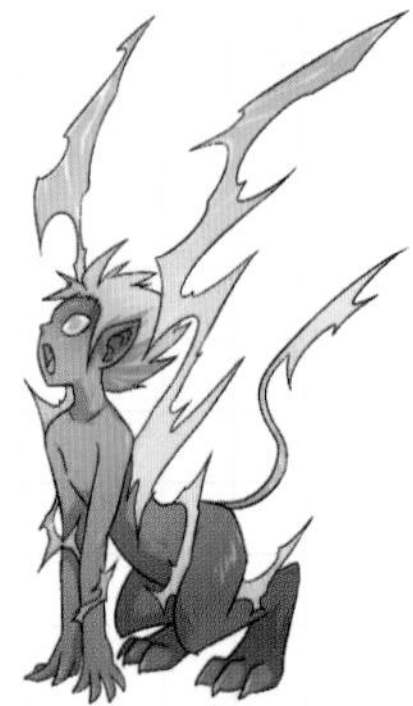

280

elemental heroes

search criteria

female. floating.
earth. nature.

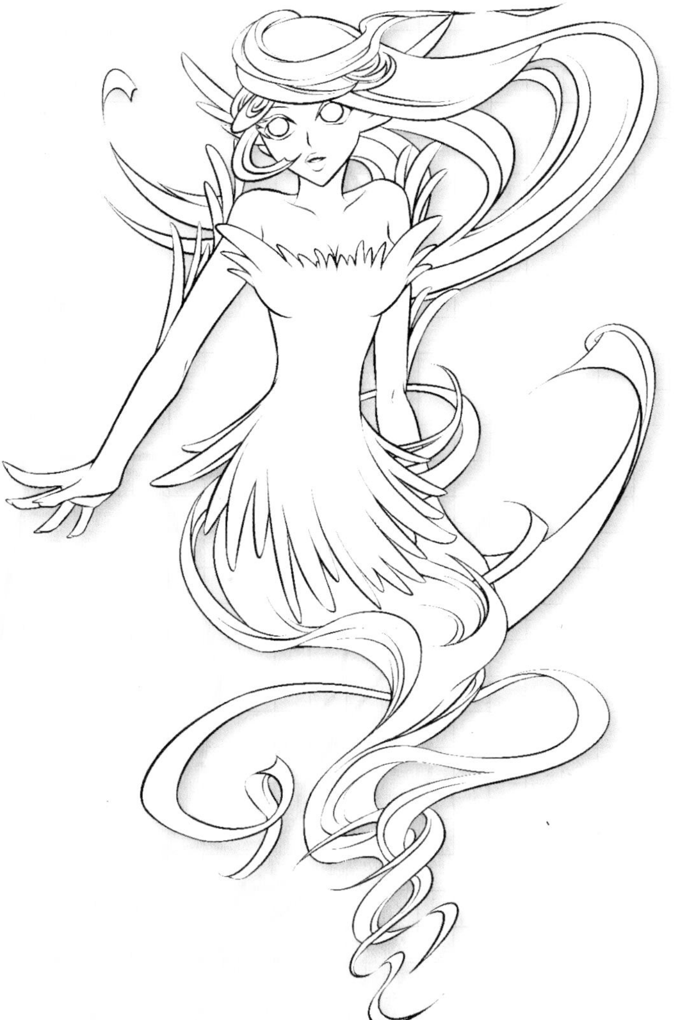

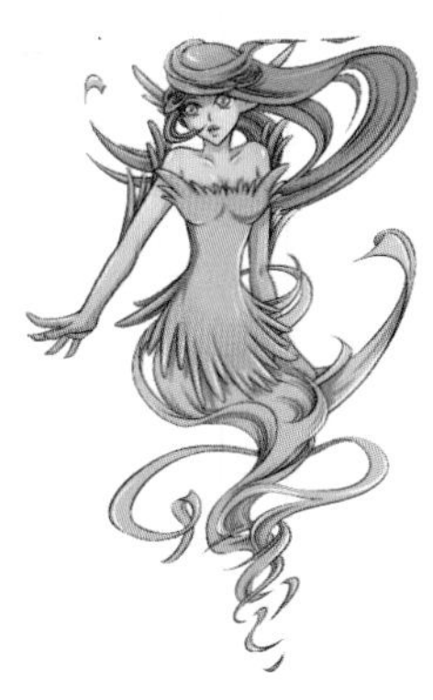

281

elemental heroes

search criteria

**female. floating.
earth. nature. tree.
wings. leaves.**

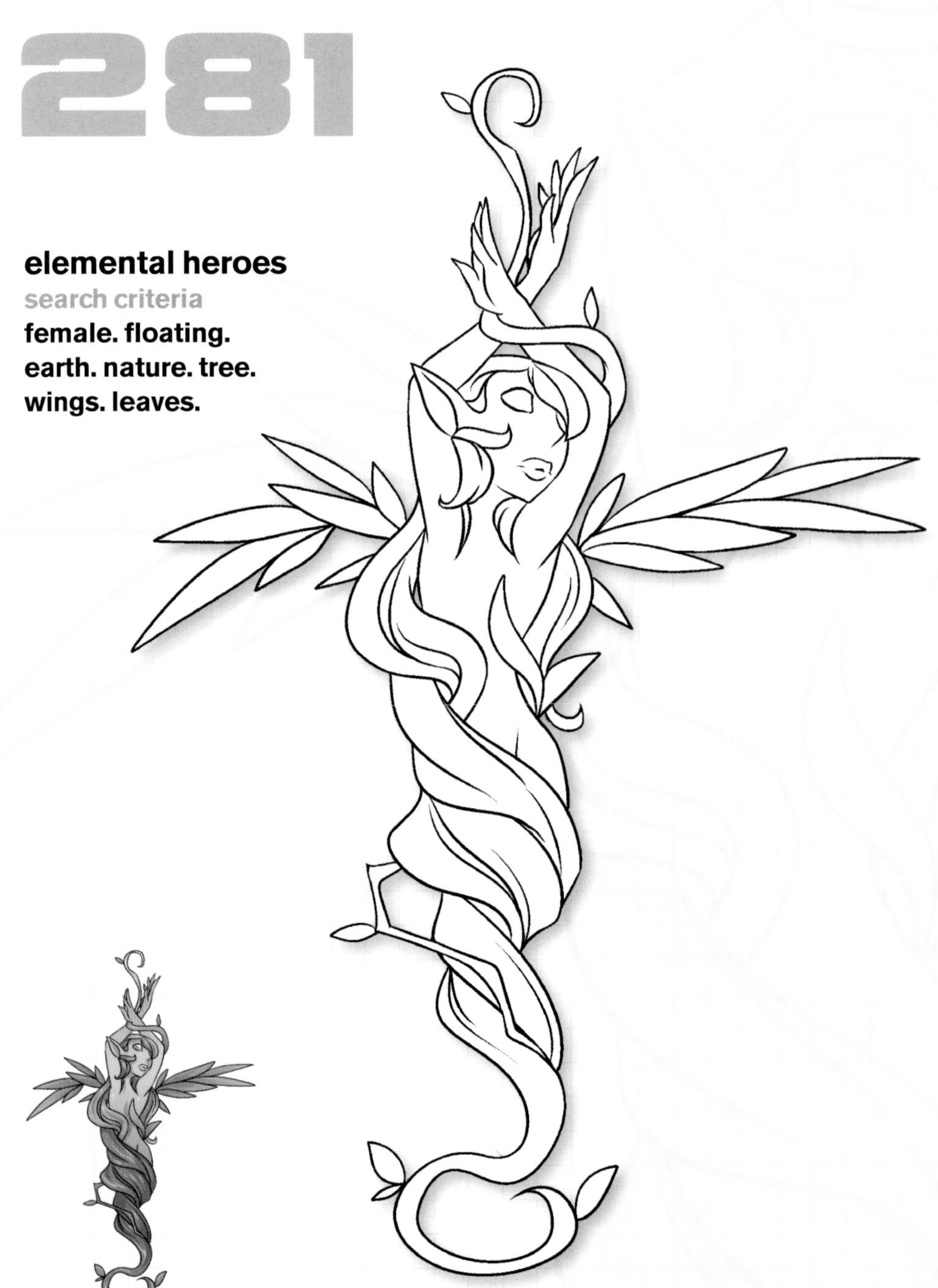

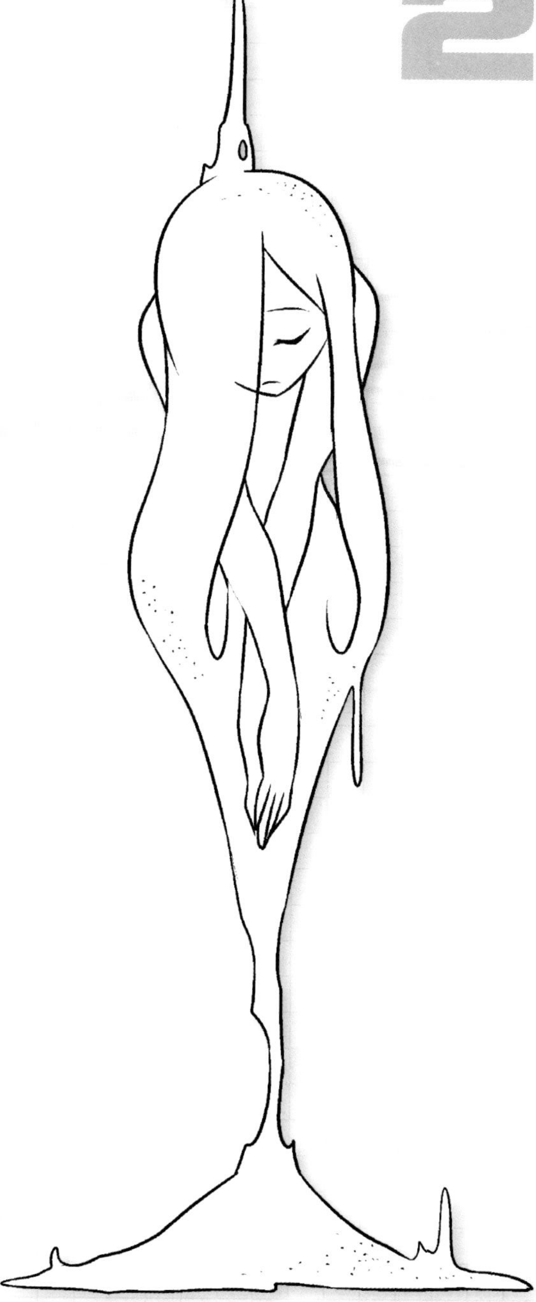

282

elemental heroes

search criteria

female. floating. nature. sand. sad.

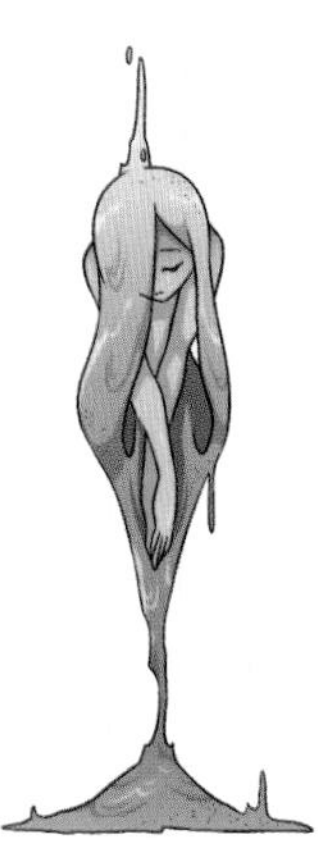

283

elemental heroes

search criteria

female. floating. flying. night. moon. spirit.

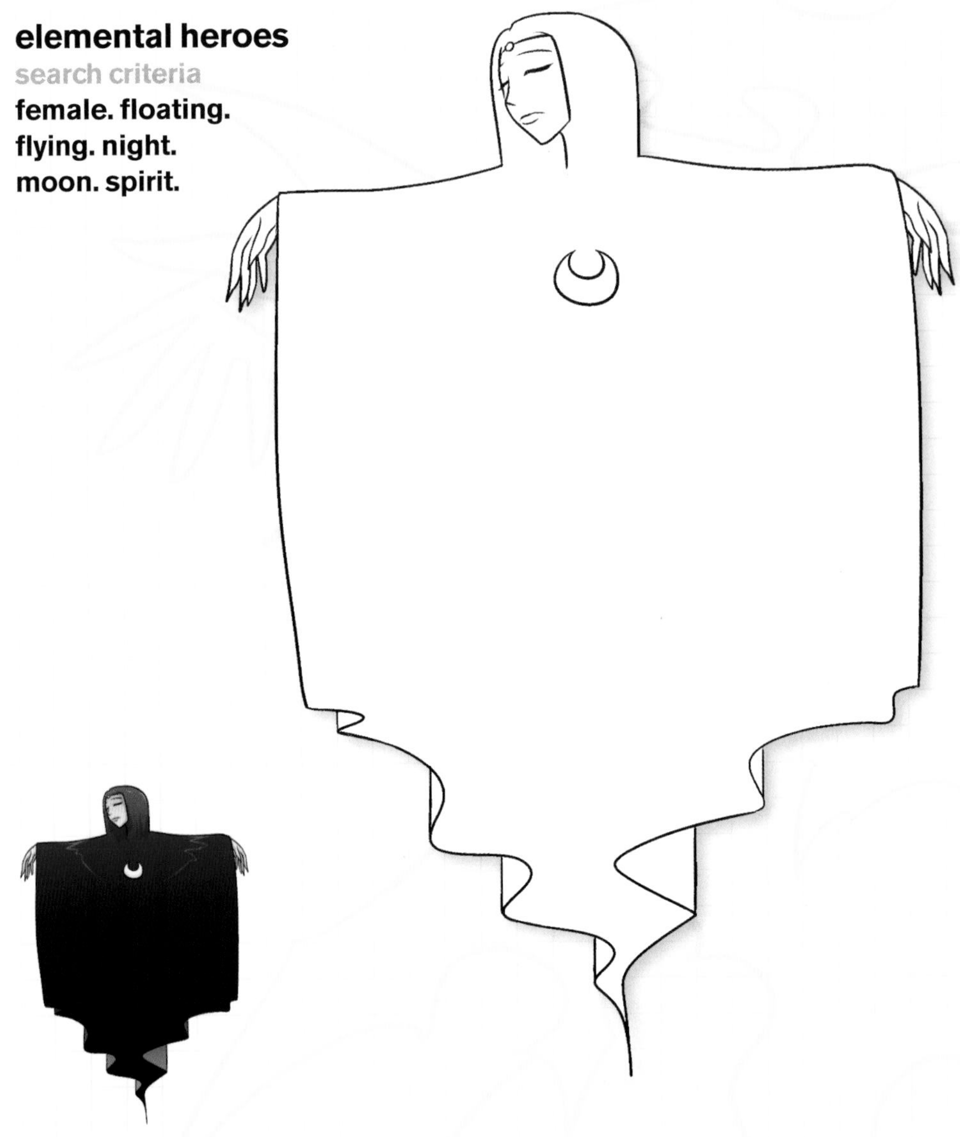

elemental heroes

search criteria

female. floating. flying. star. spirit.

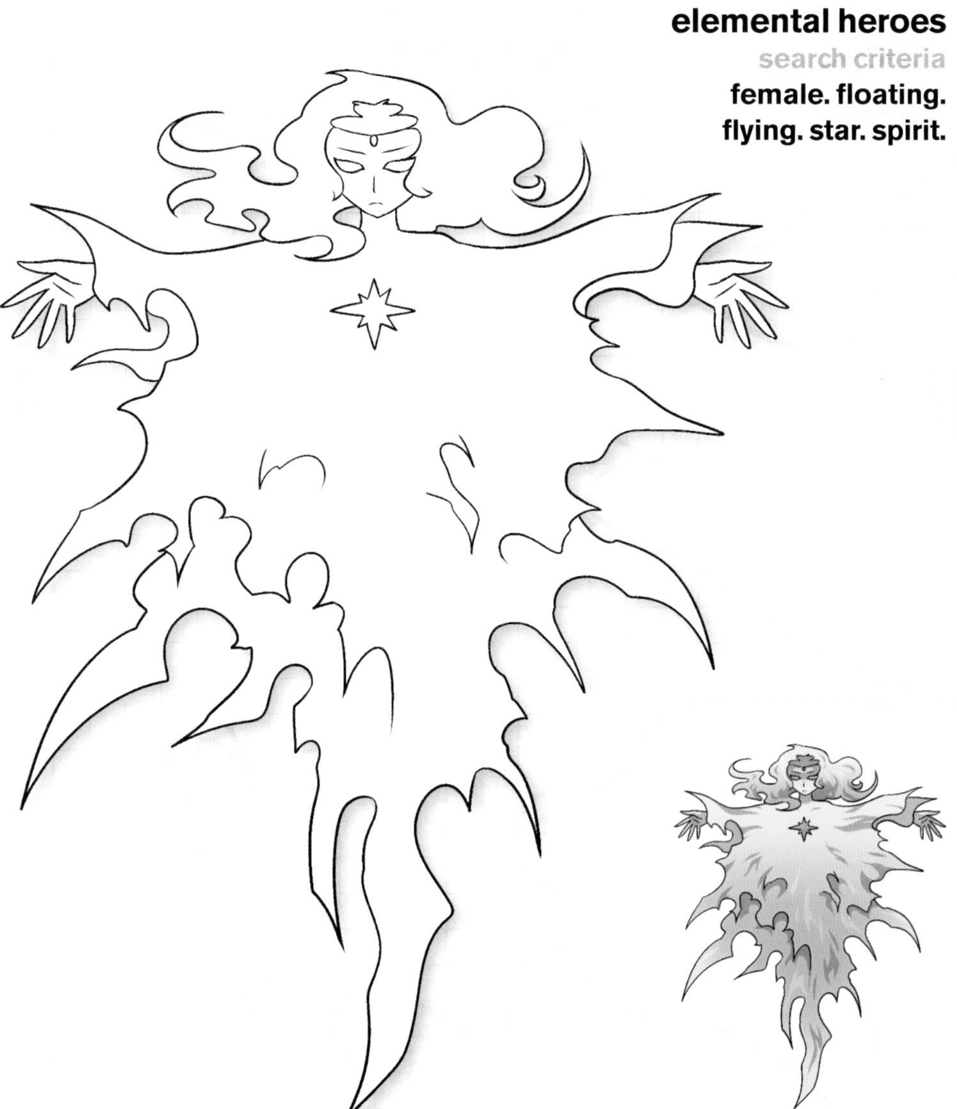

285

elemental heroes

search criteria

male. floating. flying. crystals. wings.

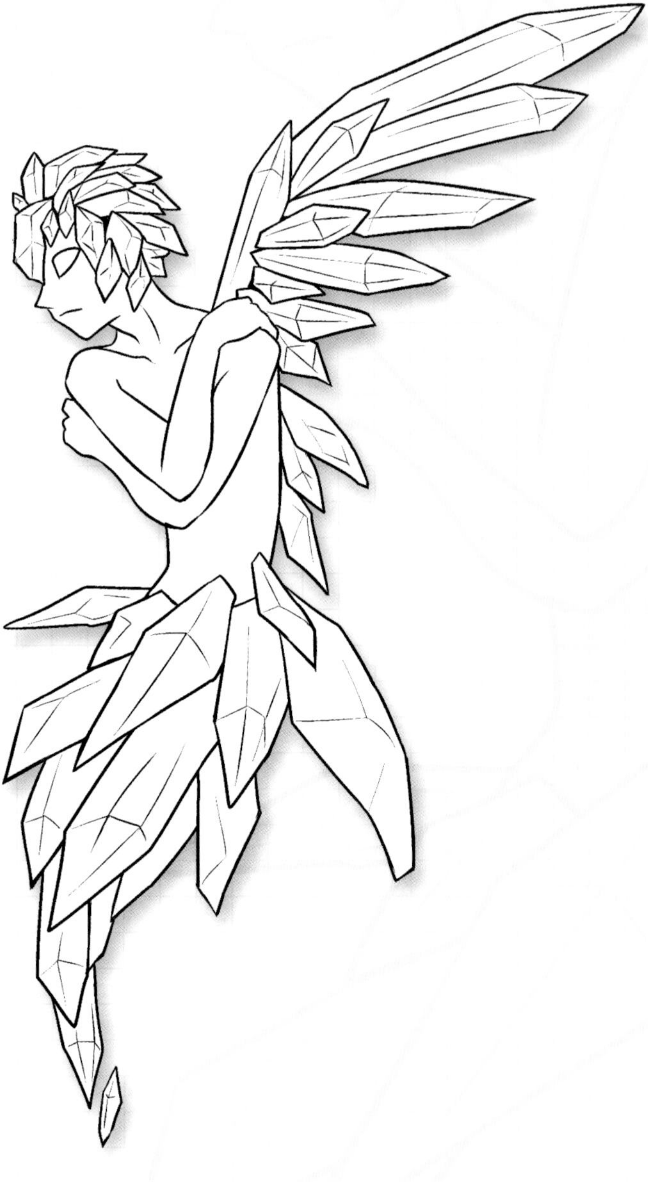

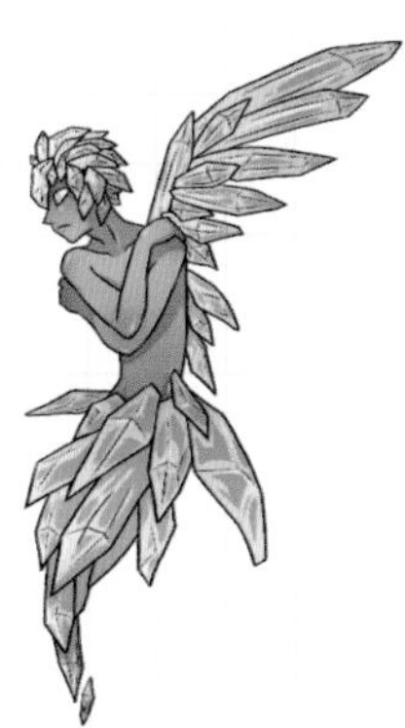

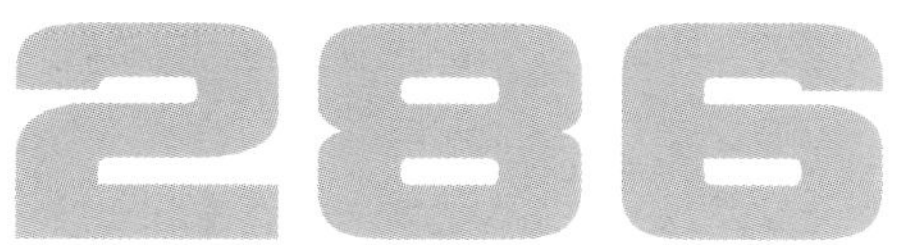

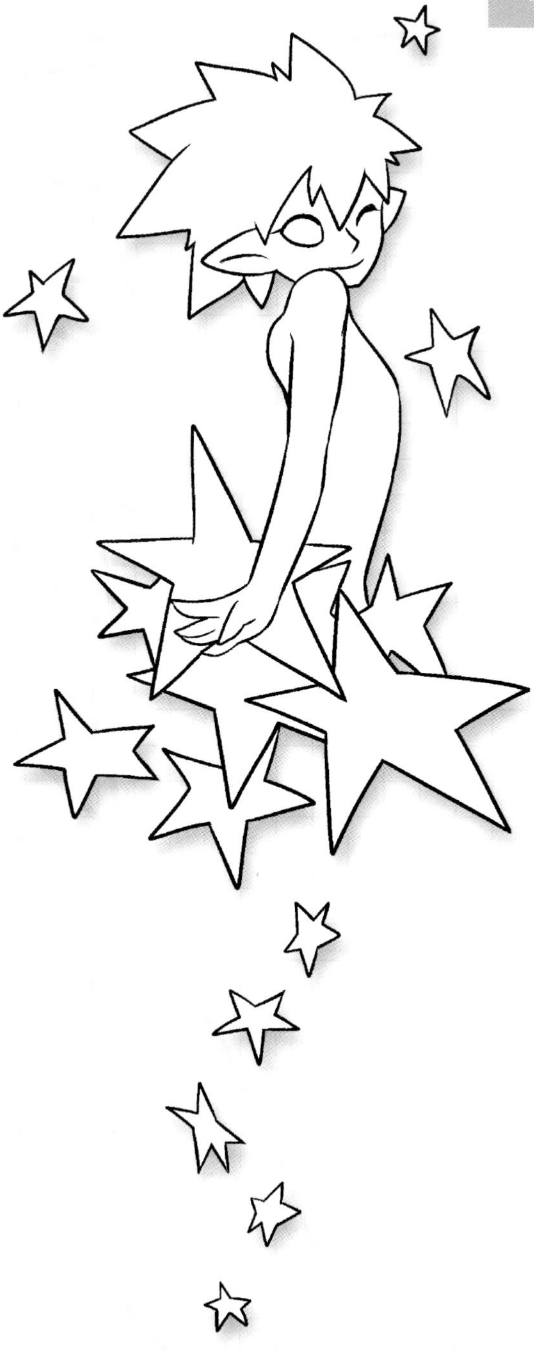

elemental heroes

search criteria

male. floating. flying. stars. boy.

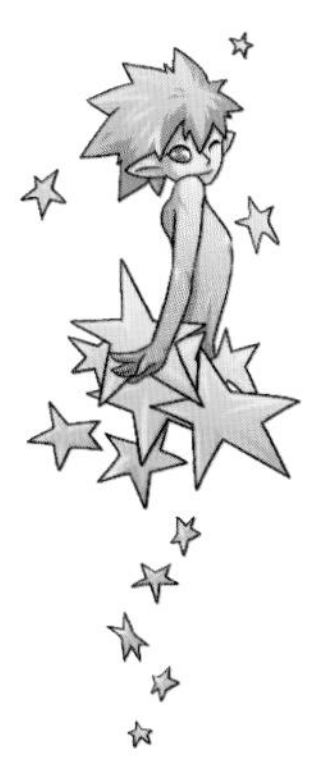

287

elemental heroes

search criteria

male. floating. flying. lightning. boy.

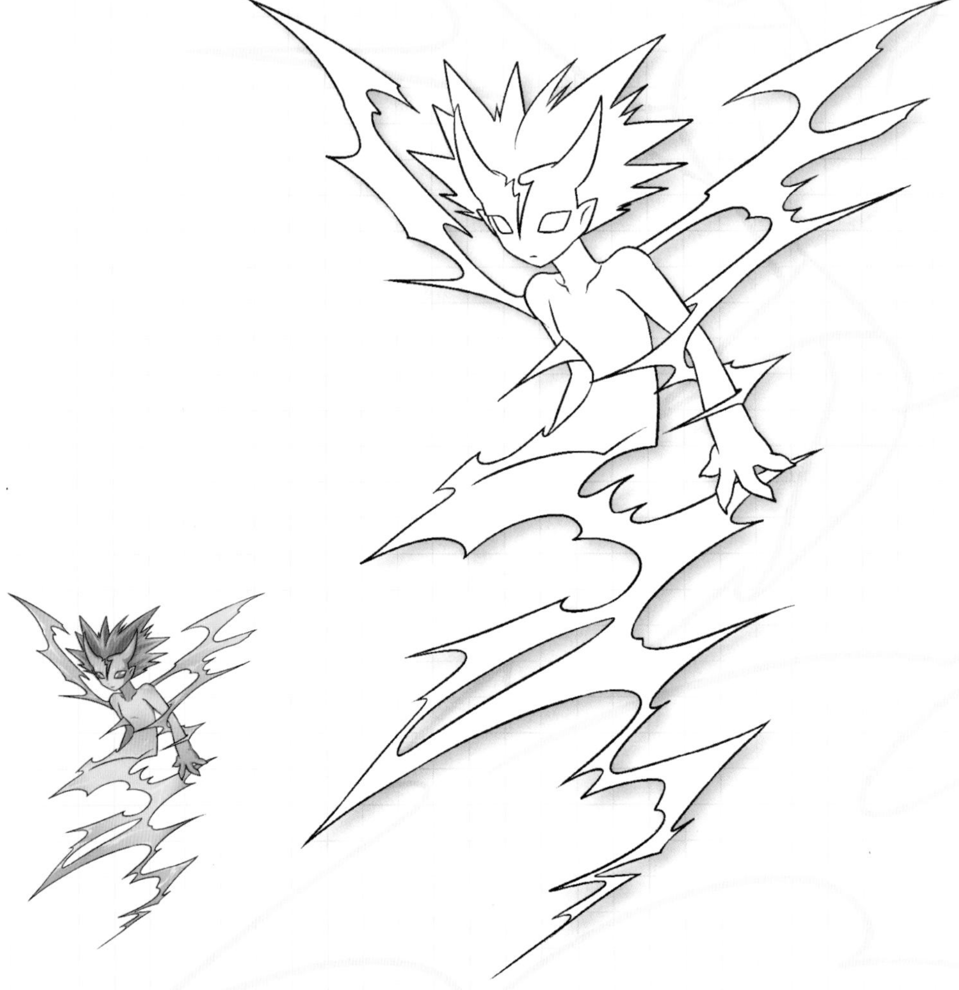

288

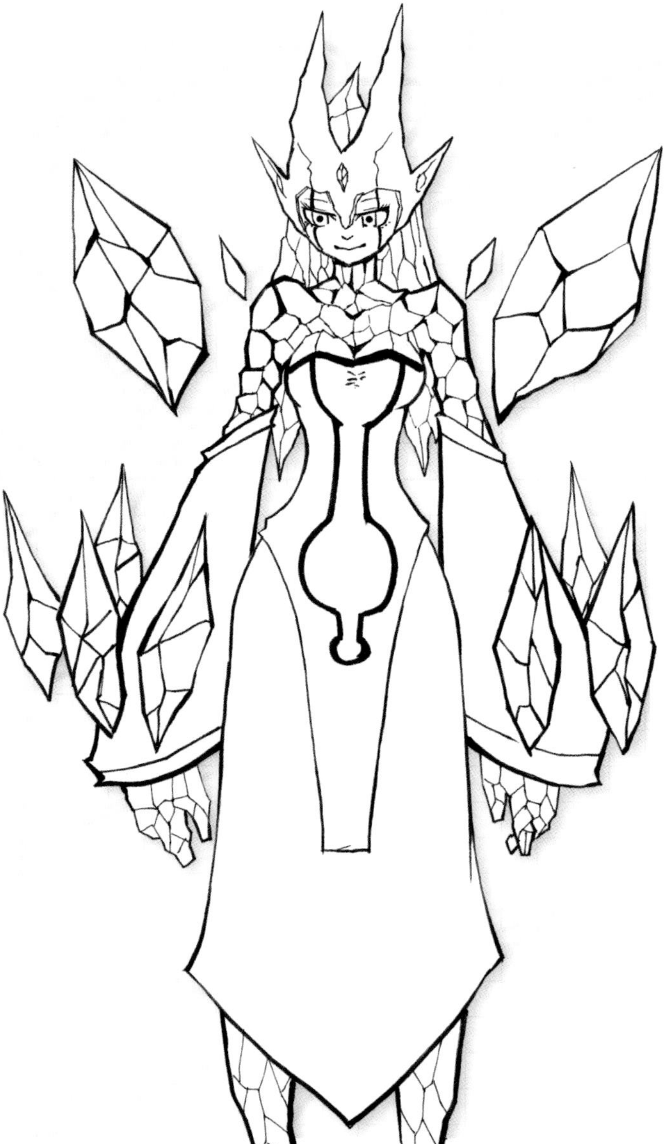

elemental heroes

search criteria

female. standing. floating. ice. queen. crystal.

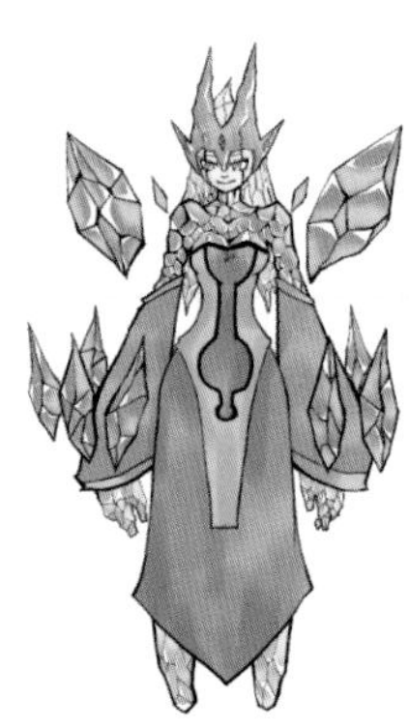

289

gothic and horror villains

search criteria

male. standing. shonen. flower. rose. lothario.

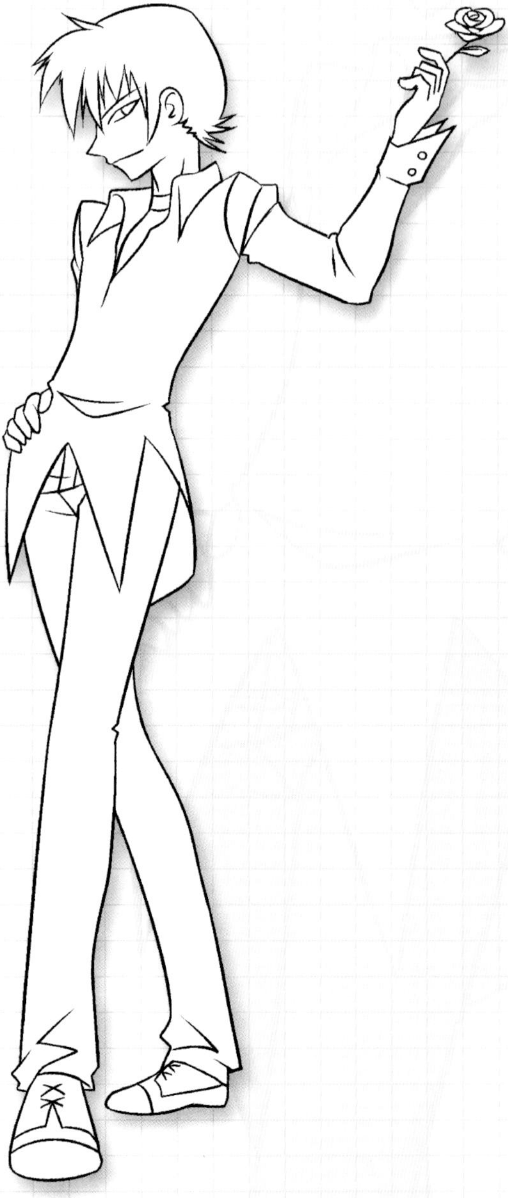

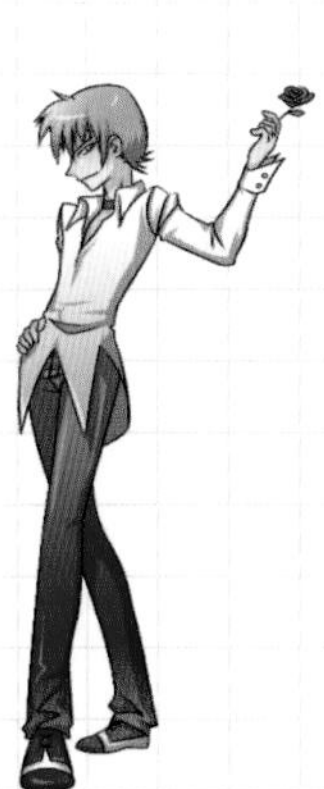

290

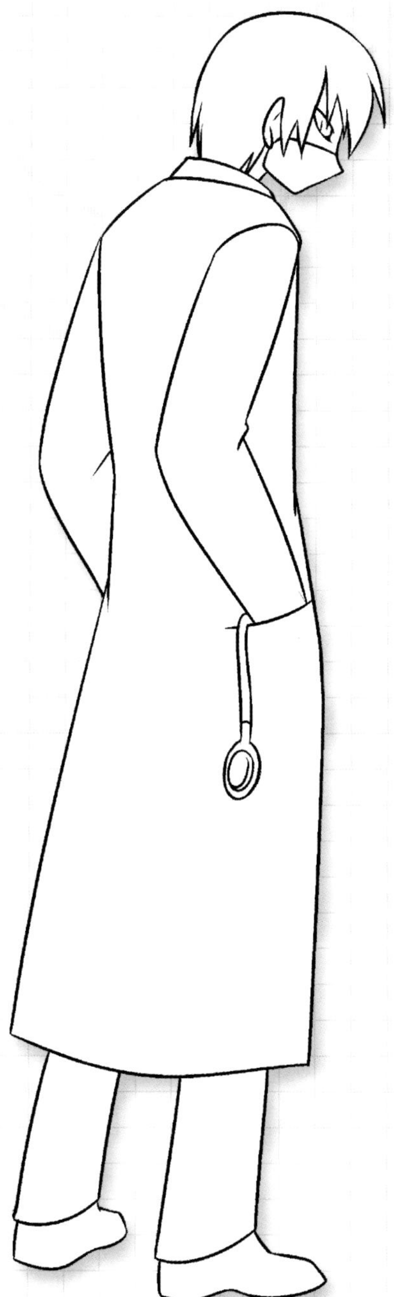

gothic and horror villains

search criteria

male. standing. side. mask. doctor. sinister. stethoscope.

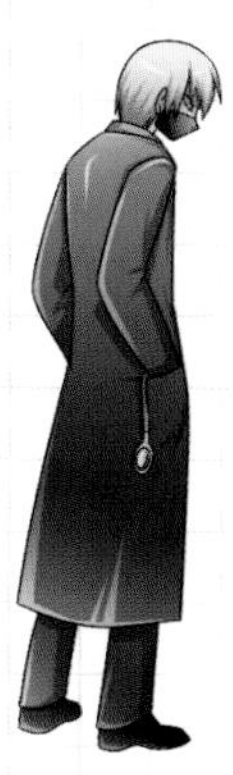

291

gothic and horror villains

search criteria

male. standing. monster. scar. frankenstein.

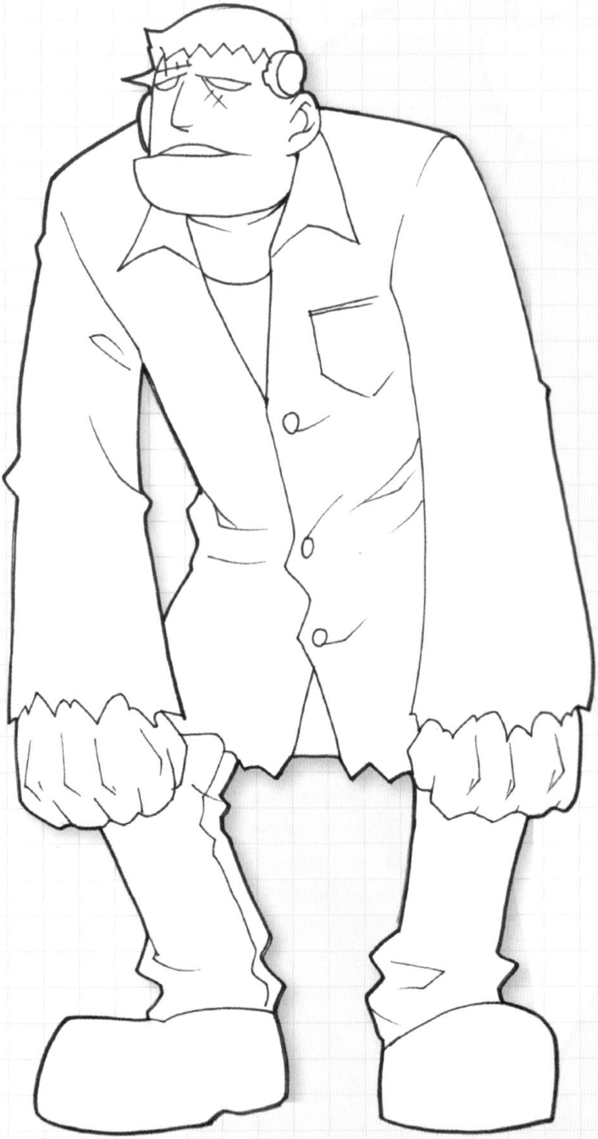

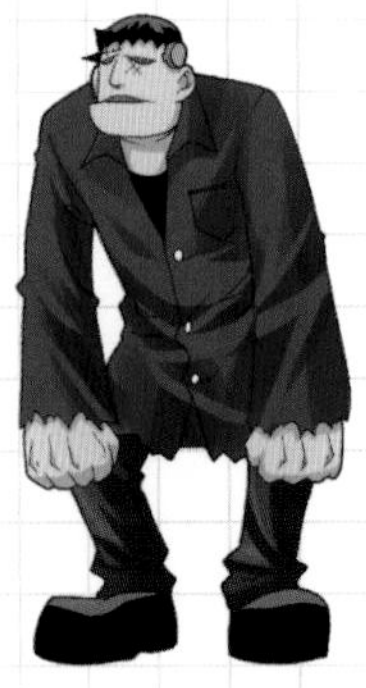

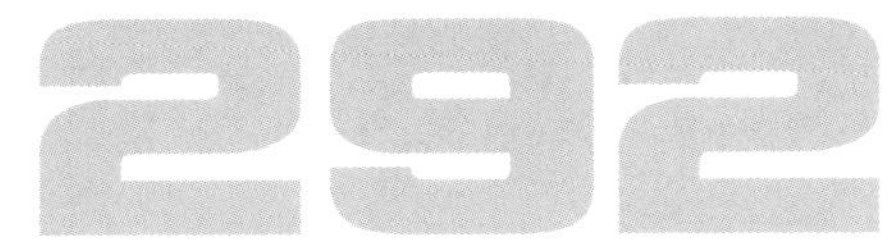

gothic and horror villains

search criteria

male. standing. cape. fang. vampire.

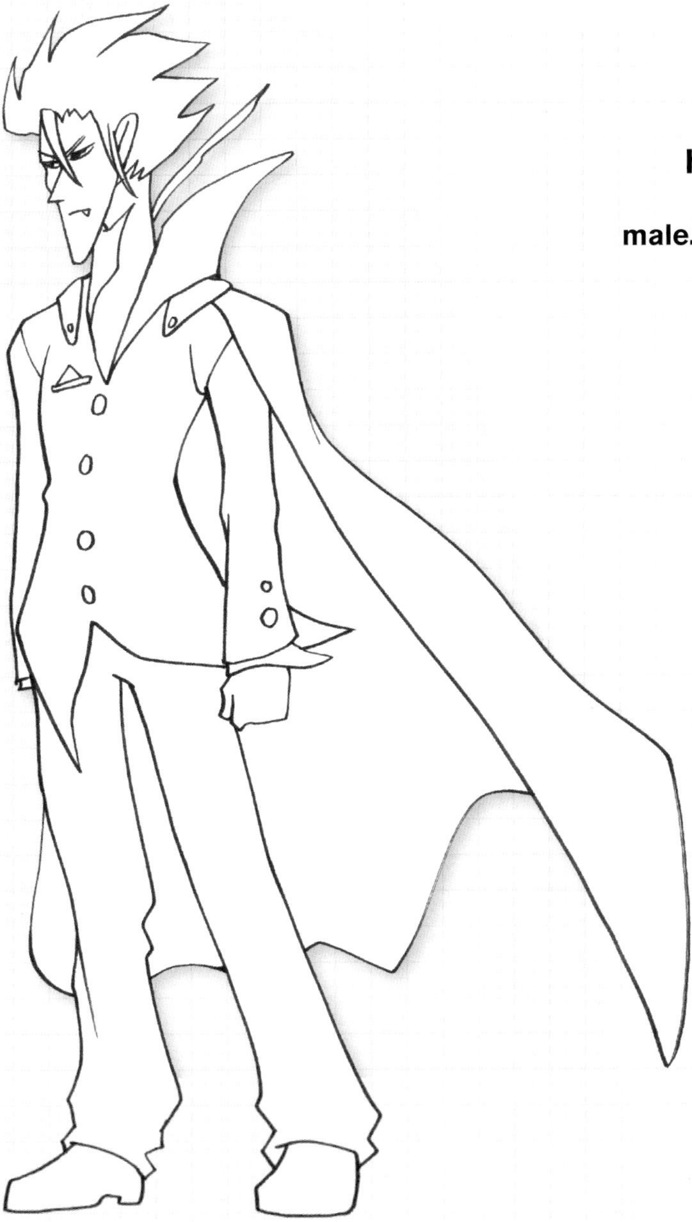

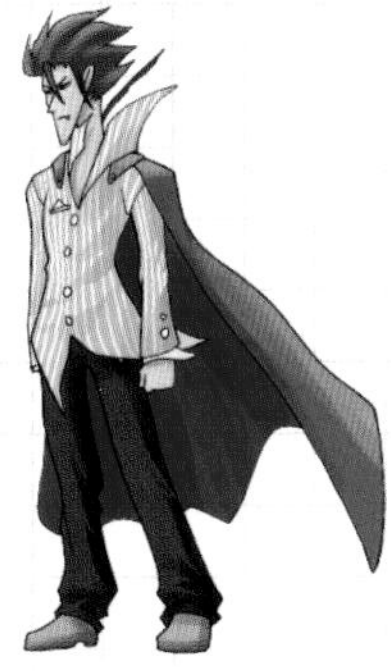

293

gothic and horror villains

search criteria

male. standing. monster. fire. evil.

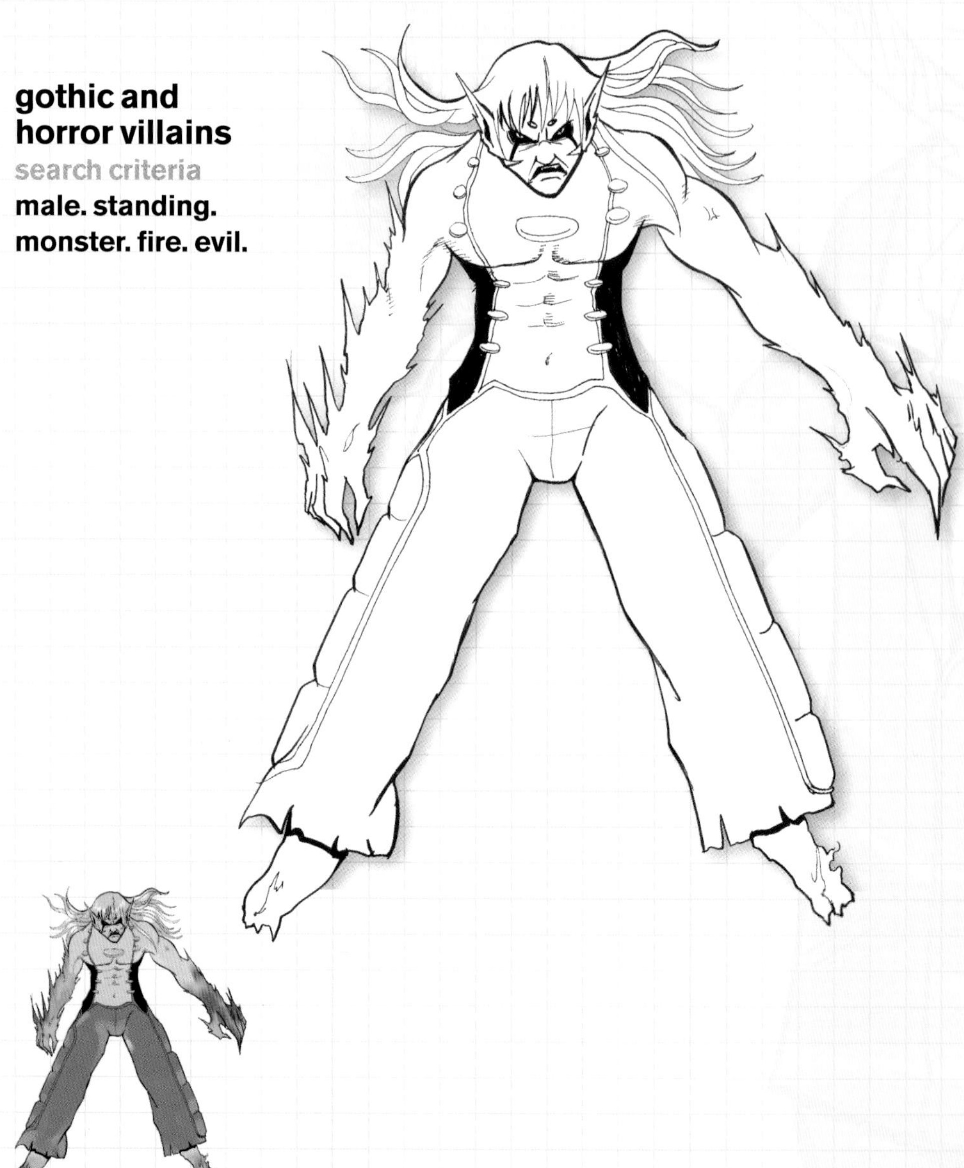

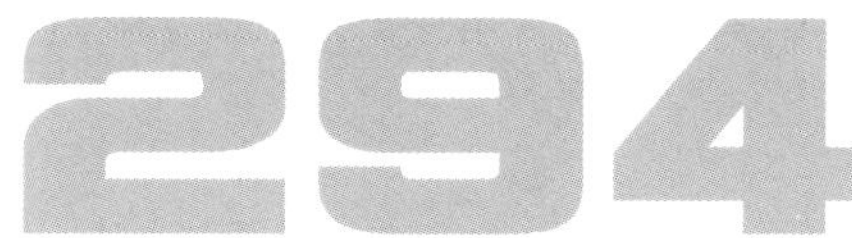

gothic and horror villains

search criteria

male. standing. fire. flames. bow.

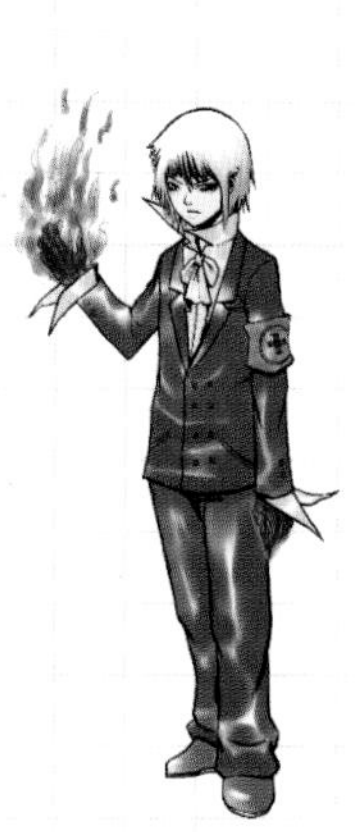

295

gothic and horror villains

search criteria

male. sitting. cape. vampire. dracula.

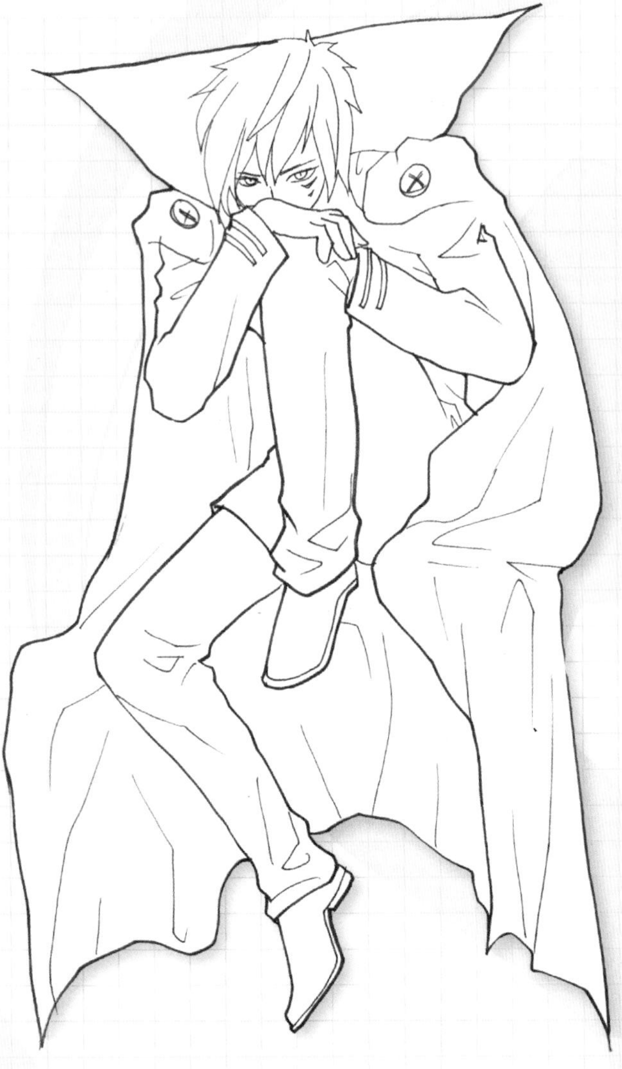

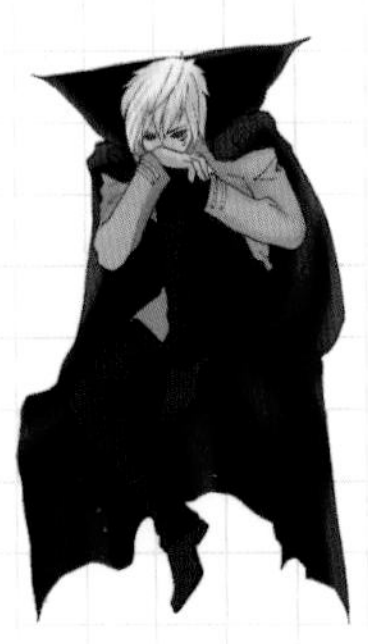

296

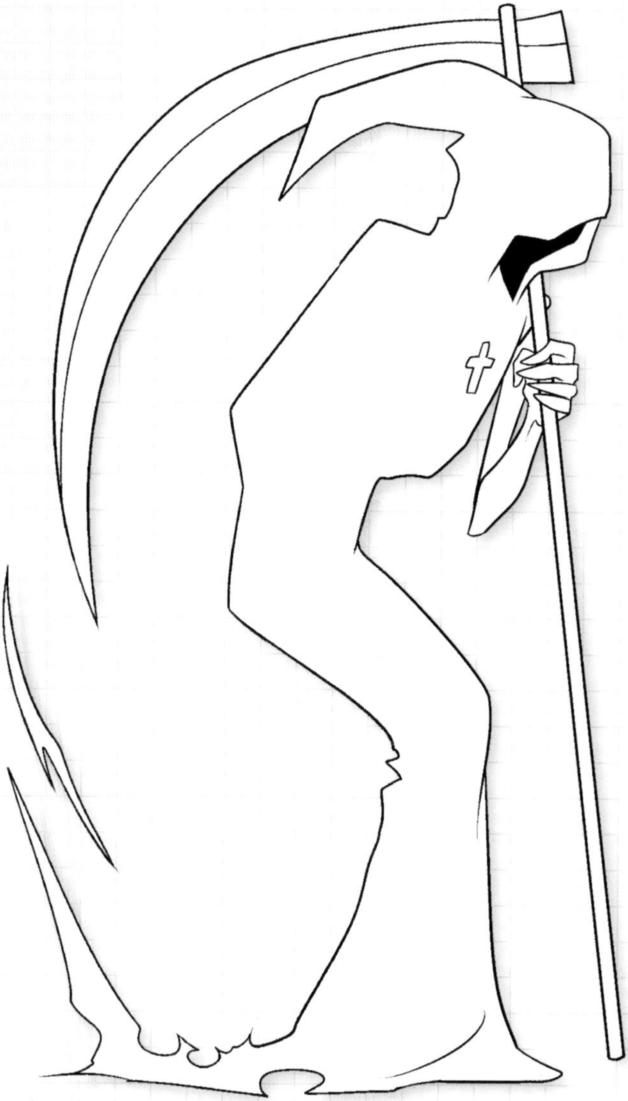

gothic and horror villains

search criteria

male. standing. side. reaper. death. scythe.

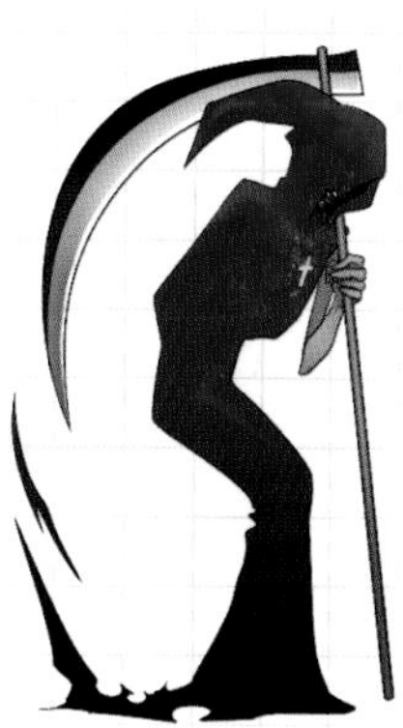

297

gothic and horror villains

search criteria

male. standing. side. cape. vampire. dracula. hat. fangs.

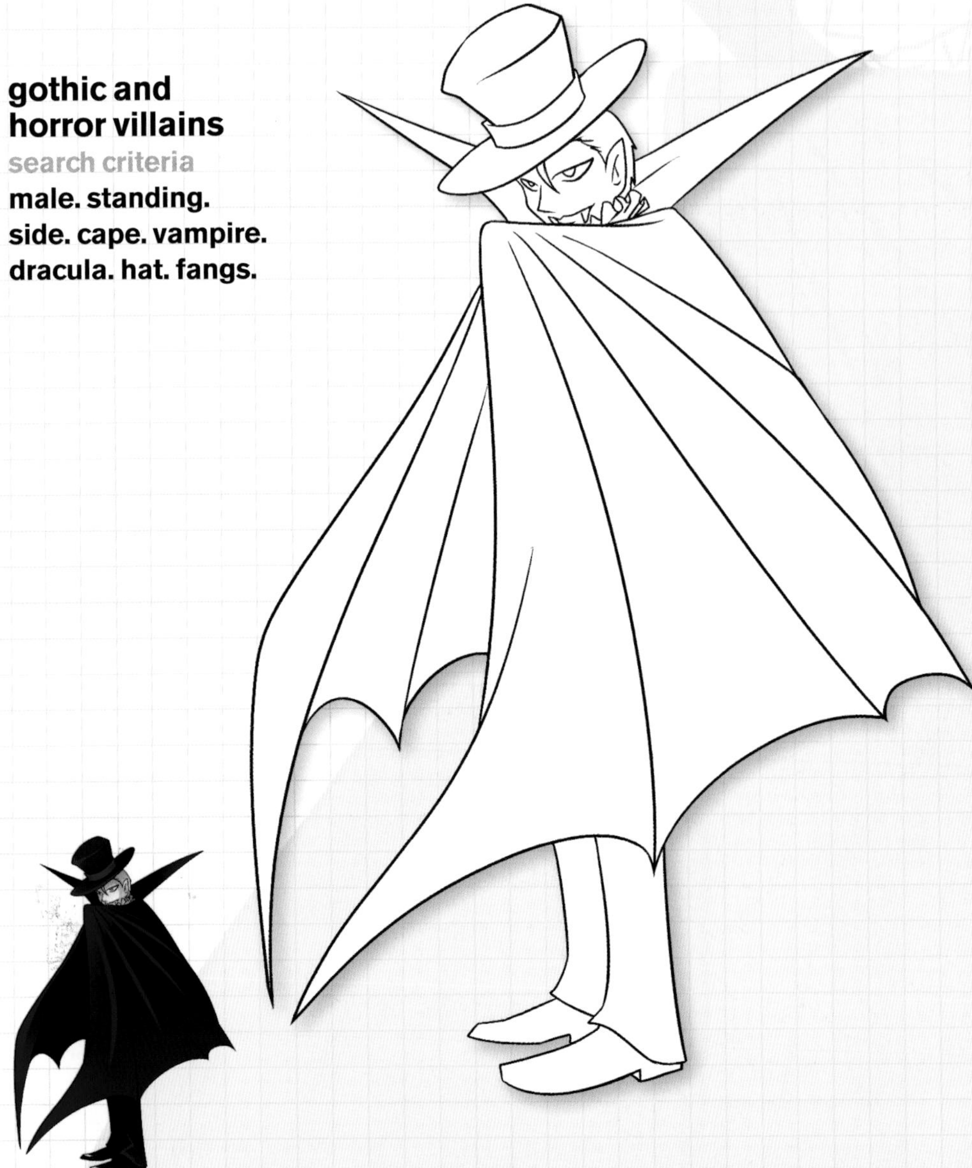

298

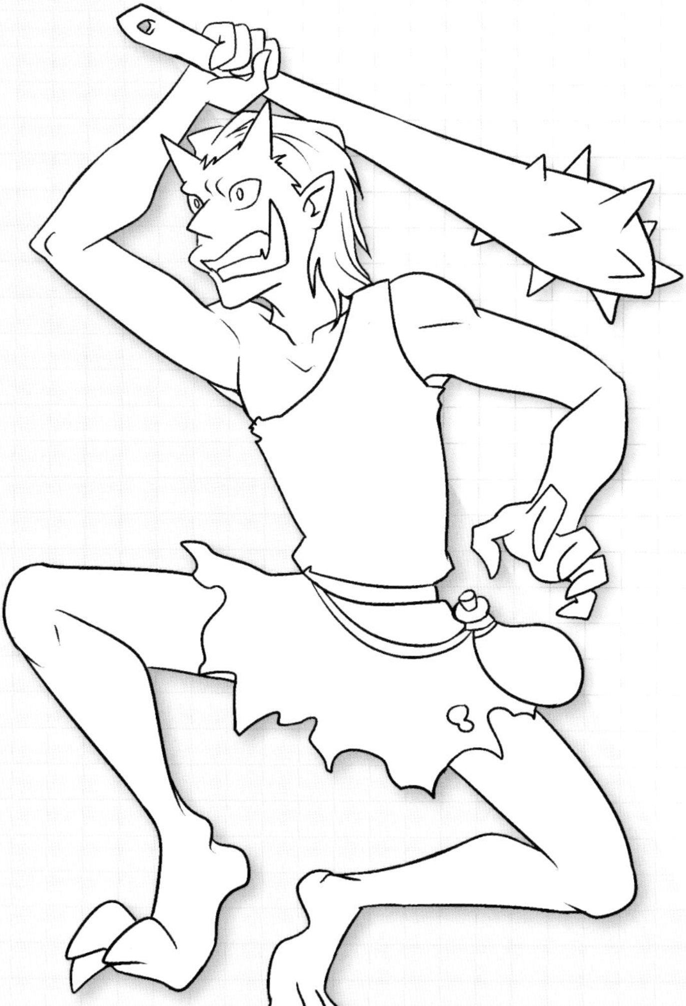

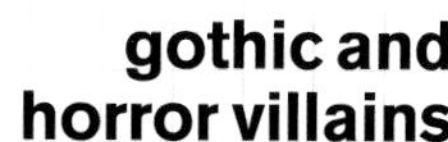

gothic and horror villains

search criteria

male. jump. posed. fang. weapon. club.

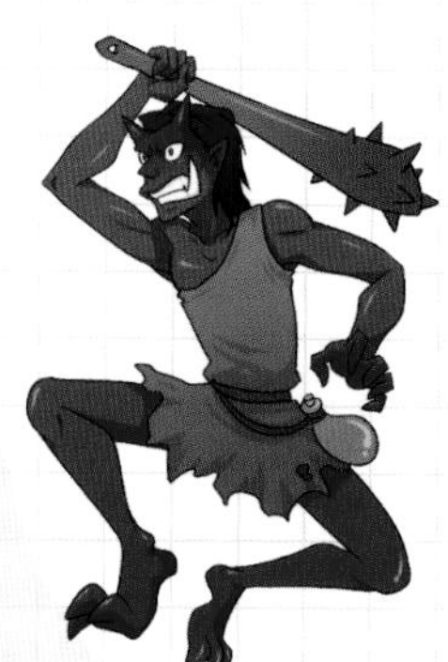

299

gothic and horror villains

search criteria

female. standing. stitches. skull. doll.

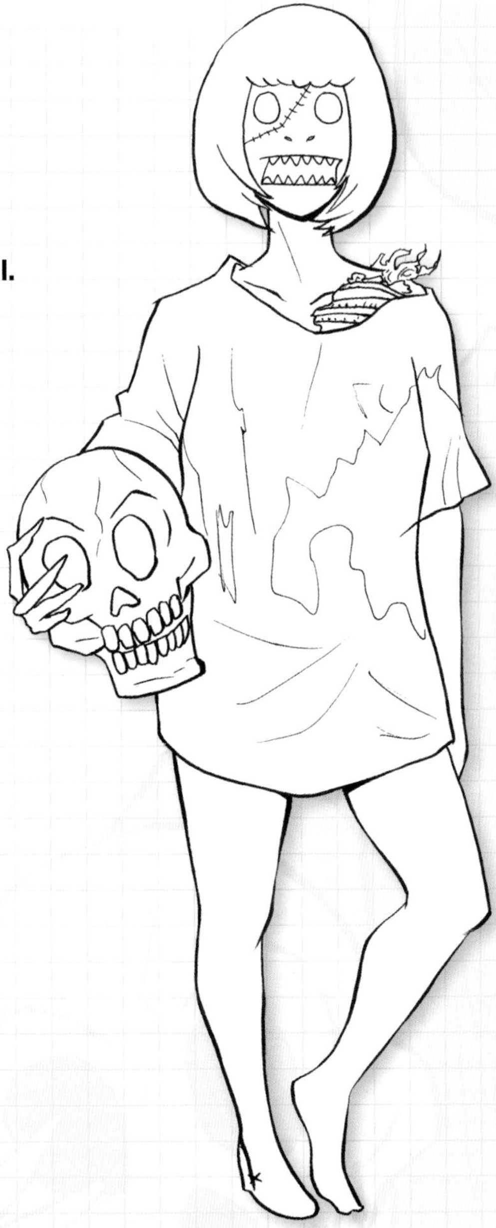

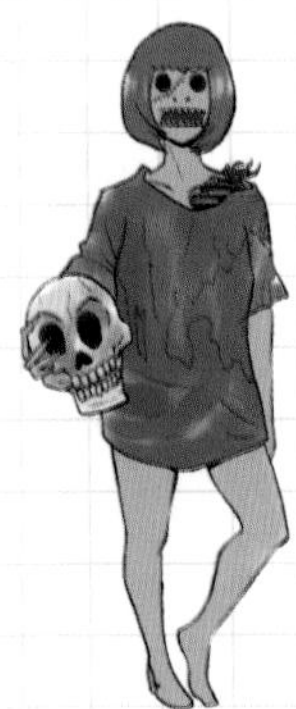

300

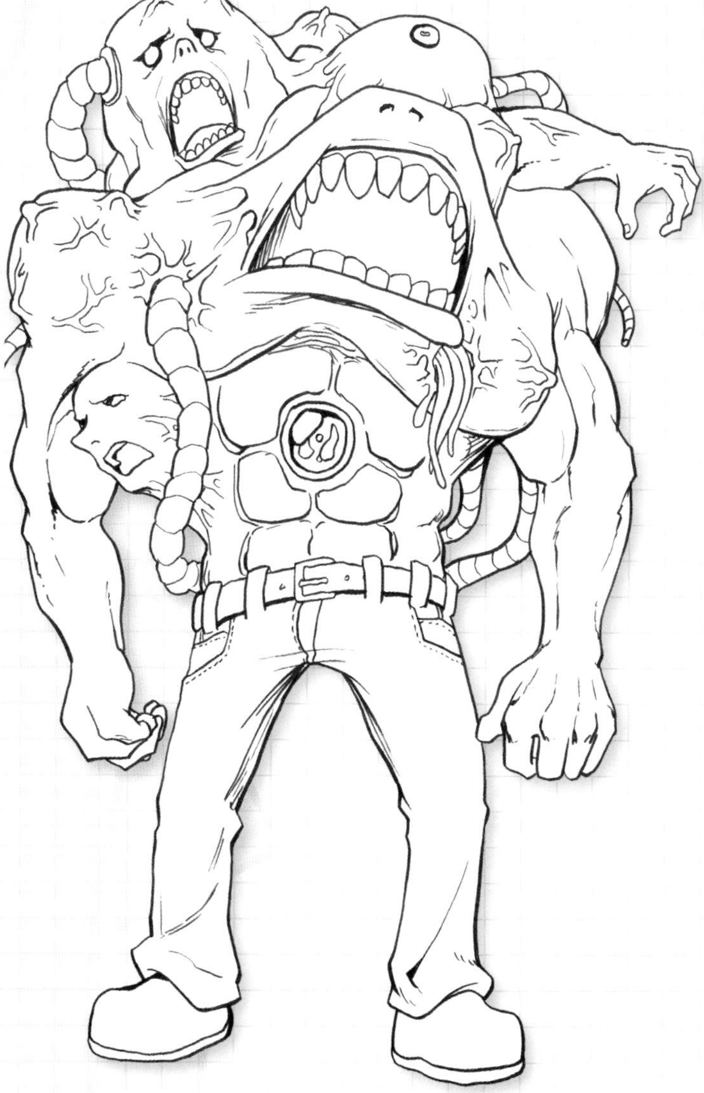

gothic and horror villains

search criteria

male. standing. monster. muscle.

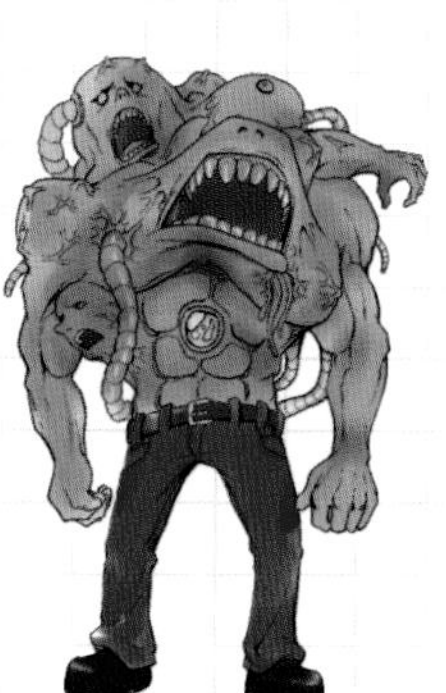

301

gothic and horror villains

search criteria

male. side. standing. monster. claw.

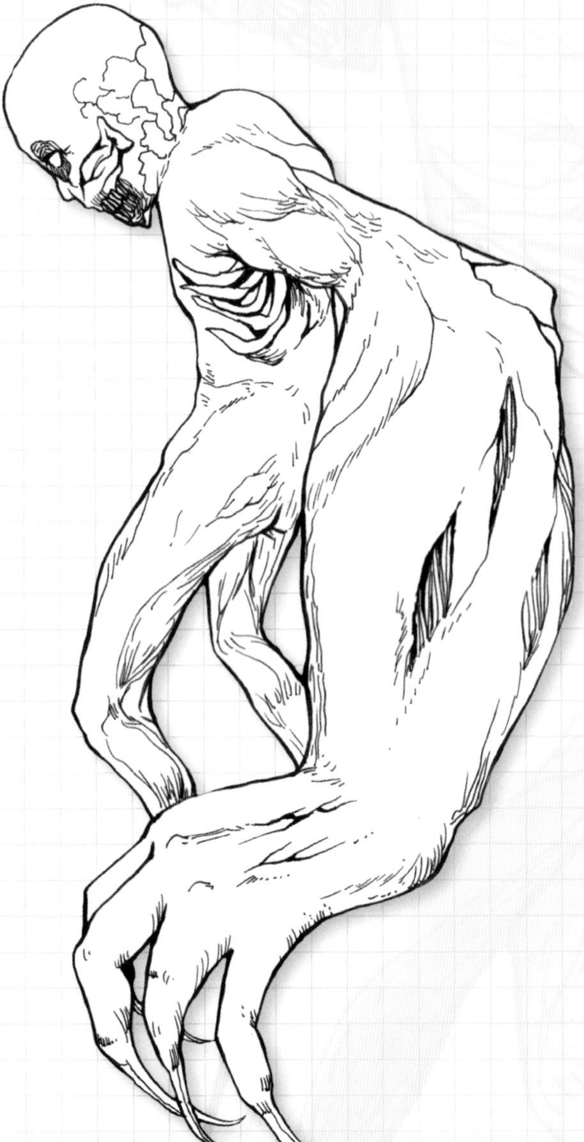

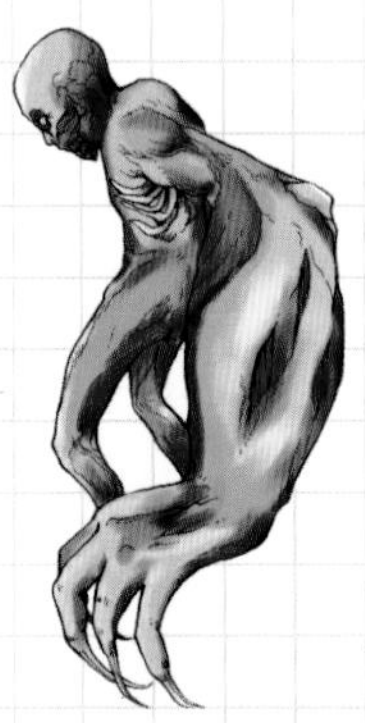

302

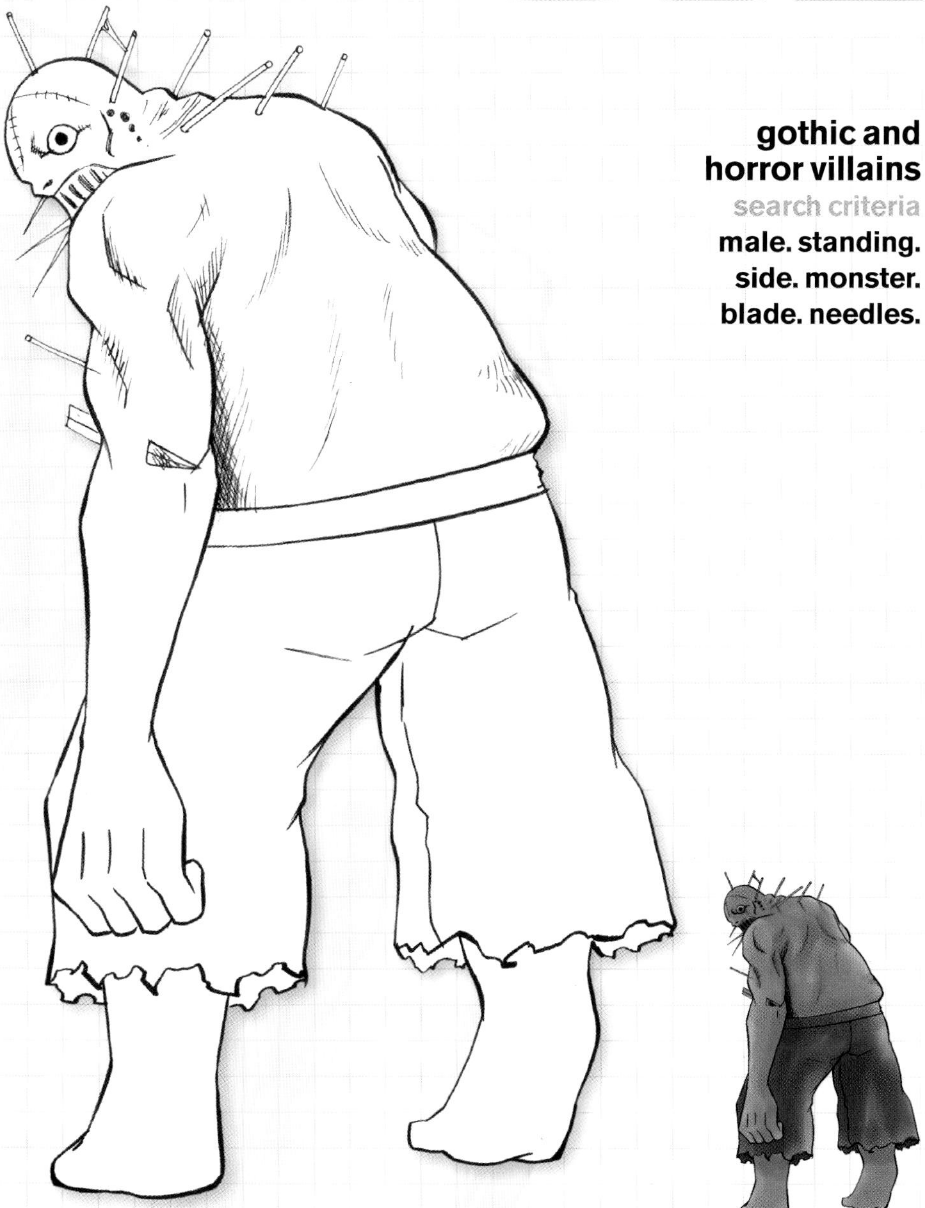

gothic and horror villains

search criteria

male. standing. side. monster. blade. needles.

303

gothic and horror villains

search criteria

male. kneeling. monster. bones. weapon. sword.

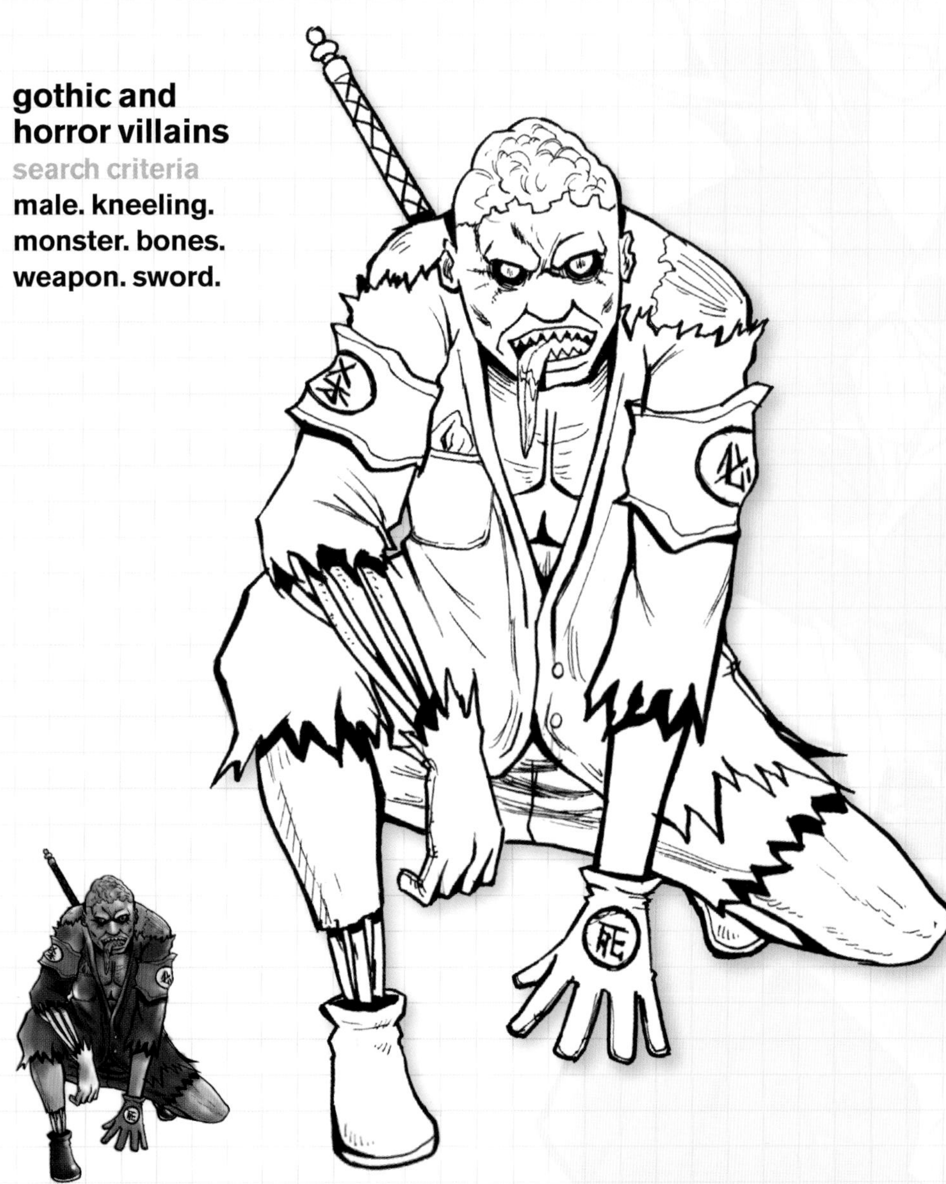

304

gothic and horror villains

search criteria

male. standing. drink. vampire. fang. dracula. cape.

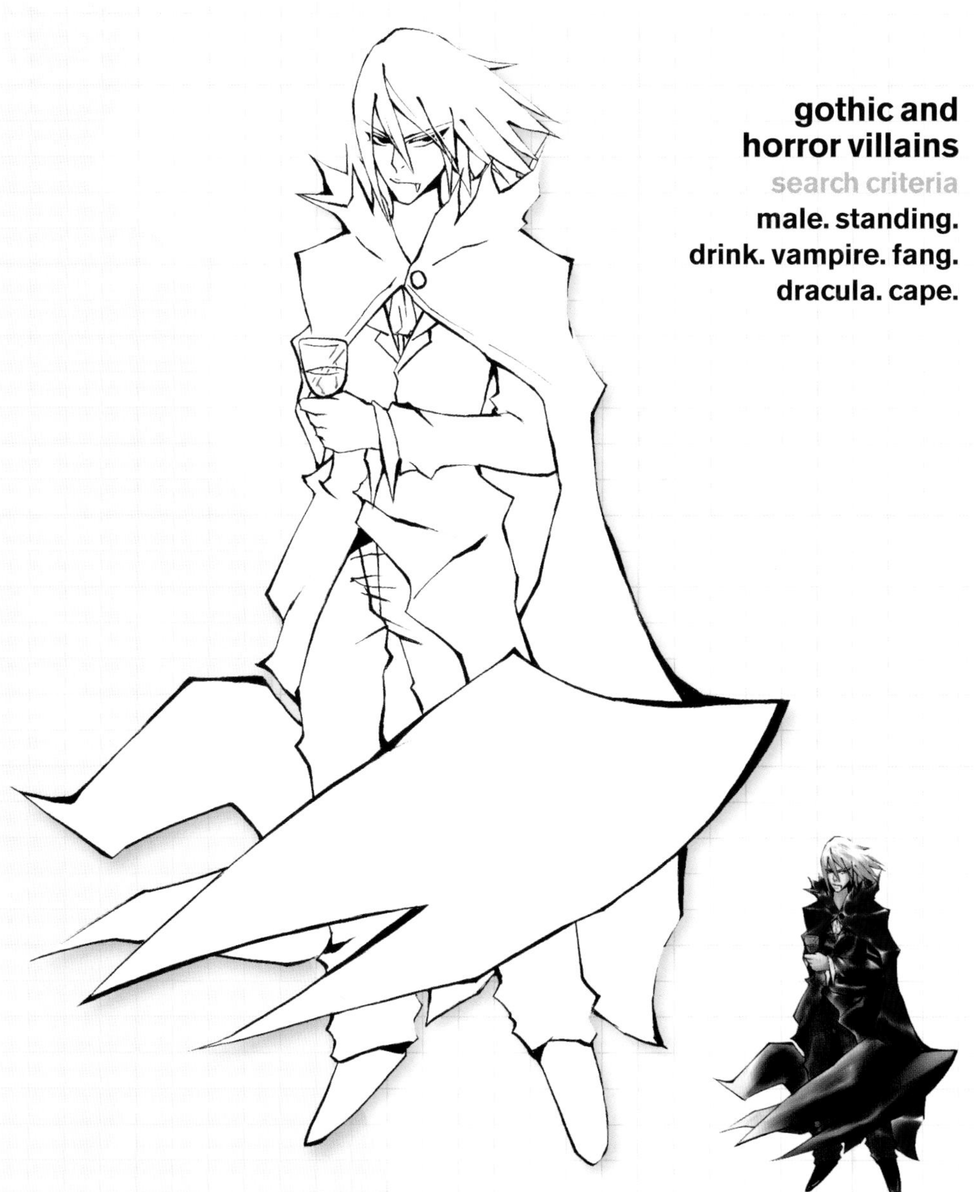

305

gothic and horror villains

search criteria

male. standing. ghost. horns. weapon. axe. demon. spirit.

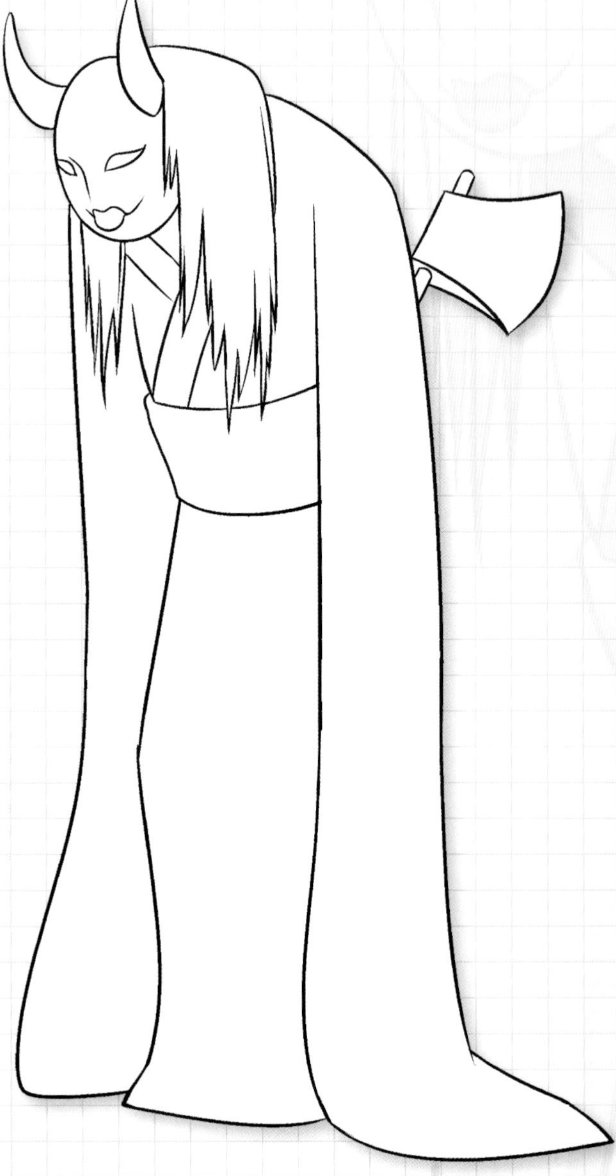

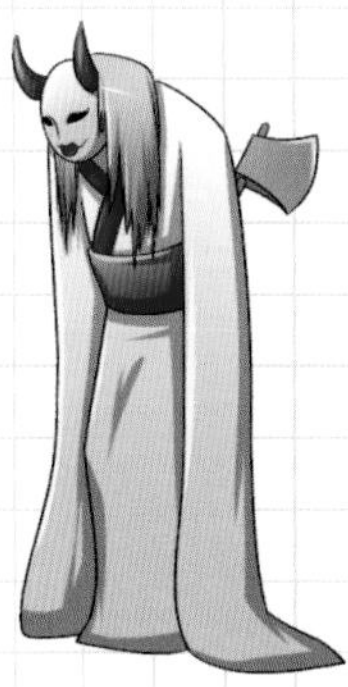

306

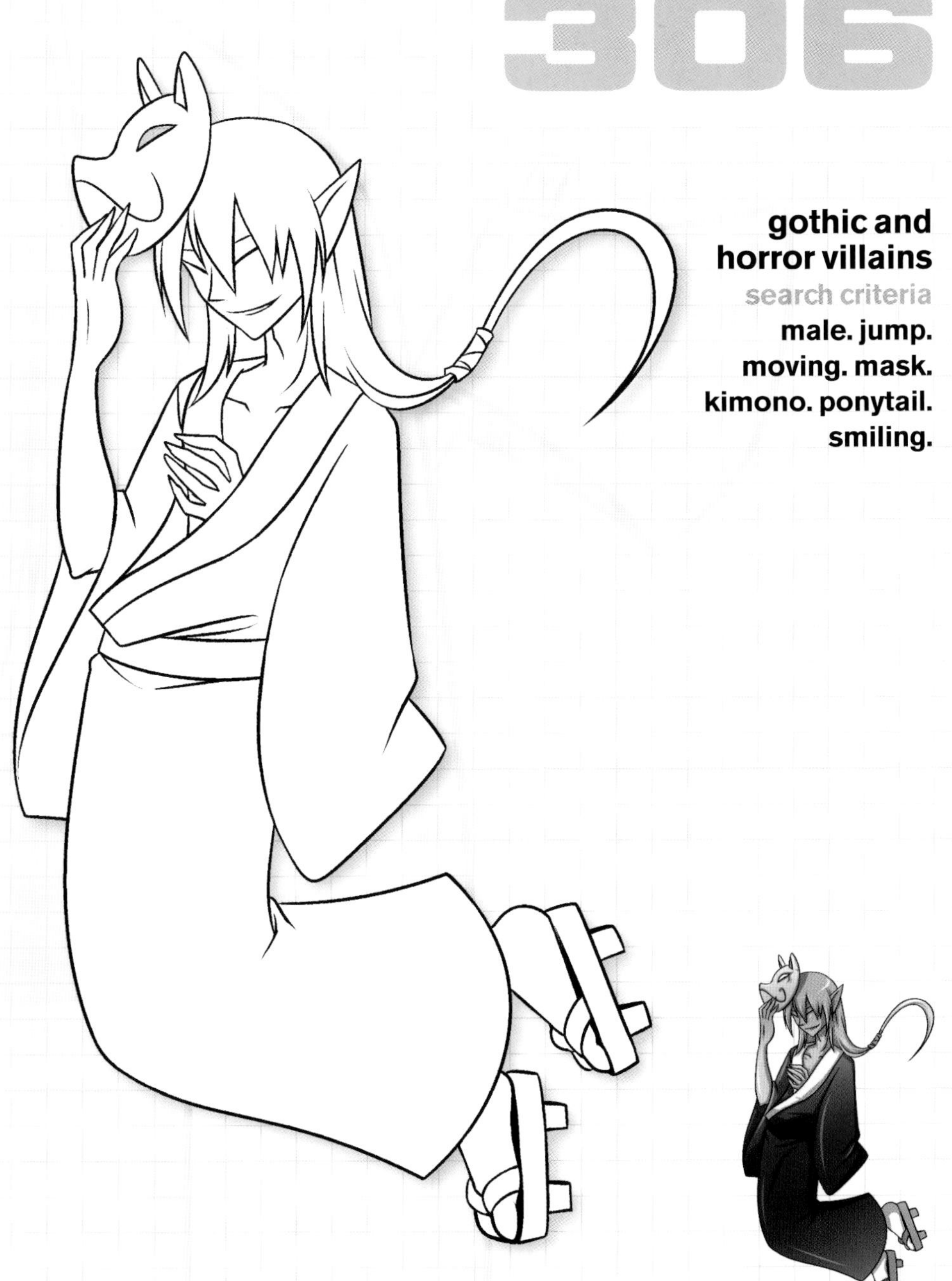

gothic and horror villains

search criteria

male. jump. moving. mask. kimono. ponytail. smiling.

307

gothic and horror villains

search criteria

male. standing. giant. cyclops. weapons. clubs.

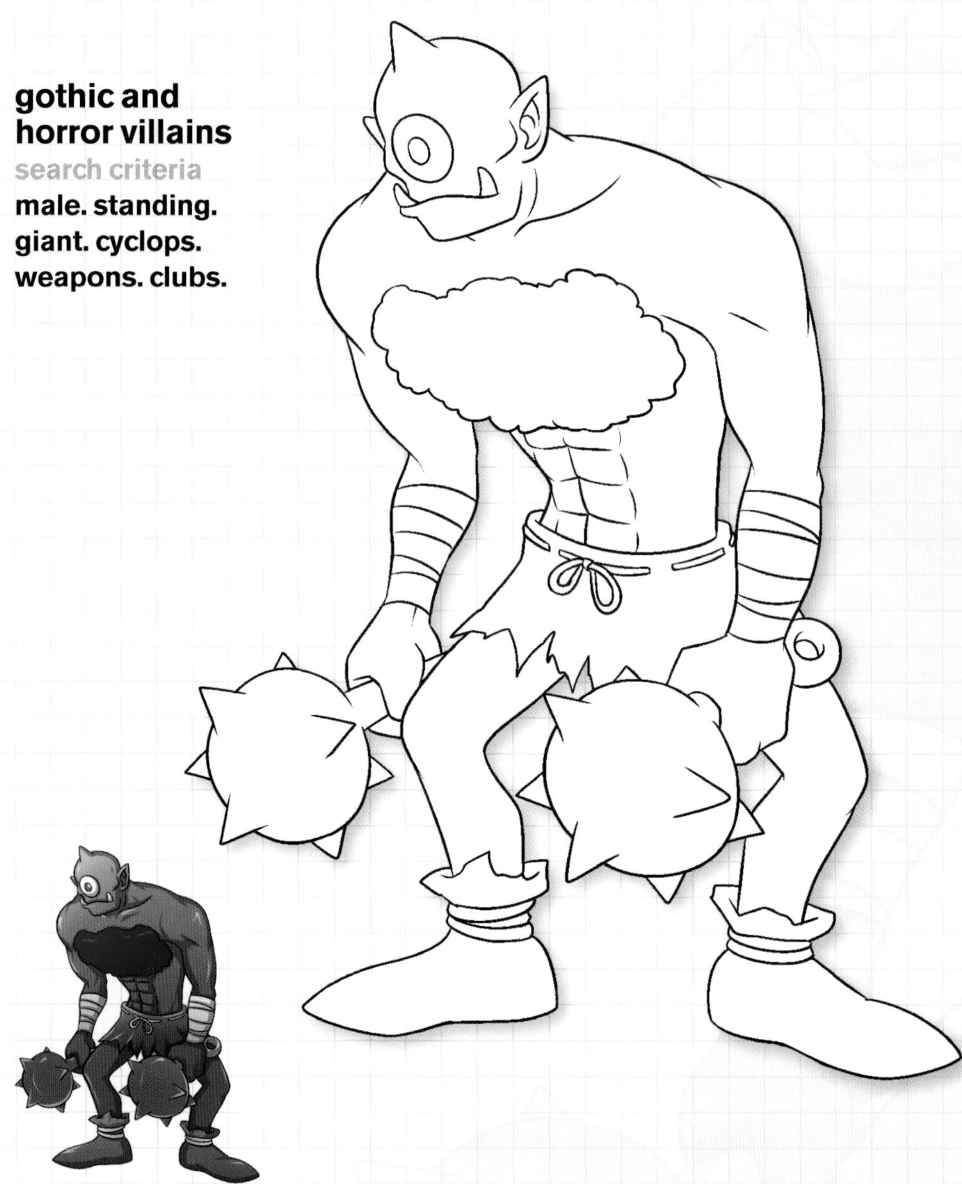

308

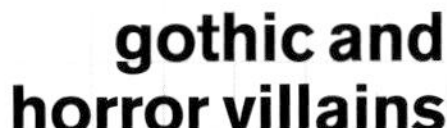

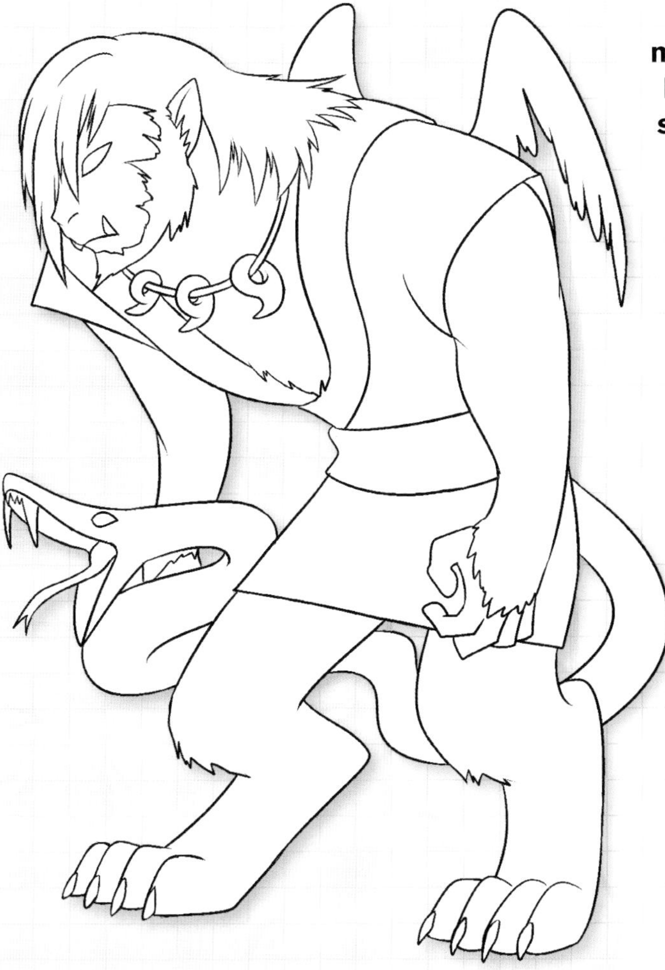

gothic and horror villains

search criteria

male. standing. wolf. beast. fangs. wings. snake. fur. necklace.

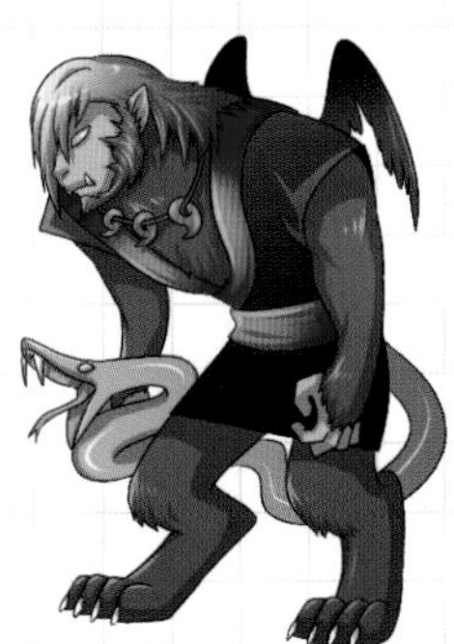

309

gothic and horror villains

search criteria

female. floating. tail. ghost. demon.

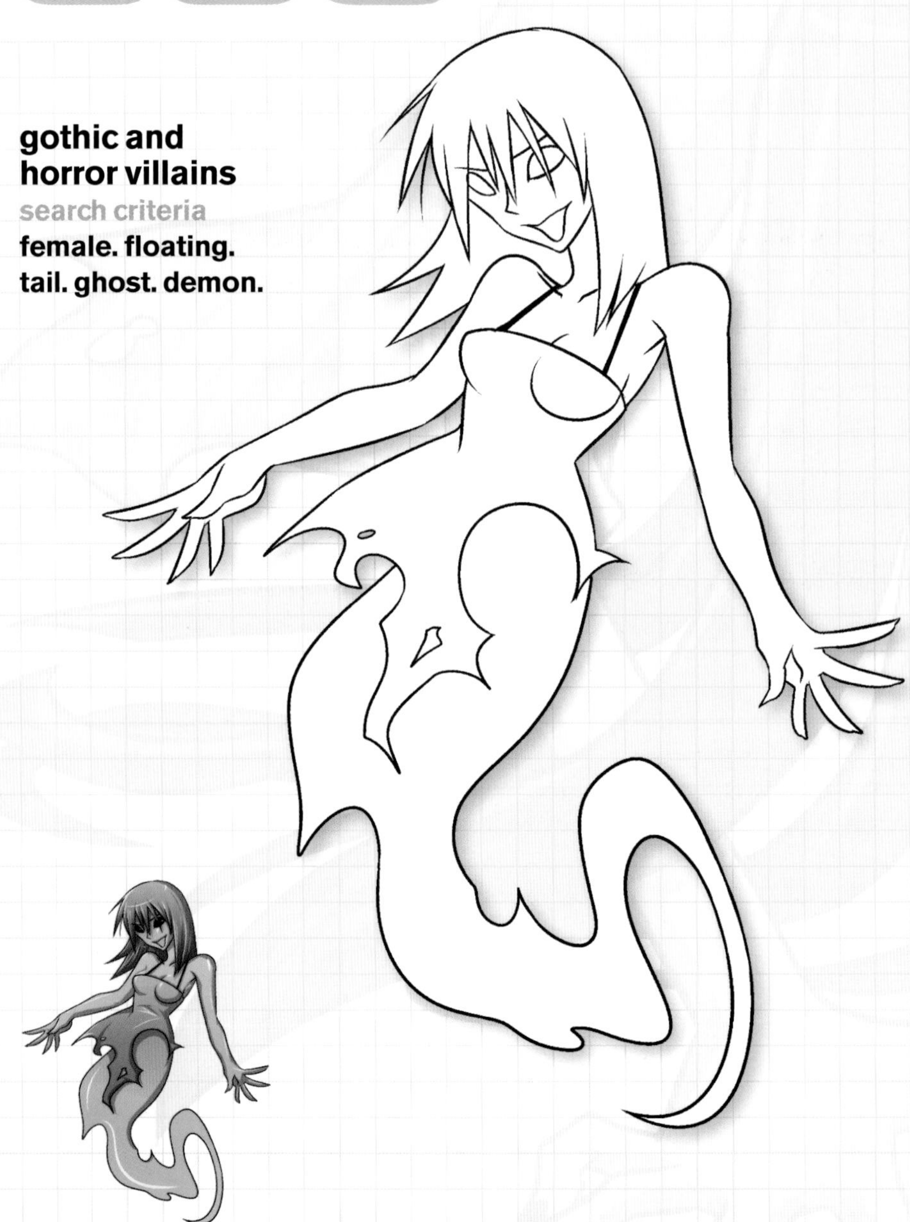

310

gothic and horror villains

search criteria

female. crawling. ghost. demon.

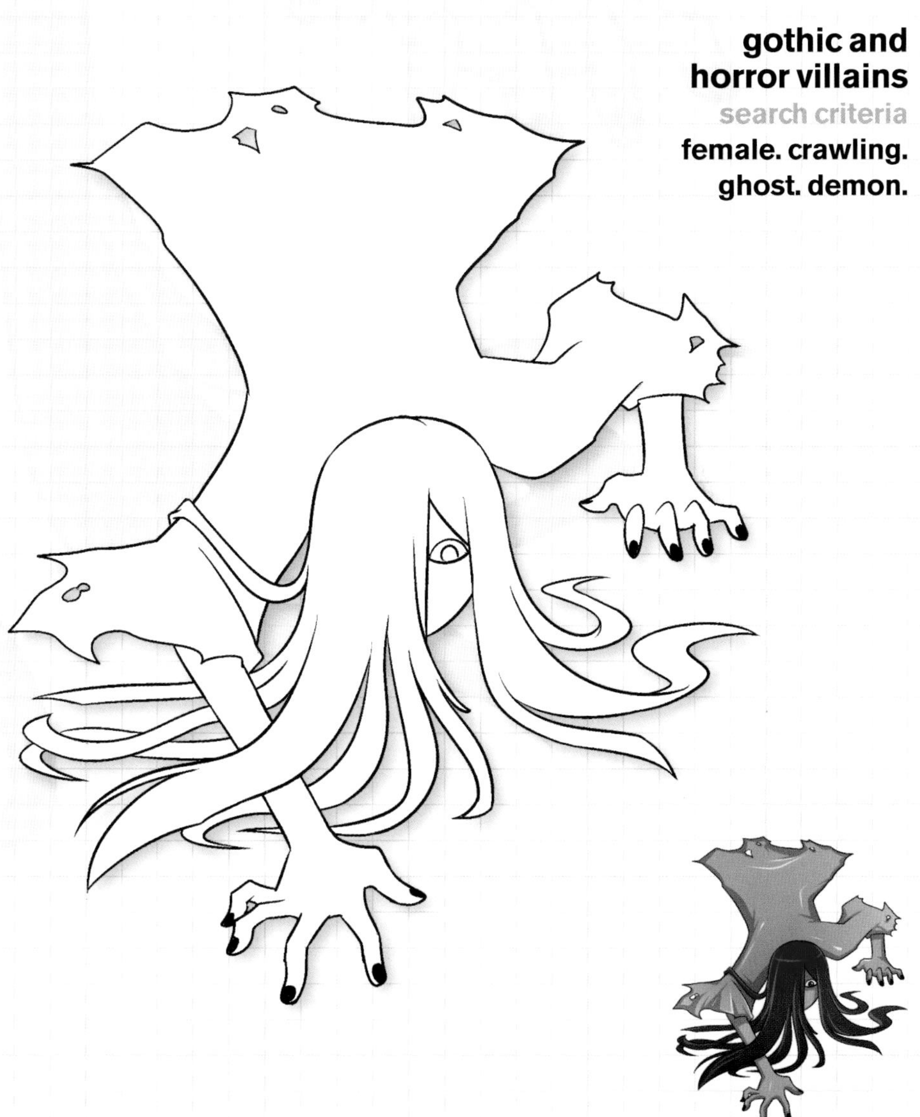

311

gothic and horror villains

search criteria

male. walking. moving. mummy. bandages.

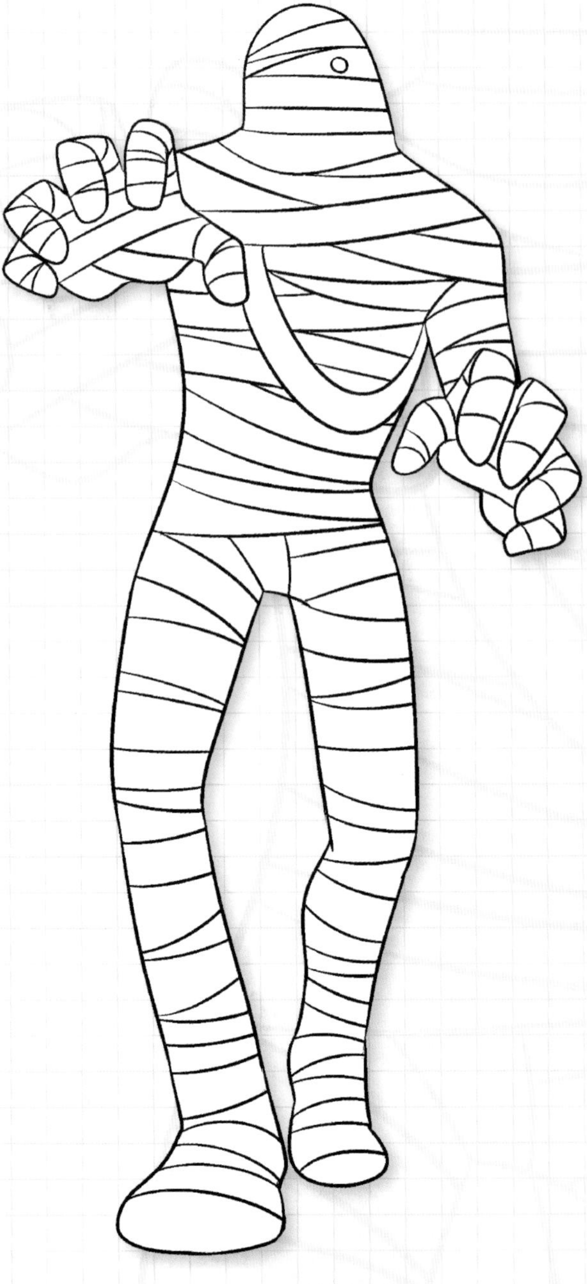

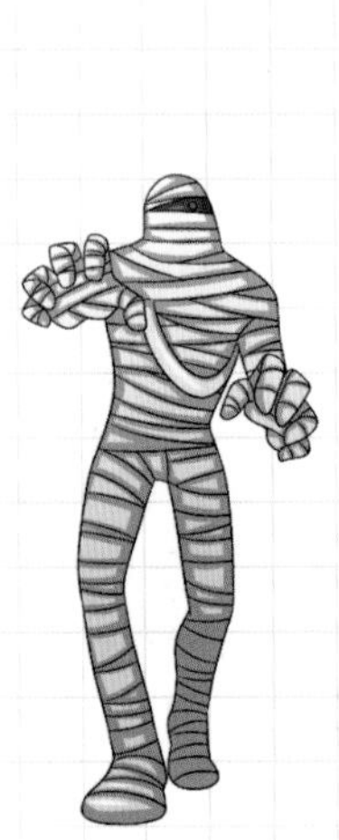

312

gothic and horror villains

search criteria

female. side. crawling. spider.

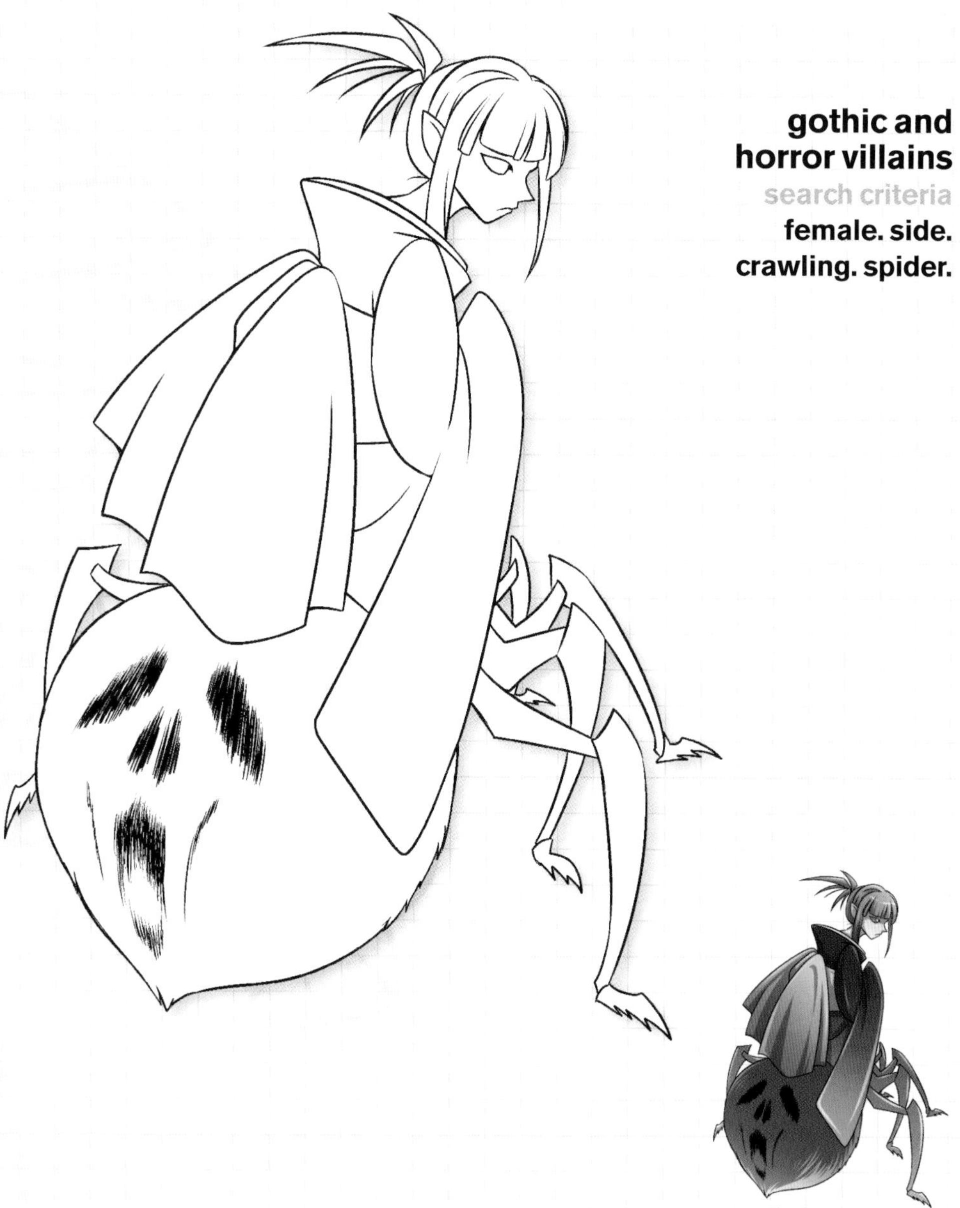

313

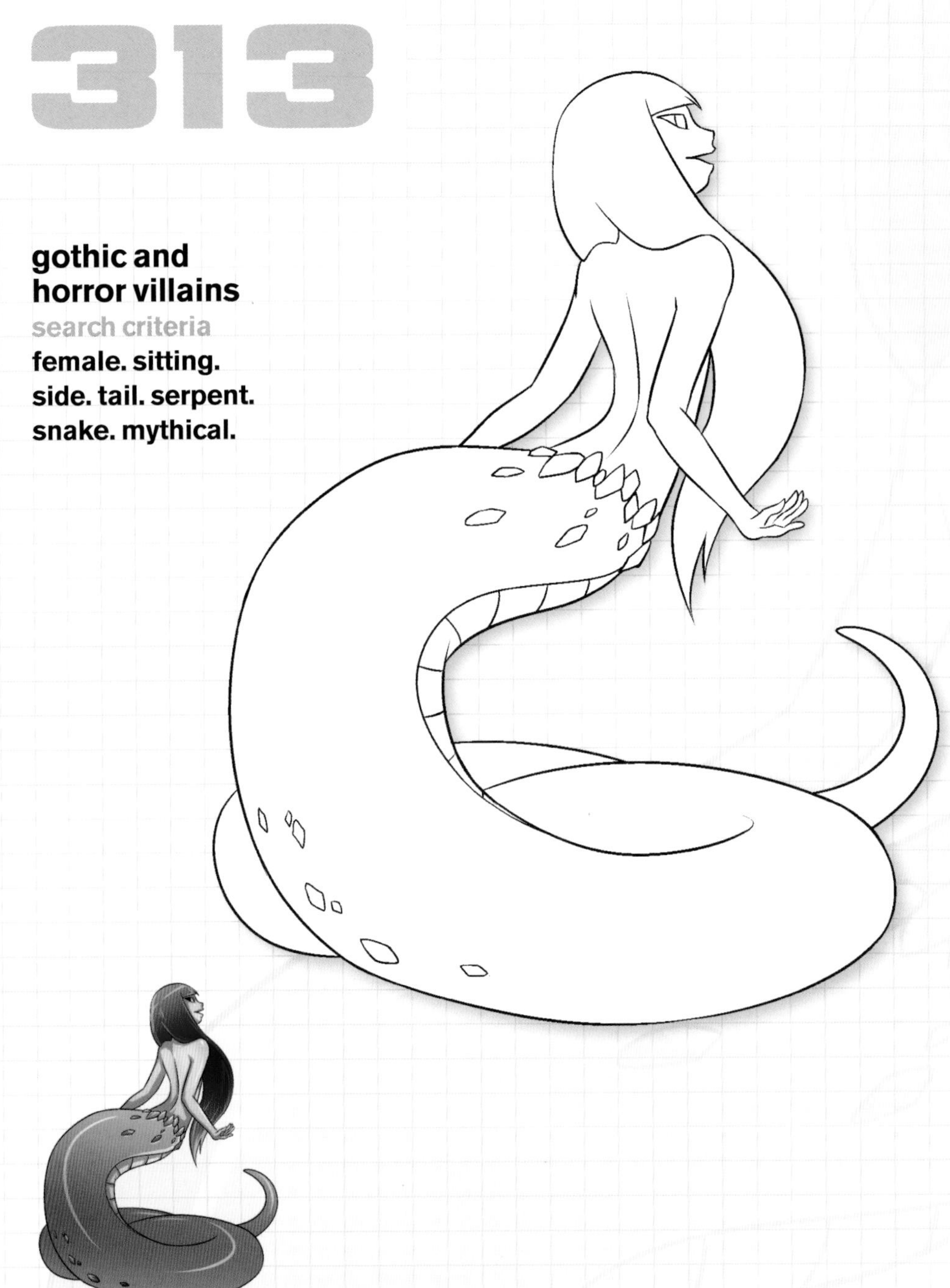

gothic and horror villains

search criteria

female. sitting. side. tail. serpent. snake. mythical.

314

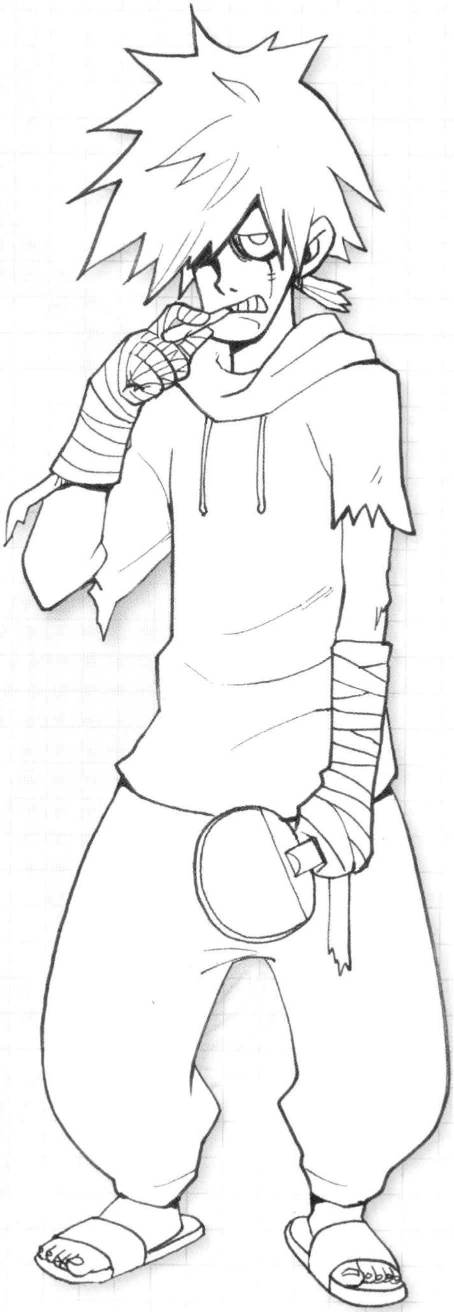

gothic and horror villains

search criteria

male. standing. bandages. scar. shonen. sport.

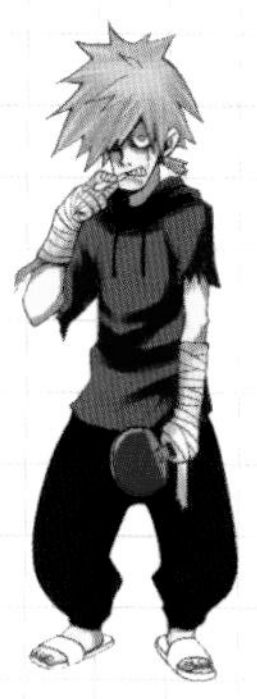

315

gothic and horror heroes

search criteria

male. standing. side. nomad. bag.

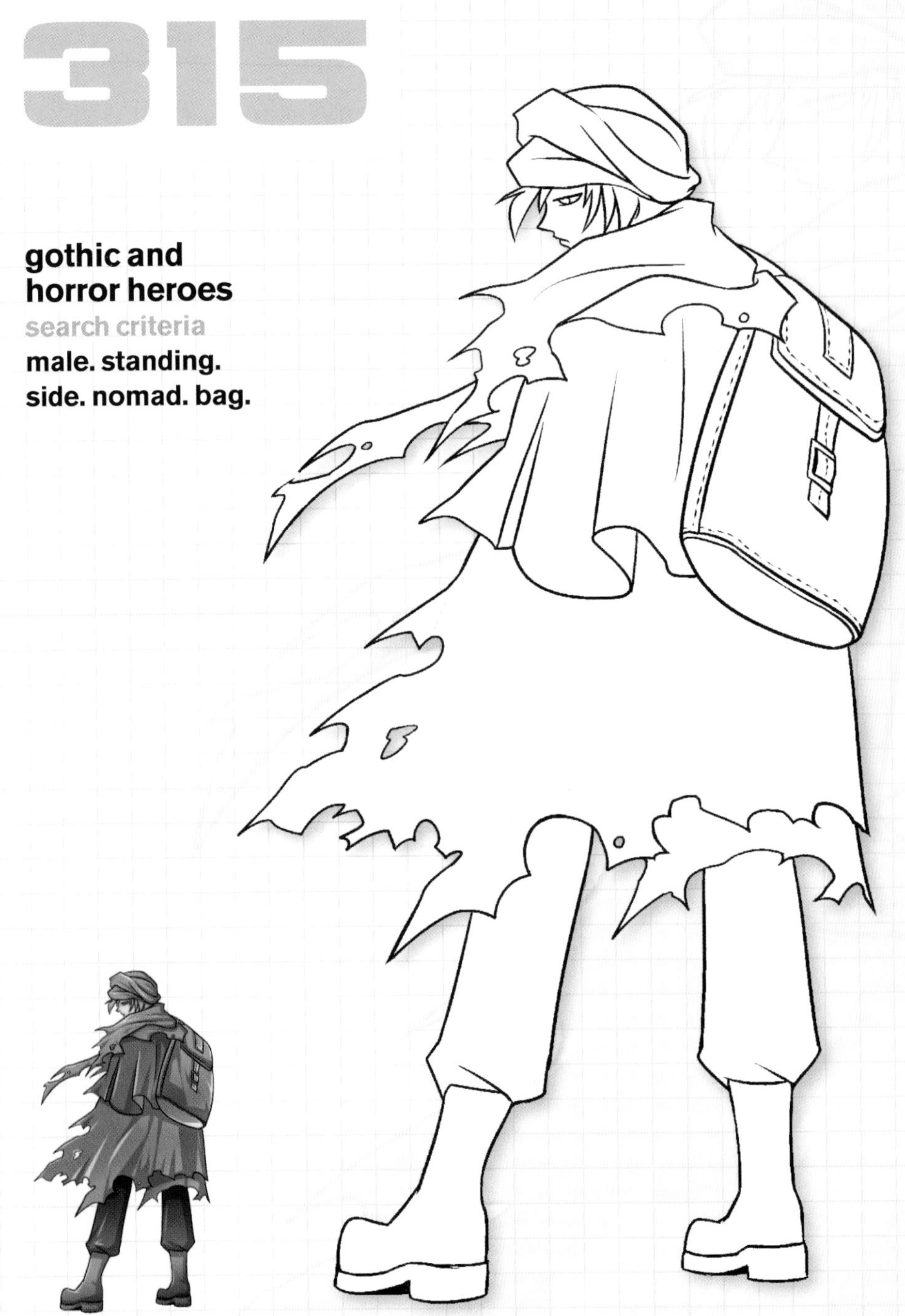

316

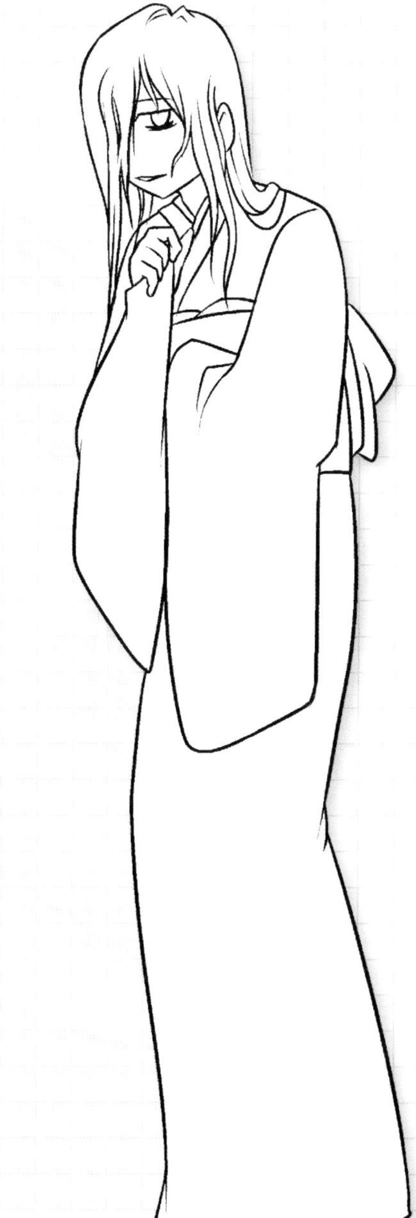

gothic and horror heroes

search criteria

female. standing. rain. water. sad. ghost. kimono.

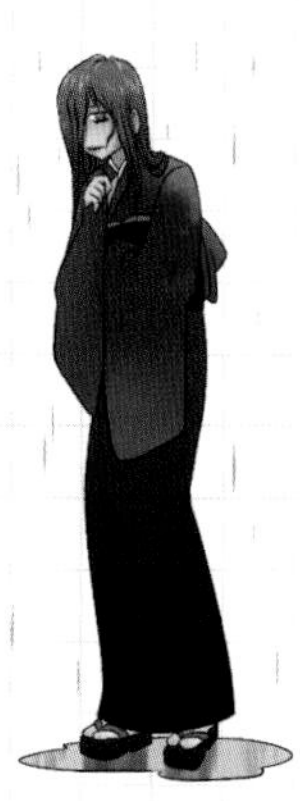

317

gothic and horror heroes

search criteria

female. jump. smiling. ghost.

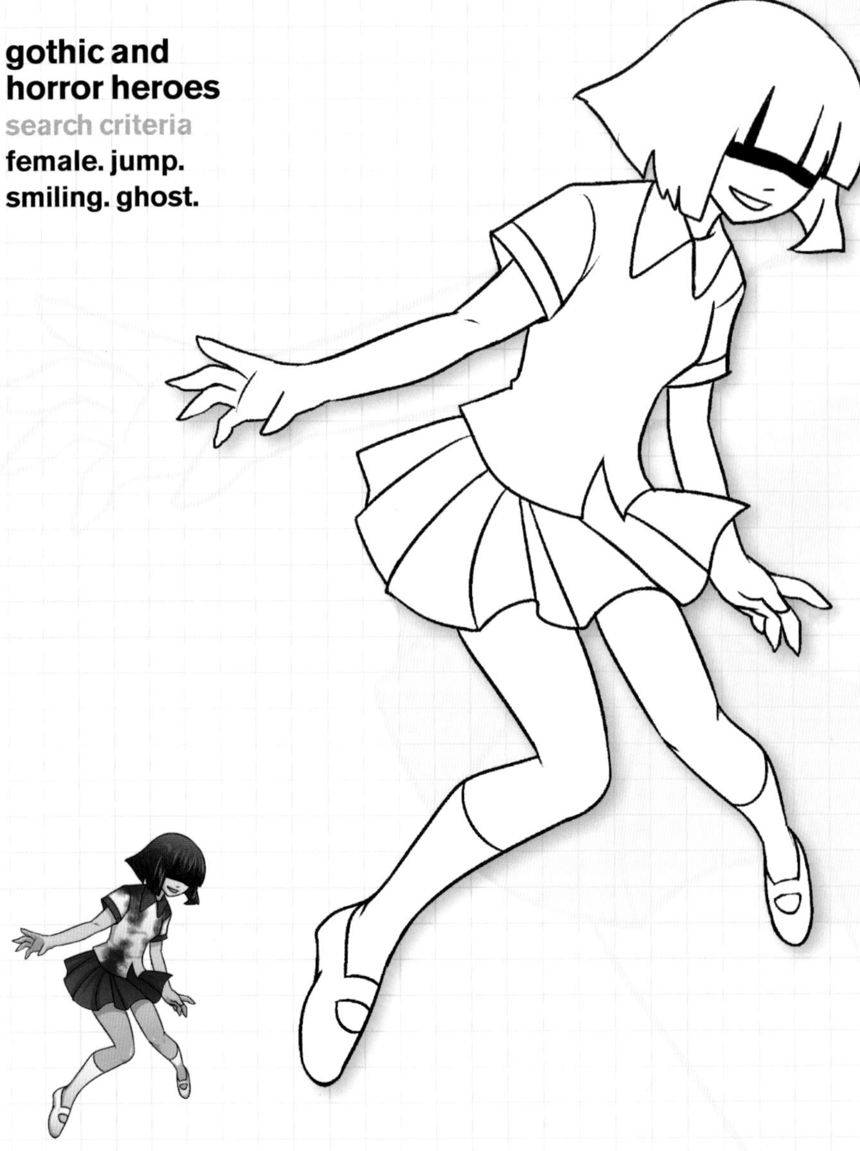

318

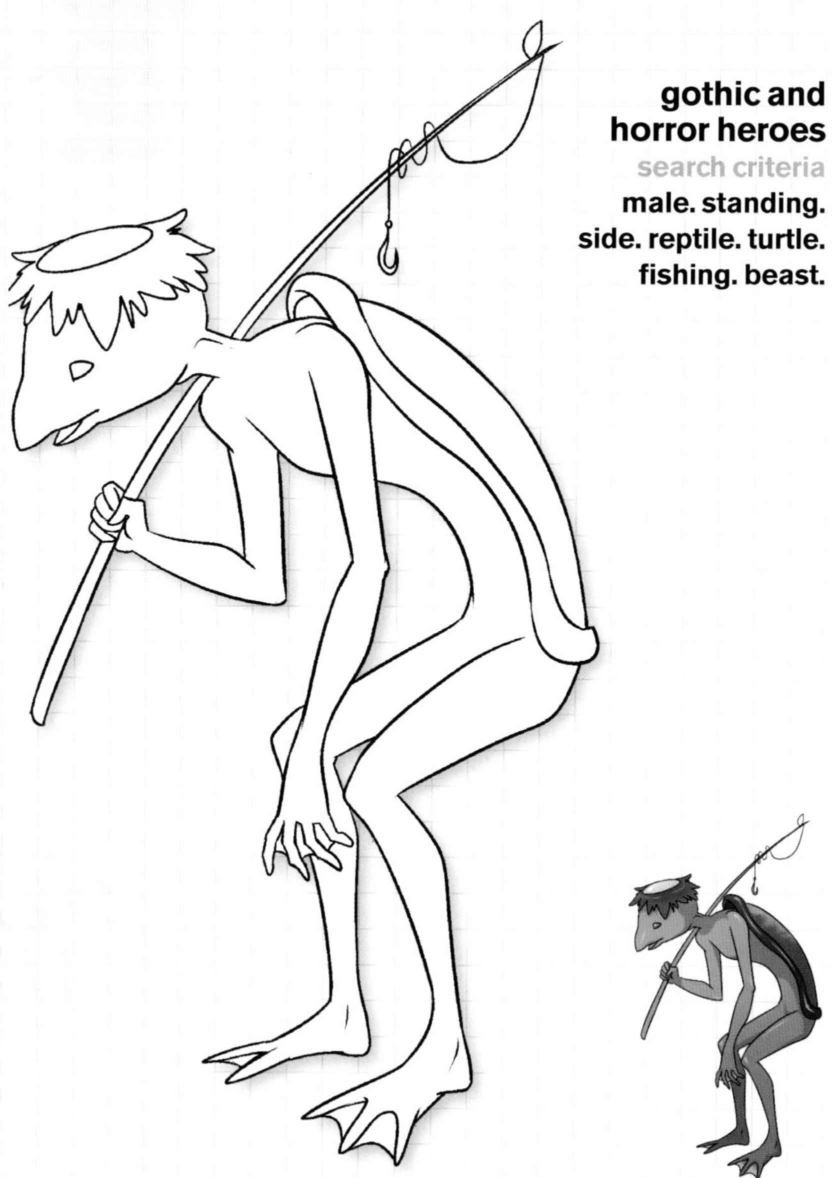

gothic and horror heroes

search criteria

male. standing. side. reptile. turtle. fishing. beast.

319

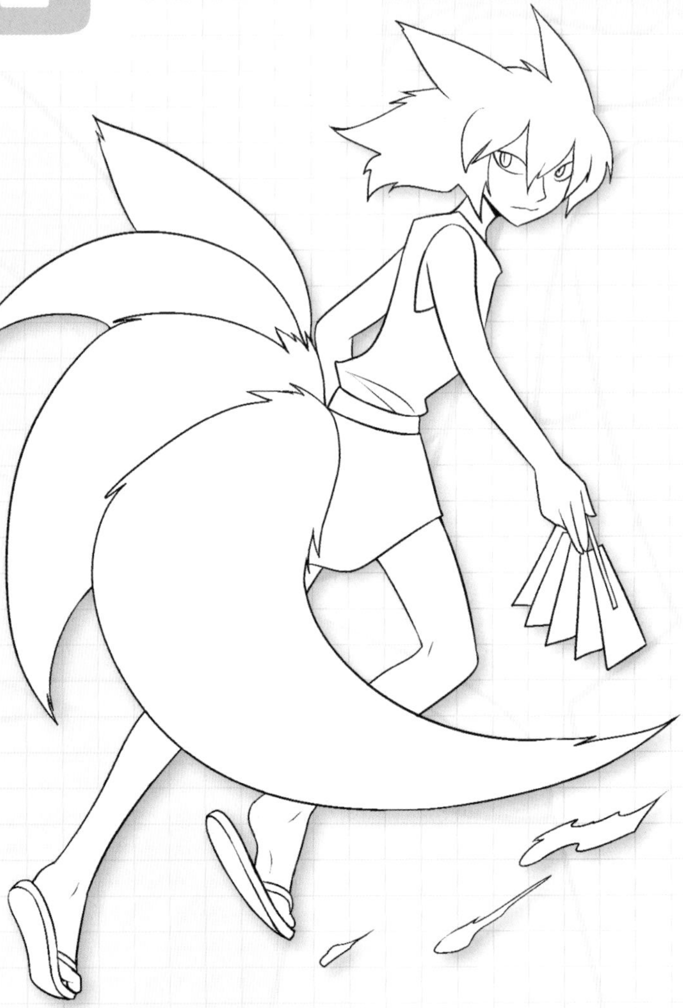

gothic and horror heroes

search criteria

female. side. running. tail. fox. fan.

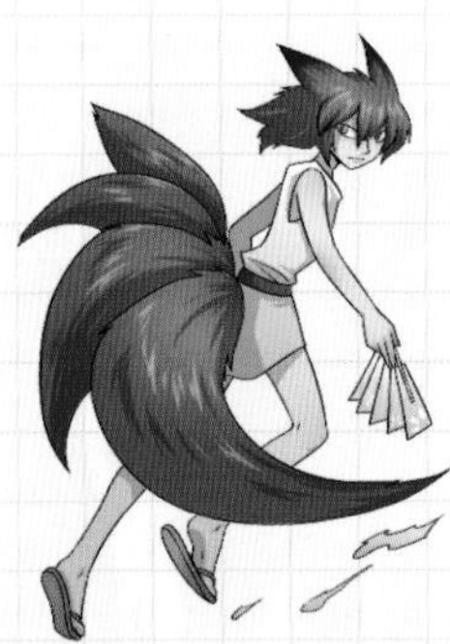

320

gothic and horror heroes

search criteria

female. standing. griffin. wings. tail. time. sand. mythical.

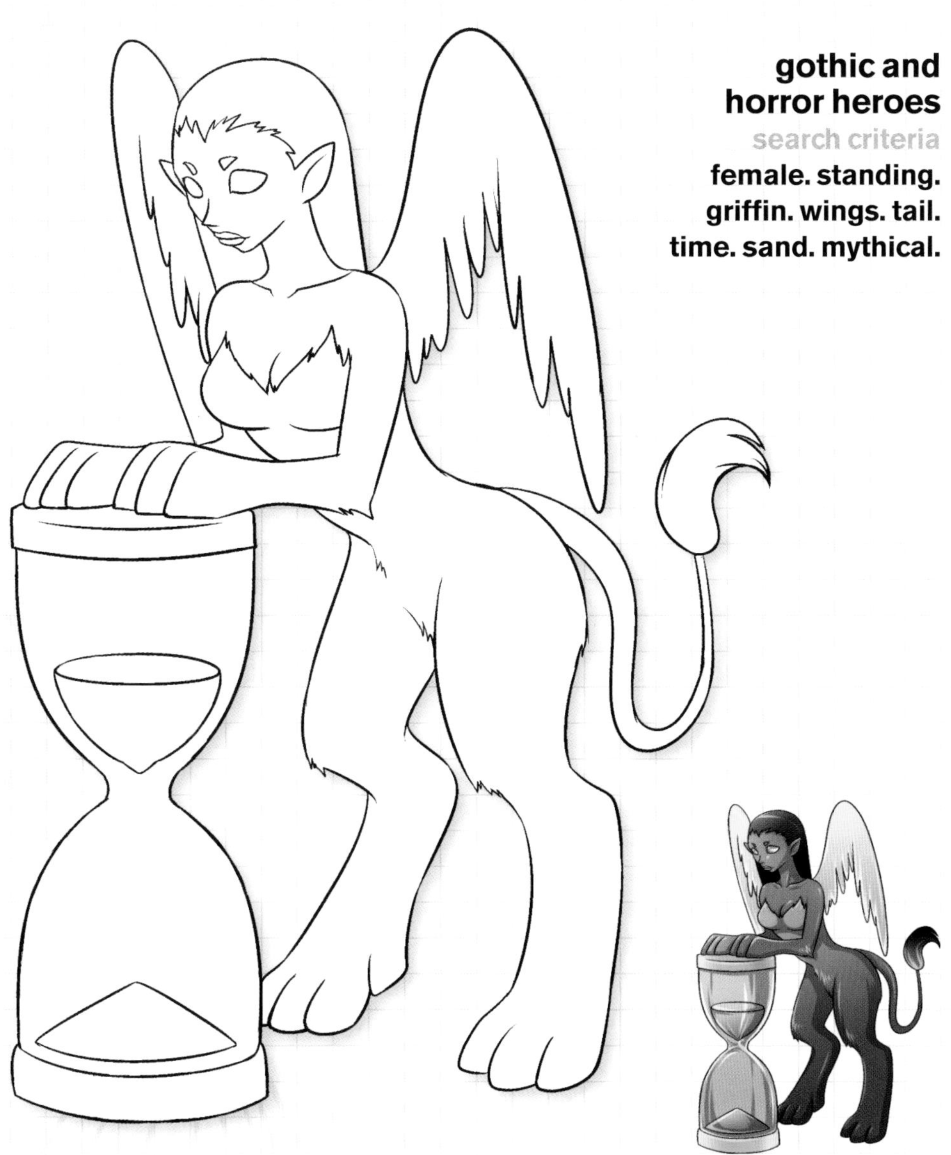

321

gothic and horror heroes

search criteria

male. floating. jump. weapons. blades. sad. boy.

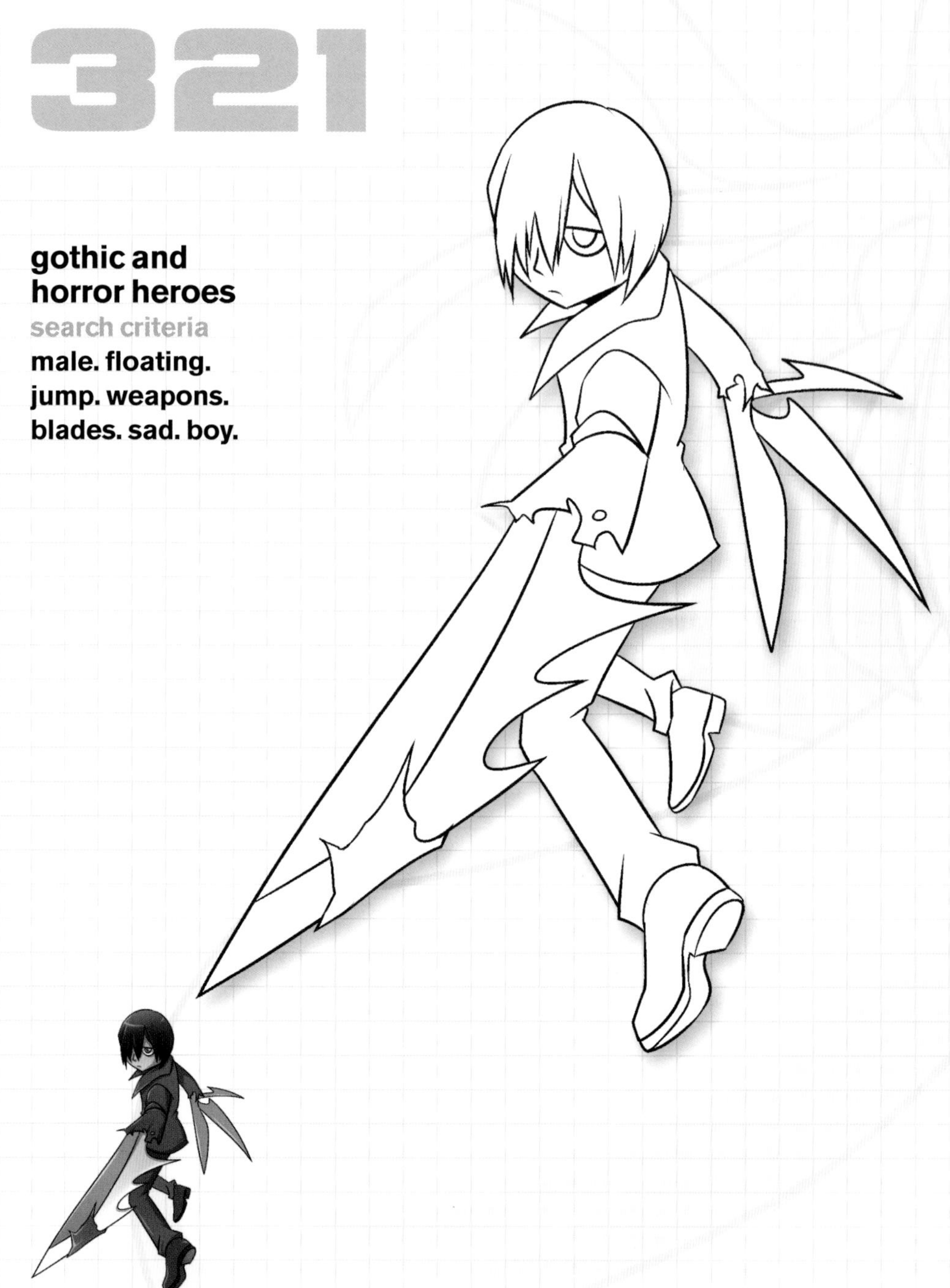

322

gothic and horror heroes

search criteria

female. running. sad. tears. water.

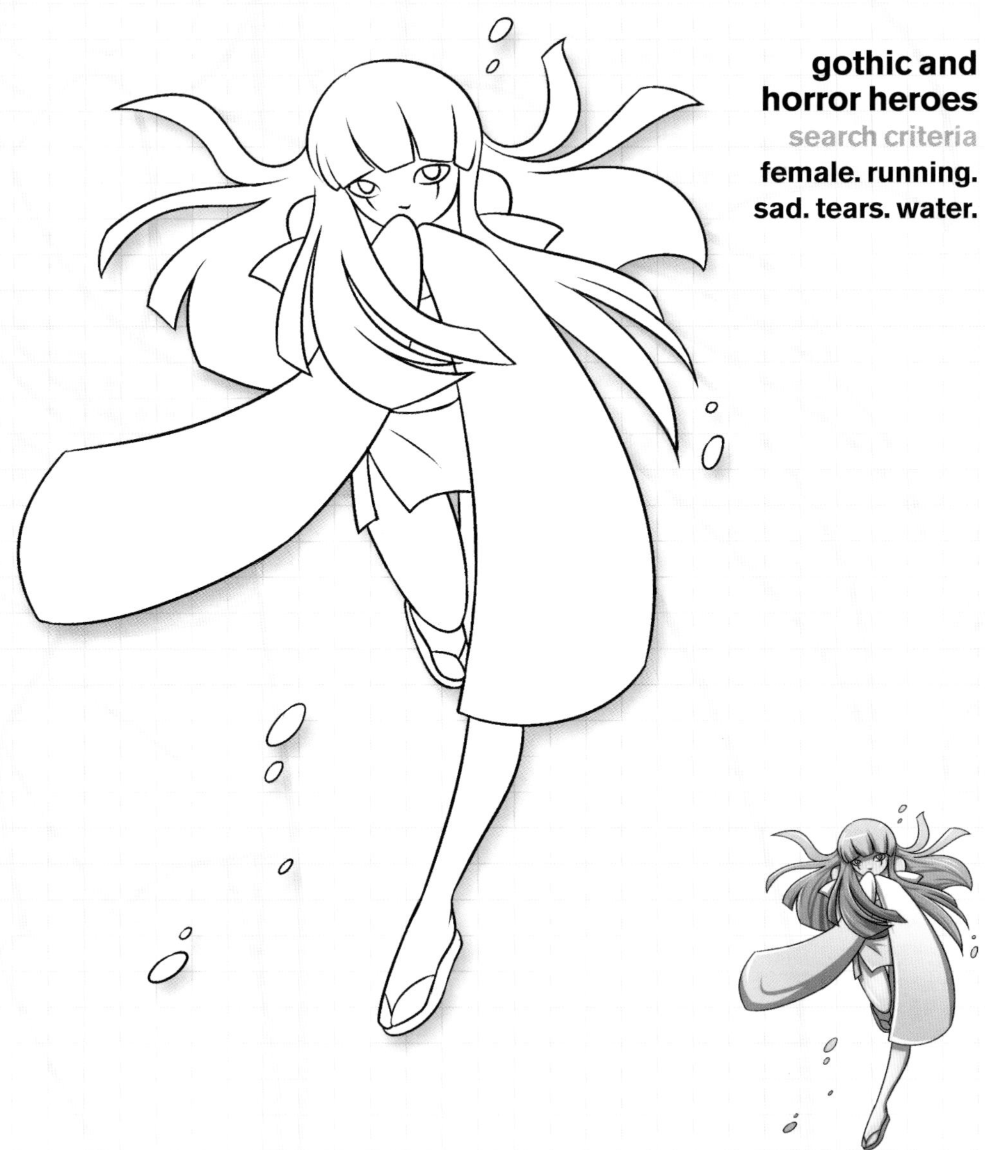

323

gothic and horror heroes

search criteria

standing. spirit. kimono. ball.

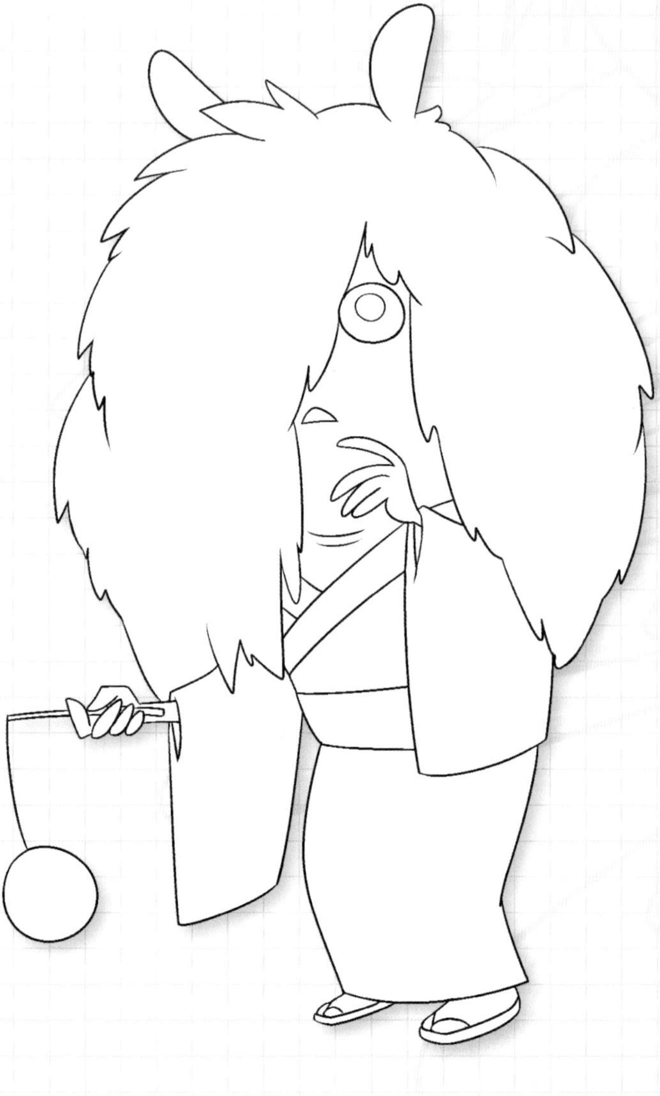

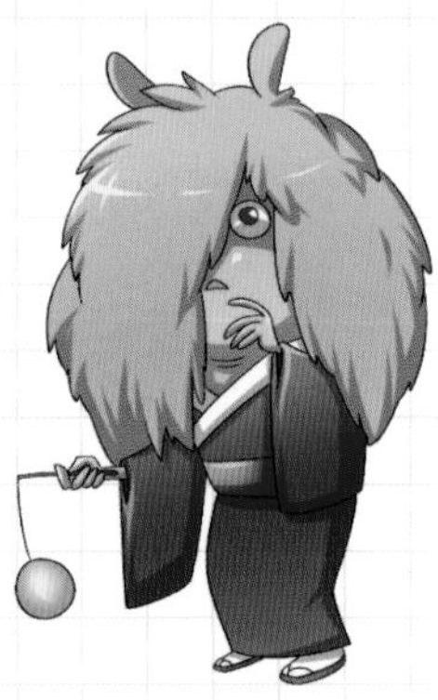

324

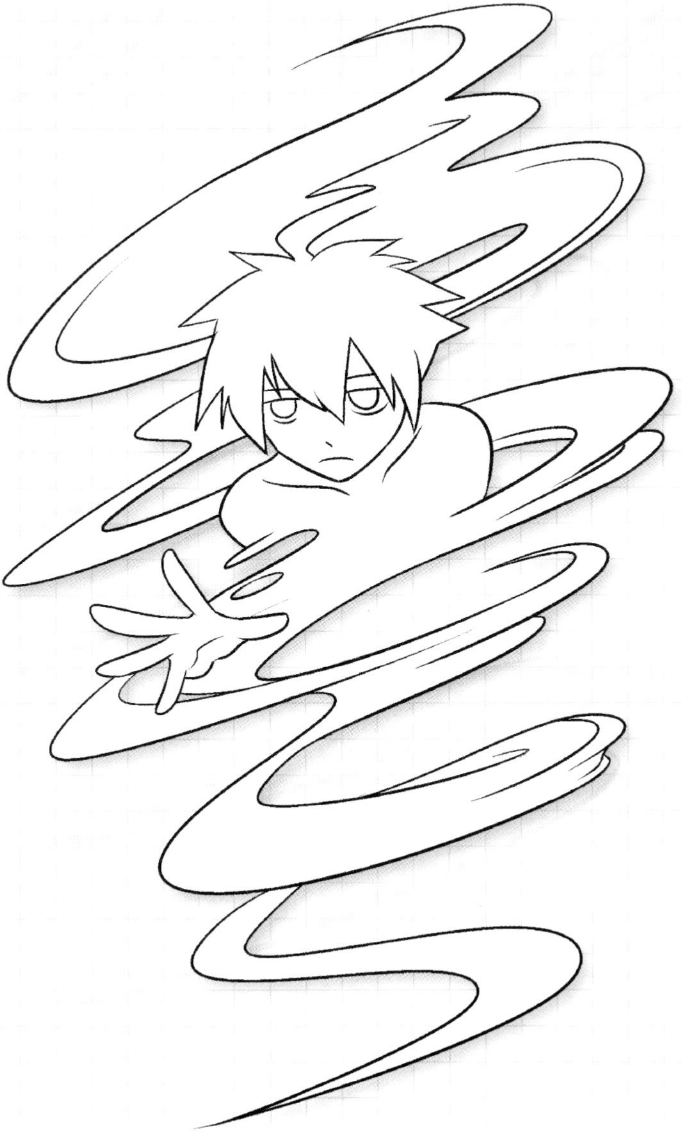

gothic and horror heroes

search criteria

male. floating. air. demon. spirit. ghost. sad.

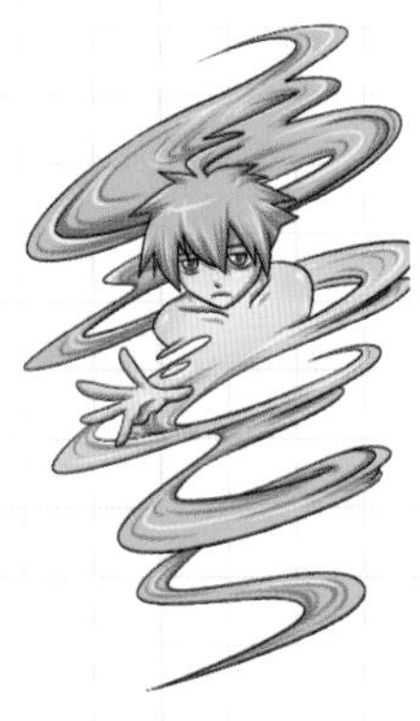

325

historical villains

search criteria

male. kneeling. hat. samurai. warrior. weapon. sword.

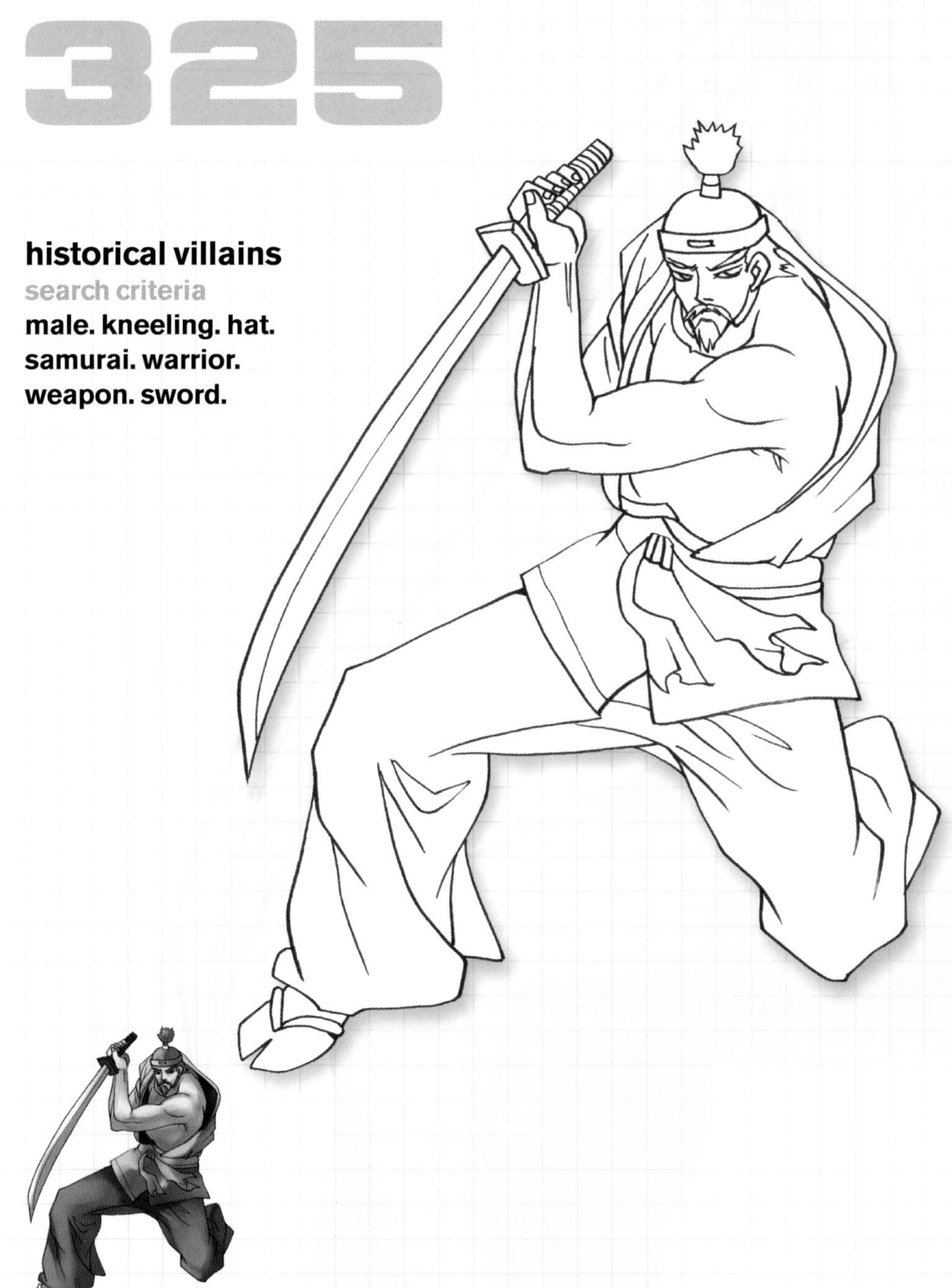

326

historical villains

search criteria

male. kneeling. side. scar. warrior. weapon. sword.

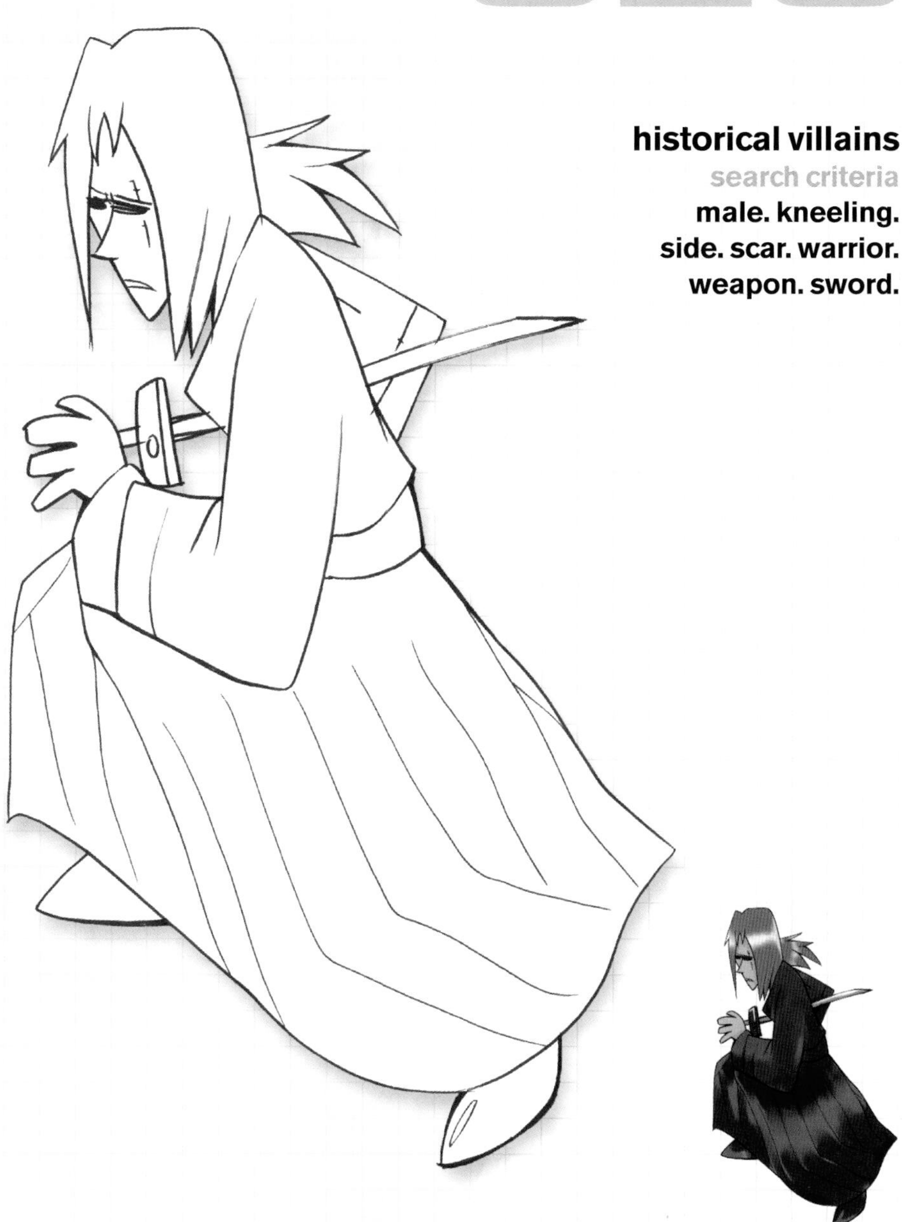

327

historical villains

search criteria

male. standing. armor. warrior. axe. weapon. knight.

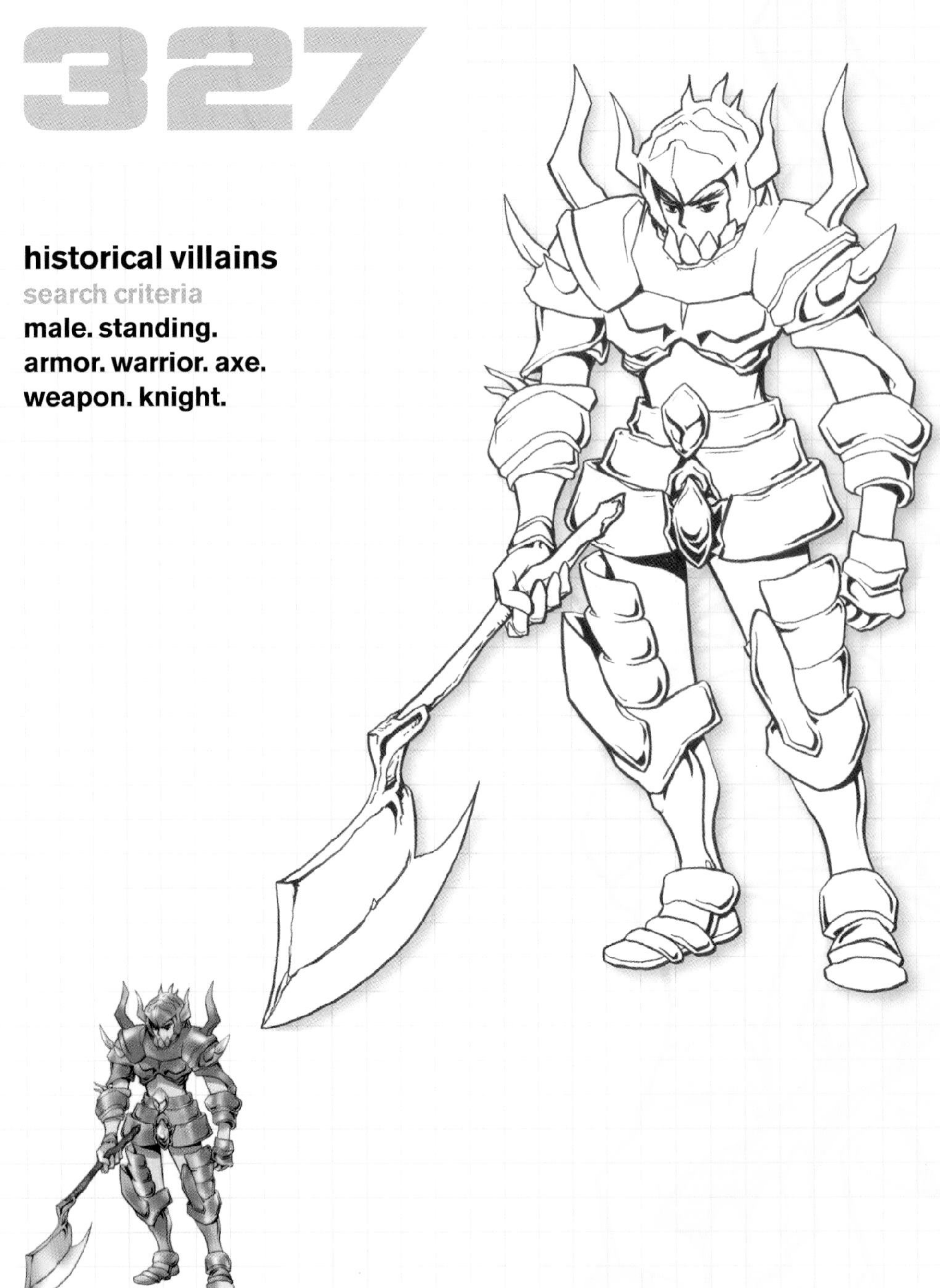

328

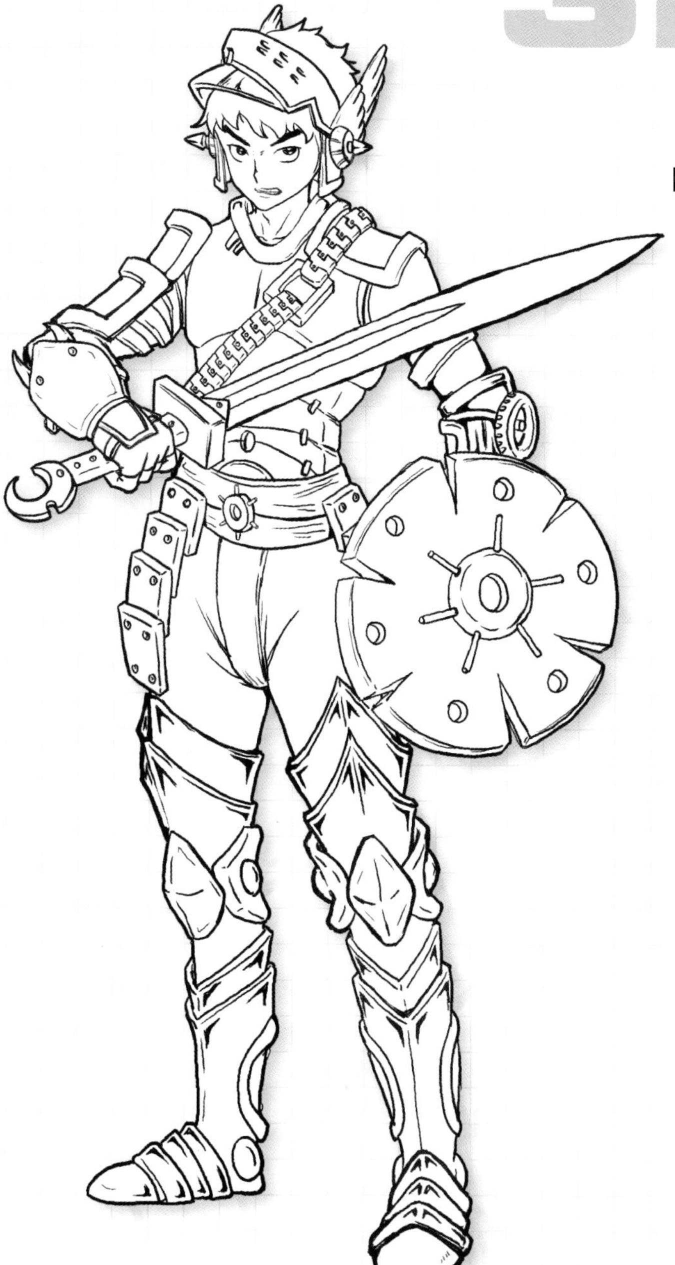

historical villains

search criteria

male. standing. armor. warrior. shield. weapon. sword. knight.

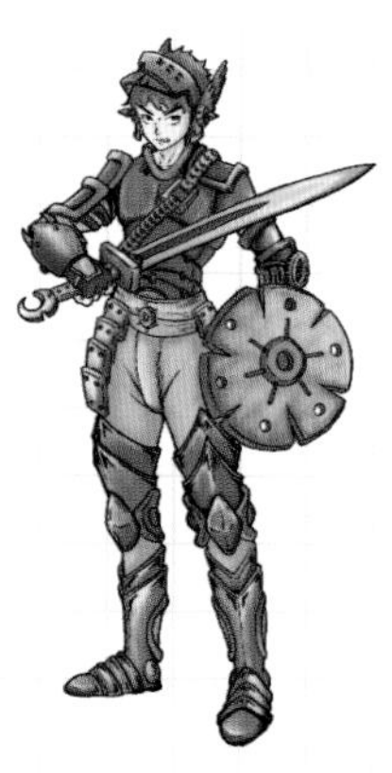

329

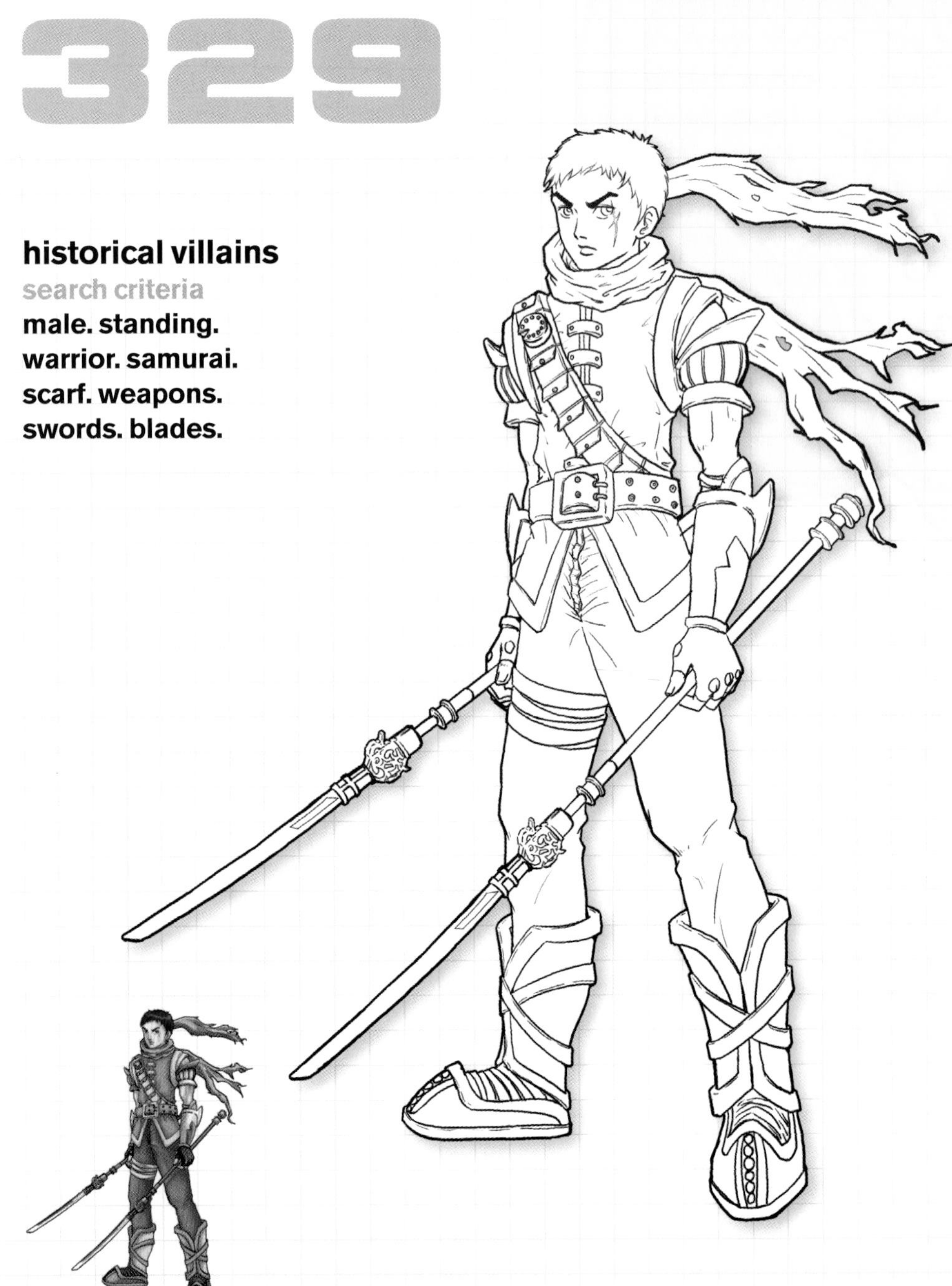

historical villains

search criteria

male. standing. warrior. samurai. scarf. weapons. swords. blades.

330

historical villains

search criteria

male. leaning. armor. attack. warrior. shield. weapon. blades.

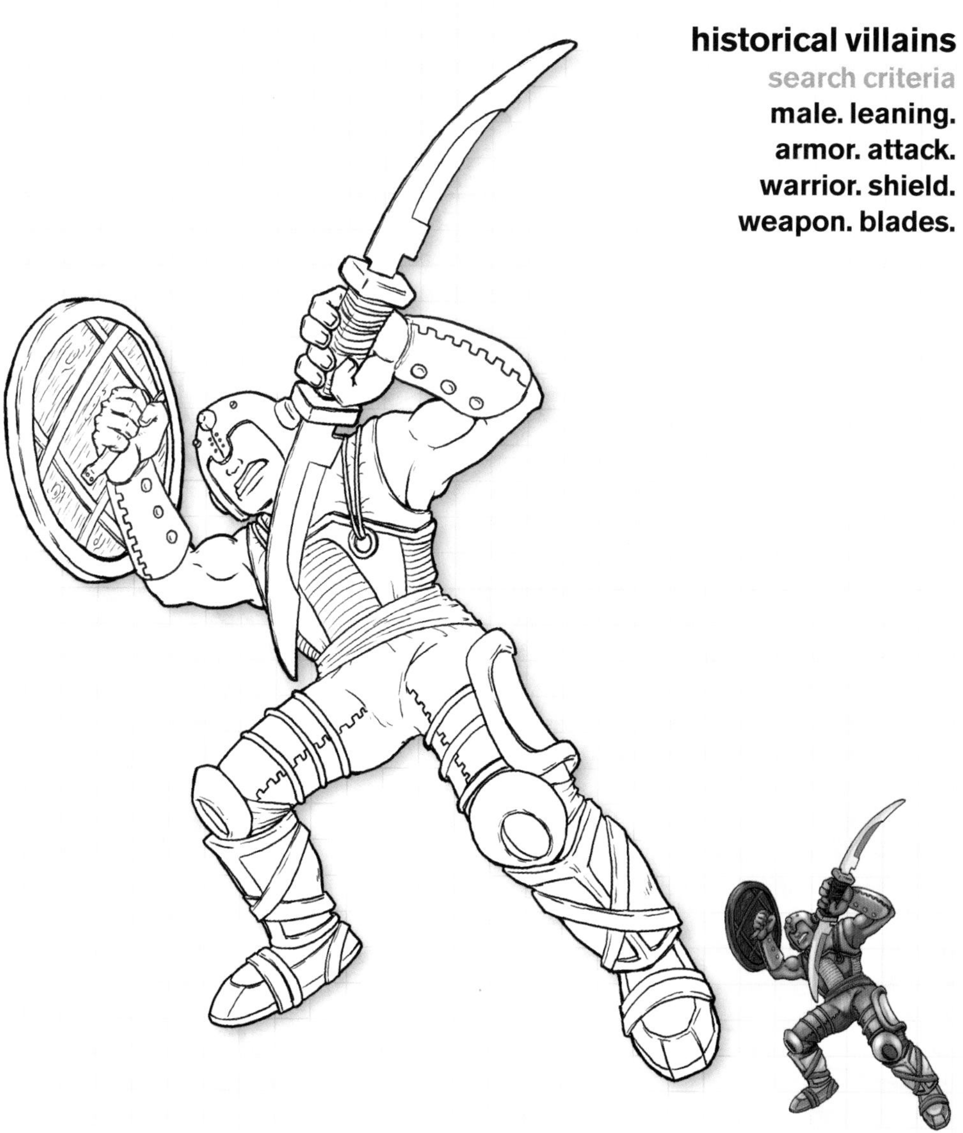

331

historical villains

search criteria

male. jump. pounce. attack. scar. ninja. weapon. stick.

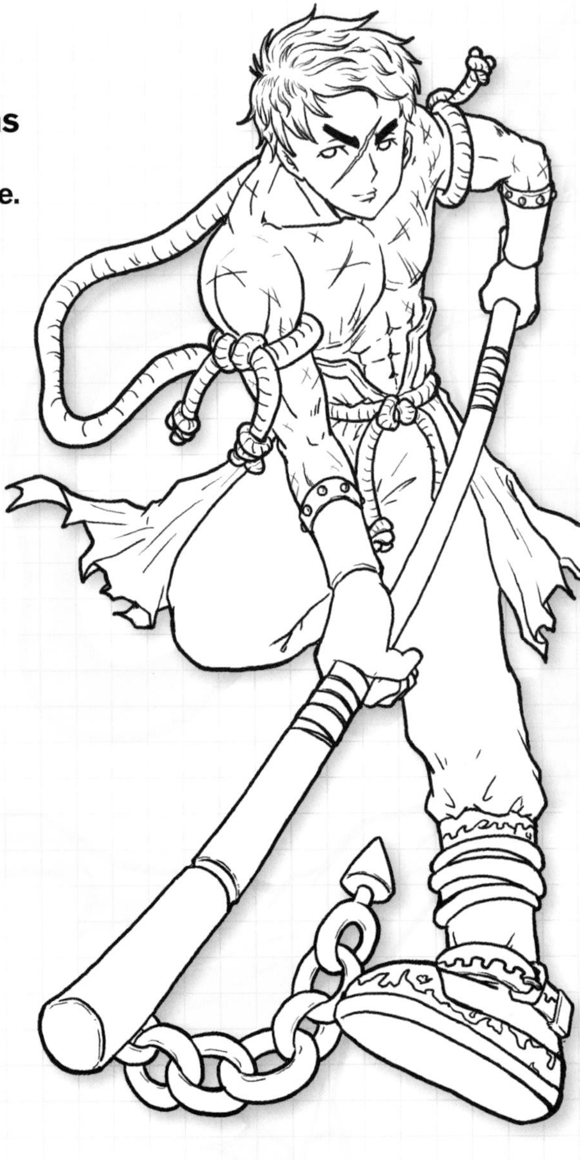

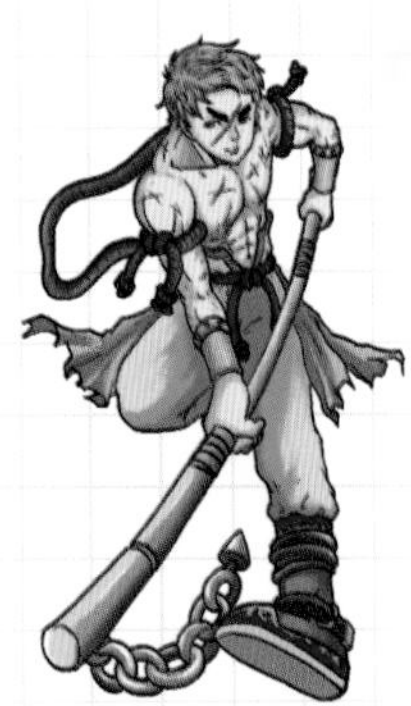

332

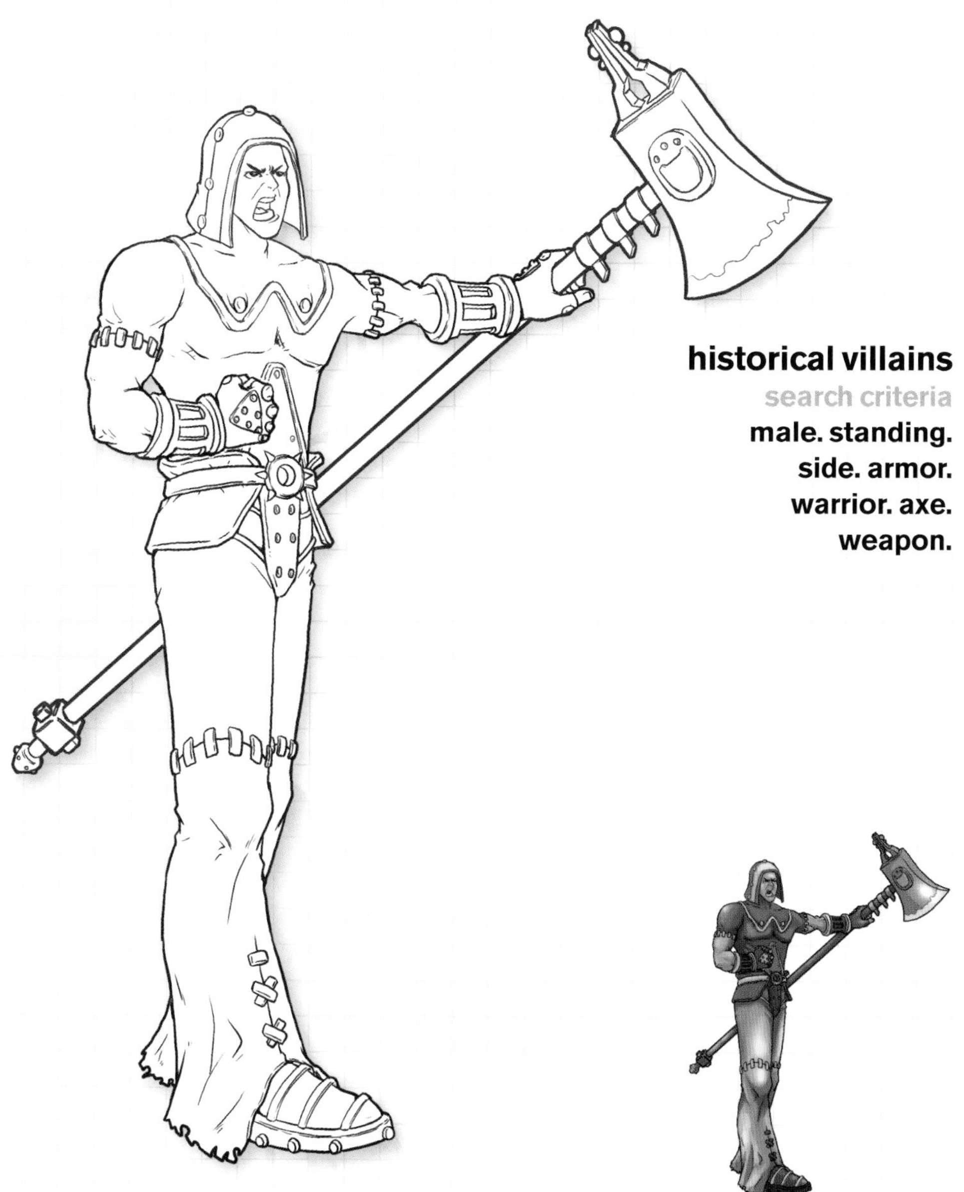

historical villains

search criteria

male. standing. side. armor. warrior. axe. weapon.

333

historical villains

search criteria

male. standing. side. armor. cape. warrior. weapon. sword.

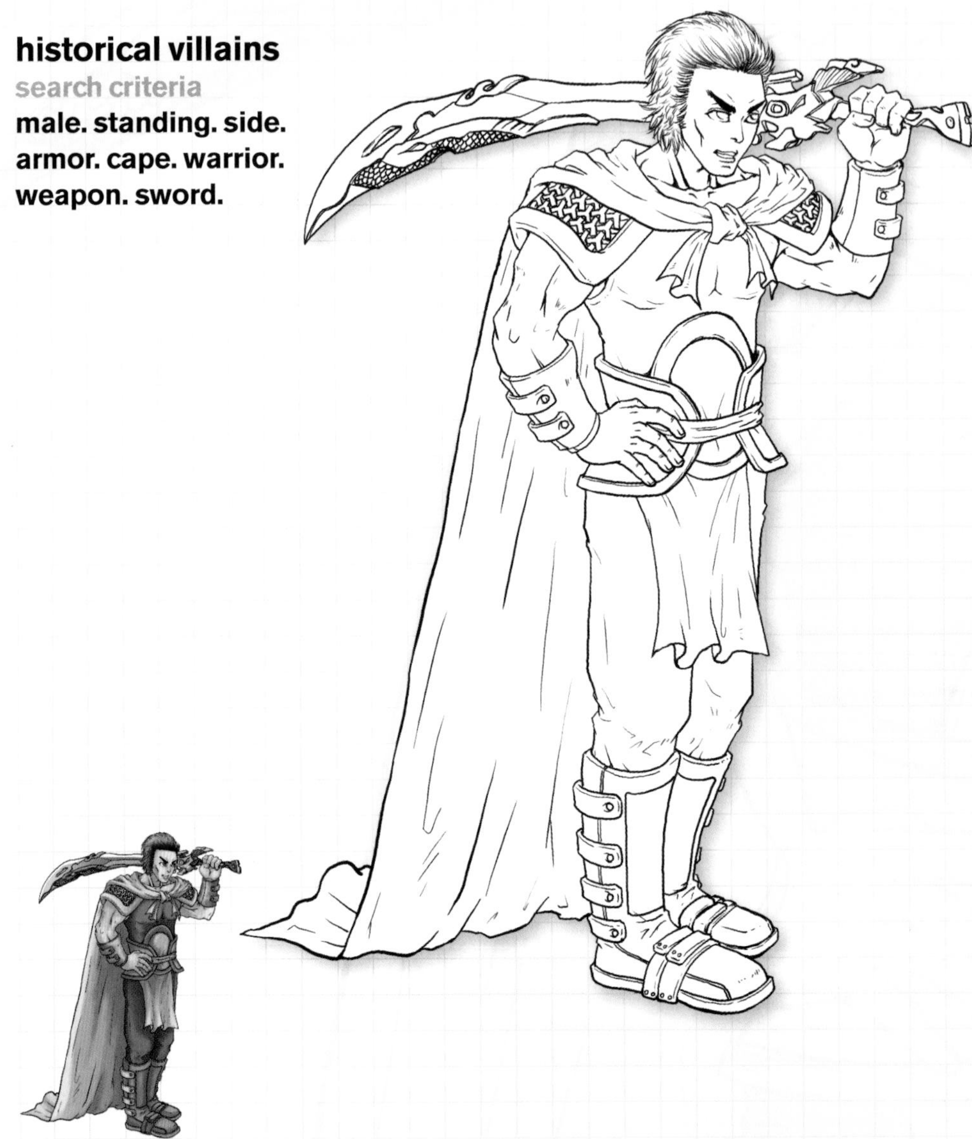

334

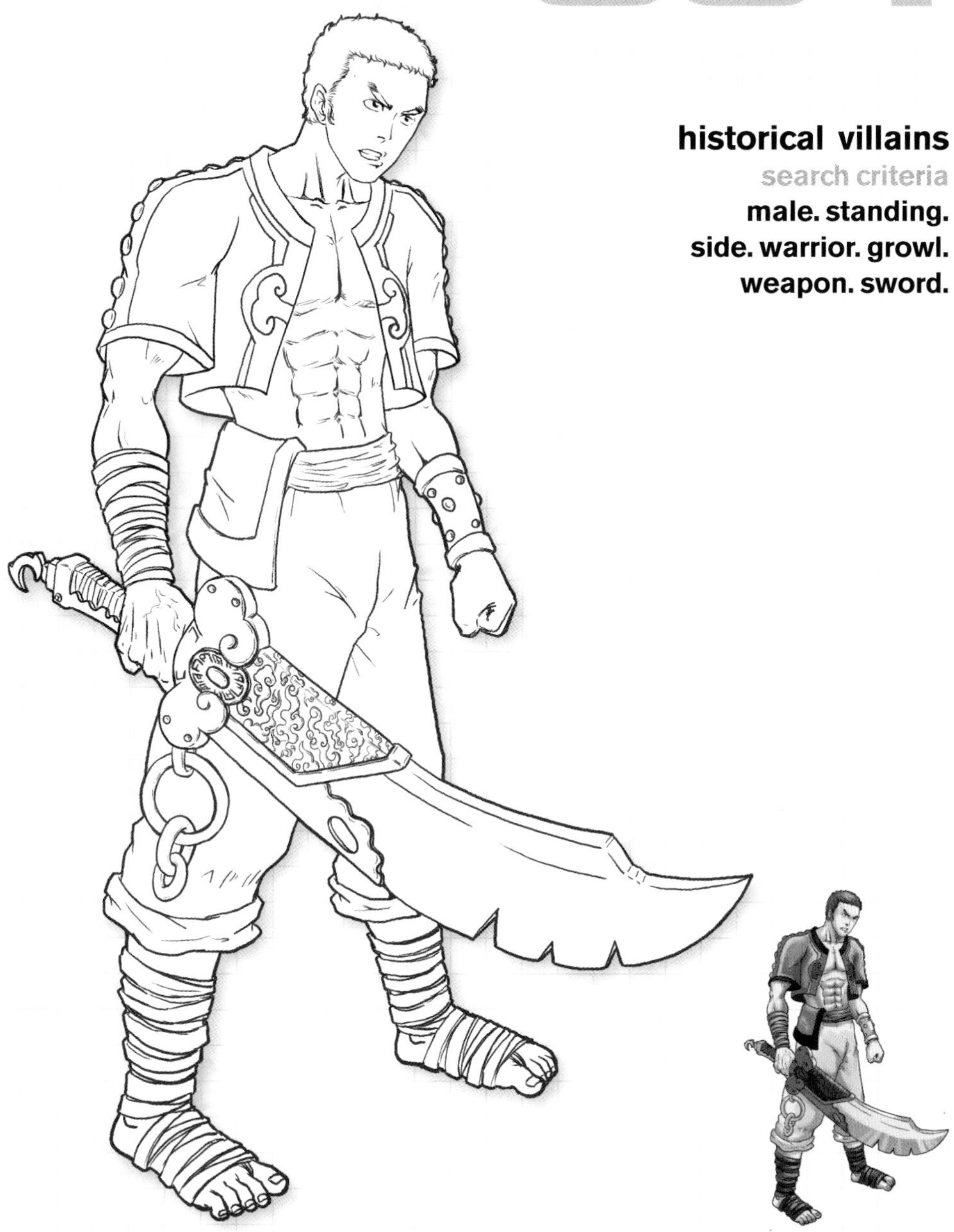

historical villains

search criteria

male. standing. side. warrior. growl. weapon. sword.

335

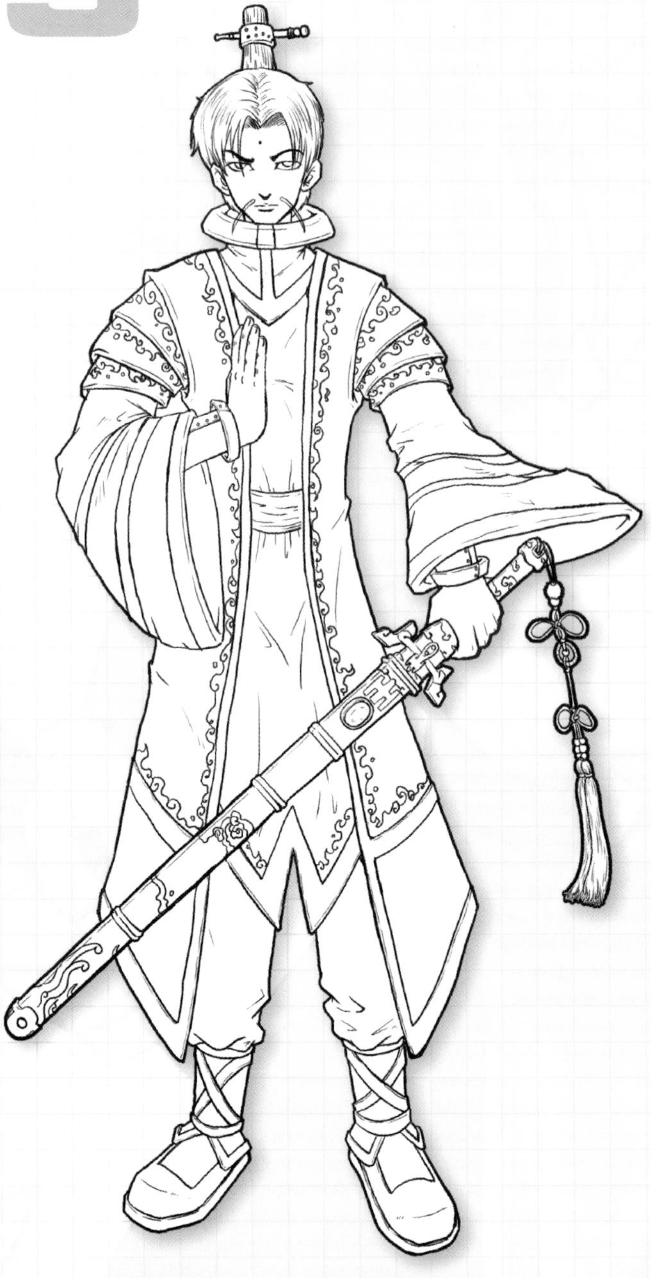

historical villains

search criteria

male. standing. warrior. samurai. weapon. sword.

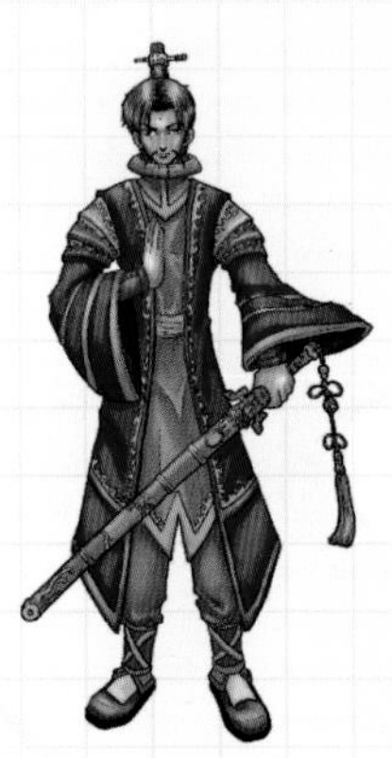

336

historical villains

search criteria

male. standing. armor. warrior. shield. viking. weapon. axe.

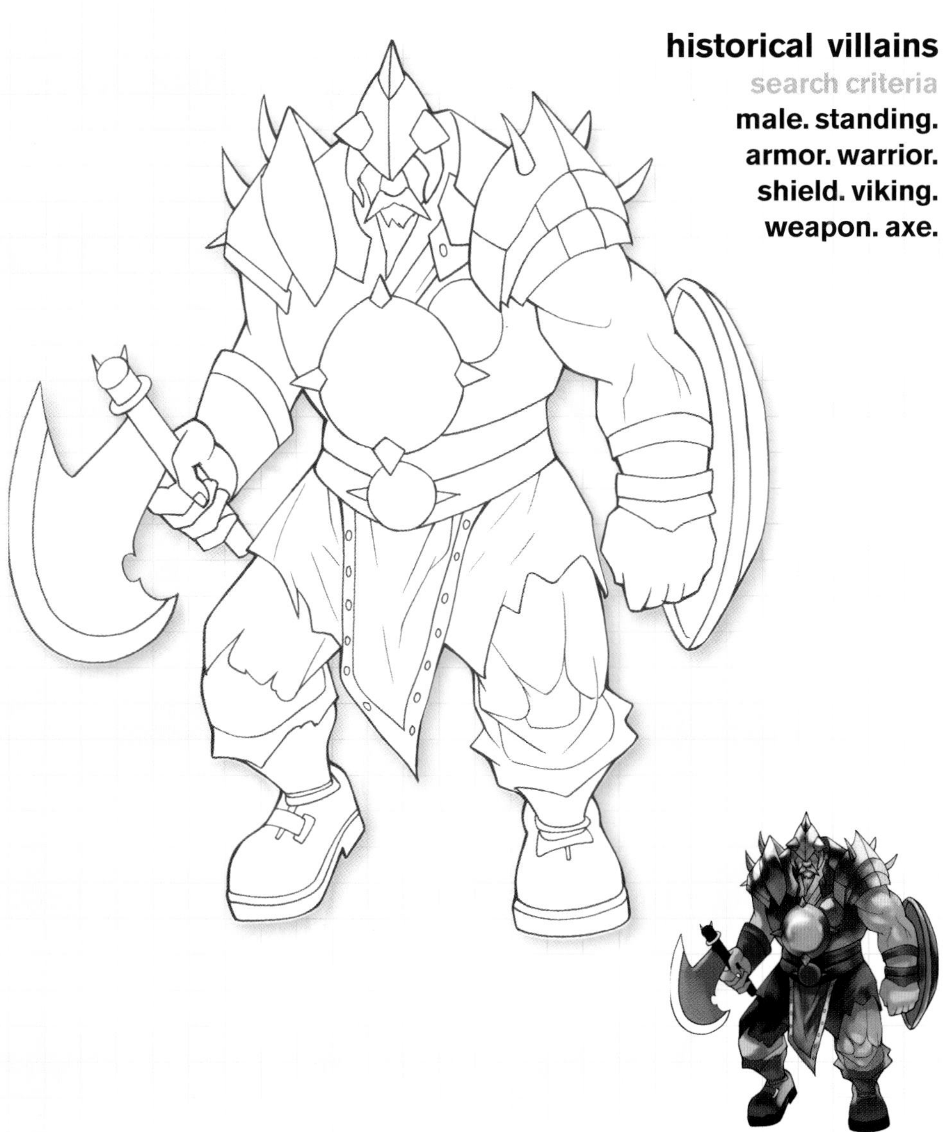

337

historical villains

search criteria

male. jump. attack. warrior. samurai. weapon. sword.

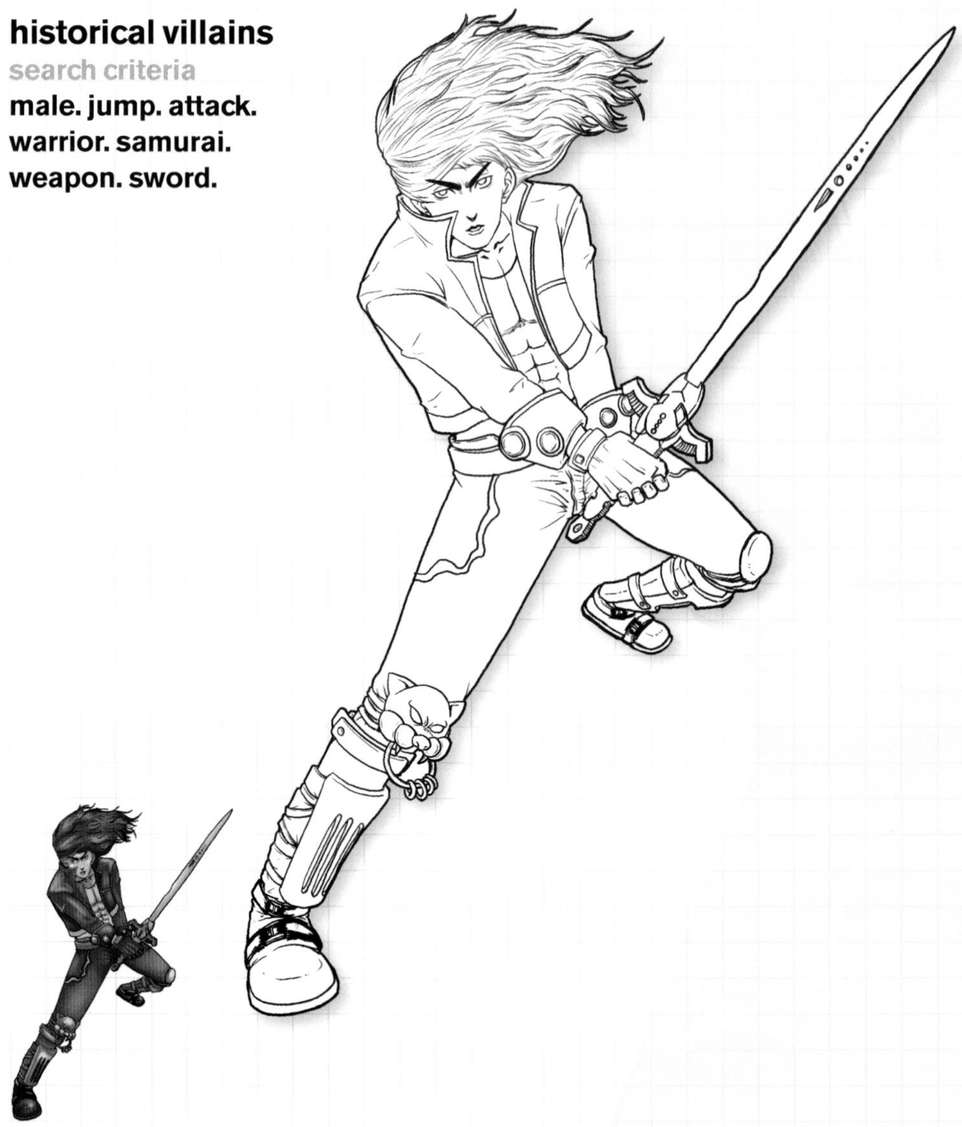

338

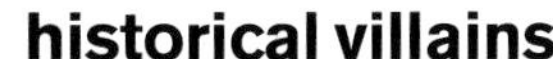

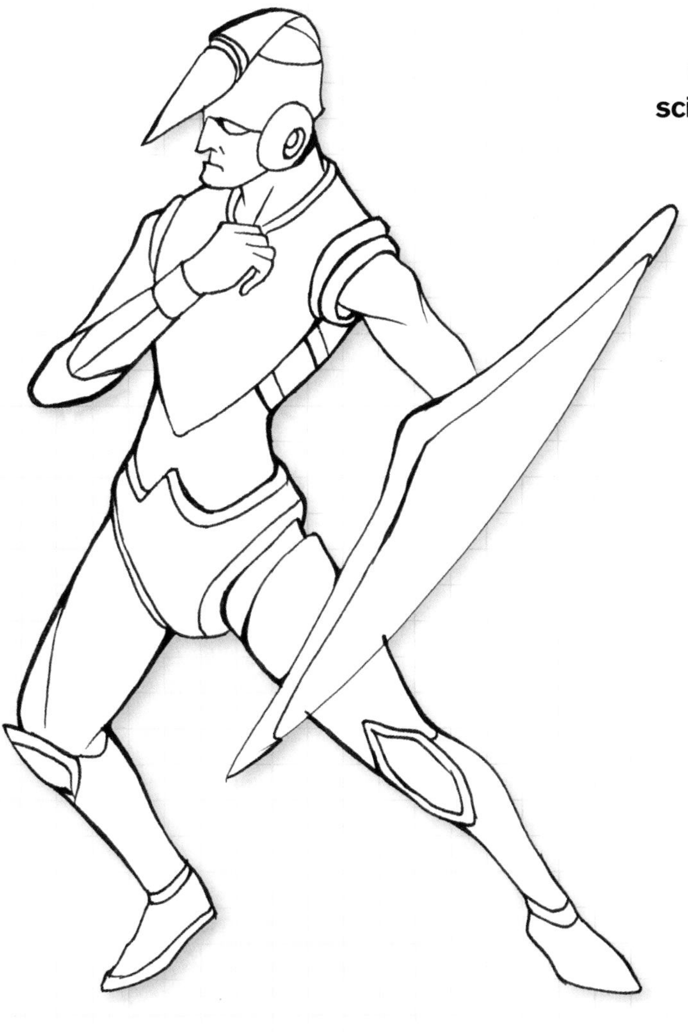

historical villains

search criteria

male. standing. futuristic. knight. sci-fi. shield. armor.

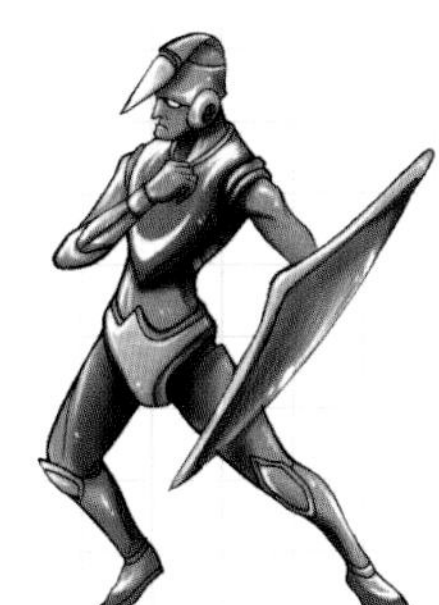

339

historical heroes

search criteria

male. standing.
knight. armor. shield.
weapon. spear.

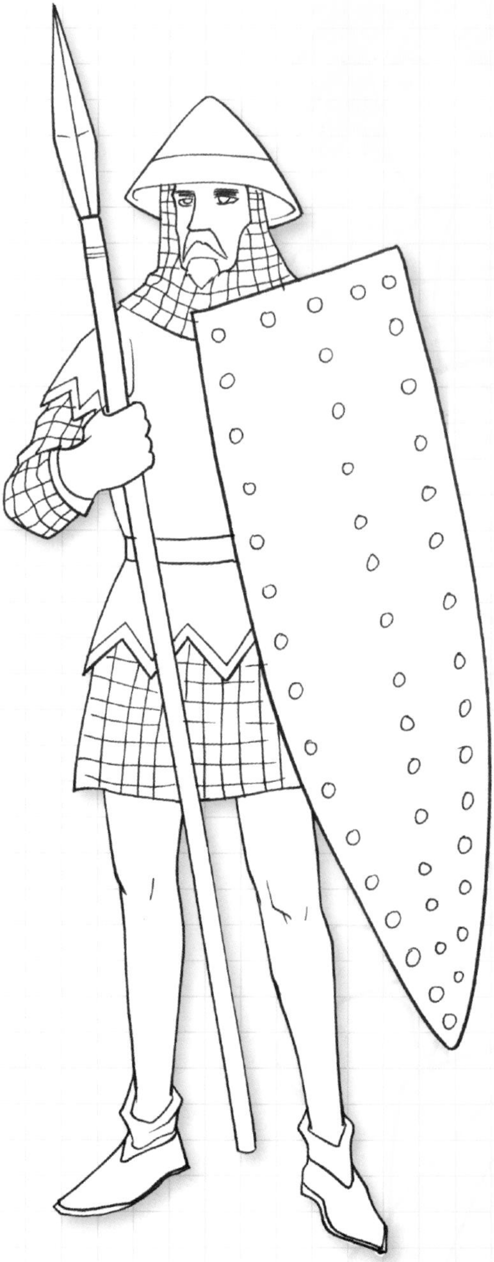

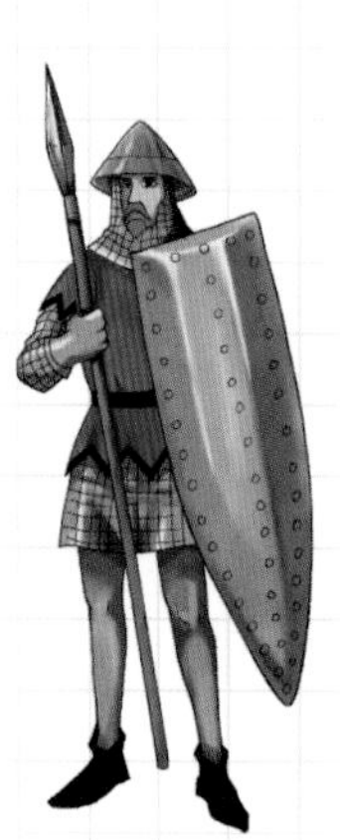

340

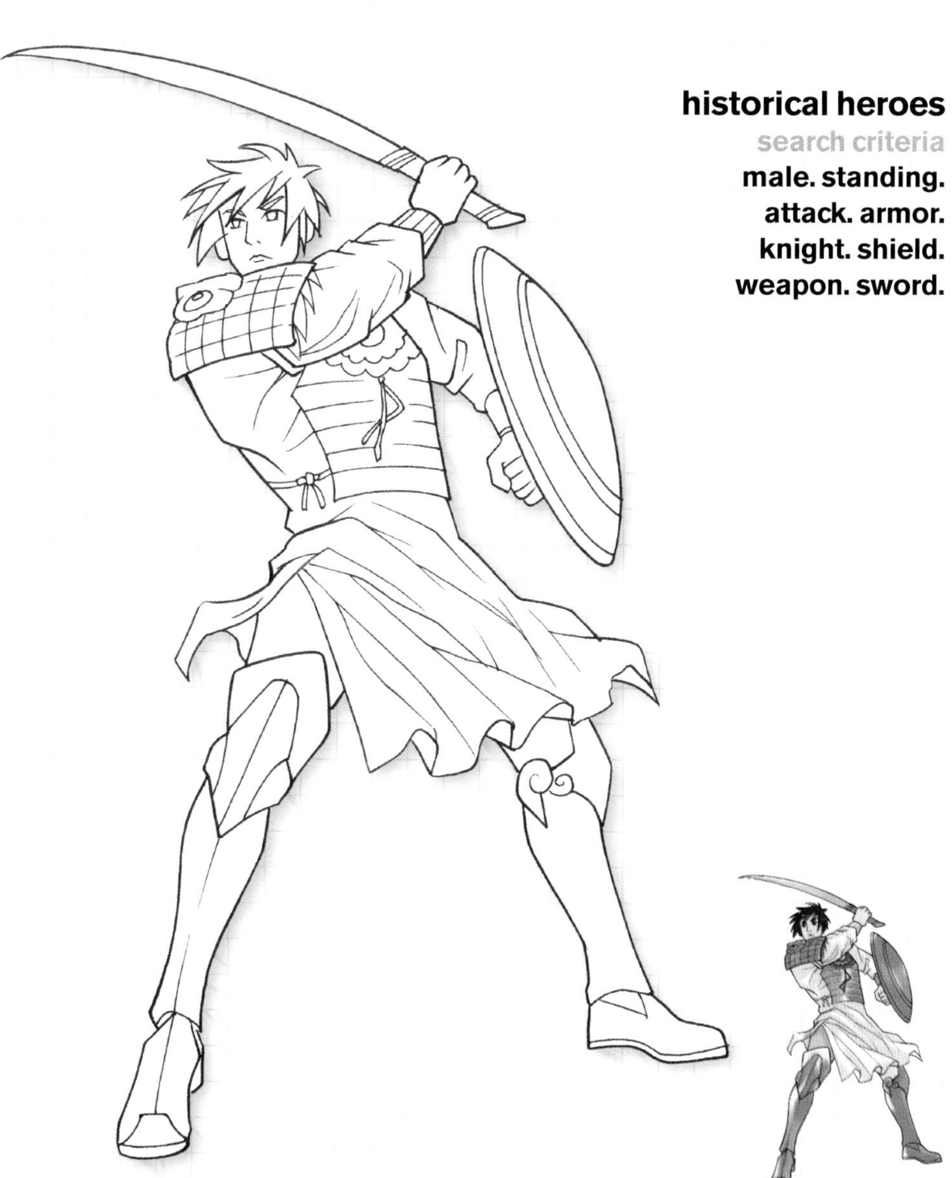

historical heroes

search criteria

male. standing. attack. armor. knight. shield. weapon. sword.

341

historical heroes

search criteria

male. standing.
armor. knight.

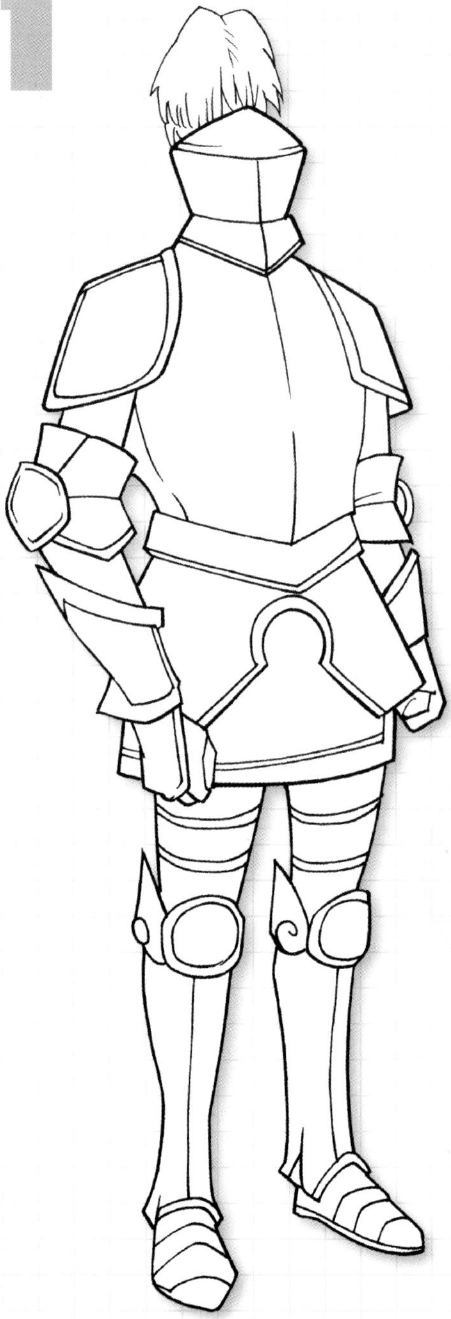

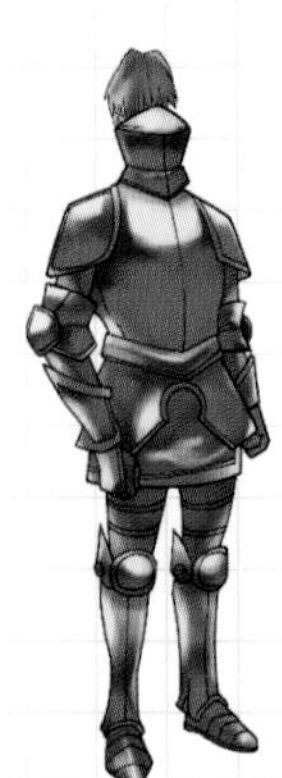

342

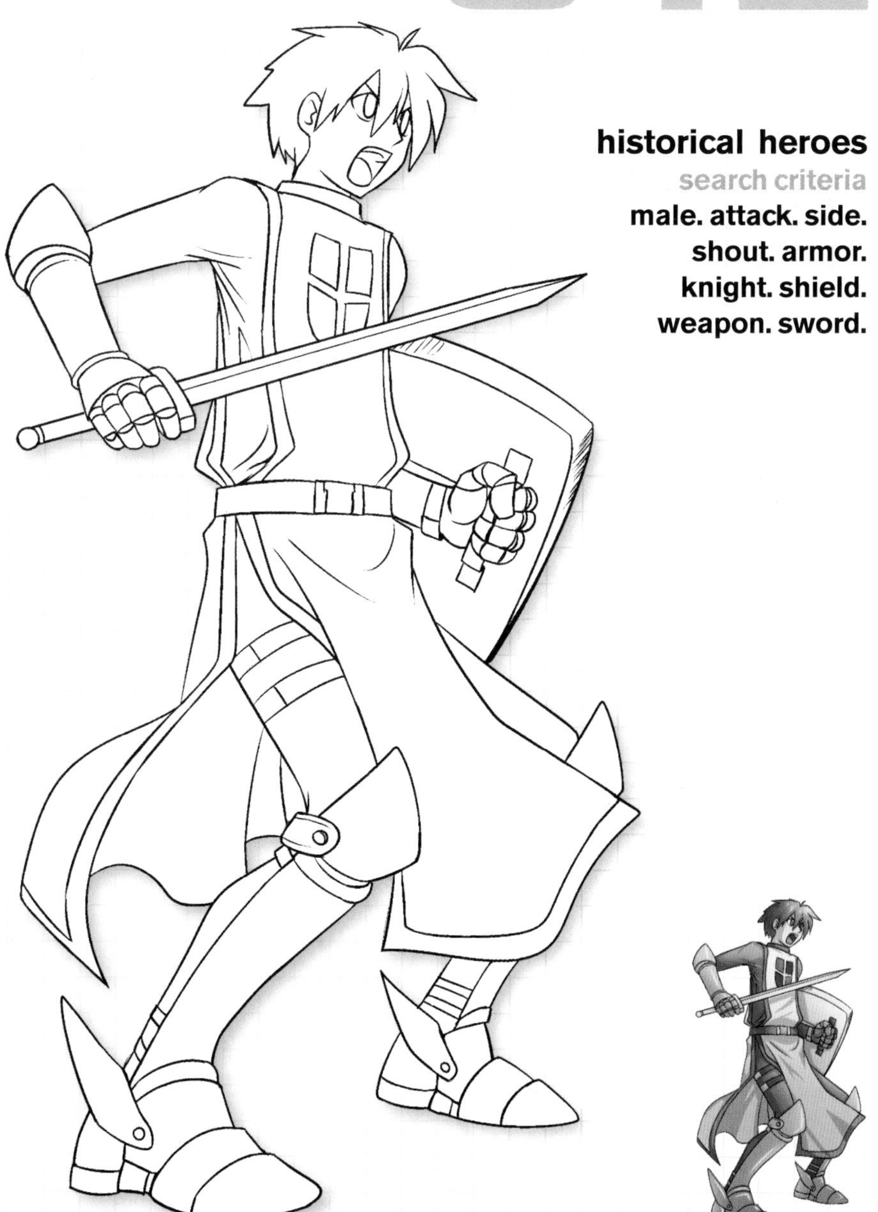

historical heroes

search criteria

male. attack. side. shout. armor. knight. shield. weapon. sword.

343

historical heroes

search criteria

male. standing. gladiator. shield. armor. weapon. sword. roman.

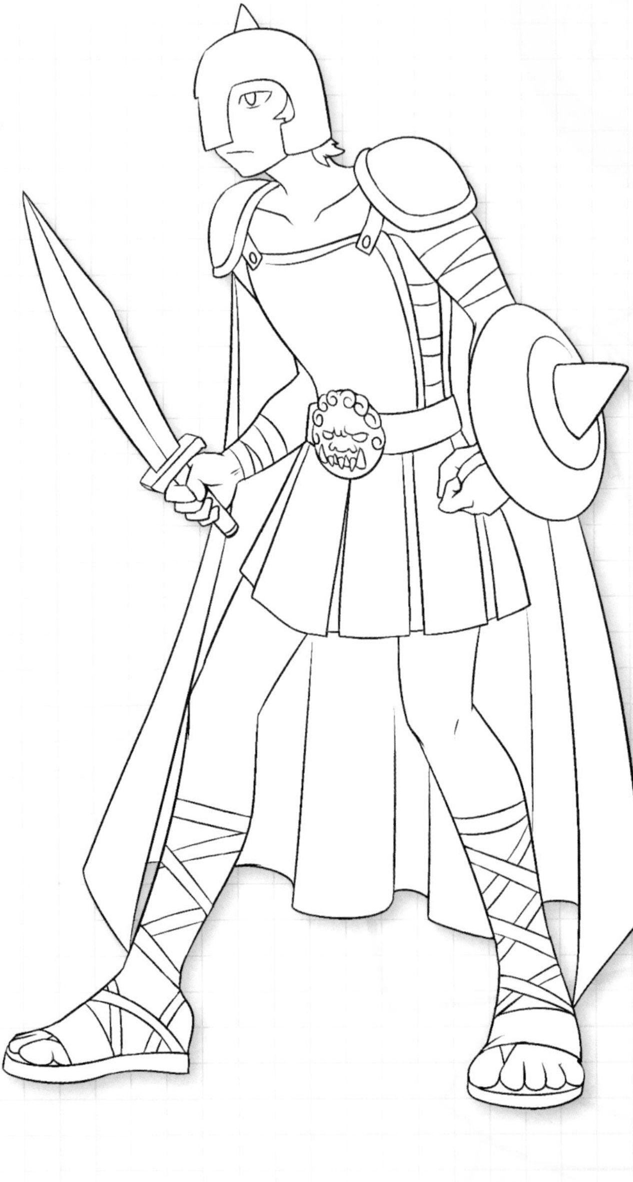

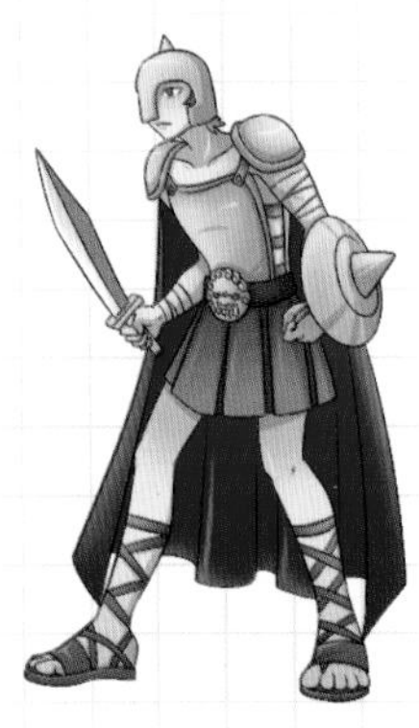

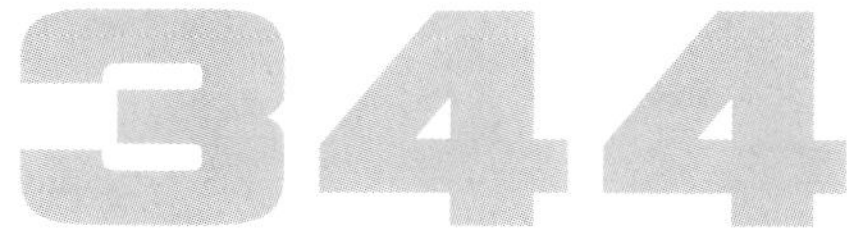

historical heroes

search criteria

female. standing.
roman. jug.

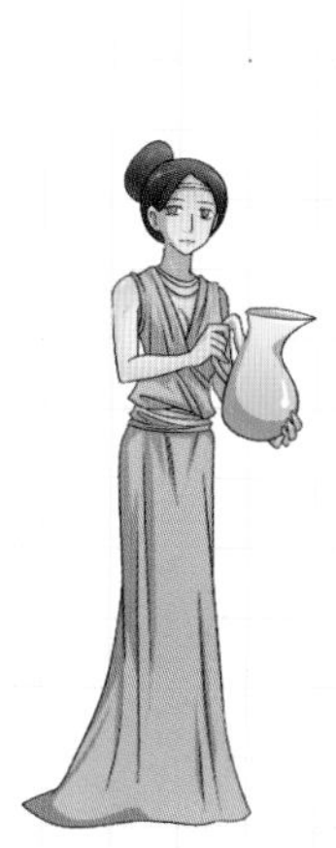

345

historical heroes

search criteria

female. standing. armor. warrior. weapon. sword.

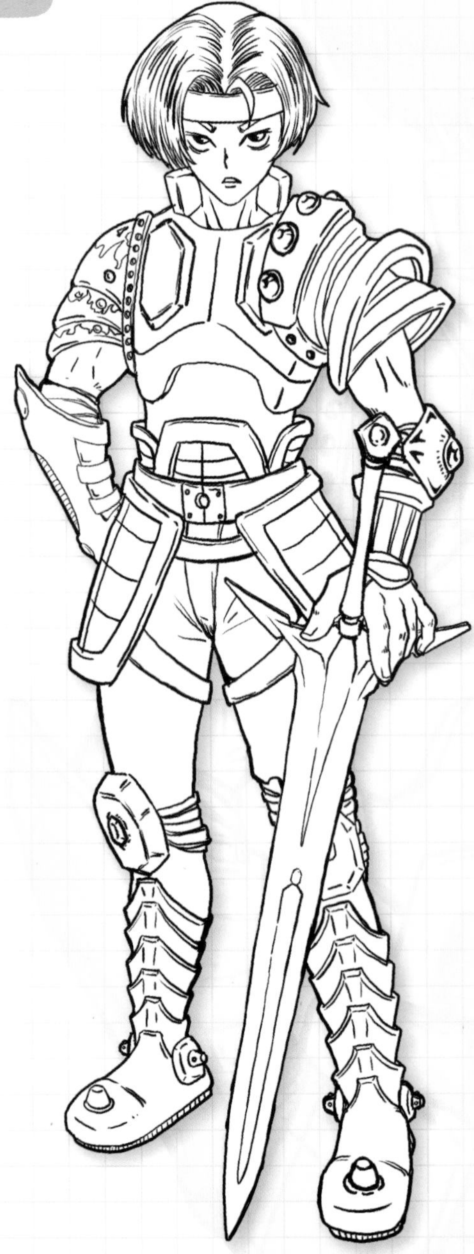

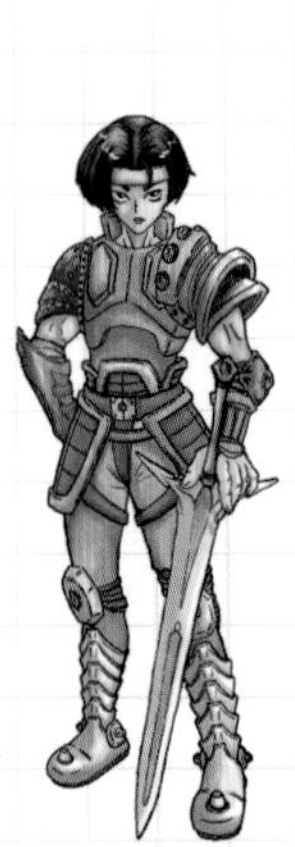

346

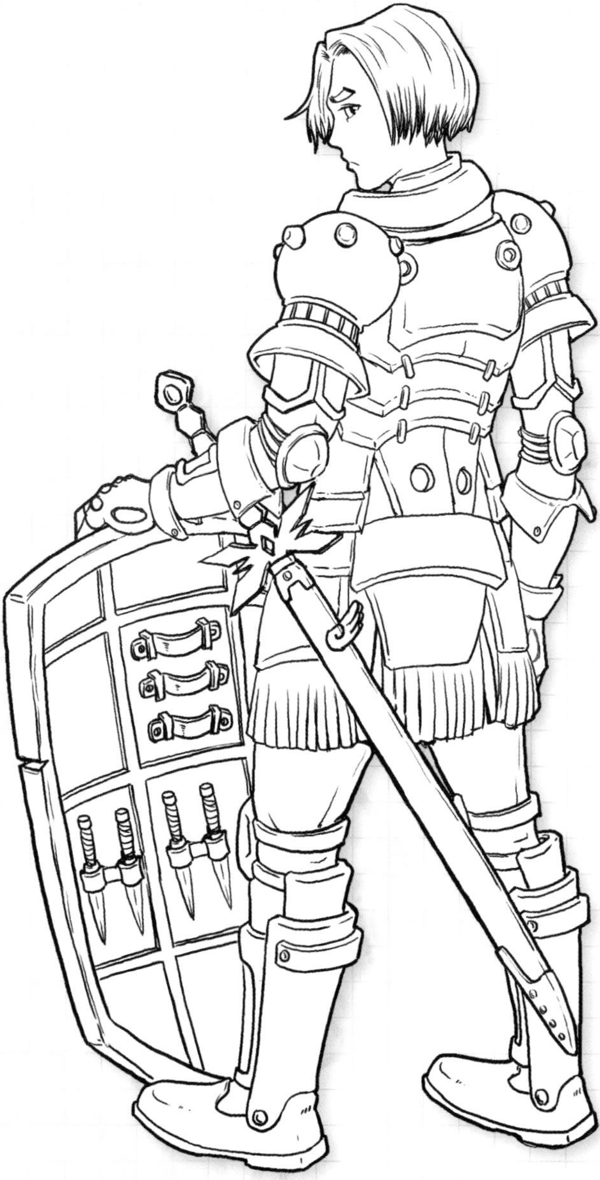

historical heroes

search criteria
male. standing. side. armor. shield. weapons. swords. warrior.

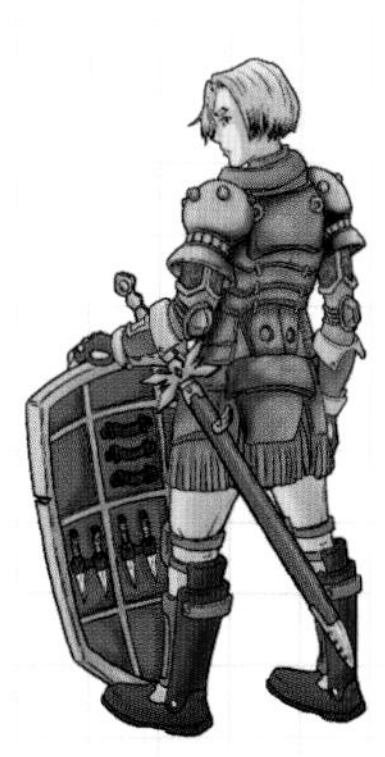

347

historical heroes

search criteria

male. standing. attack. warrior. horns. armor. weapon. sword.

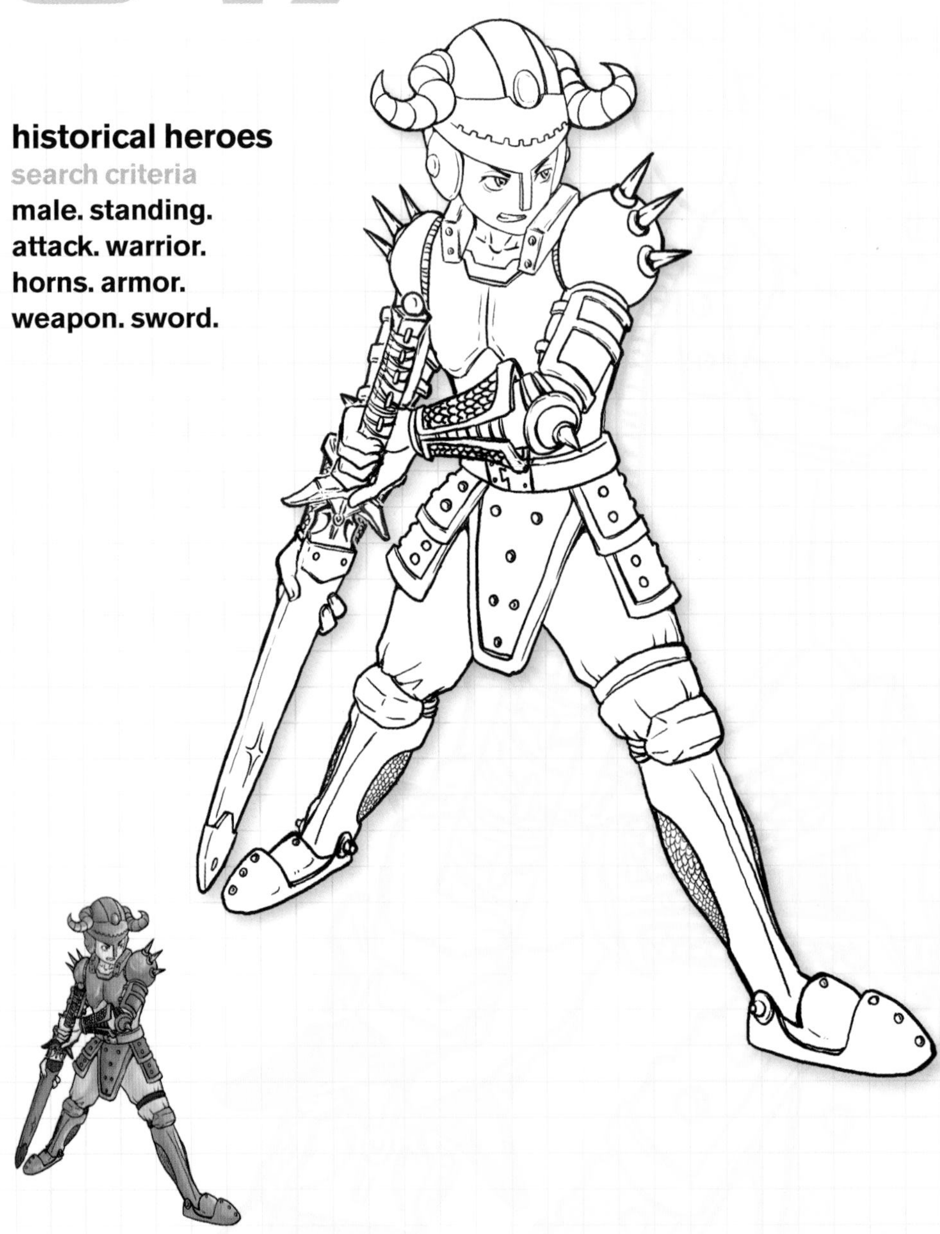

348

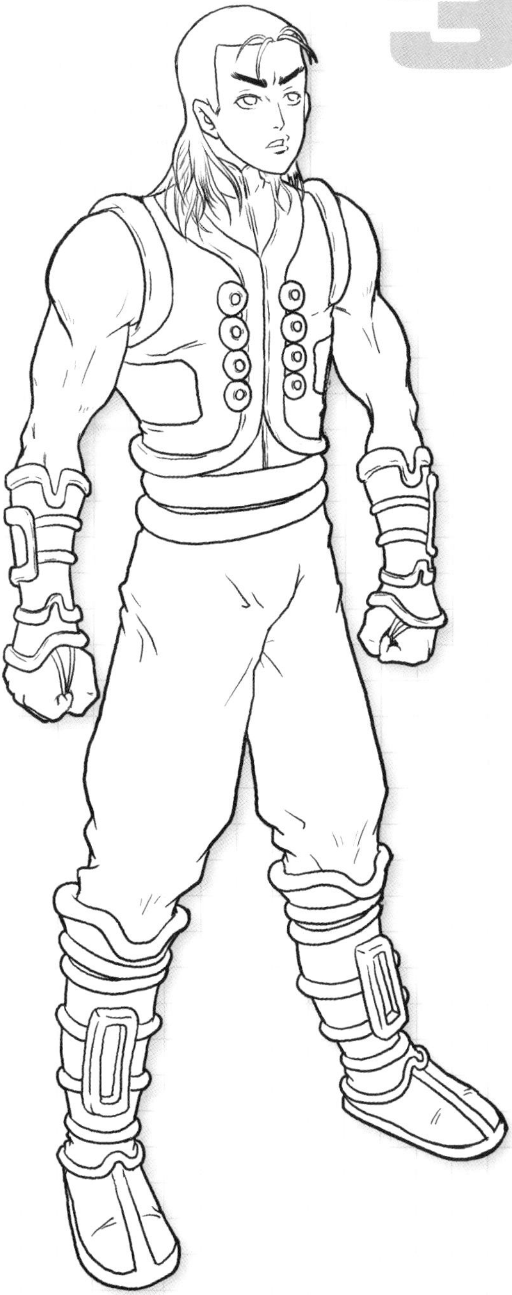

historical heroes

search criteria

male. standing. ninja. armor.

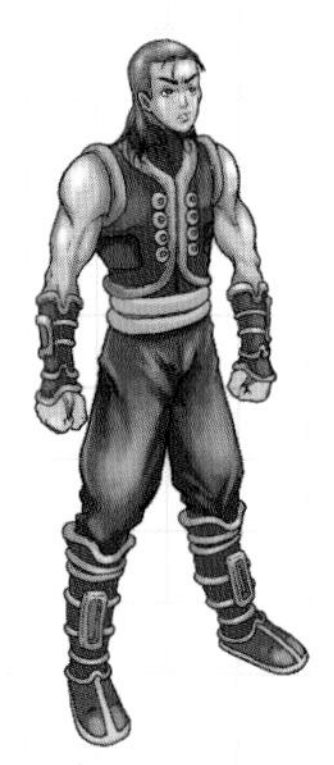

349

historical heroes

search criteria

male. leaning. warrior. shield. weapon. sword.

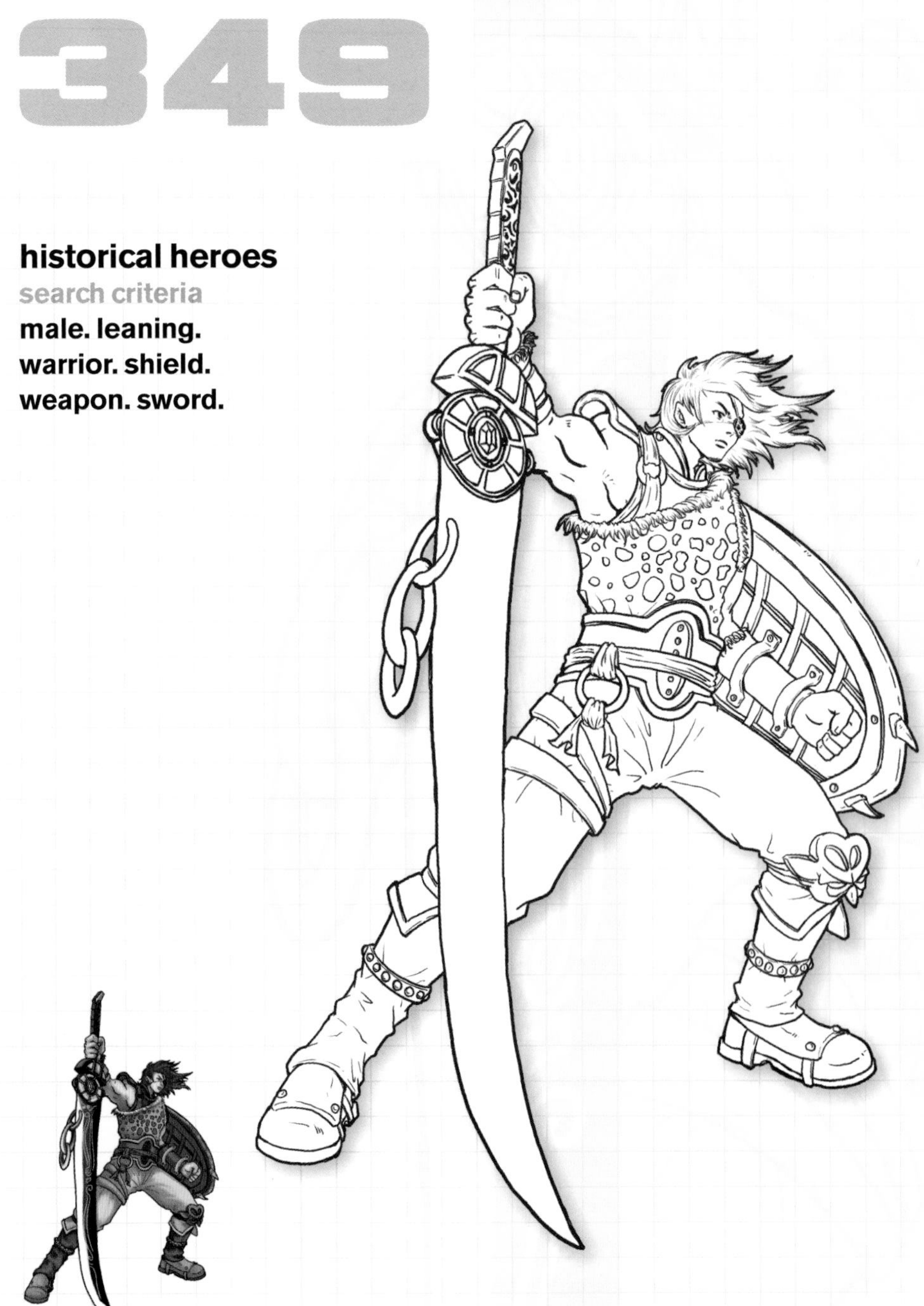

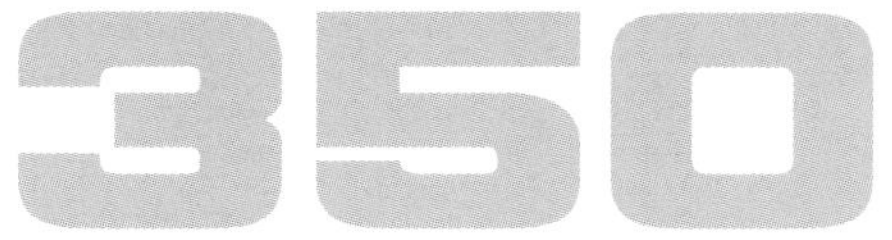

historical heroes

search criteria

male. standing. side. samurai. weapon. sword.

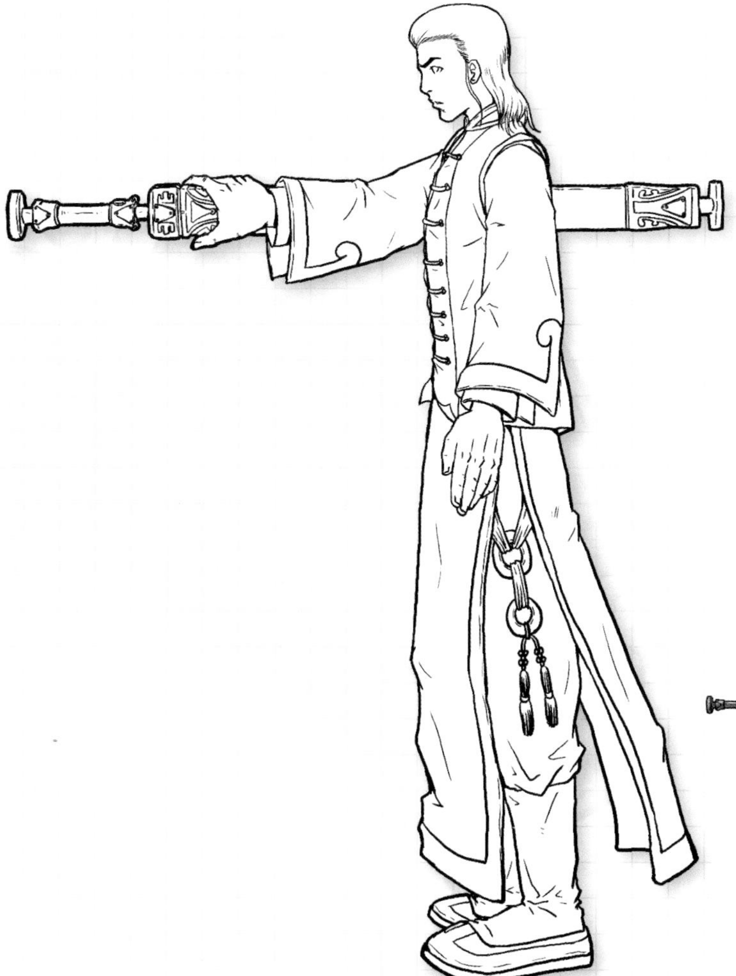

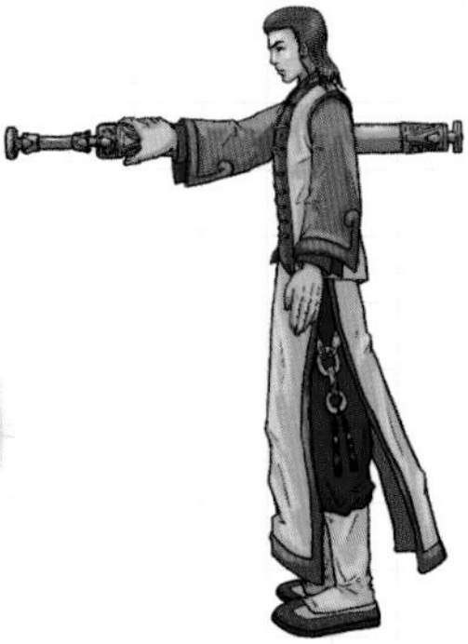

351

historical heroes

search criteria

male. standing. attack. roman. armor. weapon. axe. gladiator.

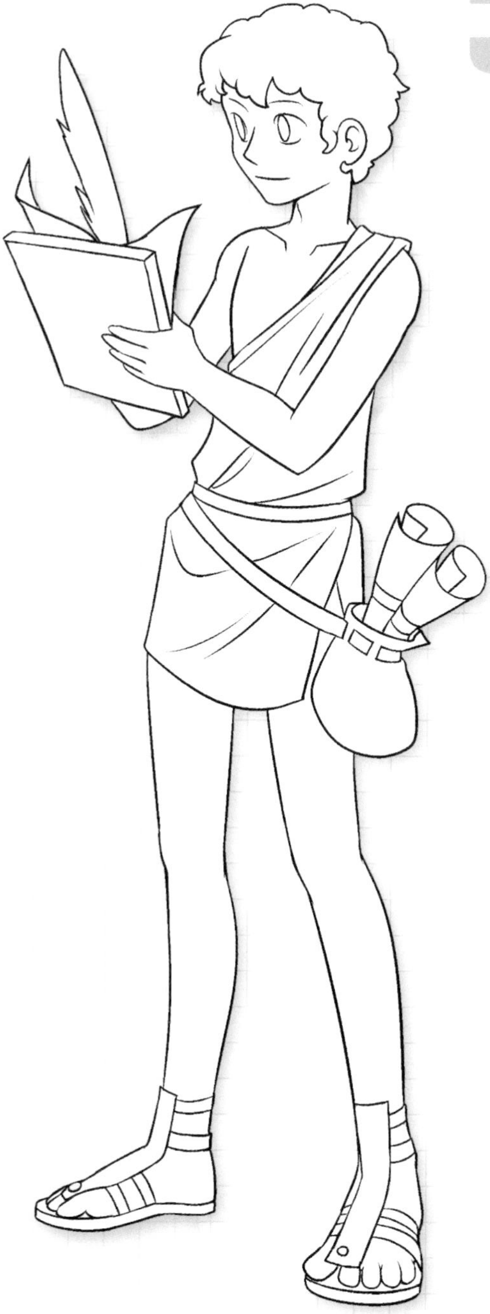

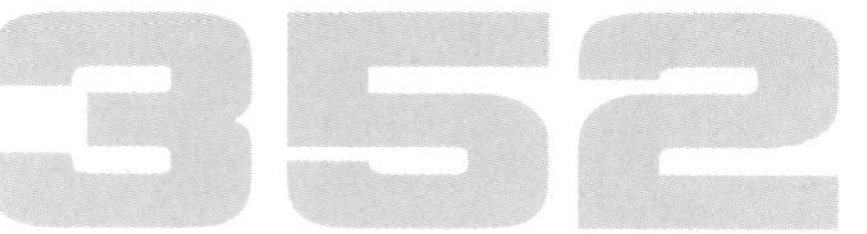

historical heroes

search criteria

male. standing. quill. writing. paper. roman. boy.

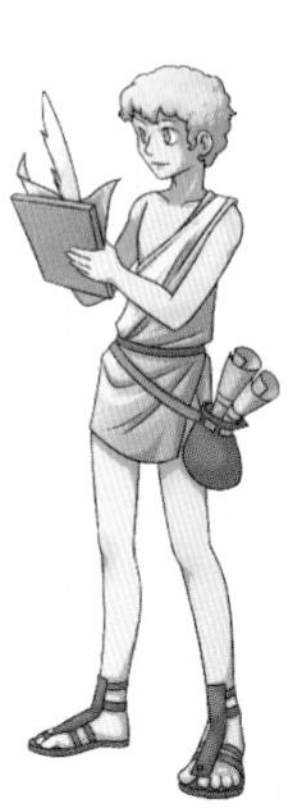

353

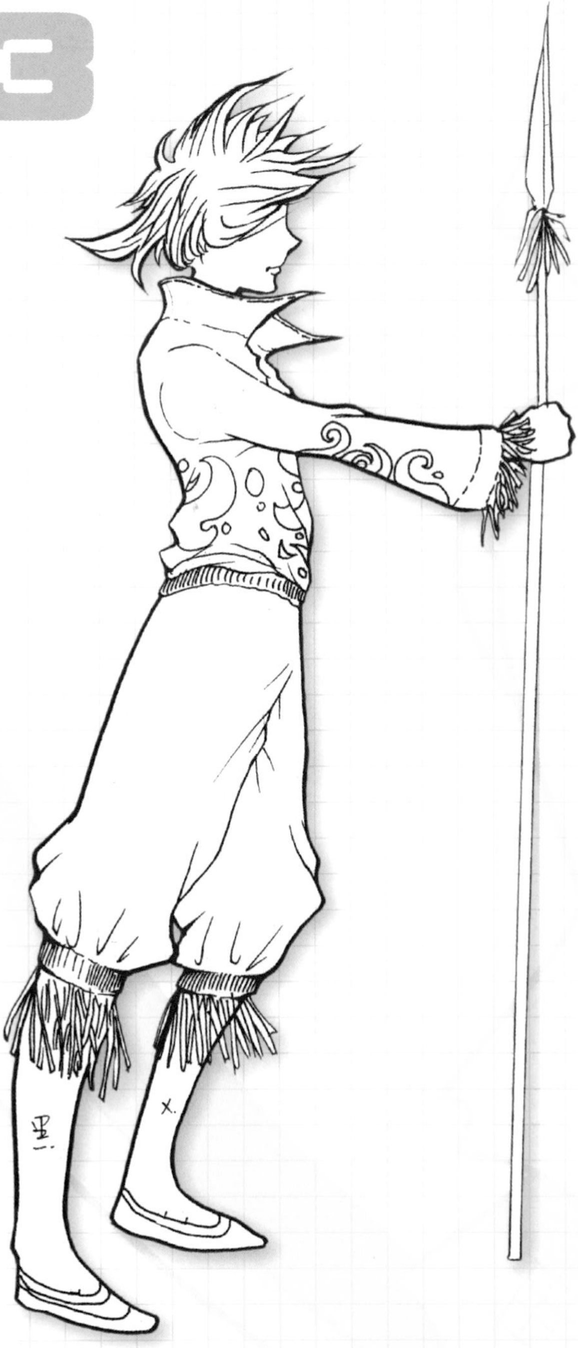

historical heroes

search criteria

male. standing. warrior. weapon. spear. tattoos.

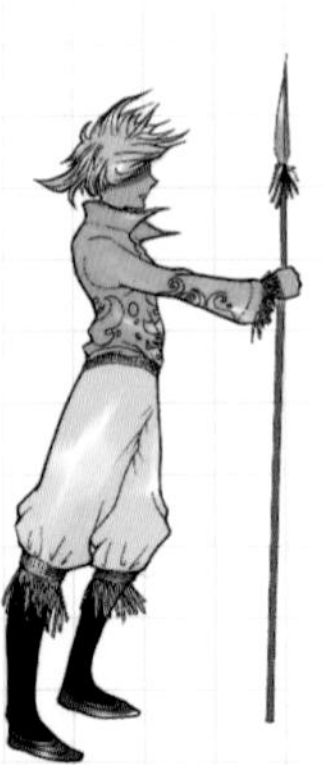

354

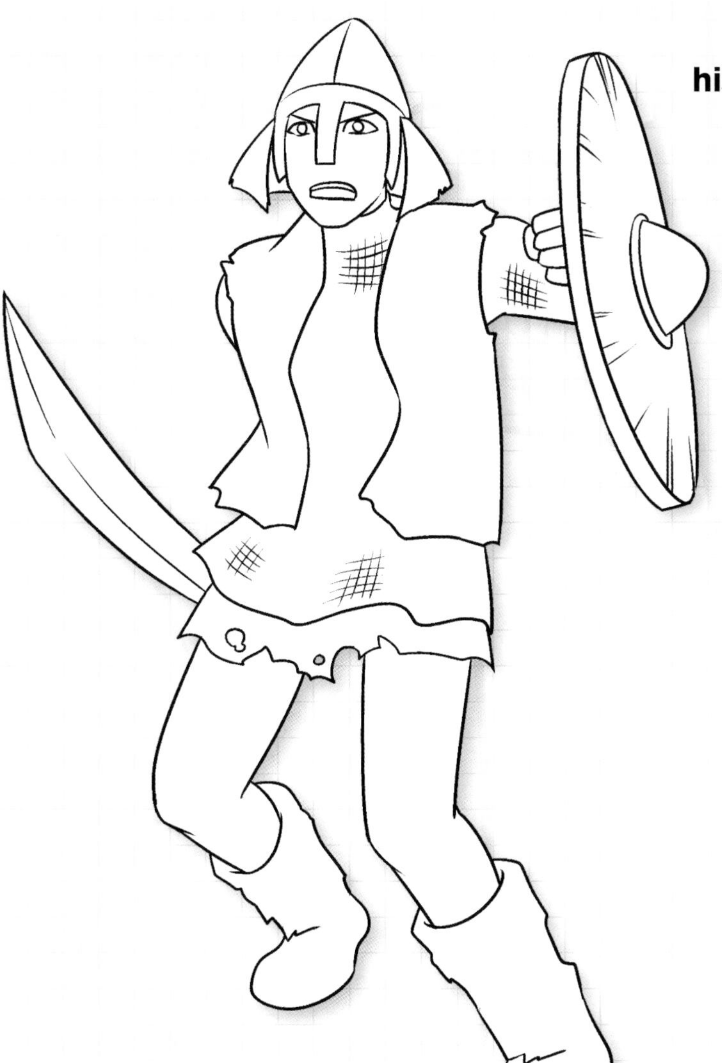

historical heroes

search criteria

male. standing. attack. knight. armor. shield. sword. shout.

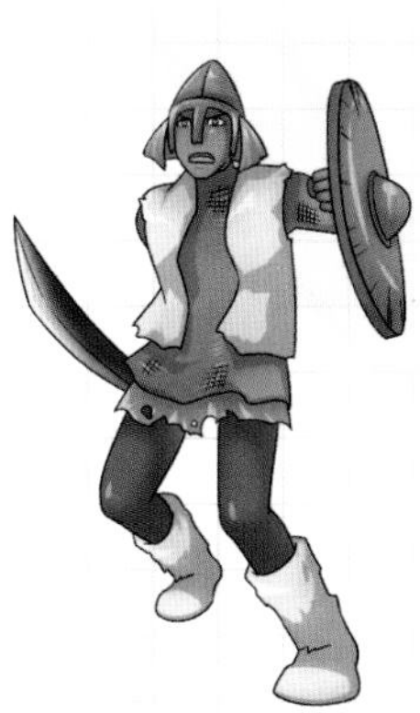

355

historical heroes

search criteria

male. standing.
book. roman. greek.

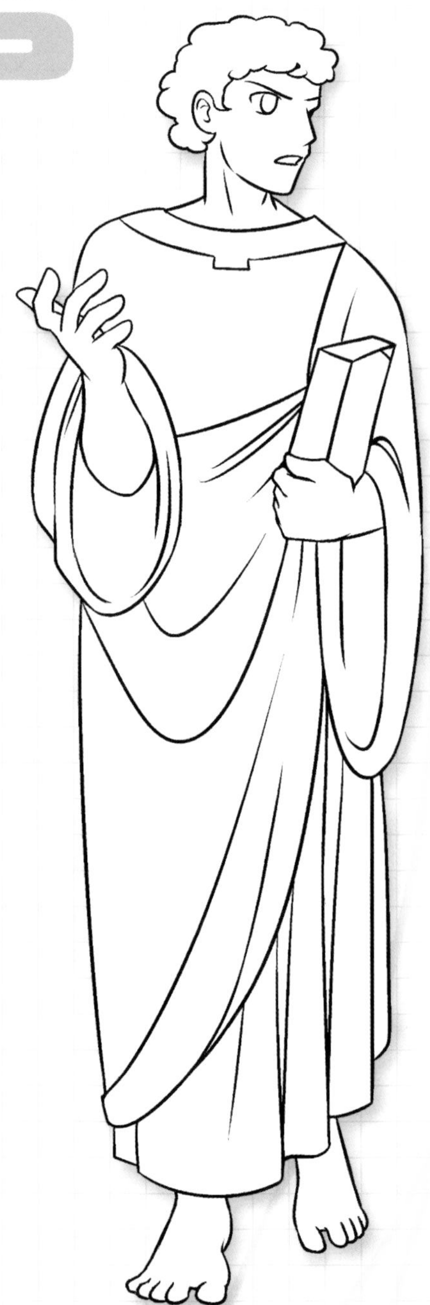

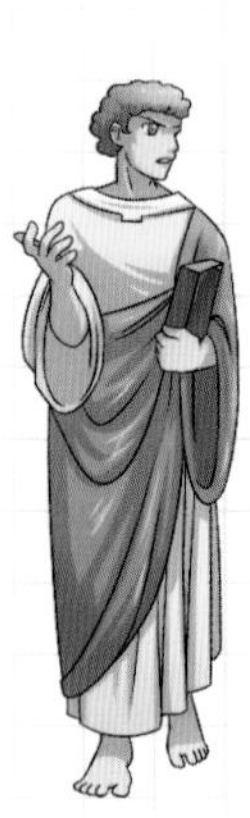

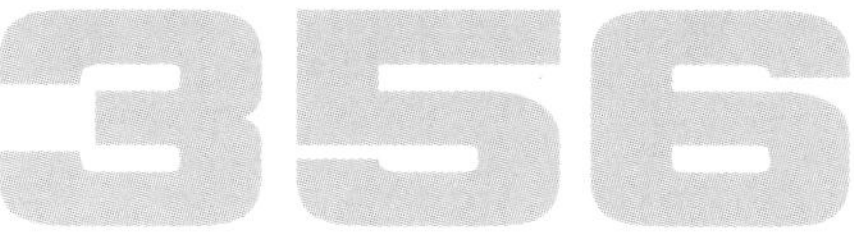

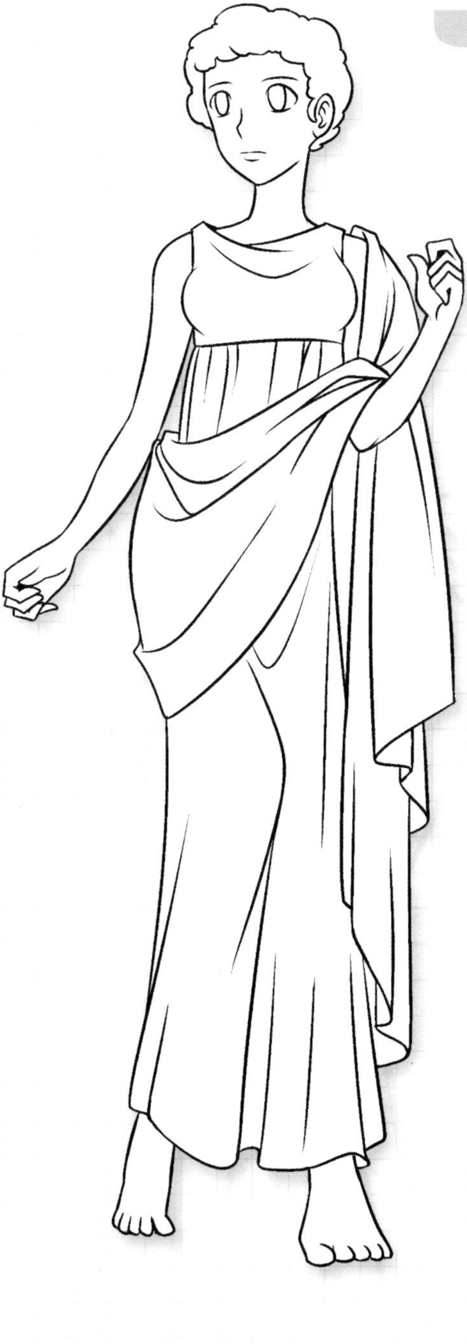

historical heroes

search criteria

female. standing. roman. greek.

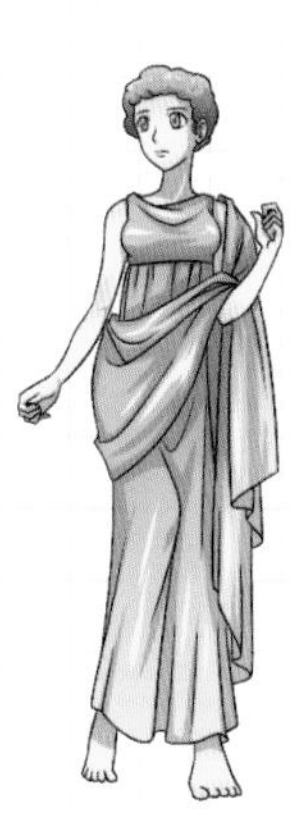

357

historical heroes

search criteria

female. standing. side. warrior. roman. shield. weapon. spear.

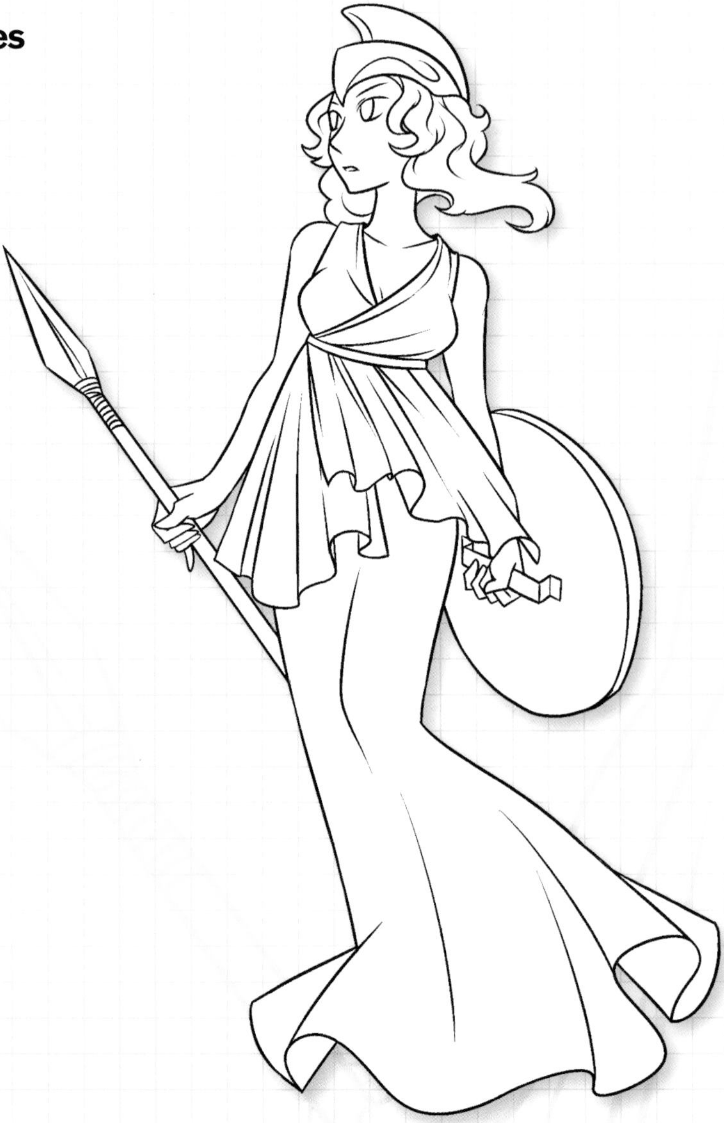

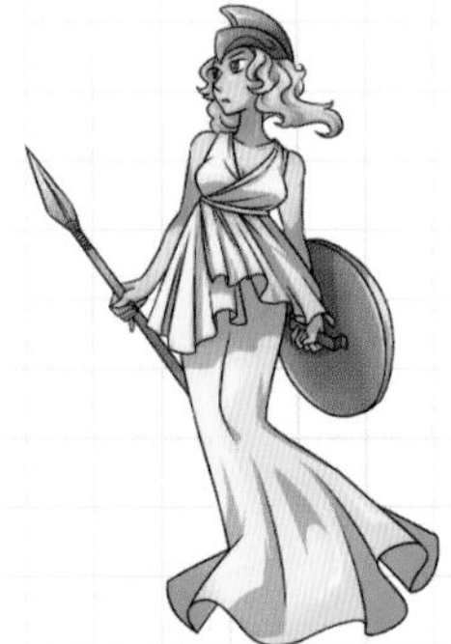

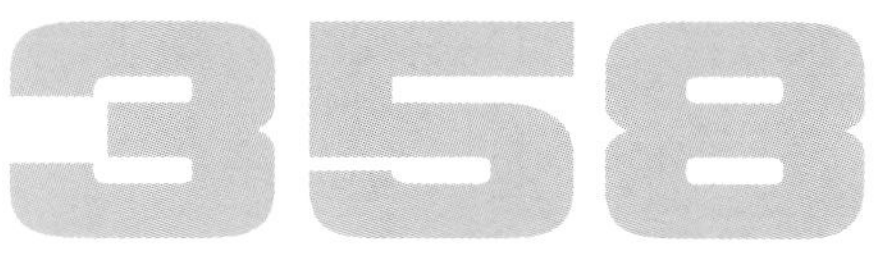

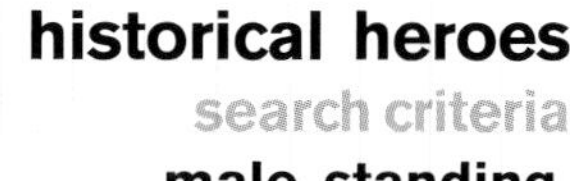

historical heroes

search criteria

male. standing. roman. boy.

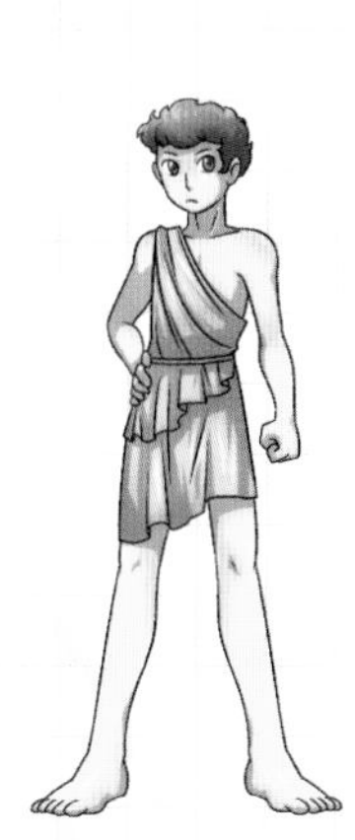

359

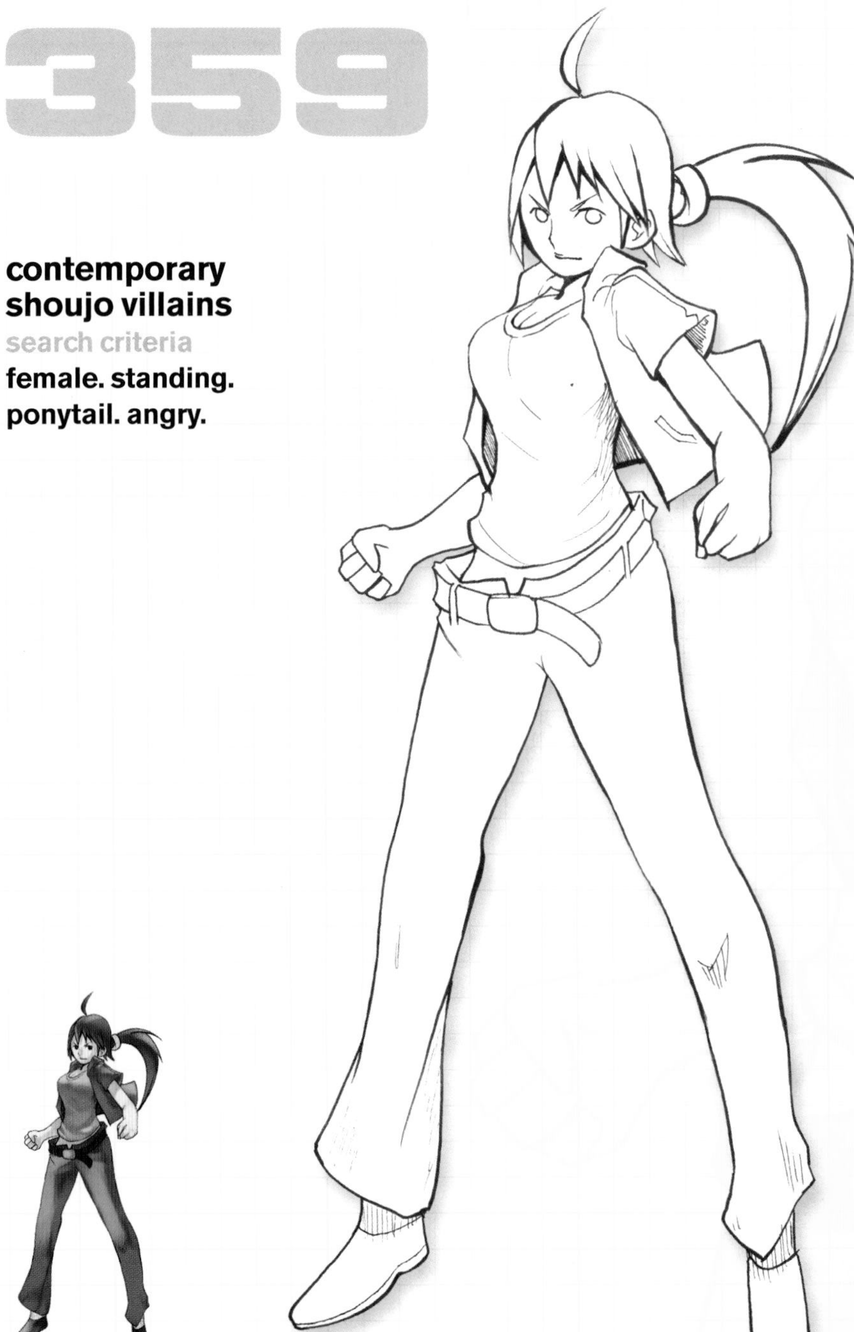

contemporary shoujo villains

search criteria

female. standing. ponytail. angry.

360

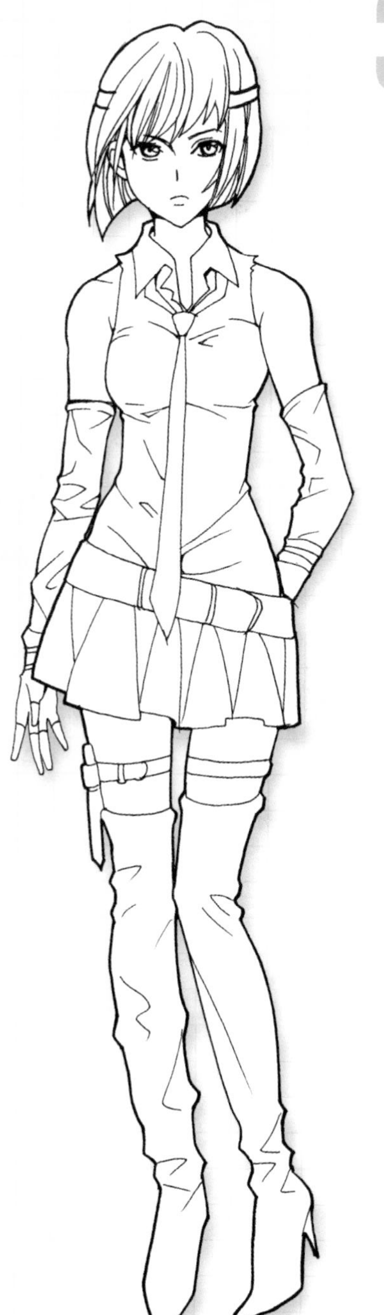

contemporary shoujo villains

search criteria

female. standing. tie. weapon. knife.

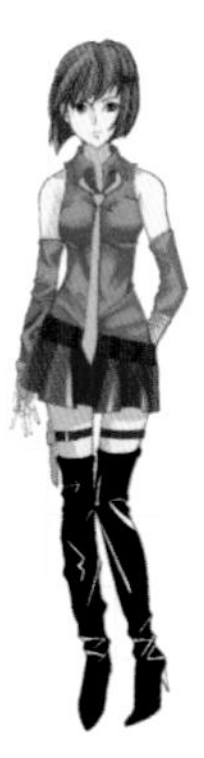

361

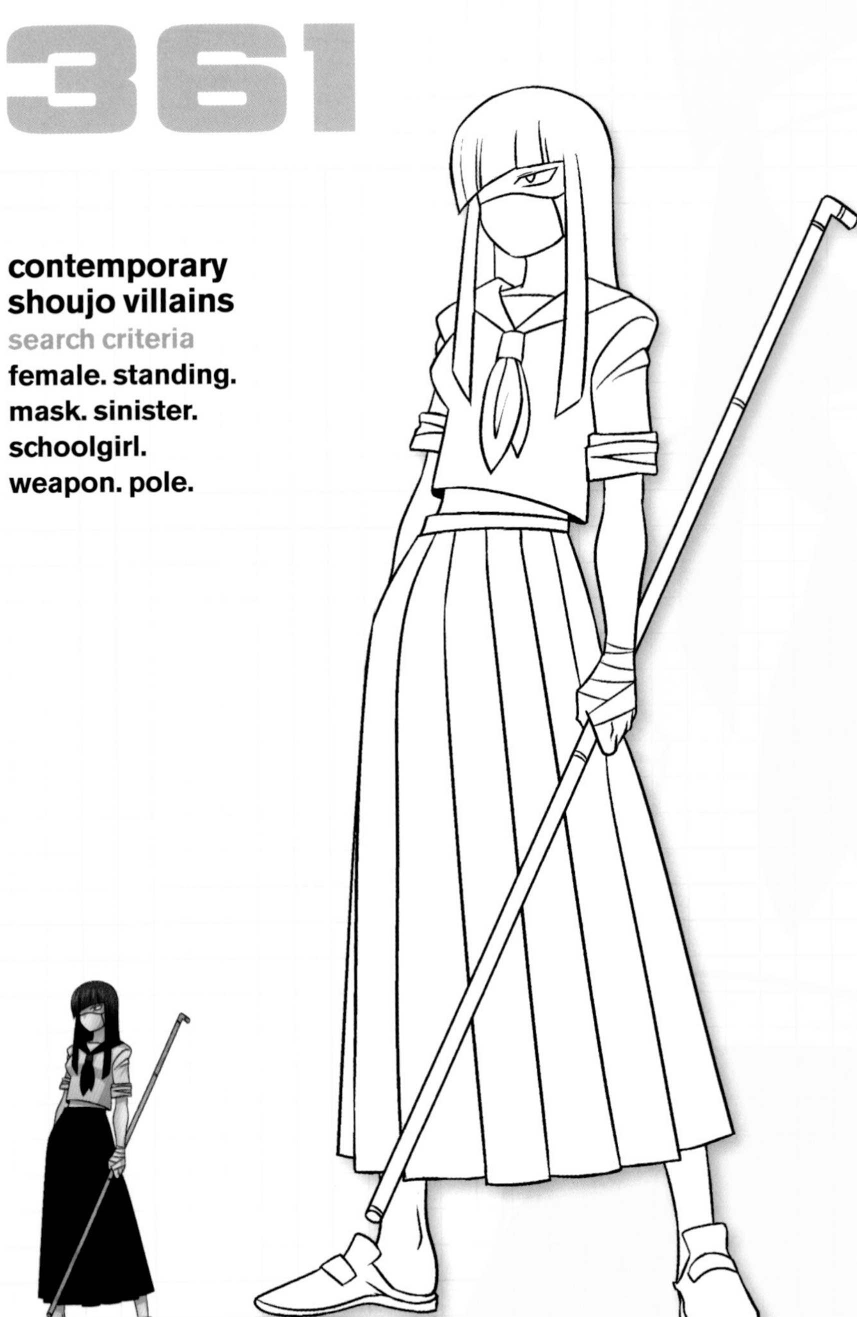

contemporary shoujo villains

search criteria

female. standing. mask. sinister. schoolgirl. weapon. pole.

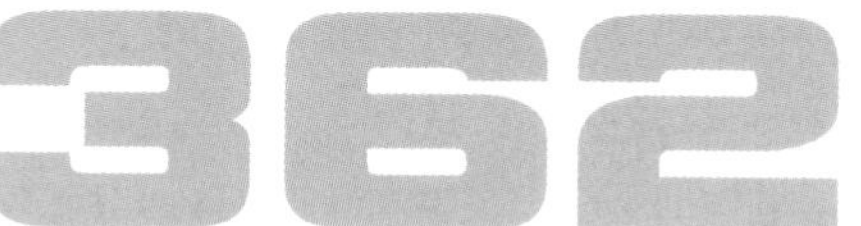

contemporary shoujo villains

search criteria

female. standing. sinister. angry. bag. catsuit.

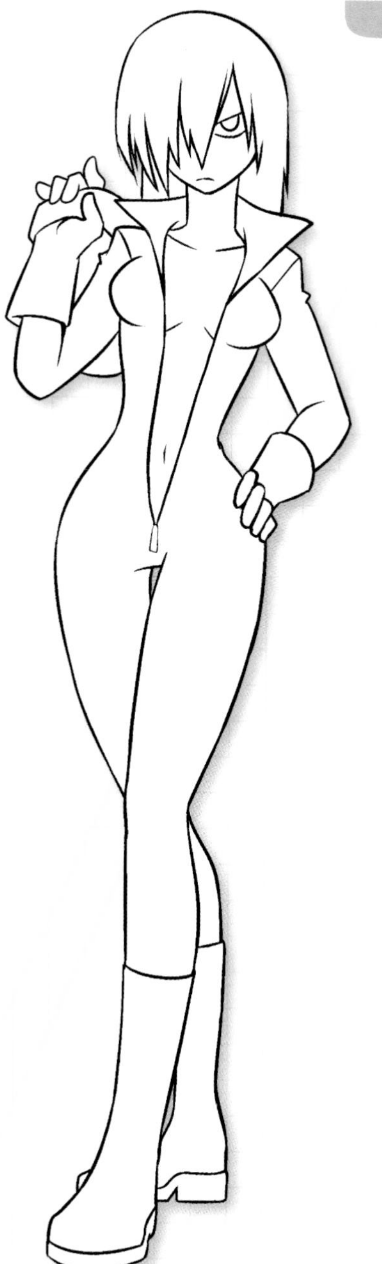

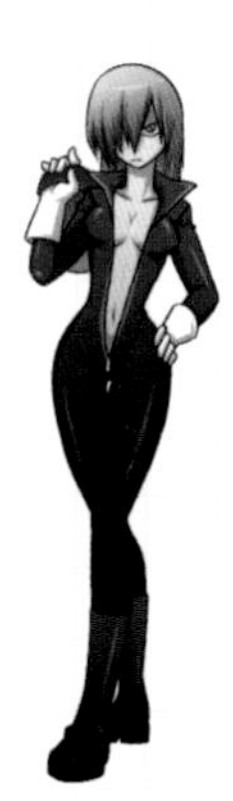

363

contemporary shoujo villains

search criteria

female. standing. side. bag. smoking. cigarette. schoolgirl.

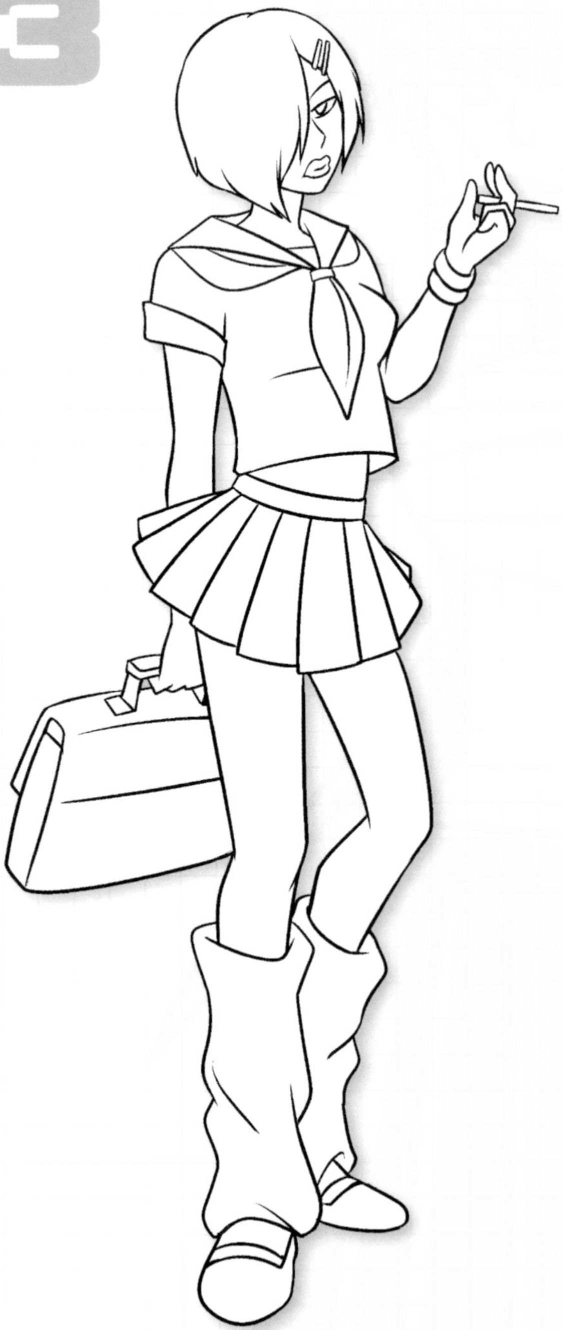

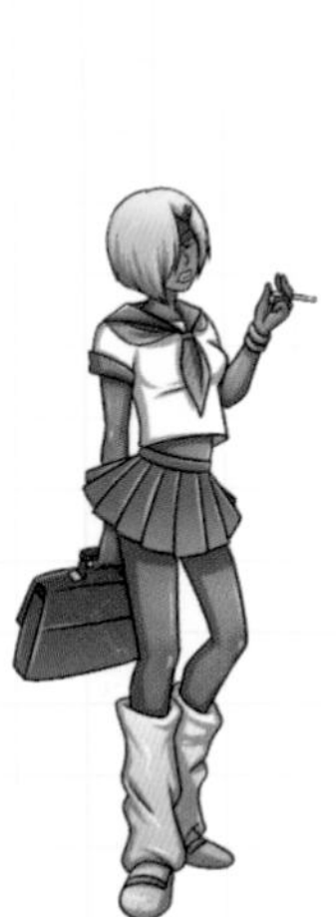

364

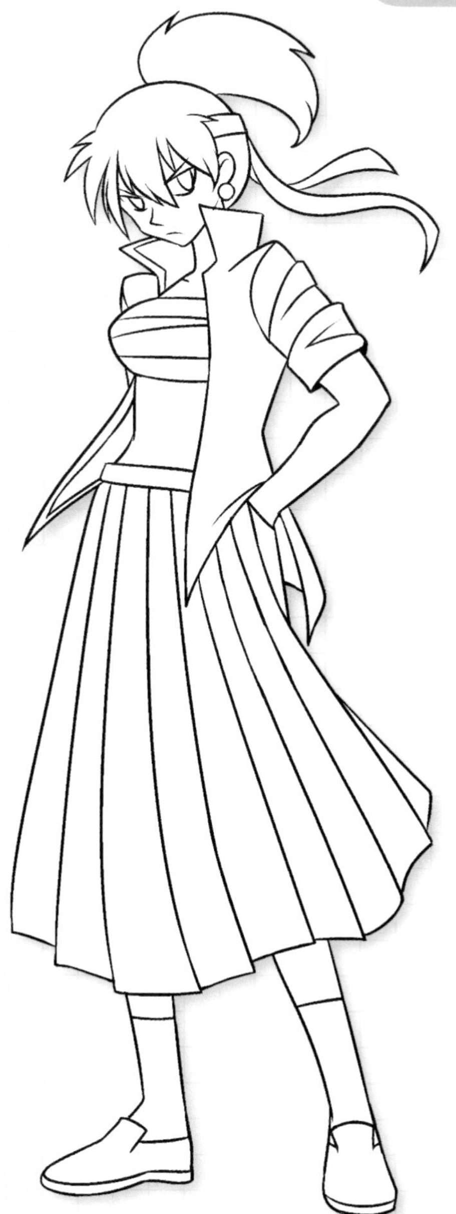

contemporary shoujo villains

search criteria

female. standing. side. angry. schoolgirl.

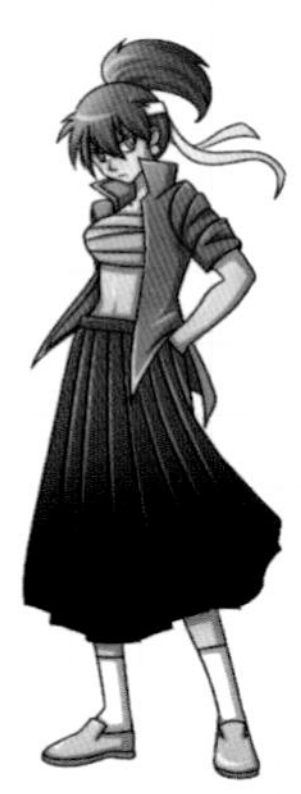

365

contemporary shoujo villains

search criteria

female. standing. side. weapons. razors. blades.

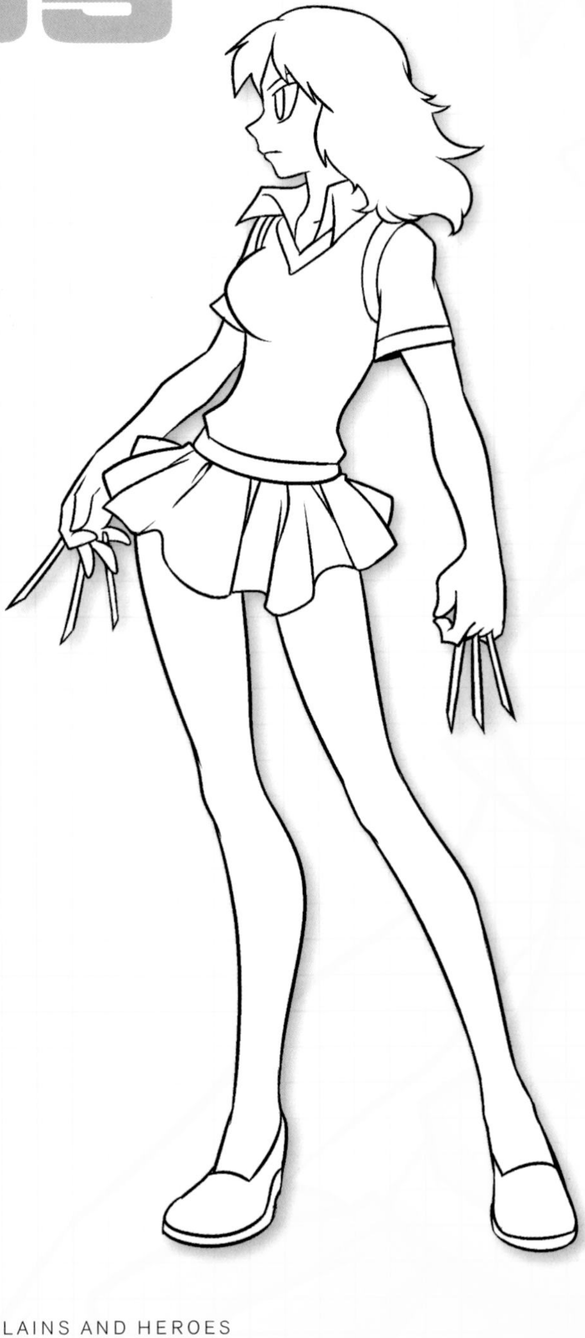

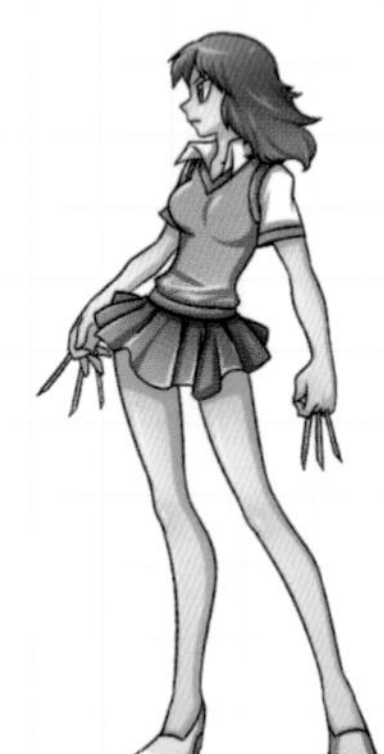

366

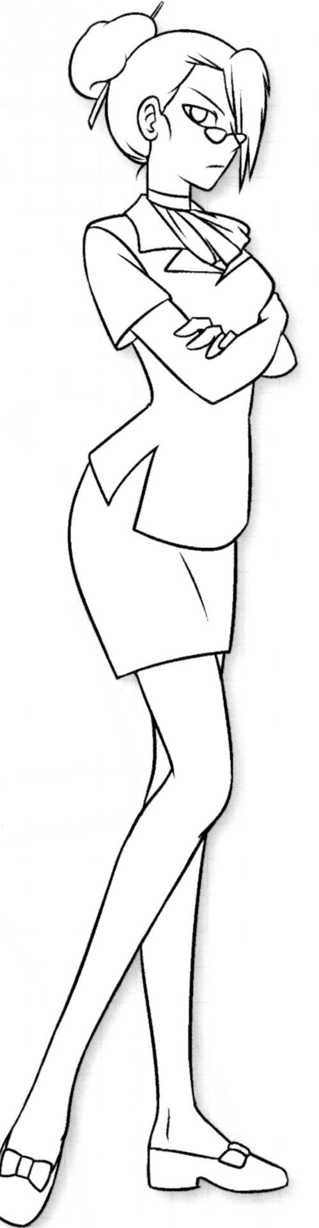

contemporary shoujo villains

search criteria

female. standing. side. glasses. angry. secretary.

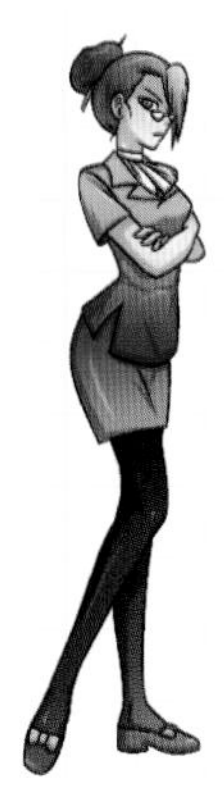

367

contemporary shoujo heroes

search criteria

female. standing. side. angry. attack. cheongsam. pigtails.

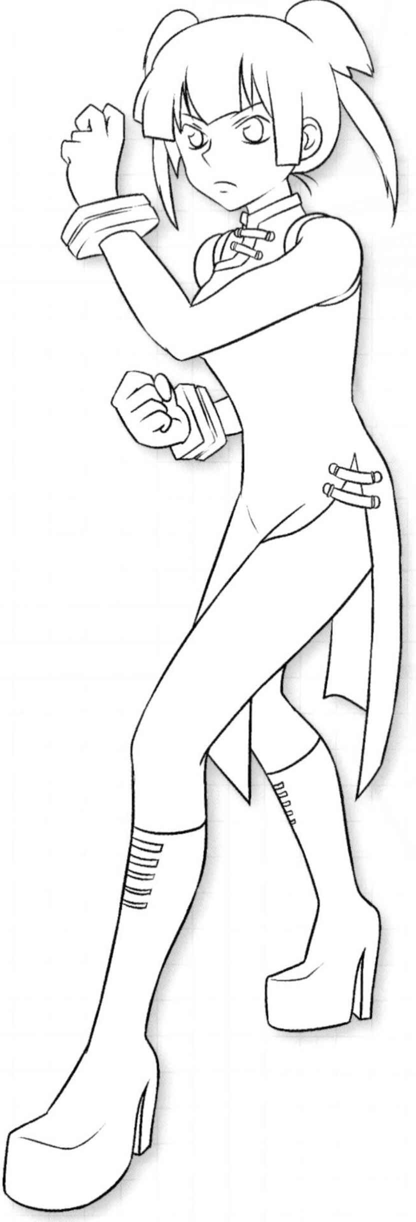

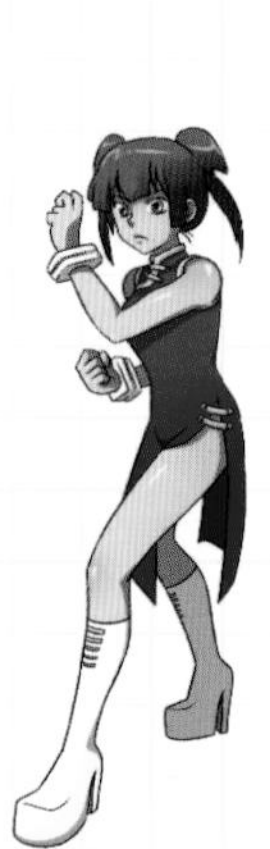

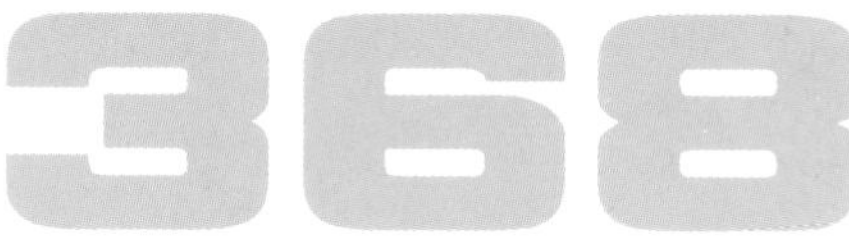

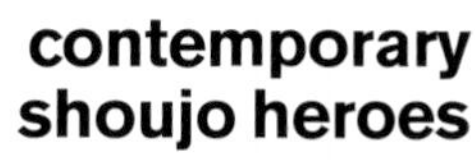

search criteria

**female. standing.
hat. bow. smiling.**

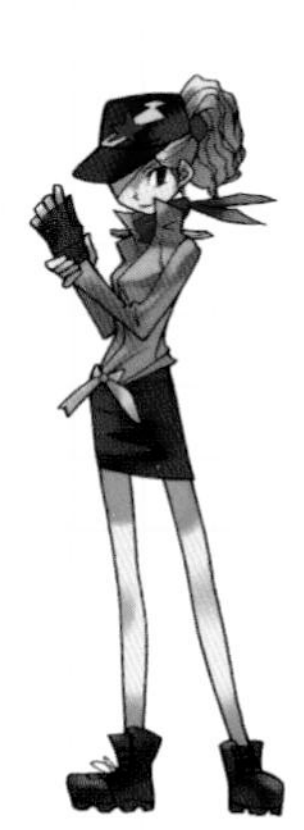

369

contemporary shoujo heroes

search criteria

female. standing. ponytail. tracksuit.

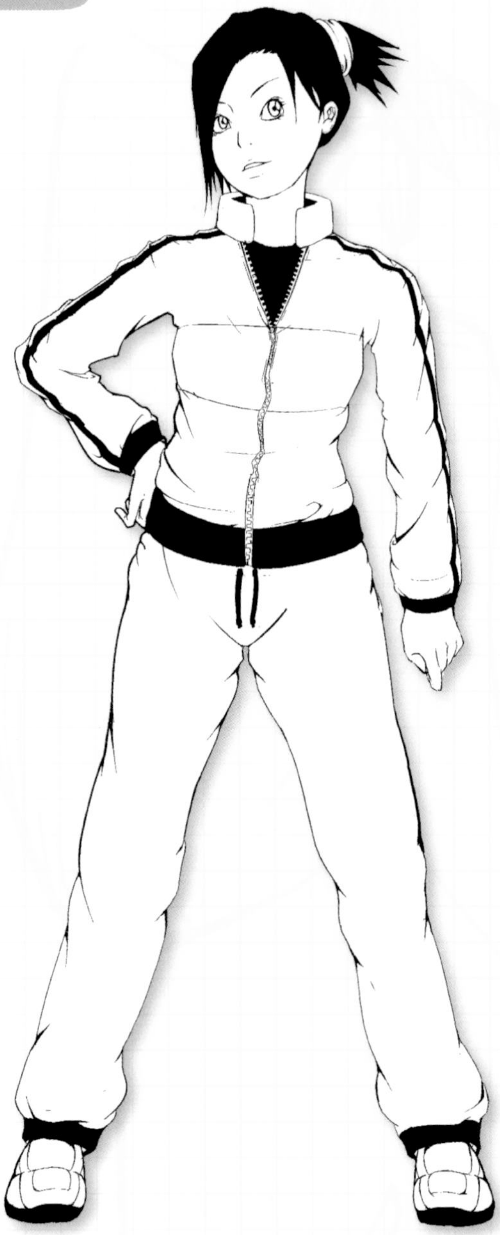

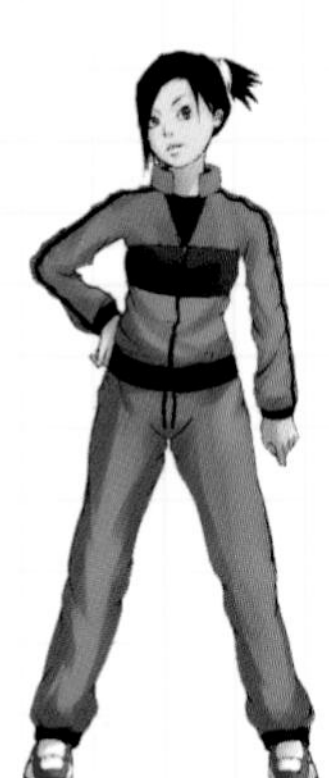

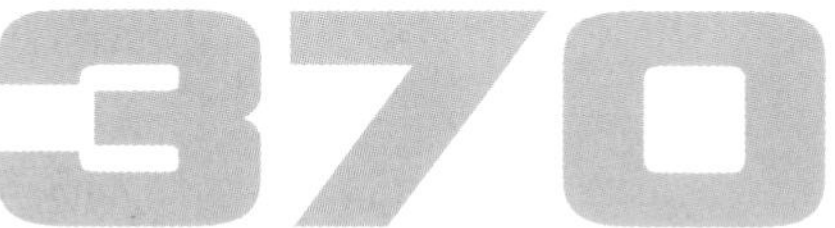

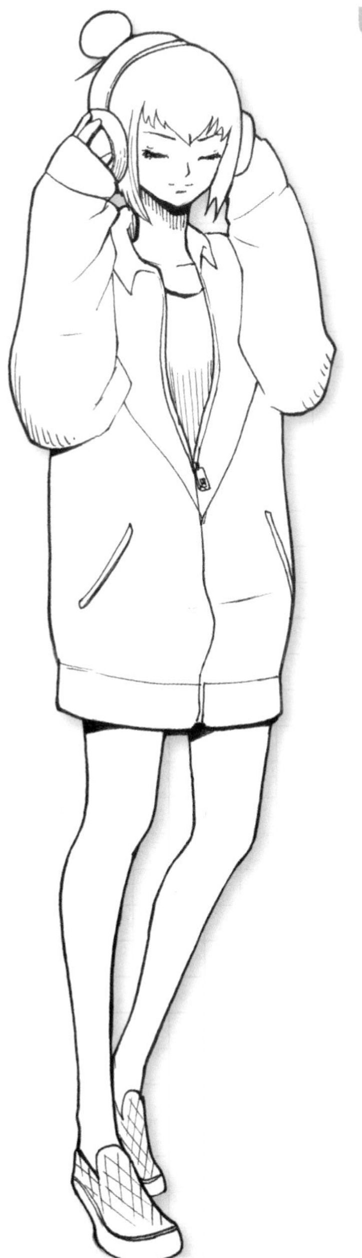

contemporary shoujo heroes

search criteria

female. standing. headphones. walking. music.

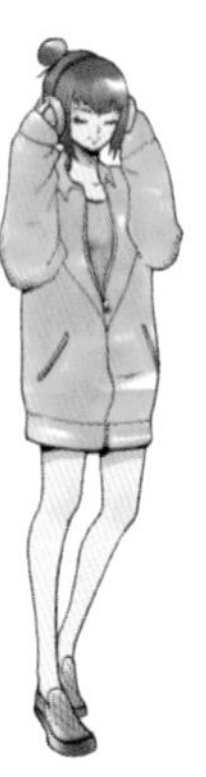

371

contemporary shoujo heroes

search criteria

female. standing. schoolgirl. watch. time. sad.

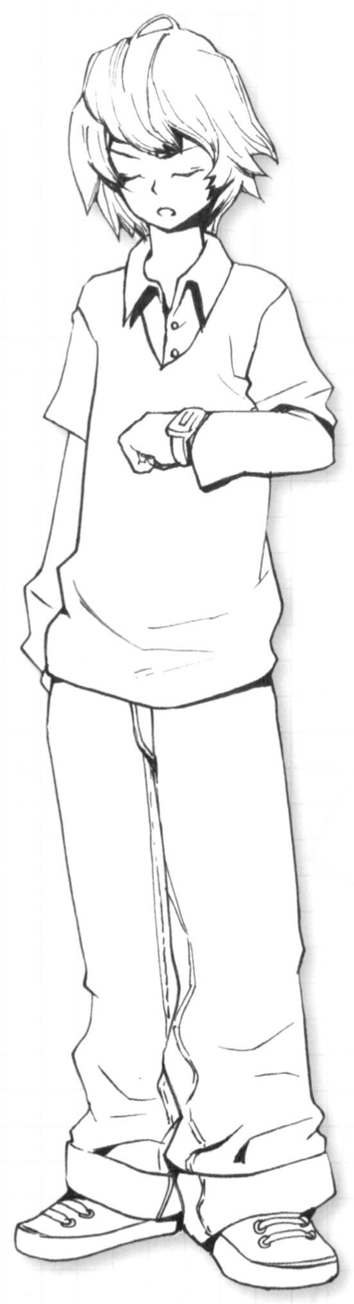

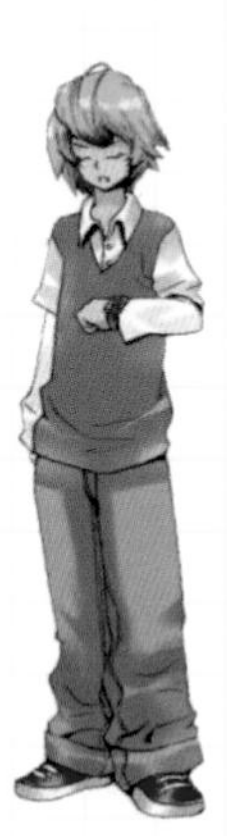

372

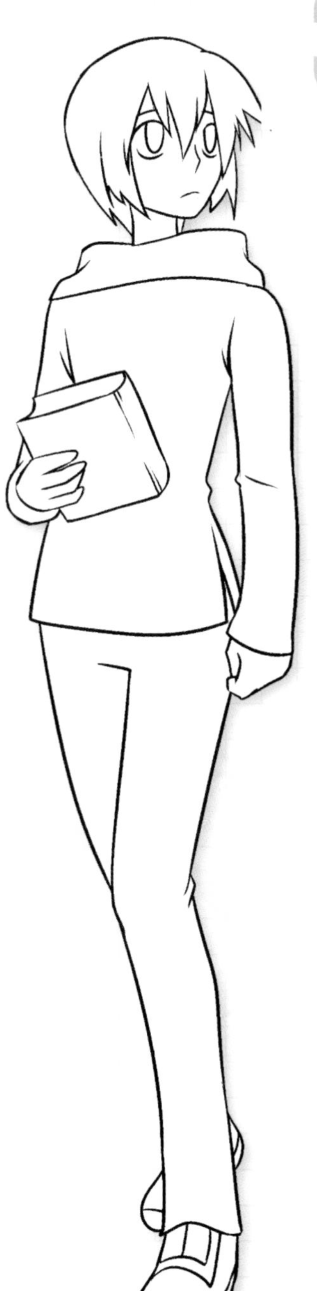

contemporary shonen heroes

search criteria

female. standing. book. sad.

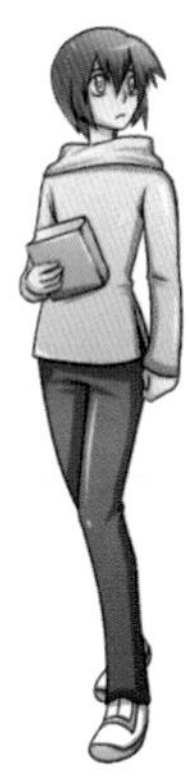

373

contemporary shoujo heroes

search criteria

female. standing. side. schoolgirl. weapon. fan.

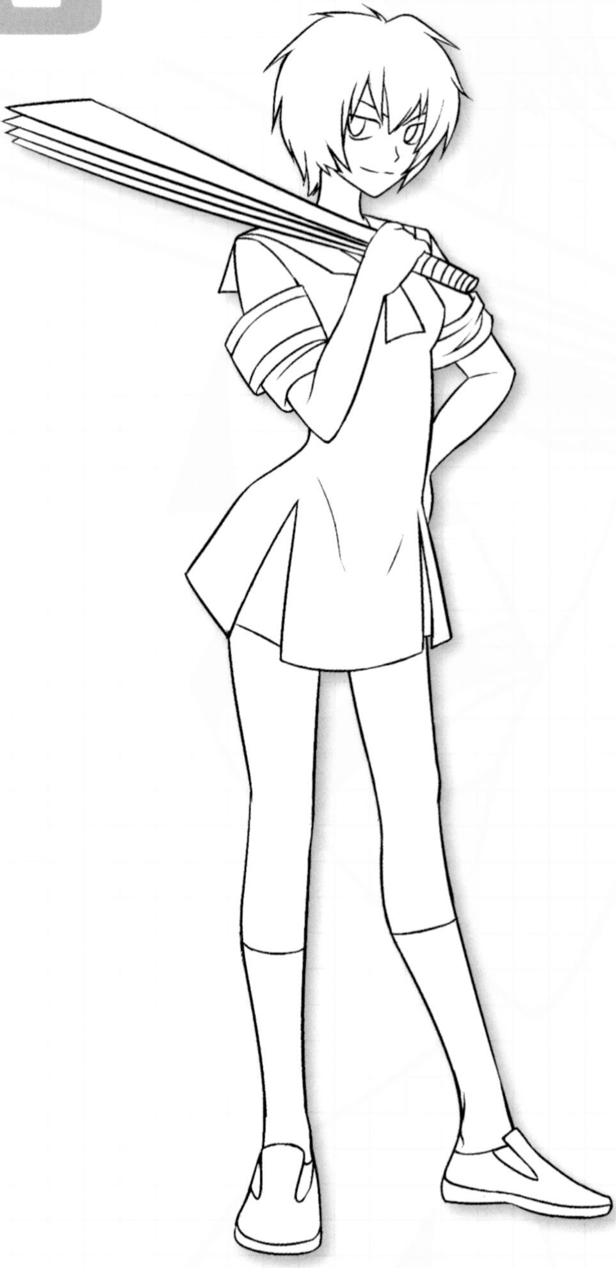

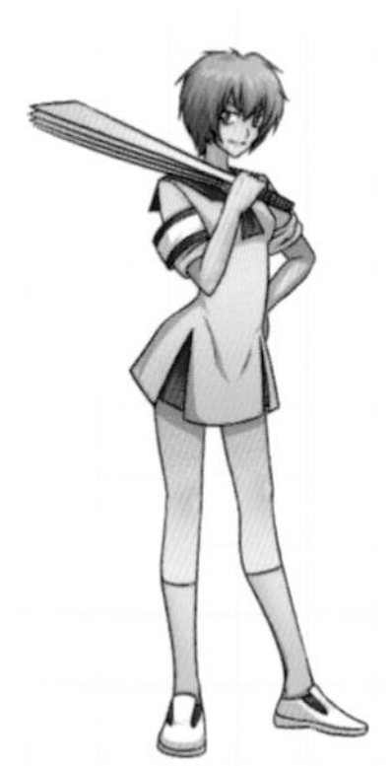

374

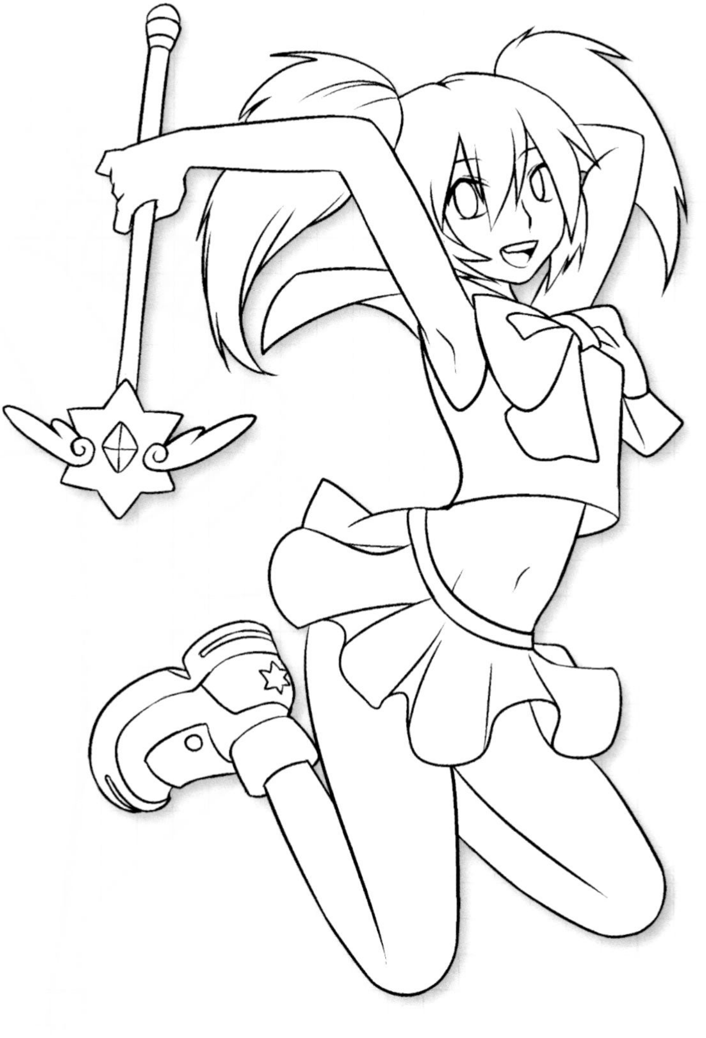

contemporary shoujo heroes

search criteria

female. jump. side. cheerleader. bow. pigtails. baton.

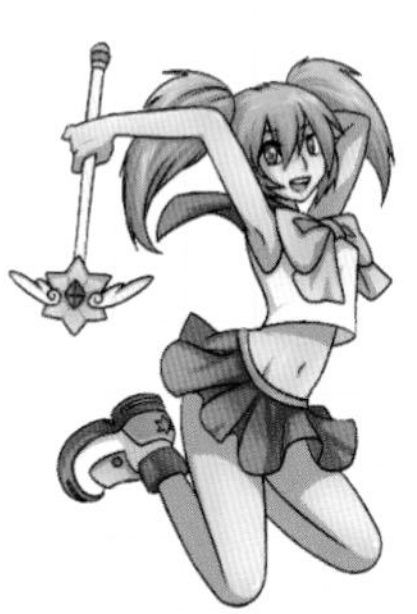

375

contemporary shoujo heroes

search criteria

female. resting. side. schoolgirl. leaning. headband.

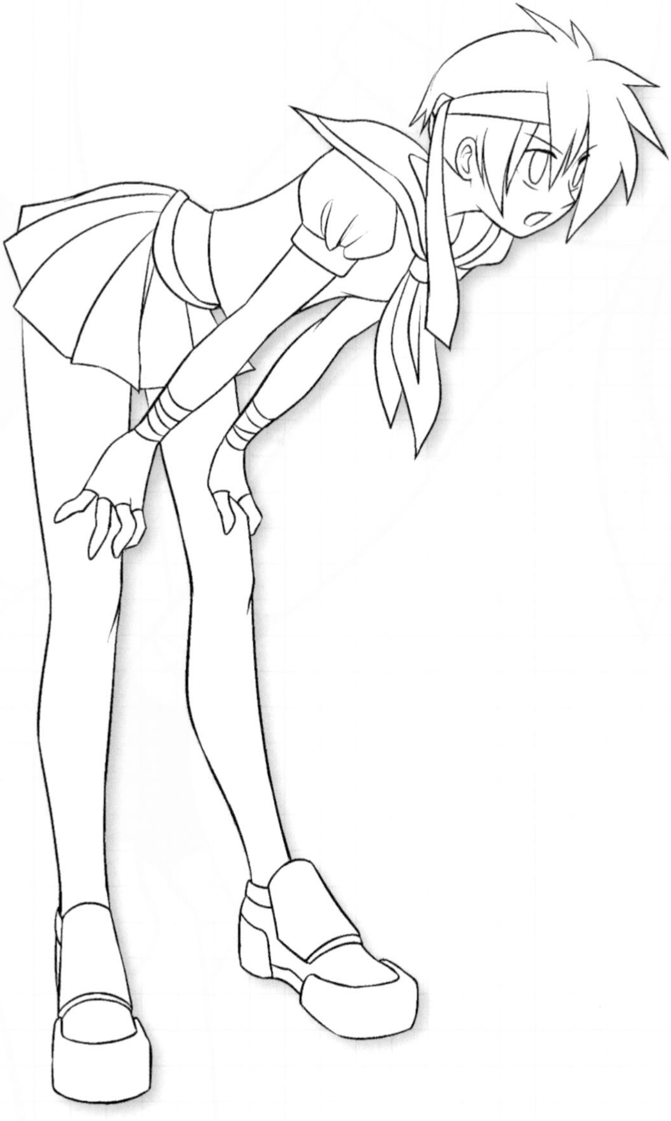

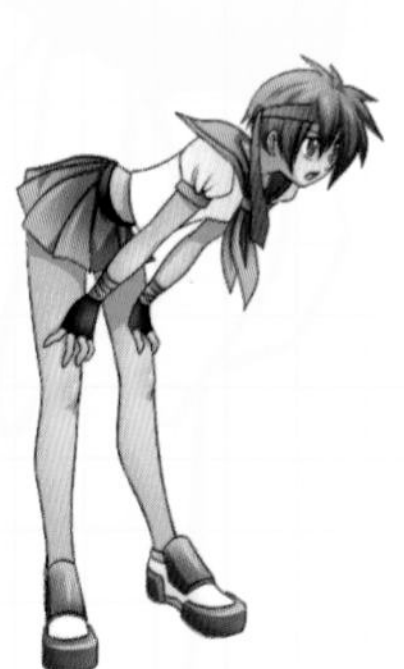

376

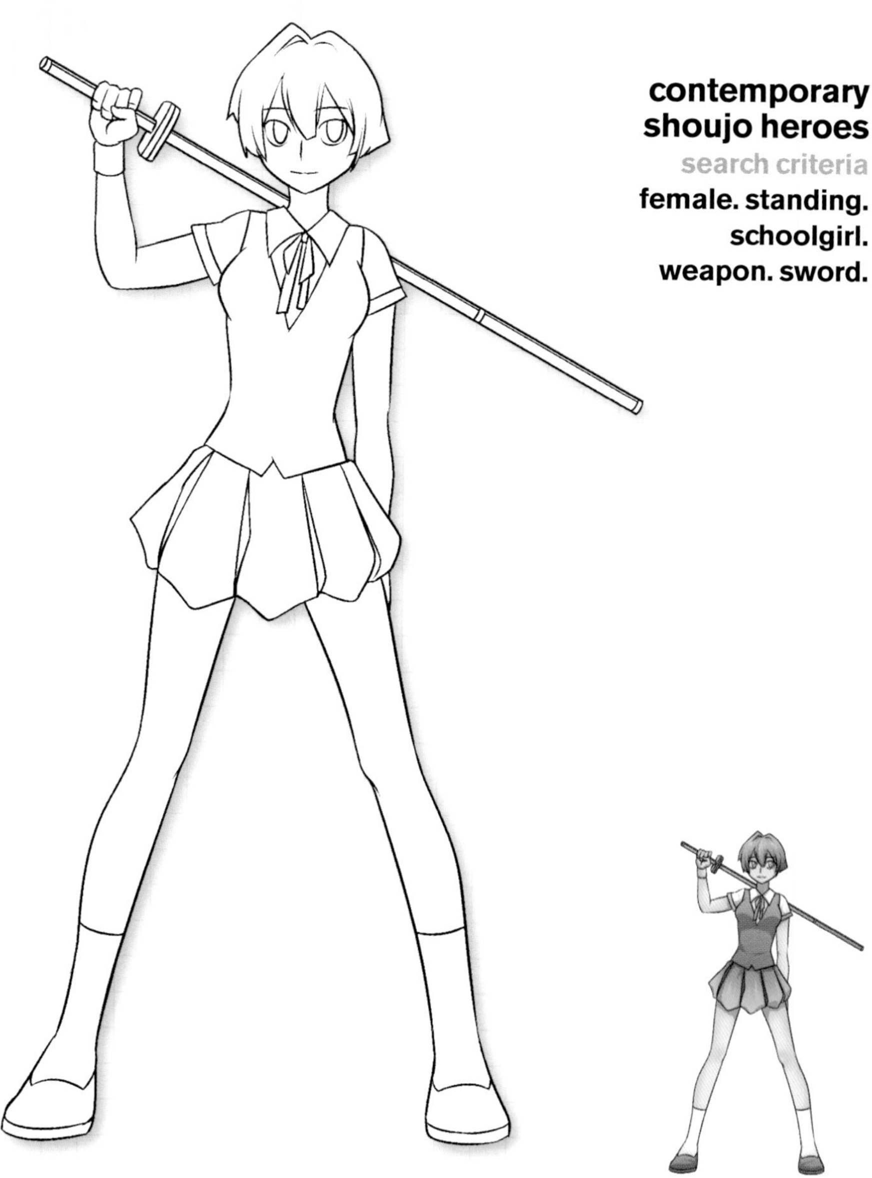

contemporary shoujo heroes

search criteria

female. standing. schoolgirl. weapon. sword.

377

contemporary shoujo heroes

search criteria

female. standing. side. hat. bow. wind. historical.

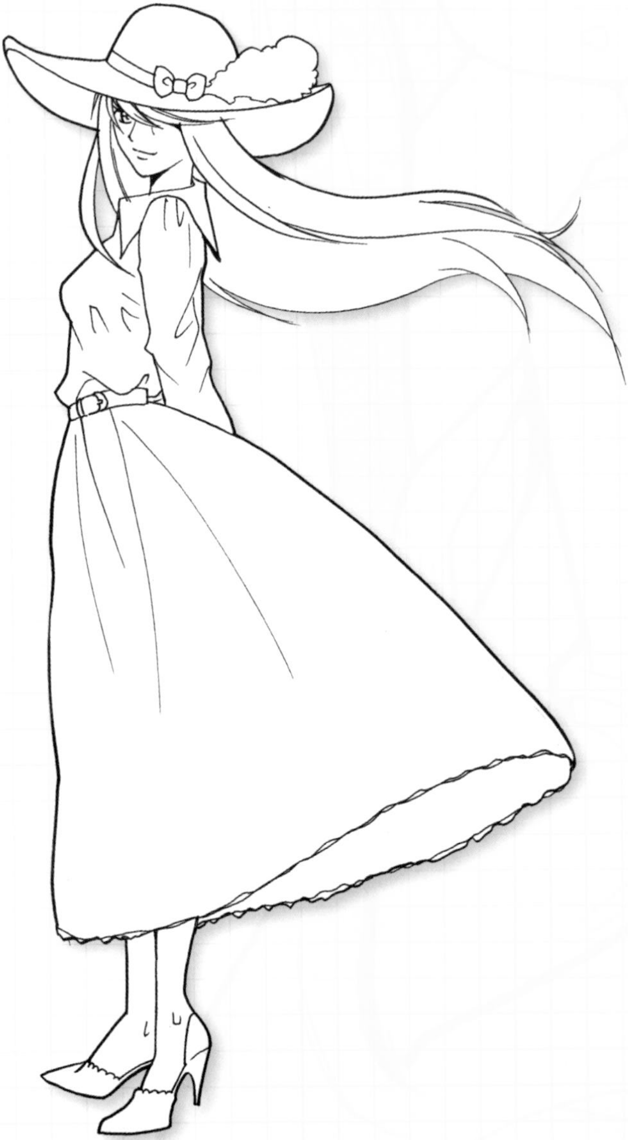

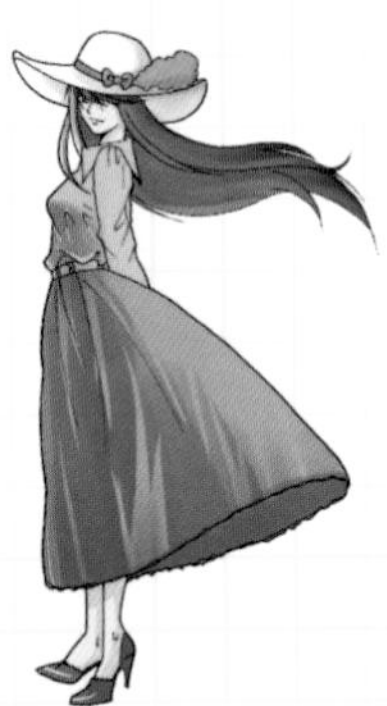

378

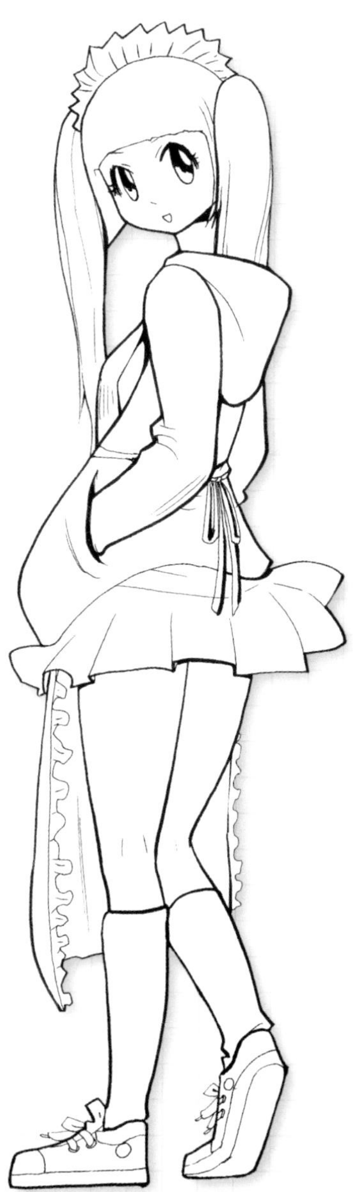

contemporary shoujo heroes

search criteria

female. standing. side. pigtails. apron.

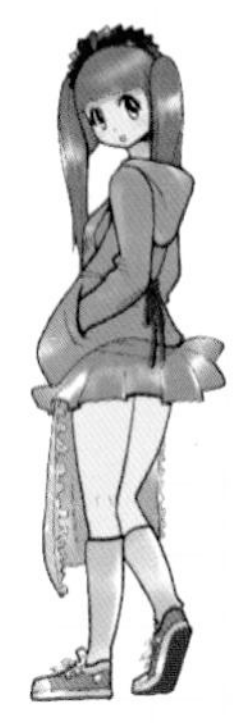

379

contemporary shoujo heroes

search criteria

female. standing. pocket. glasses.

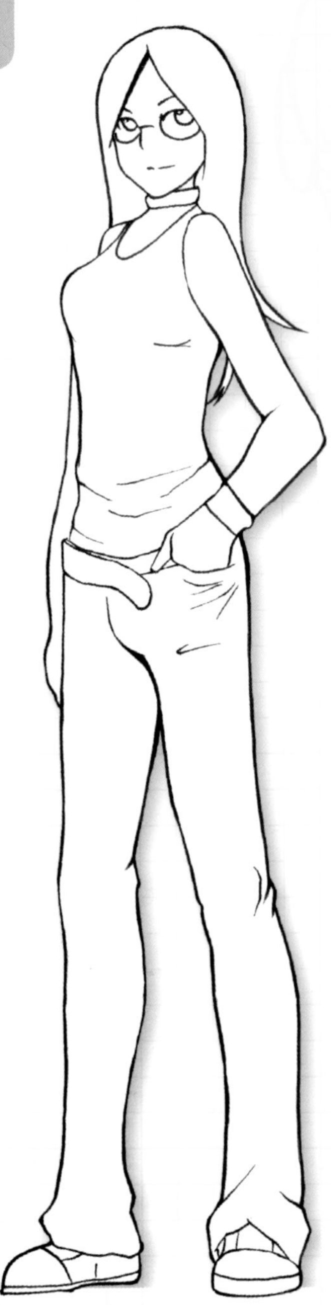

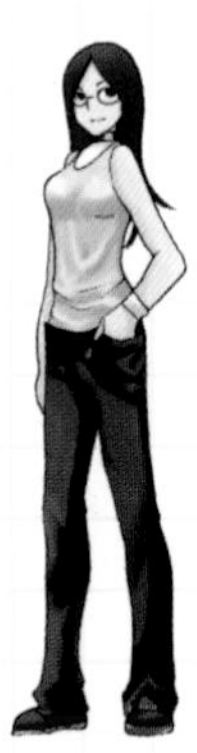

380

contemporary shoujo heroes

search criteria

female. standing. side. smiling. bow. headphones. music.

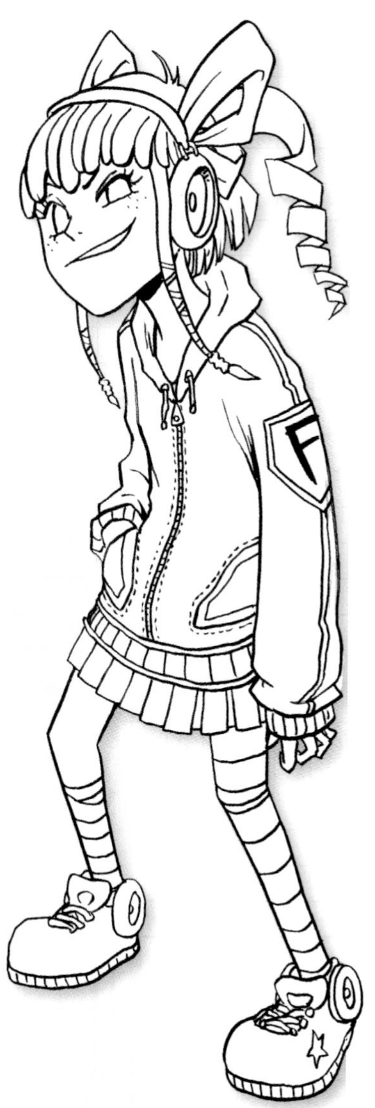

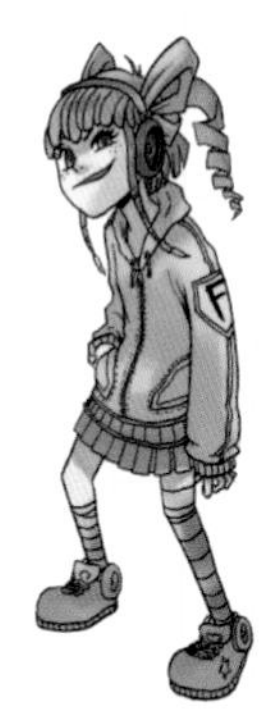

381

contemporary shoujo heroes

search criteria

female. jump. side. cheerleader. pompoms. shout.

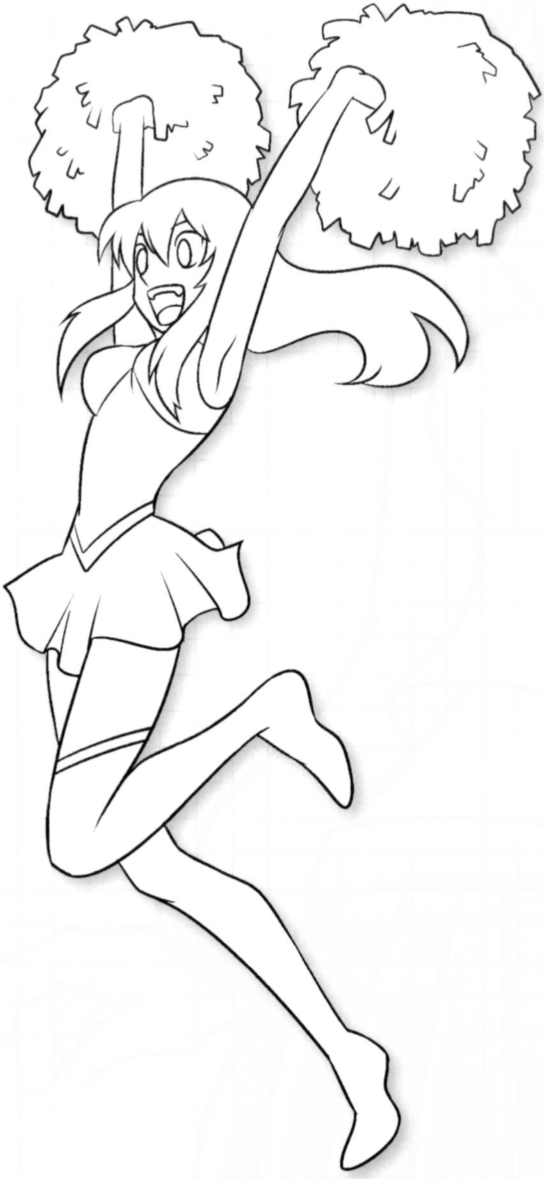

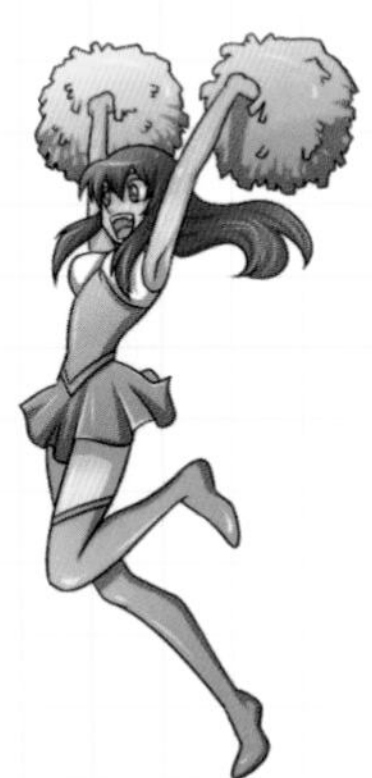

382

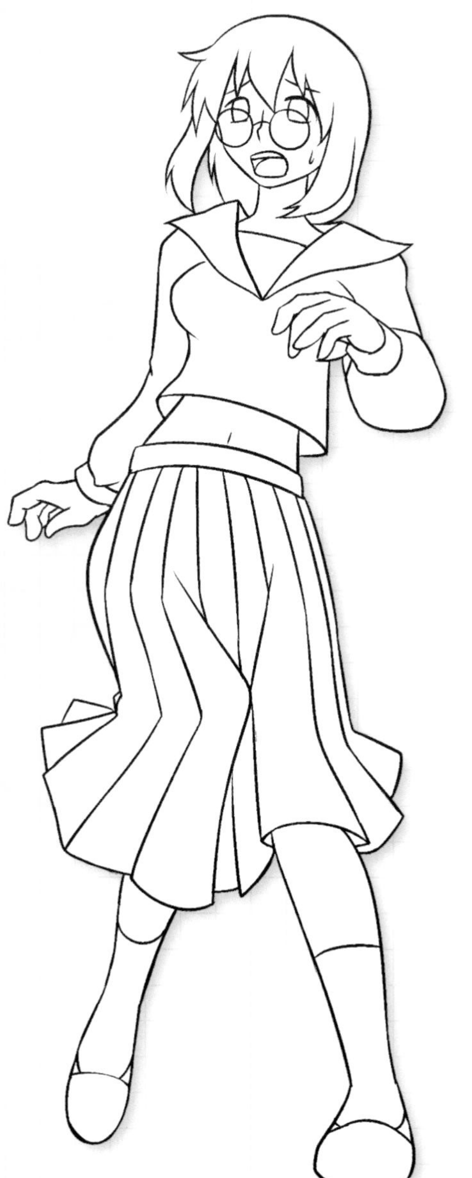

contemporary shoujo heroes

search criteria

female. running. shout. glasses. tear. sad. schoolgirl.

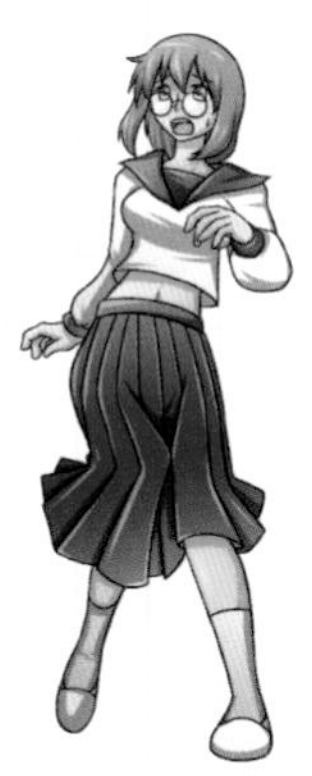

383

contemporary shoujo heroes

search criteria

female. jump. side. singing. pigtails. microphone. music.

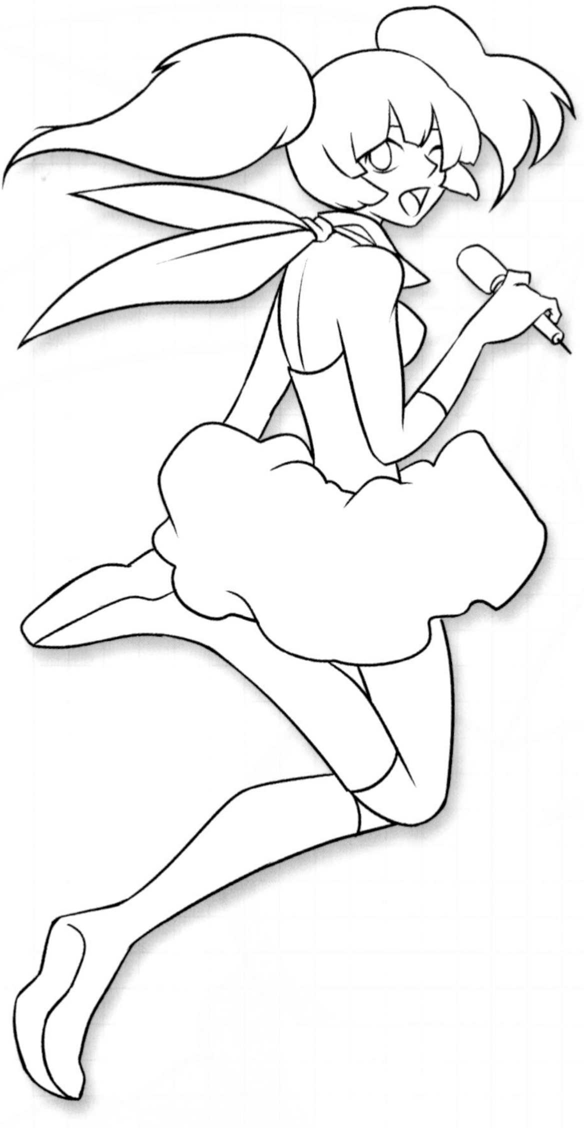

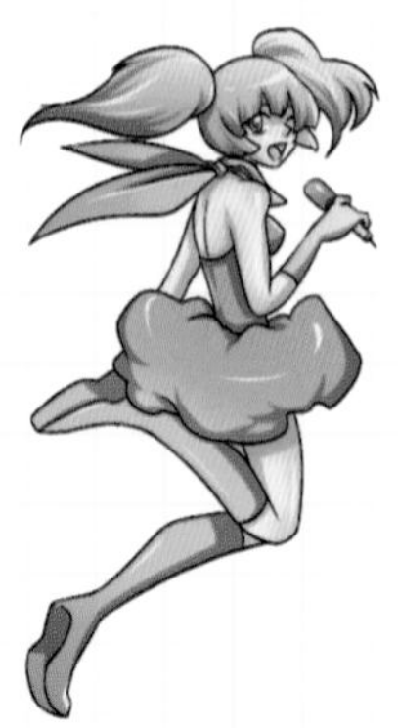

384

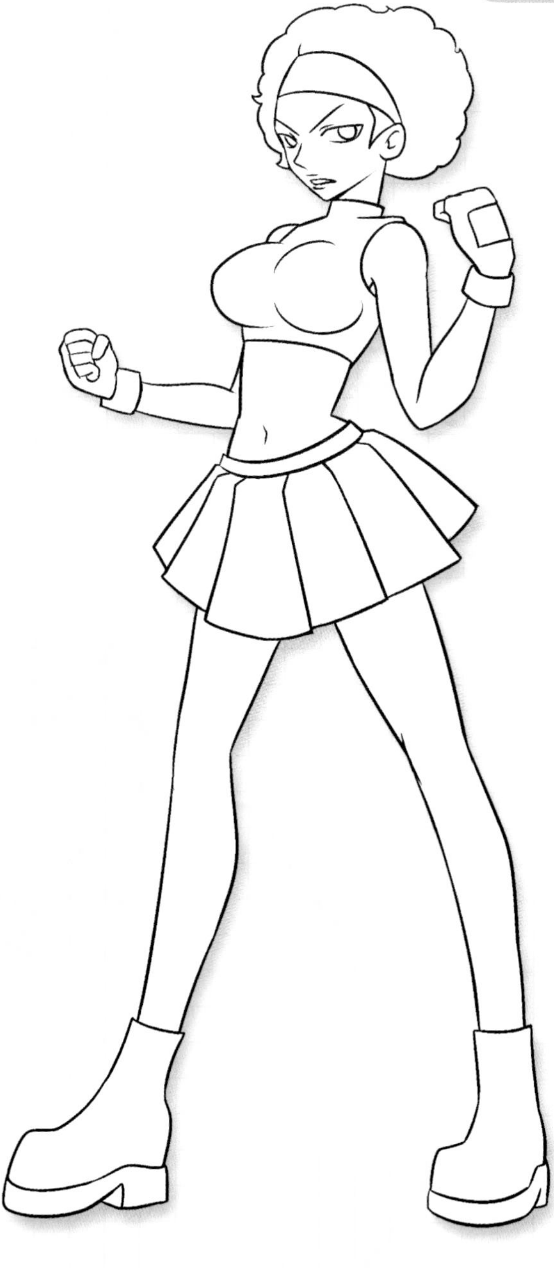

contemporary shoujo heroes

search criteria

female. standing. headband. fists. angry.

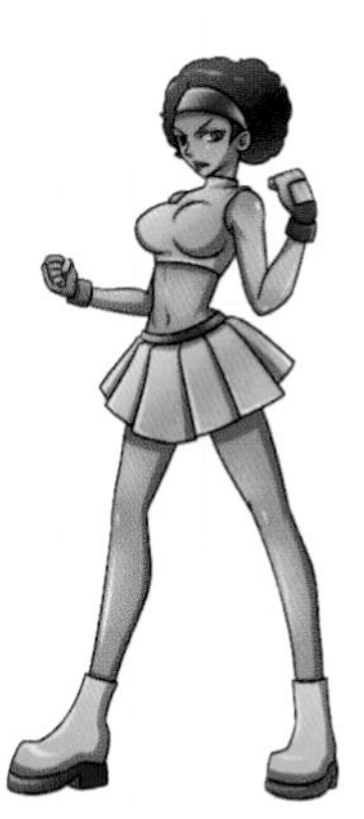

385

contemporary shoujo heroes

search criteria

female. standing. schoolgirl. tie. headband. gesture. smiling.

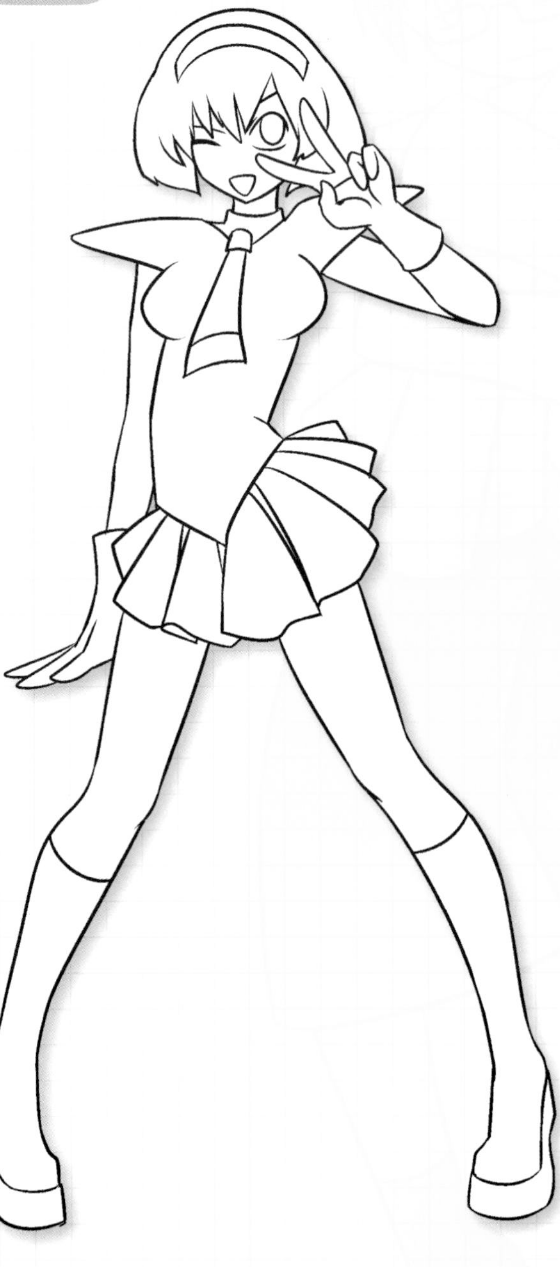

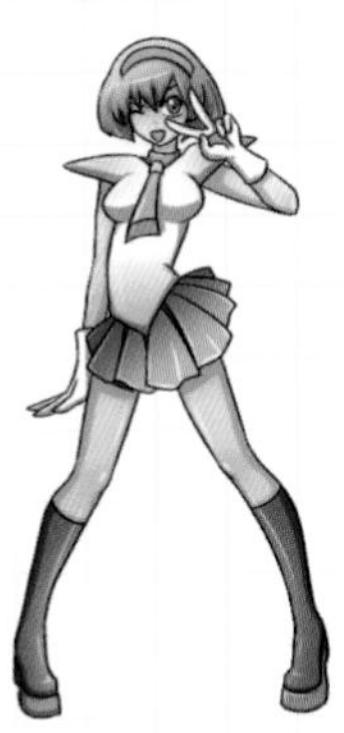

386

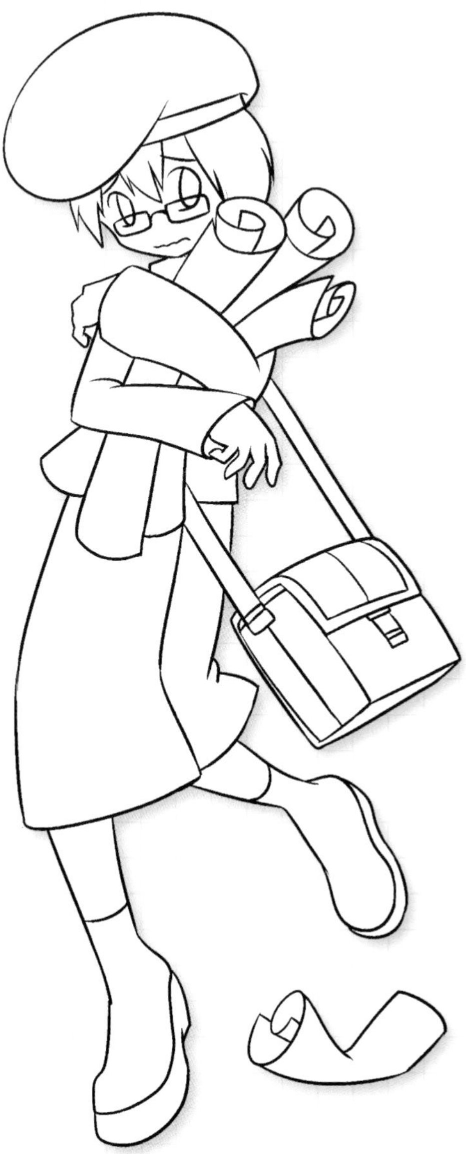

contemporary shoujo heroes

search criteria

female. walking. glasses. papers. hat. bag. sad.

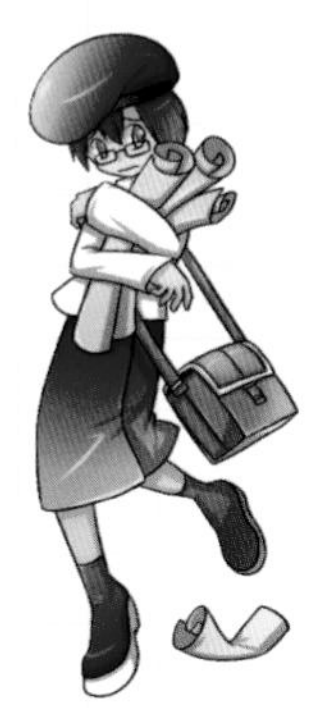

387

contemporary shonen villains

search criteria

male. standing. side. gangster. angry. eyepatch.

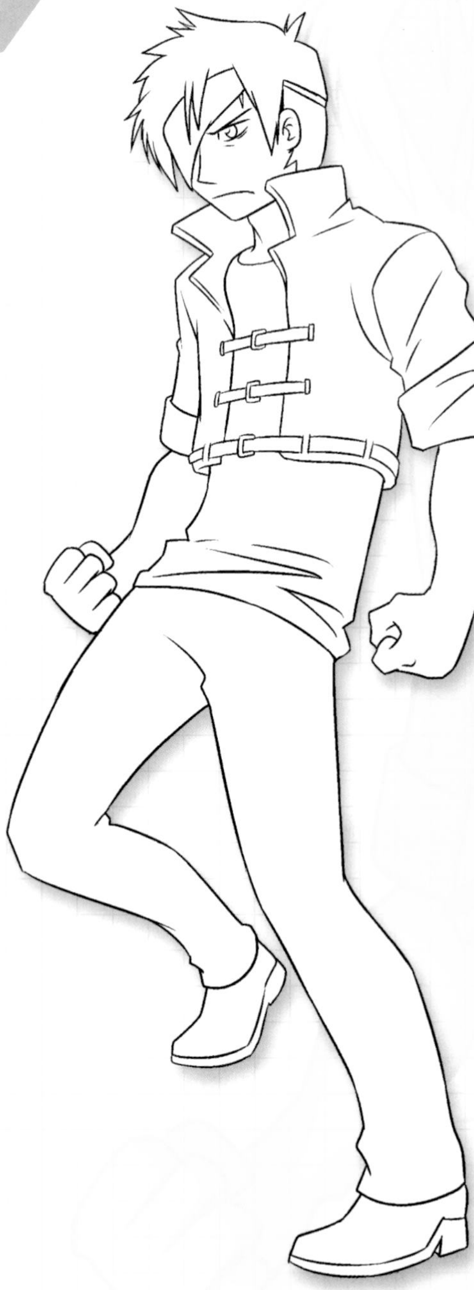

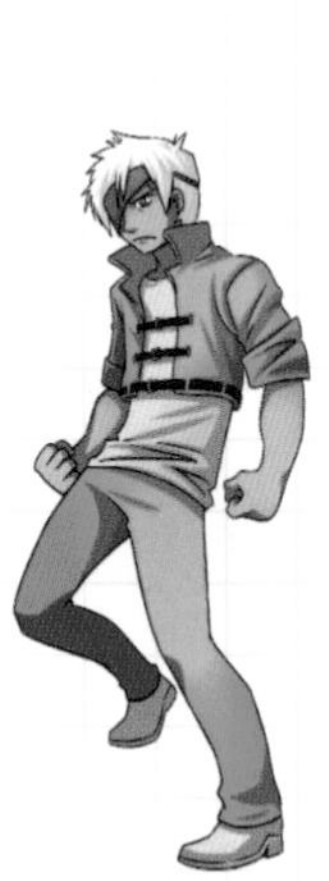

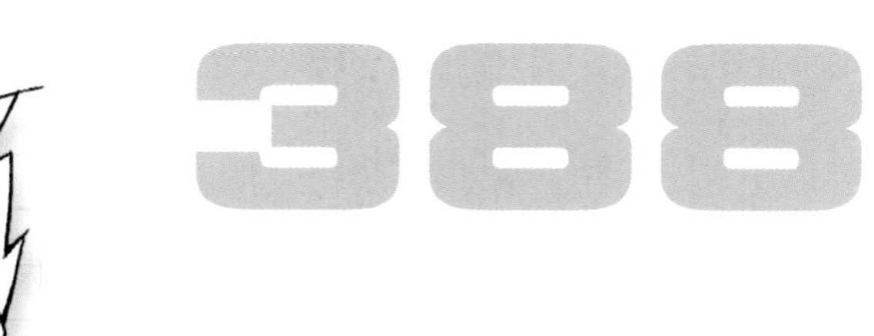

contemporary shonen villains

search criteria

male. standing. angry. gangster.

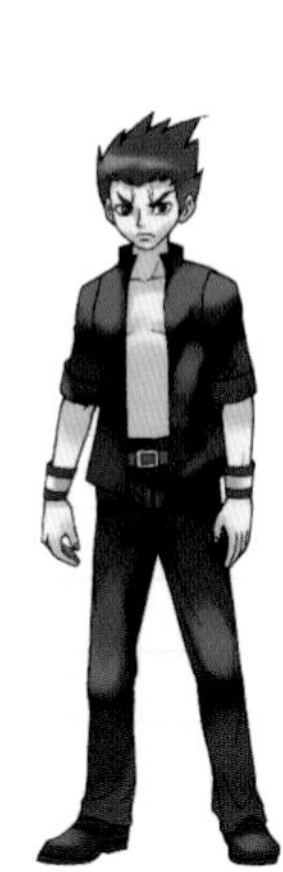

389

contemporary shonen villains

search criteria

male. crouched. headscarf. gangster.

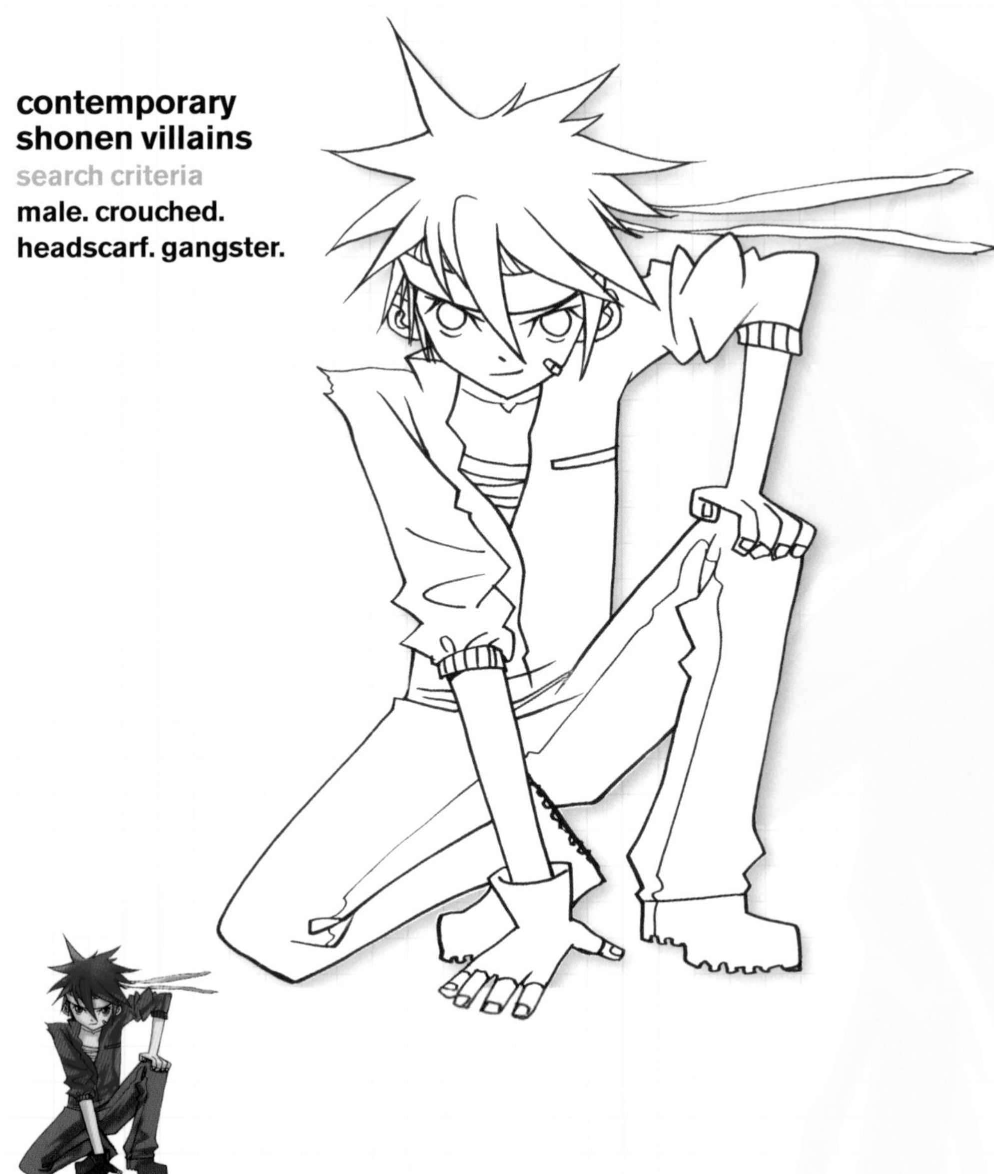

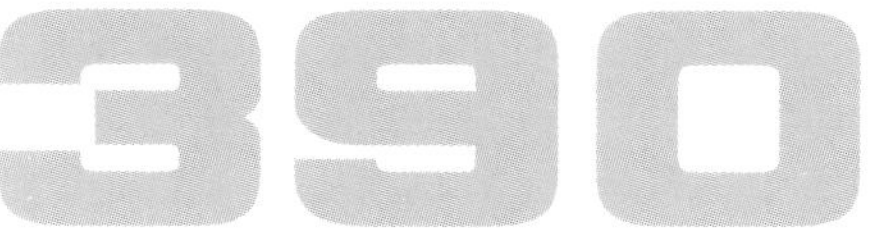

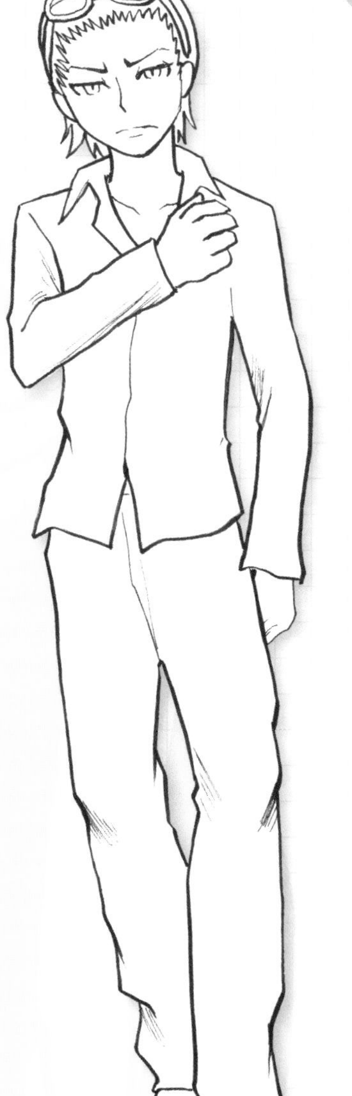

contemporary shonen villains

search criteria

male. standing. sunglasses. gangster.

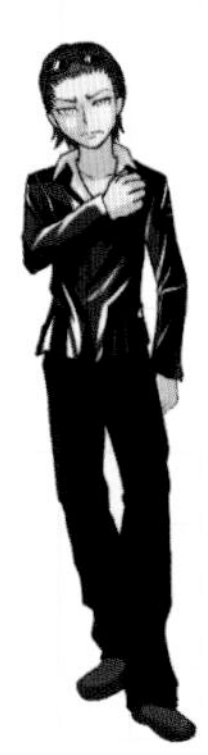

391

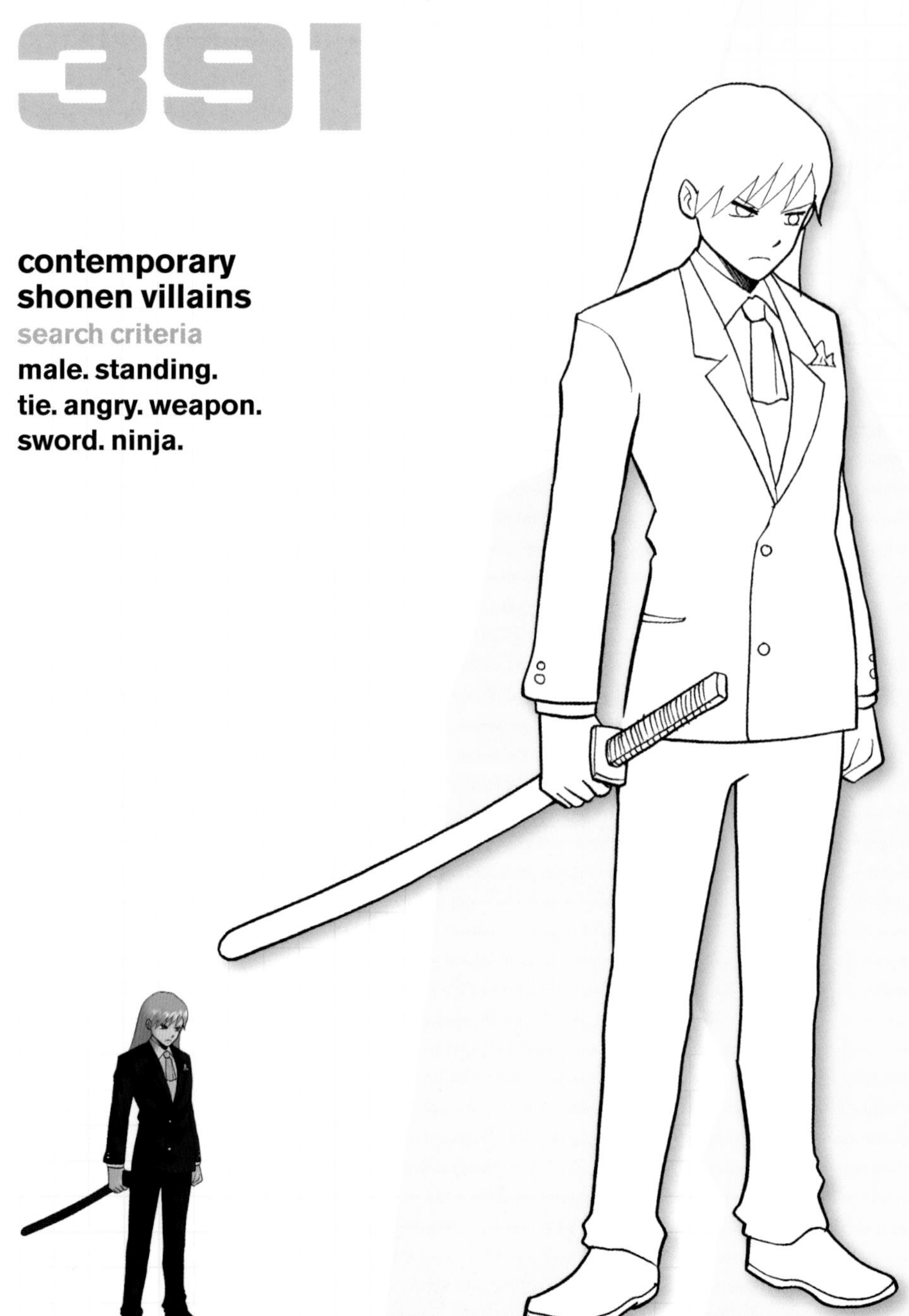

contemporary shonen villains

search criteria

male. standing. tie. angry. weapon. sword. ninja.

392

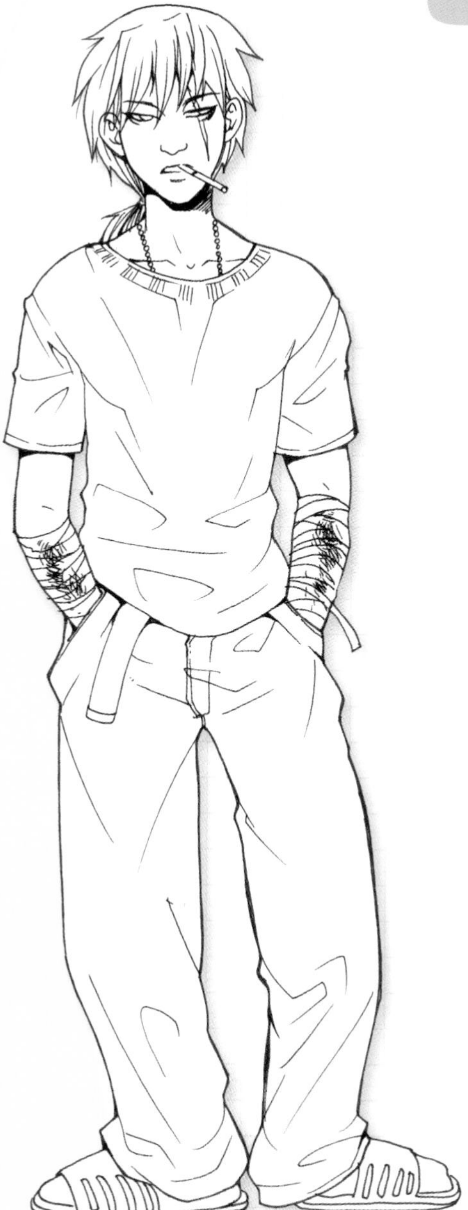

contemporary shonen villains

search criteria

male. standing. scar. smoking. cigarette. bandages. gangster.

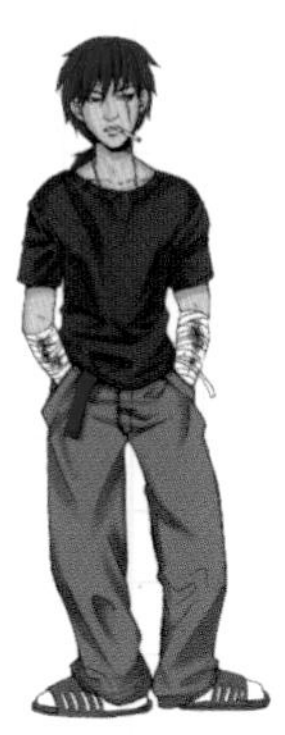

393

contemporary shonen villains

search criteria

male. standing. side. walking. smoking. cigarette. gangster.

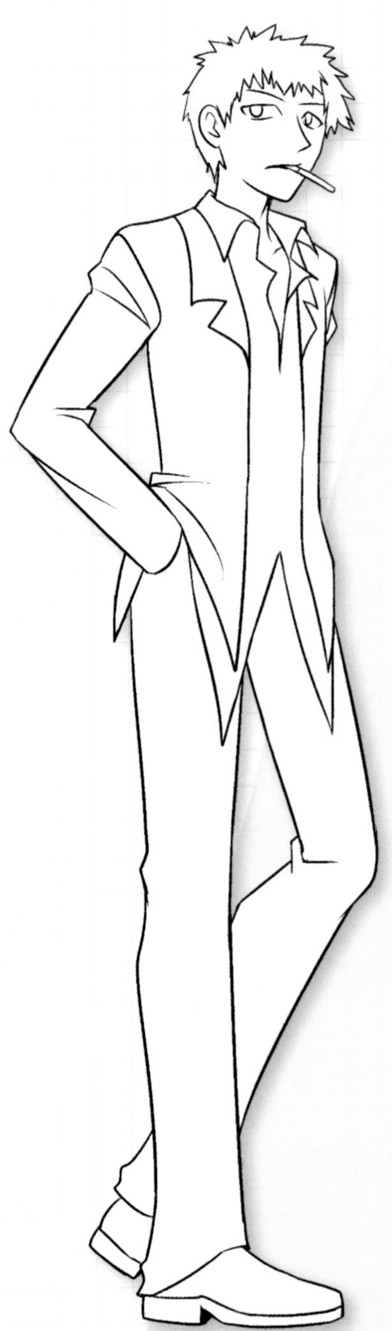

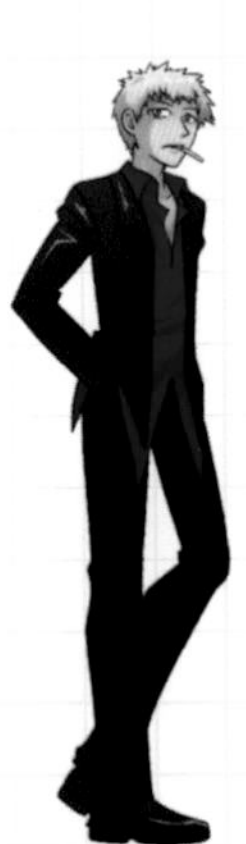

394

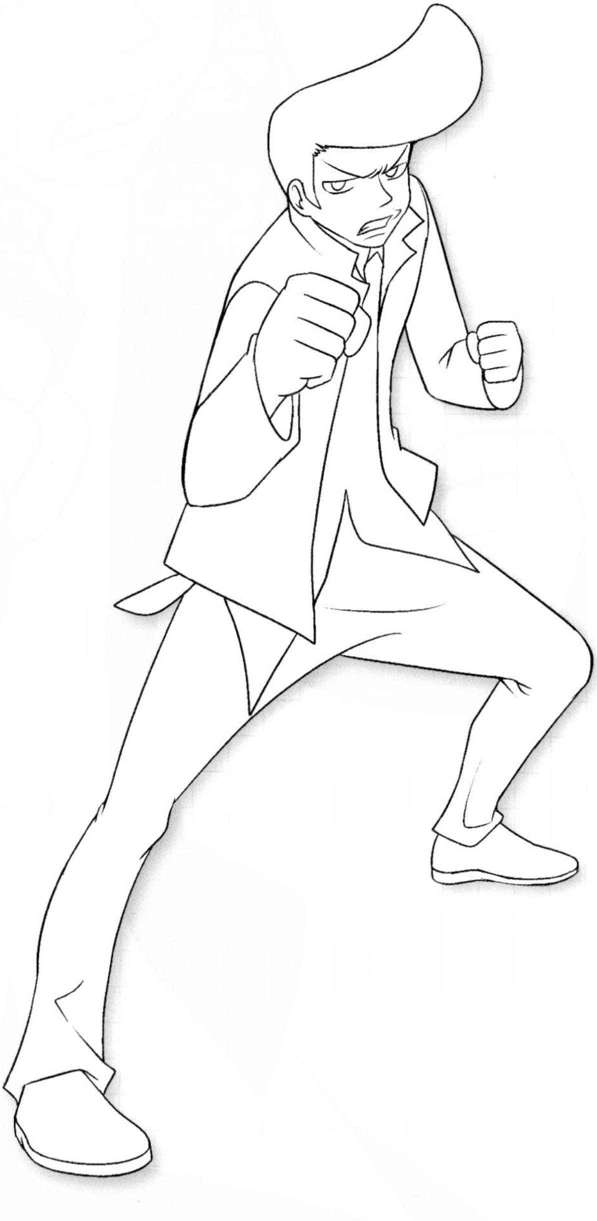

contemporary shonen villains

search criteria

male. angry. fists. punch. gangster.

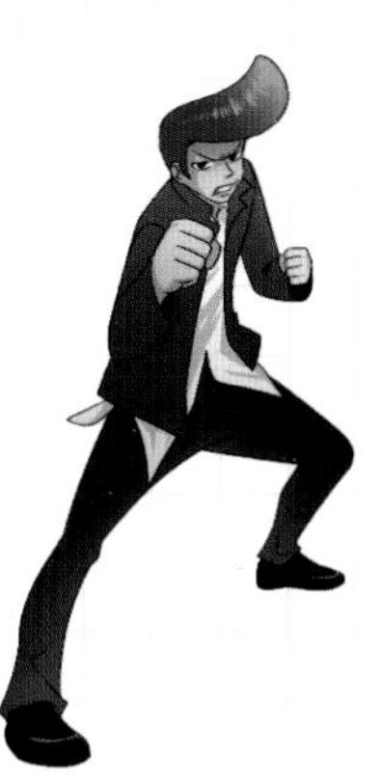

395

contemporary shonen villains

search criteria

male. standing. hat. smiling. chewing.

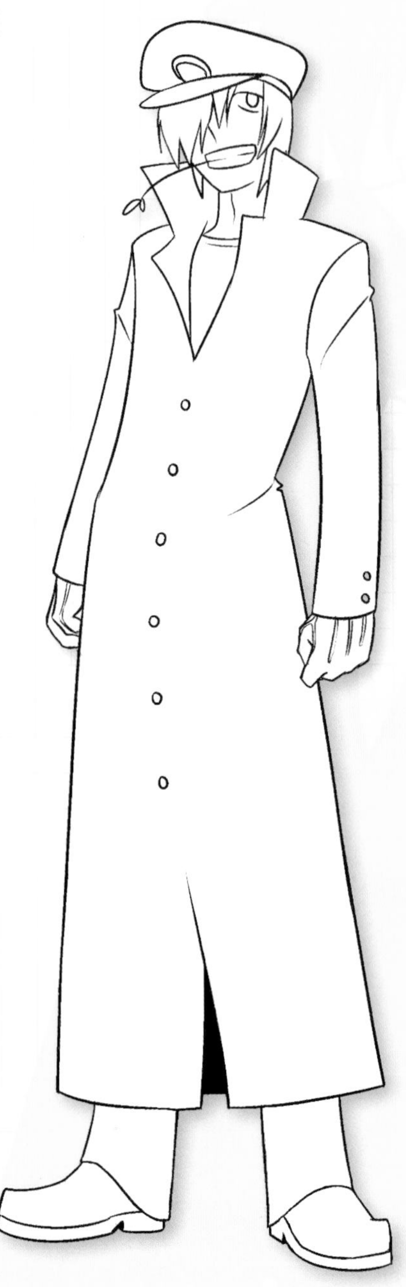

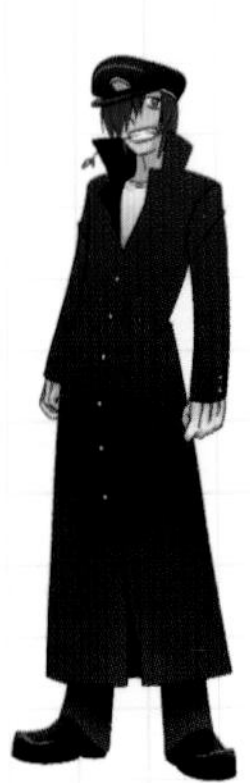

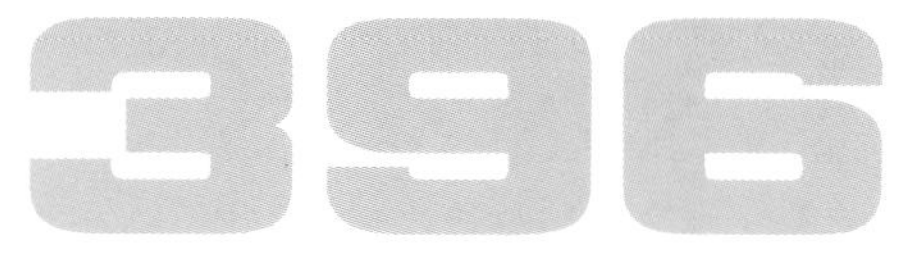

contemporary shonen villains

search criteria

male. standing. side. glasses. book. captain.

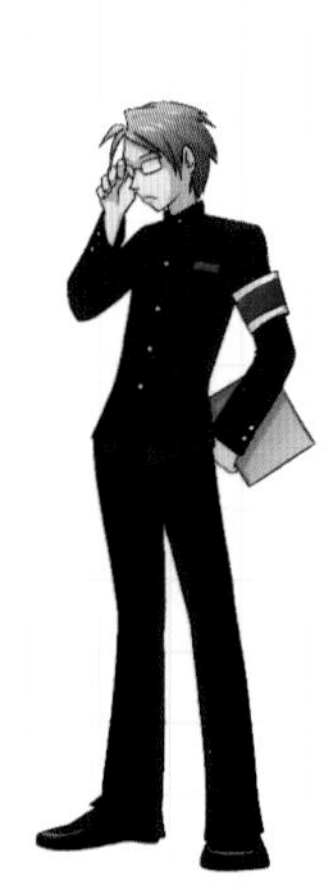

397

contemporary shonen villains

search criteria

male. standing. piercings. weapon. bat. gangster.

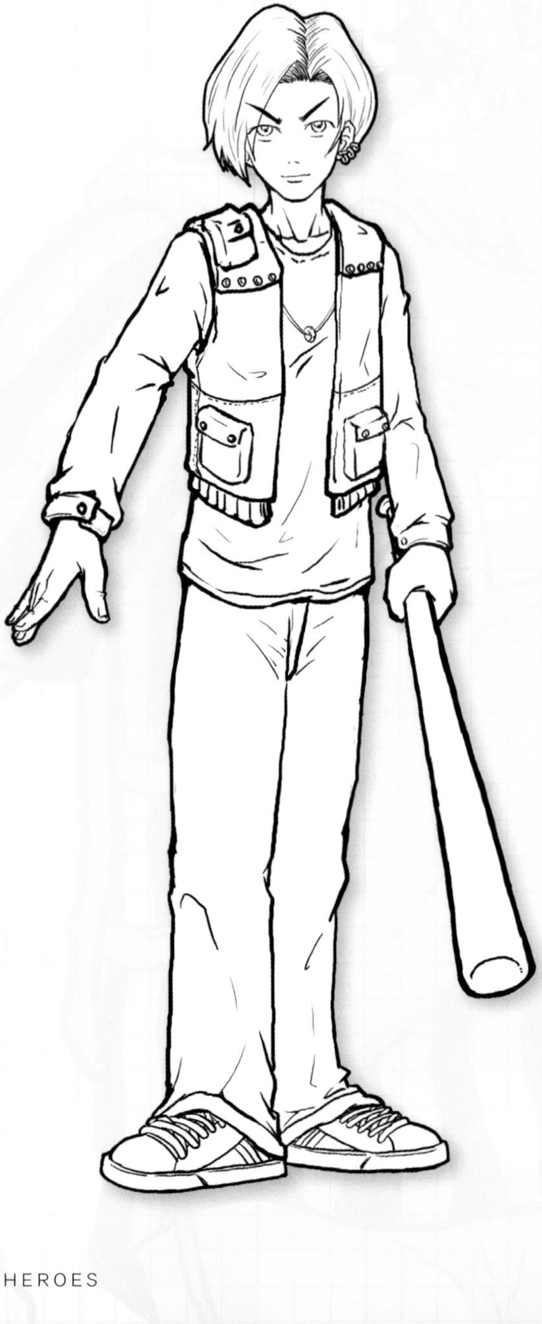

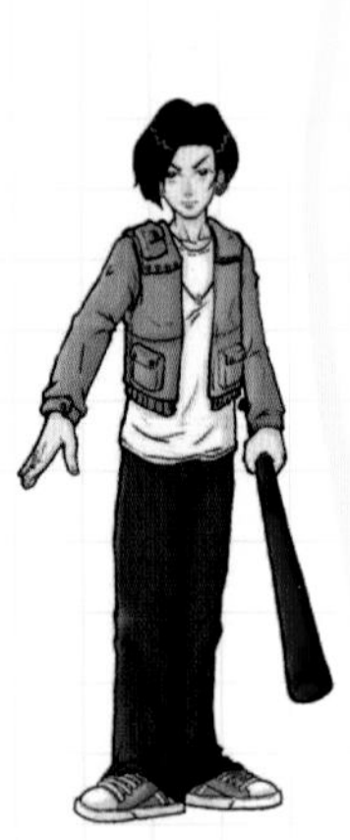

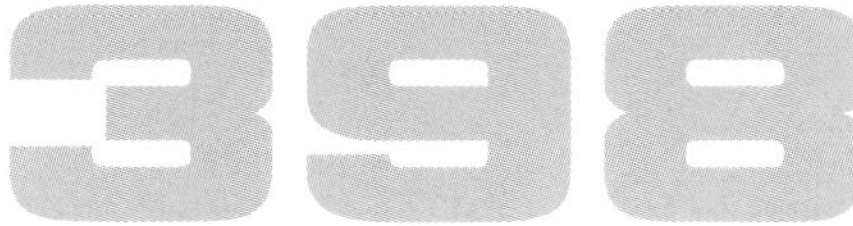

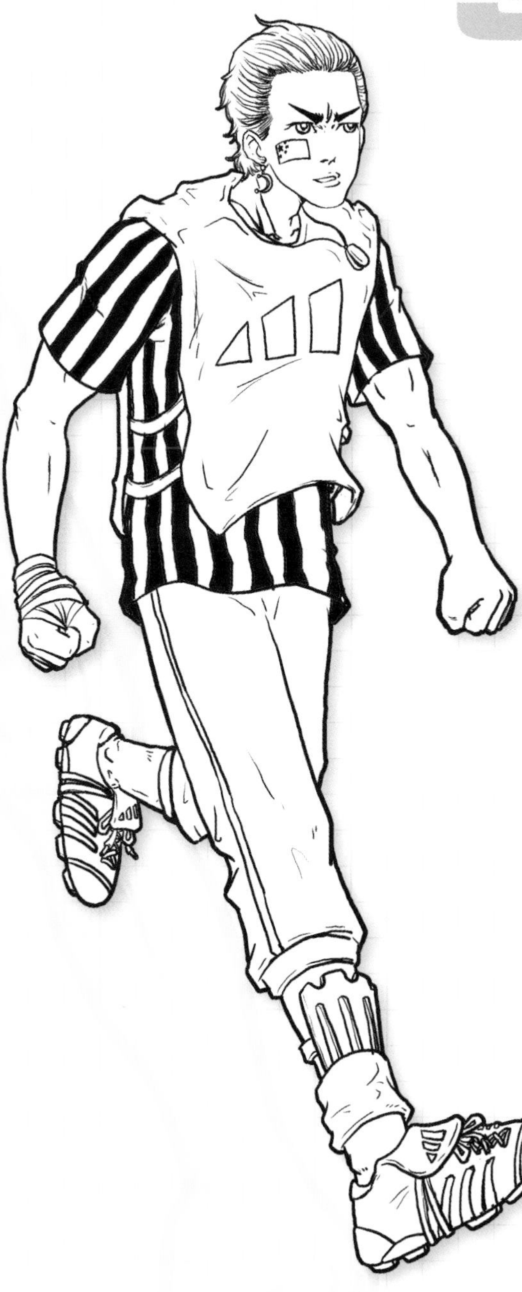

contemporary shonen villains

search criteria

male. running. side. bandages. sport. stripes.

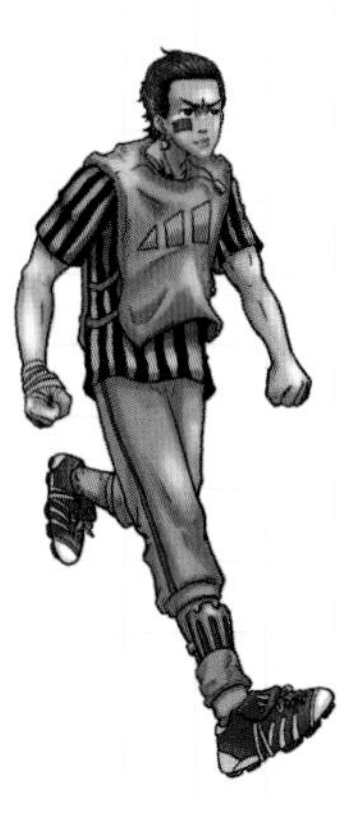

399

contemporary shonen villains

search criteria

male. sitting. hat. smoking. cigarette. gangster. piercing.

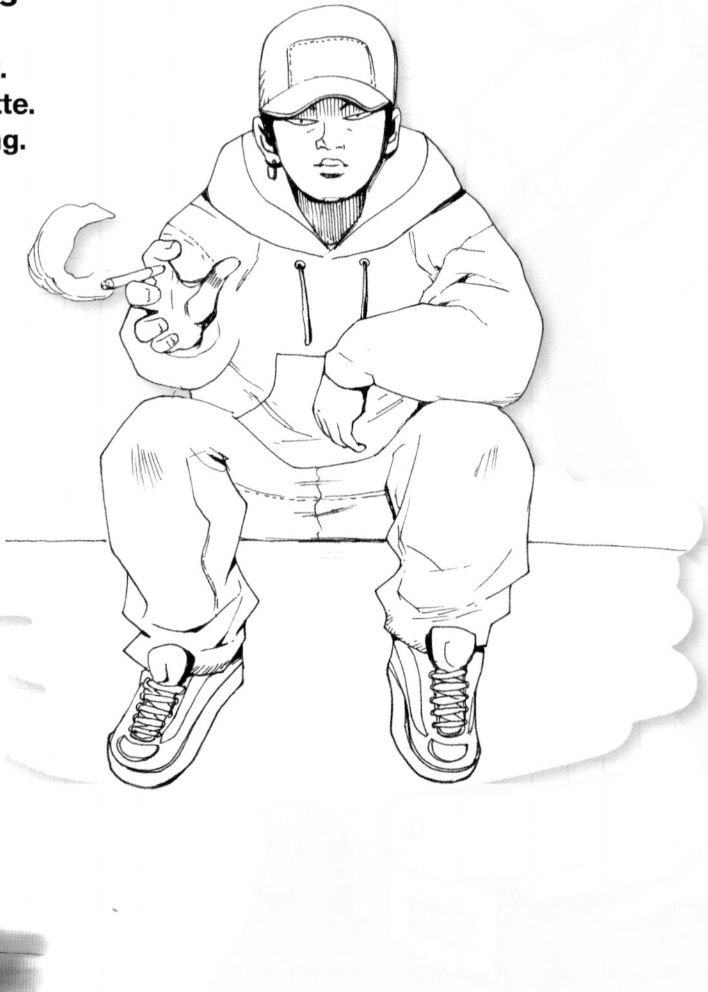

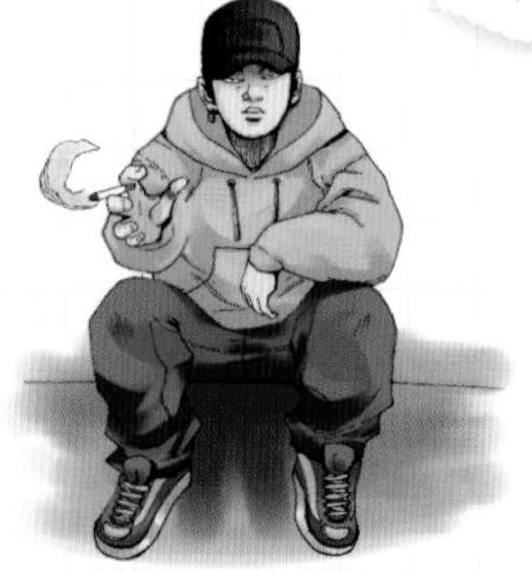

400

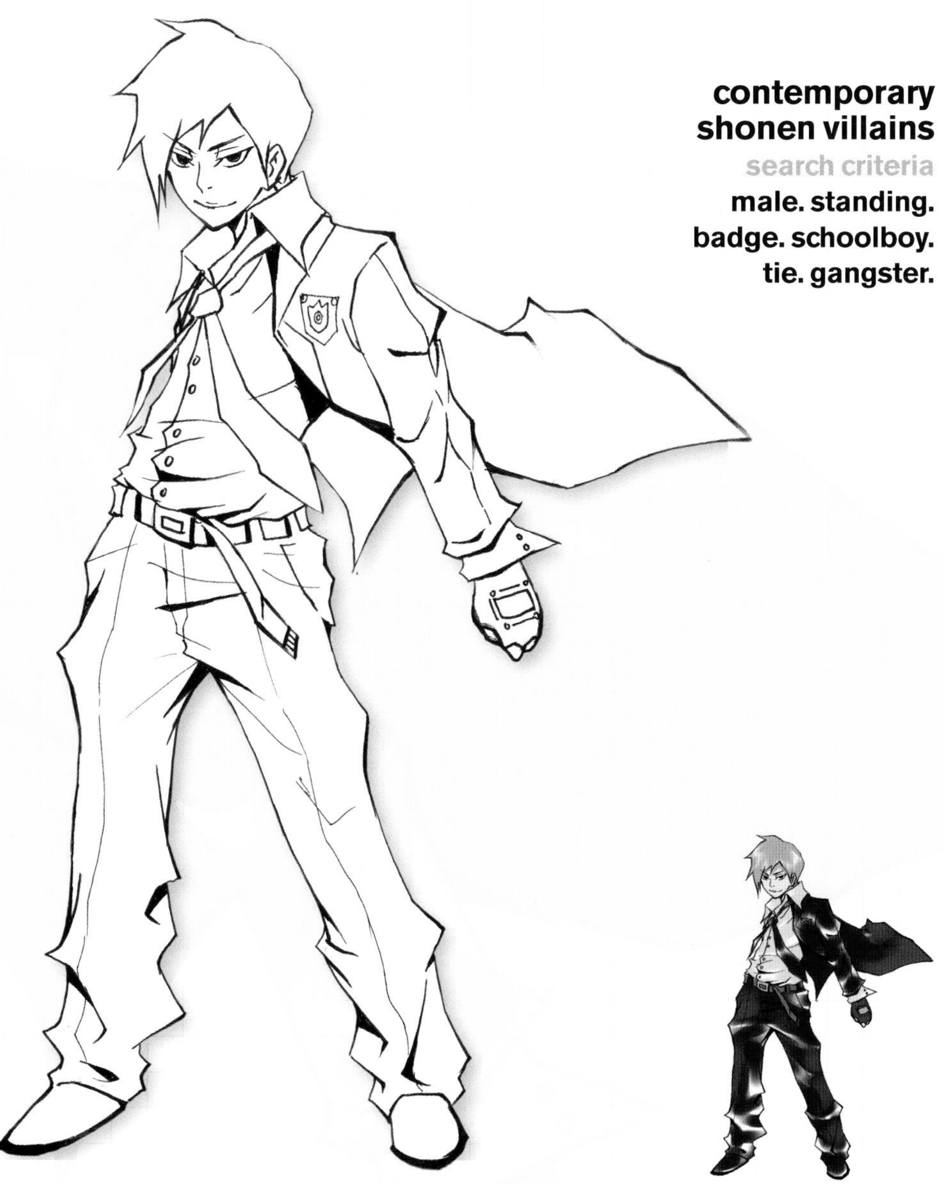

contemporary shonen villains

search criteria

male. standing. badge. schoolboy. tie. gangster.

401

contemporary shonen villains

search criteria

male. standing. side. ponytail. horse. gangster. biker.

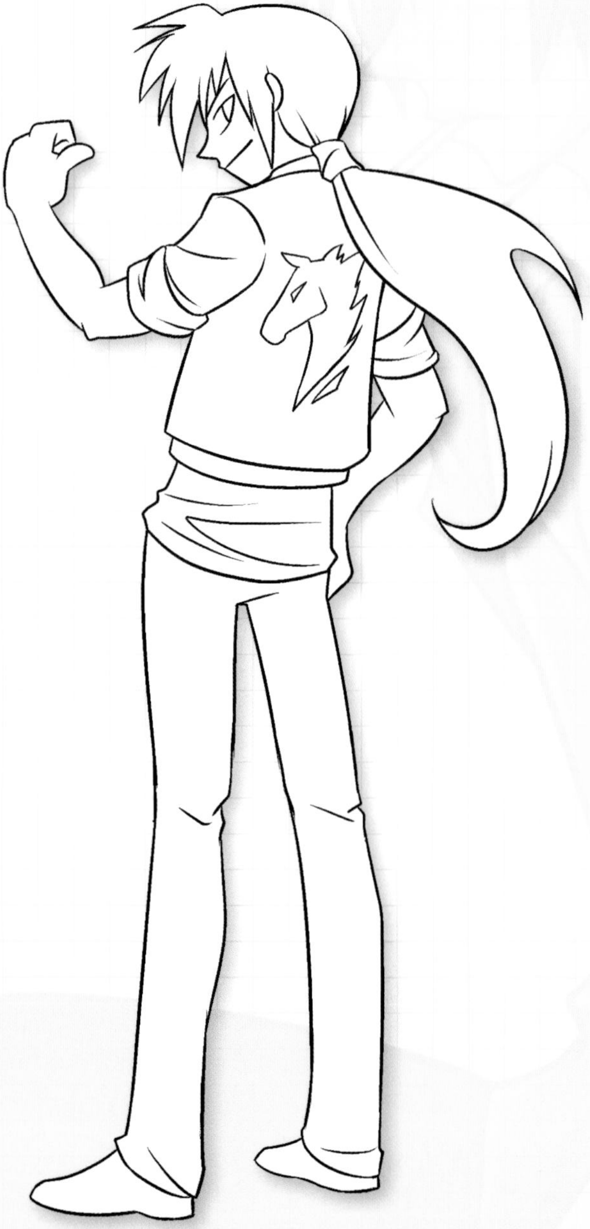

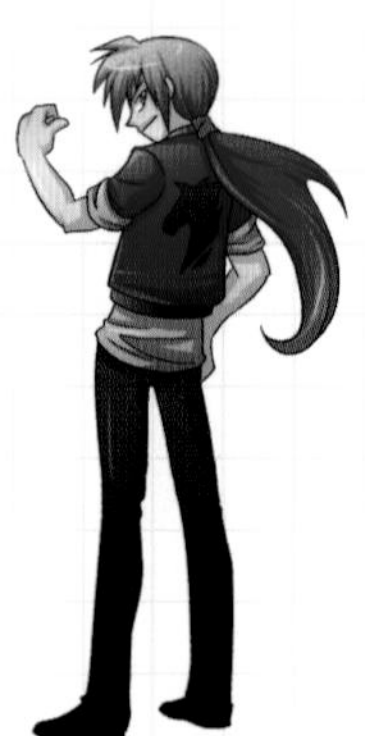

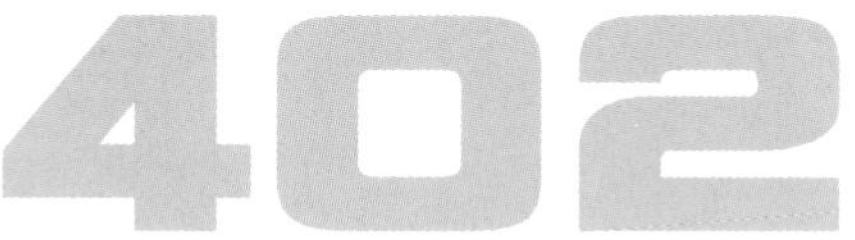

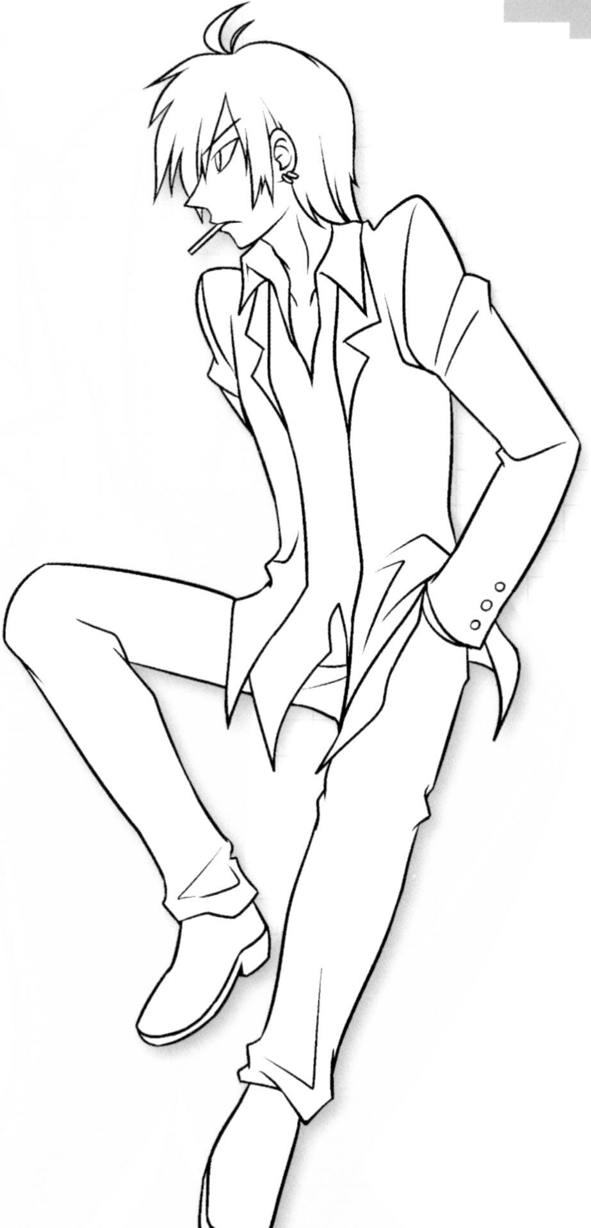

contemporary shonen villains

search criteria

male. sitting. smoking. cigarette. piercing. gangster.

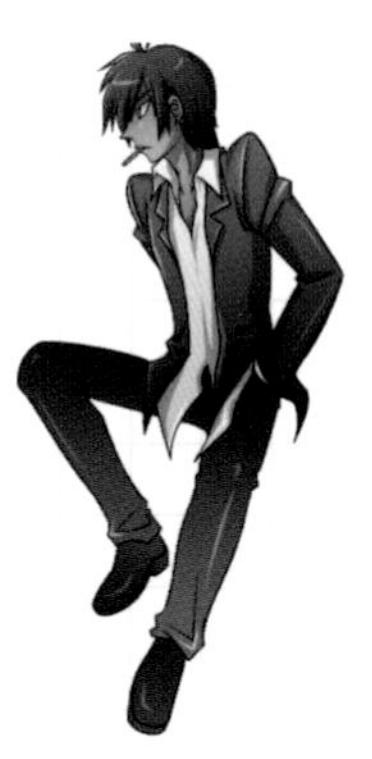

403

contemporary shonen villains

search criteria

male. standing. angry. necklace.

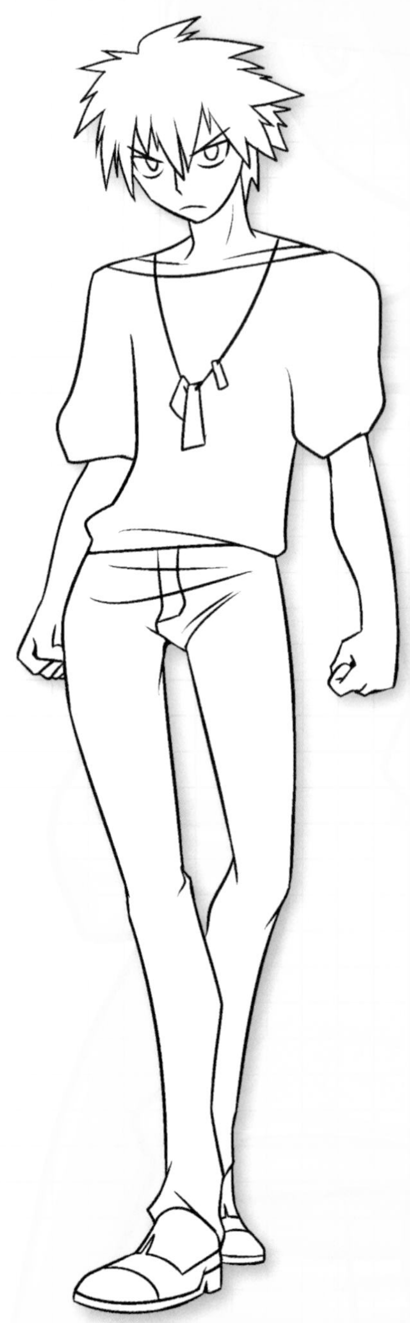

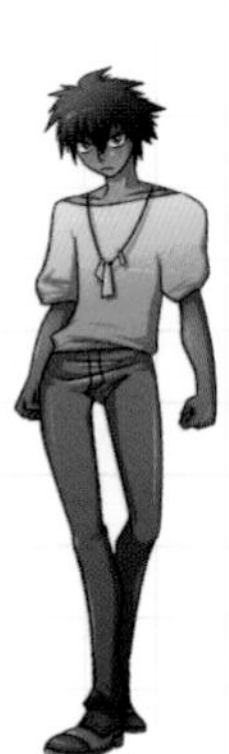

404

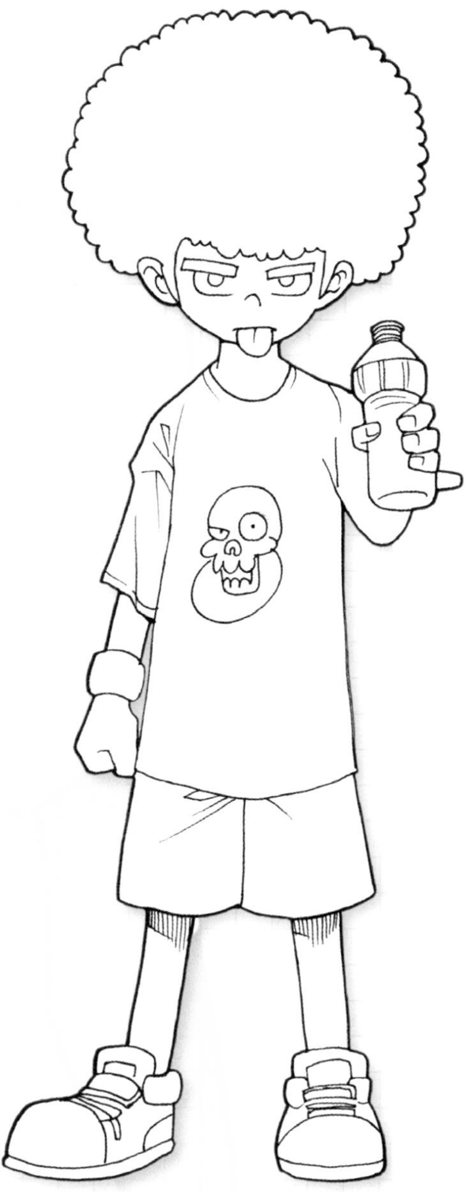

contemporary shonen villains

search criteria

male. standing. skull. prankster. goofy. bottle.

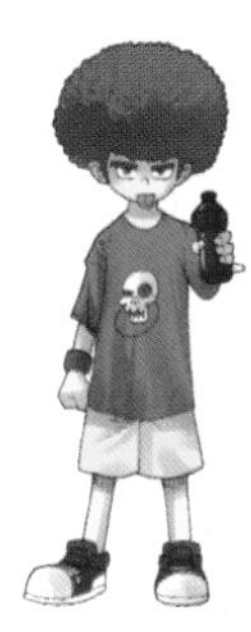

405

contemporary shonen heroes

search criteria

male. standing. side. weapon. sword.

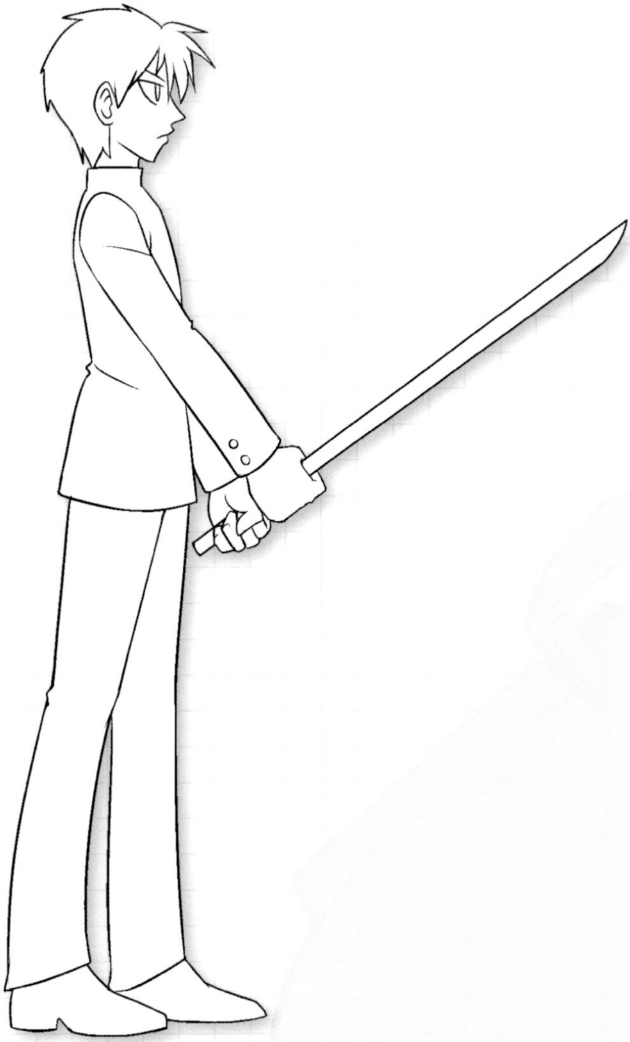

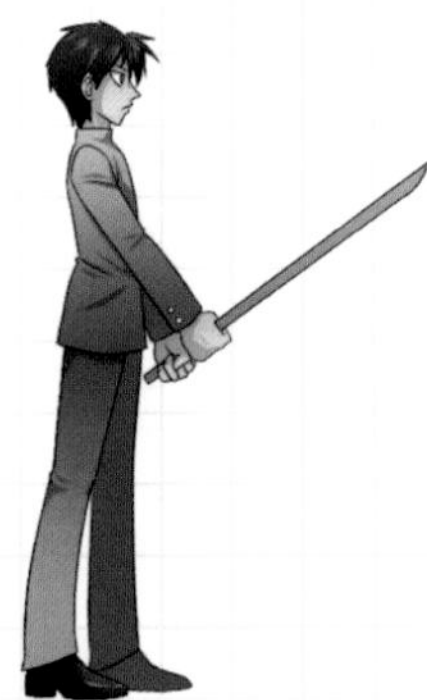

406

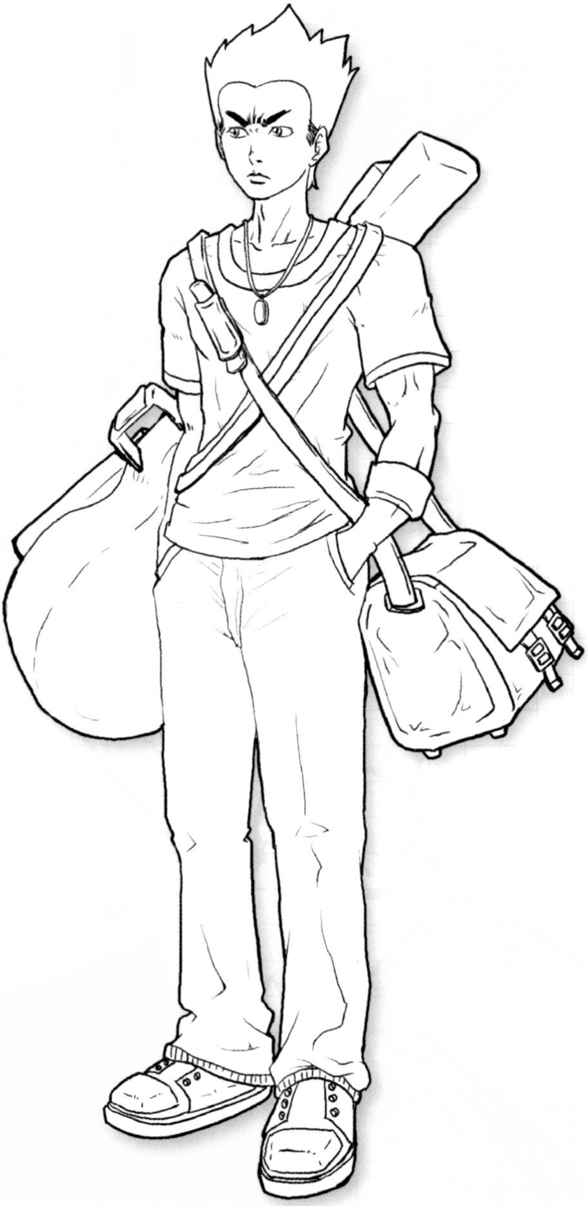

contemporary shonen heroes

search criteria

male. standing. necklace. bags. guitar. music.

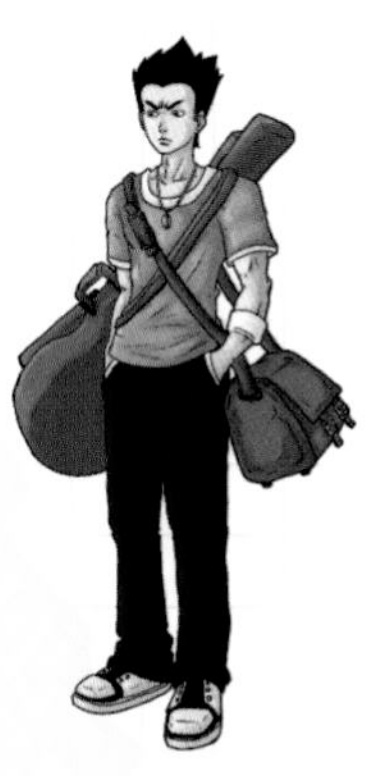

407

contemporary shonen heroes

search criteria

male. standing. side. tie. bag. schoolboy.

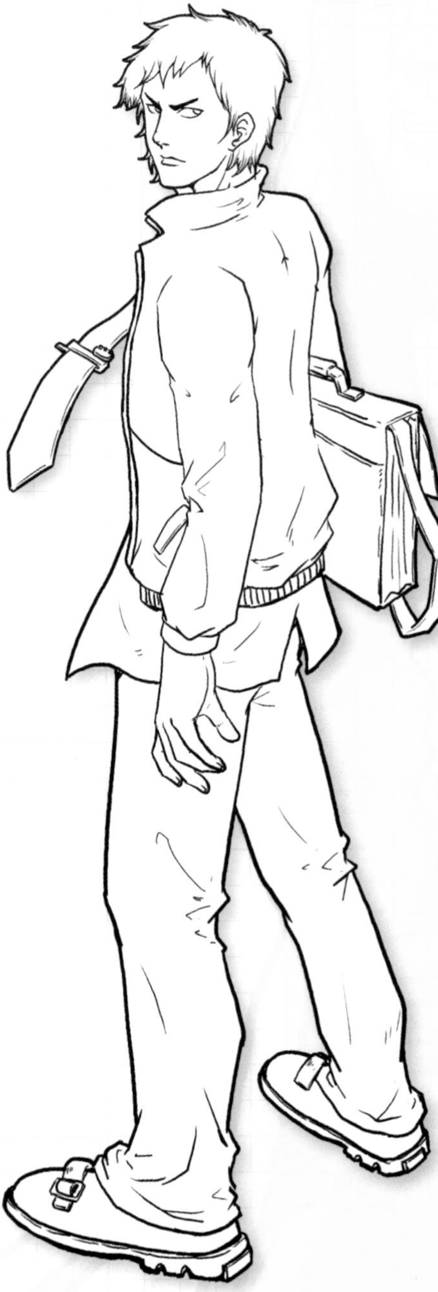

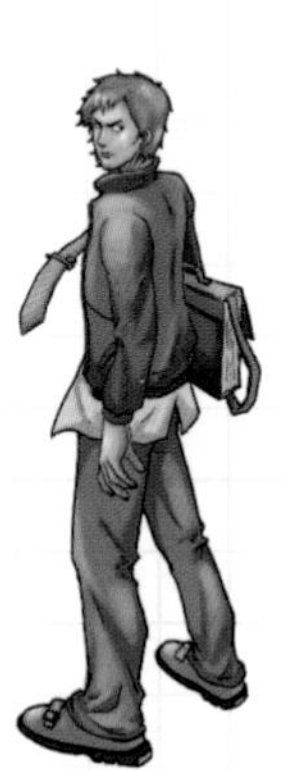

408

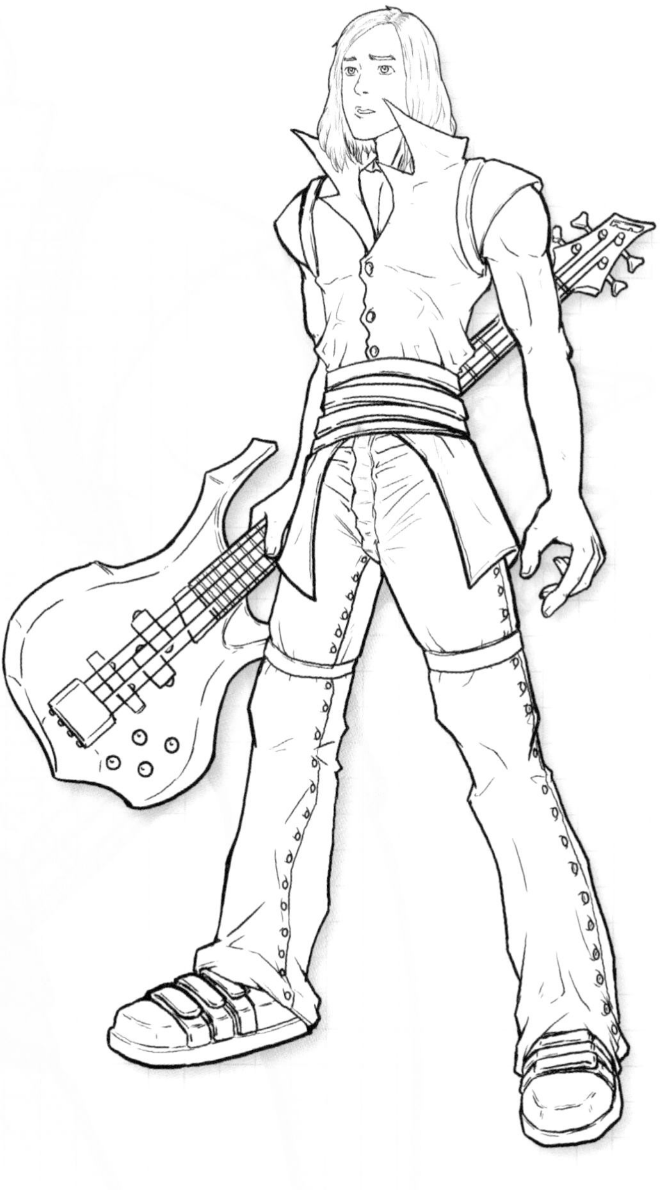

contemporary shonen heroes

search criteria

male. standing. side. guitar. music.

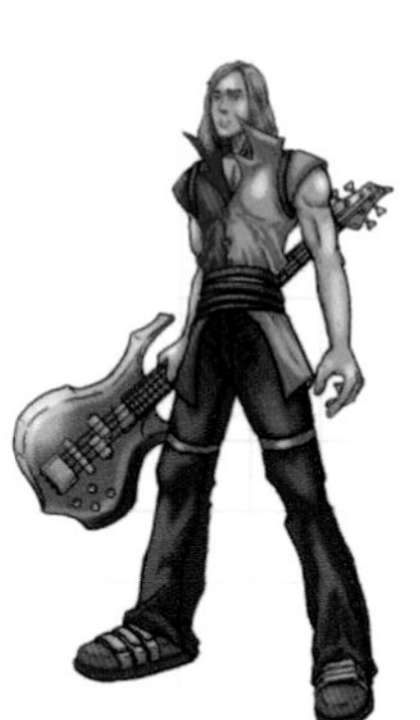

409

contemporary shonen heroes

search criteria

male. standing. smiling. chain. headband. watch.

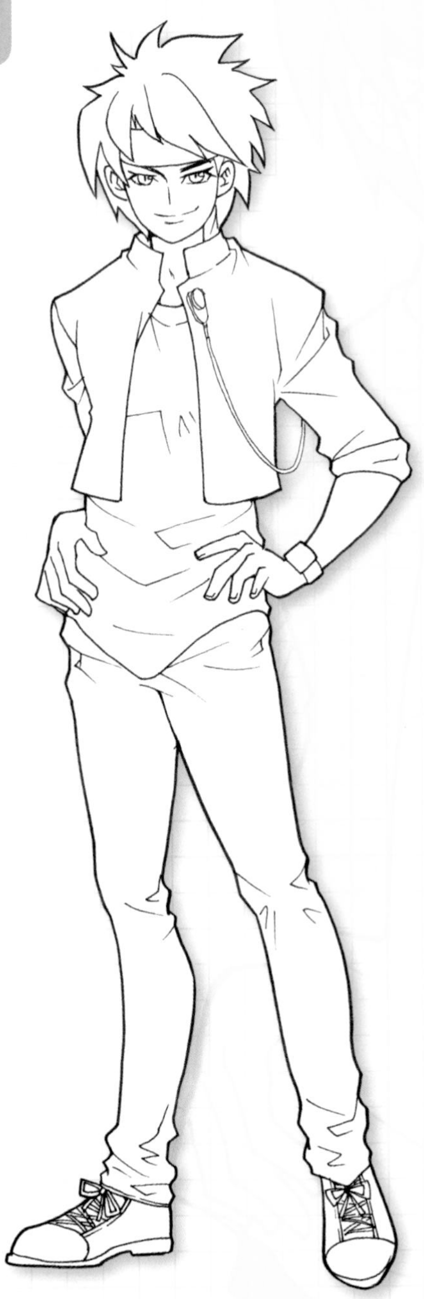

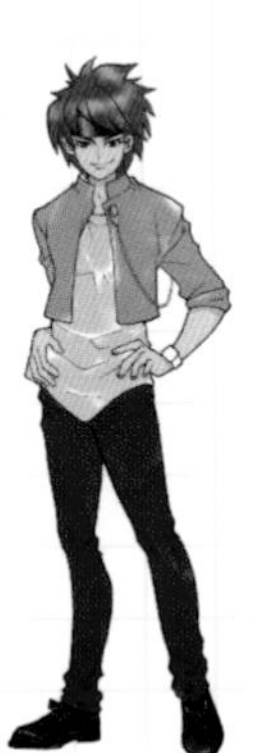

410

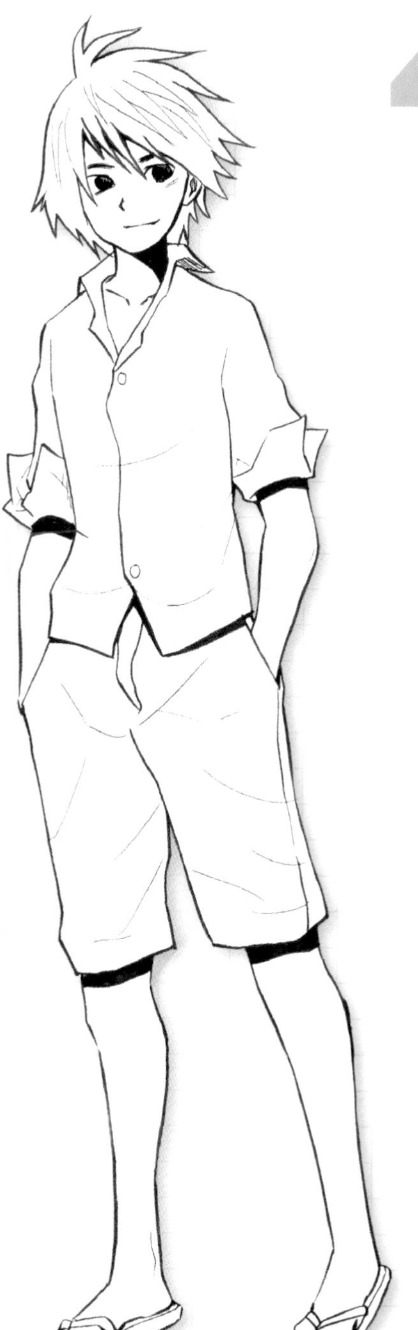

contemporary shonen heroes

search criteria

male. standing. smiling. surfer.

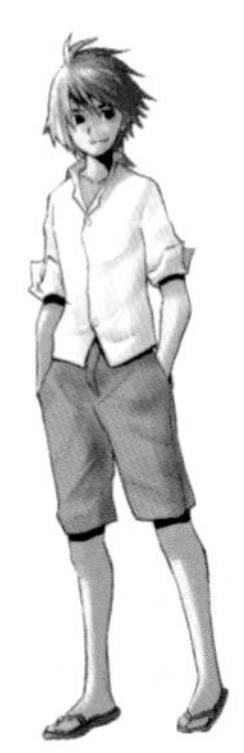

411

contemporary shonen heroes

search criteria

male. standing. fists. belts. biker. angry.

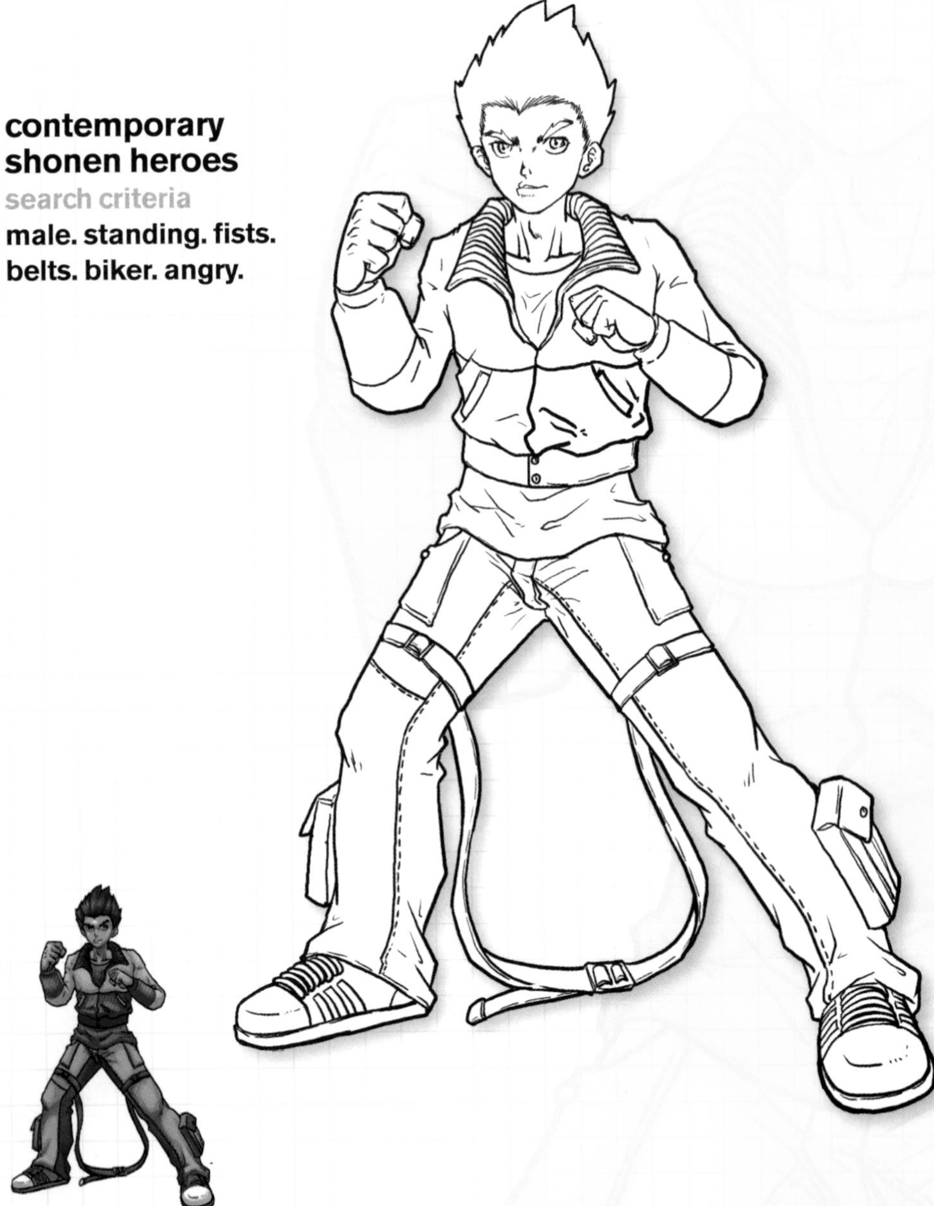

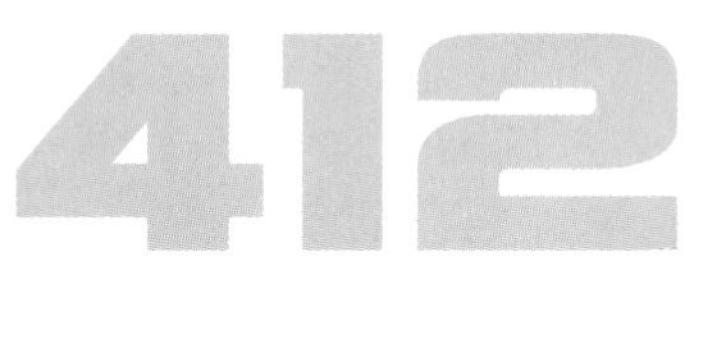

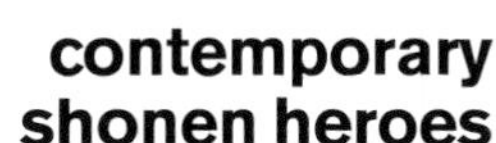

search criteria

male. standing. side. boy.

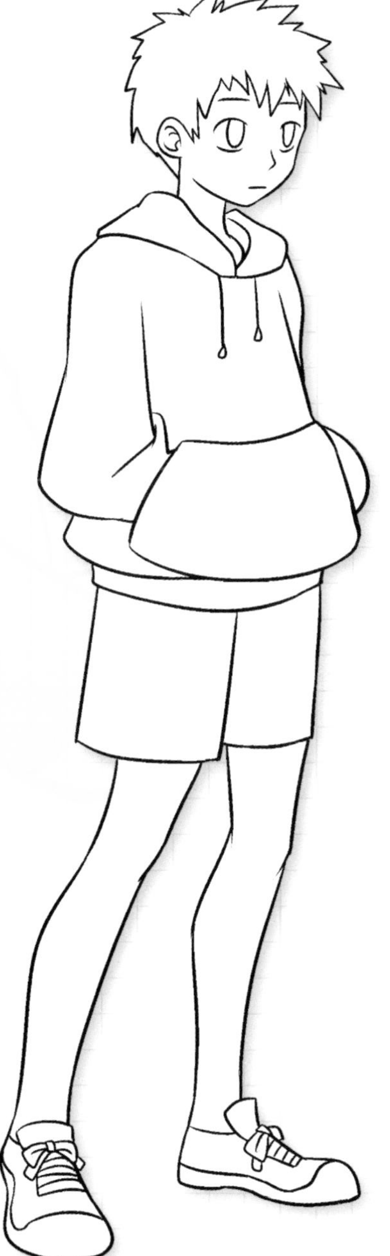

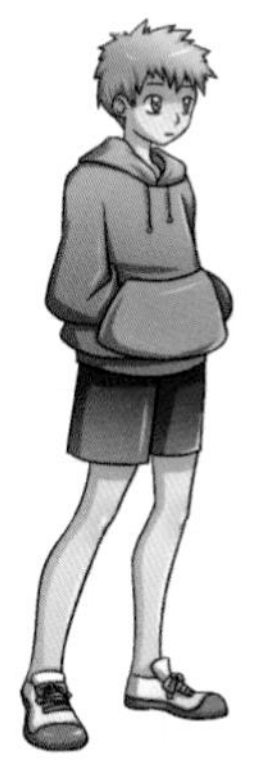

413

contemporary shonen heroes

search criteria

male. jump. running. shout. angry.

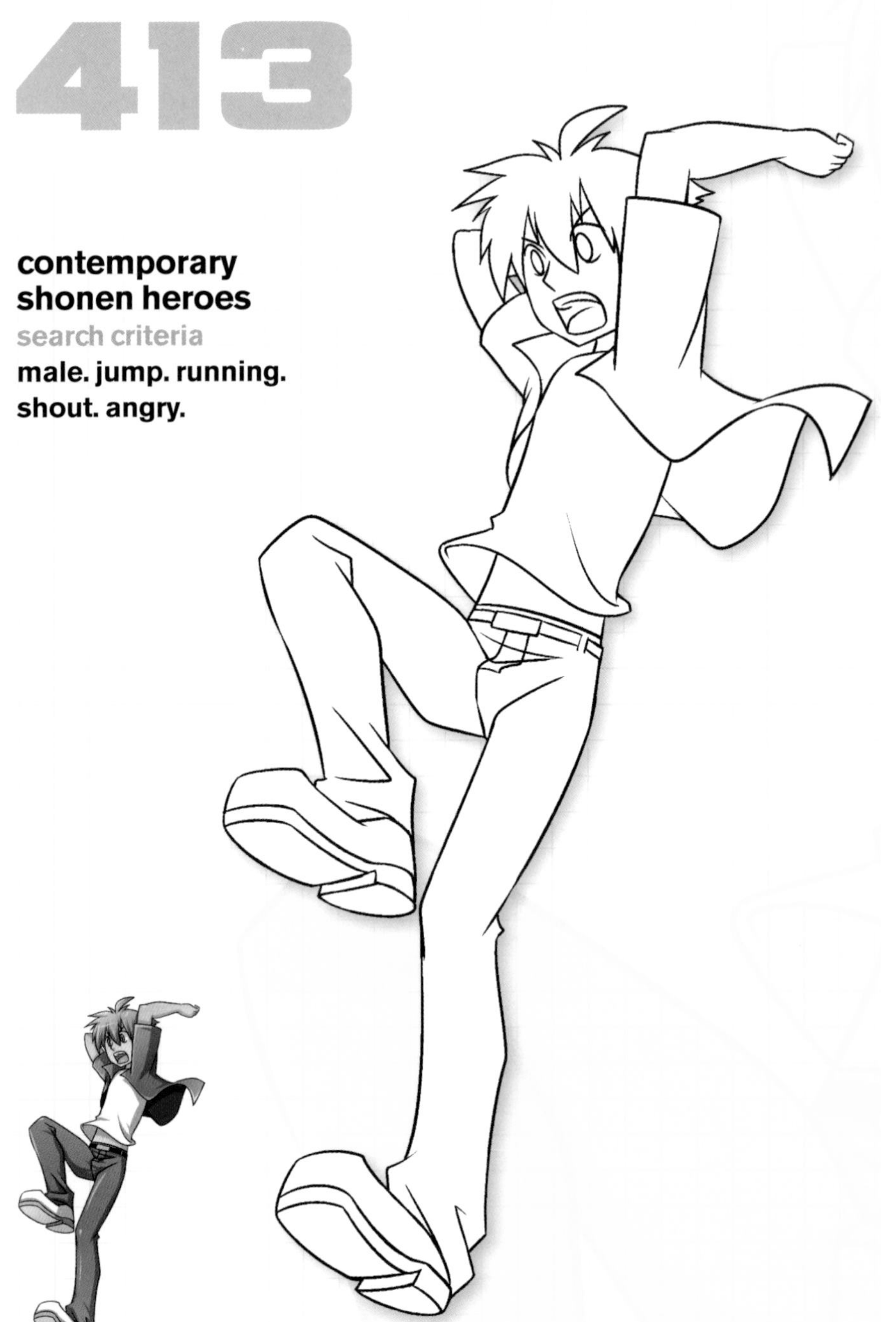

414

contemporary shonen heroes

search criteria

male. sitting. reading. book.

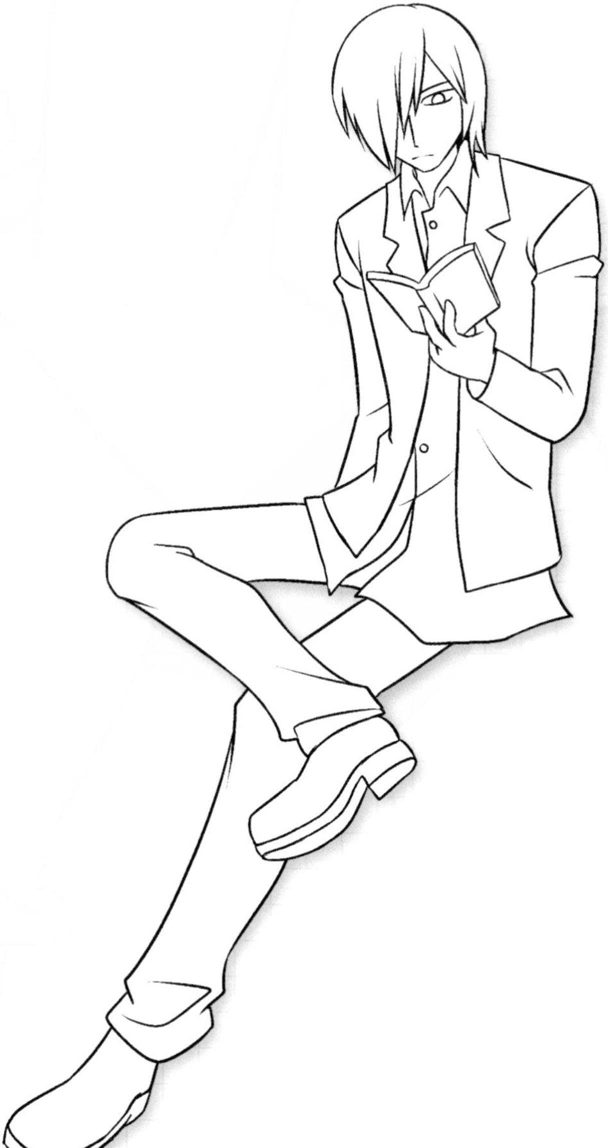

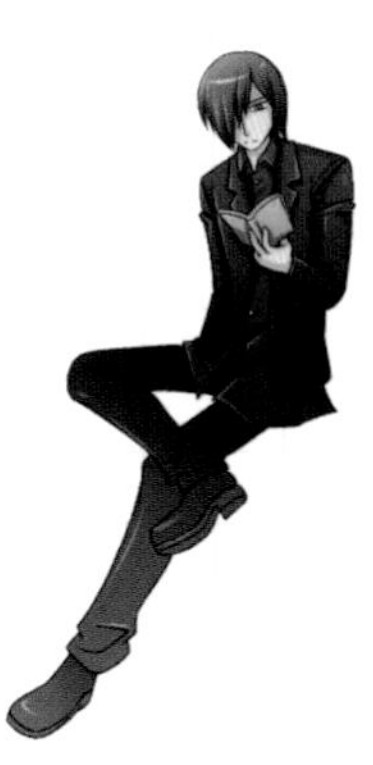

415

contemporary shonen heroes

search criteria

male. standing. leaning. side. bag. scratching. glasses.

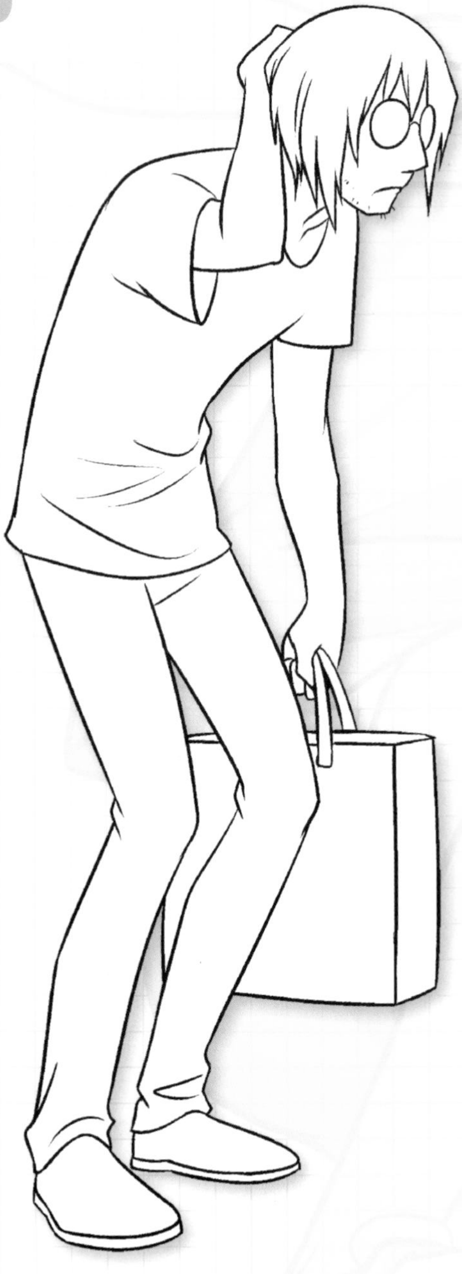

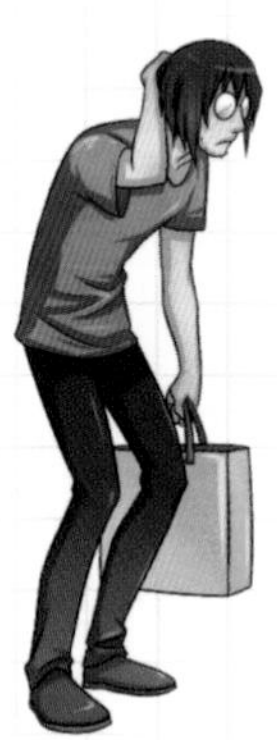

416

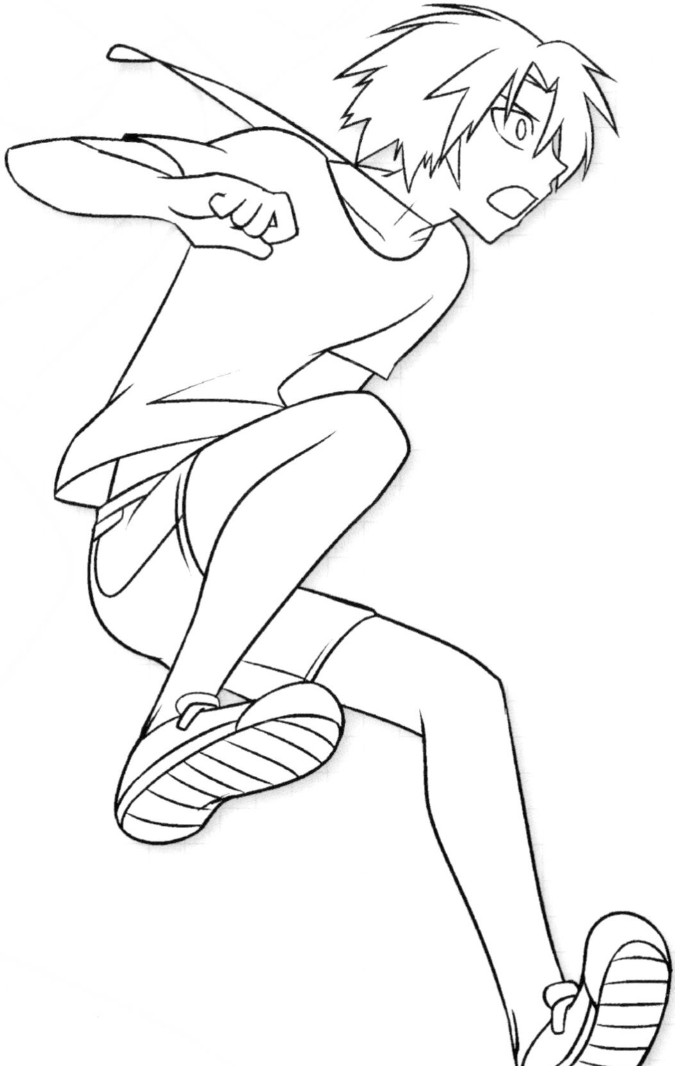

contemporary shonen heroes

search criteria

male. jump. pounce. shout.

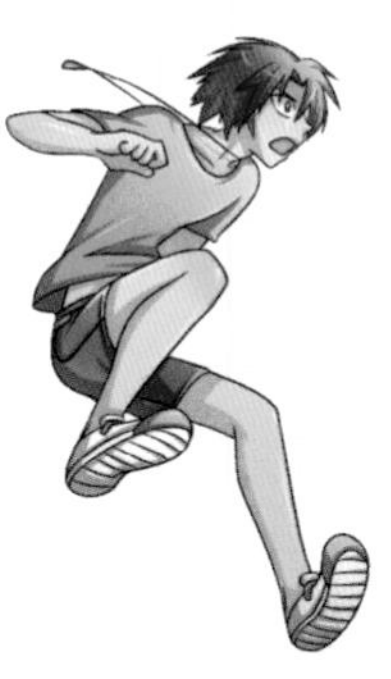

417

contemporary shonen heroes

search criteria

male. standing. side. fists. smiling.

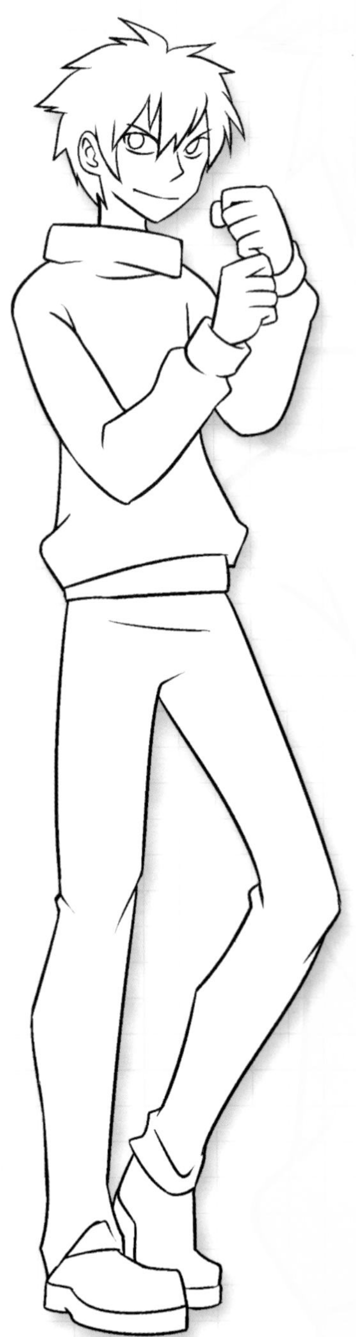

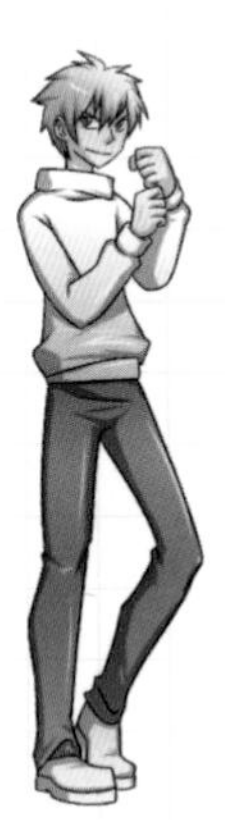

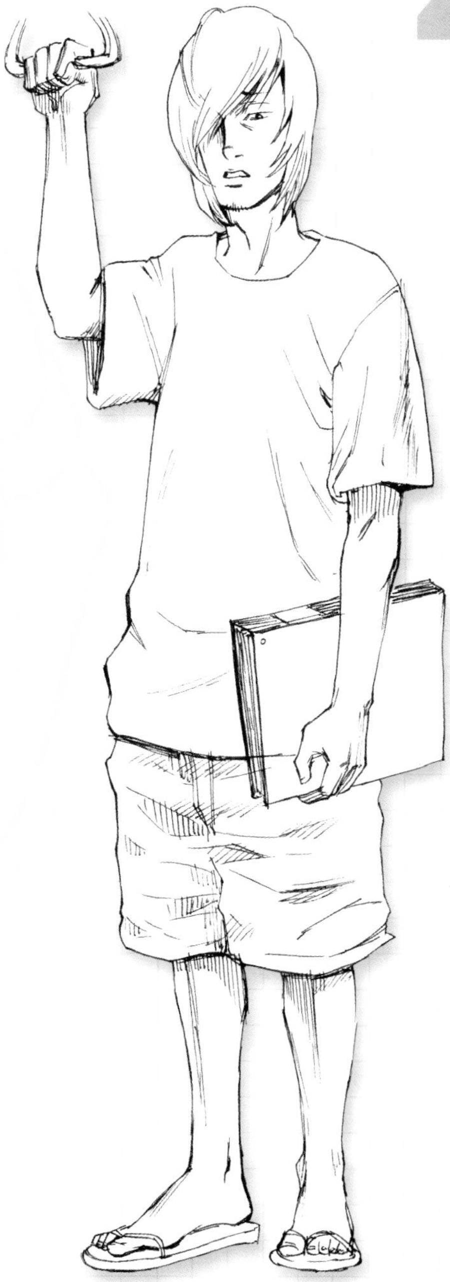

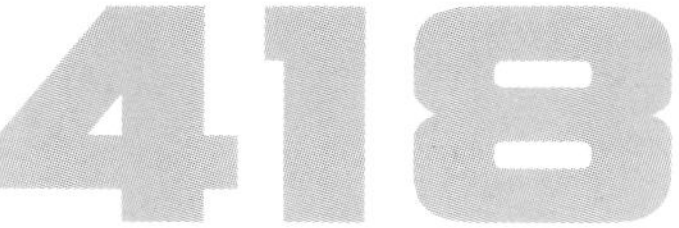

contemporary shonen heroes

search criteria

male. standing. folder. papers. schoolboy.

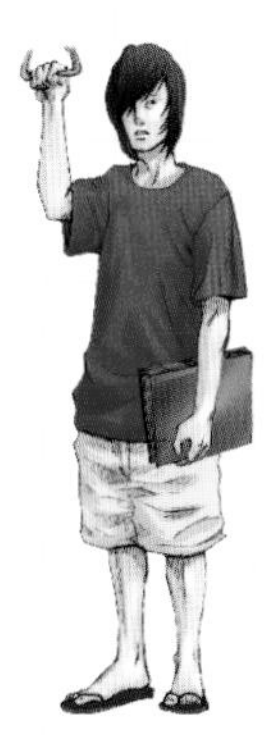

419

contemporary shonen heroes

search criteria

male. standing. pray. sad. tear.

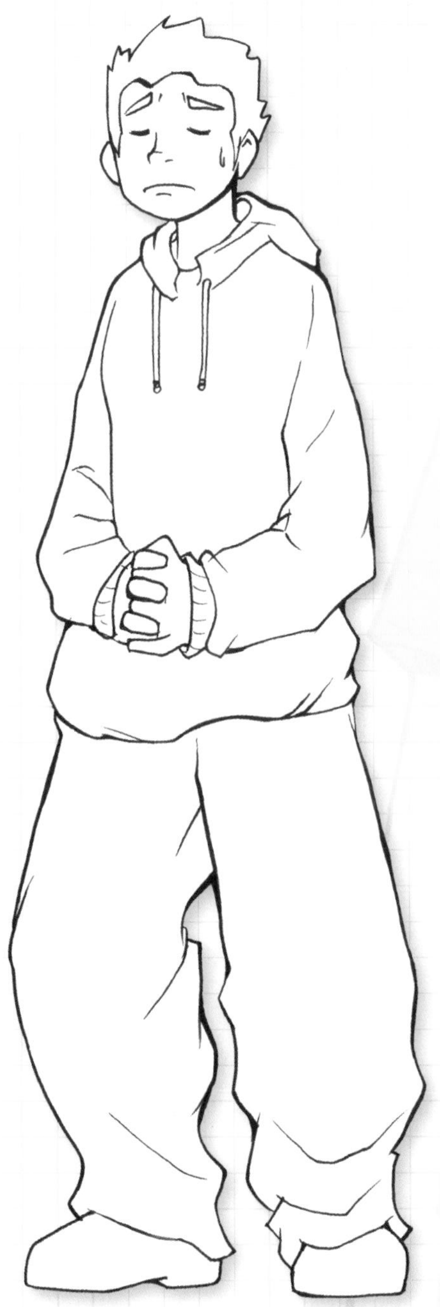

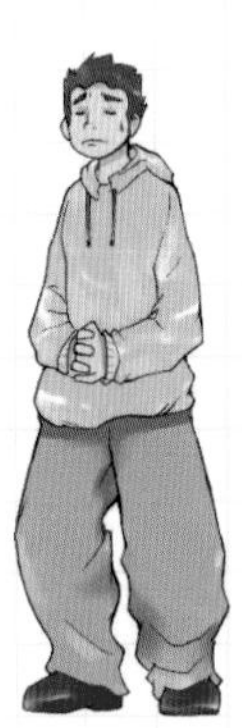

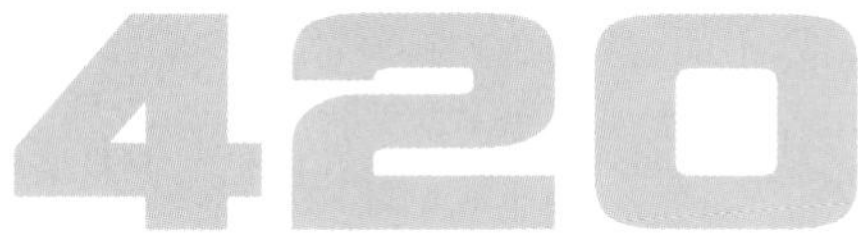

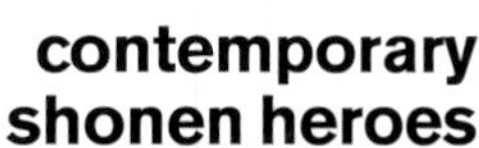

contemporary shonen heroes

search criteria

male. standing. headphones. music. glasses. smiling.

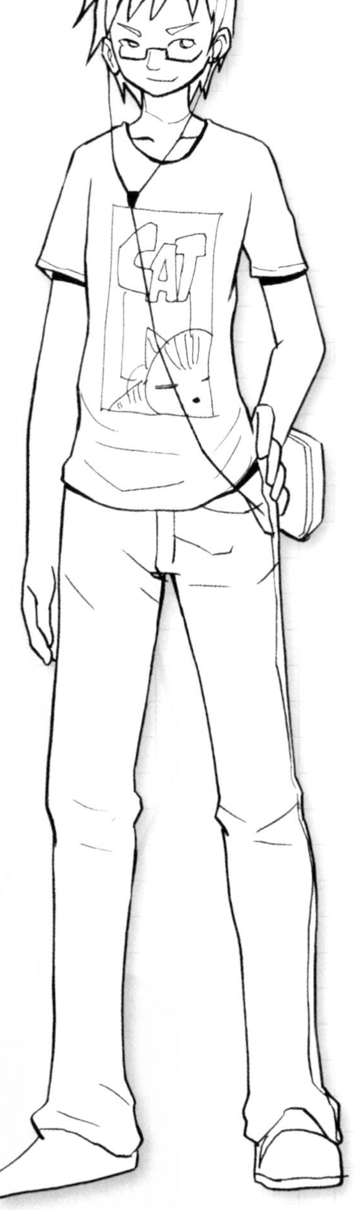

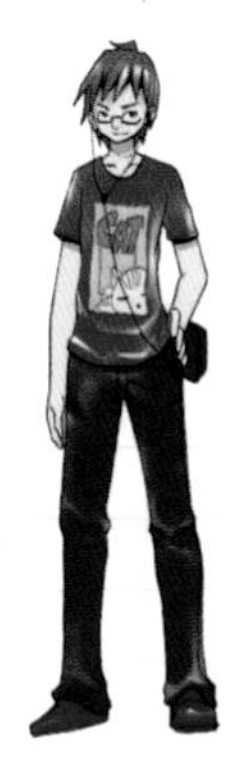

421

gangsters
search criteria
male. standing.
scar. muscle.
weapons. fists.

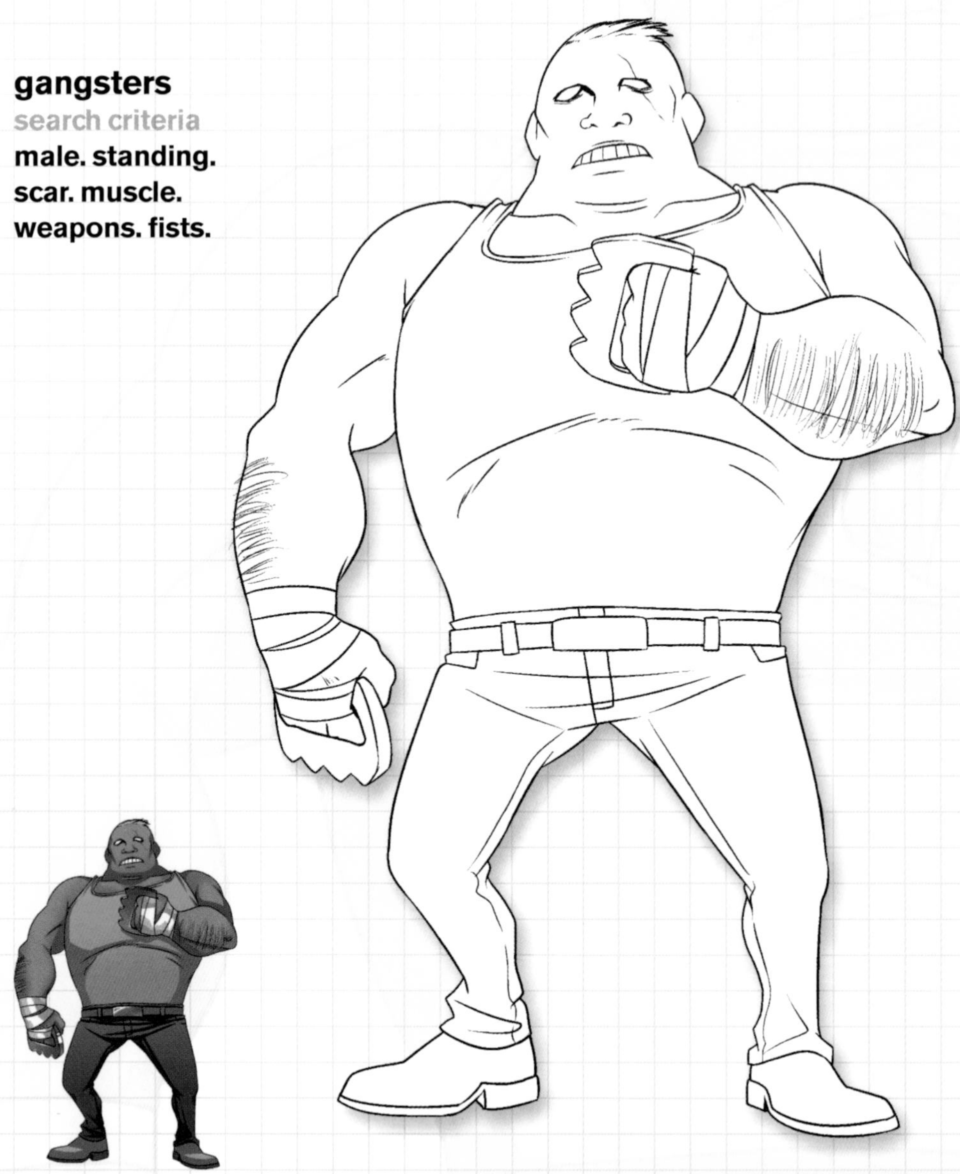

422

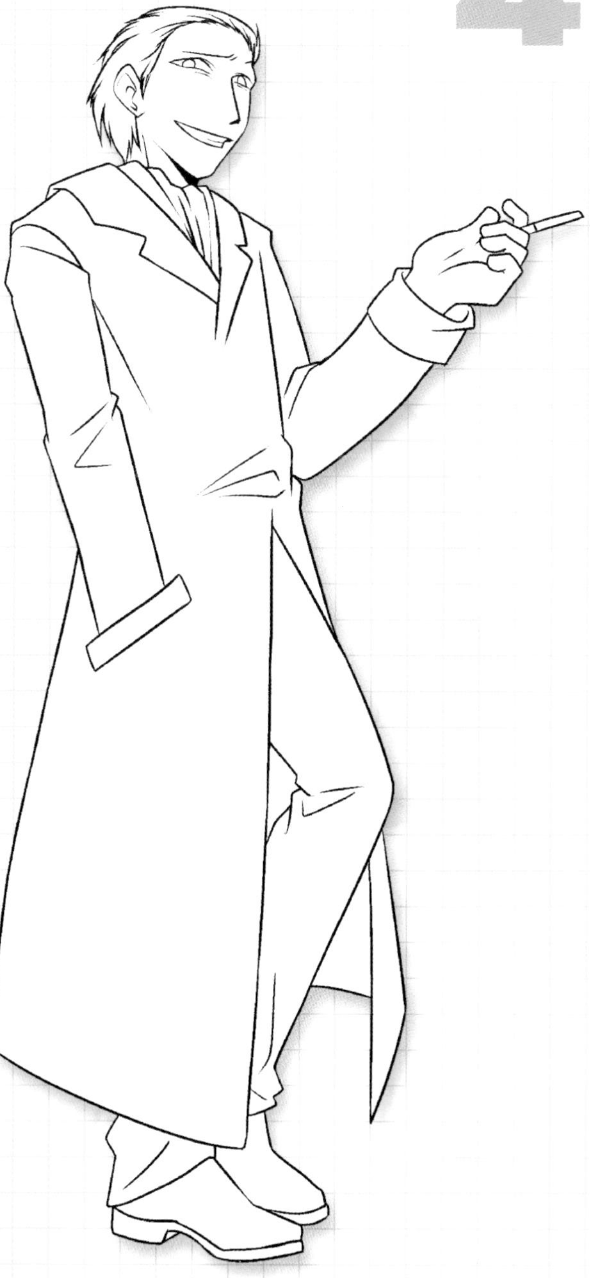

gangsters

search criteria

male. standing. side. smoking. cigarette. smiling.

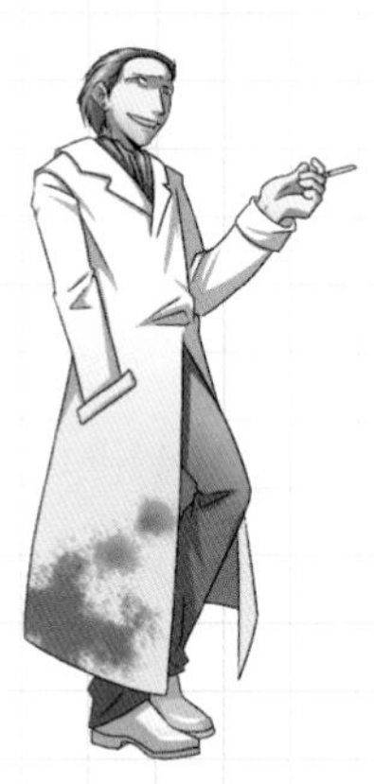

423

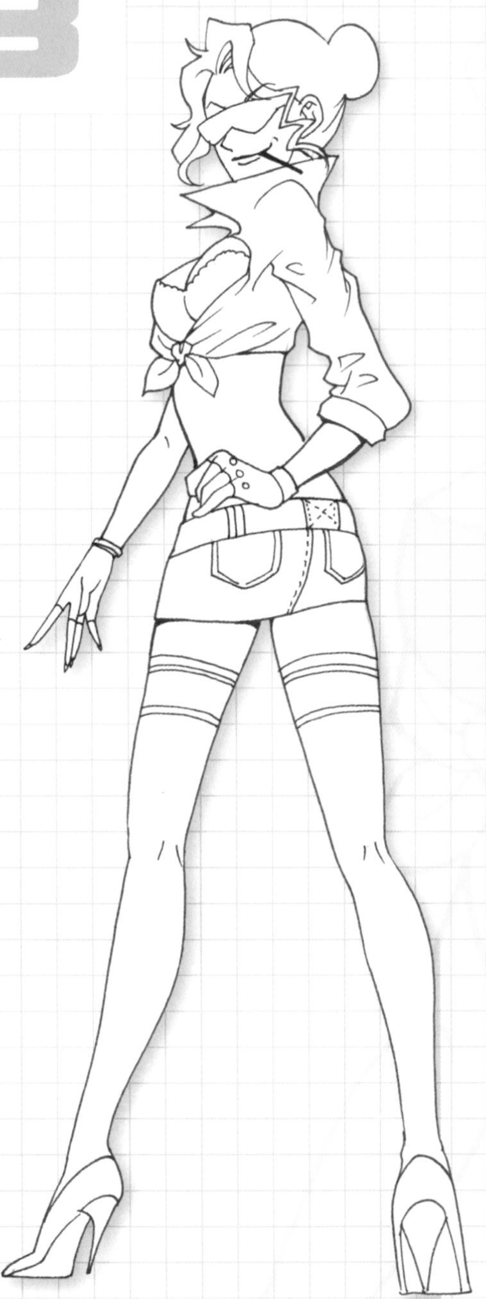

gangsters

search criteria

female. standing. side. chewing. smiling. sunglasses.

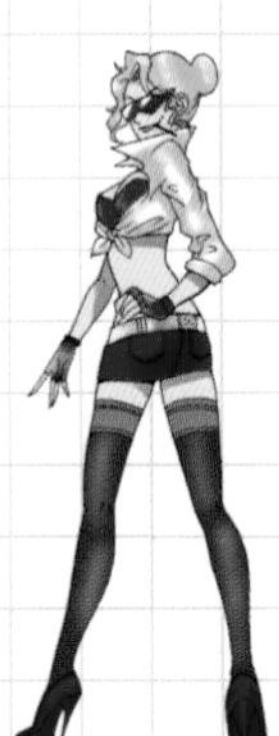

424

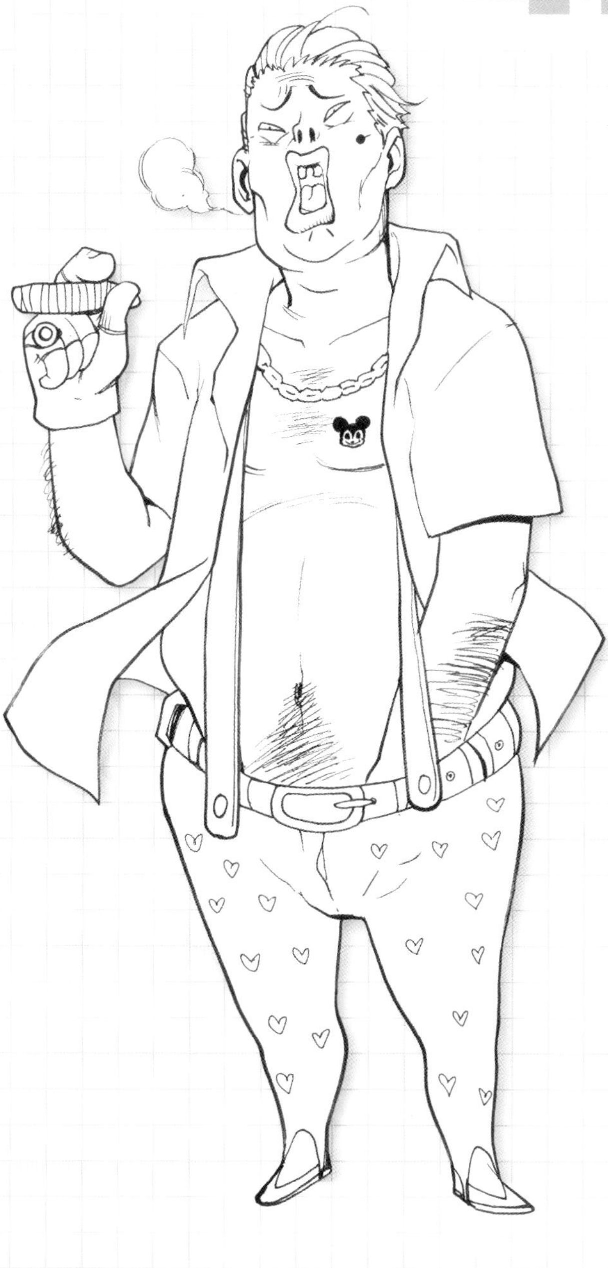

gangsters

search criteria

male. standing. smoking. cigar. tattoo. hearts.

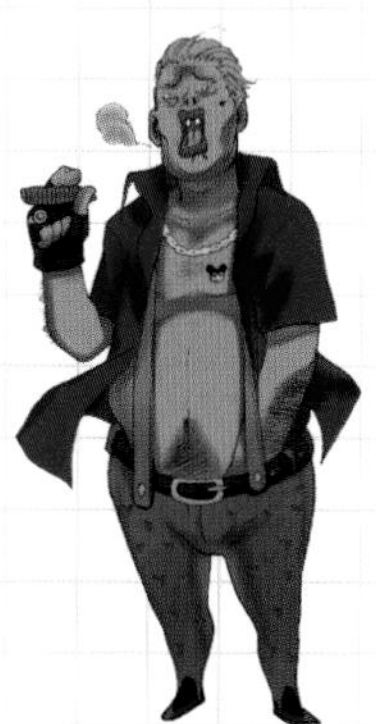

425

gangsters

search criteria

female. standing. angry. rock. goofy.

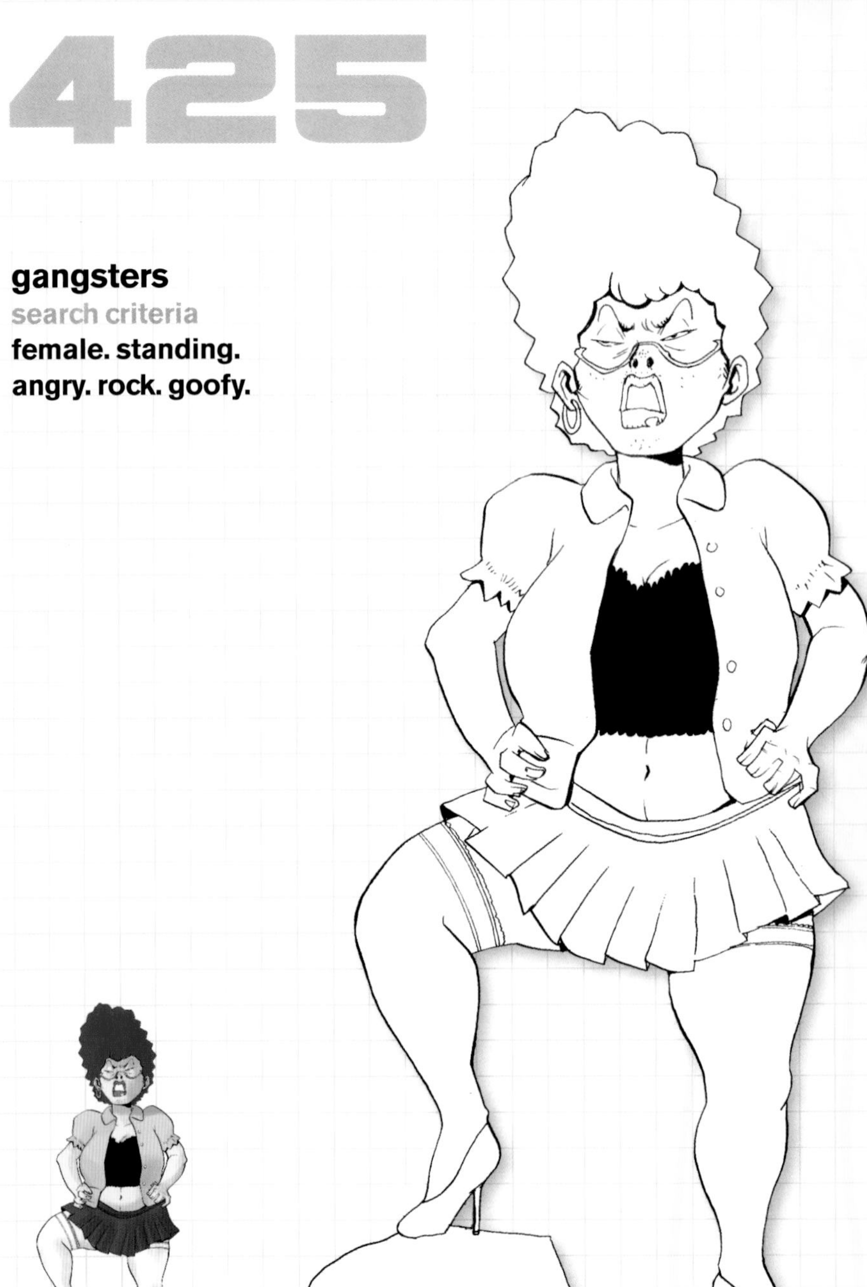

426

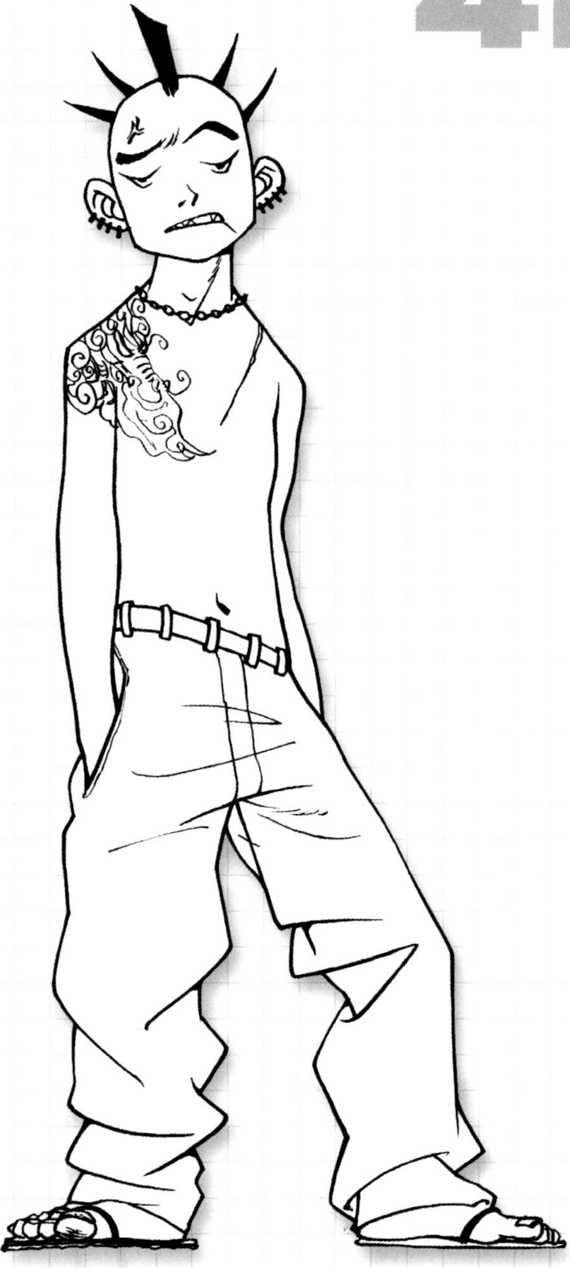

gangsters

search criteria

male. standing. piercings. punk. tattoo. chain.

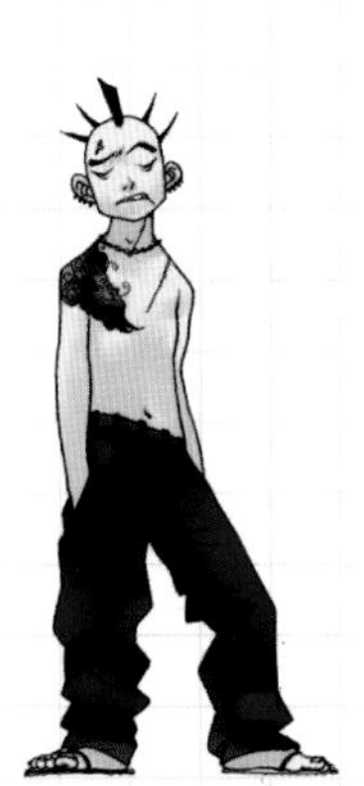

427

gangsters

search criteria

female. standing. punk. angry.

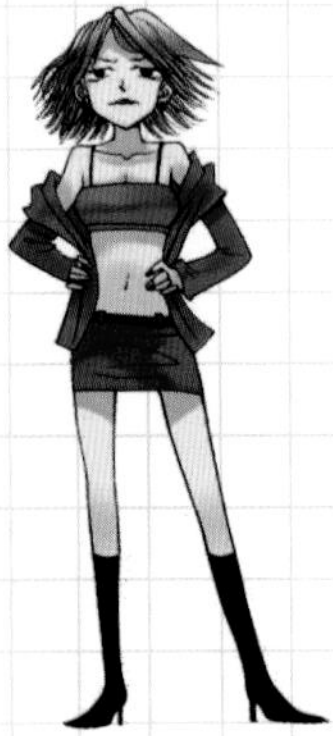

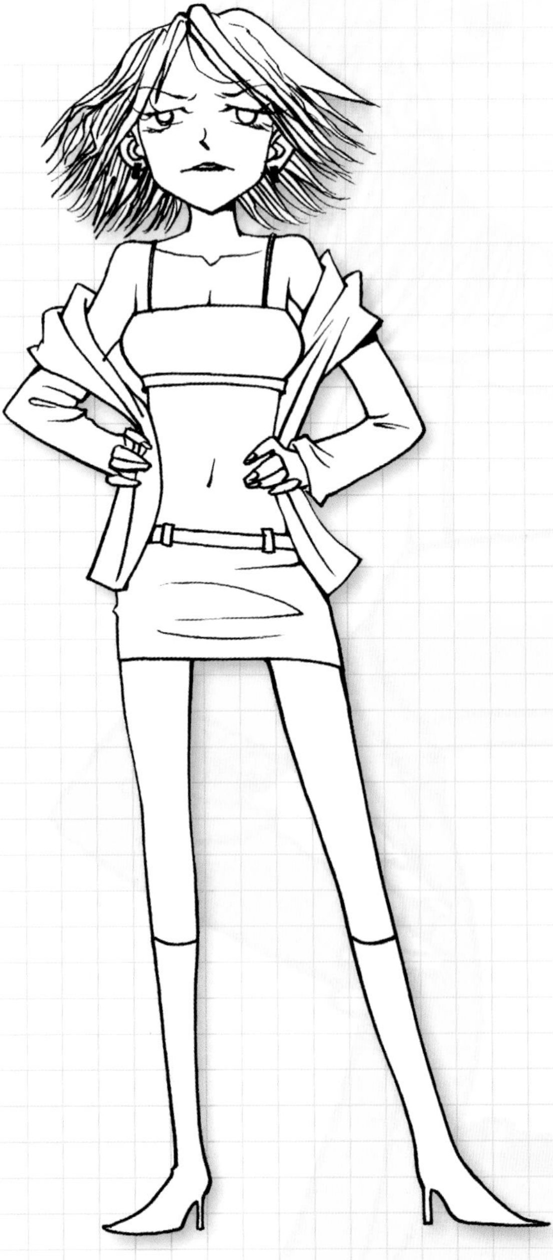

428

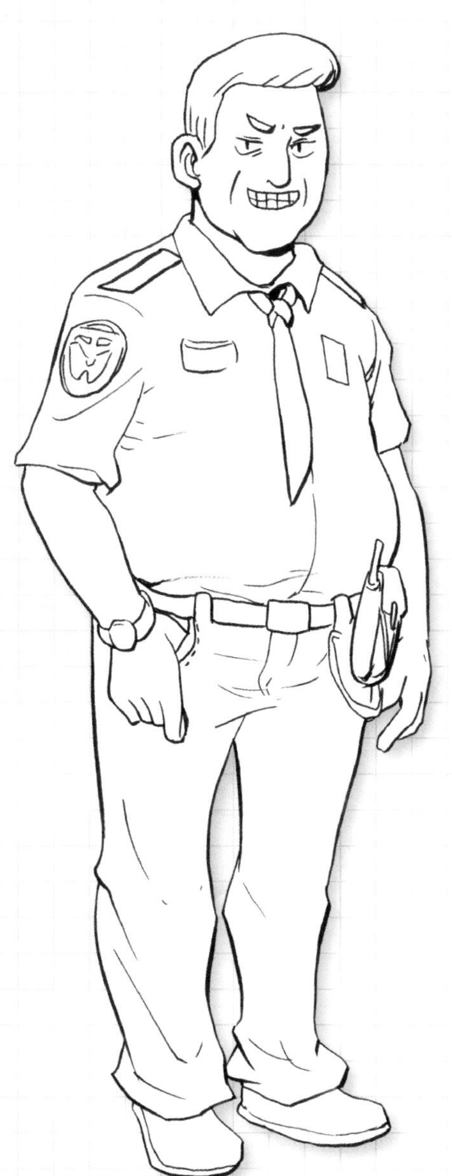

gangsters

search criteria

male. standing. badge. police. sleazy. tie. radio.

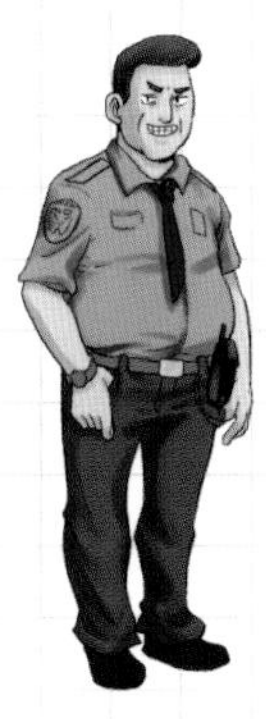

429

gangsters

search criteria

male. standing. punk. headscarf. bandages. scar.

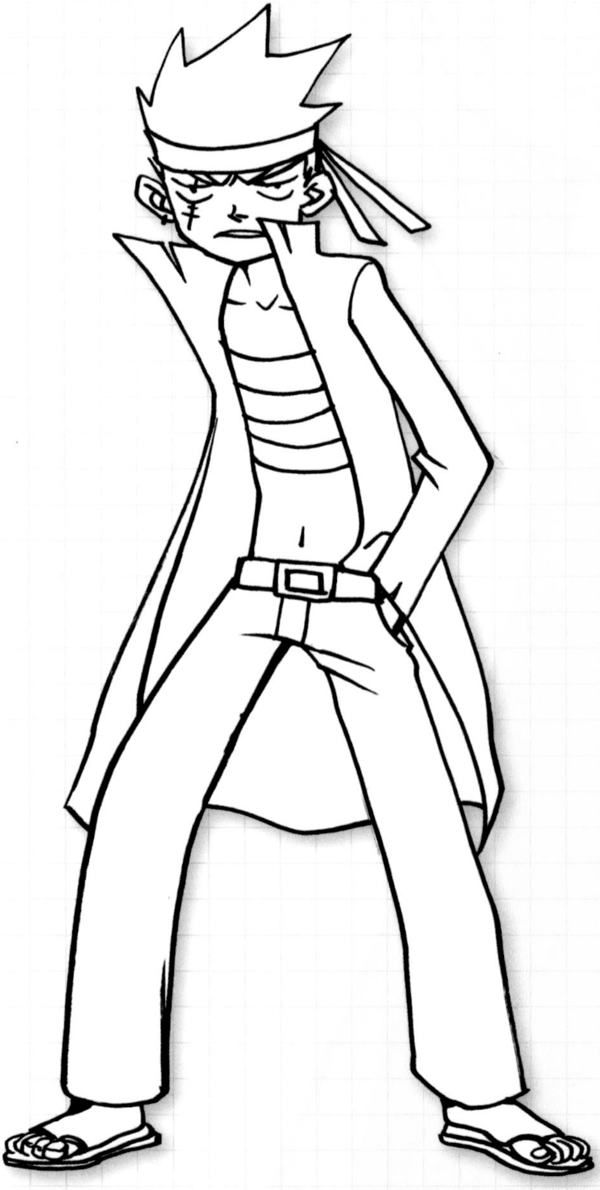

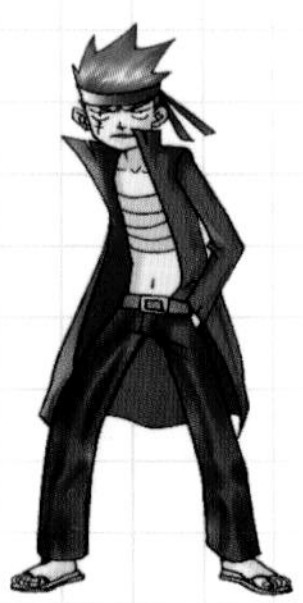

430

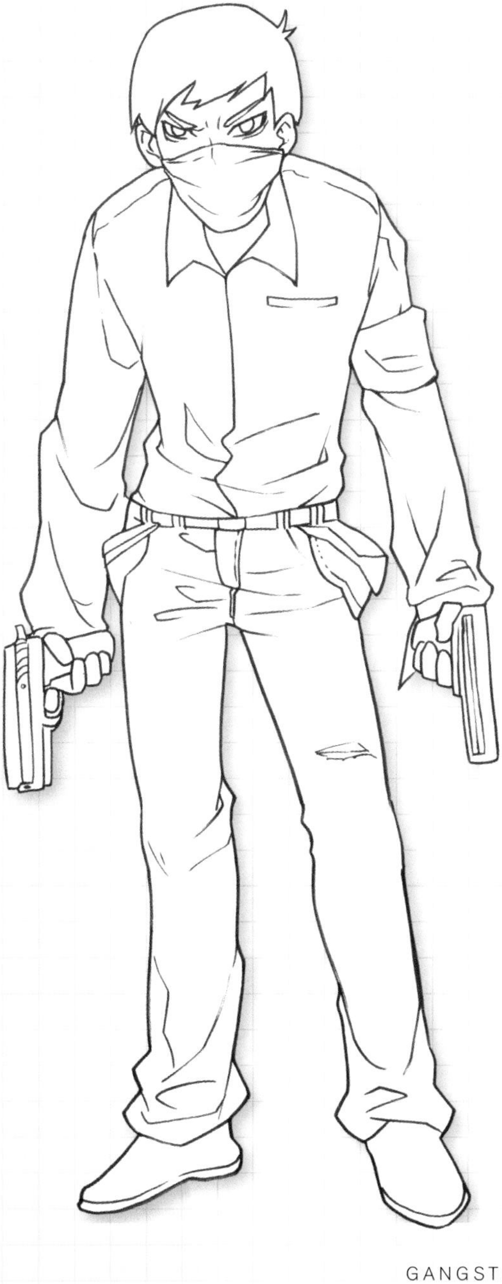

gangsters

search criteria

male. standing. mask. weapons. guns. cowboy.

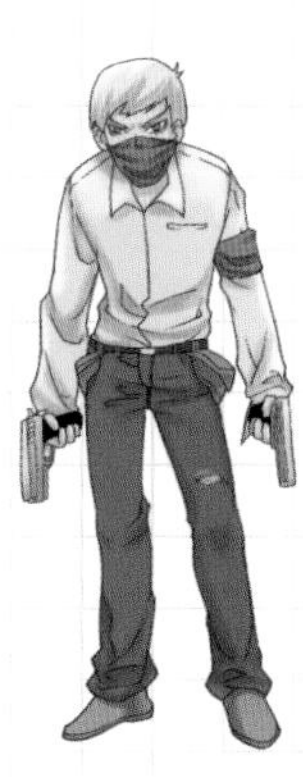

431

gangsters
search criteria
**male. sitting.
smoking. cigarette.
weapon. gun. box.
sunglasses. hood.**

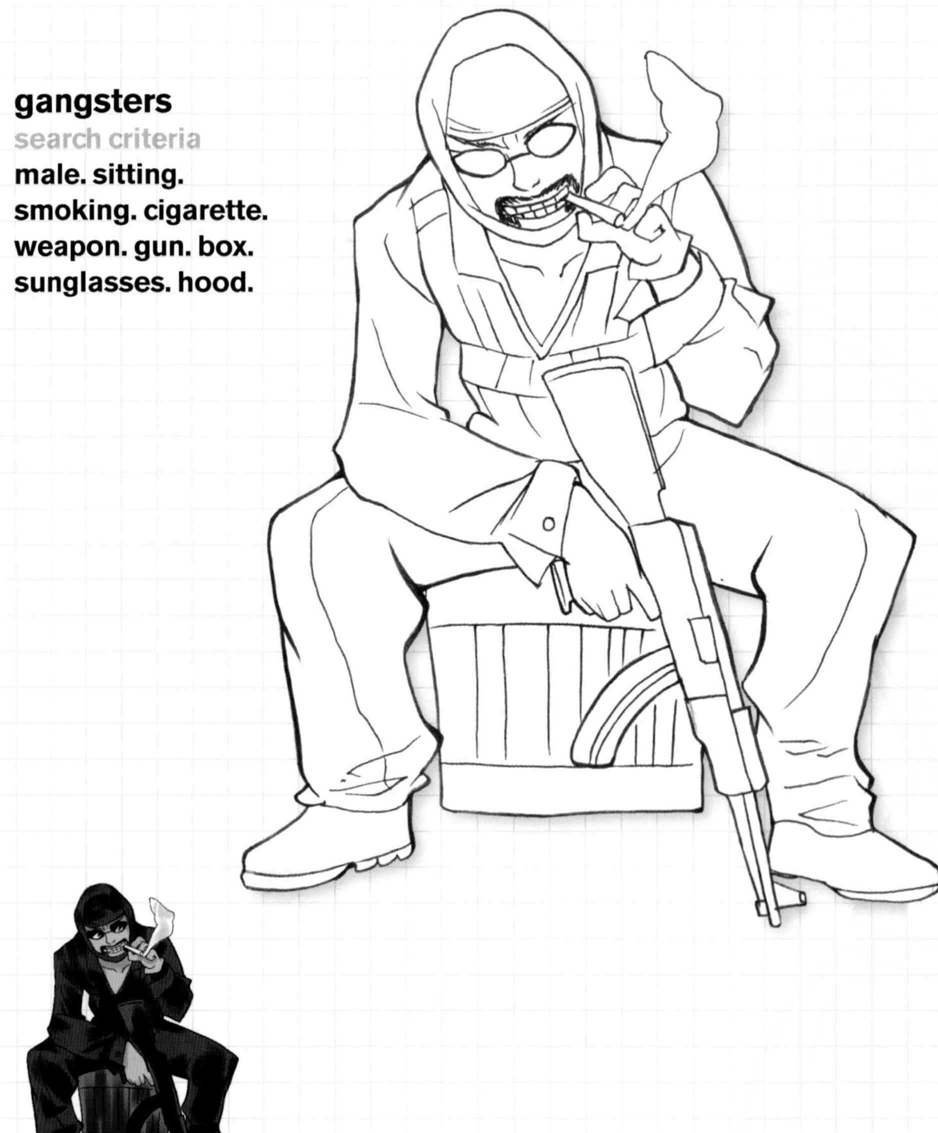

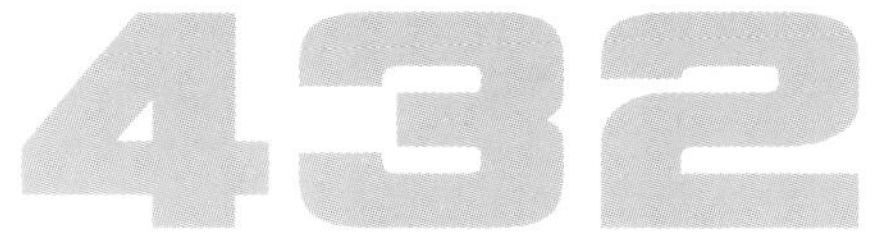

gangsters

search criteria

female. standing. side. headband. tattoo. weapon. gun.

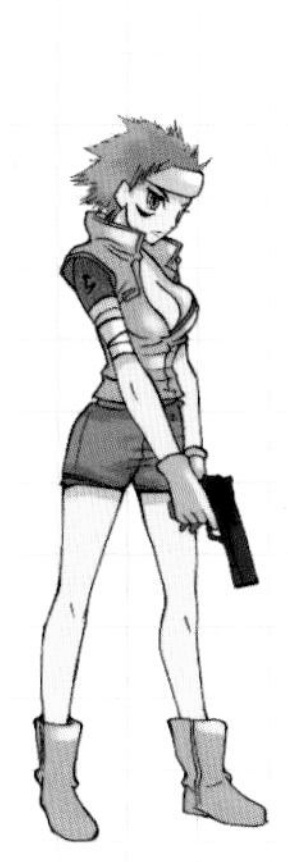

433

gangsters

search criteria

male. standing. glasses. hat. tie. weapon. gun.

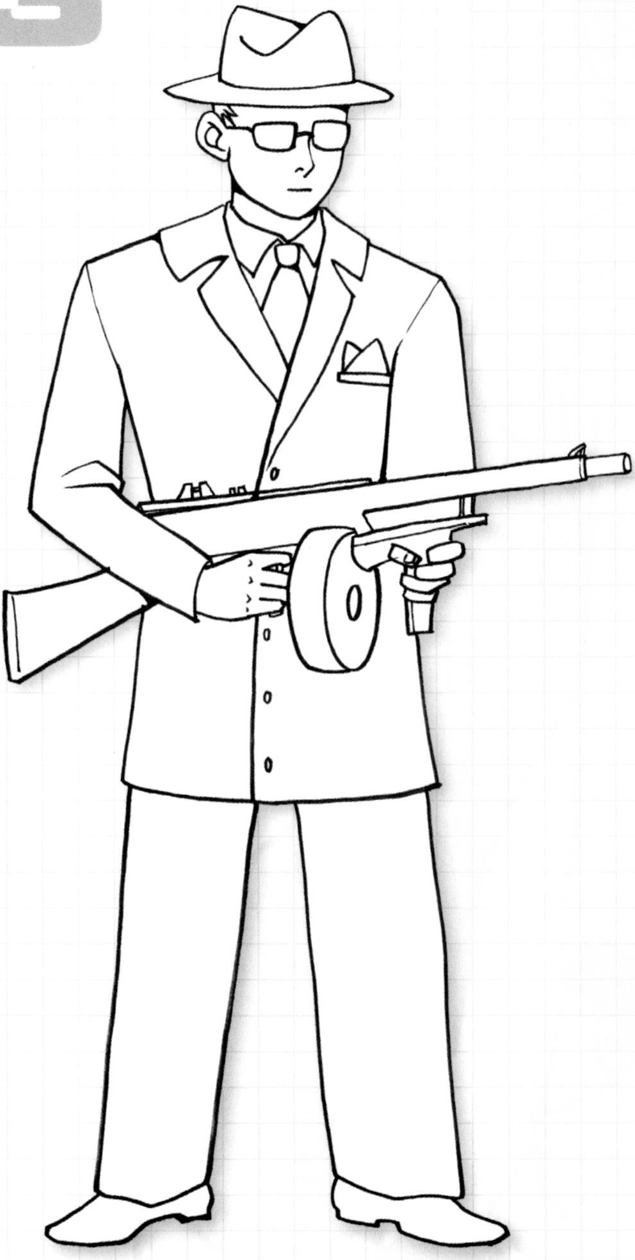

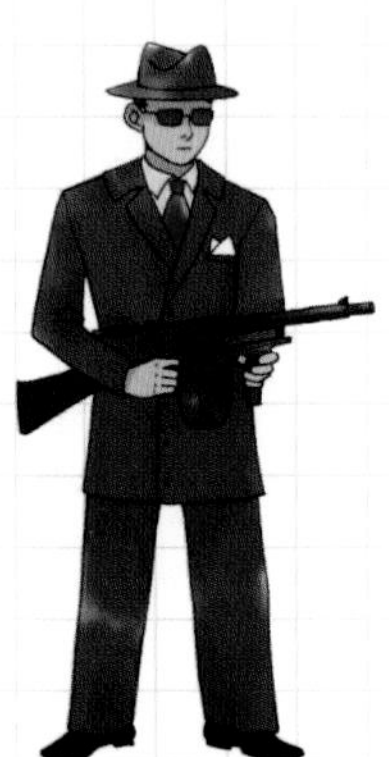

434

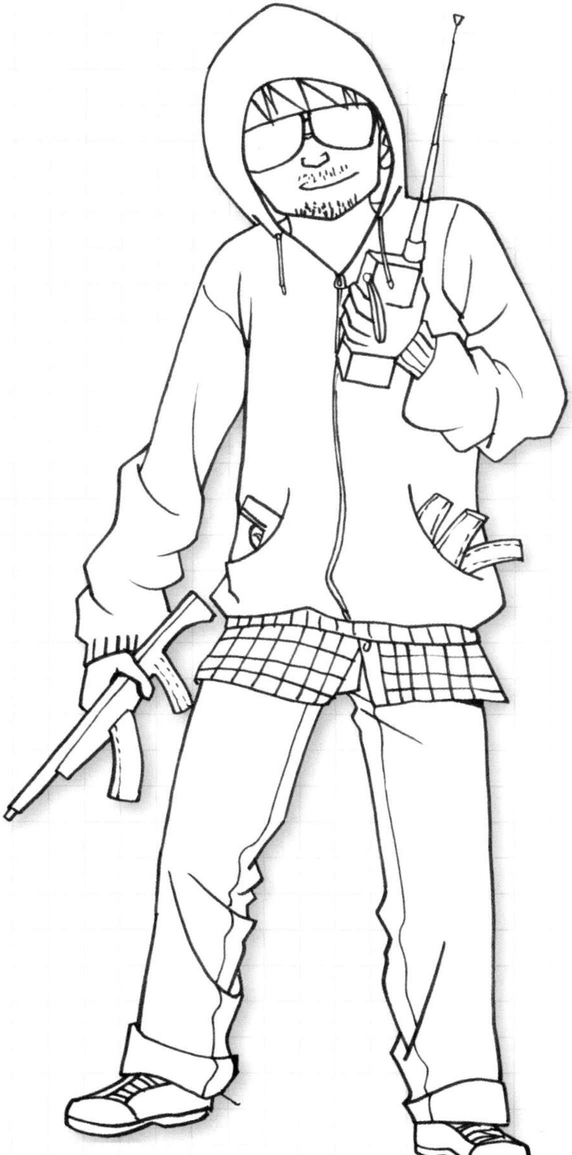

gangsters

search criteria

male. standing. weapons. guns. glasses. radio. hood.

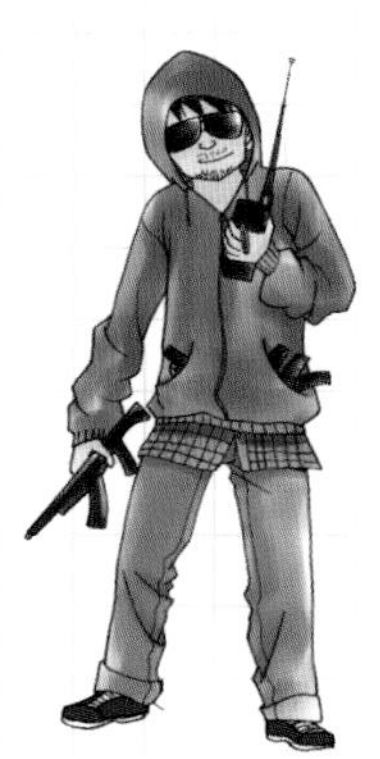

435

gangsters
search criteria
male. standing.
hat. sunglasses.
weapon. gun.
smoking. cigar.

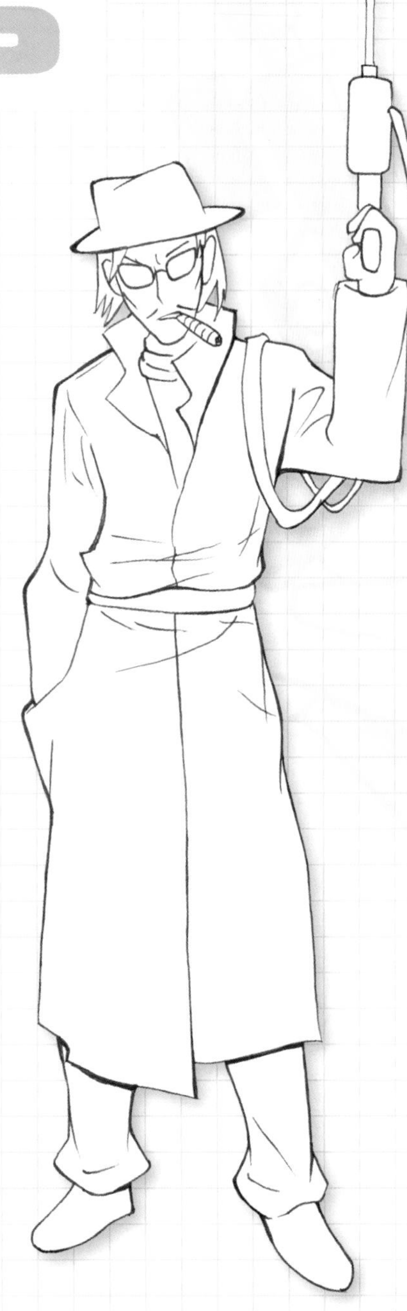

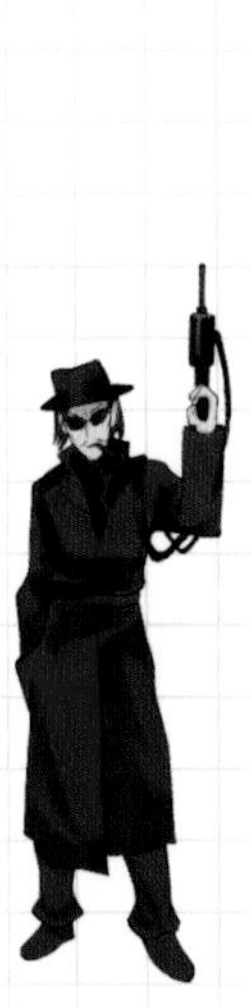

436

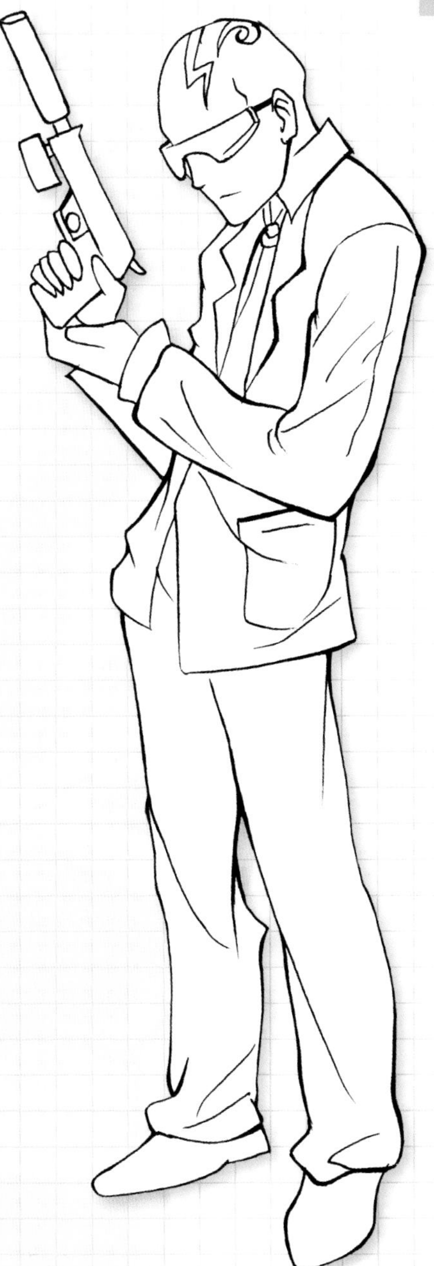

gangsters

search criteria

male. standing. side. tie. weapon. gun. sunglasses. tattoo.

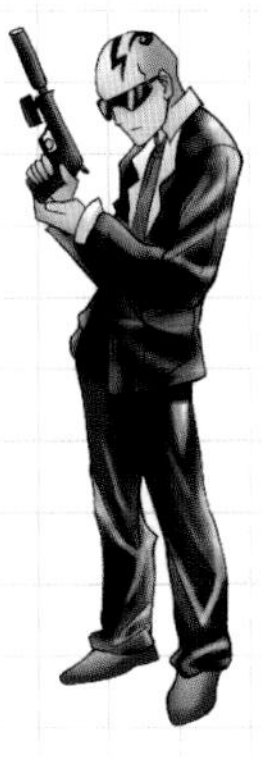

437

gangsters

search criteria

male. sitting. box. smoking. cigarette. weapon. gun. sad.

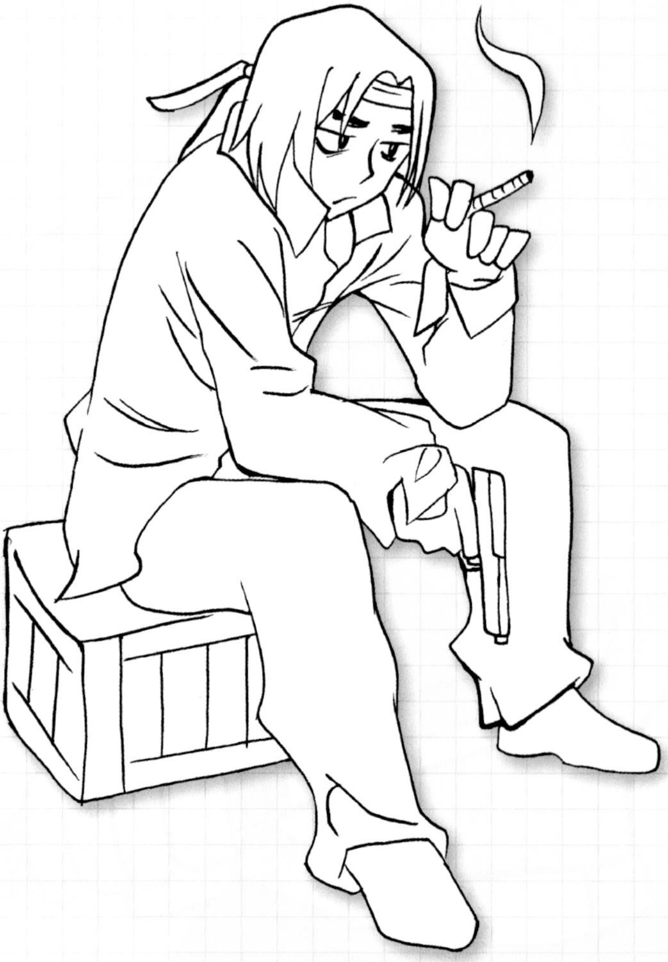

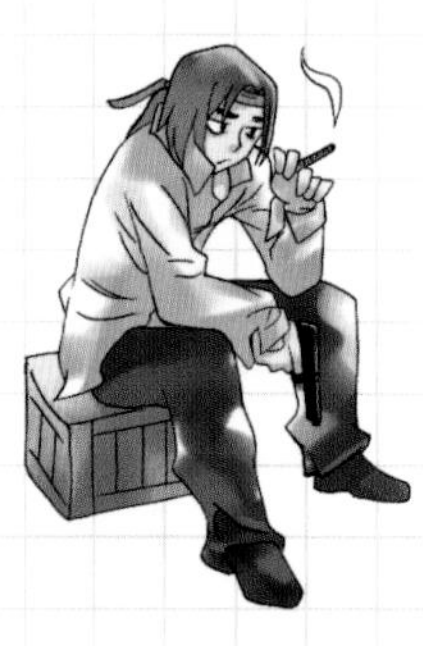

438

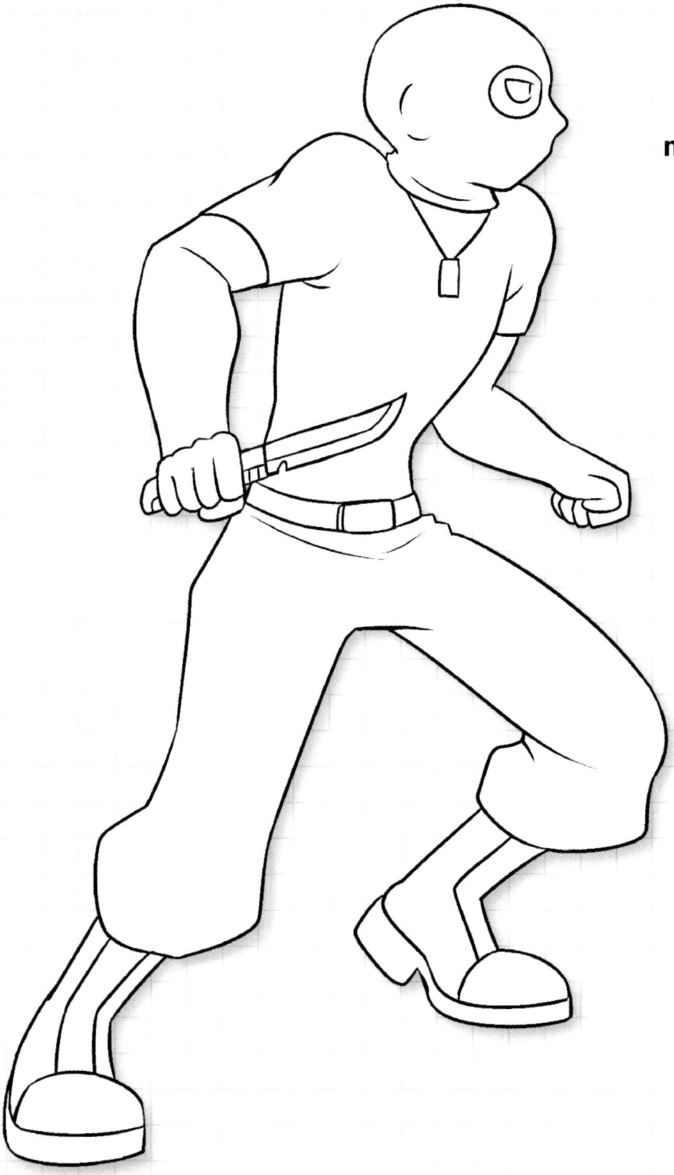

gangsters

search criteria

male. standing. side. action. necklace. mask. weapon. knife. balaclava.

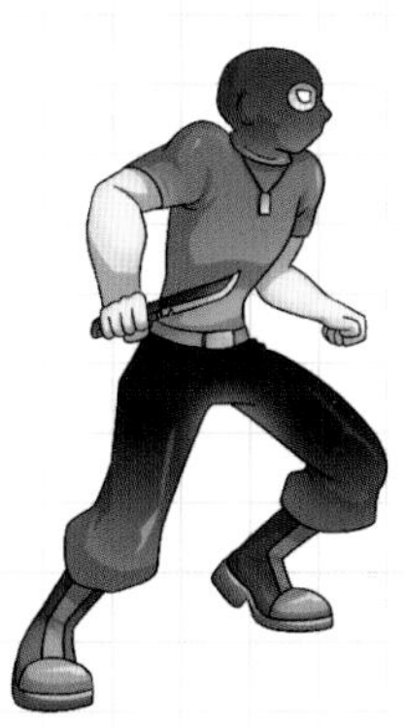

439

good guys

search criteria

female. standing. nurse. smiling.

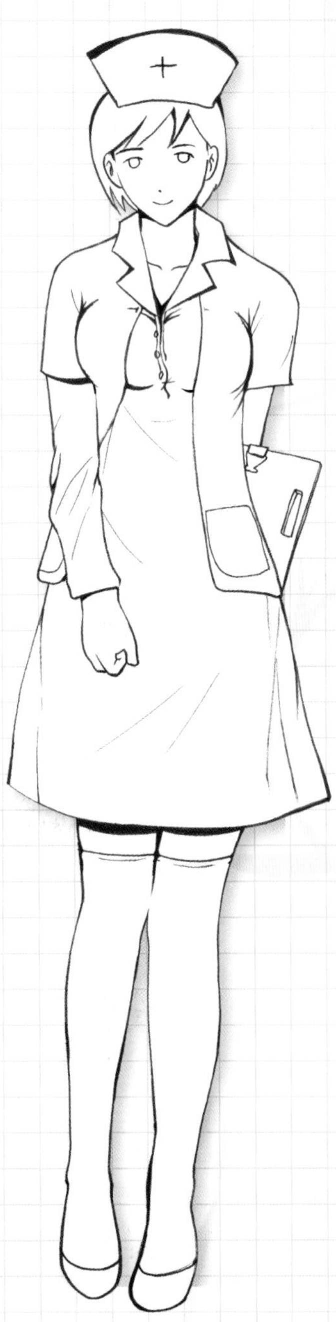

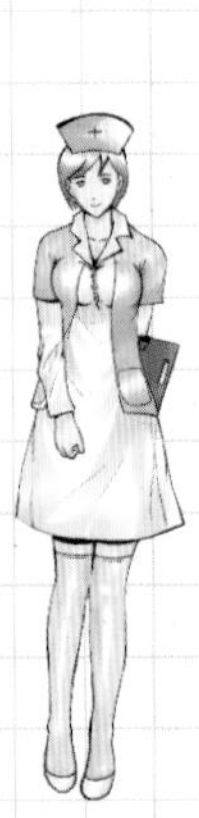

good guys

search criteria

male. standing. looking. side. hat. cowboy.

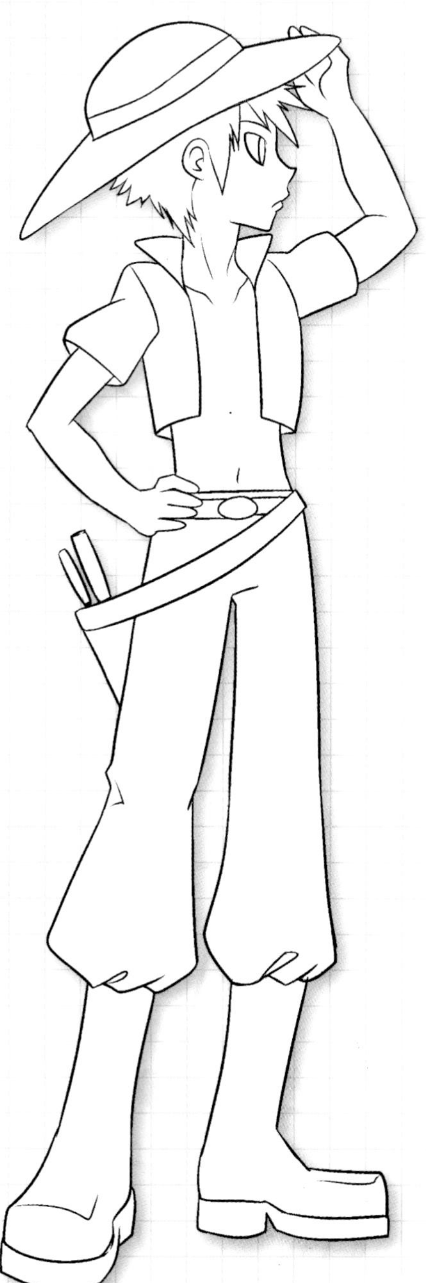

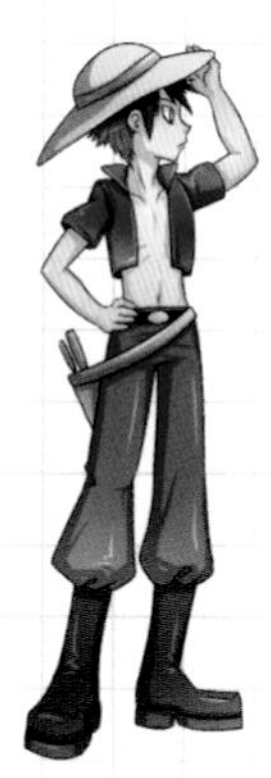

441

good guys

search criteria

male. moving.
hat. scarf. smiling.
spurs. cowboy.
weapon. gun.

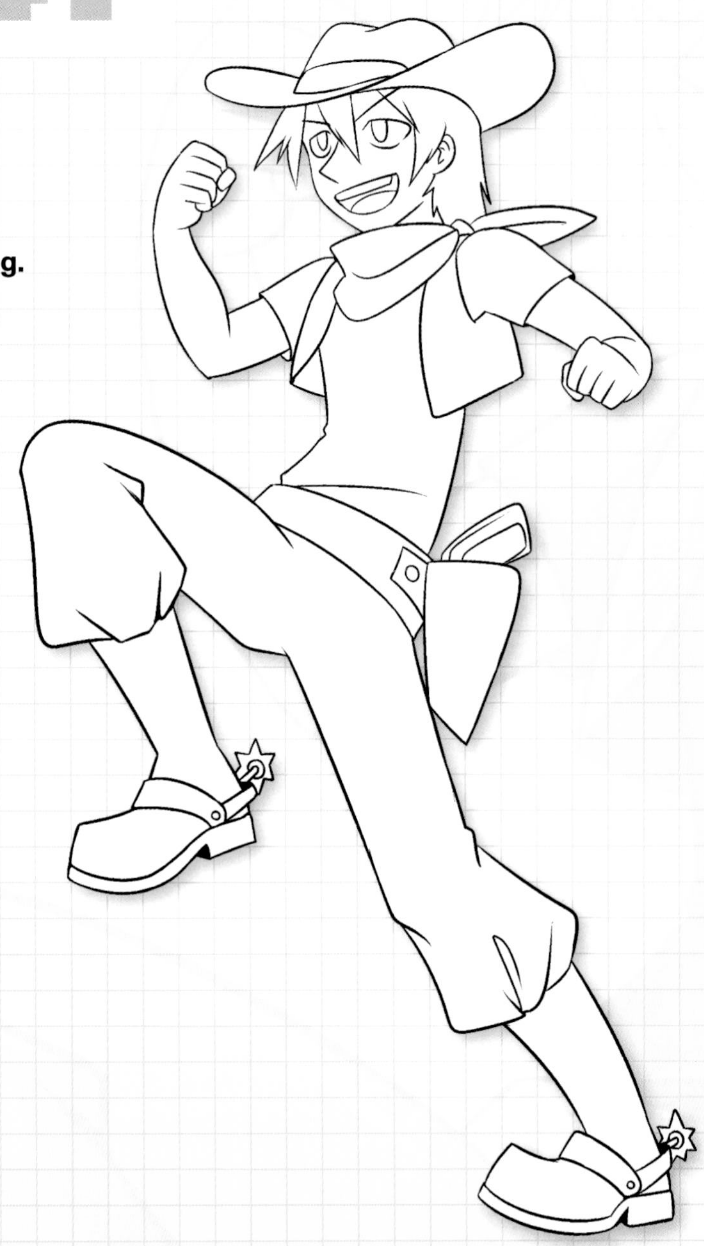

442

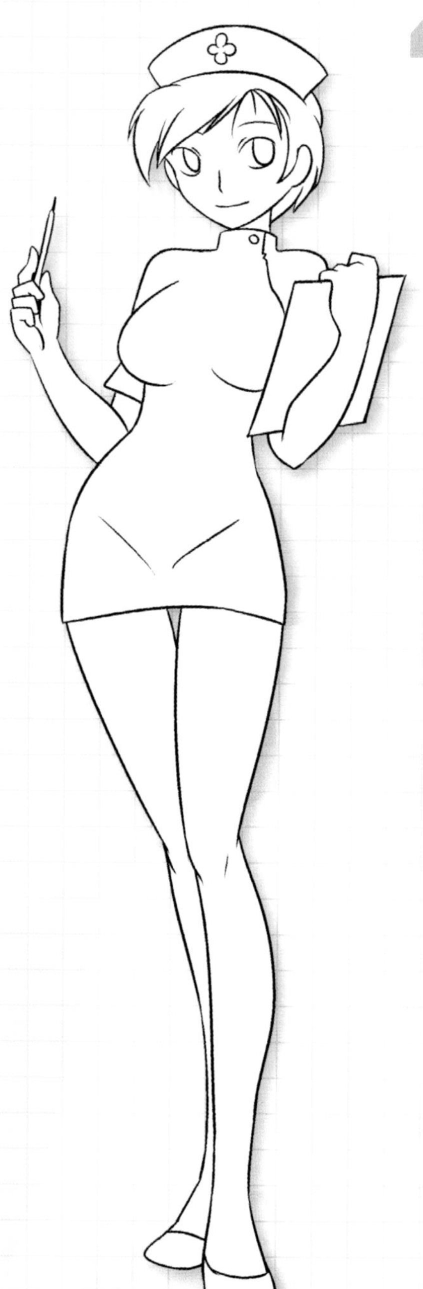

good guys

search criteria

female. standing. nurse. clipboard.

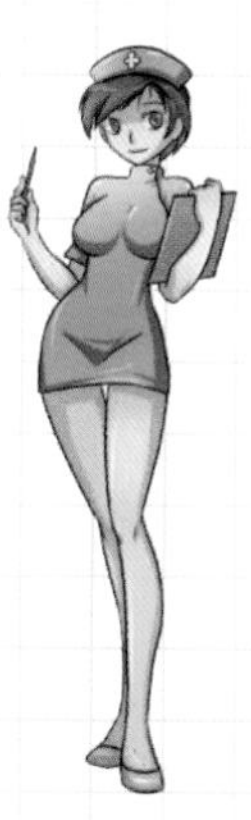

443

good guys

search criteria

female. running. smiling. apron. maid.

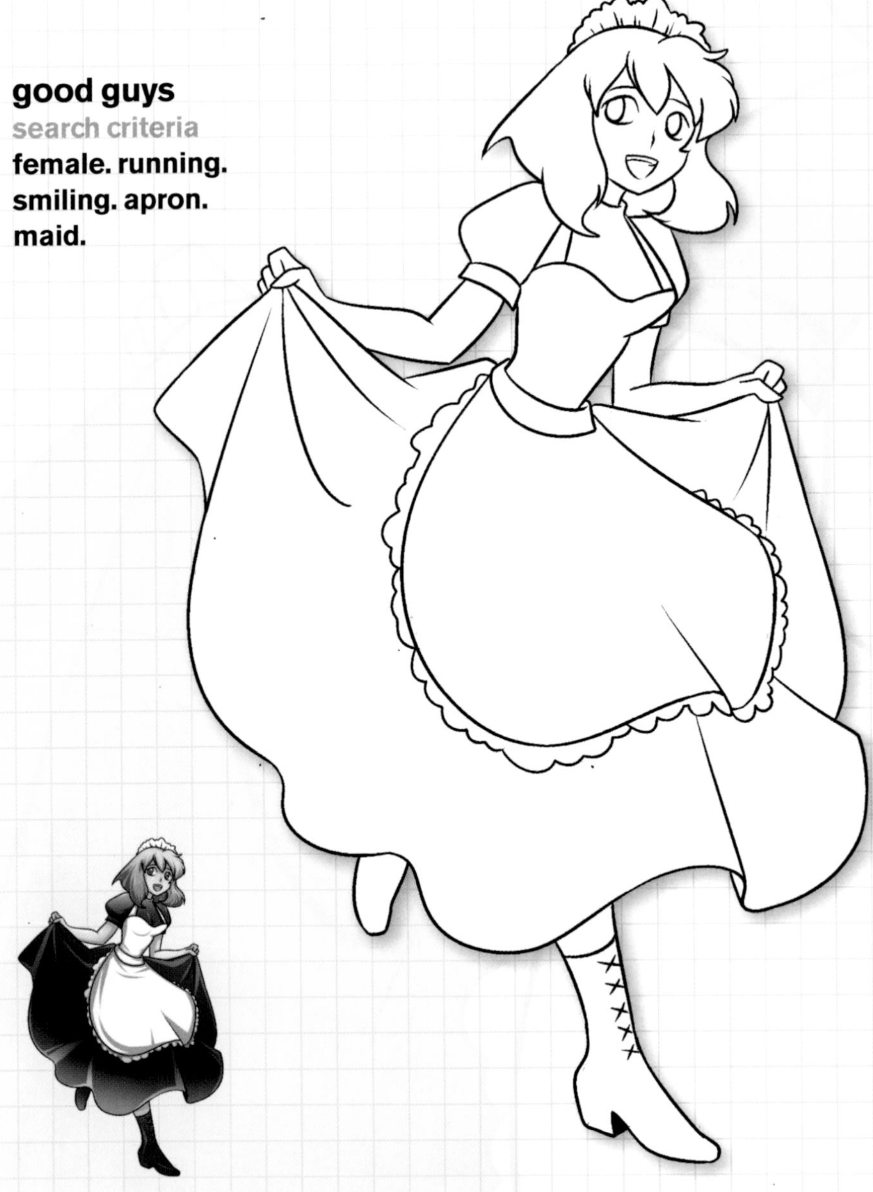

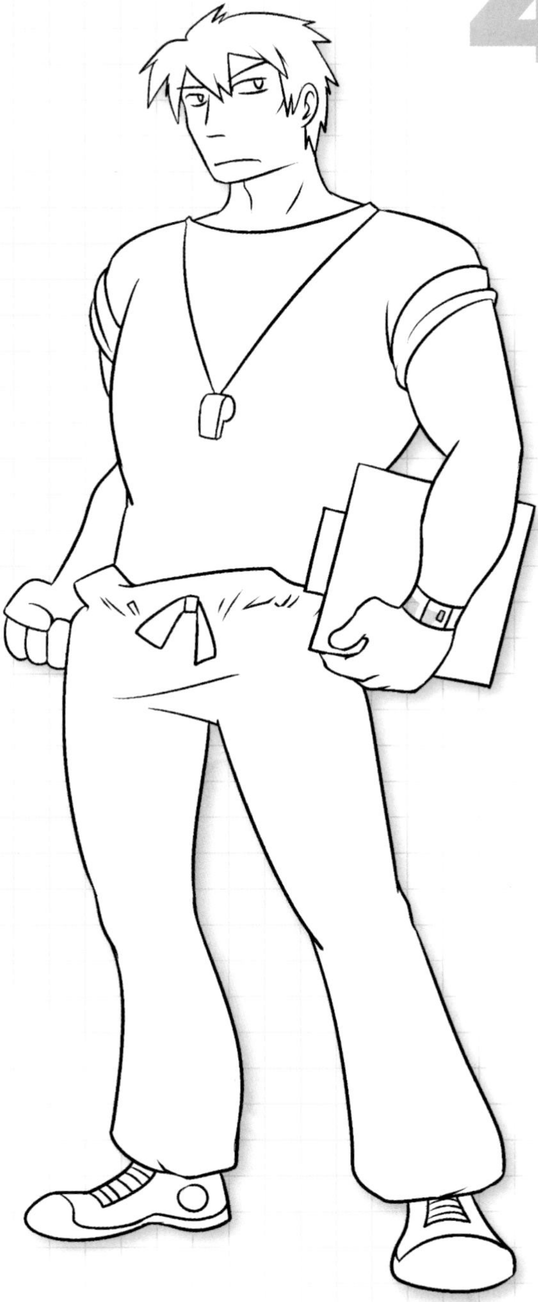

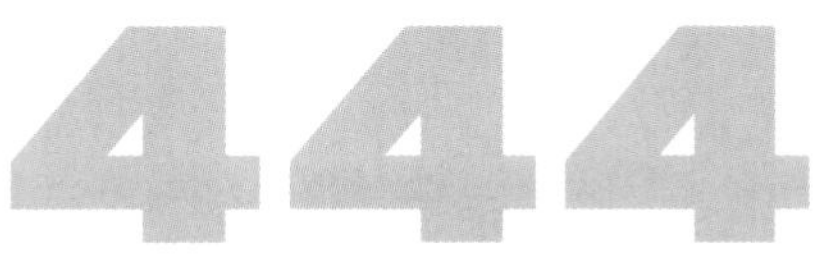

good guys

search criteria

male. standing. whistle. clipboard. watch. angry. lifeguard. rescue.

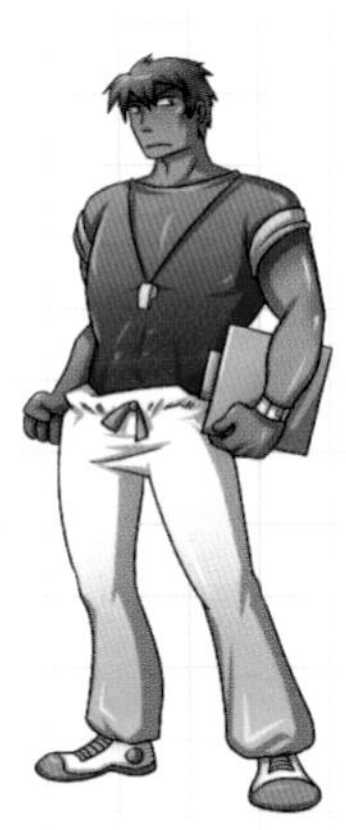

445

good guys

search criteria

male. standing. resting. cleaner. mop. deckhand.

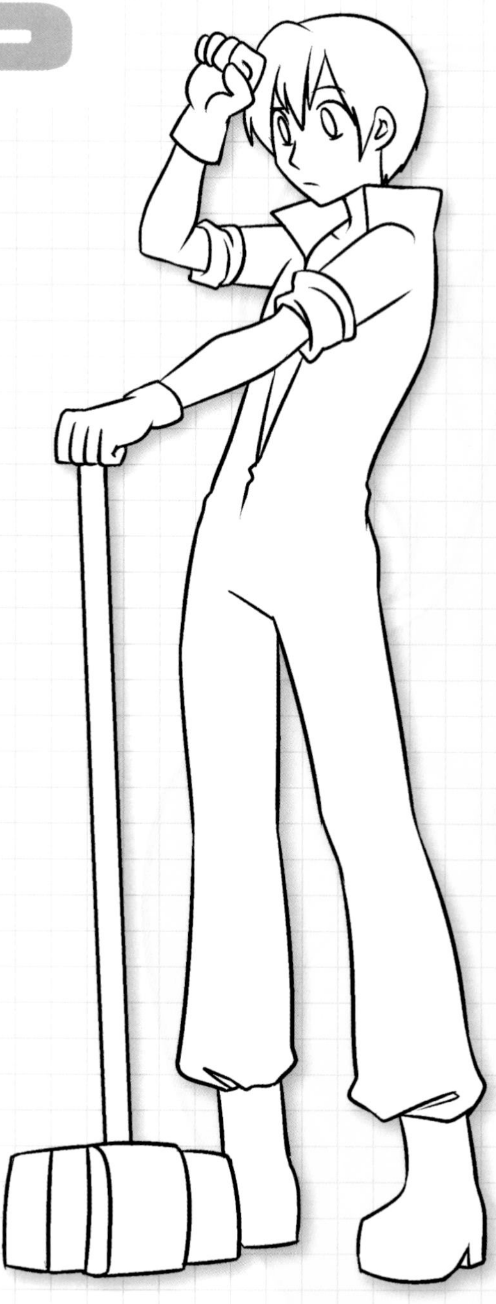

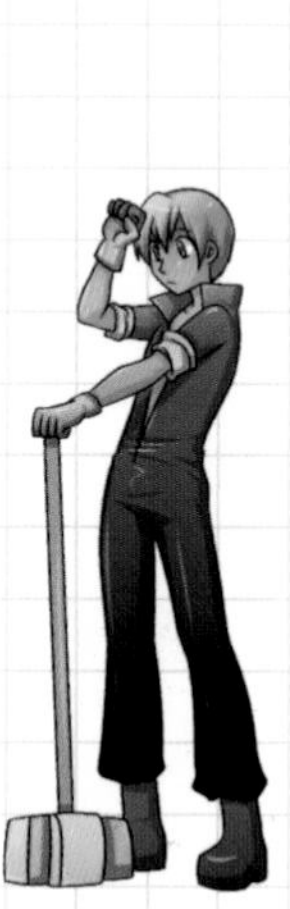

446

good guys
search criteria
female. floating. necklace. book.

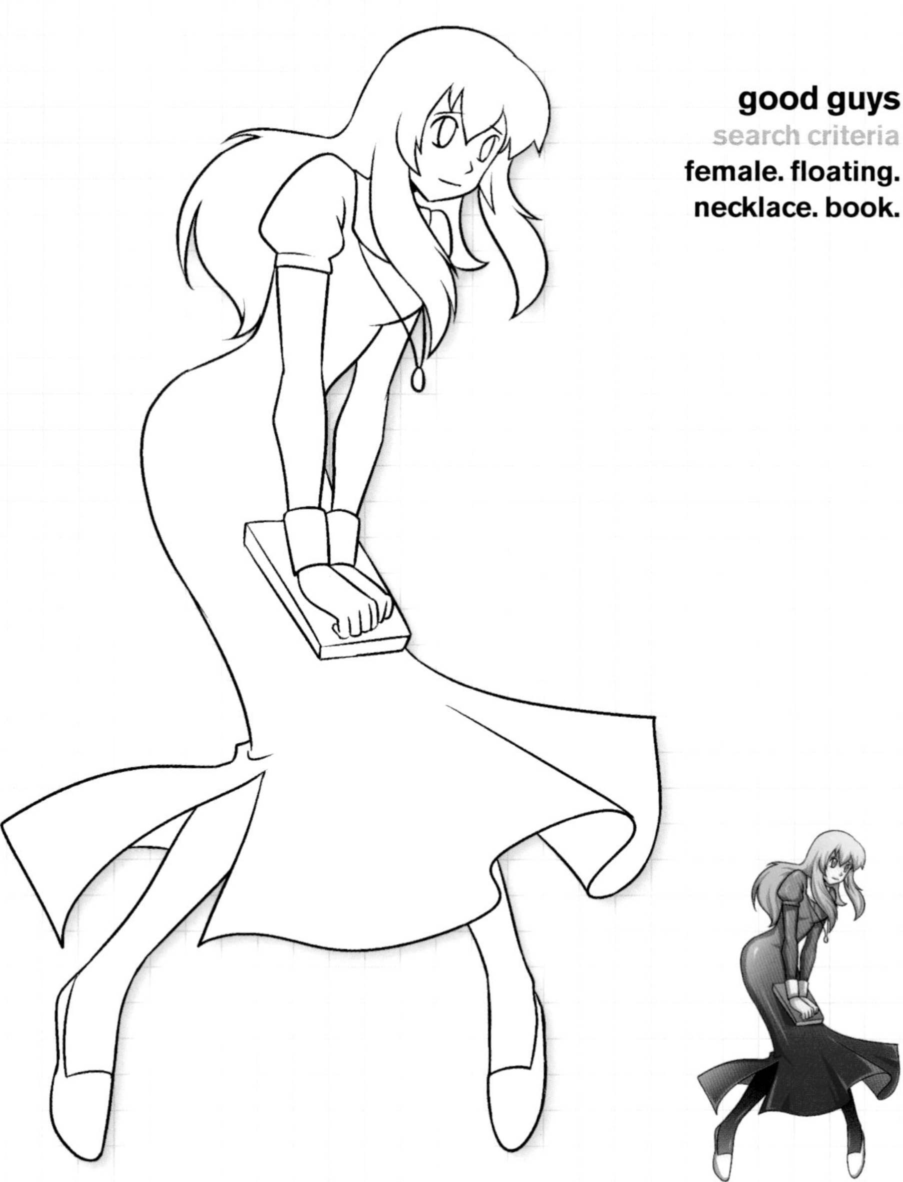

447

good guys

search criteria

female. standing. salute. gesture. hat. police. sunglasses.

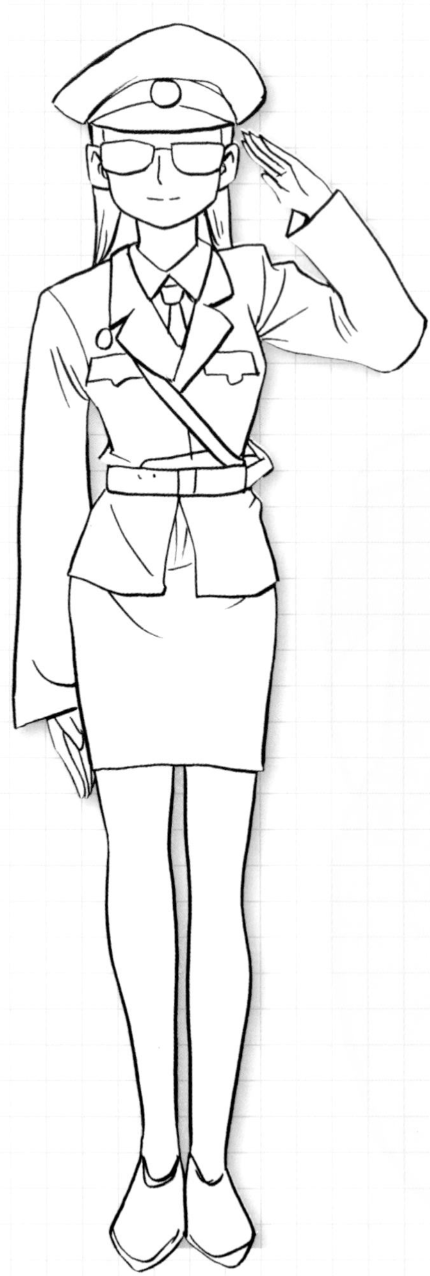

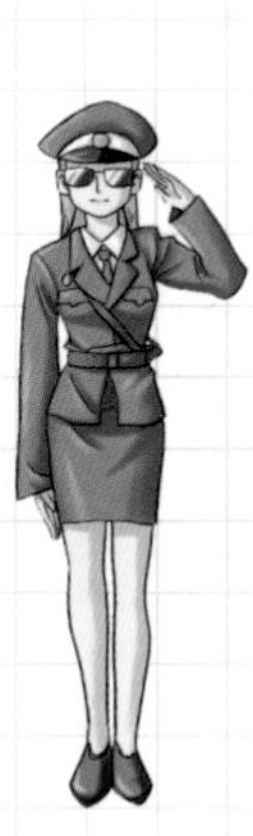

448

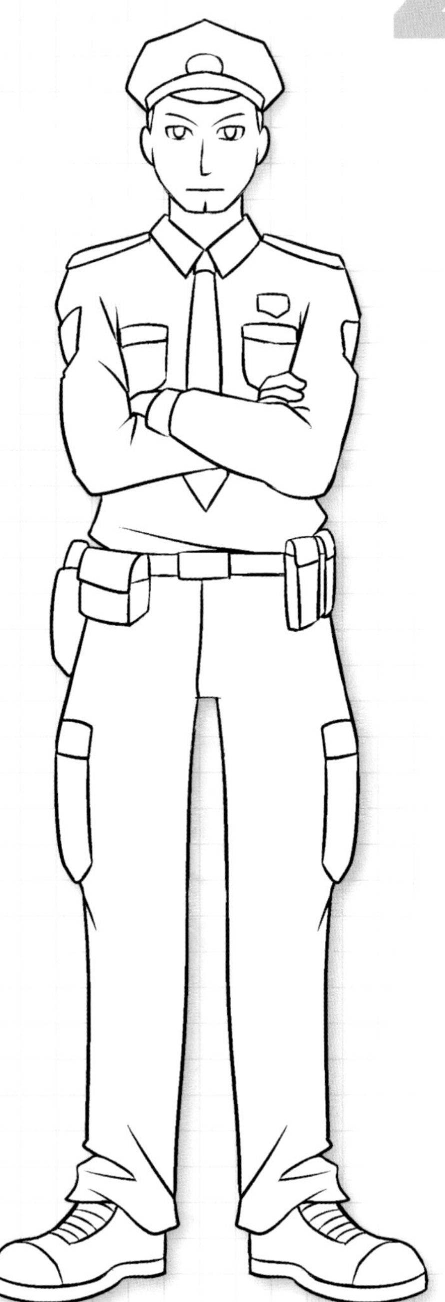

good guys

search criteria

male. standing. hat. tie. police.

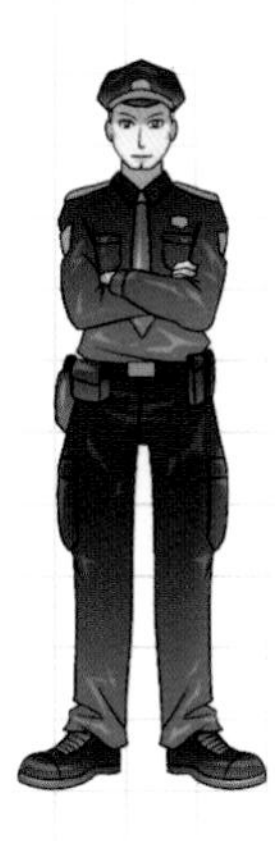

449

good guys

search criteria

**female. standing.
clipboard. tie.
police.**

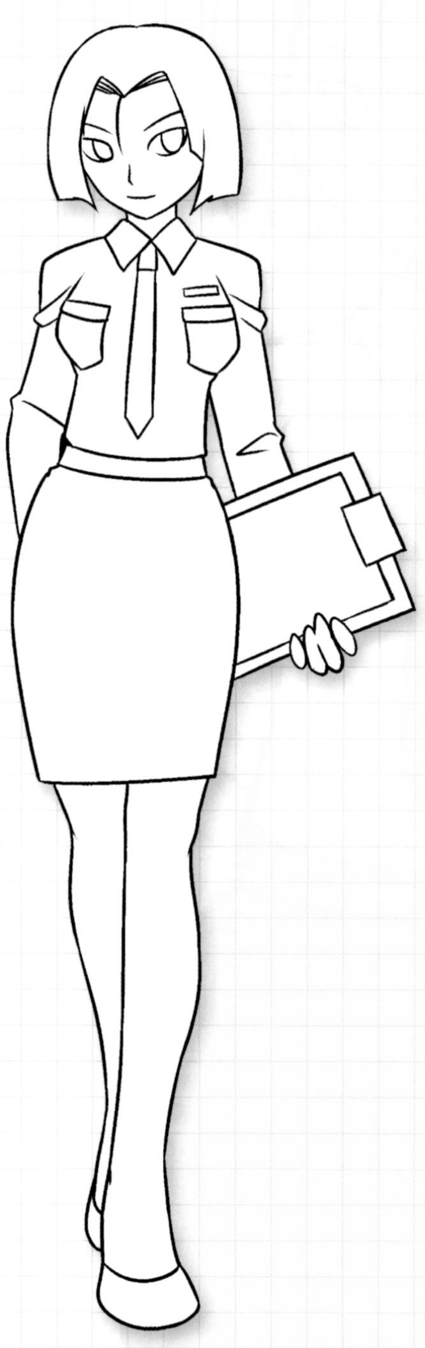

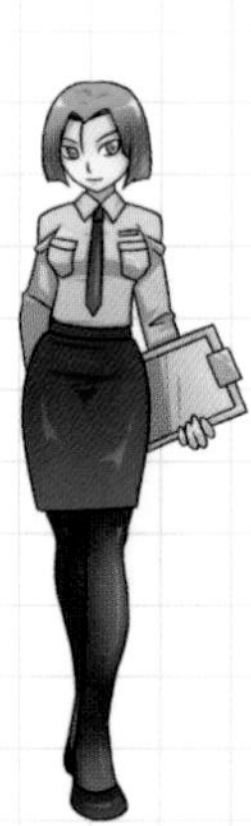

450

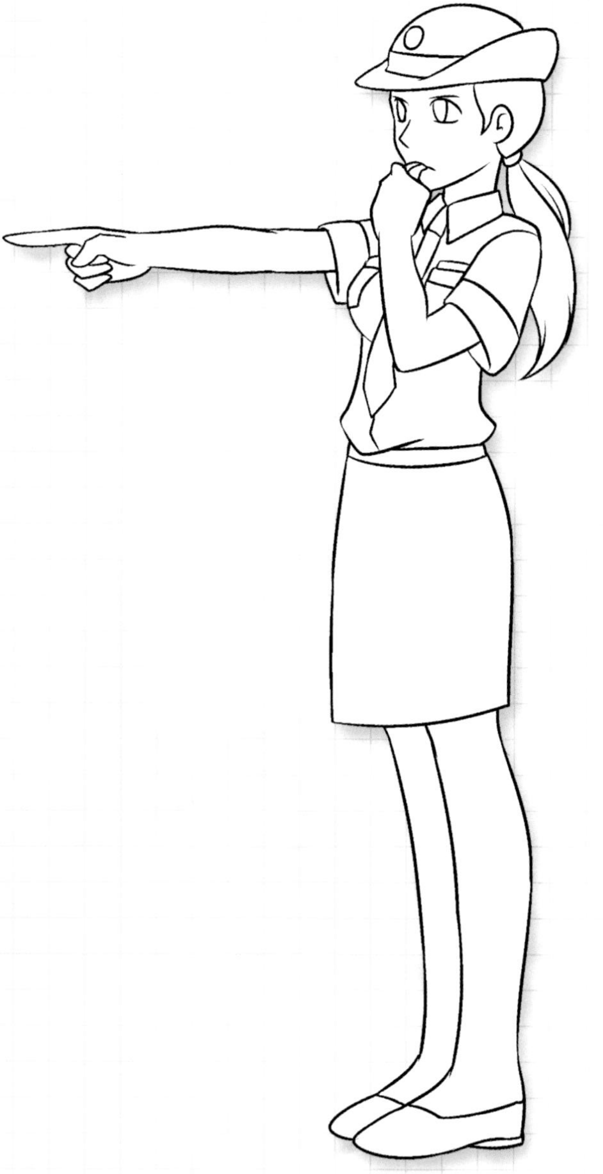

good guys

search criteria

female. standing. side. whistle. gesture. point. tie. ponytail. hat.

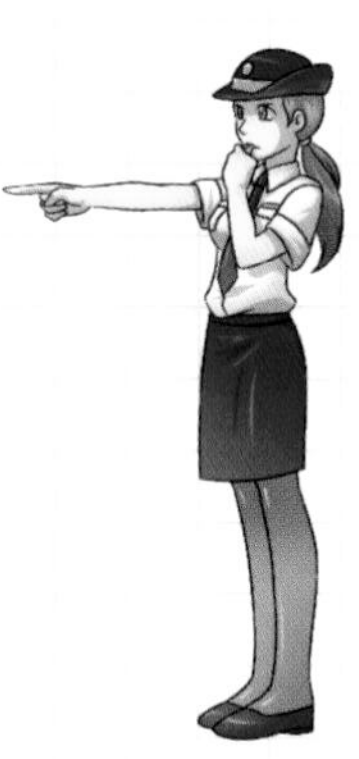

451

good guys

search criteria

female. standing. hat. salute. gesture. army.

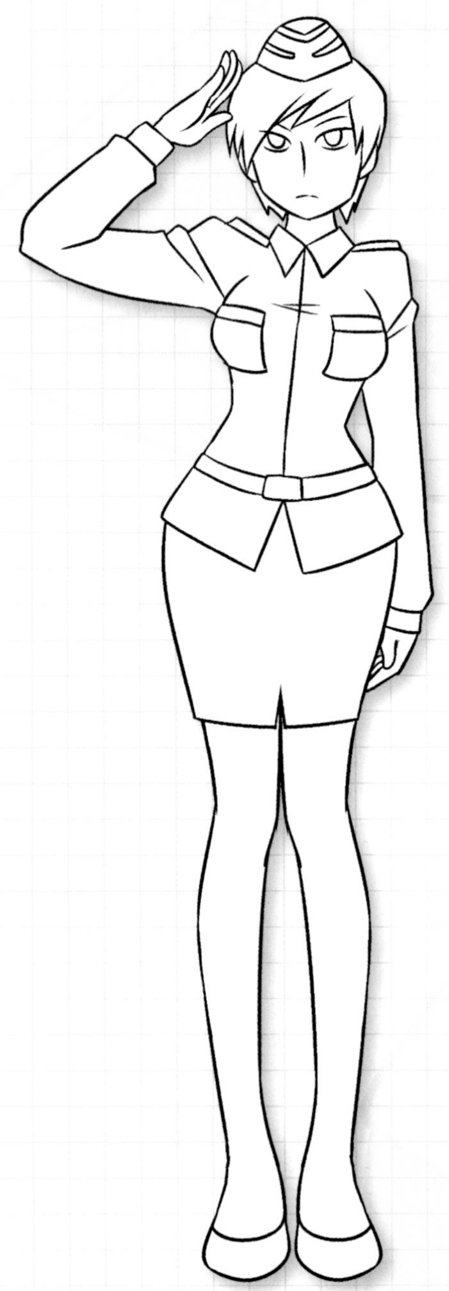

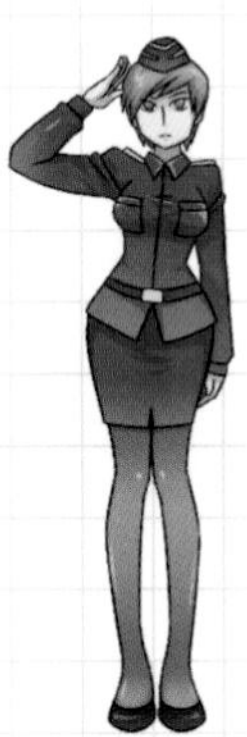

452

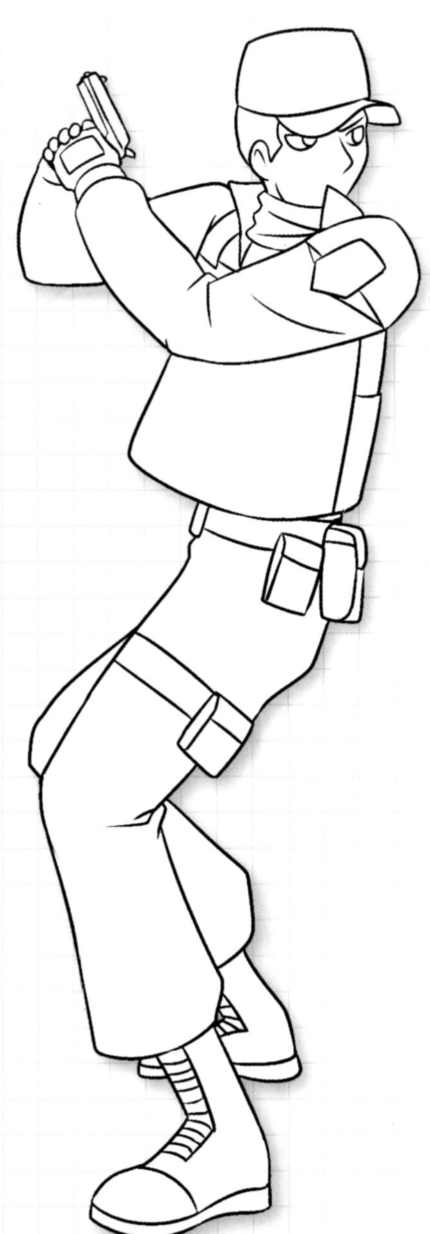

good guys

search criteria

male. standing. side. weapon. hat. gun. police.

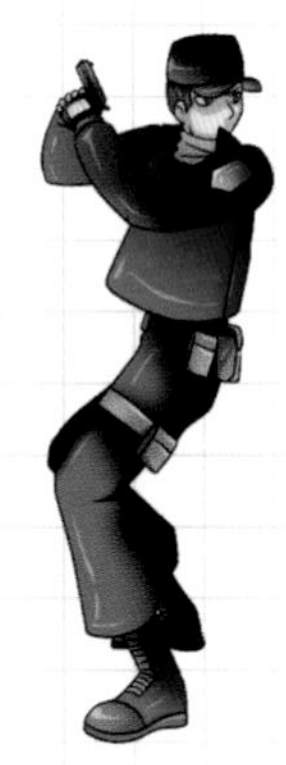

453

action villains

search criteria

male. standing. hat. glasses. weapon. gun. radio. army.

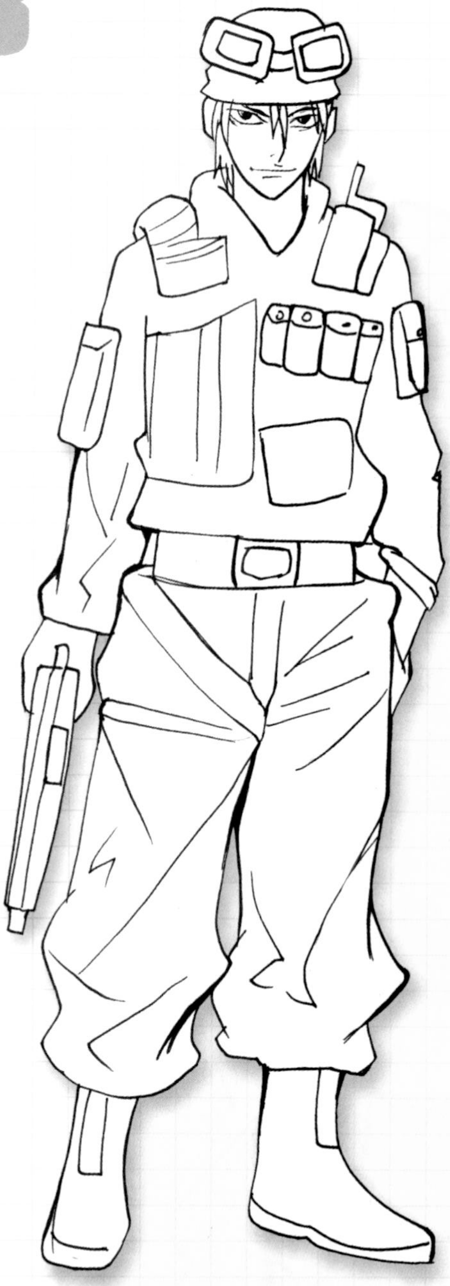

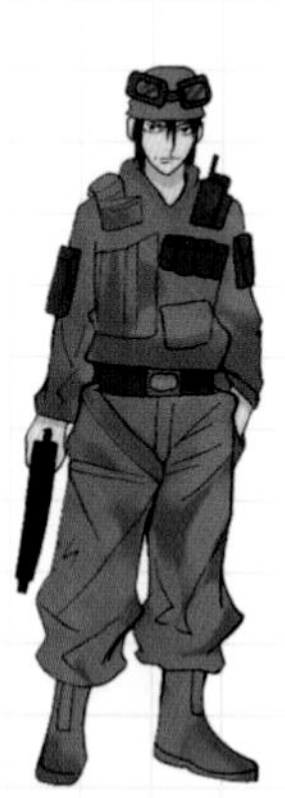

454

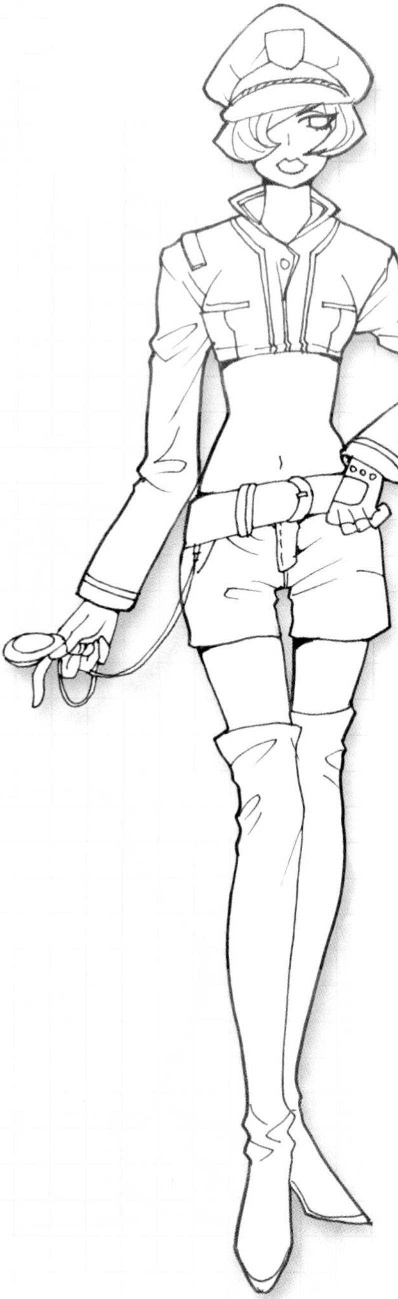

action villains

search criteria

female. standing. hat. watch. army. spy. assassin.

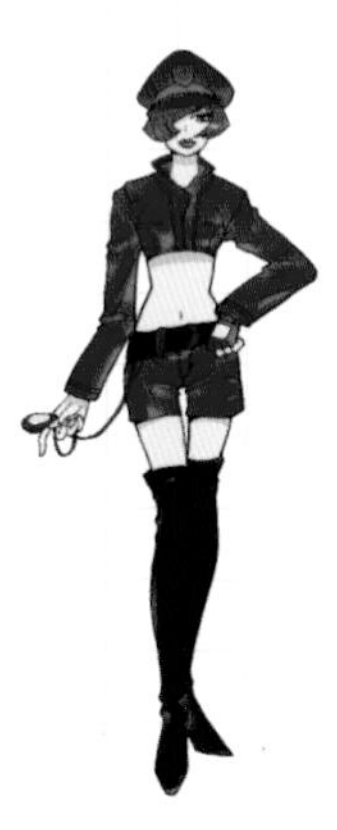

455

action villains
search criteria
female. standing. gangster. handcuffs.

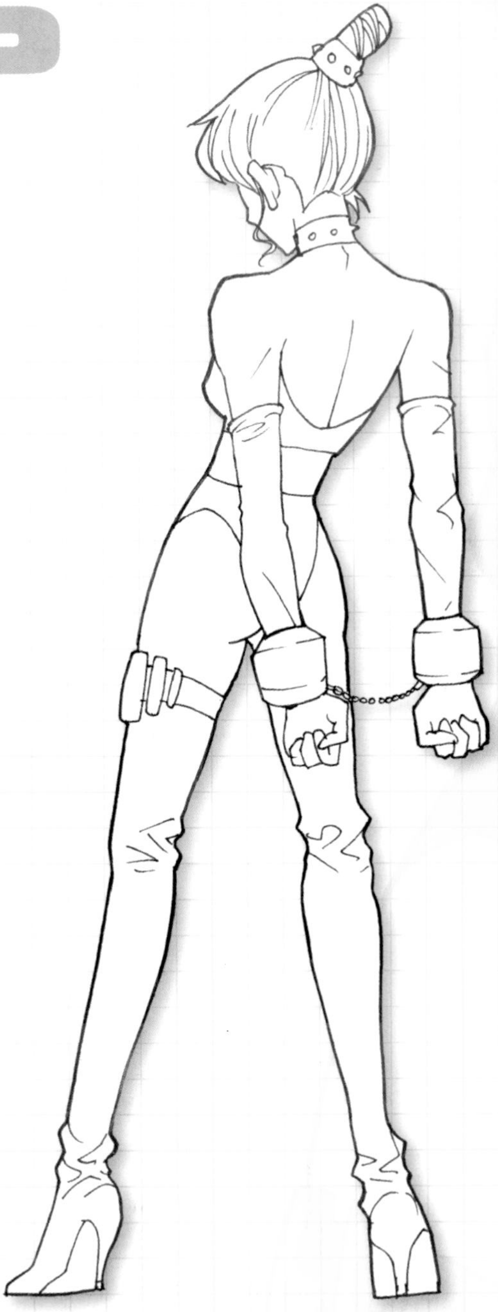

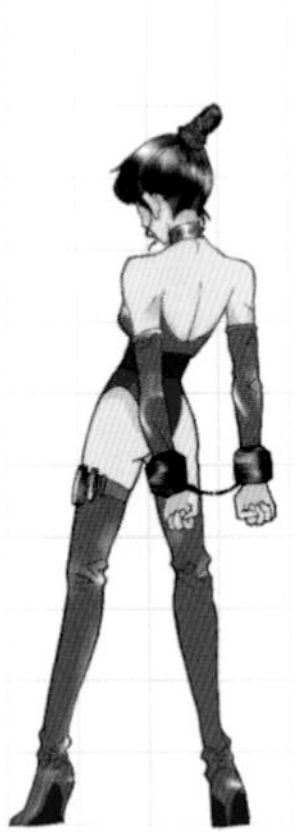

456

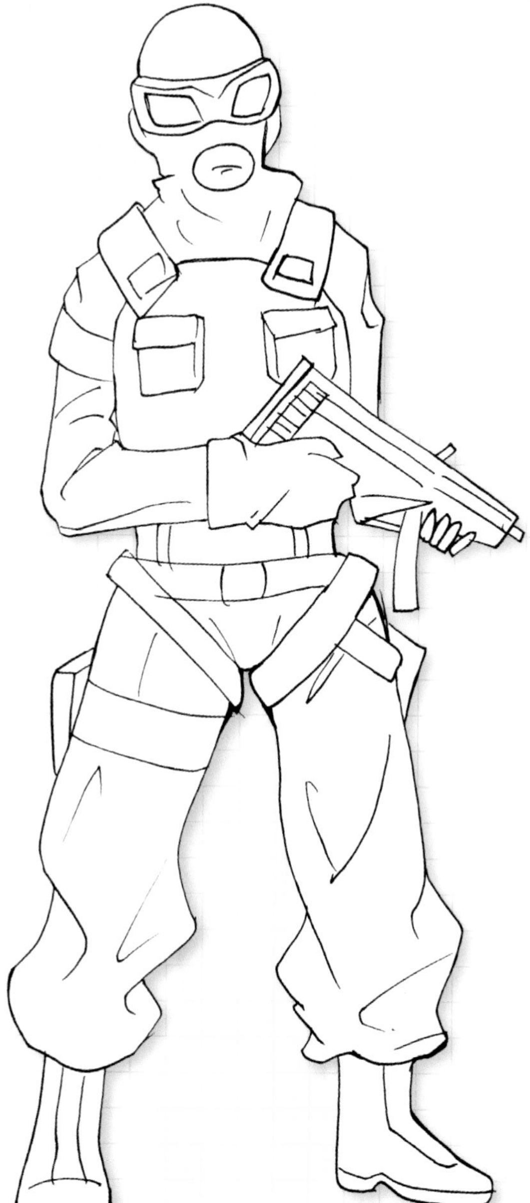

action villains

search criteria

male. standing. mask. army. weapon. gun.

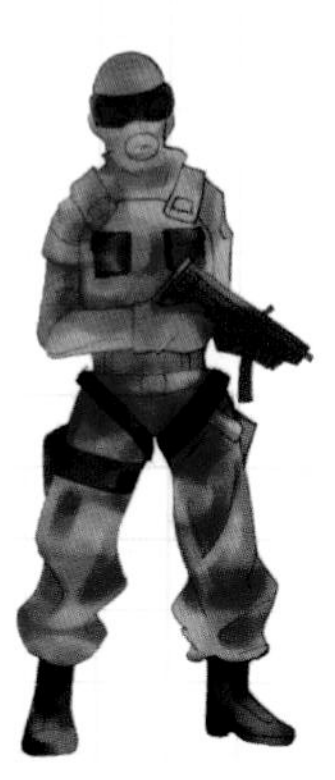

457

action villains

search criteria

male. standing. hat. sunglasses. weapon. gun. army.

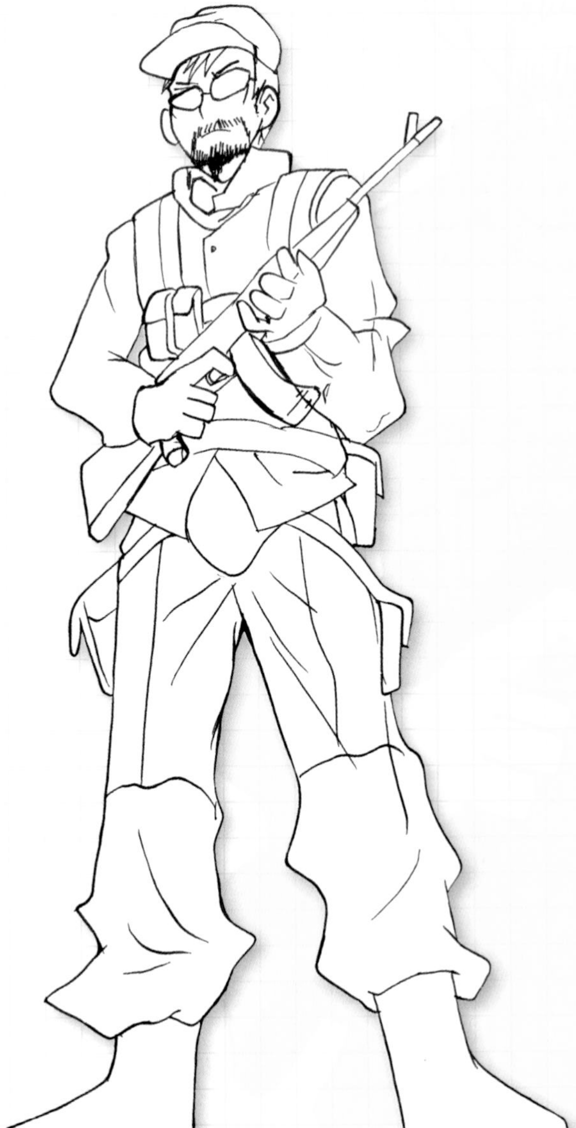

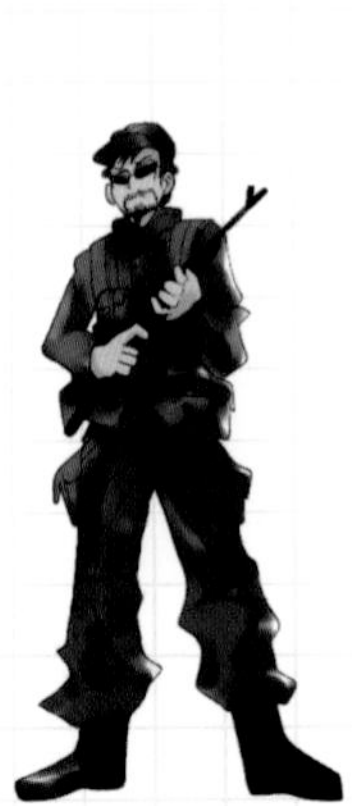

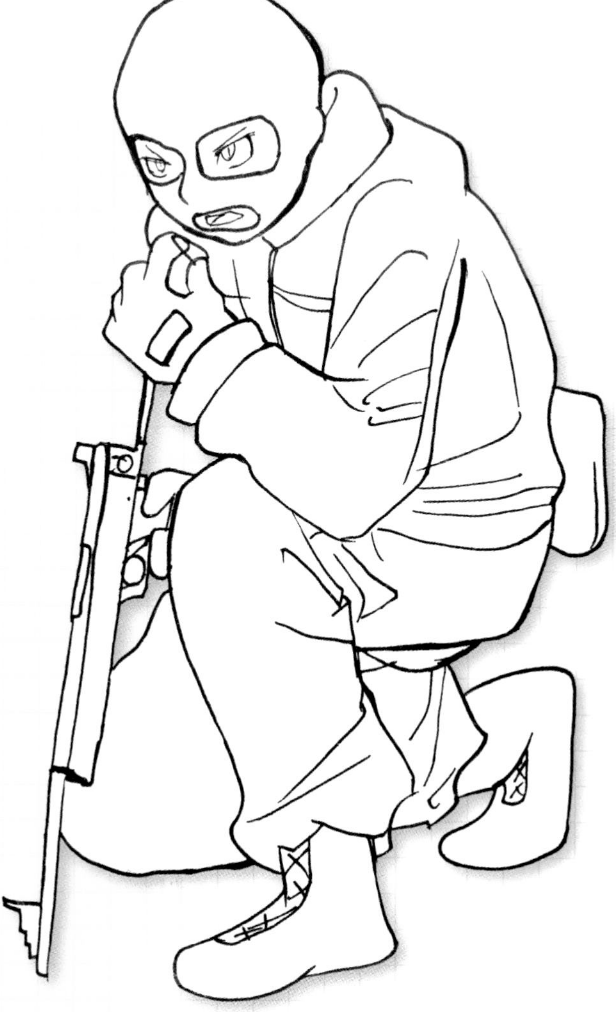

action villains

search criteria

male. kneeling. crouched. mask. balaclava. weapon. gun. army.

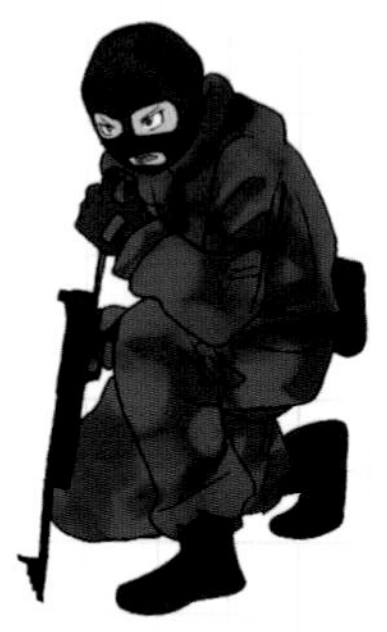

459

action villains

search criteria

male. standing. side. mask. glasses. weapon. gun. army.

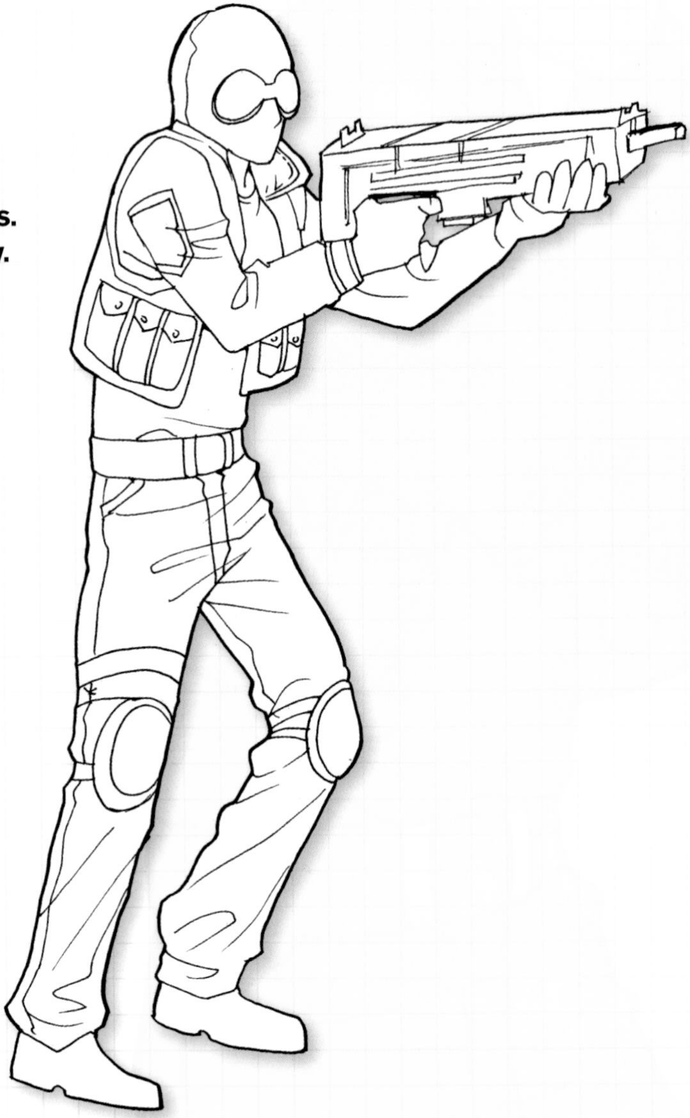

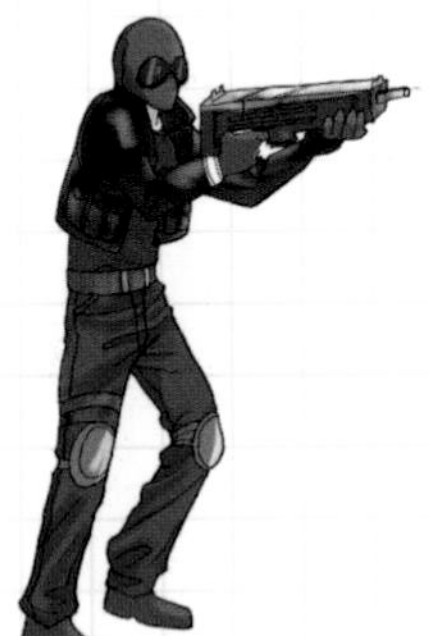

460

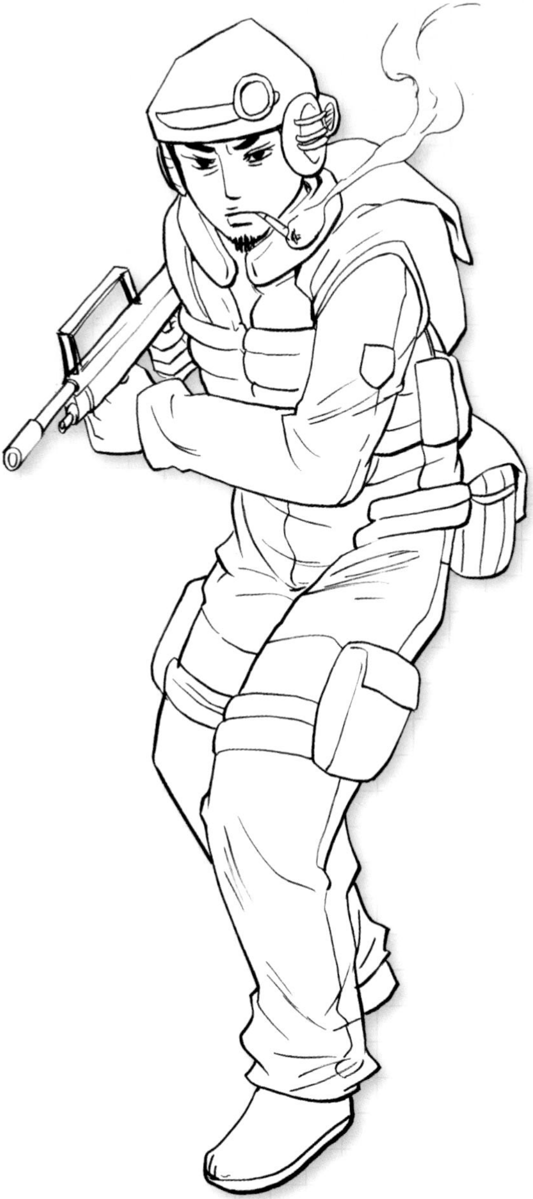

action villains

search criteria

male. standing. smoking. cigarette. helmet. weapon. gun. army.

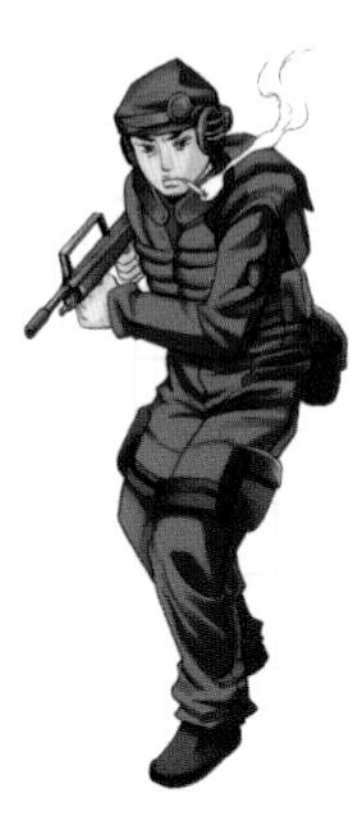

461

action villains

search criteria

male. standing. side. hat. glasses. weapon. gun. army.

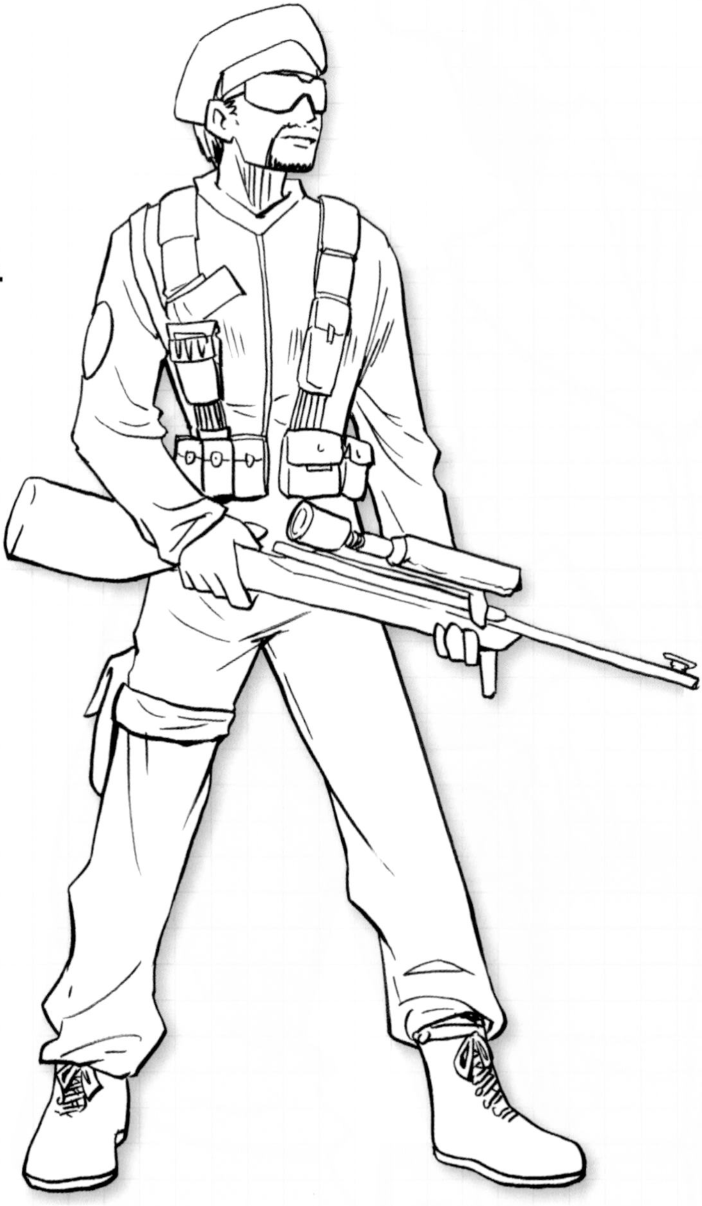

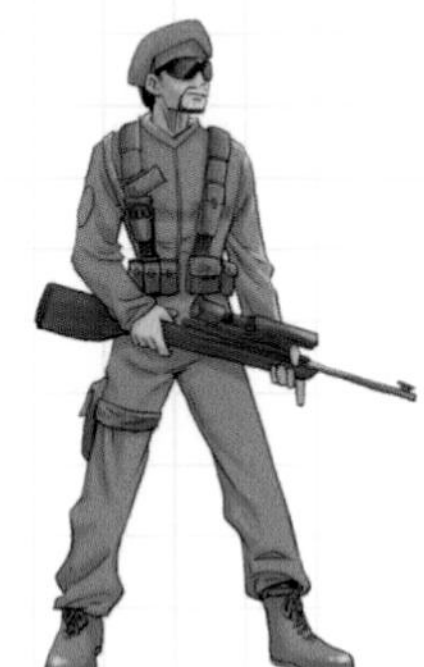

462

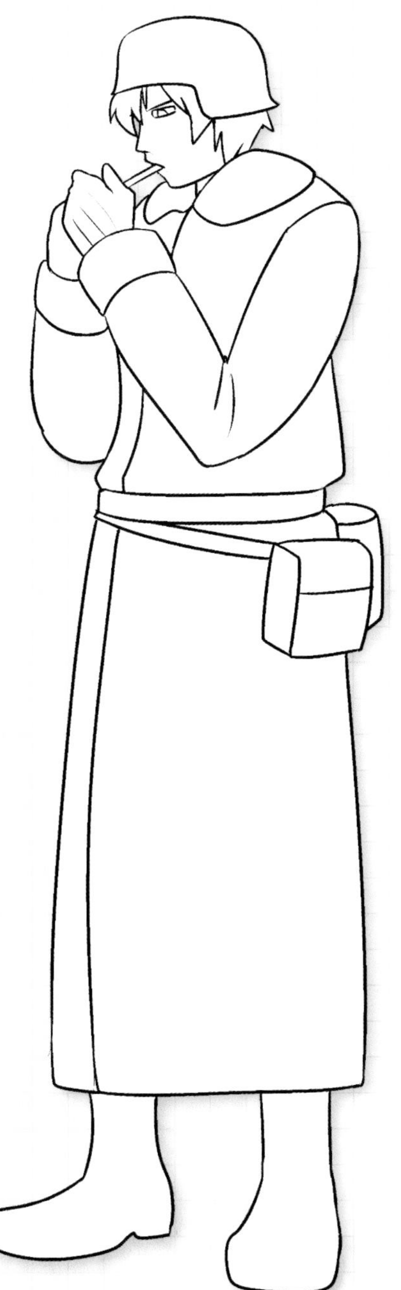

action villains

search criteria

male. standing. smoking. cigarette. helmet. spy. assassin. army.

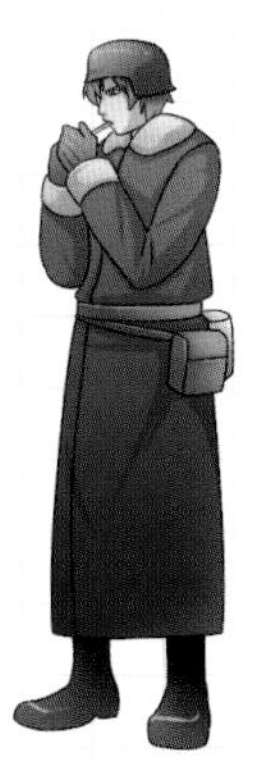

463

action villains

search criteria

male. standing. captain. hat. angry. salute. whip. army.

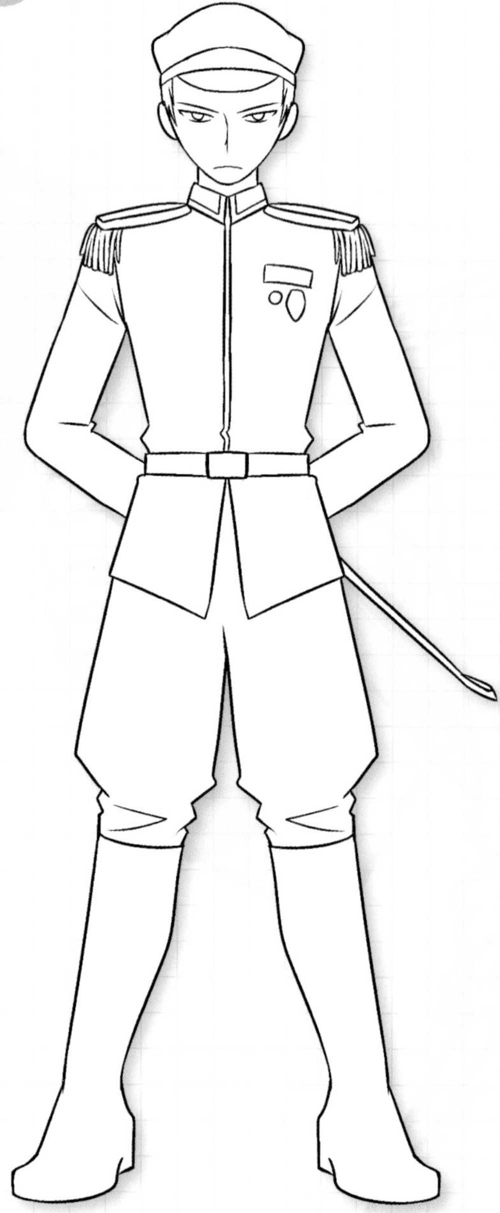

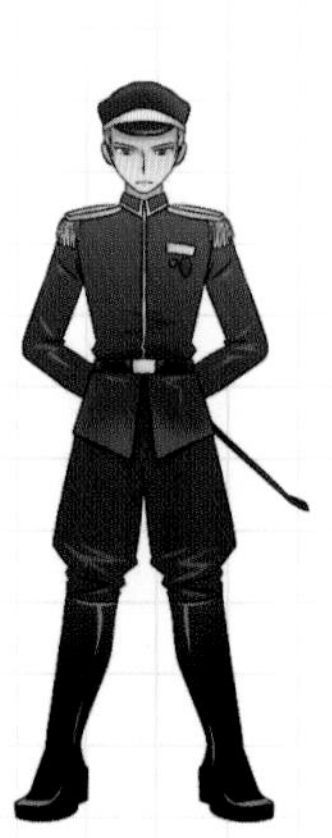

464

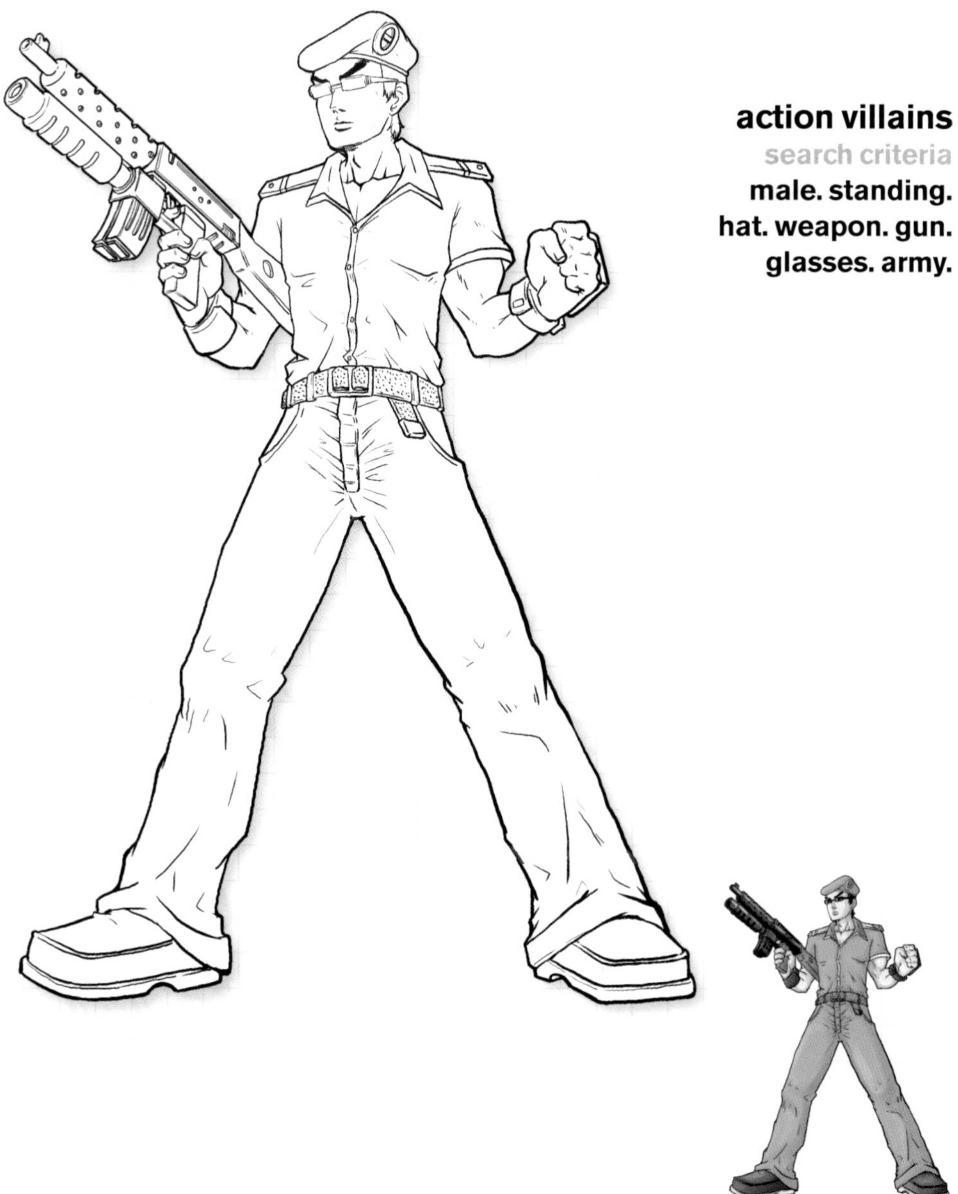

action villains

search criteria

male. standing. hat. weapon. gun. glasses. army.

465

action villains

search criteria

female. standing. side. bag. army.

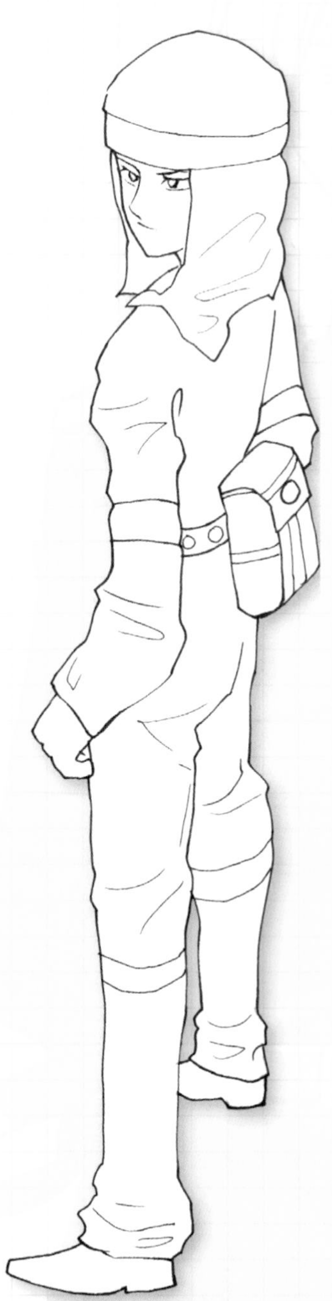

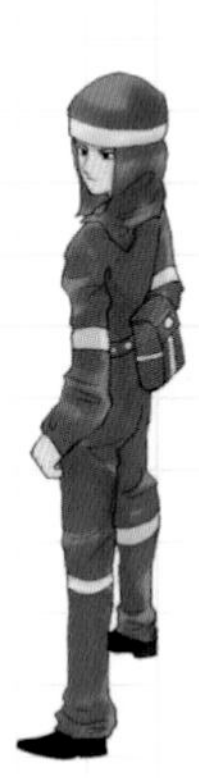

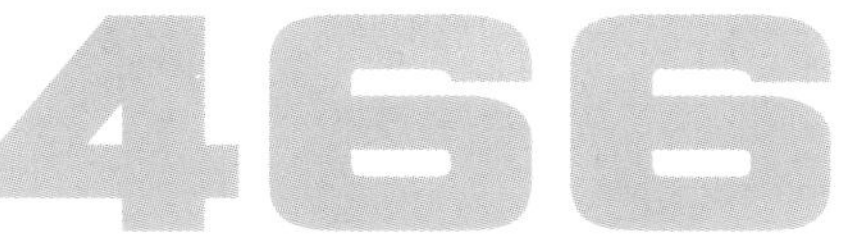

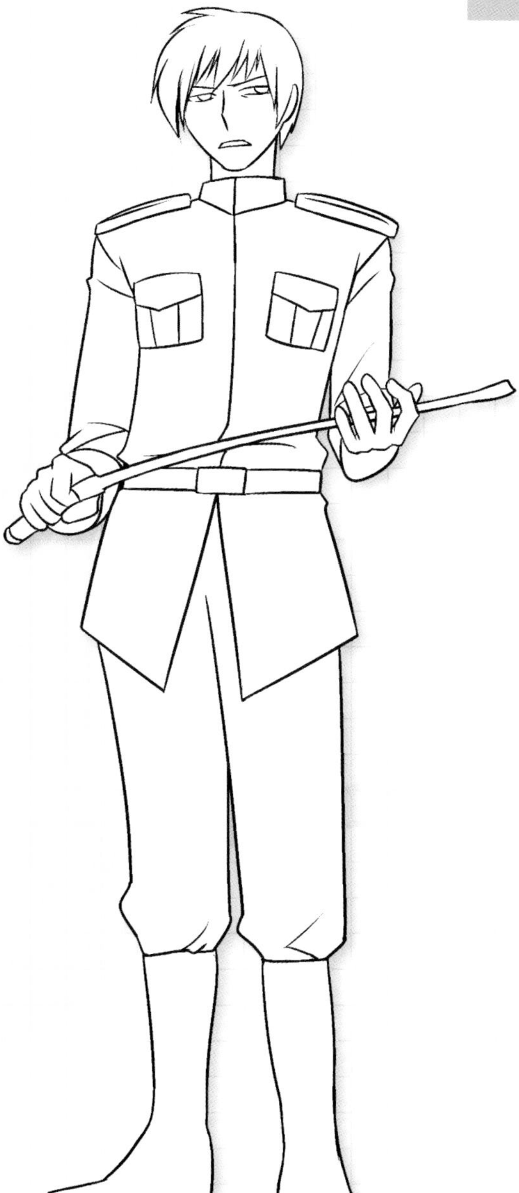

action villains

search criteria

**male. standing.
captain. whip. army.**

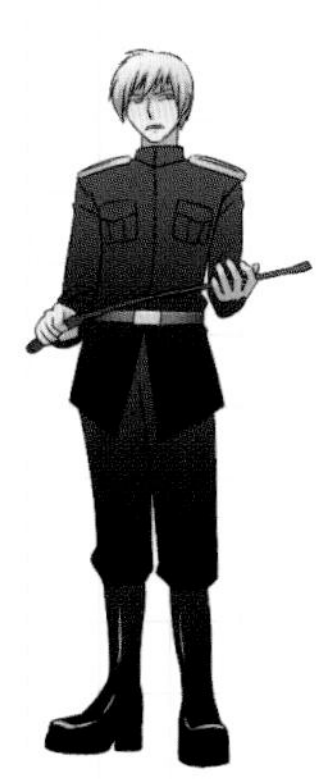

467

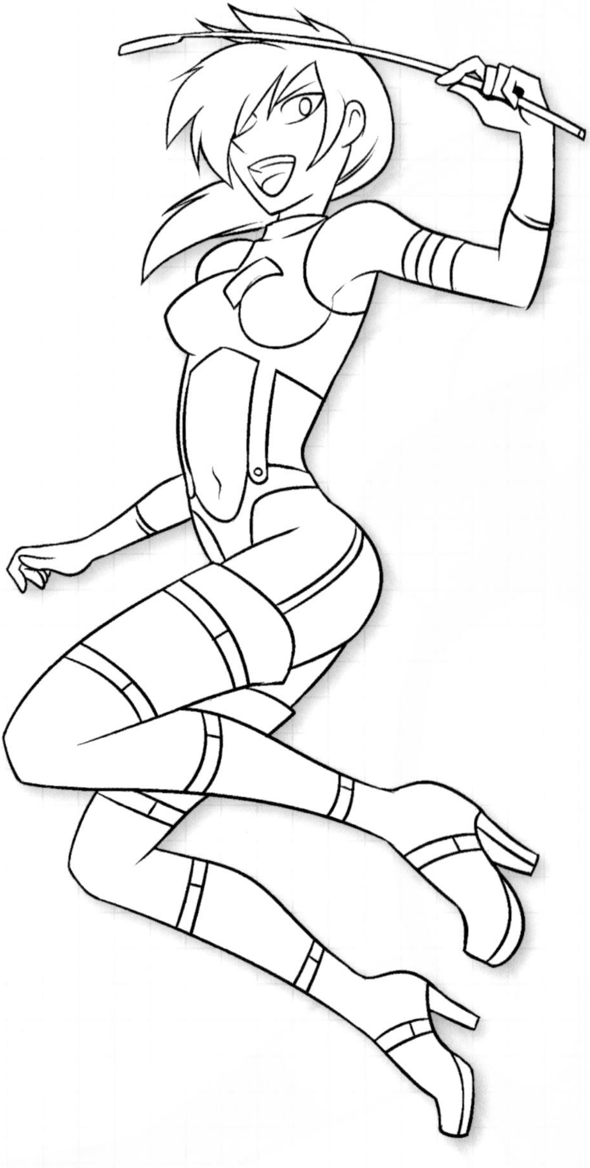

action villains
search criteria
female. jump. side. catsuit. whip. smiling.

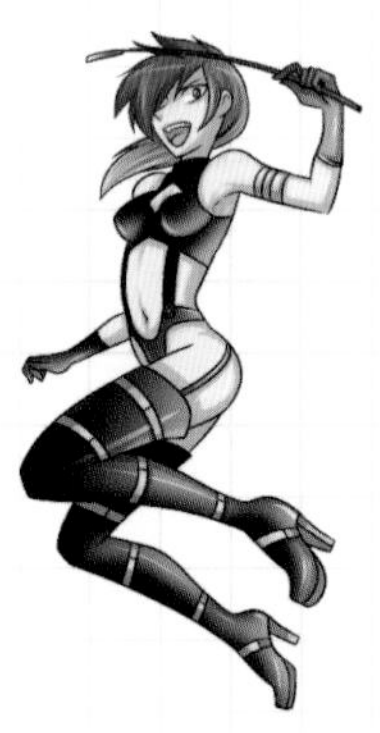

468

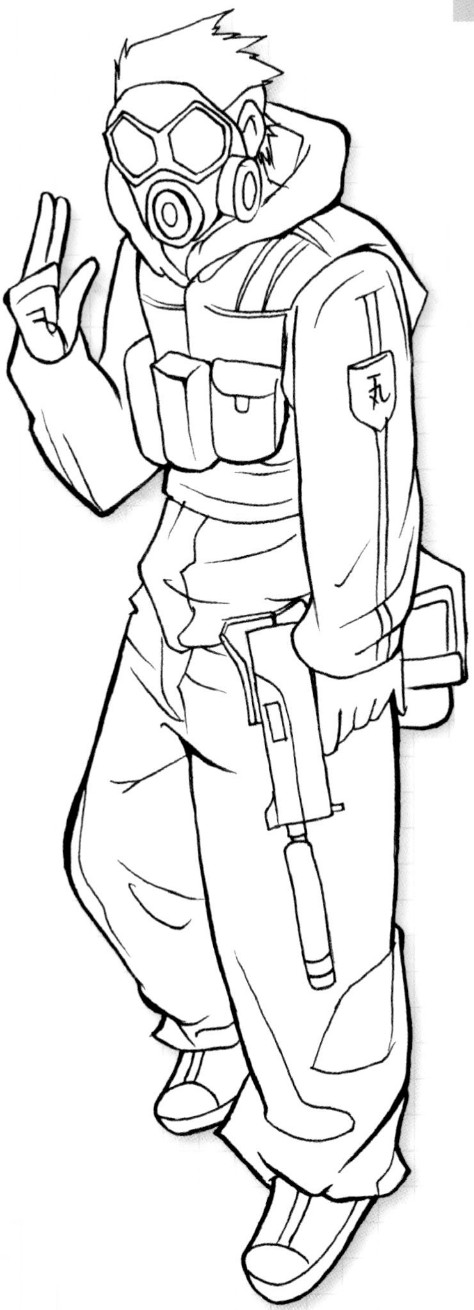

action villains

search criteria

male. standing. side. gesture. mask. gas. weapon. gun. army.

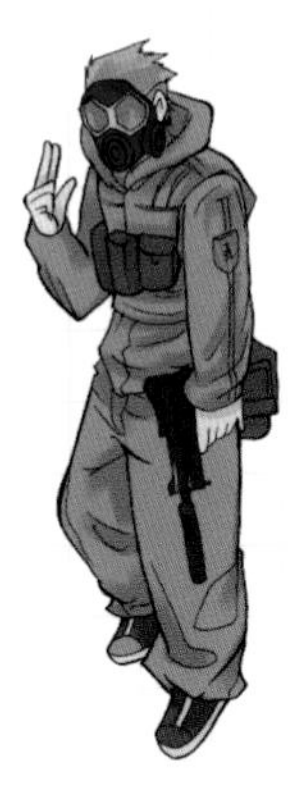

469

action villains

search criteria

male. standing.
hat. radio. weapon.
gun. army.

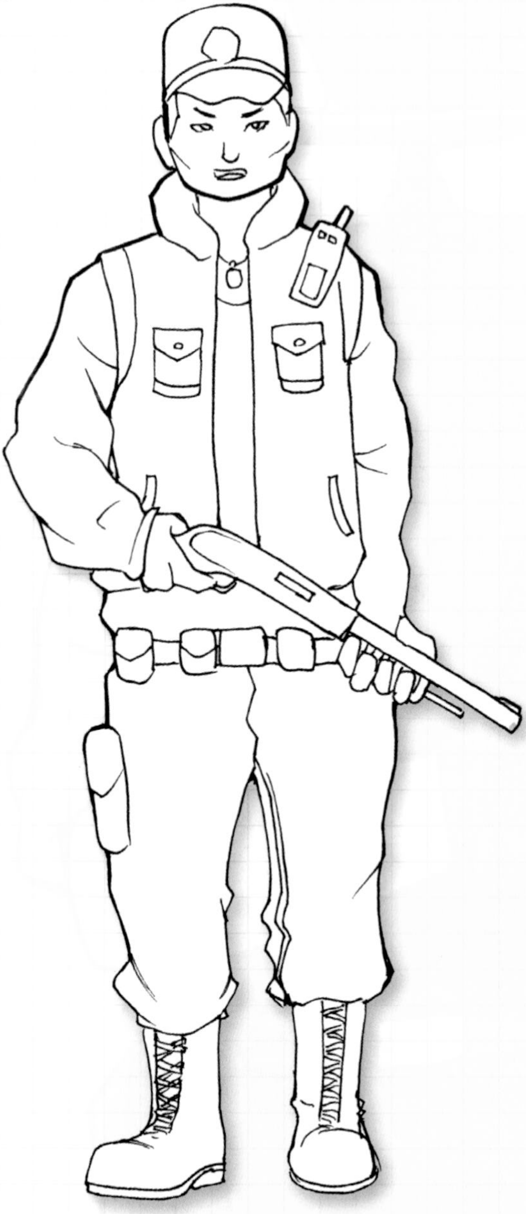

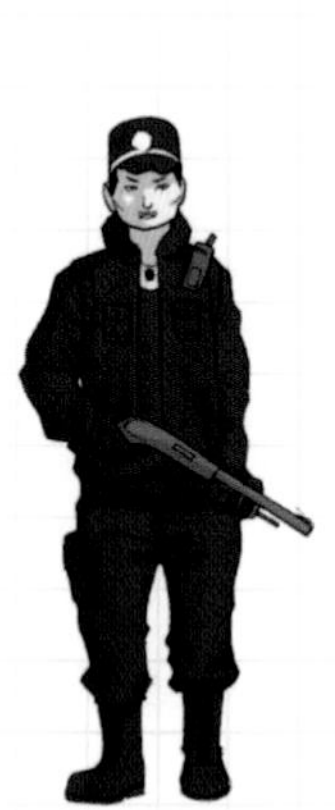

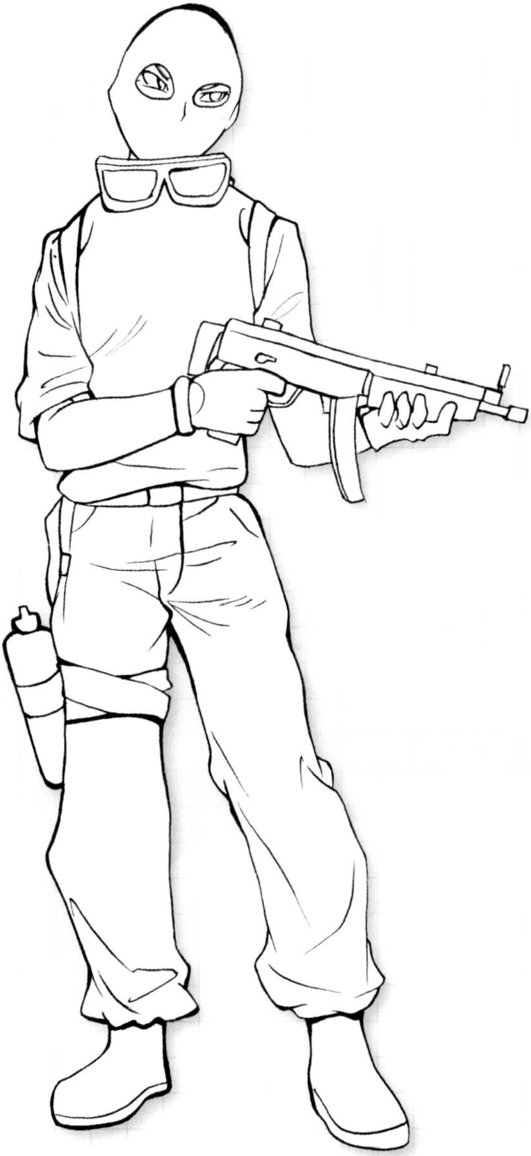

470

action villains

search criteria

male. standing. mask. glasses. weapon. gun. bottle. army.

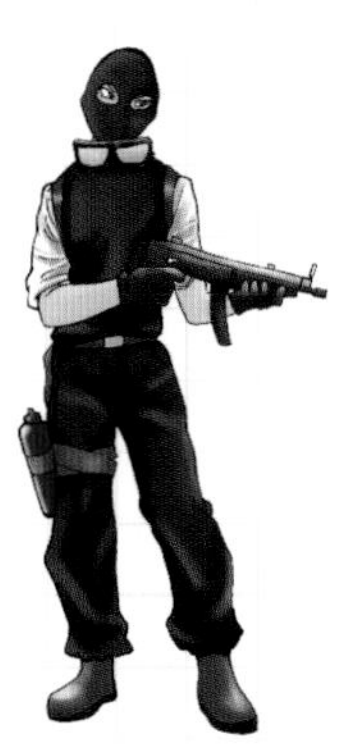

471

action villains

search criteria

male. standing. scars. muscle. weapon. gun. army. angry.

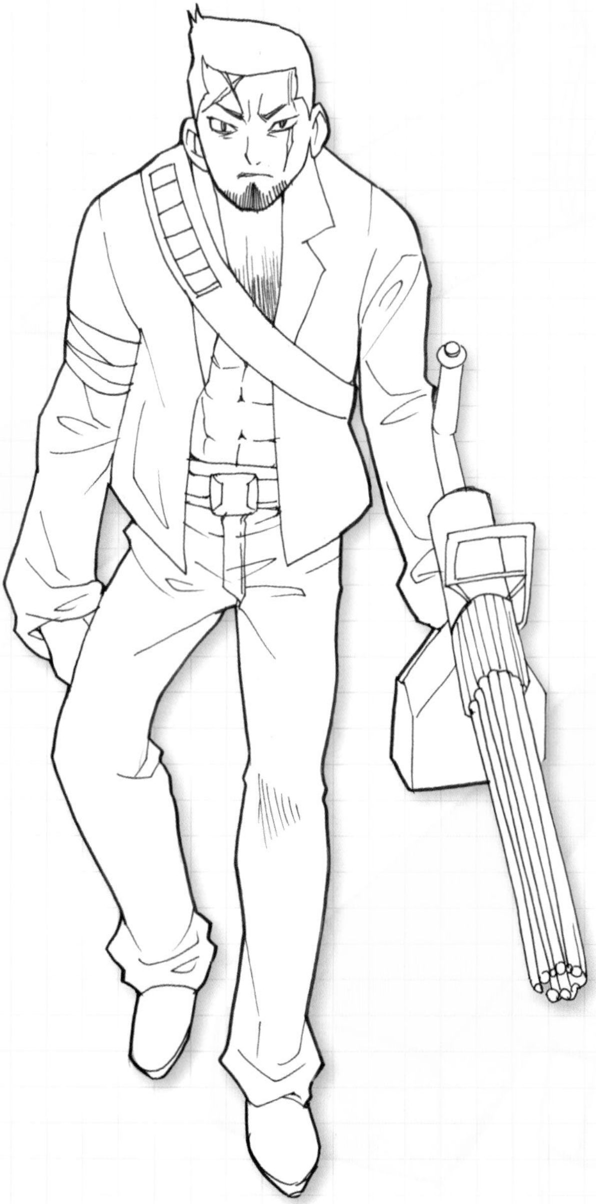

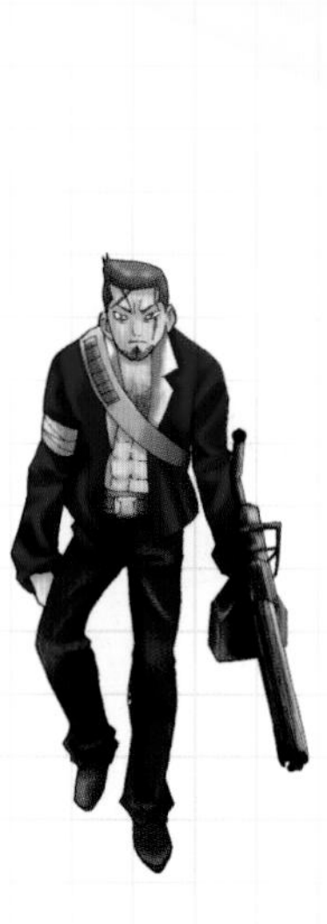

472

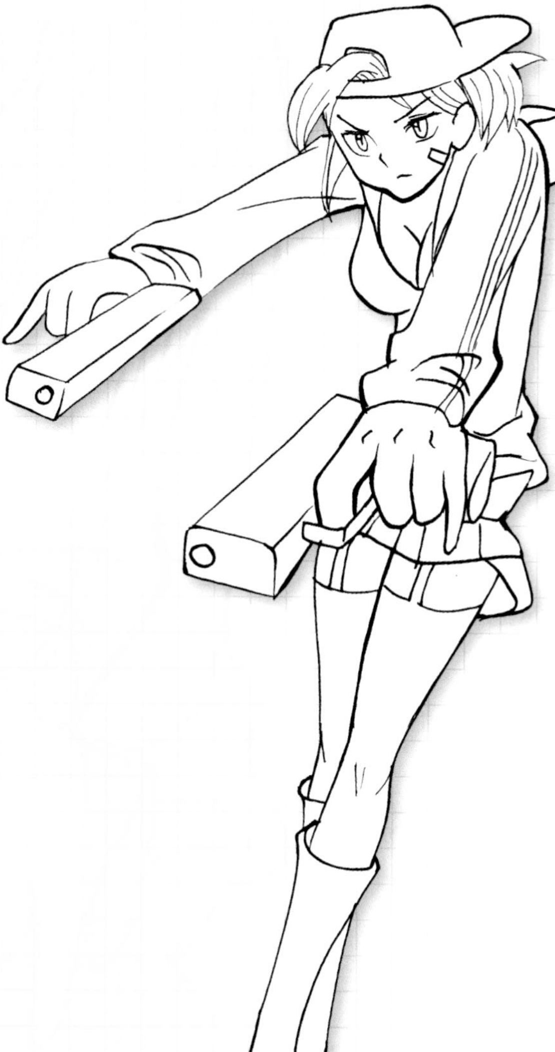

action villains

search criteria

female. standing. side. shooting. weapons. guns. hat. contemporary.

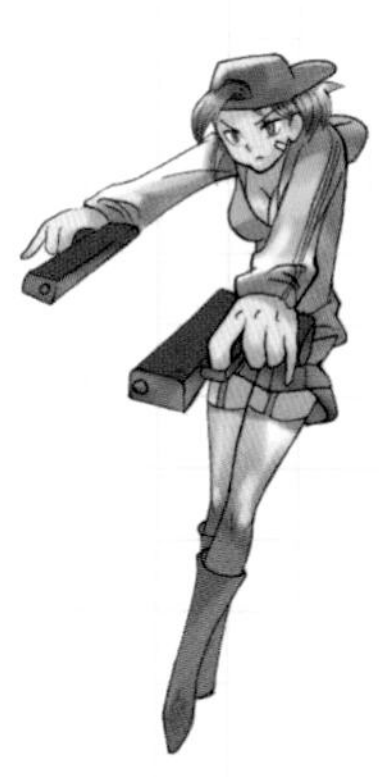

473

action villains

search criteria

male. kneeling. crouched. headscarf. mask. weapon. gun. shooting. contemporary.

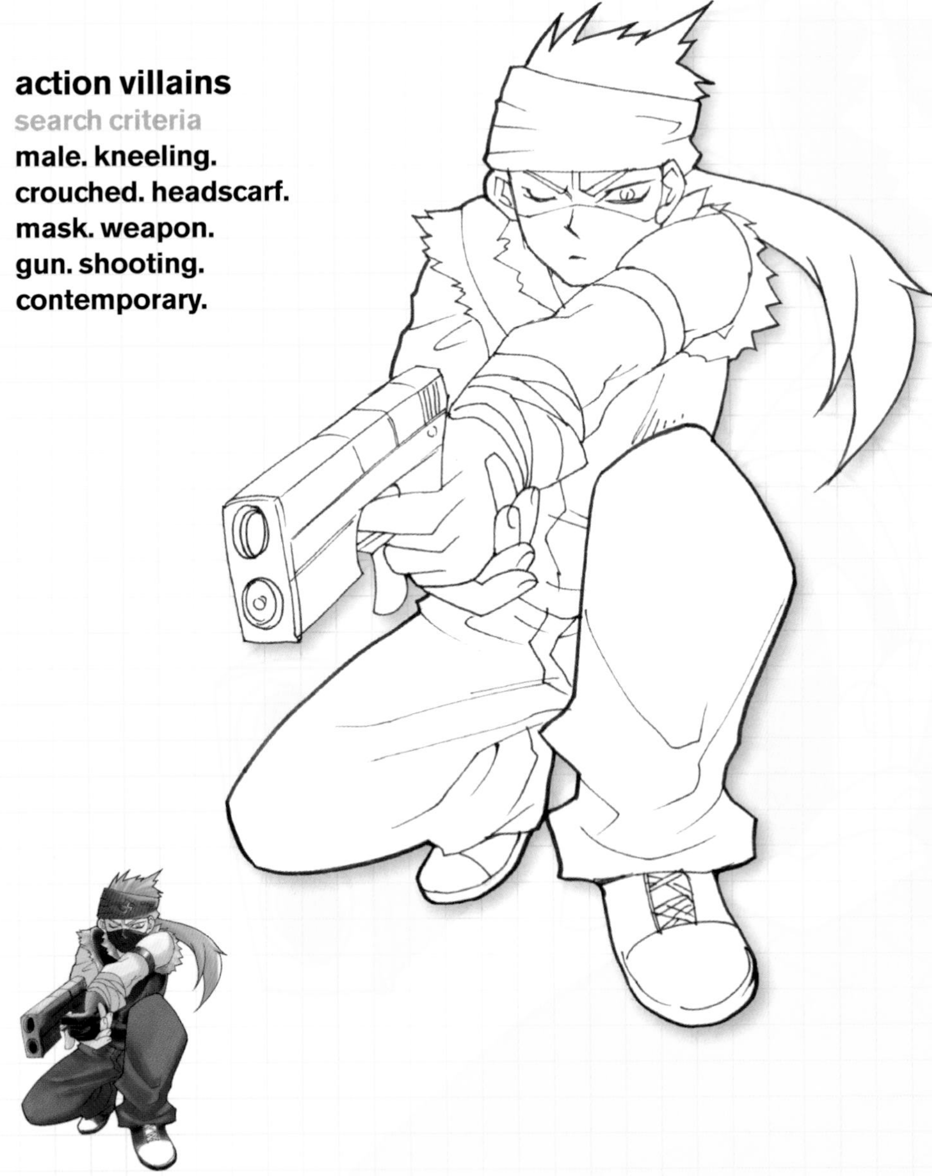

474

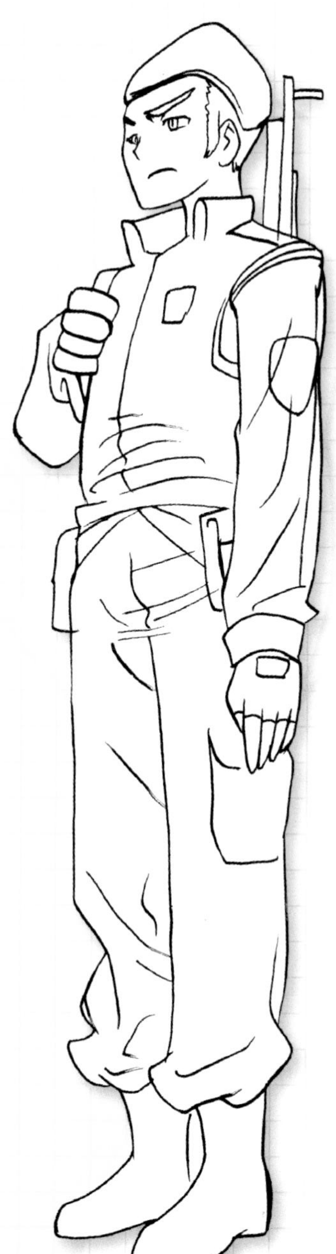

action villains

search criteria

male. standing. side. weapon. gun. army.

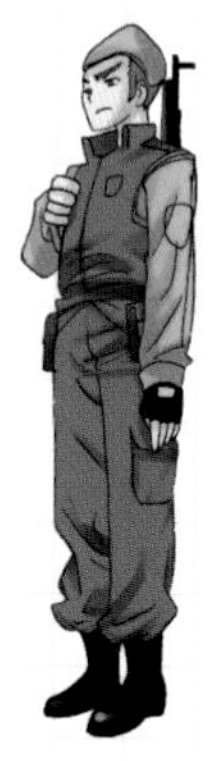

475

action villains
search criteria
male. attack. headband. army. weapon. gun.

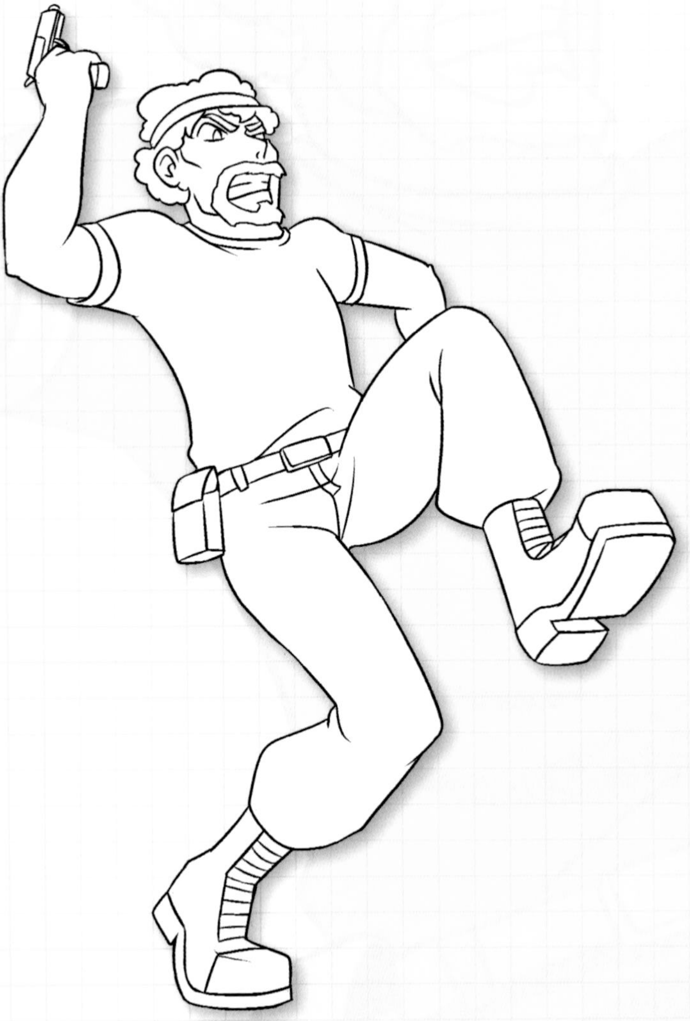

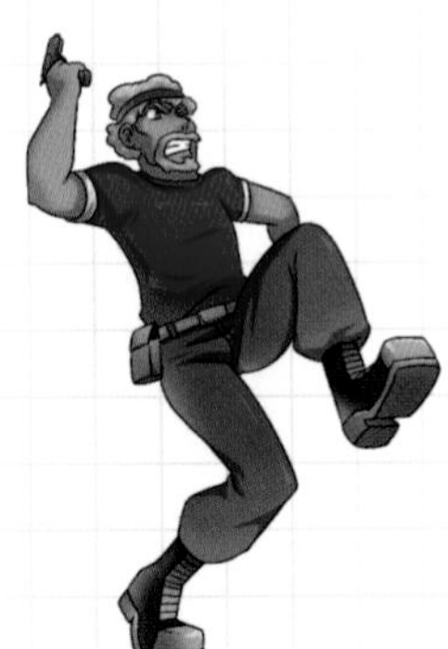

476

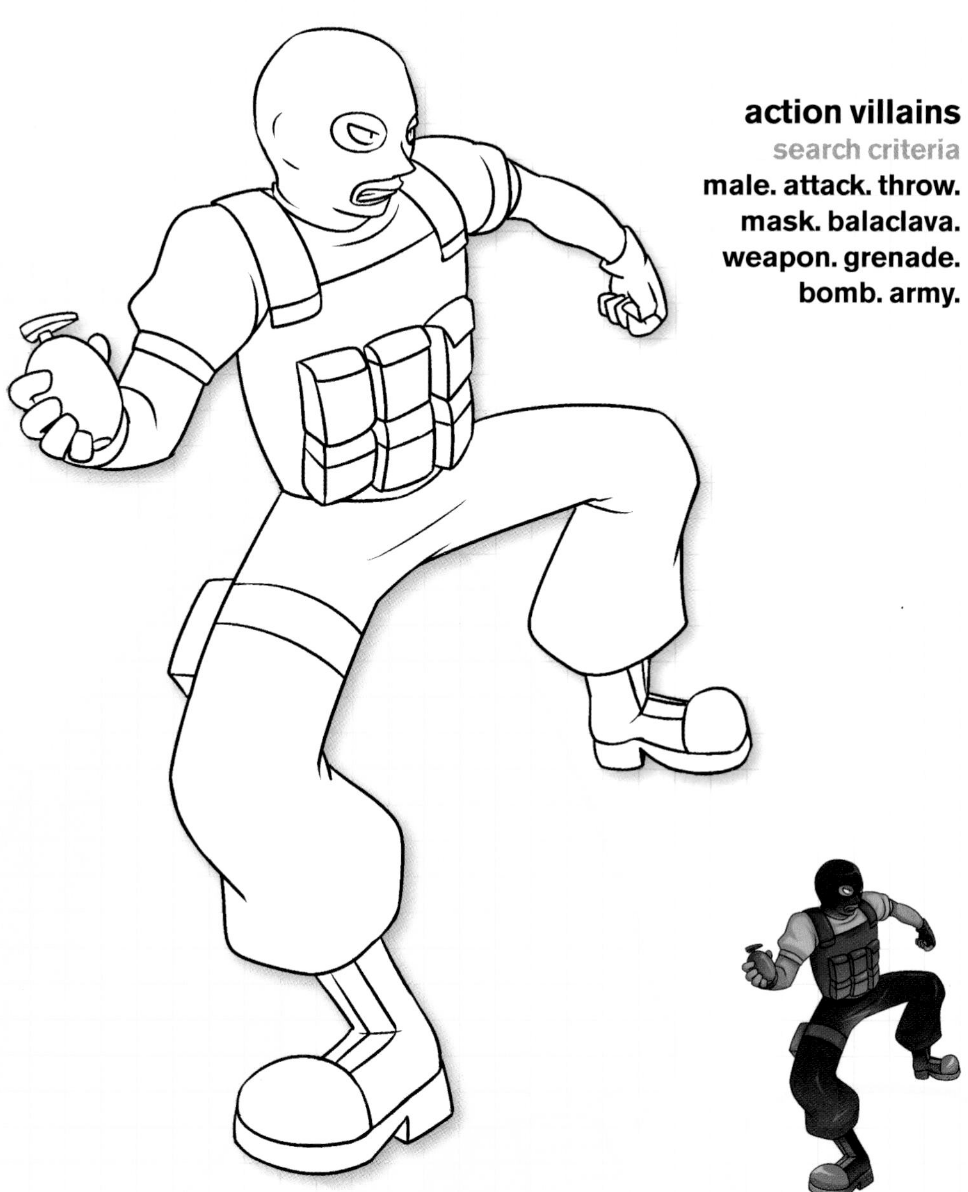

action villains

search criteria

male. attack. throw. mask. balaclava. weapon. grenade. bomb. army.

477

action villains

search criteria

male. standing. shooting. hat. weapon. gun. army.

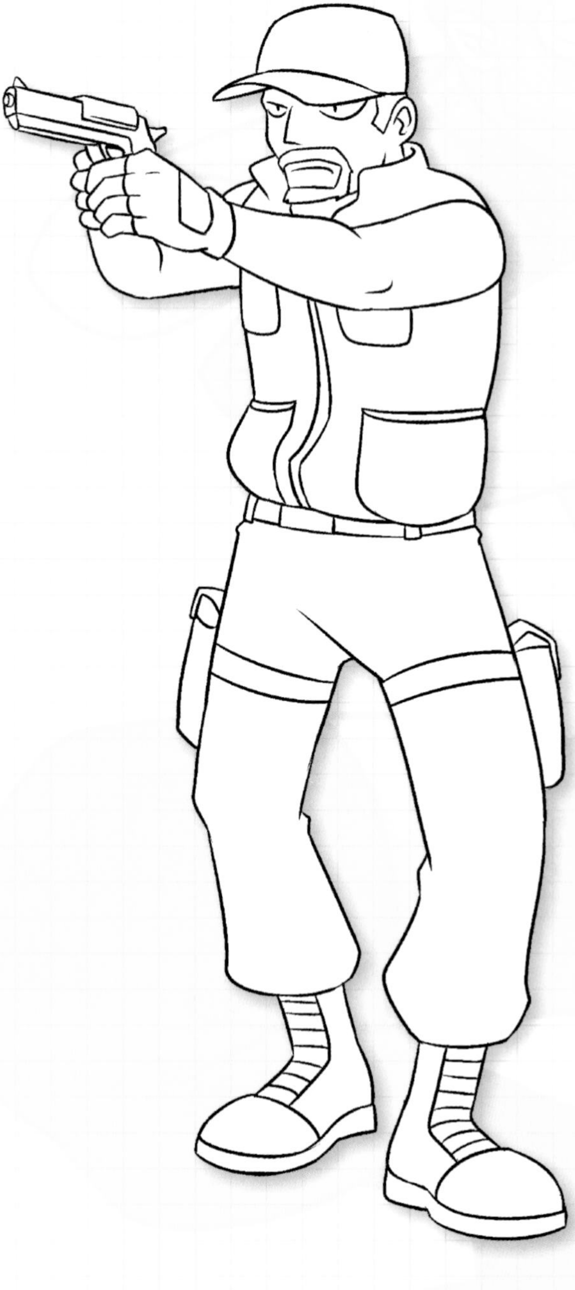

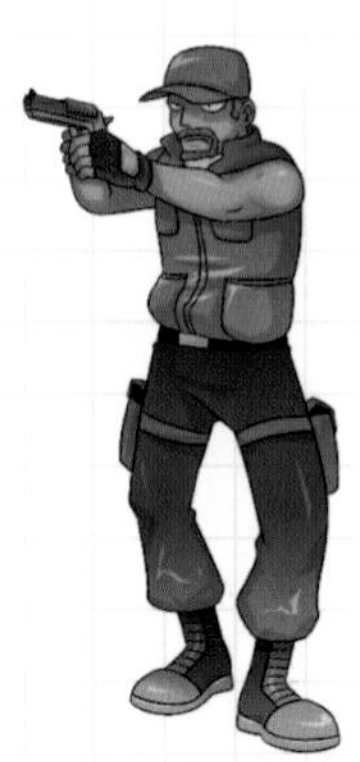

478

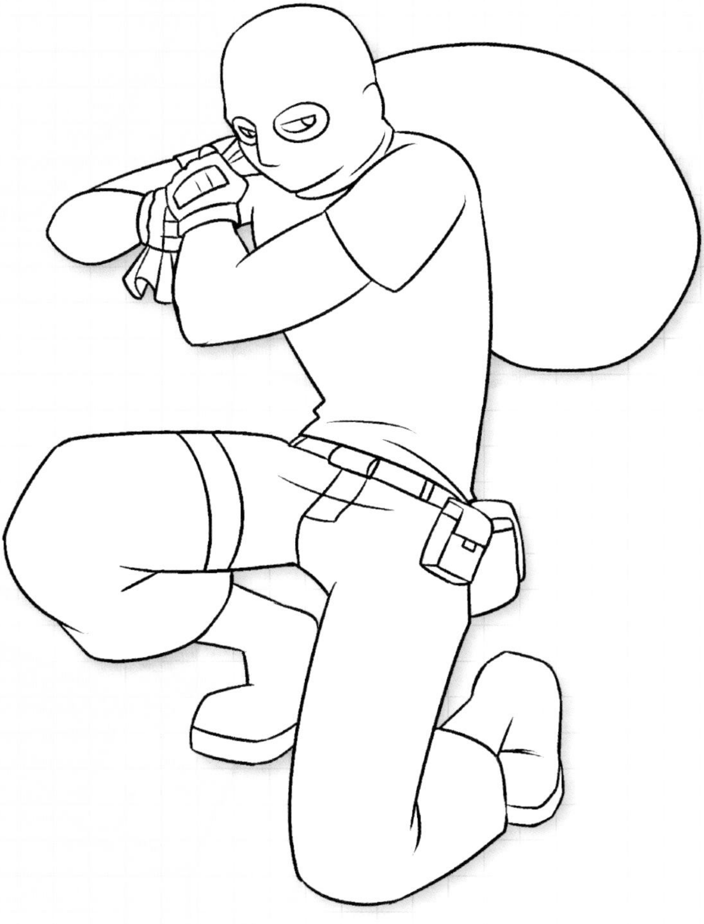

action villains

search criteria

male. kneeling. crouched. mask. balaclava. bag. burglar. army.

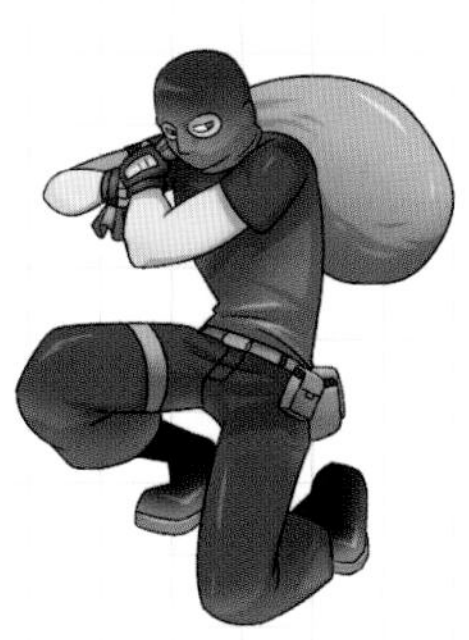

479

action heroes

search criteria

female. standing. hat. weapon. gun. army. spy. assassin.

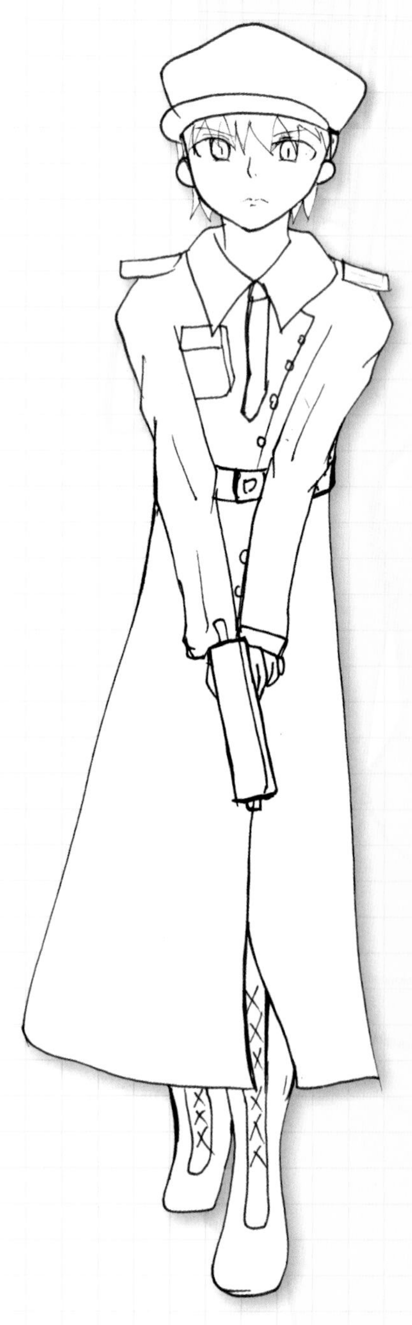

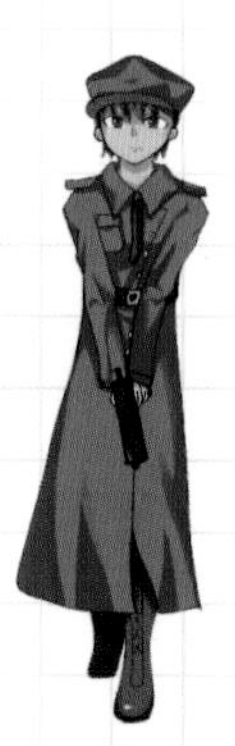

480

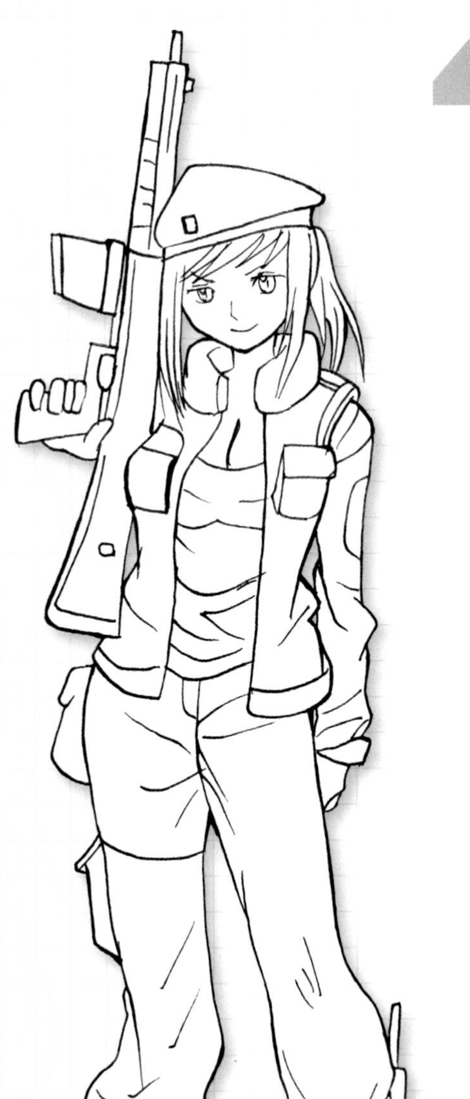

action heroes

search criteria

female. standing. hat. army. weapon. gun. smiling.

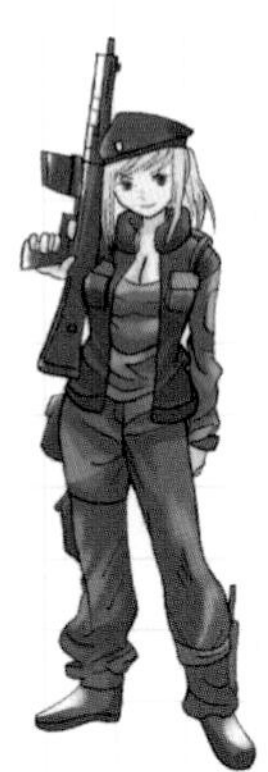

481

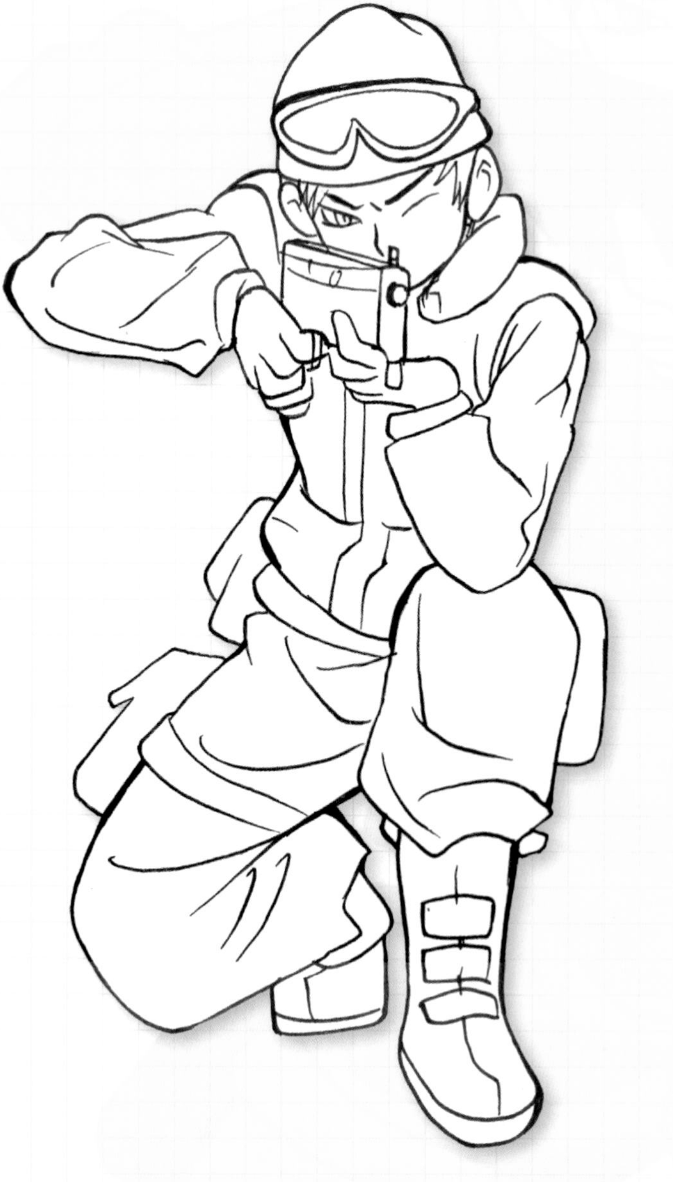

action heroes

search criteria

male. kneeling. crouched. helmet. shooting. weapon. gun. glasses. army.

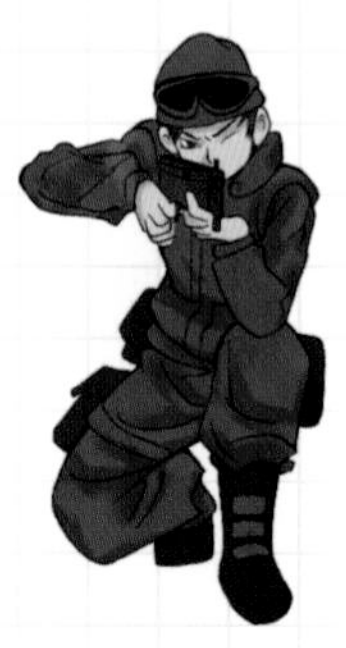

482

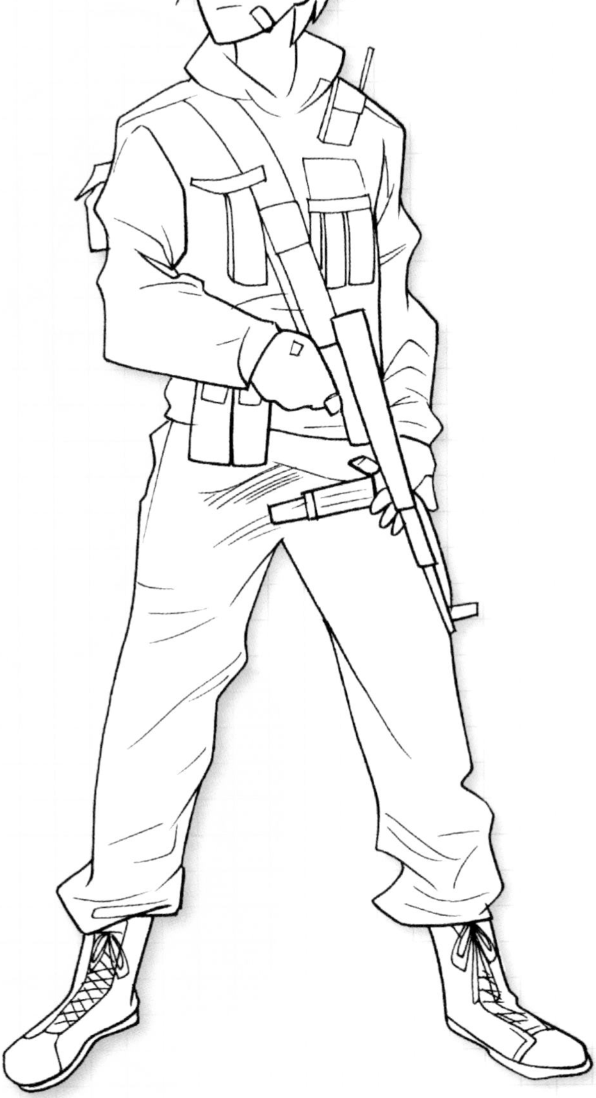

action heroes

search criteria

male. standing. hat. bandage. radio. weapon. gun.

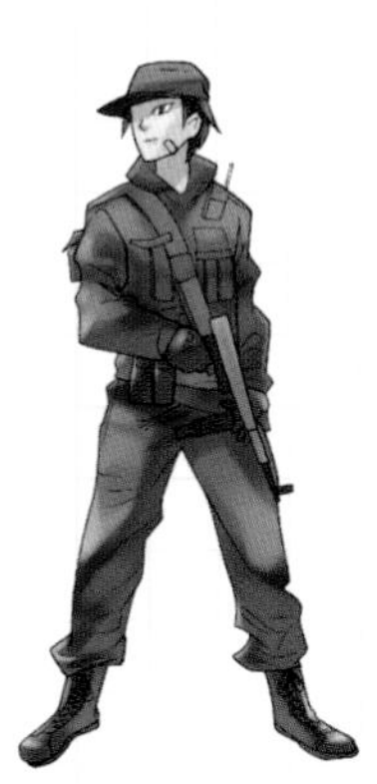

483

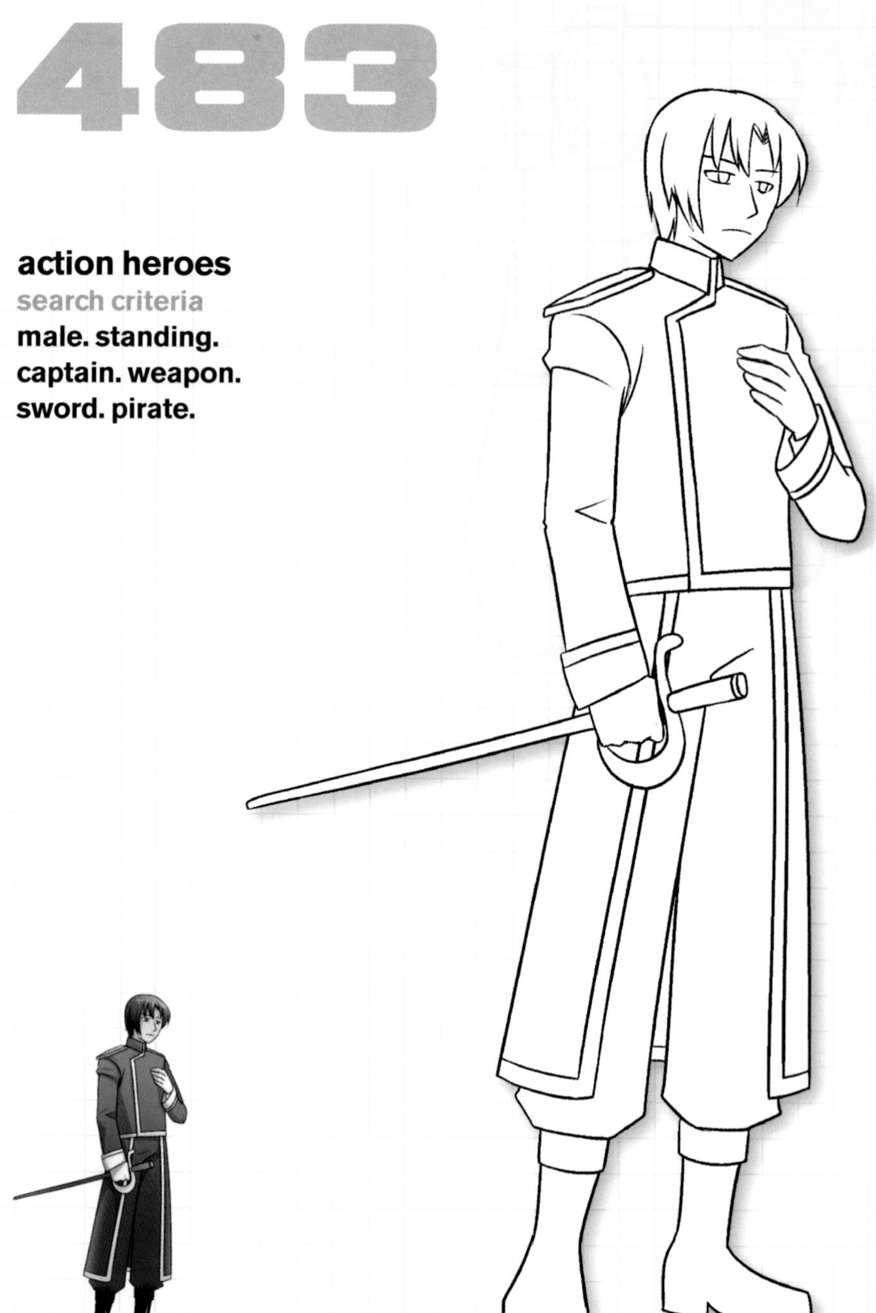

action heroes

search criteria

male. standing. captain. weapon. sword. pirate.

484

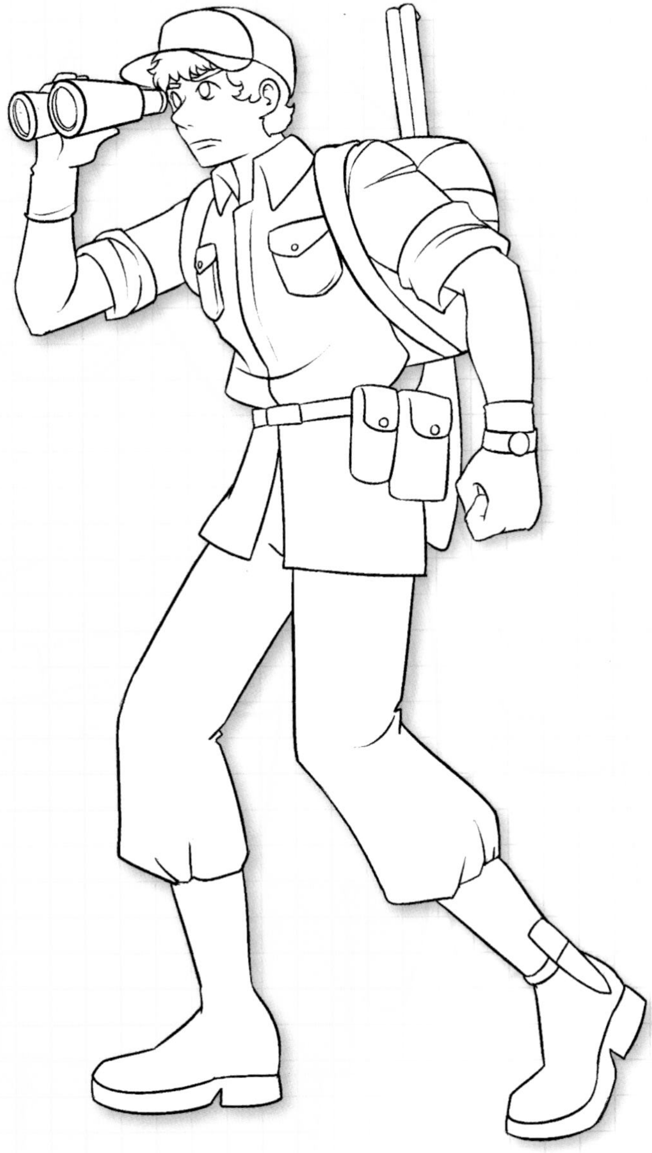

action heroes
search criteria
male. standing. side. looking. binoculars. watch. hat. explorer.

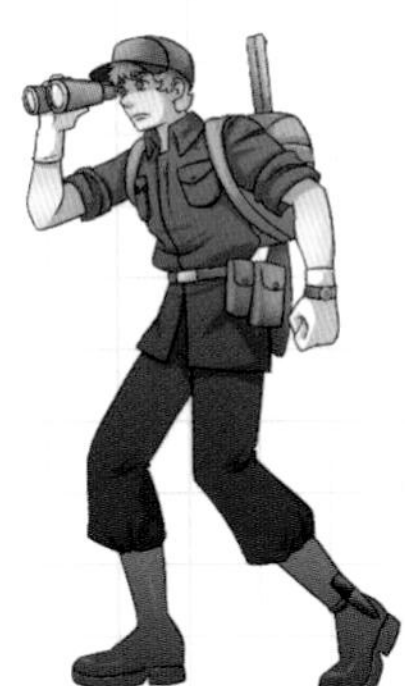

485

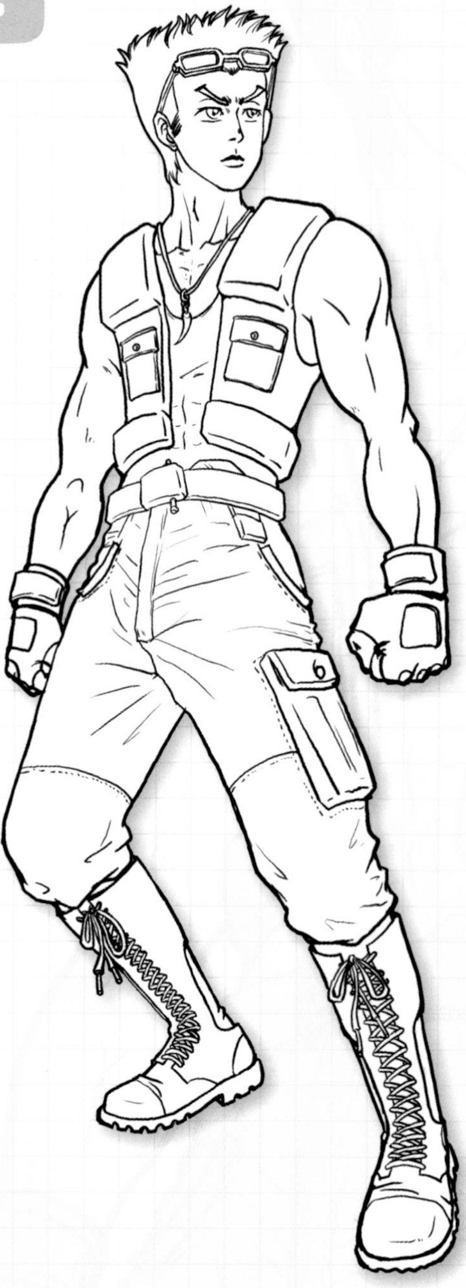

action heroes

search criteria

**male. standing.
glasses. necklace.
army. muscle.**

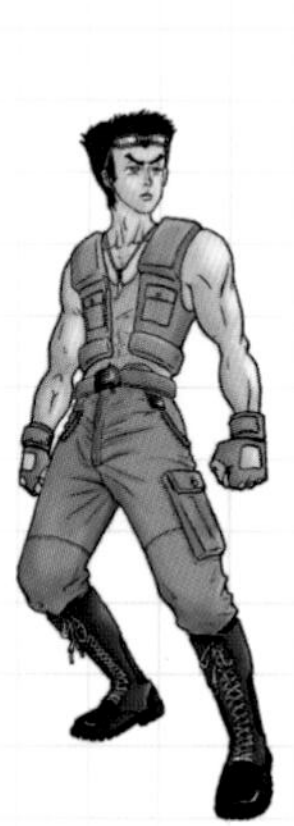

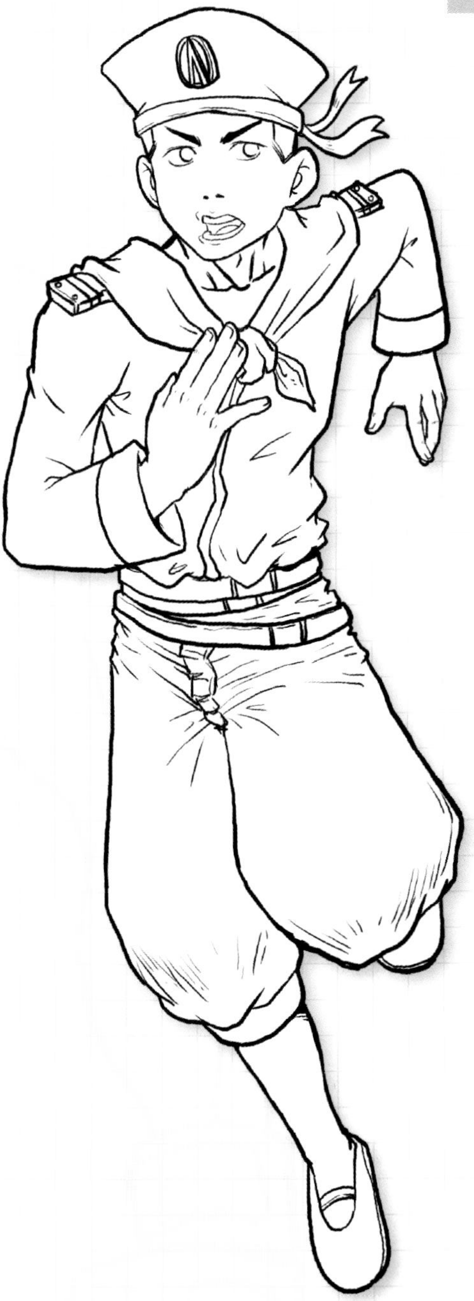

486

action heroes

search criteria

male. running.
sailor. hat.

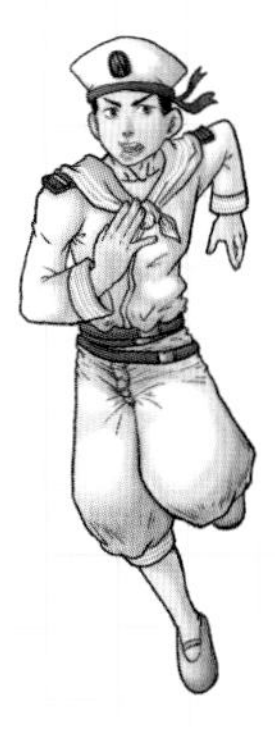

487

action heroes

search criteria

male. standing. side. armor. star. army.

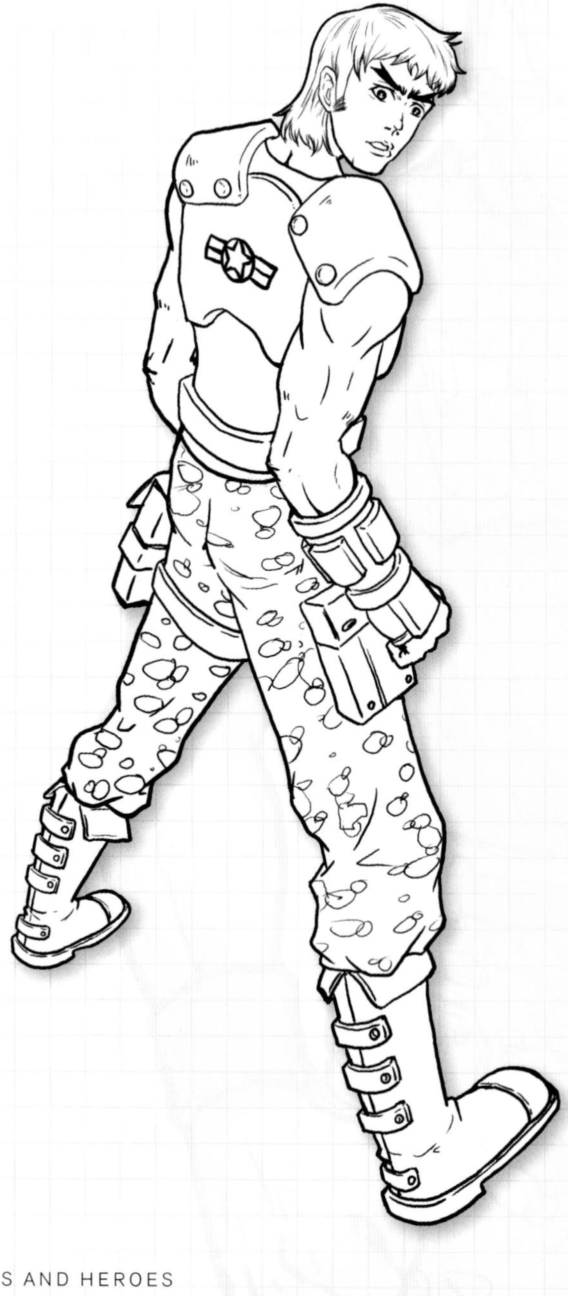

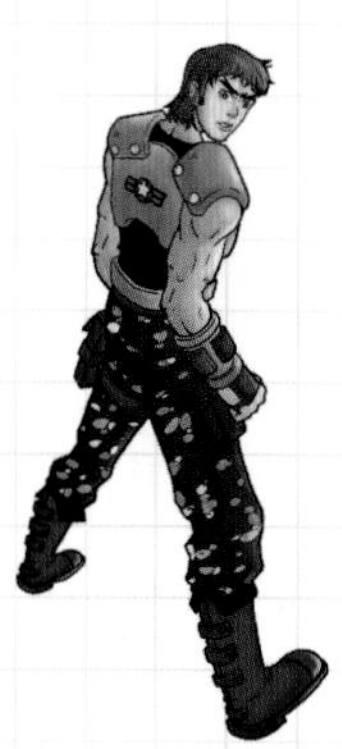

488

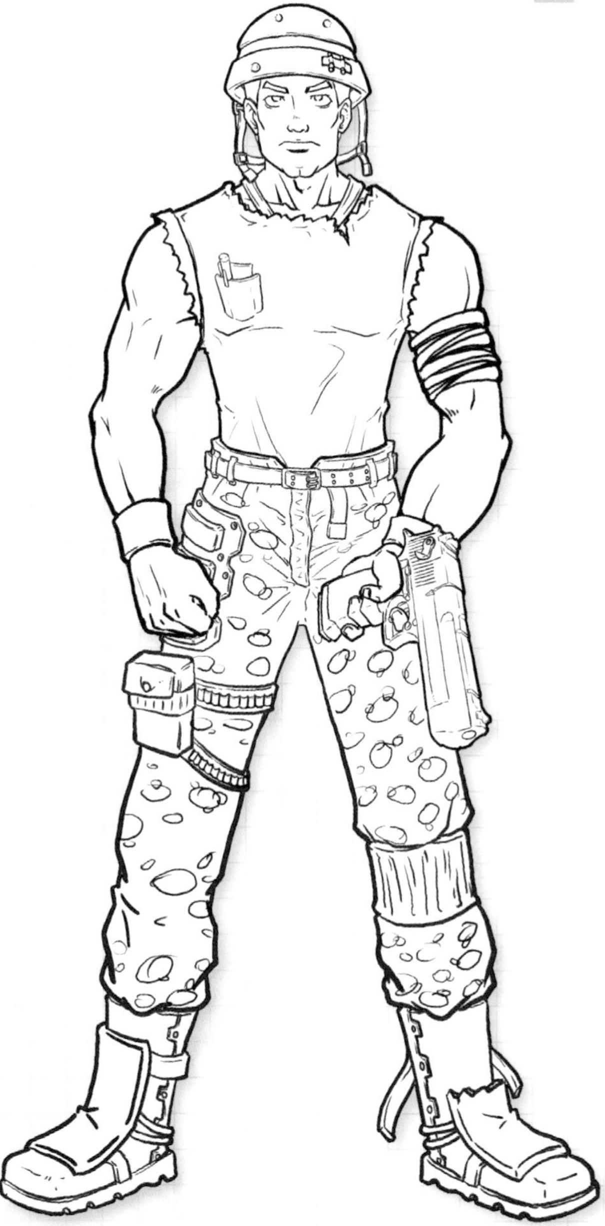

action heroes

search criteria

**male. standing.
helmet. weapon.
gun. army. captain.**

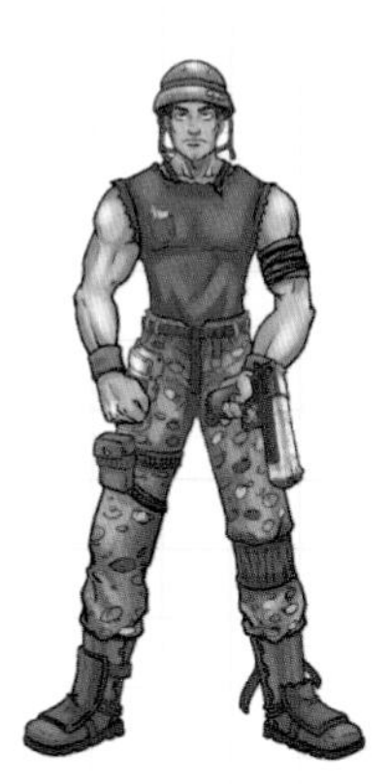

489

action heroes

search criteria

**male. standing.
captain. sailor.
clipboard. side.**

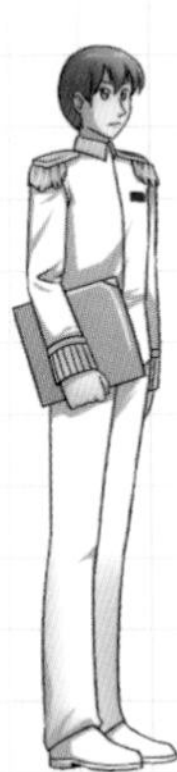

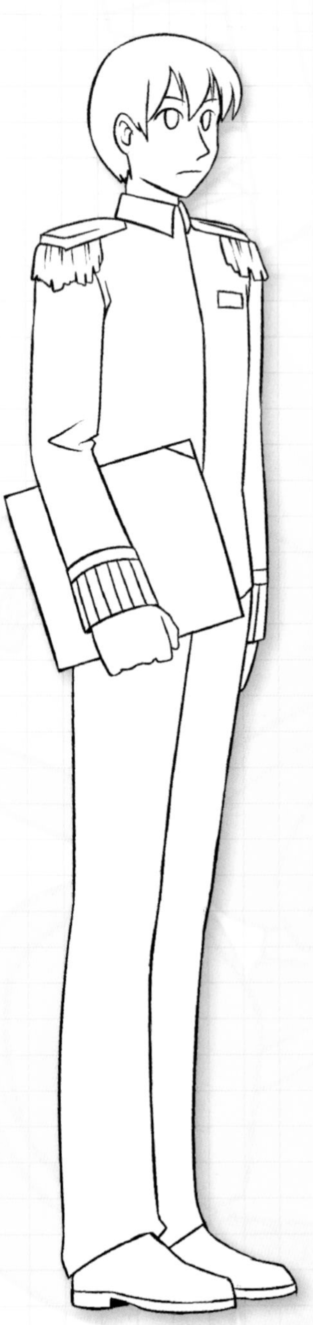

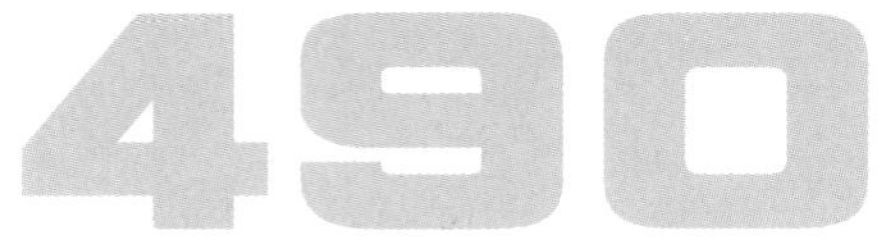

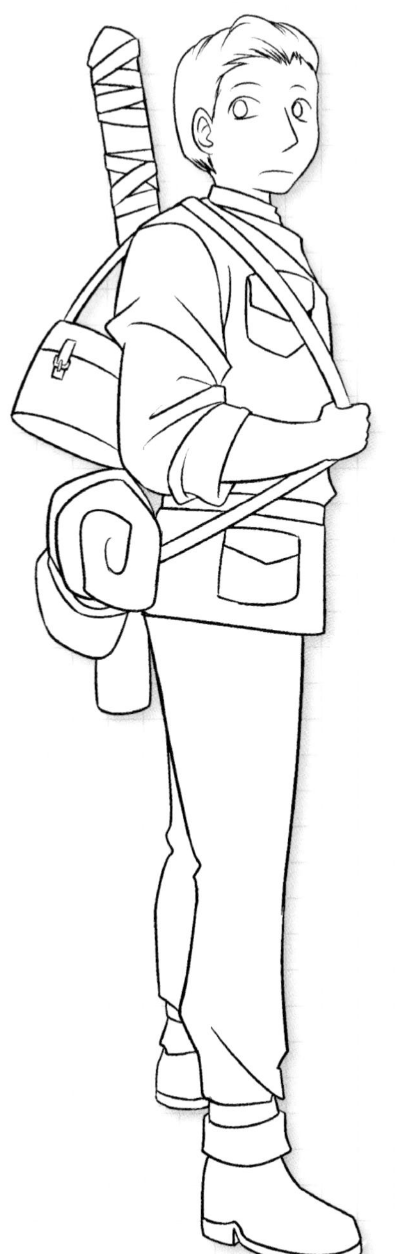

action heroes

search criteria

male. standing. side. worried. bags. explorer. army.

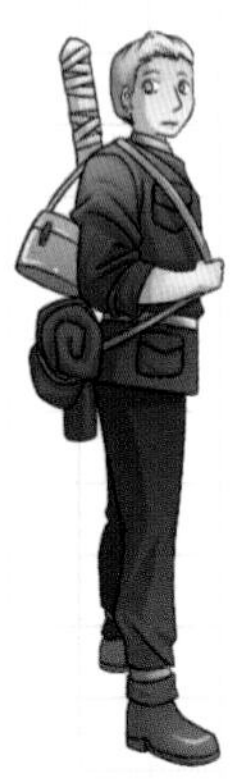

491

action heroes

search criteria

male. standing. helmet. bag. weapon. gun. spy. army.

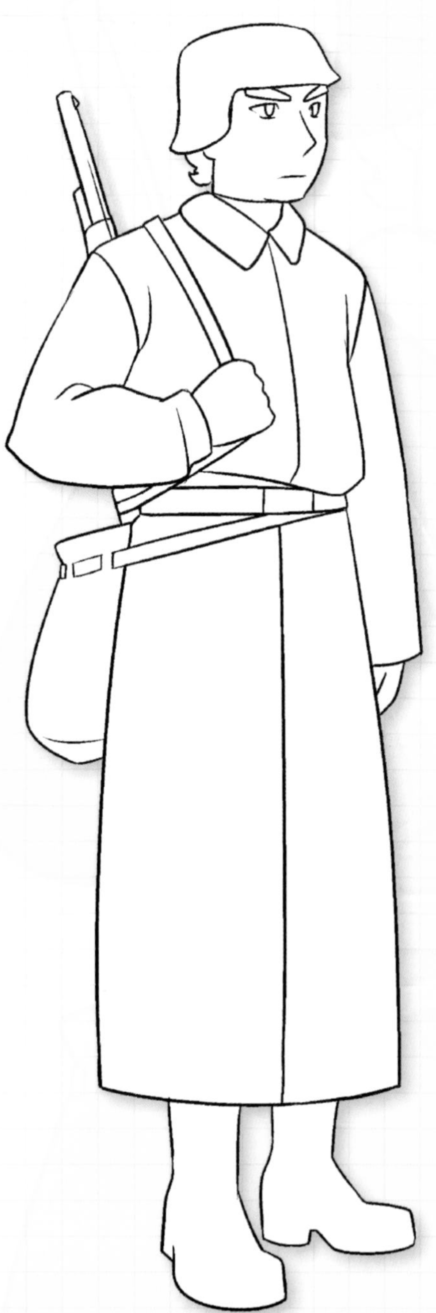

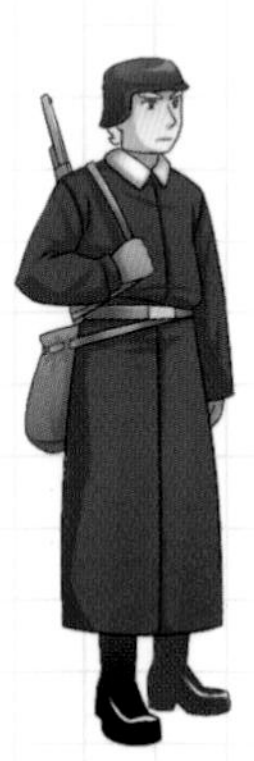

492

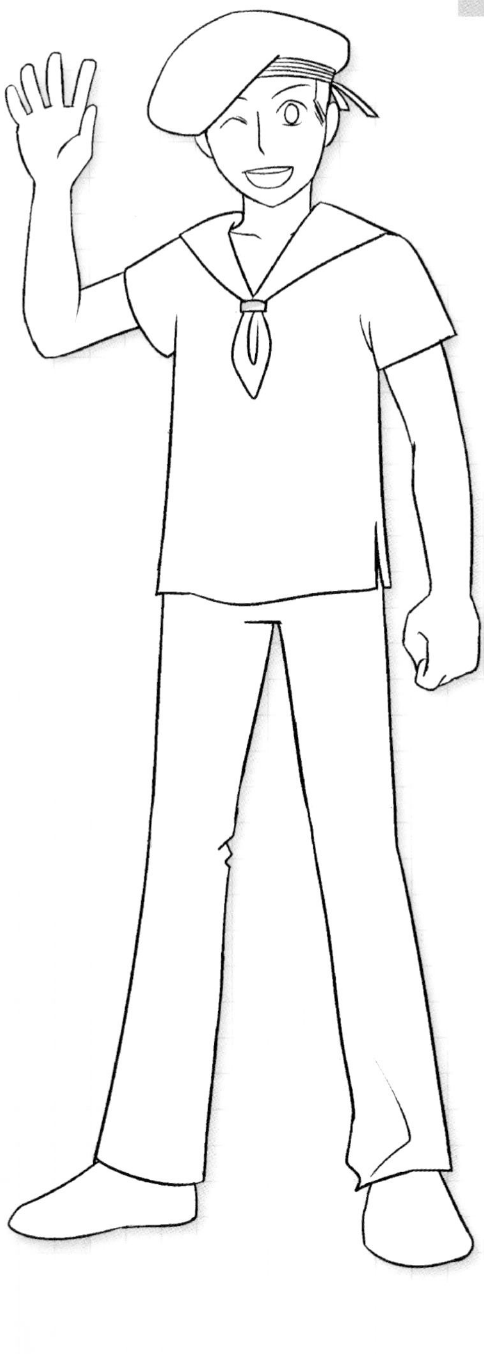

action heroes

search criteria

male. standing. waving. smiling. hat. sailor.

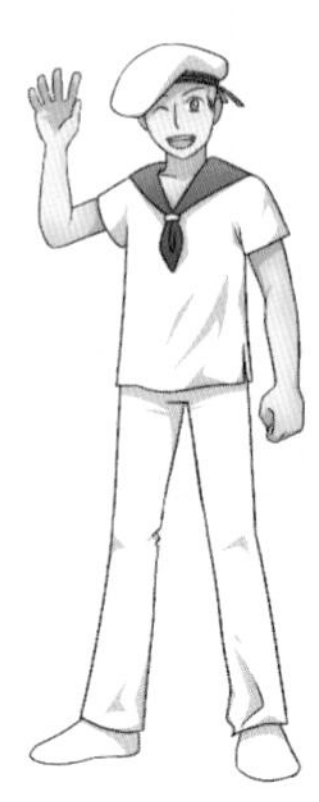

493

action heroes

search criteria

male. standing.
captain. hat. army.

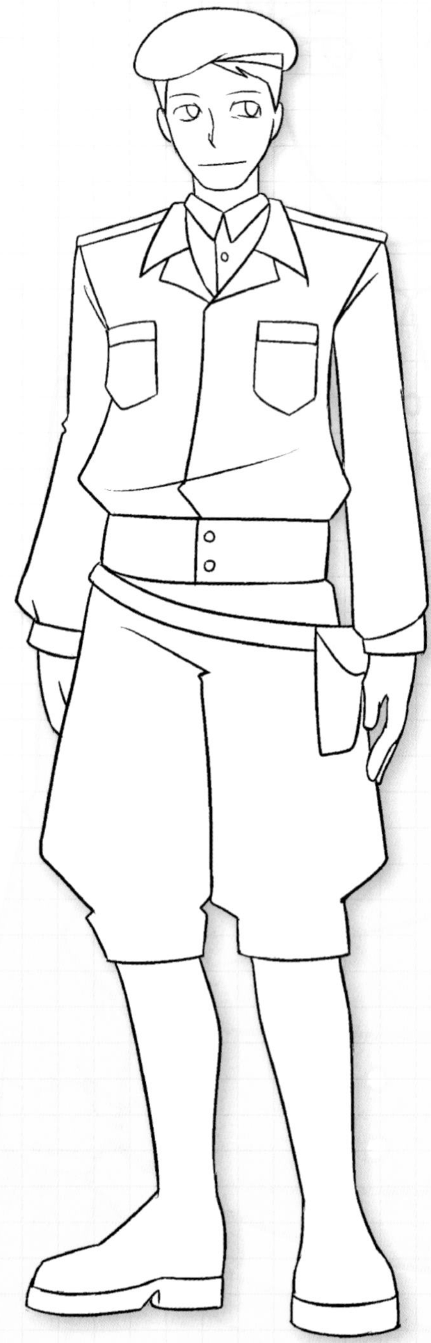

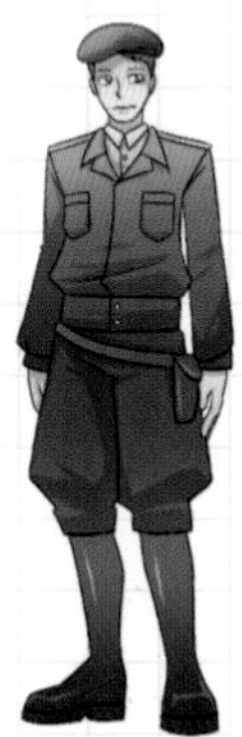

494

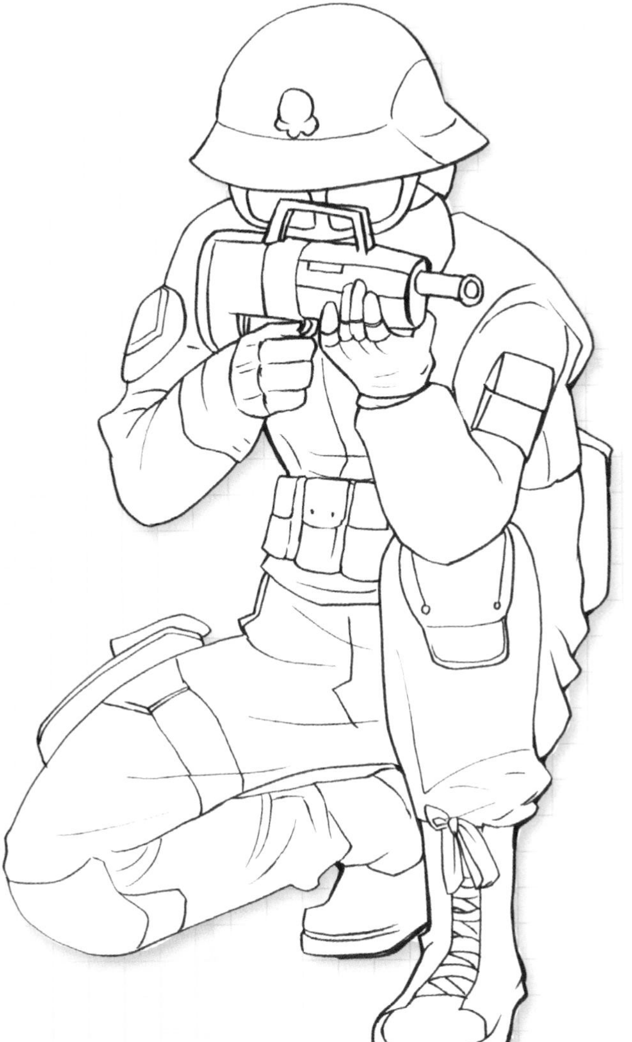

action heroes

search criteria

male. kneeling. crouched. helmet. shooting. weapon. gun. army.

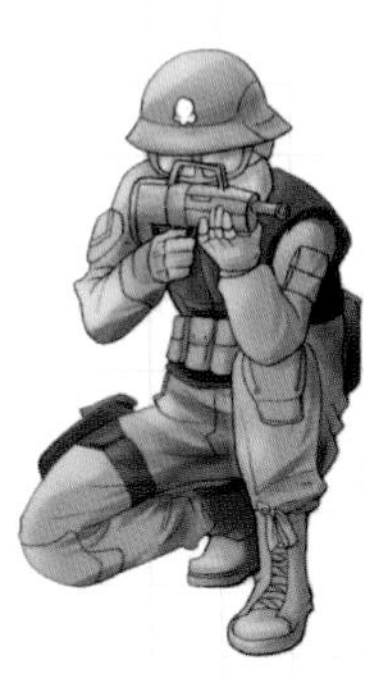

495

action heroes

search criteria

male. standing. stop. helmet. gesture. army. weapons. guns.

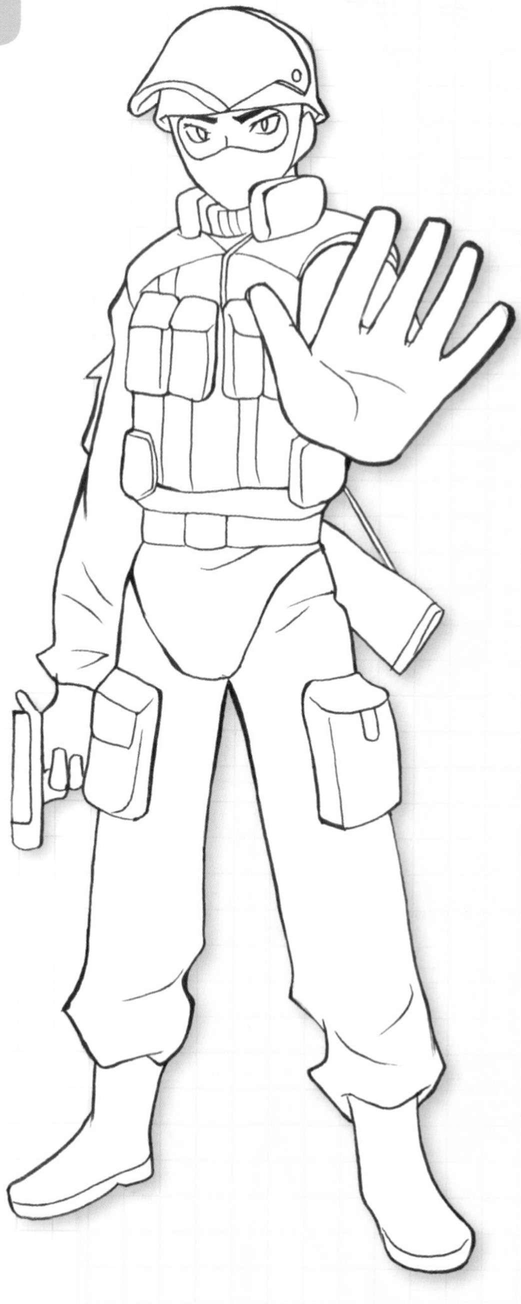

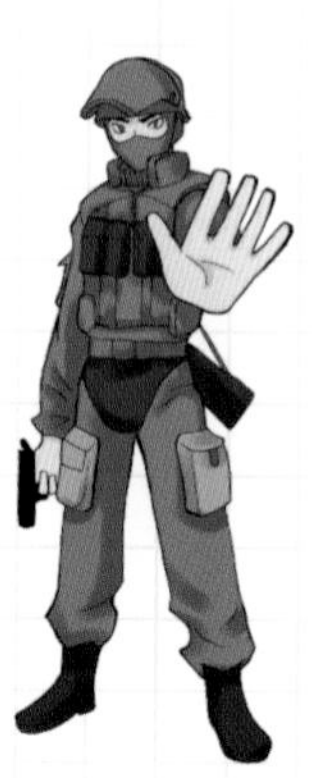

496

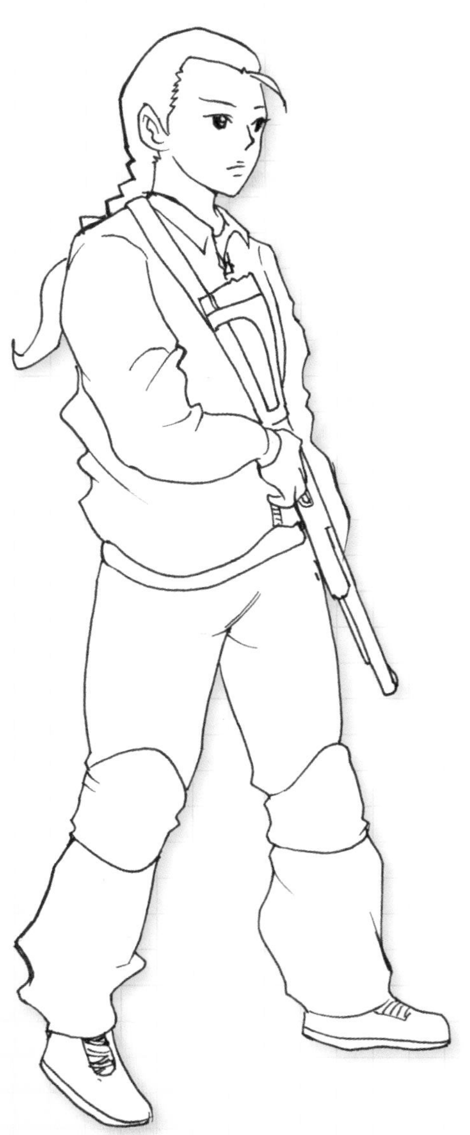

action heroes

search criteria

female. standing. side. ponytail. weapon. gun.

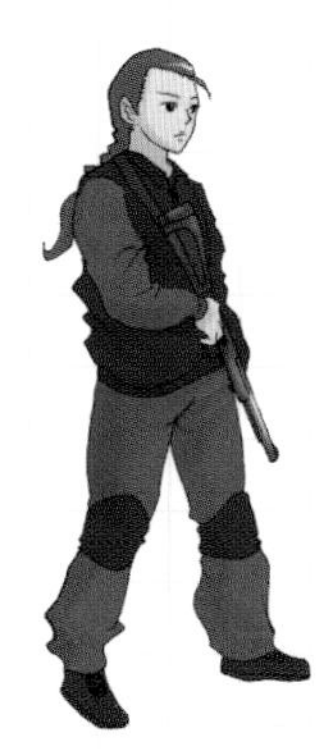

497

action heroes

search criteria

male. jump. hat. glasses. shooting. weapons. gun. army.

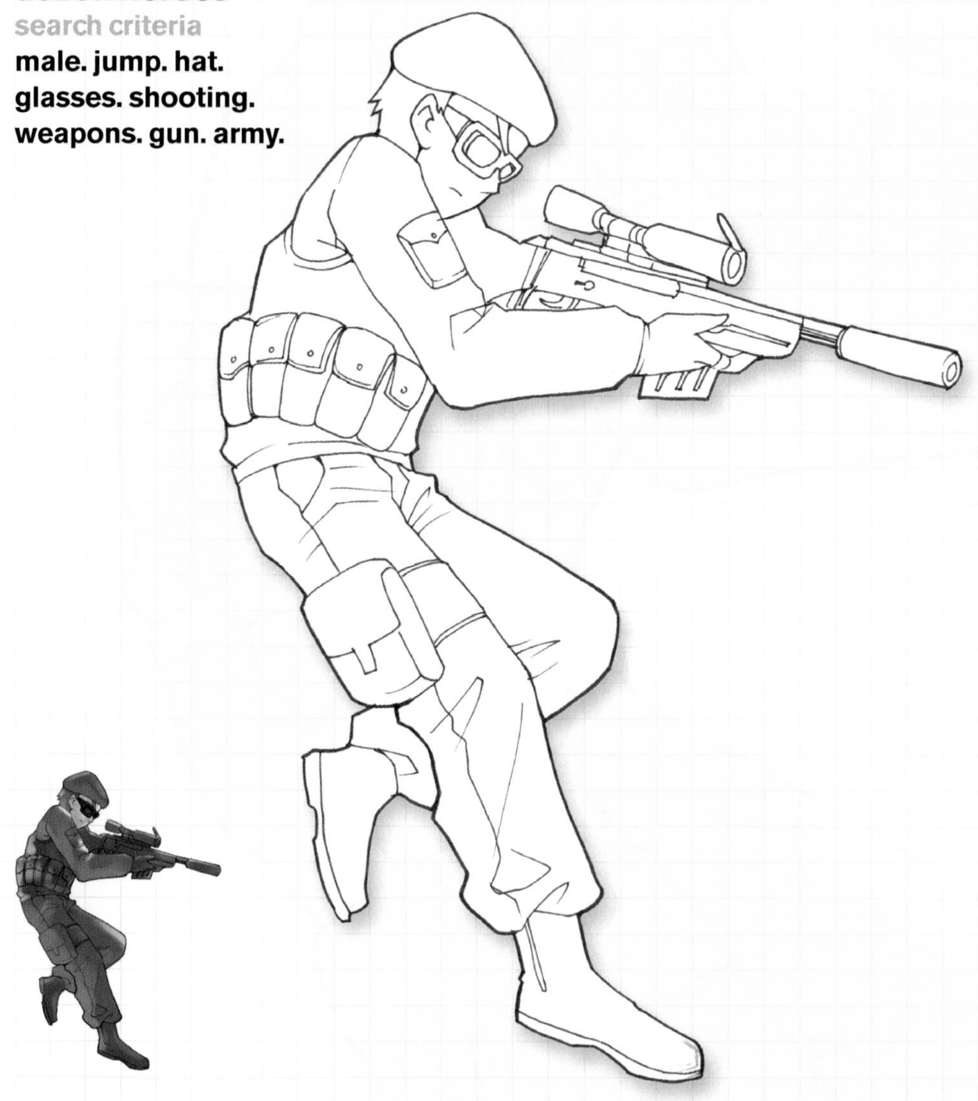

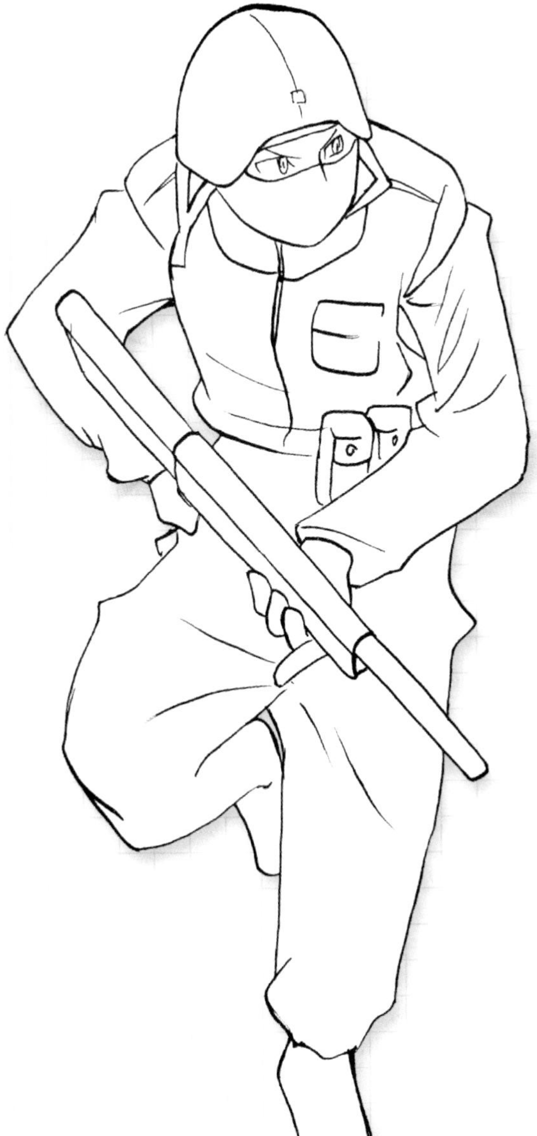

498

action heroes

search criteria

male. walking. helmet. mask. weapon. gun. spy. army.

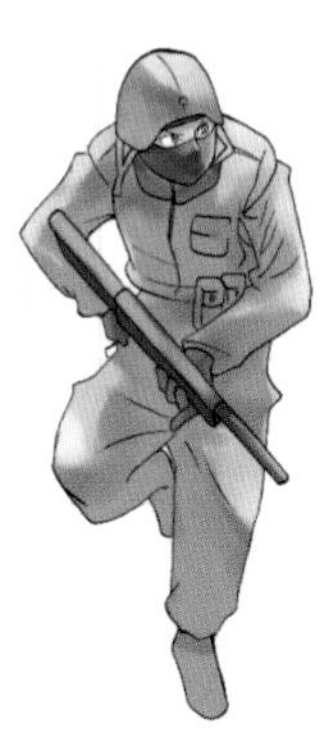

499

action villains

search criteria

female. standing.
helmet. sad. rescue.

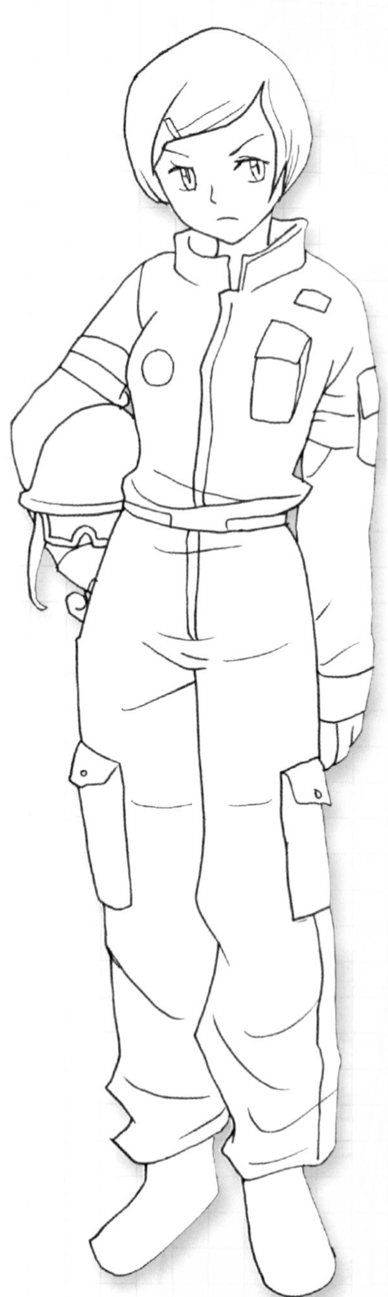

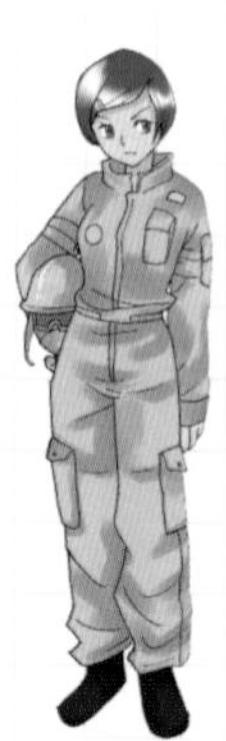

500

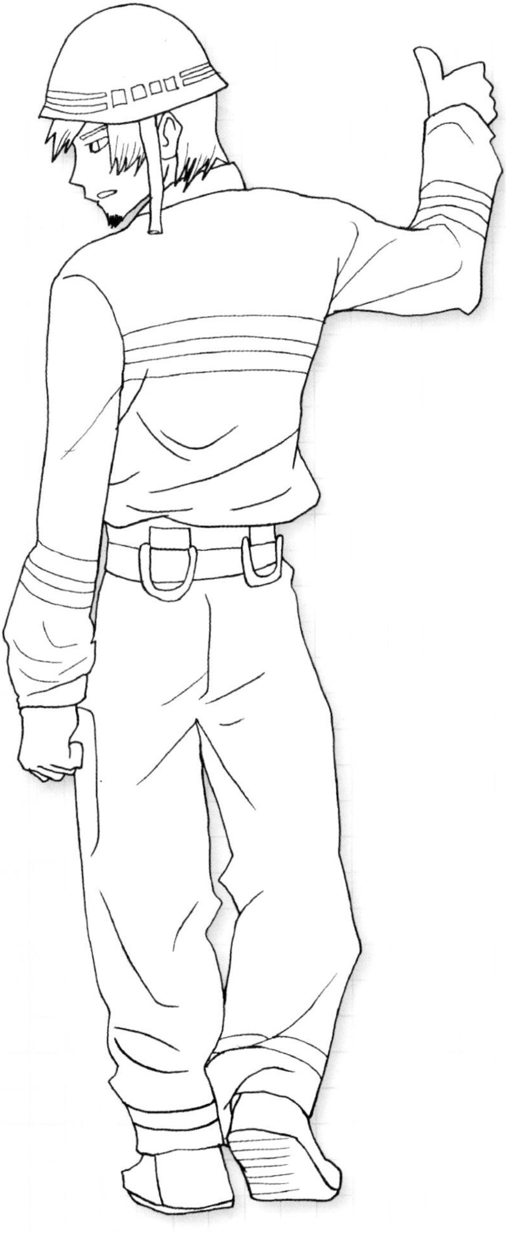

action villains

search criteria

male. standing. side. gesture. helmet. rescue.

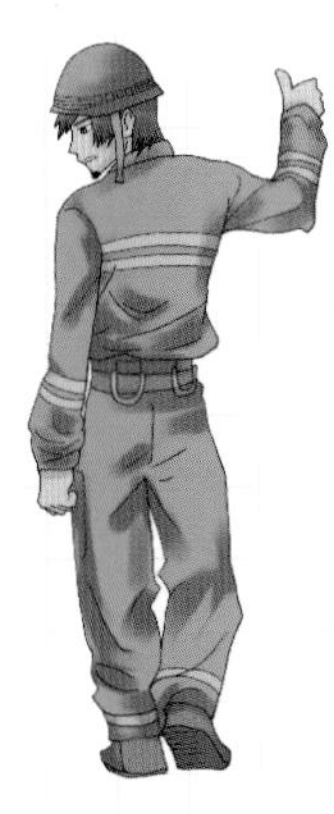

coloring basics

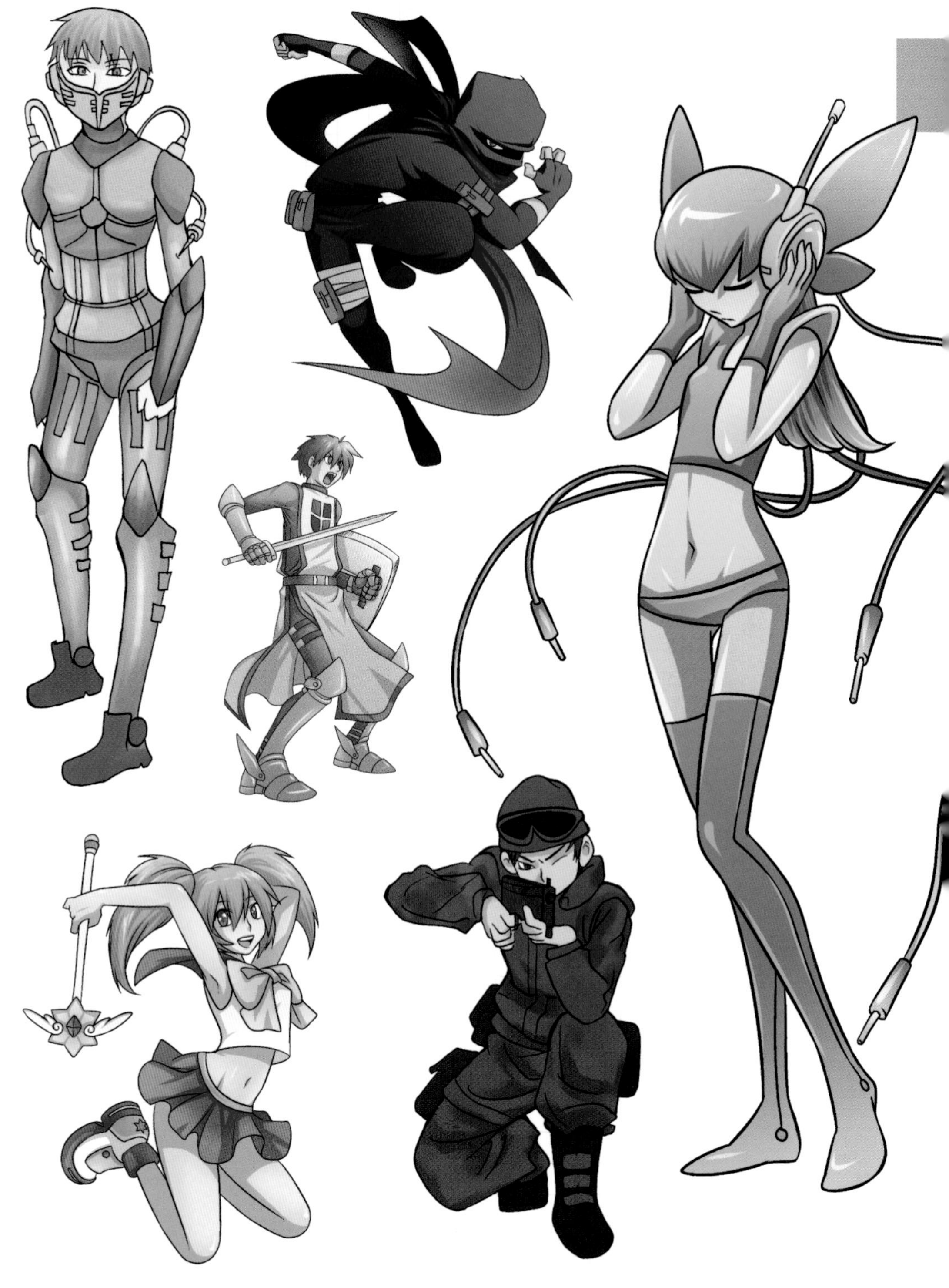

hardware

The use of computers in the production of artwork has completely revolutionized the industry, introducing a vast array of visual opportunities to artists at all levels of experience. Computers can be used solely to complement artwork produced on paper, but they can also be used as a replacement for the paper itself. Every step of the creative process can now be digitized, allowing an infinite amount of flexibility and freedom to experiment and create the best piece of artwork possible. By using your computer with some specialized image-editing software, such as Adobe Photoshop, you'll be able to capture the perfect look for the image that you are constructing. You can create artwork with just about any computer setup, but to make your life easier, you should think carefully about the hardware you choose.

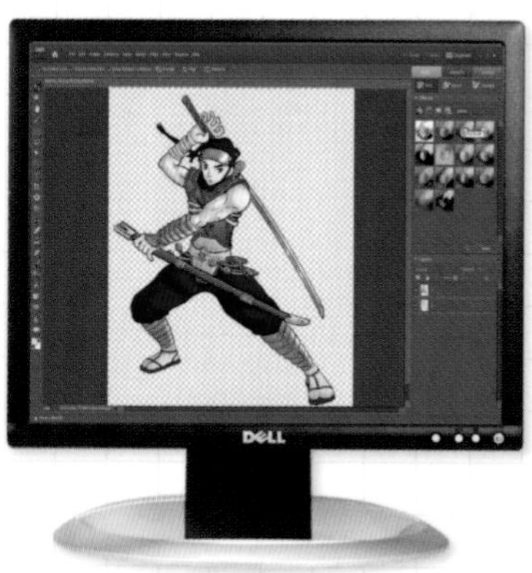

Monitor

There are two common types of computer display. The traditional type is CRT (cathode ray tube). These are the large, bulky displays of a similar design to an old-fashioned TV. The pixels are less sharp on a CRT display, but sometimes the colors can be more precise. The more modern type of display is a flatscreen type known as LCD TFT (liquid crystal display—thin film transistor). These displays are generally sharper, but are sometimes less effective for fast-moving visuals. Also, LCD displays are usually more comfortable to work on for long periods of time because of the absence of screen flicker.

The type of monitor you use doesn't make a huge amount of difference to your work, but it's worth realizing that colors may appear slightly differently on other people's screens. You can never be completely certain of other people's computer setups, so try to avoid your image relying on very subtle color differences. For example, if you add a lot of detail in a very similar color to the background or surface color, this difference might not be visible. This problem is especially noticeable with certain laptop displays.

Mouse

Every computer uses a pointing device of some sort, but it's helpful to use a decent-quality mouse if you're hoping to use it to produce artwork. You should ideally be using a modern laser or LED-based mouse, which are now quite common, as opposed to a traditional ball-based mouse (check the bottom of your mouse if you're uncertain). LED and laser mice are much more precise than their ball-based brethren, and don't jam or slow down. The only problem with them is that they sometimes become unresponsive on reflective or transparent surfaces, but this is generally not difficult to overcome.

Graphics Tablet

The graphics tablet is an extraordinarily versatile input device and is virtually essential if you are to make full and extensive use of the Airbrush tool. Graphics tablets come in a variety of sizes and different prices. Most tablets also have transparent overlays that you can use to trace over previously drawn artwork if you don't have a scanner.

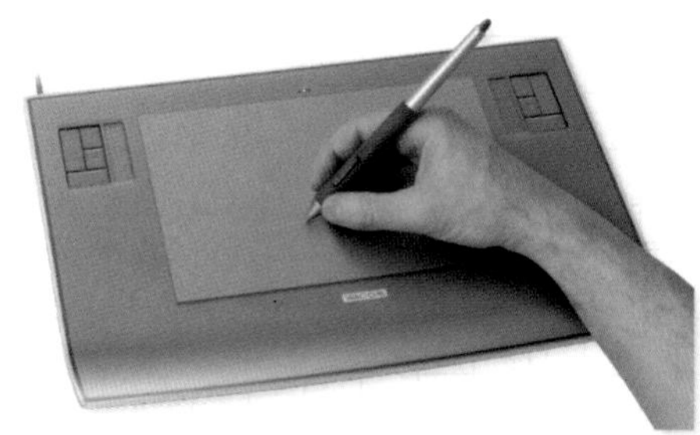

Inkjet Printer

These offer the easiest solution for printing high-quality color images. Inkjet printers are incredibly affordable, compact in size, and available to buy from a wide variety of outlets. The colors on inkjet printers can be enhanced even more with the use of specific photographic paper that enables the printer to produce finer lines and better details. It's important to realize that certain colors that are visible on screen will not be accurate when printed on paper because of the limitations of mixing the standard four inks to create the colors, though some printers offer six-color printing to increase the color fidelity. Bright purples, yellows, and certain other colors will be difficult to reproduce on paper.

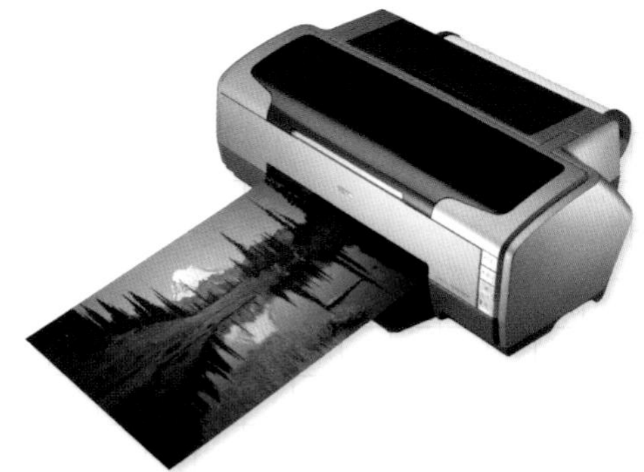

Laser Printer

Although color laser printers are still prohibitively expensive, black-and-white laser printers are the best option for printing monochrome images or documents because they are often capable of printing much finer lines than inkjets. Also, the toner they use is often waterproof and alcohol resistant. This is useful for things such as comic pages (fingers can easily smudge inkjet prints), and great for printing images that you intend to color by hand with alcohol-based markers.

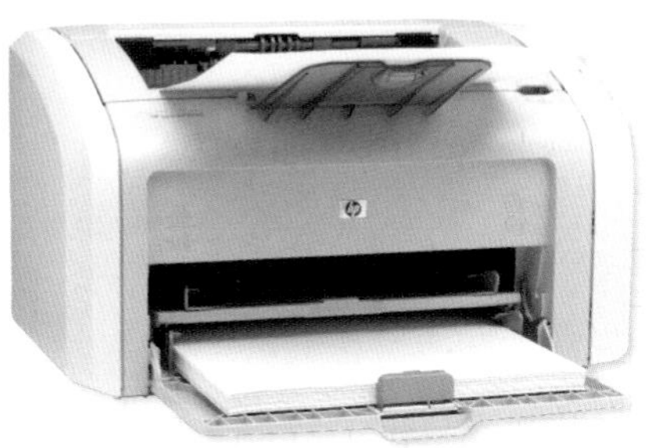

software

Photoshop has become the standard software for digital art production and photo-editing. It is used by professionals and home users alike to create artwork in a wide range of styles. The software is available for both Apple Macintosh and Windows PC machines, with only superficial differences between the two platforms, and it is available in various bundles depending upon the needs of the user.

Photoshop is also available in two different versions: The classic edition (which is now part of Adobe's Creative Suite range of software), and Photoshop Elements, a cut-down version intended for home use. The functionality removed from Photoshop Elements is quite specialized and thankfully doesn't impede the creation of manga or anime-style artwork.

Toolbar

All versions of Photoshop feature the *Toolbar*, which is placed by default on the left side of the screen. In Photoshop Elements the *Toolbar* is docked to the left side of the window as a long single column by default, but it can be undocked and placed wherever you wish within the workspace.

The *Toolbar* allows you to choose tools, as well as selecting foreground and background colors. Some of the tool icons have a small additional arrow in the bottom-right corner that indicates the presence of additional tools with related functions that will become available if you hold the mouse button down on that tool icon.

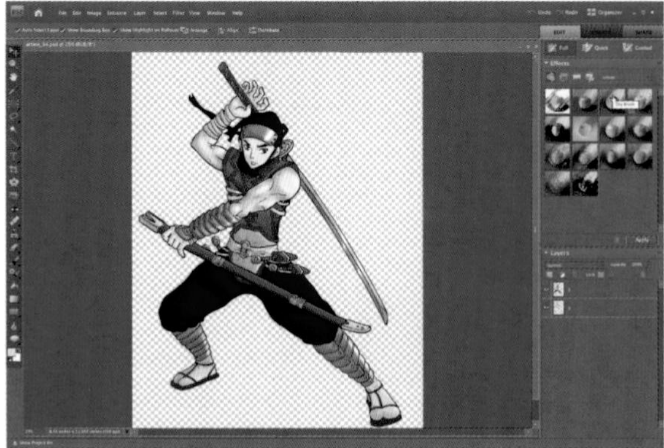

This is the standard Photoshop Elements default workspace. Although palettes are docked in a pull-out "bin" on the right side of the workspace, they can be undocked and freely placed within the work area.

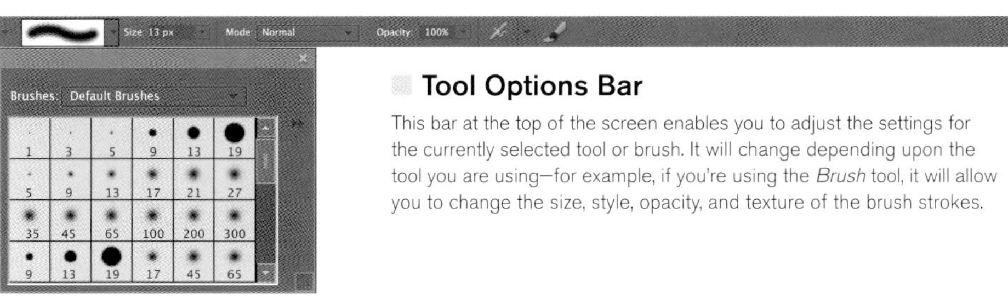

Tool Options Bar

This bar at the top of the screen enables you to adjust the settings for the currently selected tool or brush. It will change depending upon the tool you are using—for example, if you're using the *Brush* tool, it will allow you to change the size, style, opacity, and texture of the brush strokes.

Palettes

Photoshop Elements features a number of palette windows. By default some of these are in the *Palette Bin*, located on the right side of the workspace, that can be pulled open or left closed. It is possible to drag palettes from the bin into their own windows, and to combine these individual windows into one large multi-tab palette. This flexibility is useful for setting up the palettes in the most convenient layout. You can save your palette layout in the *Window* menu, or choose to reset the palettes to their default layout.

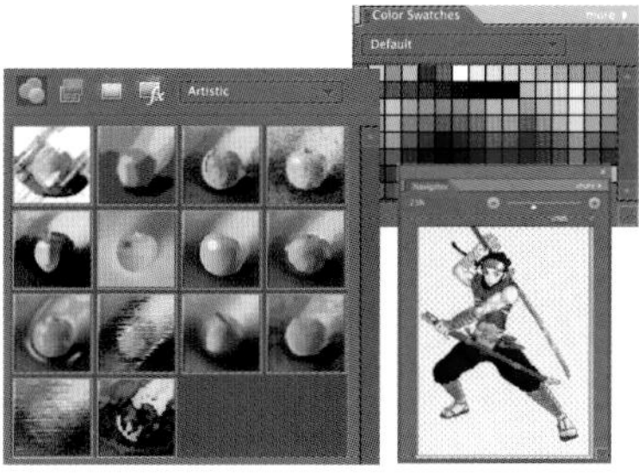

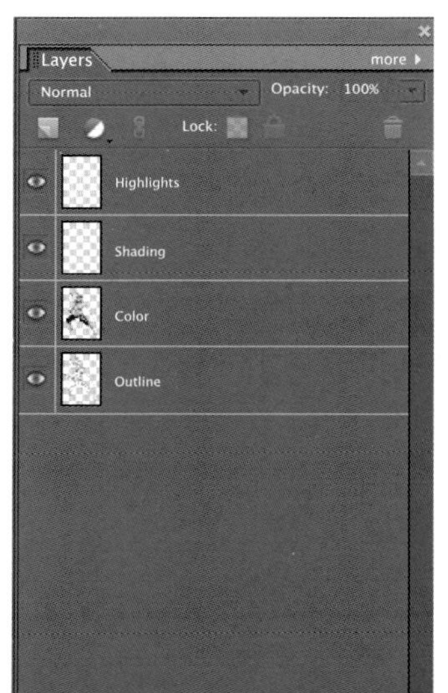

Layers Palette

The most commonly used palette is the *Layers* palette. Layers act like transparent sheets of plastic stacked on top of one another, enabling you to work on different parts of the artwork independently. In this way you can apply color and shading without risk of damaging the original line-art.

Context-sensitive menus

Like many pieces of software, Photoshop will bring up a context-sensitive menu when you right-click the mouse (Ctrl+click on a Mac). This menu will differ depending upon the currently selected tool, or whether a selection has been applied, but will always present you with useful options. Try the context-sensitive menu when performing different tasks to see the options that are available.

basic tools

Most image-editing programs have a broadly similar selection of tools. Here we will use Photoshop Elements as an example to outline their basic functions.

Navigation Tools

Move The *Move* tool enables you to select areas of the image and move the content around the screen.

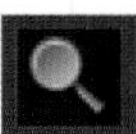

Zoom This enables you to enlarge or reduce the image on screen. This is useful when you want to see an overview of the entire artwork, or zoom in close to work on the details. Holding Ctrl/Cmd and pressing the + and – keys will allow you to zoom in quickly using the keyboard.

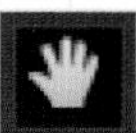

Hand The *Hand* tool is designed to move the viewable area of the image around the screen when you are zoomed in. When you have another tool selected, holding down the Space bar on the keyboard will switch to the Hand tool temporarily so you can navigate your document easily.

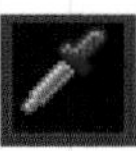

Eyedropper This tool is used to select colors from the existing image and set them as your current paint color. Set it to *Point Sample* in the *Tool Options* bar to get more accurate color selections. When using the paint tools, you can hold the Alt/Option key to temporarily select the *Eyedropper*.

Selection Tools

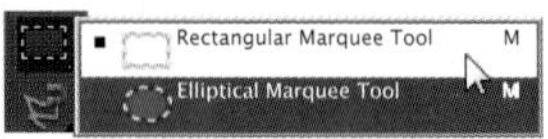

Marquee The *Marquee* tools are the simplest selection tools, enabling you to click and drag a rectangular or elliptical area of the image. Holding Shift will constrain these tools into perfect square or circle shapes respectively.

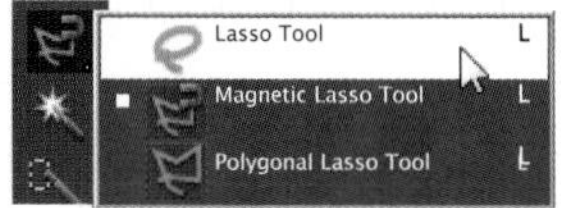

Lasso These tools allow you much greater control over the area of image you want to select. The *Freehand Lasso* allows you to draw around the area you want to select, but it can be tricky to control precisely. The *Polygonal Lasso* lets you plot a series of points to define the selection area.

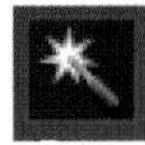

Magic Wand This tool uses the shapes and colors of the image to work out which areas of the image you wish to select. By changing the *Threshold* value, it's possible to change how much contrast the tool will use to define different areas.

basic tools

Paint Tools

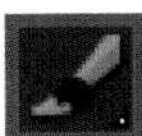

Paintbrush The standard painting tool in Photoshop, this is useful for applying color with soft edges and smooth lines. This is a great tool for applying color to an image, and the effect of brushstrokes can vary widely depending upon the chosen brush and *Tool Options* settings.

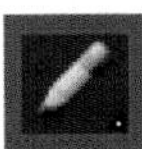

Pencil The pencil is an ultra-precise variation of the *Brush* tool, allowing pixel-perfect (or "aliased") brushstrokes. The tool sits under the *Brush* tool in the Tools palette, so you need to hold the mouse button down on it, then select the tool from the drop-down menu to switch between them. The *Pencil* tool is useful for cel-style coloring and making sure that colors are kept precise, but it can appear "jagged" when used on a low-resolution image.

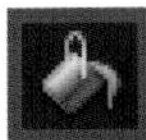

Paint Bucket The *Paint Bucket* works in a very similar way to the *Magic Wand* tool, but instead of selecting an area, it fills it with the current foreground color. Remember to select *All Layers* in the *Tool Options* bar if you're applying color to a different layer.

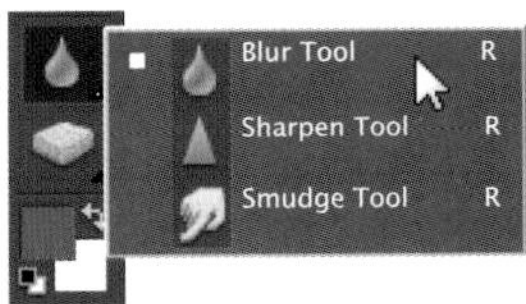

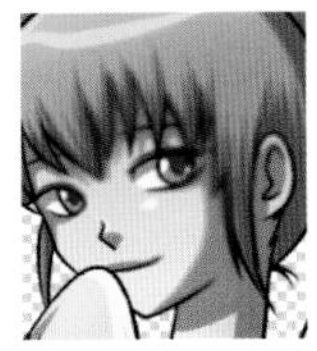

Blur

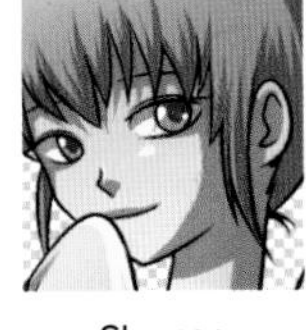

Sharpen

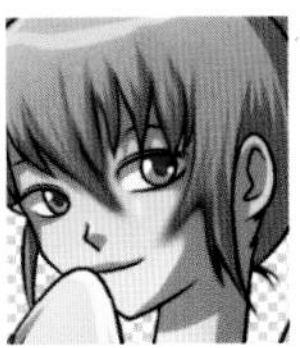

Smudge

Blur, Sharpen, and Smudge These tools adjust the colors already present in the image. *Blur* and *Sharpen* adjust the nearby contrast for the area to make the image more pronounced or fuzzy. *Smudge* allows you to move the colors around depending upon the direction you draw with the tool.

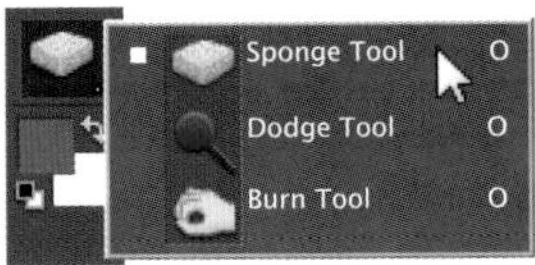

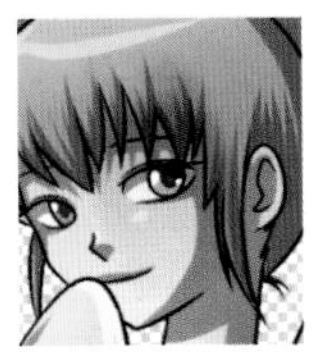

Sponge

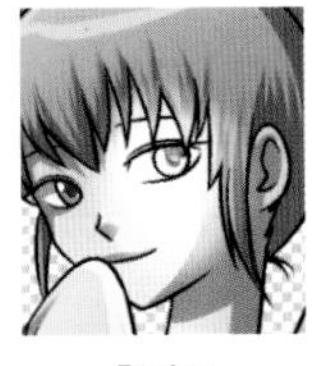

Dodge

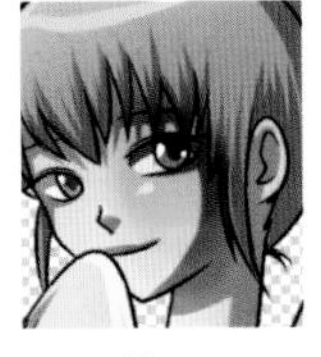

Burn

Sponge, Dodge, and Burn These tools behave like brushes, but are actually used to adjust the existing color in different ways. The *Sponge* tool is used to remove color from the image and make the image grayscale. *Dodge* fades the current color, while *Burn* makes the color darker and richer. These can be used to apply shading and highlights, but most artists prefer to use layers and other methods of shading to ensure greater control over the results.

brush tools

When coloring your manga-style artwork you will inevitably be using the *Brush* and *Pencil* tool for a significant part of the procedure because they represent the most direct method of applying colors to the image. The *Brush* tools enable you to paint directly onto the image using freehand strokes similar to a real pencil, pen, or paintbrush. You can apply color to be opaque like paint or translucent like ink, or even remove color as you would with an eraser. Your strokes can be wide like chalk, fine like pencil, or even change width dynamically like a nib pen or paintbrush. Learning how to adjust these settings will help you to achieve the best results.

Brush Toolbar

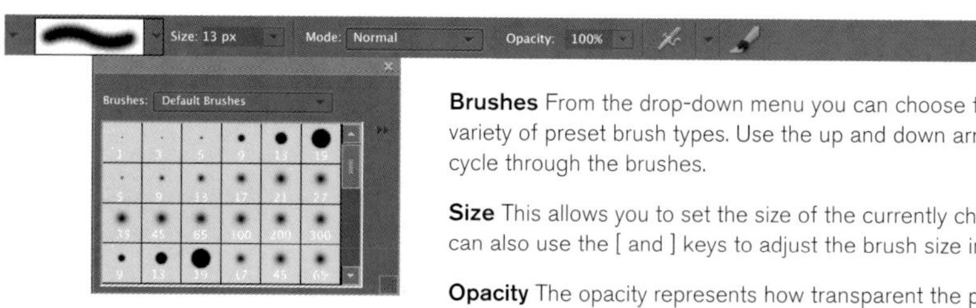

Brushes From the drop-down menu you can choose from a wide variety of preset brush types. Use the up and down arrow keys to cycle through the brushes.

Size This allows you to set the size of the currently chosen brush. You can also use the [and] keys to adjust the brush size in set increments.

Opacity The opacity represents how transparent the paint or ink will be when placed on the page. 0% is completely transparent, 50% is half-visible, and 100% is completely solid. If you want to mix colors on the page, this is an easy way to do it.

Airbrush This changes the behavior of the brush, so that holding down the brush produces a constant flow. Although this can be useful, it's generally much easier to use a brush with soft edges instead.

Brush Spacing

The *Spacing* setting in the *Tool Options* bar (found under *More Options* in Elements, and in the *Brushes* palette under *Brush Tip Shape* in Photoshop) can make a big difference to the quality of your brush strokes, but can also slow down your computer. By reducing the *Spacing*, the space between each "dot" of the stroke is reduced, creating a more realistic flow of paint. Adjust the setting to suit your needs.

Pastel brush set to 1% spacing

Pastel brush set to 50% spacing

Pastel brush set to 200% spacing

brush tools

Brush Shapes

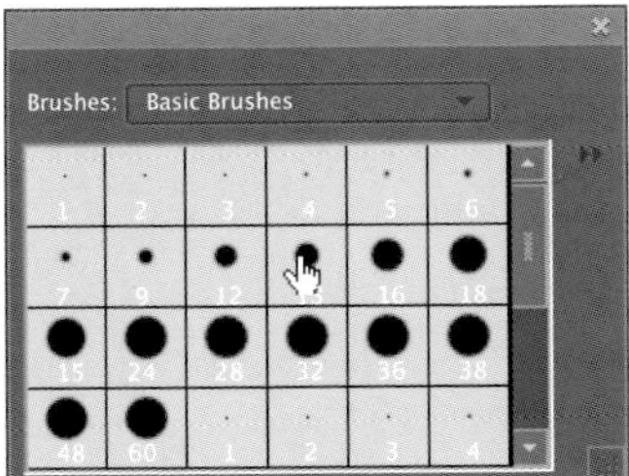

Hard brushes These brushes give a solid line where the color stops clearly at the edge of the brush stroke. They are ideal for applying base colors to an image, and defining lines and shapes.

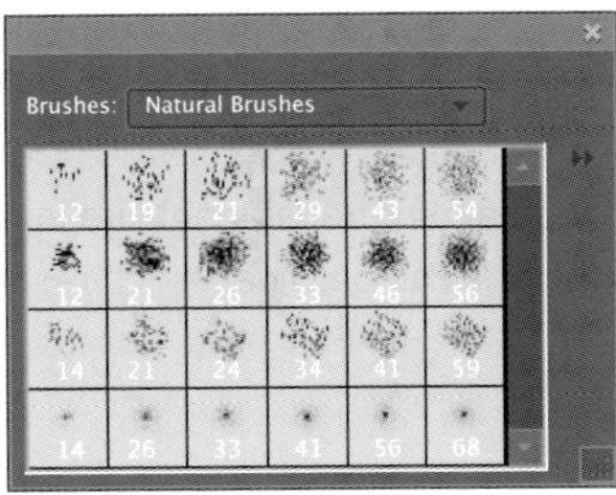

Soft brushes These brushes produce lines that fade toward the edge of the stroke. They tend to be best for applying soft, airbrush-style shading and coloring.

Natural brushes Photoshop Elements offers a range of irregular brush shapes to help recreate natural media techniques such as pastel, charcoal, or chalk. These can be useful for introducing texture into your image.

Graphics Tablet Pressure Settings

A graphics tablet allows a much greater degree of control over your digital brushes. Not only will it help you to draw precise brush strokes, but you will also be able to control the opacity or size of the brush directly depending upon the pressure of the pen against the tablet, because the pen nib is pressure sensitive. This can help you to achieve a much more natural-looking result.

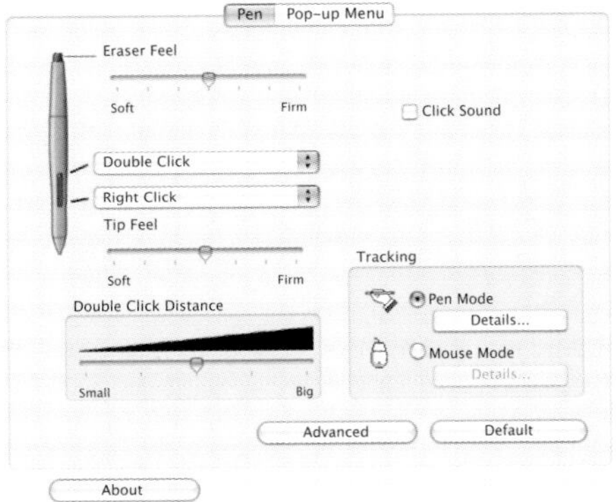

blocking in colors

With every image, whether simple or complex, it's useful to lay down basic colors before proceeding with more complicated shading. When you've mastered your basic coloring technique, you may even find that, in some cases, additional shading is unnecessary.

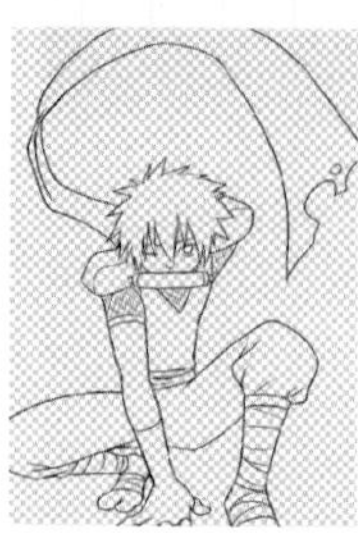

1 Start by opening an image from the CD. Change the image mode from Grayscale to RGB (*Image > Mode > RGB Color*). This will enable you to add color to the image.

Next, create a new layer containing just the outline. To do this, duplicate the original Layer 0 (*Layer > Duplicate Layer*) and name the duplicate "Outline."

With the Outline layer active, select the *Magic Wand* tool and set the *Tolerance* to 32. Make sure that *Anti-alias* and *Contiguous* are unchecked in the *Tool Options* bar—with *Contiguous* unchecked, the tool will select all instances of the color you click on.

Click in any of the white image areas, and all the white will become selected. Press Delete. Deselect (Ctrl/Cmd+D) and you will be left with just the outline.

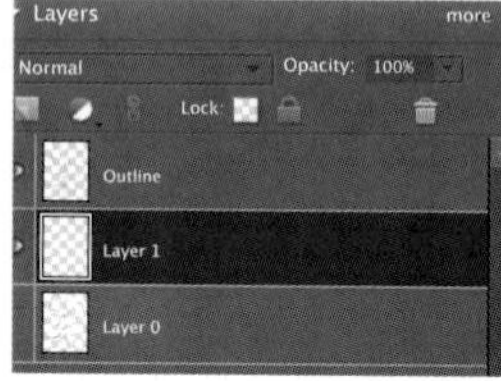

2 Rather than filling in all your colors on the original Layer 0, it is much better to create a new layer for each group of colors. This will give you much greater control over the final look of the image. To make new layers, click on the *Create a New Layer* icon at the top of the *Layers* palette, and name them appropriately by double-clicking on its name in the *Layers* palette.

On complex images, you may find that you build up a large number of layers, and it may be best to group associated colors, such as skin, together on the same layer.

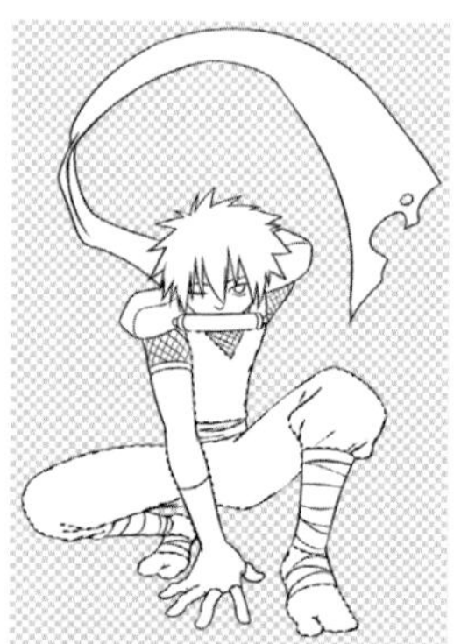

3 Now we can start blocking the basic image with flat color. Click on Layer 0 to make it active, and start selecting areas that you want to be the same color within the image. Use the *Magic Wand* tool again, but this time make sure that *Contiguous* is checked. Hold the Shift key while selecting so that you add to the previously selected areas. When all of the areas that you want to be a particular color are selected, click on your new color layer to make it active (the marching ants will remain, selecting the chosen areas).

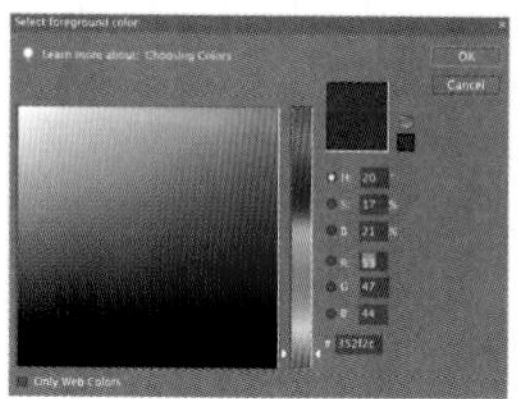

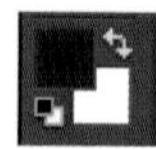

4 To choose the color that you want to fill the area with, click once on the foreground color icon in the *Toolbar* and the *Color Picker* dialog will open. From here, pick a suitable color and click *OK*—this color will now be your foreground color.

blocking in colors

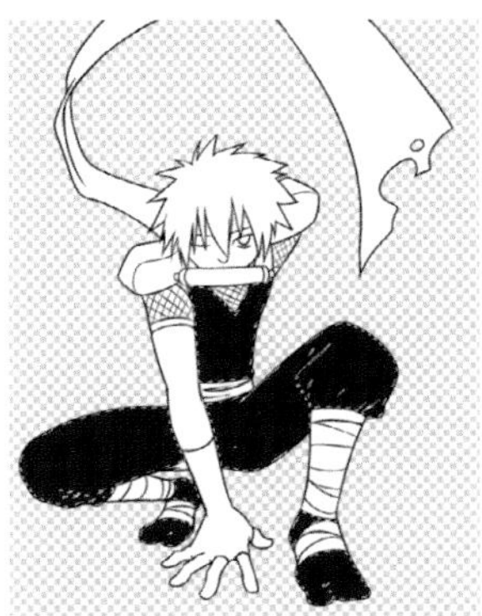

5 To fill your selection, use the *Paint Bucket* (make sure *Contiguous* is unchecked in the *Tool Options* bar). Clicking the *Paint Bucket* tool in any of the selected areas will fill them all with the foreground color. Alt/Opt+Backspace will also fill all of the selected areas with the foreground color.

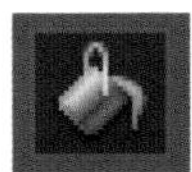

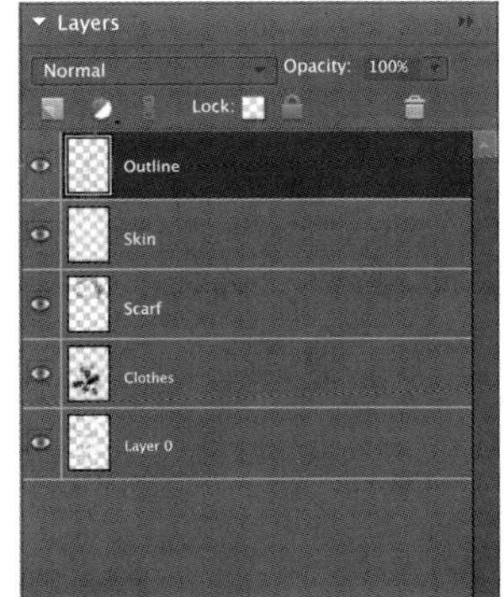

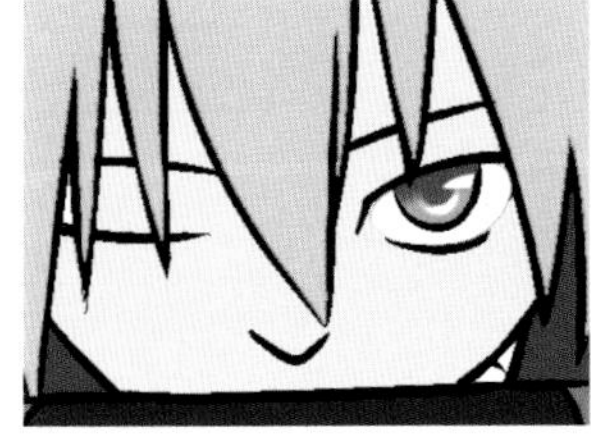

6 Zoom in to your image when making small selections, to make sure that you only select the required areas. You can also use the *Pencil* tool to fill in very small areas, or areas that are not defined by lines (such as around the eyes in this example).

7 Press Ctrl/Cmd+D to deselect. Click on Layer 0 to make it active again, and continue to work selecting and coloring on new layers. How you name the layers is up to you, but try to stick with logical names that will be easy to understand next time you come back to the file.

8 When you've finished, you will have a flat-colored figure that you can either use as is, or take to the next stage and introduce more complex lighting and shading.

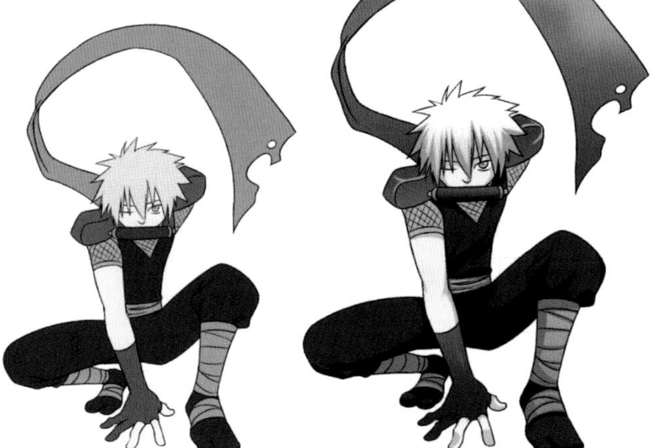

light and shade

The application of shading is one of the most distinctive aspects of anime-style artwork. The method of defining tone with a few solid stages of color developed a distinctive and iconic visual appearance that has become synonymous with Japanese anime. Shading is represented by large areas of darkened tone, while highlights are picked out with bright white or light color glints. By paying attention to the direction of light and considering the shape and volume of the body, it's easy to introduce effective shading into your artwork.

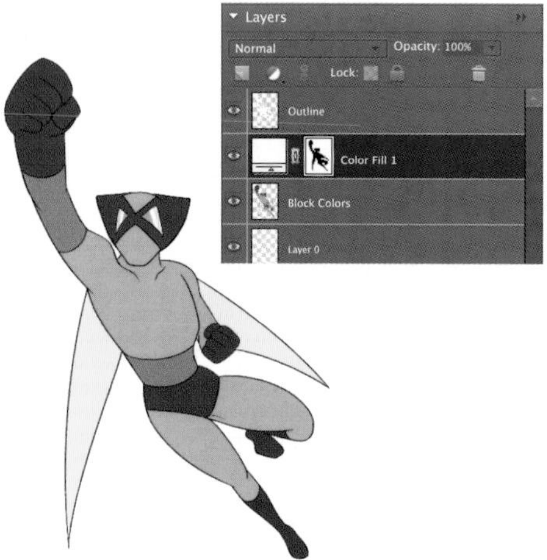

1 Start with an image that you have already blocked in with flat colors, as described on pages 520–521. It is useful to create a mask around the image to help keep the shadow color brushstrokes within the image outline. This is easy to do because our image still has the transparent Layer 0. Simply click the *Magic Wand* tool (with *Contiguous* unchecked) in the transparent (checkerboard) area of the layer to select it all.

Make a new *Solid Color* layer (*Layer > New Fill Layer > Solid Color*, or by clicking on the *Create Adjustment Layer* icon in the *Layers* palette), and fill it with white (it fills with the foreground color). Move this layer beneath the Outline layer created in the blocking stage. Make another new layer below this mask layer, and call it "Light Shading." Set its blending mode to *Multiply* by clicking on the drop-down list at the top of the *Layers* palette.

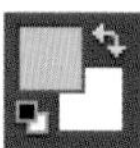

2 Choose the color you want to use for your shadows. Although you can use gray to add shading, it can result in a very dull image. It's better to use a color such as a dull orange or a faded purple. Experiment with different colors to see what suits the image and its existing colors. You can create paler shadows by choosing lighter tones of the same color.

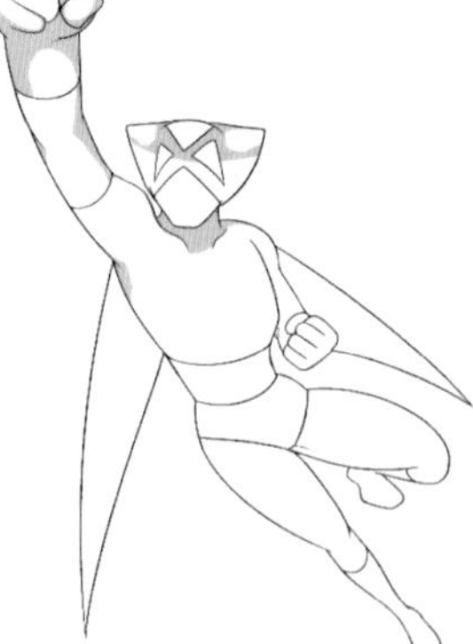

3 Make sure the Light Shading layer is active by clicking on it in the *Layers* palette. Choose a soft round brush and start painting in the shadows in your image. You can erase mistakes on the shadow layer with the *Eraser*. Try to block out all of the shadows roughly at first to get an idea of the overall look of the image, and to make sure that the light is cast evenly.

It's often helpful to hide the color layers when working on shading. You can do this by clicking the eye icons next to the color layer names in the *Layers* palette.

light and shade

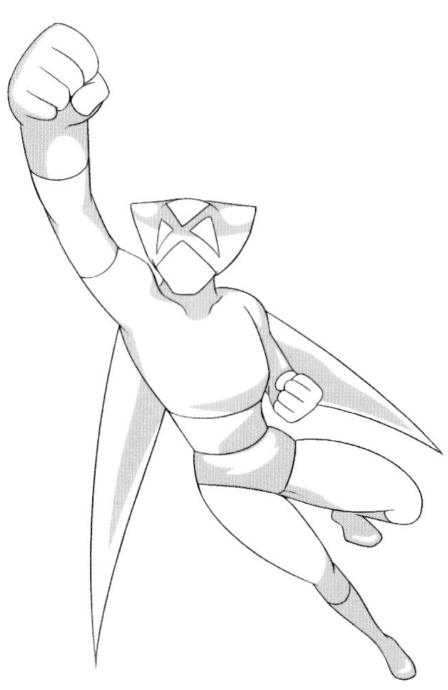

4 Continue to block in the shadow color, using different-sized brushes to fill the shadow area until you are satisfied with it. Remember that painting with white will not show up when the blending mode is set to *Multiply*, so you can use it to tidy up areas of shadow.

6 For the highlights, be sure to turn the color layers back on. Create a new layer with the blending mode set to *Normal* and place it at the top of the layer stack. You shouldn't need to make a layer mask for this layer because you'll only be creating a small number of highlights. Paint the glints of highlight in places where the main light source falls. This is best when applied only to shiny surfaces such as leather, metal, and plastic, and also hair and skin.

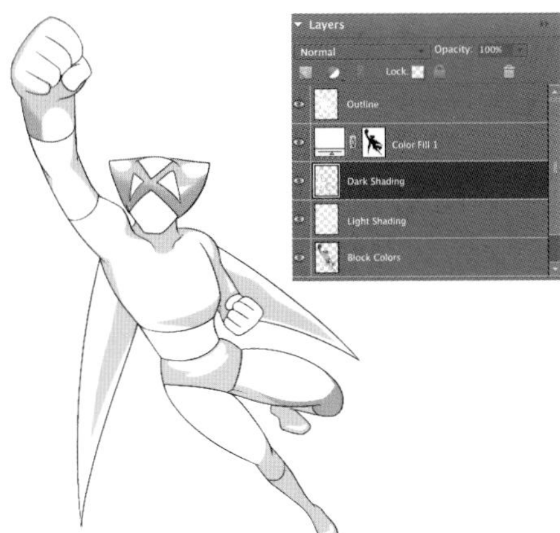

5 Make another new layer, name it "Dark Shading," and place it above the Light Shading layer. Draw with a darker color in the areas that are heavily cast in shadow, or on shiny, reflective materials. Using this darker shadow tone sparingly has a greater impact and helps to define the shape of the character.

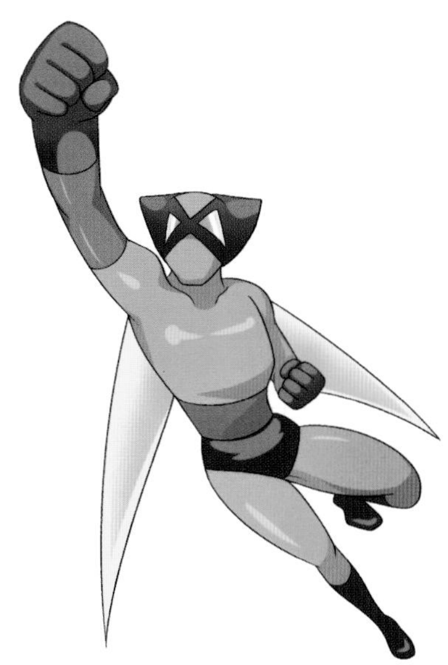

airbrush & beyond

While the traditional flat shading or "cel-coloring" style is especially iconic and commonly associated with manga and anime, it is by no means the only way in which color can be applied. With a variety of methods and styles available, it's possible to extend the cel style with airbrushing, or to completely ignore hard shading and try for something much more subtle. Depending upon the mood you want to create and the overall look of your image, you can apply any number of brush styles. When working digitally, it's possible to experiment with styles by saving multiple versions of your work, so that there's always room to try out new ideas and improve your techniques. Here are just a few examples.

Airbrush Style

The airbrush style refers to the use of gradient colors to achieve a look similar to a traditionally airbrushed image. This style can either be used to add softness to an image already painted in cel colors, or to completely replace the shading with softer lighting and gradual shading.

5	9	13	17	21	27
35	45	65	100	200	300

For the airbrush technique the use of soft brushes is crucial. These are represented in Photoshop as circles which become lighter toward the edge of the circle. The larger the brush is, the softer the gradient will be.

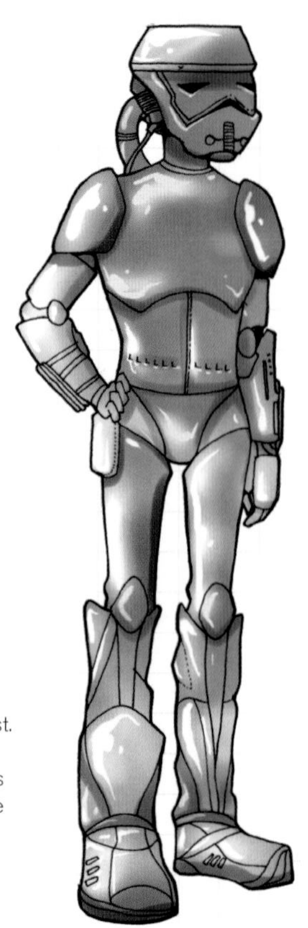

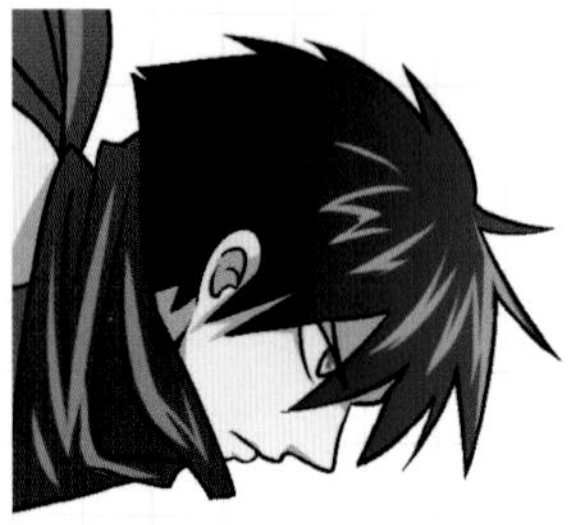

One of the simplest and most effective ways to introduce airbrushing into your artwork is to make the shading lighter beyond the initial area of contrast. This "falloff" effect helps to emulate ambient lighting and generally manages to maintain the feel of cel shading while adding a softer, more natural look.

airbrush & beyond

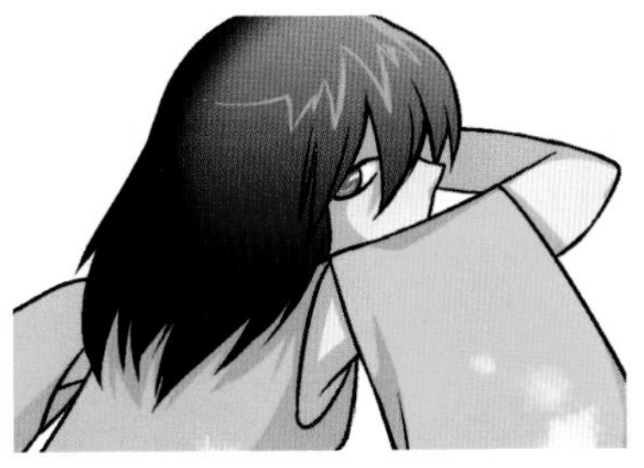

Airbrushed Highlights

Simple but natural-looking highlights can be easily created using the airbrush—just apply dabs of white in the appropriate places using the airbrush tool. Experiment with the settings, but it is essential to always use a very soft brush. When combined with the basic shadows and highlights used in block shading, the results can be very effective.

Natural Media Style

There are a number of different ways to achieve a natural media look using modern software. The natural media brushes available in Photoshop offer irregular shapes that give the impression of the tools used on canvas and paper, especially when the brush settings are handled well. By using settings like the *Multiply* blending mode, you can ensure that colors overlap and intensify in a manner similar to working with ink, while other settings can emulate paints, pencils, or even bleach. When working with these sorts of brushes, it is advisable to set the brush to a low opacity—between 5% and 40%. This helps to achieve the desirable layered look of "real" tools, and also helps to build up color with increasingly confident lines. If you are working with opaque paint-like brushes, it's still worth setting the opacity to 80–90%, so that the faintest trace of the color beneath shows through.

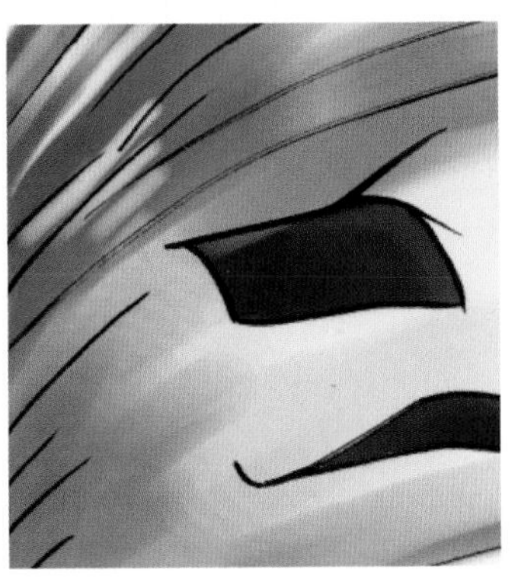

This Elemental character has been colored by using a variety of natural media brushes. The enlargement of the eye area shows how different brush types, strokes, colors, and opacity have been used to create a particular look, somewhat similar to pastel crayons.

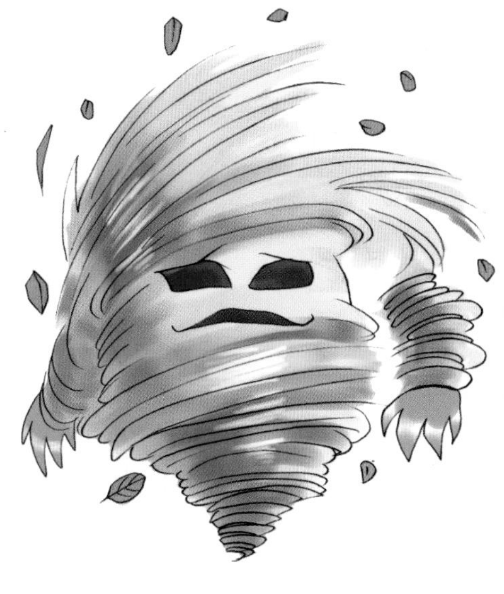

color collage

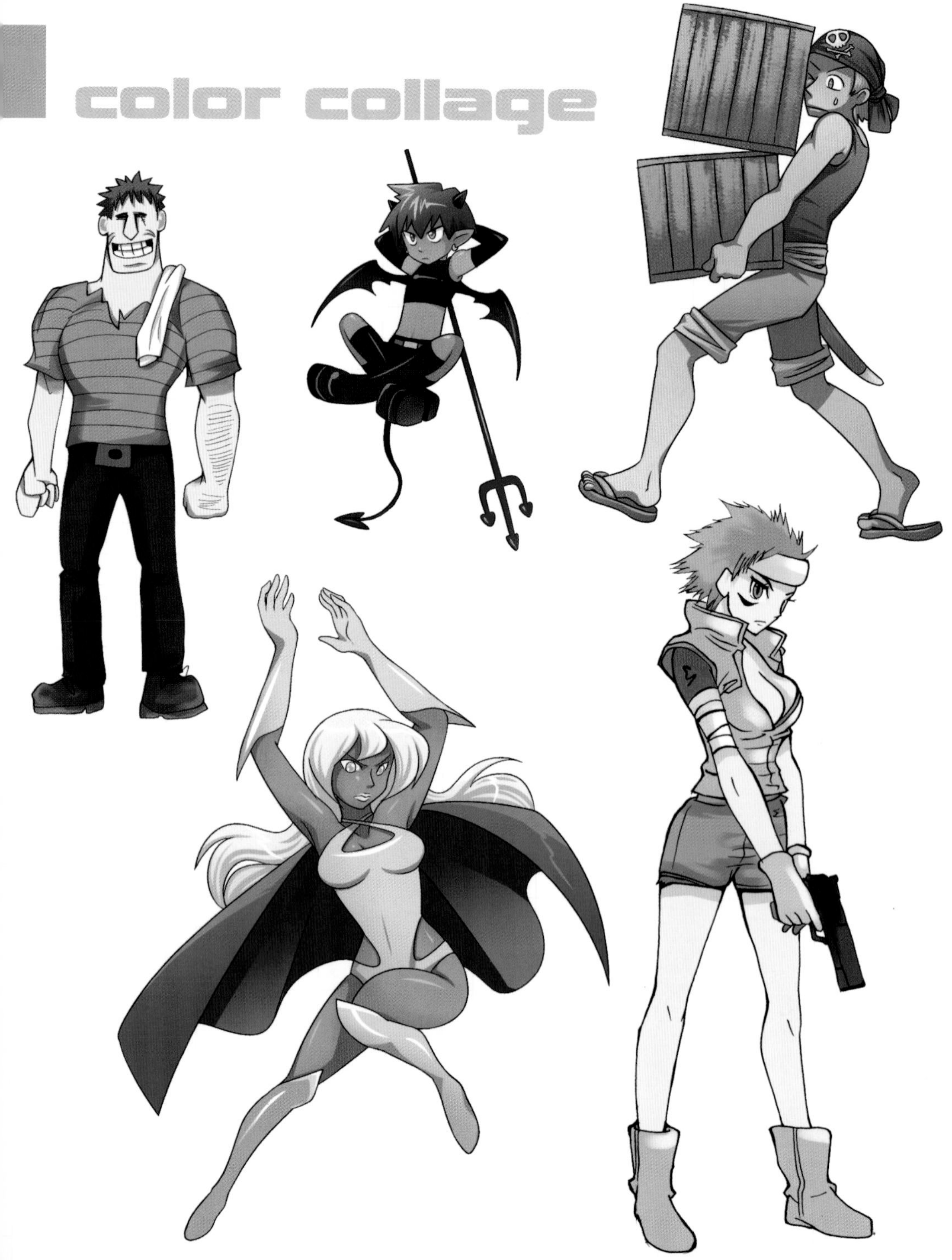

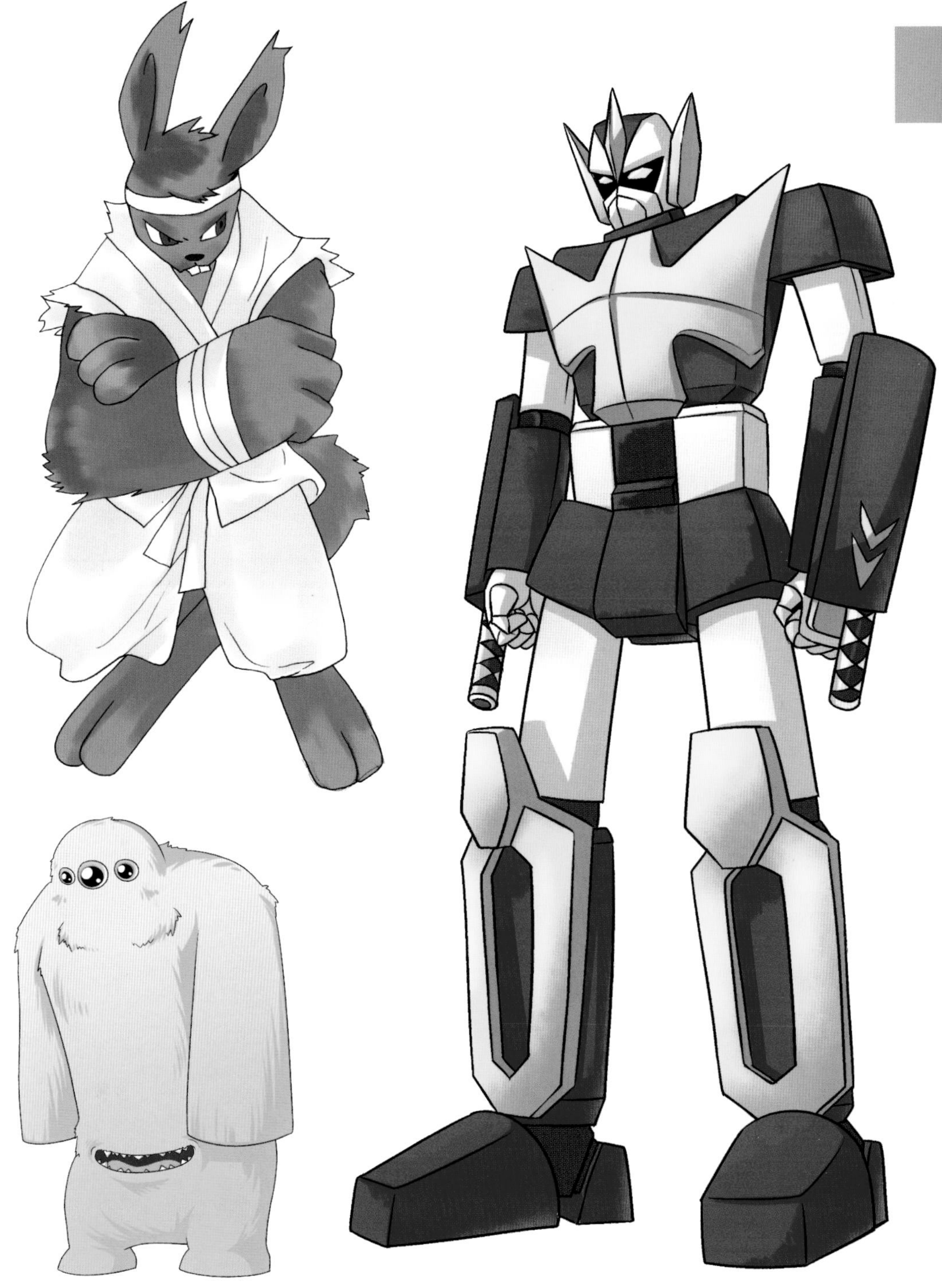

Image Gallery: 500 Manga Villains and Heroes License Agreement

The 500 Manga Villains and Heroes image gallery of digitized images ("The Images") on this CD-ROM disc ("The Disc") is licensed for use under the following Terms and Conditions, which define what You may do with the product. Please read them carefully. Use of The Images on The Disc implies that You have read and accepted these terms and conditions in full. If You do not agree to the terms and conditions of this agreement, do not use or copy The Images.

Terms and Conditions of Use

You agree to use The Images under the following Terms and Conditions:

Agreement

1. These Terms and Conditions constitute a legal Agreement between the purchaser ("You" or "Your") and The Ilex Press Ltd. ("Ilex").

2. License

You are granted a non-exclusive, non-transferable license to use, modify, reproduce, publish, and display The Images provided that You comply with the Terms and Conditions of this Agreement.

3. You may, subject to the Terms and Conditions of this Agreement:

a) Use, modify, and enhance The Images (provided that You do not violate the rights of any third party) as a design element in commercial or internal publishing, for advertising or promotional materials, corporate identity, newsletters, video, film, and television broadcasts except as noted in paragraph 4 below.
b) Use, modify, and enhance the images as a design element on a web site, computer game, video game, or multimedia product (but not in connection with any web site template, database, or software product for distribution by others) except as noted in paragraph 4 below.
c) Use one copy of The Disc on a single workstation only.
d) Copy the images to Your hard drive.
e) Make a temporary copy of The Images, if You intend to output the images by means of an output device owned or operated by a third party, such as a service bureau image setter. Such copies must be destroyed at the end of the production cycle.

4. You may not:

a) Distribute, copy, transfer, assign, rent, lease, resell, give away, or barter the images, electronically or in hard copy, except as expressly permitted under paragraph 3 above.
b) Distribute or incorporate the images into another photo or image library or any similar product, or otherwise make available The Images for use or distribution separately or detached from a product or web page, either by copying or electronically downloading in any form.
c) Use the The Images to represent any living person.
d) Modify and use The Images in connection with pornographic, libellous, obscene, immoral, defamatory, or otherwise illegal material.
e) Use The Images as part of any trademark whether registered or not.
f) Transfer possession of The Images to another person across a network, on a CD, or by any other method now known or hereafter invented.

5. Termination.

This license is in force until terminated. If You do not comply with the terms and conditions above, the license automatically terminates. At termination, the product must be destroyed or returned to Ilex.

6. Warranties.

a) Ilex warrants that the media on which The Images are supplied will be free from defects in material and workmanship under normal use for 90 days. Any media found to be defective will be replaced free of charge by returning the media to our offices with a copy of Your receipt. If Ilex cannot replace the media, it will refund the full purchase price.
b) The Images are provided "as is," "as available," and "with all faults," without warranty of any kind, either expressed or implied, including but not limited to the implied warranties or merchantability and fitness for a particular purpose. The entire risk as to quality, accuracy, and performance of The Images is with You. In no event will Ilex, its employees, directors, officers, or its agents or dealers or anyone else associated with Ilex be liable to You for any damages, including any lost profit, lost savings, or any other consequential damages arising from the use of or inability to use The Images even if Ilex, its employees, directors, officers, or its agent or authorized dealer or anyone else associated with Ilex has been advised of the possibility of such damages or for any claim by any other party. Our maximum liability to You shall not exceed the amount paid for the product.
c) You warrant that You do not reside in any country to which export of USA products is prohibited or restricted or that Your use of The Images will not violate any applicable law or regulation of any country, state, or other governmental entity.
d) You warrant that You will not use The Images in any way that is not permitted by this Agreement.

7. General

a) The Disc, The Images, and its accompanying documentation is copyrighted. You may digitally manipulate, add other graphic elements to, or otherwise modify The Images in full realization that they remain copyrighted in such modification.
b) The Images are protected by the United States Copyright laws, international treaty provisions and other applicable laws. No title to or intellectual property rights to The Images or The Disc are transferred to You.
c) You acknowledge that You have read this agreement, understand it, and agree to be bound by its terms and conditions. You agree that it supersedes any proposal or prior agreement, oral or written, and that it may not be changed except by a signed written agreement.